It is Teddy's birthday
What will Teddy wear?
One red hat with a pom-pom
What a smart teddy bear!

10

ten

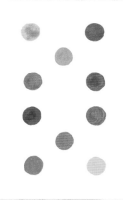

Here are ten cards for Teddy
That he will want to keep
Teddy cannot count them –
For he is fast asleep!

3  5

9 10

flowers

sun

swing

You can learn some new words
Say each one you see
And find it in the picture
With Teddy and with me.

boat

stool

bed

lamp

rug

star

pillow

Earth Friendly Home
Alternative Energy For Your Home

Published by
Starcott Media Services, Inc.
P.O. Box 54987
Cincinnati, Ohio 45254

Printed in the United States of America
First Edition
Copyright © 1999 by James T. Dulley
All rights reserved
9, 8, 7, 6, 5, 4, 3, 2, 1

ISBN 0-9625583-1-1

We recommend care and adherence to standard construction safety procedures. Wear adequate protective clothing and safety gear (approved safety eyeglasses, work gloves, breathing filter mask) when working with power and hand tools, and with building and insulation materials. If you have questions about proper safety procedures or protective clothing to wear, contact your local health department, Occupational Safety and Health Administration or Environmental Protection Agency. Neither the author nor the publisher takes responsibility for accidents that may occur during the building or use of any of the projects or products described in this book.

Introduction

Today, people are interested in lowering their housing costs and are concerned about conserving the earth's precious resources to protect the environment for future generations. By using efficient alternative energy (sun, wood, wind and the Earth), making wise informed purchases, and doing some repair and project yourself, you can save a substantial amount of money each year. Using much of the information in this book, I have cut my utility bills in my own home by more than 70% from the previous owner's utility bills while improving my comfort. I do most of the repair and home improvement projects myself.

My syndicated columns, **_$ensible Home_** and **_Cut Your Utility Bills_**, appear each week in more than 400 newspapers and magazines from coast to coast. Each column offers a different Update Bulletin which provides more comprehensive information on the weekly topic.

Earth Friendly Home has 13 chapters in which I have selected 51 Update Bulletins and the related columns. These include many alternative energy do-it-yourself projects and information on new money-saving and efficient products. The actual savings you realize from making any of these improvements or by installing various products depend on the efficiency of your current systems and your local utility rates. Always do a payback analysis before investing your time and money in a project or a product.

Before attempting any of the do-it-yourself projects, read the Update Bulletin completely. Always wear adequate protective clothing and glasses. When these projects effect any mechanical systems in your house (furnace, air conditioner, water heater, etc.), contact a contractor or technician familiar with your specific model. Some models are unique and require specific clearances and adjustments when making improvements. Be sure to check your local building and fire codes.

Proper handling of materials is essential on any home improvement project. Some materials, such as asbestos or fiberglass, require special precautions. If you think a material contains asbestos, **do not** handle it. Contact a contractor experienced with handling asbestos. Do not dust, sweep, or vacuum particles suspected of containing asbestos. This will disturb tiny asbestos fibers and may make them airborne. The fibers are so small that they cannot be seen and can pass through normal vacuum cleaner filters and get back into the air. The dust should be removed by wet-mopping procedures or by trained asbestos contractors using specially-designed "HEPA" vacuum cleaners.

Some possible asbestos-containing materials include cement pipes, wallboard and siding; asphalt and vinyl floor tile; ceiling tiles and lay-in panels; all types of insulation; and roofing felt and shingles. Special precautions should be taken during removal of the exposed or damaged asbestos-containing material. Do not disturb any material you think may contain asbestos unless you have to. Removal of the material is usually the last alternative.

When working on any electrical appliances or equipment, **always unplug it first**. If you are going to do any work on the electrical wiring in your home, **switch off** the main circuit breaker or switch before touching any wires. In addition, check to make sure the wires are not "hot" with an appropriate tester as a double safety check before touching any wires.

This book is divided into ten general topic areas with many related Update Bulletins and columns in each. The chapter topic refers to the subject of the first question of each column and its corresponding Update Bulletin. Model numbers provided are the most current as of this printing. Actual model numbers may vary with specific colors or styles. If any of the model numbers have changed, a retail dealer or the manufacturer can provide you with the new model number based on the old one shown.

If you would like to receive a free topics listing of the 150 most current Update Bulletins available, write to Starcott Media Services, Inc. at the address on the preceding page. Please include a self-addressed stamped business-size envelope with your request for the listing. You can also visit my web site at "www.dulley.com".

Table of Contents

Chapter   **Pages**

Solar Water Heating · **1 - 12**

do-it-yourself passive batch-type water heater, passive and active solar water heating kits, do-it-yourself water-type solar collector

Wind Energy · **13 - 20**

whole-house and small portable electricity-generating windmills, wind-powered turbines and other attic vents

Photovoltaics — Electricity Generation · **21 - 36**

solar-powered outdoor lighting, solar-powered attic vent fans, whole-house emergency generators, large solar cell systems

Solar Heating & Cooling · **37 - 68**

solar wall heater, solar window heater, air-type solar collector and solar Trombe wall, warm water radiant floor systems, solar chimney and whole-house fan, patio door wind/sun shield or shutter, recycled and new solar ceramic tile, attic foil/heat-blocking paint and ventilation

Wood Heating · **69 - 100**

efficient wood-burning furnaces, patio/deck heaters, pellet/corn-burning freestanding stoves and inserts, massive masonry/Finnish fireplaces, firewood selector guide, fireplace upgrade products and techniques, efficient radiant and heat-circulating fireplaces, do-it-yourself firewood dryer and cold frame

Solar Food Preparation · **101 - 108**

instructions/illustrations for solar food/flower dryer, ready-to-use and do-it-yourself solar cooker kits

Passive Solar Houses and Sunspaces · **109 - 124**

garden/greenhouse windows, passive solar house plan layouts and techniques, efficient sunroom kits, do-it-yourself greenhouse construction

Swimming Pools · **125 - 132**

solar-powered ionization purifier systems, swimming pool solar systems and pool/solar deck kits

Exterior Solar Improvements · **133 - 140**

attractive segmental retaining wall systems, patio pavers and products

Landscaping · **141 - 152**

climbing vines for shading, deciduous/flowering and evergreen dwarf shrubs, tree selector guide

Windows and Skylights · **153 - 172**

ventilated roof insulation panels for skylights and cathedral ceilings, efficient fiberglass windows, bow and bay replacement windows, tubular skylight kits, high-efficiency skylights and building a lightwell

Window Improvements · **173 - 192**

permanent winter/summer window film, insulated reflective window shutter, insulated exterior rolling shutters, retractable window awnings, removable solar window film and exterior/interior shading systems

Other Alternative Energy Topics · **193 - 204**

geothermal heat pumps, do-it-yourself gazebo kits and solar deck, purifying house plants and hydroponic information

Warm up to inexpensive solar heater

Q: My kids studied about pollution last week and they are bugging me to build a solar water heater. I would like to do a weekend project with the kids. We have a sunny spot near the house. What is the simplest low-cost design to build from scratch?

A: Your kids' concerns are legitimate. They are the ones who are going to have to breathe, eat and drink all the pollution we are creating. Using the sun to help heat your water is a good first step and sets an excellent example for your children.

A batch-type solar water heater is the simplest, yet effective, do-it-yourself design. It requires no pumps or controls and you should be able to build one over a weekend with mostly scrap materials.

This type of batch, sometimes called a breadbox, solar water heater is primarily used as a preheater for your water heater. Installing one can typically cut your water heating costs by 20%. For a typical family, these savings should provide an excellent payback of the material costs within the first year. Thereafter, the solar hot water is free.

There are many effective batch heater designs. They are usually located on the ground against a south-facing house wall. Your existing water heater water inlet is diverted to the batch heater to let the sun pre-heat the water.

Plumbing it is simple. Install two low-cost tees in the water pipe going to the water heater. Put a simple valve between them so that, when you close it, the water goes through the solar heater first. Put another valve in the pipe to the batch heater.

The simplest batch heater is basically a water tank (painted black)

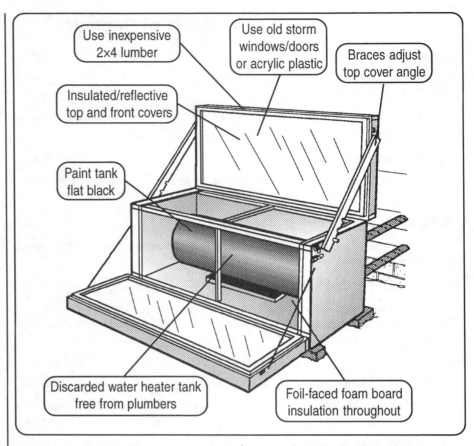

Use inexpensive 2×4 lumber

Use old storm windows/doors or acrylic plastic

Braces adjust top cover angle

Insulated/reflective top and front covers

Paint tank flat black

Discarded water heater tank free from plumbers

Foil-faced foam board insulation throughout

in a box with a clear top. As the sun shines on the tank inside the box, it continuously heats the "batch" of water inside it.

On a sunny day, water in the heater can get hot enough so that your existing water heater won't have to come on at all. On cloudy or very chilly days, close the hinged insulated covers so it does not lose heat. Depending on your climate, it should be effective for six to nine months per year.

The sides of the box should be insulated to reduce heat loss. If you really want to get fancy, install some insulated hinged covers. Close them at night to keep the water warm. Just throwing an old quilt over the clear top at night is effective too.

Total material costs can be reduced by using a discarded water heater tank from a plumber. Electric water heater tanks are best. Strip off the outer shell and insulation and paint it flat black.

If there are any old solar designers in your area, they may still have some adhesive-based selective coating foil. This can increase solar heat gain of the tank. You can use either glass, acrylic or fiberglass reinforced polyester (FRP) for the clear top.

Q: I just bought an older house that has tube and knob wiring in the attic. I want to add more attic insulation. Can I put the insulation right up against this old wiring?

A: If it is in good condition, the tube and knob wiring should be okay. You must leave an air gap around it though so the insulation does not touch it at all. This is needed for cooling. In those areas of your attic where the insulation would touch the wiring, use rigid foam insulation instead. It is more expensive, but it has greater insulation value per inch thickness so you can leave a gap.

When completed, this solar water heater will be approximately 31" high, 28" wide, and 61" long. If you happen to have an old storm window or door, you can make the solar heater any size. The size shown here makes efficient use of most standard size building materials and water tanks per diagram #3 as shown on page 3.

1) Cut four 21" long 2×4 uprights and four 53¾" long 2×4 crosspieces. Cut four 21" long 2×3 upright supports. Measure in 16½" from each end of the crosspieces and mark a line. Glue and nail these pieces together as shown in diagram #1, page 3, to form the back and the bottom of the box.

2) Cut four 24½" long and four 24" long 2×4 pieces. Glue and nail pieces together per diagram #1.

3) Make the frames for the insulating and reflective front and top lids. For the top lid, cut two 25⅛" long and two 61½" long 2×4 pieces and two 25⅛" long 2×3 pieces. Glue and nail together per diagram #1. For the front lid cut two 21" long and two 61¼" long 2×4 pieces and two 21" long 2×3 pieces. Glue and nail together per diagram #1.

4) Make two glazing frames to cover the top and the front of the box from the 1×4 lumber. Rip it to four ¾" square strips. For the top glazing frame, cut three 18" long and two 53¾" long. To assemble the glazing frame, nail through the longer strips into the shorter ones at both ends. A support is centered between the two end pieces. Mark its position and nail it in place. From the remaining ¾" strips, cut three 21" long pieces and two 53¾" long pieces. Assemble these for the front glazing frame.

5) Cut and install the insulation in the box frame. It is very important that the insulation fits tightly in the box with no gaps. Measure each side and carefully cut the pieces. It is easy to do a final trim with a utility knife. For the front lid, cut a piece of the ½" foil-faced insulation. It should measure roughly 21"x58¼". Spread adhesive on the supports and place the insulation in the

lid against the support with the reflective foil surface facing up. Tape it to the frame with strips of the foil duct tape.

6) Cut pieces of 2" foil-faced insulation to fit between the supports in the top lid. Two pieces should be roughly 15"x21" and one piece should be 25¼"x21". Spread adhesive on the supports and the ½" insulation already installed. Place pieces of 2" insulation in the lid. Allow adhesive to dry. Cover the top of the lid with plywood. The foil surface should be showing on the other side. Install insulation in the top lid and finish it the same as the front lid.

7) Insulate the box framing in the same fashion. The reflective side of the ½" insulation should face inside the box. This directs as much heat as possible on to the water tank. Seal the insulation to the lumber with the foil duct tape. With the insulation in the bottom, back, and side sections of the box frame, glue and nail the framing together to form the box. Caulk all the wood to wood joints on the inside with silicone caulking. Cut plywood pieces to cover and finish the outside of the box. Paint the exterior of the box with an epoxy marine-type paint or exterior house paint.

8) Using 2x4 lumber, make two cradle pieces to support the water tank. Cut a long shallow "V" to form the cradle. Nail these through the ½" insulation into the supports in the bottom frame section. This will position the tank about 2" above the bottom of the box.

9) Paint the water tank with flat black paint. For greater efficiency, use a special selective solar paint. The tank

should be positioned with the hot water outlet fitting directly above the cold water inlet. Since the hottest water will rise to the top, this positioning will minimize mixing of the hot and cold water. Screw a short nipple into the tank fittings and solder on 90-degree elbows. Measure the position of the elbows and drill inlet and outlet holes

---

Required Materials for Batch Solar Water Heater

lumber — 2×4, 2×3, 1×4, 1×3, 1×2 and ¼" plywood

water tank — stripped discarded water heater tank

insulation — foil-faced ½" sheet and 2" sheet

insulation — tubular foam for pipes

glazing — clear acrylic, special solar glazing, or glass

½" wood dowel, aluminum angle

caulking — silicone

weatherstripping — adhesive-backed foam

plumbing supplies — copper pipe, solder, fittings

Teflon tape and wood glue

paint — flat black or special solar paint, marine epoxy
   or exterior house paint

foamboard/panel adhesive

tape — aluminum foil duct tape

fasteners — nails, screws, strapping, butt hinges,
   brads, washers

luggage catches, 2' small link chain, staples

---

in the back of the box. Tilt the pipes slightly downward to your house so they will drain out when you want to drain it. Secure the tank in the cradles with metal strapping.

10) Rip the 1×4 lumber to ¾" strips to form ledgers to support the clear glazing. Nail these ledgers ¾" below the top and front surface of the box frame — diagram #2. Set the glazing frames in the box against the ledgers. The outside edge of the glazing frames should be flush with the surfaces of the box. For greater efficiency, you can staple clear Teflon™ film to the bottom of the glazing frames first. This produces a double-clear cover when completed. Nail the front edges of the glazing frames together to complete the box. Caulk all the joints.

11) For the clear top and the front of the

box, you can use clear acrylic, polycarbonate, fiberglass reinforced polyester (FRP), low-iron glass (this is the best for solar), or standard glass. Cut the glazing pieces to cover the entire top and front surface of box (you will have to have glass professionally cut). Lay a thin bead of caulking on frame and place the clear glazing covers in their position. Finish the edges over the glazing with an aluminum angle. Place another thin bead of caulk under the aluminum angle. Drill through the aluminum and the acrylic glazing into the wood. When using glass, screw the angle on from the sides since it is somewhat difficult to drill through glass. Secure it in place with screws every six inches. If you ever have to remove it for maintenance, you can slip a thin knife under the angle and then the glazing to cut it loose.

12) Lay the front reflective lid on the ground in front of box. Attach the butt hinges at the bottom so it will close snugly against the front cover. Lay the top reflective lid on top of the box. Attach it with the butt hinges. Drill ½" holes in the tops of the ends of the box and insert a ½" dowel. It should extend out about 2". Make two lid supports from 1x3 lumber. Cut notches in them and drill $^{17}/_{32}$ inch holes in one end. Install a short piece of the ½" dowel in each side of the top lid. Slip the lid supports over the dowels. Adjust the position of the top lid with the notches in the lid supports. Place the adhesive-backed weatherstripping around the edge of the lid so it seals against the box when it is closed.

13) Position the solar water heater as close to the south side of your house as possible. Leave adequate space to get behind it in case any work has to be done. Contact your local weather service to find the exact true solar south direction in your area. It is not the same as the south on your compass.

14) Run the inlet and outlet pipes into your water heater. Pipe it into your water heater system as shown in the plumbing diagram below. Wrap the tubular foam pipe insulation over the outdoor sections of the pipes.

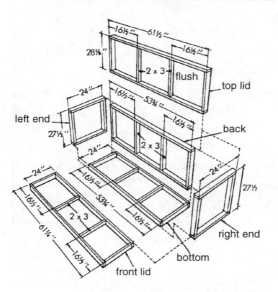

diagram #1

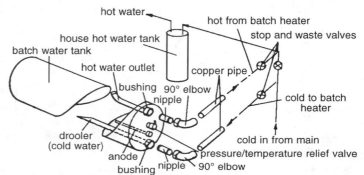

Fittings for batch water heater and to tie heater into house plumbing

Valve Settings (plumbing diagram)			
O = open C = closed	V1	V2	V3
Using solar	C	O	O
Not using solar	O	C	C

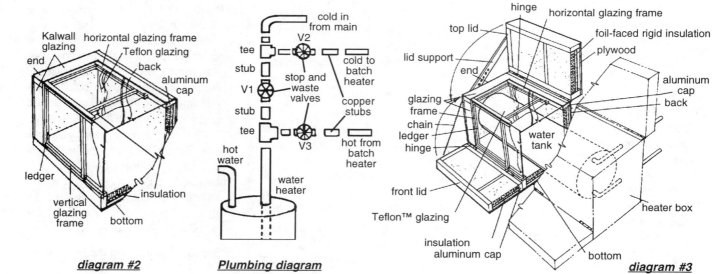

diagram #2   **Plumbing diagram**   **diagram #3**

3

Do-it-Yourself Instructions for Making a Basic Batch Solar Water Heater

When you build this batch solar water heater, make it as simple as you possibly can, using as many materials as possible that you already have on hand.

1) You will first need to get one or two water tanks depending on the size of the solar water heater you want. Two 40 gallon tanks are generally adequate. Check at your local plumbing supply outlet for old tanks.

2) Strip down the tanks to remove the outer covering and the insulation. Once you have the actual tanks, you will be able to see what has to be done. Your plumbing supply dealer can explain the details.

3) Paint the stripped tanks with two coats of flat black paint.

4) Make the basic rectangular frame using 2×4 lumber. Size it big enough for the tanks and plumbing with at least one foot clearance between the tanks. You will need that clearance to gain additional exposure to the sun. Use screws and wood glue to assemble the frame.

5) Attach the four 2×4 posts vertically at each corner of the base.

6) To support the tanks, mount two 2×4 supports vertically across the bottom of the frame base as shown in diagram #4 on page 4. Cut eight small pieces of the 2×4's to be used as the tank cradles. Nail the tank cradles to the horizontal tank supports.

7) Cover the sides and back of the box with plywood sheathing. Use the silicone caulk at all of the joints and seams to seal the box tightly.

8) Assemble the top frame using the 2×2 lumber. Cut the glazing 1" smaller than the outside dimension of the cover to allow for any thermal expansion. Lay the glazing in a bead of silicone and cover it with another bead of caulk. Then screw the corner flashing down over it to the frame.

9) Avoiding the glazing, drill clearance holes through the flashing and the top frame. These will be used for screws to mount the glazing cover to the box.

10) Cut and install the insulation in the bottom and sides of the box with the foil facing toward the inside. It is very important that the insulation fits tightly in the box with no gaps. Measure each side and carefully cut the pieces.

11) Measure the location of the water tanks in the box and make necessary plumbing to fit. You should run the inlet and outlet pipes into the back of the box.

12) Lay the water tanks in their cradles in the box. Tie the water tanks down with pipe strapping. Two straps over each tank should be adequate.

13) Cut exit holes in the bottom of the box for the pipes. Attach the pipes to the tanks. Put the weatherstripping over the top edge of the box and screw the glazing cover over that.

14) Using 2×4 lumber, make brackets to tilt the box up facing the sun. You should tilt it so that the back of the box makes an angle from the ground that is equal to your latitude angle for your area.

15) Set up the plumbing as shown in the diagram shown below. If you are using two tanks, then pipe them in series with the hot outlet from the first one to the inlet for the second one.

Materials for Batch Solar Water Heater

lumber — 2 x 2, 2×4 and ³/₈" exterior plywood
water tank — two stripped discarded
    water heater tanks
insulation — foil-faced rigid
insulation — tubular foam for pipes
glazing — clear acrylic, special solar glazing,
    or glass
caulking — silicone
weatherstripping — adhesive-backed foam
corner flashing
plumbing supplies — copper pipe, solder, fittings
Teflon tape and wood glue
paint — flat black or special solar paint,
    marine epoxy or exterior house paint
tape — aluminum foil duct tape
fasteners — nails, screws, strapping, butt hinges,
    brads, washers

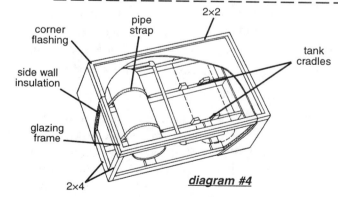

diagram #4

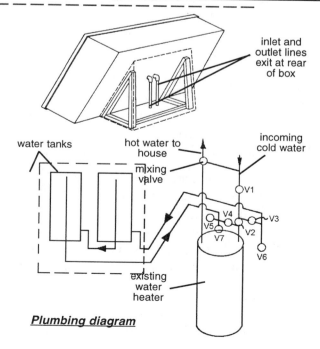

Plumbing diagram

Valve Operation (plumbing diagram)

O = open C = closed	V1	V2	V3	V4	V5	V6	V7
Solar only	O	C	O	C	O	C	C
Solar plus regular water heater backup	O	C	O	O	C	C	C
Winter shutdown	O	O	C	C	C	O	O

Solar water heater cuts utility bills year-round

Q: Does it make economic sense to install a solar water heater? I want a simple system that I can install and maintain myself to lower the cost of heating my water. What are the best types of solar water heaters available?

A: Installing a solar water heater can cut your annual utility bills by $200 or more for a typical family of four. Over the life of the solar system (many water heaters have ten-year warranties), one easily pays back its cost.

Changing technology of solar water heater is constantly improving the efficiency, appearance and ease of installation. Some collectors are so shallow that you cannot distinguish them from a flat skylight on the roof.

Many are sold as complete kits with all the components and fittings included. New solderless fittings and simple controls make installation easy for even the inexperienced do-it-yourselfer.

Evacuated tube solar collectors are one of the most efficient designs. These work like a Thermos™ bottle. The water flows in a finned copper pipe which is mounted inside a five-inch diameter glass tube.

The air is drawn out of the glass tube and sealed creating a vacuum, one of the best insulators available. Very little of the sun's heat gets wasted.

One unique evacuated tube design provides for the tubes to be rotated to face directly toward the sun. This allows the collector to be mounted flat or at any angle. It can therefore be hidden in an out-of-the-way place.

Standard flat plate solar collectors are an older, yet still effective design. With new types of foam

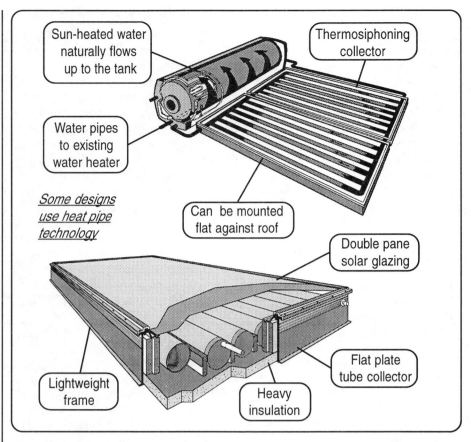

- Sun-heated water naturally flows up to the tank
- Thermosiphoning collector
- Water pipes to existing water heater
- *Some designs use heat pipe technology*
- Can be mounted flat against roof
- Double pane solar glazing
- Lightweight frame
- Heavy insulation
- Flat plate tube collector

insulation, like phenolic, and special black chrome energy absorbing paints, they are very efficient.

A hi-tech design by Thermomax uses the U.S. space program's heat pipe technology. The sun's heat is transferred to the water by means of a heat pipe. This is efficient, saves space and eliminates back flow heat loss.

Complete passive, thermosiphoning solar water heater kits (no pumps or controls) are the simplest and least expensive to install. The less dense hot water naturally circulates up to a built-in storage tank.

Active solar kits with pumps and electronic controls are most efficient and produce the greatest amount of hot water. These can either be connected to an existing water heater or to a specially designed new tank.

To simplify installation, many kits include a small solar cell panel to produce its own electricity. No standard wiring is required. This is a natural solar fit because the heat and electricity outputs are matched.

Q: There is too much glare from the lights in my kitchen. I was thinking of installing a dimmer switch, but I have never done any wiring. Is one easy to install and is it worthwhile?

A: Installing a dimmer switch is worthwhile and about your only option for overhead kitchen lighting. You must have standard incandescent bulbs, not fluorescent bulbs. Standard fluorescent bulbs cannot be dimmed.

Dimmer switches are easy to install. Always switch off the circuit breaker or remove the fuse. It is just a two-wire hookup, so following the package instructions is easy. Neatly bend the wires so they fit into the conduit box.

Manufacturers of Residential Solar Water Heating Systems

AMERICAN ENERGY TECH., PO Box 1865, Green Cove Springs, FL 32043 - (800) 874-2190 (904) 284-0552
system type - active and passive   collector type - flat plate   collector size* - 4×6 • 4×7 • 4×8 • 4×10 • 4×12
features - The collectors have a black chrome selective surface on all copper absorber plates. The box is constructed of lightweight extruded aluminum and the collectors are glazed with High-T low iron tempered glass. There are 6 systems available.

GULL INDUSTRIES, 2127 S. First St., San Jose, CA 95112 - (408) 293-3523
system type - active   collector type - flat plate   collector size - 4×8
features - The "Gull 5000C" is a retrofit system that you can hook up to your existing hot water system by using an auxiliary solar storage tank or by replacing your hot water tank with a solar storage tank that contains a back-up electric heating element. It has an anodized aluminum frame and a brushed bronze finish.

HELIOTROPE GENERAL, 3733 Kenora Dr., Spring Valley, CA 91977 - (800) 552-8838 (619) 460-3930
system type - active   collector type - flat plate   collector size - 3×8 • 4×8
features - The "Solar Sidebar" is powered with a 10 watt photovoltaic (PV) array and is installed on the side of your present water heater. The drain is removed and replaced with a new drain and the "Sidebar". From this, water lines are run to the collector and the other connection is the PV module wiring at the "Sidebar". The PV module is mounted on the side of the thermal collector. A high limit temperature sensor monitors the tank temperature and will stop solar pick-up when this temperatures is above either 180°F or 160°F. A mixing/tempering valve is installed at the heater's hot water outlet line to mix cold water with the hot if necessary. The outlet temperature will not exceed the setting of the valve.

HELIODYNE INC., 4910 Seaport Ave., Richmond, CA 94804 - (510) 237-9614
system type - active   collector type - flat plate   collector size - 4×8 • 4×10
features - The "Helio-Flo" system includes the "Gobi" collector, solar storage, pump, control, sensors, mild climate freeze protection and hardware. The "Helio-Pak" is a closed loop system with an anti-freeze/water mix and can be installed anywhere that is suitable, even in a vertical position. The "Gobi" collector is glazed, with a black-chrome selective surface on an all copper absorber.

RADCO PRODUCTS, 2877 Industrial Pky., Santa Maria, CA 93455 - (800) 927-2326 (805) 928-1881
system type - passive   collector type - flat plate   collector size - 4×8 • 4×10 • 4×12 • 11×4 • 11×6
features - The "Sunsation" is a complete kit that includes an all copper tank, bronze anodized aluminum exterior and dual heat exchangers. It is available with a 40 gallon, 60 gallon or 80 gallon tank. The "6000 Series" is a 8 or 12 gallon capacity drainback system. The heat exchange module is a factory-assembled unit that provides a heat exchanger, collector fluid reservoir, solar collector fluid circulator pump, hot water booster circulator pump and a differential temperature controller unit that is combined into one module.

SOLAHART INDUS., 939 S. 48th St., Suite 207, Tempe, AZ 85281 - (800) 233-7652
system type - passive   collector type - flat plate   collector size - one or two panels @ 3½×7
features - This is a complete system and does not require any pumps. The hot water is stored in an 80 gallon tank that is lined with two coats of vitreous enamel (glass). The tank is insulated with pressure injected high density polyurethane foam.

SOLAR DEVELOPMENT INC., 3607-A Prospect Ave., Riviera Beach, FL 33404 - (561) 842-8935
system type - active   collector type - flat plate   collector size - 4×8 • 4×10
features - These are complete kits that include everything, even a water tank. The "Now" and the "Pacemaker" systems are operated by a pump that is turned on and off by an appliance timer that is set to circulate the water throughout the day. The "Pacemaker" and "Sunraker" systems have an automatic freeze protection. A non-electric device opens when it approaches a freezing condition. When this happens, warm water from the tank passes through the collector and out of the valve. As the valve warms, it closes. A retrofit system, "Pacemaker II", is available with either 2×5 or 2×10 collectors to hook-up to your water heater. It has polyisocyanurate foam insulation under the absorber plate. The absorber plate is covered with a special black chrome coating. The "Sunstar 80" is designed for frequently freezing climates. In order to prevent freezing, the fluid that circulates is a combination of water and antifreeze that flows through a very long copper tube wrapped around the steel storage tank. It has a back-up heater if there is not enough sunshine during the day.

SUNQUEST, Route 1, Box 77E, Newton, NC 28658 - (828) 464-6419
system type - active   collector type - flat plate   collector size - 4×8 • 4×10 • 4×12 • 4×14
features - The "Fresource" is a two component system — the outdoor collector and an indoor thermal exchange appliance. You simply connect this to your existing water heater. It has a patented three-way, double wall copper heat exchanger. The clear collector cover will not crack or shatter. This system can be easily disassembled so you can take it with you if you should relocate.

SUN UTILITY NETWORK, 626 Wilshire Blvd., Suite 711, Los Angeles, CA 90017 - (800) 822-7652 (213) 623-9797
system type - active   collector type - evacuated tube   collector size - 2×8 • 4×8 • 6½×8
features - The "Sunfamily" system enclosure is made of polypropylene and all the metal parts consist of stainless steel. This protects it from rust and can be installed in salty environments. The hot water storage tube is made of stainless steel and provides a constant supply of clean hot water. The "Suntube" pipes that are connected to the header are insulated with fiberglass. These tubes can be installed on roofs, under eaves, in the garden or any place where sunlight is available. They can be installed horizontally, allowing you to integrate them into your individual surroundings.

You may need to use either one, two or three collectors, depending on your individual application.

6

THERMAL CONVERSION TECH., PO Box 3887, Sarasota, FL 34230 - (941) 953-2177
system type - passive   collector type - flat plate   collector size - 4×8
features - The "ProgressivTube" is a self-contained unit that acts as a solar collector and storage tank integrated into one piece of equipment. This unit is recommended for the sun-belt areas. See below for specifications and an illustration.

THERMOMAX, 6193 Wooded Run Dr., Columbia, MD 21044 - (410) 997-0778
system type - active   collector type - evacuated tube   collector size - 4×6 • 7¼×6
features - "Heat Pipe" operates like a radiant heating system. Solar hydronic space heating system has its own method of heat distribution. A double coil tank (a water tank with two heat exchangers) serves as water heater and heat distributor. Through a circulation pump and bottom coil solar energy heats the water in the tank. A thermostat calls for heat in a particular zone and the thermal energy is delivered through the top coil. Wwater in tank provides the household hot water demand.

ProgressivTube PT-40-CN by Thermal Technology

Glazing Gaskets — A continuous gasket made of special long life EPDM synthetic rubber is compressed by the glazing caps to seal out the weather. The inner glazing spline is made of high-temperature tolerant EPDM.

Case — The baked-on bronze acrylic finish of the hard temper extruded aluminum framewall and glazing caps assures years of attractive rust-free appearance. All rivets and bolts are aluminum or stainless steel. Aluminum back sheet .025".

Glazing — Outer glazing is tempered low-iron solar glass with 91% transmittance. Inner glazing is Teflon® film, known for its high temperature tolerance (525°F) and its long term durability and stability, transmittance 96%. The 1" air space between glazings reduces heat loss.

Fluid Connection — Inlet and outlet connections are made of nominal 1" diameter hard copper pipes. This allows for fast, leak-free plumbing hook-ups.

Absorber/Storage Tank — Constructed of copper, the 4" diameter tubes are welded to interconnecting pipes to form a series flow pattern. Tank is pressure rated to 300 psi, holds 41.13 gallons of water, coated with a high-temperature "selective" solar radiation absorption surface that maximizes heat gain and reduces heat loss.

Insulation — Rigid phenolic foam board, the most efficient insulation available, is used to maximize heat retention. Sides and ends of the unit have 1.5" board, R-value 12.5; bottom has 2" board, R-value 16.7; between tank tubes has 1.5" board, R-value 12.5.

Plumbing Diagrams for ProgressivTube PT-40-CN

Pre-Heater Solar Systems

With Electric Water Heaters

Legend
1. PT-40-CN
2. Freeze prevention valve (optional)
3. Roof jacks
4. Boiler drains — bronze
5. Pressure relief valve — 150 psi
6. 3-way ball valve — bronze
7. Check valve
8. Tempering valve (optional)
9. Conventional electric water heater
10. Temperature/Pressure relief valve — 210°F/150 psi

hot water out / cold water in / hot water inlet / hot water outlet / cold water inlet

With Gas Water Heaters

Legend
1. PT-40-CN
2. Freeze prevention valve (optional)
3. Roof jacks
4. Boiler drains — bronze
5. Pressure relief valve — 150 psi
6. 3-way ball valve — bronze
7. Check valve
8. Tempering valve — set between 140°F and 160°F
9. Conventional gas water heater
10. Temperature/Pressure relief valve — 210°F/150 psi

hot water out / cold water in / hot water outlet / cold water inlet

Direct Solar Systems

Ground Mount

Legend
1. PT-40-CN
2. Supply shut off valve — bronze gate or ball valve
3. Boiler drain — bronze
4. Pressure relief valve — 150 psi
5. Tempering valve — set between 120° and 145°F

hot out / cold in

Roof Mount

Legend
1. PT-40-CN
2. Roof jacks
3. Boiler drain — bronze
4. Supply shut off valve — bronze gate or ball valve
5. Tempering valve — set between 120° and 145°F
6. Pressure relief valve — 150 psi

hot out / cold in

Construction Section of The Gull 5000C by Gull Industries

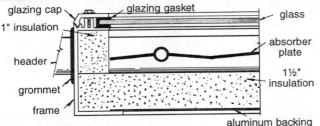

glazing cap / 1" insulation / header / grommet / frame / glazing gasket / glass / absorber plate / 1½" insulation / aluminum backing

System Placement and Sizing — The best position for a solar heating system for year-round performance is facing true south, tilted at an angle equal to the latitude of your location plus 10 degrees. However, panels which are pitched differently as much as plus or minus 15 degrees or which face east or west of south but up to 15 degrees will not severely hamper performance.

300 Series System by Solahart

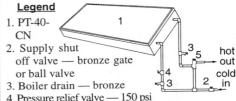

- Collectors are insulated with fiberglass for maximum heat retention/performance.
- The storage cylinder is protected from harsh water with two coats of Primaglaze vitreous enamel plus a sacrificial anode.
- Superior quality solar glass provides better performance, protection and appearance.
- Maximum absorption of solar energy is achieved by the large collectors designed to collect more heat and transfer it more efficiently.
- A sealed jacket is around tank. The closed circuit fluid flows from the solar panels around the outside of the tank and transfers its heat to the water in the tank. The result is hot water free from the sun.
- The cylinder is insulated in its tough aluminum case by pressure injected high density polyurethane foam. Your water stays hotter — longer.

The system types described for tropical regions are the "D", "DPV" and "FF". For hard freezing climates the "I", "IPV" and "DB" are shown. These systems can be sized to accommodate any load with maximized energy savings and design life.

Direct (Open Loop) Systems
"D" System — Diagram #1
(Differential Control)

This is the type of system most common in the Southern United States and Tropical Climates. As illustrated in diagram #1, the system consists of solar collector(s) installed on the roof and a hot water storage tank usually located in the garage or utility room. An alternating current (A/C) pump circulates the water from the tank up to the collector and back. This system is referred to as direct because the sun's heat is transferred through the collector directly to the potable water. No antifreeze solution or heat exchanger is required.

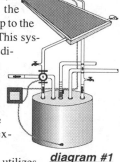

diagram #1

The "D" System utilizes a differential control to sense the temperature differences between water leaving the collector and the coldest water in the bottom of the storage tank. The control turns the pump on when the water in the collector is about 20°F warmer than the water in the tank. Similarly, the pump is turned off when the temperature variation is approximately 5°F. This process ensures that the water is always being heated while the pump is operating.

A thermally operated valve is installed at the collector to provide freeze protection where required. This valve will open to let warm water flow through the collector whenever temperatures approach freezing. As an alternative, the collector can be manually drained by closing the isolation valves and opening the drain valves (located above the storage tank).

Direct PV System (PV Drive)
"DPV" System — Diagram #2

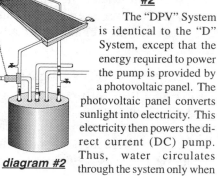

The "DPV" System is identical to the "D" System, except that the energy required to power the pump is provided by a photovoltaic panel. The photovoltaic panel converts sunlight into electricity. This electricity then powers the direct current (DC) pump. Thus, water circulates through the system only when

diagram #2

the sun is shining.

The DC pump and photovoltaic panel are suitably matched to ensure proper performance. The pump starts when there is sufficient solar radiation available to heat the thermal collector. It shuts off later in the day when the available solar energy diminishes. As in the "D" System, a thermally operated valve provides freeze protection or the collector can be manually drained.

Indirect (Closed Loop) Systems
"I" System — Diagram #3
(Differential Control)

The "I" System is designed to accommodate climates where freezing weather occurs more frequently. Instead of water flowing through the collector, an antifreeze solution is circulated. A heat exchanger is located within the storage tank. This maximizes the heat transfer from the antifreeze solution to the coldest water in the storage tank.

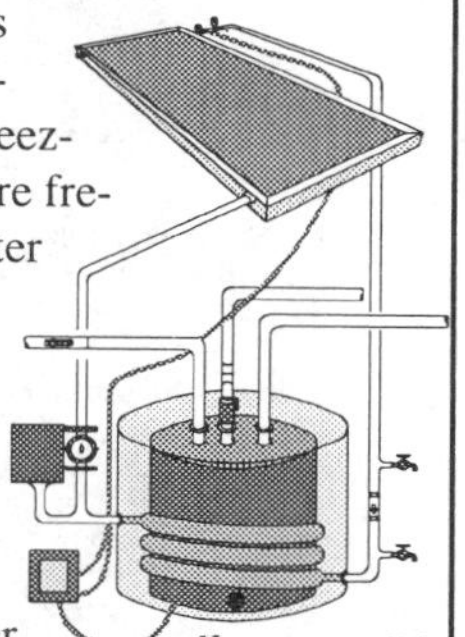

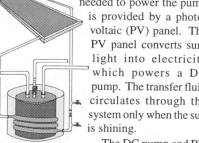

diagram #3

The "I" System is known as an indirect pumped system because the heat transfer solution, i.e., antifreeze is pumped through the collector in a closed loop. It never comes in direct contact with the potable water in the storage tank. The closed loop includes the collector, connecting piping, pump, expansion tank and heat exchanger. In this design, the large heat exchanger coil wraps around the perimeter of the storage tank.

As in the "D" System, the differential control determines when the pump should be activated and deactivated.

Indirect PV System (PV Drive)
"IPV" System — Diagram #4

The "IPV" System is similar to the "I" System except that the energy needed to power the pump is provided by a photovoltaic (PV) panel. The PV panel converts sunlight into electricity which powers a DC pump. The transfer fluid circulates through the system only when the sun is shining.

The DC pump and PV are suitably matched to ensure optimum performance. The pump starts when there is sufficient solar radiation available to heat the thermal collector. The pumping speed increases with the increase in the amount of

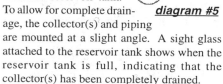

diagram #4

sunlight. This produces a flow rate matched to the level of heat transfer required. The system then shuts off when the available solar energy diminishes.

Drainback System
"DB" System — Diagram #5
(Drainback)

"DB" (Drainback) System provides a reliable method for ensuring that the collectors and their pipelines never freeze. This is done by removing all the water from the collector(s) and piping when the system is not producing heat. Freeze protection is provided when system is in drain mode. Each time the pump shuts off, the water in the collector(s) and piping drains into the insulated reservoir tank. To allow for complete drainage, the collector(s) and piping are mounted at a slight angle. A sight glass attached to the reservoir tank shows when the reservoir tank is full, indicating that the collector(s) has been completely drained.

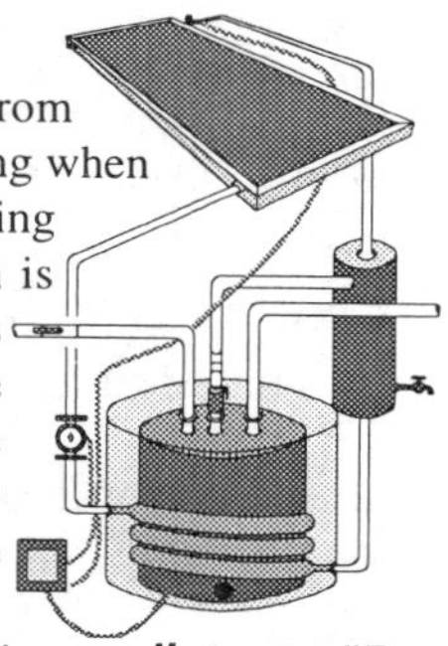

diagram #5

The differential control of the "DB" System activates the pump using the same strategy as the "D" System. The solution, distilled water or antifreeze, circulates in a closed loop never coming in direct contact with the potable water in the storage tank. The closed loop includes the collector, connecting piping, pump, reservoir tank and heat exchanger. The heat exchanger wraps around the perimeter of the storage tank, heating the potable water in tank.

Thermosiphon System "FF"
System — Diagram #6 (Free Flow)

The "Free Flow" (FF) System is widely accepted throughout the world today. It is automatic, simple and reliable. Diagram #6 illustrates a typical system.

All "Free Flow" Systems have their collector(s) positioned lower than their tank(s). As the sun heats the water in the collector, it "rises" into the tank in the same way that a hot air balloon "rises" in the air. The cold water in tank then "sinks" into collector. These events create a continuous process which results in a full tank of hot water by the end of the day.

"Free Flow" System does not require a pump or control. Cold water flows directly to the thermosiphon tank on roof where the water is heated. Solar heated water then flows from the thermosiphon tank to ground level where it is ready to use.

diagram #6

Home solar system is easy to construct

Q: I have some scrap building materials around and I want to build several low-cost solar collectors. I want two of them for heating our water and our house and one for the swimming pool. What design is best?

A: Although slightly more difficult to build than simple air-type solar collectors, water-type collectors are much more effective and versatile. Using scrap materials, you can build them for about $100 each. Super-efficient, hi-tech solar collector kits, like evacuated tubes, are available too.

A simple do-it-yourself water-type solar system can cut your water heating costs in half and add months of swimming pool use. Do not alternate the use of one collector between a pool and domestic water heating for health reasons.

Water-type solar collectors circulate water (antifreeze solution in cold climates) to absorb and transfer the sun's heat. Plain old water is one of the best solar storage and transfer media available.

Swimming pool solar collectors are easiest to make because they circulate pool water directly through the collector. Since the pool water is usually cooler than the air, heavy insulation and a glass cover are seldom needed.

In contrast, when heating domestic water, the water temperature must be raised much higher than the air temperature. Insulation is needed on the back of the collector with single or double pane glazing on the top.

If you can repair a bathroom faucet, you should be able to build your own solar collector. Special electric water heater tanks, with built-in solar heat transfer coils, are available from major manufacturers.

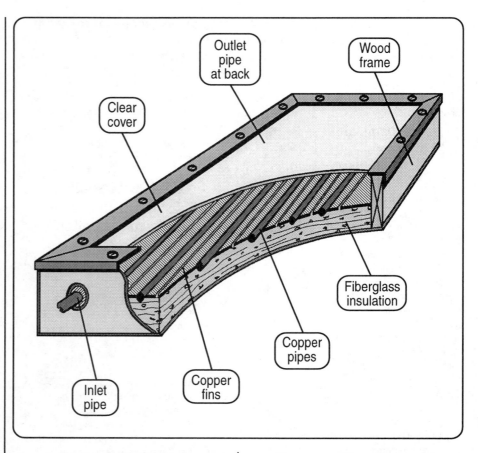

A thermosiphoning solar system design does not require a pump to circulate the water. An insulated storage tank is located above the collector so the solar-heated water (hot water is less dense) naturally flows up to it.

A simple active water-type collector consists of a shallow insulated box with a clear cover. When it is completed, locate it in a sunny location on the ground instead of on the roof. This provides easier access for cleaning the glass or plastic top. The plumbing is also easier to attach.

Make a shallow collector box frame from 2x6 pressure-treated lumber and plywood. Lay fiberglass insulation batts in the bottom of the box. This blocks heat loss out the back of the collector. Use easy-to-cut clear acrylic plastic or glass for the top. Make sure all the joints are caulked.

Run small copper pipes, painted flat black, vertically in the collector. Attach the pipes to larger horizontal (header) pipes at each end. For more efficiency, solder flat copper fins to the copper collector pipes.

Q: My neighbor is a cleaning nut. She even cleans off the light bulbs in her lamps and claims it saves electricity. Is there really any point to dusting light bulbs?

A: Actually, your neighbor may not be the nutty one in your neighborhood. Just a fine layer of dust on a light bulb can reduce the light output by 20%. This often forces you to switch on another lamp for adequate lighting.

Gently wipe off each light bulb with a damp cloth every several weeks. Unplug the lamp before wiping it. Make sure the bulb has been off for at least five minutes so that it is cool or the glass may crack.

Do-It-Yourself Instructions for Making a Water-type Solar Collector

This type of solar collector utilizes a header/riser panel design. Copper pipes and absorber plates are energy efficient and copper is fairly easy to work with. The glazing cover can be made of many materials - glass (tempered and annealed or low-iron tempered and annealed), acrylic, polycarbonate, fiberglass reinforced polyester, or polyvinyl fluoride. Check with local plastic material suppliers for the non-glass glazing materials.

1) A good collector size is 96" by 48" outside dimensions. Lumber and other materials for this size are easy to find.

2) Make the frame for the solar collector using 2×6 lumber. Standard lumber will work, but pressure-treated lumber is best. When using pressure-treated lumber, follow the suppliers guidelines for handling and safety precautions. You might want to consider treating the lumber after assembly. Therefore, the treating chemicals won't reduce the adhesion power of any glues that you use. Using dowels at the corner joints will increase the strength.

3) Nail and glue the plywood base on to the bottom of the frame. Drill several small weep holes in the back of the frame to let any moisture escape. Paint the inside and outside of the frame. Cut a wood center support to fit across the frame. This supports the glazing in the center of the frame. Do not nail it into place yet.

4) You need eight copper riser pipes and two header pipes. Make the header pipes using ¾" copper pipe and the risers using ½" copper pipe. The header pipes should be cut to lengths of about 4⅛" long to fit between the ¾" × ¾" × ½" tees. The riser pipes should be about 90 inches long. This will allow for expansion as the pipes heat in the sun. If they are too long, the header pipe will be too close to the inside of the frame. Trial assemble all the pipes together in the collector frame to make sure they fit properly.

5) Make the eight absorber plates using

Required Materials

2x6 pressure-treated lumber
2x4 lumber
1/4" plywood
1/2" type M copper pipe (risers)
3/4" type M copper pipe (headers)
.010 or .020 copper sheet
3/4" x 3/4" x 1/2" tees
3-1/2" foil-faced fiberglass
    or mineral wool insulation
1-1/2" aluminum screws
2-1/2" threaded aluminum nails
glass or clear acrylic sheet
aluminum angle
rubber washers
silicone caulking

.020" copper sheet metal. They should be about 88" long and 5¼" wide after they are formed with the groove for the riser pipe. Trim one of the center

How to form absorber plate

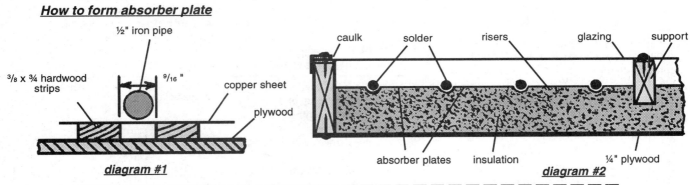

³/₈ x ¾ hardwood strips   ½" iron pipe   ⁹/₁₆ "   copper sheet   plywood

diagram #1

caulk   solder   risers   glazing   support

absorber plates   insulation   ¼" plywood

diagram #2

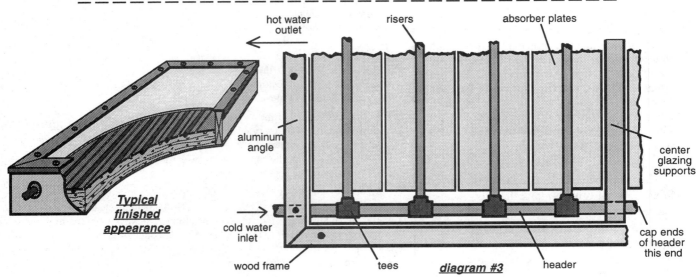

hot water outlet   risers   absorber plates

aluminum angle

Typical finished appearance

cold water inlet

wood frame   tees   *diagram #3*   header

center glazing supports

cap ends of header this end

absorber plates narrower to leave clearance for the center wood support for the glazing. An easy way to form the groove is to make a simple 8-foot long wood jig. See diagram #2 on page 10. Press a ½" steel pipe down to form the groove in the copper.

6) Clean the copper risers and the grooves in the absorber plates with steel wool. Place the riser pipes in the plates. Using a propane torch, sweat solder into the joint attaching the risers to the plates. Make sure you get a continuous bead of solder connecting the two pieces. This is essential for good heat transfer from the absorber plates to the water in the risers.

7) Solder the tees and header pipe pieces to the riser/absorber plate assemblies. Cap off one end of both header pipes (same end of each). The other ends are the inlet and outlet that extend out the holes in the sides of the frame.

8) When the entire piping system is soldered and assembled, pressure test it with water and resolder any leaky spots.

9) Paint the copper assembly with high-temperature flat black paint to increase the solar heat gain. A flat black barbecue or automotive engine paint should work.

10) Use 3½" foil-faced fiberglass or rock wool insulation batts in the bottom of the frame. Install the insulation with the foil facing upward. Staple the edges of the foil facing to the sides of the frame. This keeps it from settling when the collector is mounted up on an angle to face the sun. Seal the joints of the foil facing with duct tape.

11) Drill holes in the side of the frame for the inlet and outlet header pipes. Gently, slip the inlet and outlet pipes through the holes in the sides of the frame and lower the absorber assembly into the frame on top of the insulation. Using pipe strapping, secure the header pipes to the sides of the frame. Seal the gap between the inlet and outlet pipes and the frame.

12) Nail the wood support for the glazing across the center of the collector. You may have to notch it to clear the header pipes. Lay a bead of caulk along the top edge of the frame and the center support. Place the glazing on top of the frame. Lay another bead of caulk on top of the glazing and place aluminum angle over that. If plastic glazing is used, you can drill through that and nail it on from the top.

13) If you use glass, screw (don't nail) on the angle pieces from the sides. Since the glass may get broken and need to be replaced, use gaskets or weatherstripping instead of caulk. Low-iron content glass allows the most solar energy to pass through, but it is more expensive. Check with a solar designer or system dealer in your area to find a local source.

This is a representation of the skyspace for a site at 36° north latitude according to the solstice azimuth angles. If you're studying your site primarily for space heating you're probably interested in finding shadow makers in the lower half of the skyspace band. For year-round domestic water heating, you should look for objects throughout the band, particularly those nearest to true south, where at solar noon insolation peaks.

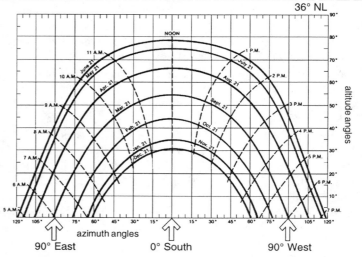

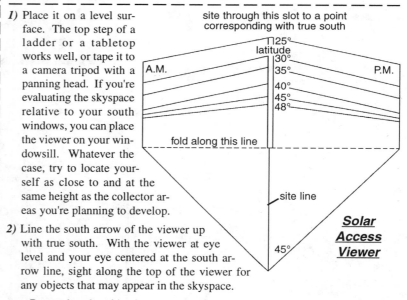

This typical chart shows the position of the sun in the sky for various times of the day and days of the year. The azimuth angles are how far from true solar south that the sun is. The altitude angle is the height of the sun in the sky. This chart is for 36° latitude. For more northern areas (greater latitude angle), the sun will be lower year-round. For southern areas, the sun will be higher in the sky.

1) Place it on a level surface. The top step of a ladder or a tabletop works well, or tape it to a camera tripod with a panning head. If you're evaluating the skyspace relative to your south windows, you can place the viewer on your windowsill. Whatever the case, try to locate yourself as close to and at the same height as the collector areas you're planning to develop.

2) Line the south arrow of the viewer up with true south. With the viewer at eye level and your eye centered at the south arrow line, sight along the top of the viewer for any objects that may appear in the skyspace.

Remember that this viewer is not a precision tool and is meant to help you make a rough survey of your skyspace. Use a compass to locate the solar azimuth at 9:00 A.M. and use the viewer to sight the altitude. Note any objects protruding above your line of sight, since they will shade your collector in the morning. Then repeat the process, rotating through south to the west, correlating azimuth and altitude as many times as you need to see where shadows will be.

Thermosiphon Water Heaters

Thermosiphon systems consist of a solar collector panel to absorb solar heat and a separate storage tank, either built-in at the top of the collector or placed inside the house, to hold solar-heated water. The solar collector is faced true south at an angle equal to the latitude. It must be mounted at least a foot below the storage tank to permit thermosiphoning - upward movement of water by natural convection. When the water in the collector is heated, it becomes less dense and rises to the top of the storage tank. At the same time, cool water from the bottom of the tank flows into the bottom of the collector.

Although thermosiphon systems can be quite efficient and supply 40 to 60 percent of your hot water, two problems keep them from being used more often. First, because storage tank must be installed above collector, it is often placed on an upper floor or high in attic above the roof rafter. In some cases, roof or flooring may have to be reinforced because water tanks are quite heavy. Of course, collectors can be placed on the ground if an adequate site is available.

In an indirect (or closed-loop) system, an antifreeze solution is pumped through a heat exchanger, where it gives up its heat to the house water supply.

Second, thermosiphon collectors in their simplest form contain no safeguard against freezing. This is important because water remains in the collector whenever convection stops (during sunless periods). If this water freezes, it can expand with enough force to burst the piping of the tank. Freezing can be prevented by using movable insulation, an antifreeze/water solution, or by installing a valve allowing the water to be drained at night. But operating a thermosiphon water heater is cheaper and easier in areas where freezing does not occur. If used elsewhere, the simplest solution is to drain them before the first frost.

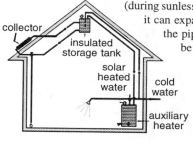

In a thermosiphoning system, cold water flows from the bottom of the tank to the bottom of the collector, and returns to the tank when warmed.

Active Systems

Unlike passive systems, active domestic hot water systems use electrically driven pumps and valve to control the circulation of the heat absorbing liquid. This allows a greater degree of flexibility than their passive counterparts since the hot water storage tank does not have to be above or near the collectors. Also, active systems are designed to operate all year round without any danger of freezing.

All systems fall within four main categories — draindown, drainback, indirect and phase change.

Draindown

In a draindown system, water is pumped from the hot water storage tank up to the collectors and back again. It derives its name from the electrically-powered draindown valve which is the key to its freeze protection system. When the sun is out, the valve is open and the pump circulates water through the pressurized solar loop. When there is not enough solar gain and the outdoor temperature drops near 32°F (in clear, dry climates, night sky radiation can draw enough heat from collectors to cause freezing at an ambient temperature of 40°F), a sensor signals the central controller to close the valve. This causes the pressure in the loop to drop, and all the water in the collectors and the exposed plumbing empties out through a special opening into a house drain. When the temperature rises above 32°F, the draindown valve will open and the pump will once again begin circulating the water.

Drainback

When the temperature falls near the freezing point the drainback system, like the draindown one, empties its collectors of water to avoid free[z] damage. The difference betwe[en] the two is that the water that for[ms] in the collectors in the drainba[ck] system empties back into a holdi[ng] tank and is saved. Another diffe[r]ence is that the loop between the holding tank and the collectors is not pressurized. Therefore, when the thermostat signals the pump to turn off, the water drains by force of gravity. No electric valves are used which might fail.

In a pumped draindown unit, solar heated water flows to the storage tank for direct use by the household. When the pump shuts off, whatever water remains in the collector drains away by gravity flow.

Recommended Glazing Systems									
Type of Material	Thick-ness	Weight/area (lb./sq. ft.)	% Solar Transmittance	Thermal Expansion	Max. Temp. °F	Estimated Life (yrs)	Trans-parent	Trans-lucent	Notes
Standard Float Glass	3/16"	2.4	84	0.47	400	very long	x		Excellent esthetic quality; large double and triple-glazed units heavy, but otherwise easy to install.
Low-iron Glass	3/16"	2.4	91	0.47	400	very long	x	x	
Acrylic (Plexiglas)	1/8"	.7	93	4.0	180	20	x		High transmittance; lightweight; does not yellow. Scratches easily; may become brittle with age; large thermal expansion.
Polycarbonate (Lexan)	1/8"	.75	87	3.3 to 4.0	270	10	x	x	High-impact strength. Large thermal expansion; some yellowing with age.
Fiberglass Reinforced Plastic	.025" to .04"	.25	81 to 85	1.36	160 to 225	15		x	Available in 4' & 5' wide rolls, and double-glazed panels.
Films (Tedlar)	4 mil	.03	92	2.8	150	5		x	High transmittance; low cost. Recommended for inner glazings only.
Films (Teflon)	1 mil	.02	96	5.9	300	25	x	x	

Capture the wind's power for free electricity

Q: I have always been intrigued by generating my own electricity with a windmill. Are there any residential-size units available that I could use in my backyard? Can I sell any excess electricity it generates back to my utility company?

A: There are many sizes of electric-generating windmills available for residential use. Some inexpensive tiny models are portable and weigh only 13 pounds. These are also ideal for a backyard workshop, garage, when camping out or on boats or RV's.

One tiny model, Air Wind, has a 45-inch diameter rotor (blade) and can be mounted on a roof. It produces a maximum of 300 watts and starts producing electricity in only a 5-mph wind.

Another 20-pound portable windmill quickly collapses to be carried under your arm. It uses a 41-inch one-piece natural poplar rotor. With a direct-drive generator (no gears needed), it is practically maintenance free.

Depending on your budget, you can install a small windmill to produce just a fraction of the electricity your family requires or a larger one to supply most of your electric needs. Once installed, it produces free electricity for many years.

At times when your windmill produces more electricity than you need, some utility companies will purchase the extra electricity. If it is a small amount, they often allow your electric meter to just run in reverse. If you produce a lot of extra electricity, they will buy it, but it will be bought at a discounted price.

All windmills have overspeed protection for high-wind, stormy weather. Some automatically tilt back in high wind and others rotate

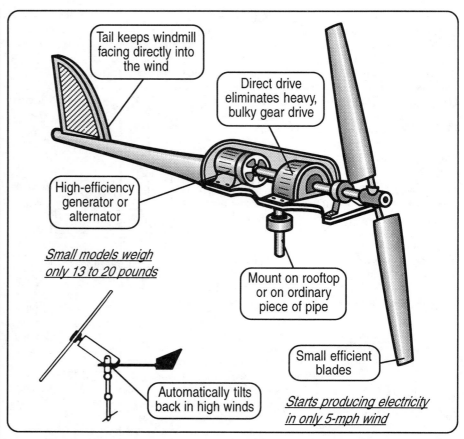

Tail keeps windmill facing directly into the wind

Direct drive eliminates heavy, bulky gear drive

High-efficiency generator or alternator

Small models weigh only 13 to 20 pounds

Mount on rooftop or on ordinary piece of pipe

Small efficient blades

Automatically tilts back in high winds

Starts producing electricity in only 5-mph wind

out of the wind. A typical whole-house residential-size windmill has a rotor blade diameter of 20 feet and a rated output of about 10,000 watts of electricity. An automatic computerized "brain" controls the electricity output and frequency to match your utility company's output.

A small windmill can power refrigerators, lights, TV's, power tools, etc. The ideal system attaches to car-type batteries and includes a small solar photovoltaic (PV) panel. On calm, sunny days, the PV panel powers the system.

Before you invest in a larger whole-house windmill, check the typical wind conditions in your area to determine its feasibility. Just a small increase in wind speed from 10 to 18 mph can quadruple the electricity output.

If you have an electric water heater, the electricity from the wind-

mill can be used to heat the water. This is a very inexpensive method to capture the excess electricity that is not currently being used.

Q: Each spring, I spray (and waste) a lot of water trying to flush out my gutters. I'm older and I do not like getting up on a ladder. Is there any simple way to clean them without using all that water?

A: There is a low-cost do-it-yourself water-saving gutter cleaner. Buy enough thick-wall 3/4-in. PVC pipe to reach one foot over your gutter.

Glue a hose coupling onto one end. Glue on two 90-degree elbows with a short straight piece in between them. Glue another short piece to the end elbow to form a "J" shape. Glue a cap on the end.

Drill four holes in one side of the cap. These spray water out the side to quickly clean the gutter of clogs and debris.

There are many sizes of windmills available from small portable to large whole-house models. The following pages list the major windmill manufacturers and information about their products. Since the price of installing a windmill increases with its size, choose the smallest one that will meet your needs.

Large whole-house systems will produce more electricity than you can sometimes use. Check with your local utility company about its policy on buying back excess electricity that your windmill produces.

Another option for storing the excess electricity is to use it to heat your hot water. The diagram opposite shows a schematic of how this is set up. A bank of lead-acid batteries can also be used to store the electricity. Electricity from the batteries runs through an inverter first so it can be used to operate common household appliances.

Using an array of solar cells (photovoltaics) is a good fit with a windmill. On sunny days, the solar cells produce electricity even when the wind is calm.

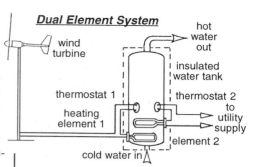

Dual Element System

Manufacturers of Whole-House and Portable Windmills

ATLANTIC ORIENT CORP., PO Box 1097, Norwich, VT 05055 - (802) 649-5446

model - "AOC 8/12"	rated power - 12,000 watts	voltage output - 12 to 24 volt	weight - n/a
start up wind speed - 7 mph	rated wind speed - 25 mph	number of blades - 3	rotor diameter - 24 ft.
model - "AOC 15/50"	rated power - 50,000 watts	voltage output - 12 to 24 volt	weight - n/a
start up wind speed - 8 mph	rated wind speed - 28 mph	number of blades - 3	rotor diameter - 45 ft.

BERGEY WIND POWER, 2001 Priestly Ave., Norman, OK 73069 - (405) 364-4212

model - "BWC 850"	rated power - 850 watts	voltage output - 12 to 24 volt	weight - 86 lbs.
start up wind speed - 8 mph	rated wind speed - 28 mph	number of blades - 3	rotor diameter - 8 ft.
model - "BWC 1500"	rated power - 1500 watts	voltage output - 12 to 120 volt	weight - 168 lbs.
start up wind speed - 8 mph	rated wind speed - 28 mph	number of blades - 3	rotor diameter - 10 ft.
model - "BWC Excel"	rated power - 10,000 watts	voltage output - 48 or 120 volt	weight - 1050 lbs.
start up wind speed - 7.5 mph	rated wind speed - 29 mph	number of blades - 3	rotor diameter - 23 ft.

LAKE MICHIGAN WIND & SUN, 1015 County Rd "U", Sturgeon Bay, WI 54235 - (920) 743-0456
This company specializes in the repair and re-manufacture of residential size wind systems. The company can supply parts for almost any residential wind generator. The company is a distributor for small wind systems.

NORTHERN POWER CORP., PO Box 999, Waitsfield, VT 05673 - (802) 496-2955

model - "HR-3"	rated power - 3000 watts	voltage output - 48 volt	weight - 880 lbs.
start up wind speed - 8 mph	rated wind speed - 28 mph	number of blades - 3	rotor diameter - 16 ft.

SOUTHWEST WINDPOWER, 2131 N. First St., Flagstaff, AZ 86004 - (520) 779-9463

model - "Air Wind Module"	rated power - 300 watts	voltage output - 12 to 60 volt	weight - 13 lbs.
start up wind speed - 6 mph	rated wind speed - 28 mph	number of blades - 3	rotor diameter - 45 in.
model - "Windseeker 502"	rated power - 500 watts	voltage output - 12 to 180 volt	weight - 20 lbs.
start up wind speed - 5 mph	rated wind speed - 30 mph	number of blades - 2	rotor diameter - 5 ft.
model - "Windseeker 503"	rated power - 500 watts	voltage output - 12 to 24 volt	weight - 20 lbs.
start up wind speed - 5 mph	rated wind speed - 30 mph	number of blades - 3	rotor diameter - 5 ft.

TRILLIUM WINDMILLS, 1843 Marchmont Rd., RR #2, Orillia, Ontario, L3V, 6H2, Canada - (800) 787-8470

model - "Furlmatic 910"	rated power - 150 watts	voltage output - 12 or 24 volt	weight - 38 lbs.
start up wind speed - 4 mph	rated wind speed - 36 mph	number of blades - 6	rotor diameter - 3 ft.

WIND BARON CORP., 2101 North 4th. St., Suite 218, Flagstaff, AZ 96004 - (520) 774-6341

model - "Wind Baron 750"	rated power - 750 watts	voltage output - 12 to 48 volt	weight - 38 lbs.
start up wind speed - 6 mph	rated wind speed - 30 mph	number of blades - 3	rotor diameter - 6.17 ft.

WINDBUGGER, PO Box 259, Key Largo, FL 33037 - (305) 247-2868

model - "Windbugger"	rated power - 250 watts	voltage output - 12 to 24 volt	weight - 40 lbs.
start up wind speed - 5 mph	rated wind speed - n/a	number of blades - 3	rotor diameter - 4.2 ft.

features - This self-contained unit is all aluminum weather tight marine grade construction. The pole mount rotates 360°.

WINDPOWER TECH., INC., 1135 Lakeshore Rd., Grafton, WI 53024 - (414) 375-3660
This company specializes in advanced high-tech components and fiberglass rotors for many wind systems. They are a distributor and sell new and used systems. The company also sells a complete line of generators, inverters, towers, controls and monitoring equipment.

WINDTECH INTN'L, L.L.C., 1899 Powers Ferry Rd., Ste. 200, Atlanta, GA 30339 - (914) 232-2354

model - "Oasis 3" start up wind speed - 5 mph water draw - 500 gal./hr. from depth of 30 ft. in 7 mph windspeed
model - "Oasis 7" start up wind speed - 5 mph water draw - 2000 gal./hr. from depth of 30 ft. in 7 mph windspeed

These are water-pumping windmills, designed to pump water in wind speeds as low as 2 mph to 8 mph from depths reaching 4,000 feet. These systems can be used for irrigation, land reclamation or drinking water in remote areas. The installation of the "Oasis" windmill is very easy with the bolt-together assembly of standard steel components.

WIND STREAM POWER SYSTEMS, PO Box 1604, Burlington, VT 05402 - (802) 658-0075

model - "Windstream" rated power - 300 watts voltage output - 12 to 14 volt weight - 20 lbs.
start up wind speed - 8 mph rated wind speed - 29 mph number of blades - 2 rotor diameter - 41.5 in.
features - This a portable windmill that quickly collapses and is easily carried under the arm by one person. The rotor is a one-piece blade and is constructed of natural poplar.

WIND TURBINE INDUSTRIES CORP., 16801 Industrial Circle SE, Prior Lake, MN 55372 - (612) 447-6064

model - "Jacobs 23-10" rated power - 10,000 watts voltage output - 180 volt weight - 1400 lbs.
start up wind speed - 8 mph rated wind speed - 26 mph number of blades - 3 rotor diameter - 23 ft.
model - "Jacobs 23-12.5" rated power - 12,500 watts voltage output - 180 volt weight - n/a
start up wind speed - 8 mph rated wind speed - 26 mph number of blades - 3 rotor diameter - 23 ft.
model - "Jacobs 26-15" rated power - 15,000 watts voltage output - 180 volt weight - n/a
start up wind speed - 8 mph rated wind speed - 26 mph number of blades - 3 rotor diameter - 26 ft.
model - "Jacobs 26-17.5" rated power - 17,500 watts voltage output - 180 volt weight - n/a
start up wind speed - 8 mph rated wind speed - 26 mph number of blades - 3 rotor diameter - 26 ft.
model - "Jacobs 29-20" rated power - 20,000 watts voltage output - 240 volt weight - 2300 lbs.
start up wind speed - 8 mph rated wind speed - 25.5 mph number of blades - 3 rotor diameter - 29 ft.

WORLD POWER TECH., 19 Lake Ave. N., Duluth, MN 55802 - (218) 722-1492

model - "Mariner H500" rated power - 500 watts voltage output - 12 or 24 volt weight - 29 lbs.
start up wind speed - 7.5 mph rated wind speed - 29 mph number of blades - 3 rotor diameter - 4.9 ft.
model - "Whisper 600" rated power - 600 watts voltage output - 12 to 240 volt weight - 47/49 lbs.
start up wind speed - 7 mph rated wind speed - 25 mph number of blades - 2 or 3 rotor diameter - 7 ft.
model - "Whisper 1000" rated power - 1000 watts voltage output - 12 to 240 volt weight - 65/70 lbs.
start up wind speed - 7 mph rated wind speed - 25 mph number of blades - 2 or 3 rotor diameter - 9 ft.
model - "Whisper H1300" rated power - 1300 watts voltage output - 12 to 240 volt weight - 64/69 lbs.
start up wind speed - 8 mph rated wind speed - 29 mph number of blades - 2 or 3 rotor diameter - 8 ft.
model - "Whisper 3000" rated power - 3000 watts voltage output - 24 to 240 volt weight - 155/170 lbs.
start up wind speed - 7 mph rated wind speed - 25 mph number of blades - 2 or 3 rotor diameter - 14.8 ft.
model - "Whisper H500" rated power - 8500 watts voltage output - 48 to 240 volt weight - 480/520 lbs.
start up wind speed - 8 mph rated wind speed - 29 mph number of blades - 2 or 3 rotor diameter - 20 ft.

BWC 1500 Specifications — by Bergey Windpower

Start up wind speed	7.5 mph (3.4 m/s)
Cut in wind speed	7.0 mph (3.1 m/s)
Rated wind speed	29.0 mph (13.0 m/s)
Rated power	10 kilowatts
Cut out wind speed	None
Furling wind speed	35 mph (15.63 m/s)
Max design wind speed	120 mph (53.6 m/s)
Type	3 Blade upwind
Rotor diameter	23.0 ft (7.0 m)
Weight	1050 lbs (477 kg)
Blade pitch control	Powerflex®
Overspeed protection	Autofurl™
Gearbox/Belts	None, Direct Drive
Temperature range	-40° to +140°F (-40° to +60°C)
Generator	Permanent magnet alternator
Output form	3 Phase AC, variable frequency
With VCS-10	Regulated DC, 48v - 120v
With Powersync® Inverter	Nominal 240 VAC

The BWC Excel Wind Turbine System

The BWC Excel is a 10 kilowatt wind turbine designed to supply most of the electricity for an average total electric home in areas with an average wind speed of 12 mph. In remote locations, it can charge batteries for stand-alone applications or pump water electrically without the need for batteries. Simple and rugged, the BWC Excel is designed for high and automatic operation in adverse weather conditions. It is available in three versions.

BWC Excel-S — a 240 VAC, 60 Hz interconnect system. Includes the (50Hz optional), 10 utility in-Powersync® Inverter.

BWC Excel-R — a 120 VDC (48 VDC optional) remote battery charging system. Includes the VCS-10 Control System.

BWC Excel-PD — a 30 AC system that can drive submersible or surface-mounted pumps. Includes the PCU-10 Control System.

11.5 ft. (3.5 m)

15.7 ft. (4.8 m)

Siting and Towers — Windstream Power Systems

Siting the Wind Generator — The Windstream should be securely mounted in clear air, well away from or above any obstructions such as trees or buildings, to avoid turbulence and loss of power. **Towers** — The Windstream is designed to be mounted on a threaded 48 mm OD (1½ inch schedule 40) pipe, but can be erected on almost any pipe, pole, or lattice (TV type) tower. The mounting structure must be securely guyed, to prevent vibration. **Tower Height** — The tower should be as high as practical in any installation, at least 3m (10 ft.) higher than any nearby obstructions. For boats, RVs and other portable applications, the basic 3m tower can be used alone. The velocity of the wind increases with its height above ground, so the higher the tower, generally the more energy is available from the wind.

turbulence from buildings or trees
tilt-up mast on RV
guyed lattice tower
stern mount on boat

Annual Percentage Frequency of Wind by Speed Groups and the Mean Speed

State and Station	0-3 mph	4-7 mph	8-12 mph	13-18 mph	19-24 mph	25-31 mph	32-38 mph	39-46 mph	47 mph and over	Mean speed mph
ALABAMA										
Birmingham	27	22	30	17	3	1	*	*	*	7.9
Mobile	10	28	38	20	6	1	*	*	*	10.0
Montgomery	31	29	27	12	2	*	*			6.9
ALASKA										
Anchorage	28	35	25	11	2	*	*	*		6.8
Cold Bay	4	9	18	27	21	14	5	2	*	17.4
Fairbanks	40	35	19	5	1	*	*			5.2
ARIZONA										
Phoenix	38	36	20	5	1	*	*			5.4
Tucson	18	35	30	14	3	1	*			8.1
ARKANSAS										
Little Rock	12	30	39	16	2	1	*			8.7
CALIFORNIA										
Burbank	52	26	18	4	1	*	*			4.5
Fresno	30	41	22	7	1	*				6.1
Los Angeles	28	33	27	11	1	*	*	*		6.8
Oakland	26	28	28	16	2	1	*	*		7.5
Sacramento	15	28	31	18	5	1	*	*		9.3
San Diego	28	38	28	6	*	*				6.3
San Francisco	16	21	26	22	11	3	*	*		10.6
COLORADO										
Denver	11	27	34	22	5	2	*	*		10.0
CONNECTICUT										
Hartford	13	26	32	24	6	1	*			9.8
DELAWARE										
Wilmington	15	31	30	19	4	1	*	*		8.8
FLORIDA										
Jacksonville	10	33	35	18	3	*	*	*		8.9
Miami	14	30	34	20	2	*	*			8.8
Orlando	18	28	32	17	4	1	*			8.6
Tallahassee	33	36	23	7	*	*	*			6.1
Tampa	9	31	40	16	2	*	*			8.8
GEORGIA										
Atlanta	13	24	36	21	6	1	*	*		9.7
Augusta	36	29	25	9	1	*	*			6.3
Macon	10	26	46	16	2	*	*			8.9
Savannah	12	34	37	14	3	1	*			8.4
HAWAII										
Honolulu	9	17	27	32	12	2	*			12.1
IDAHO										
Boise	15	30	32	18	4	1	*			8.9
ILLINOIS										
Chicago	8	22	33	27	8	2	*	*		11.2
Moline	14	23	32	24	7	2	*			10.0
Springfield	7	22	28	27	12	3	1	*		12.0
INDIANA										
Evansville	19	23	32	21	5	1	*			9.1
Fort Wayne	9	23	33	25	8	2	*			10.9
Indianapolis	9	22	34	26	7	2	*	*		10.8
IOWA										
Des Moines	3	17	38	29	10	3	1	*		12.1
Sioux City	10	20	31	25	10	4	1			11.7
KANSAS										
Topeka	11	19	30	27	10	2	*	*	*	11.2
Wichita	4	12	30	31	16	5	1	*	*	13.7
KENTUCKY										
Lexington	8	25	39	22	6	1	*	*		10.1
Louisville	17	28	31	20	3	1	*	*		8.8
LOUISIANA										
Baton Rouge	17	29	34	17	3	*	*			8.3
New Orleans	16	27	32	19	5	1	*			9.0
Shreveport	12	26	37	21	4	1	*			9.5
MAINE										
Portland	10	30	33	22	4	1	*			9.6
MARYLAND										
Baltimore	7	24	39	22	6	2	*	*		10.4
MASSACHUSETTS										
Boston	3	12	33	35	12	4	1	*		13.3
MICHIGAN										
Detroit	8	23	37	26	5	1	*	*		10.3
Grand Rapids	14	23	32	25	5	1	*			9.8
MINNESOTA										
Duluth	6	15	33	31	11	4	1	*		12.6
Minneapolis	8	21	34	28	9	2	*			11.2
MISSISSIPPI										
Jackson	33	25	26	14	2	*	*			7.1
MISSOURI										
Kansas City	9	29	35	23	5	1	*			9.8
St. Louis	10	29	36	21	5	1	*			9.3
Springfield	4	13	34	32	13	3	*	*		12.9
MONTANA										
Great Falls	7	19	24	24	15	9	3	1		13.9
NEBRASKA										
Omaha	12	17	29	28	11	3	*			11.6
NEVADA										
Las Vegas	18	26	25	20	8	3	1	*		9.7
Reno	52	20	13	10	4	1	*			5.9
NEW JERSEY										
Newark	11	25	34	24	5	1	*			9.8
NEW MEXICO										
Albuquerque	17	36	26	13	5	2	*	*		8.6
NEW YORK										
Albany	23	24	27	21	4	1	*	*		8.6
Buffalo	5	17	34	28	13	3	*	*		12.4
New York	6	17	35	28	10	3	1	*		12.0
Rochester	8	22	34	25	9	2	*	*		11.2
Syracuse	14	27	30	23	5	1	*			9.7
NORTH CAROLINA										
Charlotte	11	36	26	13	2	*	*			7.9
Greensboro	20	32	31	14	2	*	*			8.0
Raleigh	18	32	31	14	2	1	*			7.7
NORTH DAKOTA										
Bismarck	14	20	27	24	12	3	1	1		11.2
Fargo	4	13	28	31	15	7	2			14.4
OHIO										
Akron	7	25	25	26	5	1				10.4
OHIO										
Cincinnati	11	27	36	22	4	1	*	*	*	9.6
Cleveland	7	18	35	29	9	2	1	*	*	11.6
Columbus	26	23	29	18	4	1	*	*		8.2
OKLAHOMA										
Oklahoma City	2	11	34	34	13	6	1	*	*	14.0
Tulsa	9	24	34	26	7	1	*	*		10.6
OREGON										
Portland	28	27	25	16	4	1	*	*		7.7
Salem	25	32	28	13	2	*	*			7.1
PENNSYLVANIA										
Philadelphia	11	27	35	21	5	1	*	*		9.6
Pittsburgh	12	26	34	22	4	1	*	*		9.4
RHODE ISLAND										
Providence	11	20	32	28	7	2	*	*		10.7
SOUTH CAROLINA										
Charleston	12	28	35	19	4	1	*	*		9.2
Columbia	25	35	26	12	2	*	*			7.0
SOUTH DAKOTA										
Huron	10	18	29	29	10	3	1	*		11.9
Rapid City	15	22	28	21	10	4	1	1		11.0
TENNESSEE										
Knoxville	29	29	25	12	4	1	*			7.5
Memphis	14	26	34	20	5	1	*	*		9.4
Nashville	27	31	25	14	2	*	*			7.2
TEXAS										
Amarillo	5	15	32	32	12	4	*	*		12.9
Corpus Christi	11	16	26	33	12	2	*	*		11.9
Dallas	9	21	32	28	9	1	*	*		11.0
El Paso	10	22	32	22	9	4	1	*		11.3
Ft. Worth	4	14	34	34	10	3	*	*		12.5
Houston	6	18	36	28	10	2	*	*		11.8
San Antonio	18	23	32	22	4	1	*			9.3
UTAH										
Salt Lake City	12	33	36	14	4	1	*	*		8.7
VERMONT										
Burlington	24	28	28	22	2	*	*			8.3
VIRGINIA										
Norfolk	14	23	30	25	6	1	*	*		10.2
Richmond	14	37	33	11	1	*	*			7.8
Roanoke	31	22	23	17	5	2	*			8.3
WASHINGTON										
Seattle	13	16	35	26	8	2	*	*		10.7
Spokane	17	38	27	14	3	1	*			8.1
WASHINGTON D.C.	11	26	35	22	5	1	*			9.7
WEST VIRGINIA										
Charleston	29	37	25	8	1	*	*			6.2
WISCONSIN										
Green Bay	8	22	32	26	10	2	*	*		11.2
Madison	15	22	30	23	7	2	*	*		10.1
Milwaukee	8	17	31	30	11	3	*	*		12.1
WYOMING										
Casper	8	16	27	27	13	7	2	*	2	13.3

Let the wind cool your attic for free

Q: I can feel a lot of heat radiating down from the bedroom under the attic. It actually feels very warm to the touch. Will those turbine types of attic vents help to cool the attic down? What makes the turbine spin?

A: Turbine attic vents can be extremely effective and energy efficient because they use absolutely no electricity. The wind blowing past the turbine vent causes it to spin, which will help cool your attic for free.

By properly ventilating your attic, you can actually lower its peak temperature by 40 to 50 degrees. This not only lowers your air-conditioning and utility costs; it also makes you more comfortable. It will increase the life of the roofing materials and structural lumber in your attic.

A great advantage of turbine vents is that they spin with the wind blowing from any direction. This is important because the prevailing wind direction changes from spring through fall and from day-to-day. Gable vents are not very effective when the wind blows from the front of your house.

The centrifugal action of the spinning turbine blades creates a nimbus of low pressure in its center. This low pressure area, along with the natural tendency of hot air to rise, draws the hot air out of the attic.

You should locate the turbine vents (you will generally need more than one) as near as possible to the peak of your roof. This allows them to catch the wind from all directions without interference from the roof. The attic air is also hottest at the roof peak. It is also important to space them properly along the roof for effective ventilation.

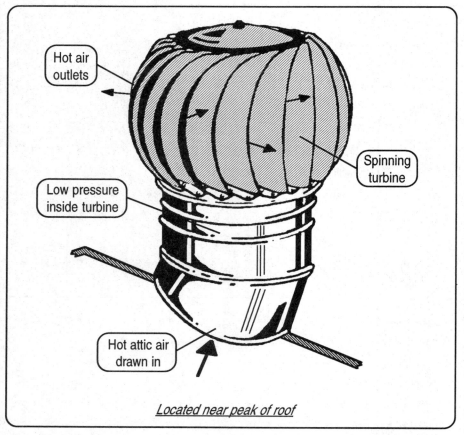

Hot air outlets

Spinning turbine

Low pressure inside turbine

Hot attic air drawn in

Located near peak of roof

Turbine vents are generally available in 12-inch and 14-inch diameter sizes. For a 1,500 square foot attic, you will need two 14-inch turbine vents. This provides the recommended 1 to 2 cubic feet per minute (cfm) of air flow for each square foot of attic floor area.

You will also need about five square feet of net-free vent inlet area. The ideal location for the inlet vents is in the soffits under the roof overhang. These create an air flow pattern over the attic insulation, thus cooling the attic floor.

Another effective attic vent option is using a combination of a ridge vent and soffit vents. Several manufacturers offer ridge vents that are only a couple of inches high and are covered with shingle material. From the ground, they are barely perceptible. Like turbine vents, they are very easy to install yourself. Be sure to use a safety harness when you are on a roof.

Q: I am planning a new room addition and I want to add rigid foam insulation to the walls when I remodel. I want to use a type that does not contain chlorofluorocarbons that hurt the ozone layer. Are there any new types available on the market?

A: Chlorofluorocarbons (CFC's) are suspected of contributing to the destruction of the Earth's ozone layer. This has very serious long-term health consequences for people, animals, and plants

Polystyrene rigid foam insulation board does not use chlorofluorocarbons as the foaming agent in its production. Generally; pentane and a flame modifying agent are used. CFC's are typically found in urethane, isocyanurate, and some phenolic types of rigid foam insulation.

You should be able to buy attic turbine vents at most building supply and home center outlets. You may have to contact the manufacturers of the continuous ridge vents for the names of local dealers. When installing a ridge vent, you should have about one square foot of vent area for each 300 square feet of attic floor area.

How to Size Turbine Ventilation Systems

Square Feet of Attic Floor Area	Number of Turbine Vents Required	Turbine Vent Size in Inches	Min. Sq. Ft. of Inlet Louver Area Required	Min. Number*/Size (inches) of Eave Vents
1200	2 each	12	4.0	9 ea. 8×16
1500	2 each	14	5.0	12 ea. 8 ×16
1800	3 each	12	6.0	14 ea. 8×16
2100	3 each	14	7.0	16 ea. 8×16
2400	4 each	12	8.0	18 ea. 8×16

* Use twice the number of 4×16-inch eave vents.

Placement of Ventilators

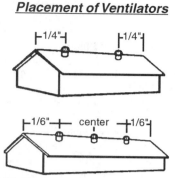

Manufacturers of Continuous Ridge or Soffit Vents

AIR VENT INC., 7700 Harker Dr., Suite A, Peoria, IL 61615 - (800) 247-8368 (309) 692-6969
   product - "Shinglevent II" — $30 for 10 foot section

BENJAMIN OBDYKE, 65 Steamboat Dr., Warminster, PA 18974 - (800) 458-2309 (215) 672-7200
   product - "Roll Vent" — $50 for 20 foot roll

COBRA VENTILATION CO. (GAF), 1361 Alps Rd., Wayne, NJ 07470 - (800) 688-6654
   product - "Cobra Ridge Vent" — $45 for 20 foot roll

COR-A-VENT INC., PO Box 428, Mishawaka, IN 46544 - (800) 837-8368 (219) 255-1910
   product - "Cor-A-Vent" — $12 for 4 foot section

LOMANCO, PO Box 519, Jacksonville, AR 72078 - (800) 643-5596 (501) 982-6511
   product - "SOV-4" — $20 for 4 ft. section

TRIMLINE ROOF VENTILATION, 7425 Laurell Ave., Minneapolis, MN 55426 - (800) 438-2920 (612) 540-9700
   product - "Fastline" — $50 for 20 foot roll

Shinglevent II by Air Vent, Inc. External Baffle Design

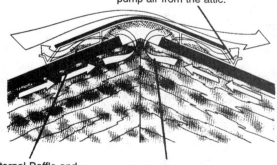

External Wind Baffle creates negative pressure above the ridge to pump air from the attic.

External Baffle and Weather Filter help protect against entry of rain, snow, dust and insects.

Air Flow through the attic space removes moisture-laden air and heat build-up.

• An end plug helps seal vent against weather and insects. • The wind baffle creates negative air pressure above ridge, pumping heat and moisture from the attic. Also deflects wind-blown elements away from filter. • A weather filter helps prevent entry of rain, snow, dust and insects. • It is molded of high-impact co-polymers that are flexible in cold temperatures, stable in heat. Colorfast pigments prevent fading. • The cap shingles are easy to install with slot width guides imprinted on vent. Rounded profile is designed to eliminate cap shingle cracking.

SOV-4 Shingle Over Vent by Lomanco

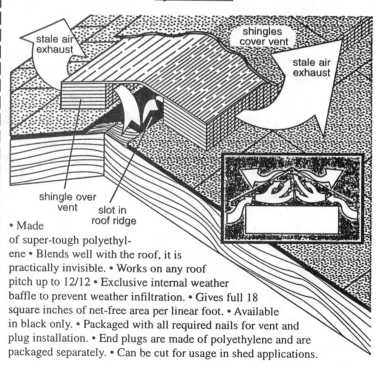

stale air exhaust

shingles cover vent

stale air exhaust

shingle over vent

slot in roof ridge

• Made of super-tough polyethylene • Blends well with the roof, it is practically invisible. • Works on any roof pitch up to 12/12 • Exclusive internal weather baffle to prevent weather infiltration. • Gives full 18 square inches of net-free area per linear foot. • Available in black only. • Packaged with all required nails for vent and plug installation. • End plugs are made of polyethylene and are packaged separately. • Can be cut for usage in shed applications.

• Low profile shingle over ridge vent system that is virtually invisible. • Won't crush when nailed, so it creates a smooth, even ridge line. • 20 foot E-Z Roll is easy to roll out and installs fast. • Features the Trimline "Clear Flow" vent design — won't clog or deteriorate like other roll vents. • Tested and patented ventilation system provides the most natural, effective attic ventilation available. • Certified ventilation per linear foot. • Roll includes 3 pull-apart endcaps. • No fabric overwrap or filters to mess with. • No cans, fittings, wraps or connectors. • Eliminates waste — every piece can be used. • Adjusts to any roof pitch. • Rounded peak reduces shingles stress and cracking. • Optional wind deflector eliminates moisture infiltration. • Won't crack or dent. • Won't damage from hail or ice. • Easy to transport and handles. • ⅝" thick, 11¼" wide.

Fastline™ E-Z Roll-Out Shingle Over Ridge Vent System by Trimline

optional wind deflector

foam endcap

Amount of Required Ventilation — The Fastline™ ridge vent has a net-free ventilation area of 12.5 square inches per lineal foot. To operate properly, there must be at least 25% to 50% more soffit ventilation than the number of square inches utilized in the ridge. As an example, for 1000 square inches of ventilation in the ridge, at least 1250 to 1500 square inches of ventilation products available on the market can be utilized. Consult your local building inspector or building supply dealer to learn the correct ventilation level required for your area or application.

Ridge Preparation for Installation — The amount of ventilation is controlled by the length of slot cut along the roof ridge. A 3½" slot should be cut at the ridge, or approximately 1¾" on each side of the center line of the ridge, equalling the amount of lineal ventilation that is required for the attic. For example, if 750 square inches of ridge ventilation is necessary, and since there are 12.5 square inches of ventilation per lineal foot of the ridge vent, it would be necessary to cut 60 lineal feet of ventilation slot. If the total roof line is 75 feet, then there would be 15 feet of ridge line which is not slotted.

The slot may be precut on a new roof prior to installation of any shingles. Or in a retrofit, the slot can be cut from the pre-shingled roof using a circular saw with a carbide tip blade. (Protective eye goggles should be worn during this process.) Once the slot is cut and any overlapping shingles covering the slot are trimmed and removed, the ridge is ready for vent installation.

Wind Deflector — Trimline™ offers an optional wind deflector. In areas of high wind accompanied by rain or snow, installation of the wind deflector is recommended to prevent moisture infiltration. Manufactured from aluminum, this baffle will not rust, and if desired, may be painted to match the color of the shingle or trim of the house.

Installation Instructions for Roll-Out Shingle Over Ridge Vent

1) — Cut a 3½" slot (1¾" on each side) along the ridge(s) either before or after shingling roof. Length of slot should be determined by the amount of required ventilation. A minimum of 6" must be left uncut on each end of the ridge.

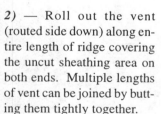

2) — Roll out the vent (routed side down) along entire length of ridge covering the uncut sheathing area on both ends. Multiple lengths of vent can be joined by butting them tightly together.

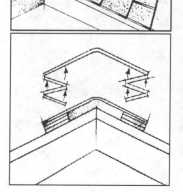

3) — Fold in a "Z" pattern the precut, hinged vent strips, on each side of the vent, on one end of the ridge. Pull apart a 5¼" section of precut foam strip and caulk into place on ridge end of vent between the two blocks of folded side vent strips.

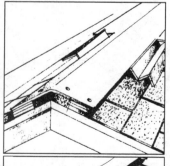

4) — Form vent and place over one end of the ridge. Nail end of vent into place, also nailing through foam end cap on the ridge end. Repeat folding step #3 on other end of vent, form and nail.

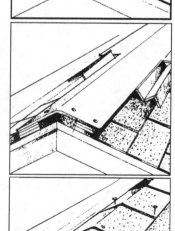

5) — Fold and nail every 24" the remaining section of the vent. If wind deflectors are to be installed, slide them under the sides of the vent prior to nailing. Install additional ridge vents as needed to complete the ridge.

6) — Install ridge shingles directly over the trimline "Roll Out" vent.

Provided by Trimline

Recommended Net-Free Vent Area for Attic — sq. in.

Attic Length in Feet	Attic Width in Feet										
	20	22	24	26	28	30	32	34	36	38	40
20	192	211	230	269	288	307	326	348	365	384	403
24	230	253	276	300	323	346	369	392	415	438	481
28	269	296	323	349	376	403	430	484	511	538	564
32	307	338	369	399	430	461	492	522	553	584	614
36	346	380	415	449	484	518	553	588	622	657	691
40	384	422	461	499	538	576	614	653	691	730	768
44	422	465	507	549	591	634	676	718	760	803	845
48	461	507	553	599	645	691	737	783	829	876	922
52	499	549	599	649	699	749	799	848	898	948	998
56	538	591	645	699	753	807	860	914	967	1021	1075
60	576	634	691	749	807	864	922	979	1037	1094	1152

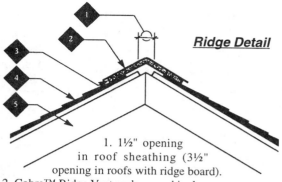

Ridge Detail

1. 1½" opening in roof sheathing (3½" opening in roofs with ridge board).
2. Cobra™ Ridge Vent under cap shingles.
3. 5/8" nominal space between cap shingle and roof shingle.
4. Roof shingle on sheathing.
5. Roof truss.

Manufactured by Cobra Ventilation Co.

Turbine Ventilators Manufactured by Lomanco

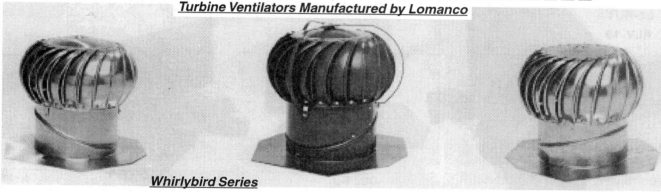

Whirlybird Series

- Permanently lubricated upper and lower ball bearings that ensure long life and no maintenance.
- All-aluminum rust-free construction.
- Rigid spider-type structure.
- Riveted at every connection.
- 21 air-foil curved vanes with rolled vane edges to deflect water.
- Exclusive vari-pitch base adjusts to 12/12 roof pitch.
- Large flashing for easy installation.
- Tested to withstand winds of 147 m.p.h..
- Lifetime warranty — transferable.

- Easy installation.
- Reduces energy bills.
- Reduces winter ice build-up.
- Big Whirly — 14" is the same as the Whirlybird, but moves up to 37% more air.
- 8" turbine and base units available. Design differs slightly.
- Internally braced series offered in black, brown, weathered bronze, and white baked enamel finishes, as well as mill finish.
- Externally braced series offered in black, brown, and weathered bronze baked enamel finishes, as well as mill finish.

GT-12 and GEB-12 Galvanized Turbines

- 0.25 stamped glvanized steel.
- Permanently lubricated ball bearings.
- Fits any roof pitch to 7/12.
- GT-12 is an internally braced 12" turbine.
- GEB-12 is an externally braced 12" turbine.
- Lifetime warranty — nontransferable.

Cutaway of Ball Bearing System

Model Number	C.F.M. at Wind Velocity of			Approximate Shipping Weight
	5 mph	8 mph	15 mph	
BIB-12	347	542	962	6 lbs.
BEB-12	347	542	962	6½lbs.
BIB-14	415	741	1342	7½ lbs.
BEB-14	415	741	1342	7½ lbs.
TIB-12	347	542	962	4 lbs.
TEB-12	347	542	962	4½ lbs.
TIB-14	415	741	1342	4½ lbs.
TEB-14	415	741	1342	5 lbs.
GT-12	347	542	962	9 lbs.
GEB-12	347	542	962	10 lbs.
IB-8 (Top)	95	172	329	4.12
VP-8 (Base only)	—	—	—	2.50

Molded and fully machined raceways — not merely molded. Concentric to .0015 for low drag and quiet operation.

Dupont Delrin® inner and outer bearing rings — the longest lasting and smoothest polymer ball bearing material available.

200 Grade 302 series stainless steel balls for low turning resistance and high resistance to moisture

Self-lubricated Turcite® bearing cage.

Ultrasonically welded and sealed bearing cap.

Unique Turcon® permanently seals lubricant in and dirt and moisture out.

Brighten your night with lights

Q: We need more outdoor security, landscaping and patio accent lights. I tried a wireless solar-powered light several years ago, but I was not satisfied with it. Are the new solar lights any better?

A: If you were dissatisfied with solar-powered (no wiring required) outdoor lights several years ago, there have been many design improvements. These improvements make them brighter and provide a longer on-time at night.

The most important improvements are in the solar cell (converts sunlight into electricity) technology, the batteries and the light bulbs used. Some of the new solar cells provide up to 1.5 watts of electricity in full sun.

These new higher-efficiency solar cell panels are inconspicuously built into the top of the light. All the solar-powered lights have electric eyes to automatically switch them on at night.

It is difficult to distinguish the new solar-powered accent lights from standard electric. Typical styles include coach, tier, pagoda, down and portable lanterns. Solite also manufactures contemporary lights, called Space and Flyeye, with a high-tech look and unique lighting patterns.

Several manufacturers have switched from nicad to tiny maintenance-free sealed lead acid batteries, the type used in your car. These batteries hold a greater charge and operate well in varying outdoor conditions.

Many new solar-powered lights now use fluorescent bulbs. These are about four times brighter using less electricity. This gives more hours of light at night even during cloudy weather.

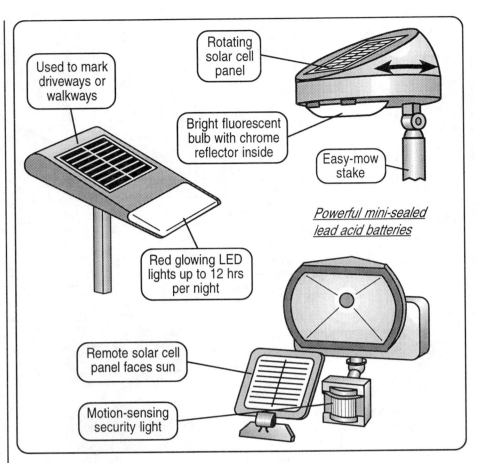

Used to mark driveways or walkways

Rotating solar cell panel

Bright fluorescent bulb with chrome reflector inside

Easy-mow stake

Powerful mini-sealed lead acid batteries

Red glowing LED lights up to 12 hrs per night

Remote solar cell panel faces sun

Motion-sensing security light

One design, Pathmarker, uses an LED that glows red. It provides up to 12 hours of on-time each night. It is ideal for marking the edges of a driveway, walkway, etc. It has a tamper-resistant stake to deter theft. Some other accent lights have an "easy-mow" stake base that easily slips out.

For security and convenience, a wireless motion-sensing solar floodlight is effective. When it detects motion, up to 75 feet (adjustable sensitivity), the floodlight automatically comes on. The floodlights have either a fluorescent or a standard bulb.

It can be adjusted to stay on for up to one minute after no more motion is detected. With the powerful battery and brief on-time, it will continue to operate for weeks. It can come on up to 120 times on a single charge, without any sunny days.

Several new designs have a rotating solar panel. This will allow you to adjust the solar panel so it will face toward the sun year-round. Some models have two-level intensity light switches. The lower brightness setting almost doubles the hours of light.

Q: I bought a house and found that it had urea formaldehyde wall insulation installed eight years ago. Should I have it removed?

A: According to the U.S. Consumer Product Safety Commission, the majority of the formaldehyde outgassing occurs in the first year. After eight years, the level of formaldehyde gas in your house should not be higher than any other house without it.

If you are still concerned, buy do-it-yourself formaldehyde gas test kits. Some kits have in-home analysis and others require that the test sample be sent to a lab for more accurate analysis.

Many new solar-powered outdoor lights have more powerful solar cells, batteries and better bulbs for extended hours of light each night. The on-time chart to the right is for Intermatic's solar light. It is shown to indicate the relative differences in on-time for various areas of the country. For example, there are more hours of daylight in June in the north than in the south. Average amount of cloud cover in your area is also a factor to consider when determining if a solar light will meet your needs.

Two-level lights, with a high/low switch can extend the on-time when set to the low light brightness. These two-level lights are ideal for decks or patios. You may sometimes want shorter-period, brighter light for entertaining and longer-period, dimmer light for general security.

Motion-sensing solar lights are a perfect fit with solar energy. These can light up to 130 cycles on a single charge. This will easily handle one to two weeks without any bright sun to recharge the battery. With a remote solar panel and a long wire, you can mount the panel so it is exposed to the most sun. See page 24 for details on the model that I use on my house.

Fluorescent bulbs provide only slightly longer on-times than incandescent bulbs, but they are much brighter. Typically, for the same amount of electricity used, a fluorescent bulb will produce three to four times more light. Replacement fluorescent bulbs cost twice as much as incandescent bulbs, but they last many times longer, saving money in the long run. Sealed lead acid batteries are most effective in all types of climates and temperature conditions. They also hold a charge for a long time.

Average Nightly Output	
City	Hours of Light Output in June
Atlanta	5
Boston	5
Chicago	5½
Honolulu	5¼
Los Angeles	5¾
Miami	4½
New Orleans	5¼
New York	4¾
Phoenix	7½
Seattle	5¼
Washington, D.C.	5¼

When solar panel faces the sun in areas which are completely unshaded, light output will be 30% to 50% less in winter months.

Styles of Solar-Powered Lights

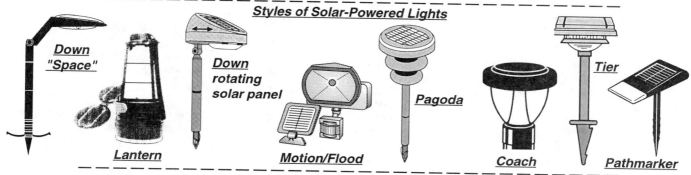

Down "Space"

Down rotating solar panel

Lantern

Motion/Flood

Pagoda

Coach

Tier

Pathmarker

Solite™ — Flyeye Style

Model SW-123A is a solar-powered fluorescent outdoor light with a flyeye style space age design. It lights up your garden, walkway, driveway or any place you choose. There are no wires to install, no utility bills cost. It uses solar energy to power and charge the built-in battery during the day and turn its fluorescent light ON automatically at dusk, day after day, night after night.

Features
- Up to Six Hours of Light — Using high-efficiency, long-life fluorescent lamp
- Independent Light Source — Using the power of the sun
- Convenient Lighting — In your backyard, walkway and driveway, year round
- Built-in Light Sensor — Turns lamp "ON" automatically at dusk, and "OFF" at day time
- Discharge Control System — Turns lamp "OFF" before battery runs down for increased battery life
- Electronic Ballast Circuit — Controls lamp turn-on cycle for extended lamp life
- External Charge Jack — Using optional 9V/140mA wall mount adaptor, to charge the unit
- Over Charge Protection — Protect the battery and extend its service life
- Mounting — Mounted on post for your garden or wall
- Mounting Poles — Adjustable height PVC pipe
- Light Reflector — High gloss electroplated reflector for maximum efficiency

Specification (nominal values)
- Power Source — Built-in rechargeable sealed lead acid battery, 6V/4.0Ah
- Power Consumption — 0.9 watt at 6.0 volt operating voltage, in "HI" mode 0.72 watt at 6.0 volt operating voltage, in "LO" mode
- Light Source — 4W fluorescent lamp
- Battery Life — Over 2 years before replacement
- Lamp Life — Over 1 year before replacement
- Solar Panel — High power Sanyo solar panel
- Solar Power — Approx. 1.0 watt at full sun
- Housing — High grade ABS plastic and high quality acrylic ultra-violet stabilized transparent cover
- Operating "Power" Mode — Selectable: "AUTO" turns light ON at dusk and OFF at day time. "OFF" turns light OFF for shipment or for battery recharging/replacement.
- Light "Intensity" Mode — Selectable: "HI" for maximum intensity. 6V/150mA. 80 Lux @ 1 ft. "LO" for maximum lighting time. 6V120mA. 60 Lux @ 1 ft.

Fluorescent Outdoor Solar Light Model SW-123A

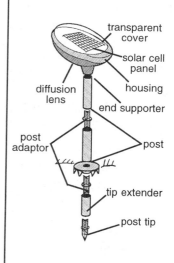

transparent cover

solar cell panel

diffusion lens

housing

end supporter

post adaptor

post

tip extender

post tip

Manufacturers of Solar-Powered Outdoor Lights

ALPAN INC., 425 I Constitution Ave., Camarillo, CA 93012 - (800) 233-1106 (805) 383-8880

<u>model</u> - "18754" <u>style</u> - pathmarker <u>on-time</u> - 12 hours <u>bulb</u> - red LED <u>battery</u> - ni-cad
<u>features</u> - LED soft red glow, 8-inch stake, deck mount option available, silicon cell with polycarbonate lens

<u>model</u> - "18752" <u>style</u> - tier <u>on-time</u> - 6 hours <u>bulb</u> - fluorescent <u>battery</u> - ni-cad
<u>features</u> - single crystal solar cell, polycarbonate lens, 12-inch adjustable stake, deck mount option available

<u>model</u> - "18756" <u>style</u> - pagoda <u>on-time</u> - 5/9 hours <u>bulb</u> - fluorescent <u>battery</u> - ni-cad
<u>features</u> - single crystal solar cell, polycarbonate lens, high/low switch, 12-inch adjustable stake, deck mount available

<u>model</u> - "18758" <u>style</u> - coach <u>on-time</u> - 5/9 hours <u>bulb</u> - fluorescent <u>battery</u> - ni-cad
<u>features</u> - single crystal solar cell, polycarbonate lens, high/low switch, pole or surface mountable

<u>model</u> - "18761" <u>style</u> - motion/flood <u>on-time</u> - 130 cycle/chg <u>bulb</u> - fluorescent <u>battery</u> - lead acid
<u>features</u> - remote solar panel with 14 feet of cord, range of 40 feet, sensitivity arc of 110°, up to two weeks of operation with no sunshine, adjustable sensitivity control, light fixture swivels front to back and left to right for positioning

<u>model</u> - "18759" <u>style</u> - portable lantern <u>on-time</u> - 3 hours <u>bulb</u> - incandescent <u>battery</u> - ni-cad
<u>model</u> - "18807" <u>style</u> - portable lantern <u>on-time</u> - 4/8 hours <u>bulb</u> - fluorescent <u>battery</u> - ni-cad
<u>model</u> - "18760" <u>style</u> - portable lantern <u>on-time</u> - 4 hours <u>bulb</u> - fluorescent <u>battery</u> - ni-cad
<u>features</u> - "18759" — compact and lightweight, "18807" — twin tube operates for 8 hours on one tube or 4 hours on two tubes, "18760" — prismatic lens gives 360° light distribution, high/low switch, blinking control function with a yellow signal cap and a powerful searchlight for emergency situations

BRINKMAN CORP., 4215 McEwen Rd., Dallas, TX 75244 - (800) 468-5252

<u>model</u> - "SL-1" <u>style</u> - tier <u>on-time</u> - 5 hours <u>bulb</u> - incandescent <u>battery</u> - ni-cad*
<u>features</u> - two section ground stake, deck/wall mounting bracket

<u>model</u> - "SL-2" <u>style</u> - down <u>on-time</u> - 5 hours <u>bulb</u> - incandescent <u>battery</u> - ni-cad
<u>features</u> - two section, easy-mow ground stake, deck/wall mounting bracket

<u>model</u> - "SL-3" <u>style</u> - down <u>on-time</u> - 7 hours <u>bulb</u> - incandescent <u>battery</u> - lead acid
<u>features</u> - 350° rotating solar panel, two section riser with easy-mow ground stake, deck/wall mounting bracket

<u>model</u> - "SL-4" <u>style</u> - pagoda <u>on-time</u> - 5/8 hours <u>bulb</u> - incandescent <u>battery</u> - ni-cad
<u>features</u> - high/low switch, two section ground stake, deck/wall mounting bracket

<u>model</u> - "SL-5" <u>style</u> - down <u>on-time</u> - 7 hours <u>bulb</u> - fluorescent <u>battery</u> - lead acid
<u>features</u> - 350° rotating solar panel, two section, easy-mow ground stake, deck/wall mounting bracket

<u>model</u> - "SL-6" <u>style</u> - pagoda <u>on-time</u> - 5 hours <u>bulb</u> - fluorescent <u>battery</u> - lead acid
<u>features</u> - two section ground stake and wall mounting bracket

<u>model</u> - "SL-7" <u>style</u> - motion/flood <u>on-time</u> - 120 cycle/chg <u>bulb</u> - incand./halogen <u>battery</u> - lead acid
<u>features</u> - twin adjustable flood lights, remote solar panel with 15 feet of cord, shielded motion sensor with automatic temperature control, adjustable from 3 to 75 foot range, lights turn off 1½ minutes after motion stops

HEATH ZENITH, 2701 Industrial Dr., Bowling Green, KY 42102 - (502) 745-7700

<u>model</u> - "SL7001" <u>style</u> - motion/flood <u>on-time</u> - 120 cycle/chg <u>bulb</u> - halogen <u>battery</u> - lead acid
<u>features</u> - amorphous solar panel, detects motion up to 60 feet in a sensitivity arc of 100°, remains on for 30 seconds once no further motion is detected, operates up to 15 days without direct sunlight, swivel adjustment for easy positioning of sensor, adjustable sensitivity control to motion detected

INTERMATIC, Intermatic Plaza, Spring Grove, IL 60081 - (815) 675-2321

<u>model</u> - "LZ6" or "LZ3" <u>style</u> - tier <u>on-time</u> - 5 hours <u>bulb</u> - incandescent <u>battery</u> - ni-cad
<u>features</u> - high-impact polymer, thermo-formed reflector, prismatic lens, 2-year warranty, "LZ6" is for table-top use, kits available with ground stakes, risers, wire and solar collector unit

SOLAR WIDE, INC., 245 Carlton Terrace, Teaneck, NJ 07666 - (201) 836-3877

<u>model</u> - "SW-134A" <u>style</u> - pagoda <u>on-time</u> - 7 hours <u>bulb</u> - fluorescent <u>battery</u> - ni-cad
<u>features</u> - two section ground stake, crystal solar panel, ABS plastic and polycarbonate dome cover

<u>model</u> - "SW-137A" <u>style</u> - pagoda <u>on-time</u> - 5 hours <u>bulb</u> - fluorescent <u>battery</u> - lead acid
<u>features</u> - two section ground stake, crystal solar panel, ABS plastic and polycarbonate dome cover

<u>model</u> - "SW-121A" <u>style</u> - down "Space" <u>on-time</u> - 5 hours <u>bulb</u> - fluorescent <u>battery</u> - ni-cad
<u>features</u> - two section ground post, mount on post/wall, acrylic transparent cover, high/low switch, hinged for seasonal angle

<u>model</u> - "SW-123A" <u>style</u> - down <u>on-time</u> - 6 hours <u>bulb</u> - fluorescent <u>battery</u> - lead acid
<u>features</u> - high/low switch, ultraviolet stabilized transparent cover, flyeye design

<u>model</u> - "SW-124B" <u>style</u> - down <u>on-time</u> - 5 hours <u>bulb</u> - fluorescent <u>battery</u> - lead acid
<u>features</u> - crystal solar panel, built-in wall mounting bracket, two section ground stake, high/low switch

<u>model</u> - "SW-125B" <u>style</u> - down <u>on-time</u> - 4 hours <u>bulb</u> - fluorescent <u>battery</u> - lead acid
<u>features</u> - rotating solar panel, hinged for seasonal angle, ABS plastic and polycarbonate transparent cover, crystal solar cell, external jack for optional 9-volt wall charger

* ni-cad stands for nickel-cadmium

Determine a satisfactory spot to mount the unit. The only constraints are that it must be mounted onto a solid wood surface where the fully adjustable solar module will get plenty of direct sunlight. Mounting on other surfaces is possible with the use of anchors.

Pre-installation Checking Procedure

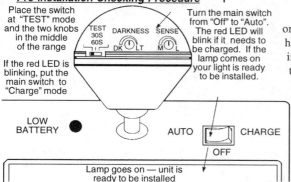

Place the switch at "TEST" mode and the two knobs in the middle of the range

If the red LED is blinking, put the main switch to "Charge" mode

Turn the main switch from "Off" to "Auto". The red LED will blink if it needs to be charged. If the lamp comes on your light is ready to be installed.

LOW BATTERY

TEST 30S 60S — DARKNESS (DK L LT) SENSE (M L)

AUTO / CHARGE / OFF

Lamp goes on — unit is ready to be installed

It is important to note the solar module should always face south in the northern hemisphere, angled at about 60 degrees toward the sun. You can mount it under an eave with one or two arm extensions, on a wall, or under an eave with the solar module mounted on the remote mount. The solar module can be tilted to one side or the other.

How to Mount Under an Eave or on a Wall

1) Use the mounting bracket as a template to mark the 5 holes for drilling. The 2 center holes should be drilled using a 1/8" drill while the 3 outside holes require a 5/32" drill. Attach the mounting bracket using the two 1¼" wood screws in the center holes.

2) Without solar module arm mounted, slide the main unit onto the mounting bracket's plastic clips. This allows the Sensor Light™ to be briefly held in place while the three 3" wood support screws are installed.
IMPORTANT: The clips are to aid in the mounting process only. Do not leave the light hanging by the clips alone without the three 3" wood support screws installed as it may fall off the mounting bracket. Make sure the motion sensor is rotated so the "Top" marking is up.

3) The next step is to assemble and mount solar module/solar module arm. Solar module may be mounted using one or both pieces of the arm extension and knuckle provided. The solar module should be angled to the south. The average angle relative to the horizon should be about 60 degrees. Lay out the pieces on a table or flat surface and temporarily assemble them, estimating the angles necessary to achieve the desired configuration.

4) Assemble the solar module/solar module arm in the desired configuration using the #10 machine screws and then place on the unit

using a #10 machine screw. Do not over tighten. Route the wire from solar module along top surface of arm extensions using the cable routing clips. Plug the connector into the power receptacle located on the side of the unit.

Mounting the Solar Module with the Remote Mount

If you are mounting the light on a north face of your home or have a large number of sun blocking obstacles, you may want to use the optional remote mounting bracket to install the solar module. If your roof faces south, you can mount the solar module directly onto the remote mount; otherwise, you will need to use the solar module arm and knuckle to have adequate adjustability.

1) First, mount the main unit on to the desired surface — eave or wall mounting as previously described.

2) Using the 1" wood screws supplied, fasten the remote mount to the desired surface. Make sure this surface is strong enough to support the weight of the solar module.

3) If you are mounting the module on a roof, we suggest using weather-proof caulking around the remote mount to assure a water tight seal.

4) Remove the cable storage door and remove enough cable to stretch between the main unit and the module. Make sure the cable is not pulled too tightly to allow for some movement.

5) The cable between light and the solar module should no be altered or installed in any manner that will cause it to fray or break.

Final Adjustment and Starting Up

After you have successfully mounted your light, you are almost ready for carefree operation with a few final steps:

1) Initial 3 day charge — on the main body of the unit, there is a rocker switch with 3 positions — Auto, Off, Charge. The "Auto" position is for normal operation. The "Off" position is for shipping or extended periods of nonuse — the unit is not operational. The "Charge" position is for the initial 3 day charge of the battery before the final adjustment and the first use. The unit can charge but it is not operational in this mode. For now, turn the rocker switch on the main unit to "Charge". In this position, the solar module will charge the battery without activating the unit. Leave the switch in this position for 3 sunny days to ensure the battery has a full charge prior to motion sensor adjustment and normal operation. Low Battery Indicator — Located on the opposite side of the unit from the 3 position rocker

marked "Low Battery". This indicator will blink if battery voltage falls below a predetermined level required for normal operation. If, while in use, this indicator starts to blink, make sure solar panel is getting plenty of direct sunlight and allow the unit to charge back up. You may, however, need to repeat step 1 if there is little available sunlight and the unit is getting a lot of use.

2) How to adjust the motion sensor — After the initial 3 day charge, turn the switch on the main body of the unit to "Auto". On the motion sensor, there is a Test/30 sec/60 sec switch. The "Test" position for adjusting the motion sensor allows the light to function during daylight hours. The "30 sec" allows the unit to run for approximately 30 seconds after you have left the area. The "60 sec" allows the unit to run for approximately 60 seconds after you have left the area. For now, turn switch to "Test".

3) Adjusting the motion sensor position — Point the motion sensor to face the area you want to detect motion in. Keep in mind the motion sensor detects motion in a span of 120 degrees horizontally and 90 degrees vertically. **Important:** Rotate the motion sensor so the controls are pointing down and the "Top" marking is up to keep the lens in the proper orientation.

4) Adjusting darkness control — The bottom middle knob of motion sensor is the "Darkness" control which controls the level of darkness outside when the unit becomes functional. For now, leave darkness control in middle position. If, in daily operation, unit turns on when it is too light outside, turn control toward "Dark". However, if the light is not activating during night time because of a street light or bright house light, turn the control toward "Light".

5) Adjusting the sensitivity control — The outer knob on the bottom right of the motion sensor is the "Sensitivity" control which controls how sensitive the unit is in detecting motion. Initially, put this control in the middle position. If the unit is not sensitive enough, turn this control to "More". If you want to filter out detection of animals or shorten the range of detection, turn this control toward "Less".

6) Final adjustment of the Test/30 sec/60 sec switch — Depending on how long you wish the unit to stay lit after you leave the area, turn the slide switch on the bottom of the motion sensor to "30 sec" or "60 sec".

7) Adjustment of lamp housing — Point lamp housing to face area you wish to illuminate.

Solar fan cools your attic for free

Q: It seems like I can feel the heat blasting down from the ceiling. It is really uncomfortable in the bedrooms. My budget is limited, so I have to make any improvements myself. What do you suggest?

A: The blasting heat is not just your imagination. A roof can reach over 150 degrees in the sun. This intense heat radiates through the attic insulation to the ceiling below. It is not only uncomfortable but it drives up your air-conditioning costs.

Even after the sun goes down, the lumber and insulation in the attic are still hot. This can continue to radiate heat down well into the evening making sleeping uncomfortable.

A combination of attic ventilation and reflective foil is most effective. The foil blocks the roof's heat from reaching the attic floor and the ventilation exhausts the hot attic air. Adequate attic ventilation is also important in the winter for moisture removal.

Since you plan to do the job yourself, consider installing a solar-powered attic vent fan kit. These solar fans are ideal attic ventilators because, as the sun gets more intense, they run faster. Better yet, they operate for free.

Solar fan kits are available as integral units (solar panel built into the top) or as a remote fan and solar panel kit. **There is no dangerous electrical wiring or complicated controls to attach.**

Just cut a hole in the roof and slip the attached flashing under the shingles. This is ideal for lower-pitched roofs with no attic access, because the entire installation procedure can quickly be done on top

Solar cell panel is built into top

Strong rigid plastic cover blocks rain, has shingle-like look

Hot air is exhausted by solar fan

Simple, no-wiring installation

Very hot air is drawn from the attic below

Remote system is used when roof does not face in the proper direction

Do-it-yourself kits include fan, solar cell panel, cover and long wire

of the roof.

Integral units are effective and some models are designed to simulate shingles. These units are best if your roof faces south or southwest. If you do not have the proper roof exposure, choose a remote kit. This allows you to face the solar panel toward the sun.

If the thought of cutting a hole in your roof scares you, try a new interior ridge ventilator. These kits use a perforated 14-inch duct under the entire length of the roof peak. A solar or electric fan at the end draws the hot air out.

If you are handier with tools, you can install a standard roll-type ridge exhaust vent. There are many designs to choose from at most home centers. You should also install some inlet air vents in the soffits.

For the greatest heat reduction, staple special reinforced-aluminum foil under the roof rafters. It is commonly available in four-foot-wide rolls for quick installation. If you can staple, you can easily do it yourself.

Q: I am planning to build a concrete planter near the house for summer cooling and a slab for winter solar heating. What is the proper consistency for the wet concrete for this application?

A: Your idea of a planter and slab is fine, but position the slab so that it is shaded by the plants in the summer. The plants will help to cool your house. In the winter, they will die back and allow the sun through.

The proper amount of water is critical. Mix the concrete so that, if you make a groove in it with a trowel, it holds its shape with a smooth surface. If the groove surface is rough, add a little more water.

Manufacturers of Electric-Powered Attic Vent Fans

BUTLER VENTAMATIC CORP., PO Box 728, Mineral Wells, TX 76068 - (800) 433-1626
    <u>type</u> - roof or gable mount   <u>cfm range</u> - 700 to 1650
    <u>features</u> - The "NRG" series has a limited lifetime warranty on all parts.

CERTAINTEED VENTILATION, 3000 W. Commerce St., Dallas, TX 75212 - (800) 527-1924
    <u>type</u> - roof or gable mount   <u>cfm range</u> - 1050 to 1620
    <u>features</u> - Five- or ten-year, limited, transferable warranty. With automatic thermostat, some models have auto humidistat.

KOOL-O-MATIC CORP., 1831 Terminal Rd., Niles, MI 49120 - (616) 683-2600
    <u>type</u> - roof or gable mount   <u>cfm range</u> - 770 to 1830
    <u>features</u> - Some models are built into a cupola, come complete with thermostatic control and horse or rooster weathervane.

LEIGH, PO Box 1150, Holland, OH 43528 - (800) 528-1411
    <u>type</u> - roof or gable mount   <u>cfm range</u> - 1170 to 1650
    <u>features</u> - Equipped with adjustable thermostat, optional humidistat

NUTONE, Madison and Red Bank Rds., Cincinnati, OH 45227 - (800) 543-8687
    <u>type</u> - roof or gable mount   <u>cfm range</u> - 900 to 2090
    <u>features</u> - Custom colors available on selected roof fans to blend and match with your roof shingles — wood tone, forest green, polar white, smoke gray, shadow black or brick red. Accessories — humidity control, automatic heat sensor or auto, adjustable thermostat.

PATTON (RIVAL CO.), 800 E. 101 Terrace, Suite 100, Kansas City, MO 64131 - (800) 334-4126
    <u>type</u> - roof or gable mount   <u>cfm range</u> - 1040 to 1620
    <u>features</u> - The roof-mounted models have bug and bird screen protection.

SOLAR ATTIC INC., 15548 95th Circle NE, Elk River, MN 55330 - (612) 441-3440
    <u>description</u> - The "Solar Attic Ridge Ventilator" is designed to control ventilation of the attic. It can also be used to collect attic heat and to redistribute this heat to another location. Available in standard or customized lengths. It is a fully automated system that works as follows — the electronic control senses the temperatures of 40°F, 70°F and 90-105°F. When the attic peak temperature (where control is positioned) drops to 40°F, the control senses a winter condition which activates a humidistat. The humidistat then vents the attic whenever the humidity exceeds a preset (adjustable) Rh% (typically set to 35% Rh). As an alternative, the humidistat can be set to the on position and the ventilator would then simply vent the attic any time the temperature is below 40°F. When the attic reaches 70°F, the humidistat is disengaged. Ventilation, then, only occurs when the attic temp exceeds 90-105°F setting (adjustable.) This provides you with fully automated winter and summer ventilation.

Specifications

Nominal air flow — 900 cfm
Blower — Inline 14" Assembly
Fan — Axial Inline 12" Diameter
Duct Size — 14" Noninsulated Flexible
Duct Length — 25 feet (standard)
Air Discharge Method — Gable (typical)
Distance To Air Discharge — 10 feet max
Power Requirements — 115 vac
Full Load Amperage — 1.9 amps
Operating Current — Nominal 1.5 amps

Operating Costs — $2.00 to $8.00 per month
Automatic or Manual
Optional — Custom duct lengths & discharge
Complete with an inline blower unit which is matched to a 25 foot length of custom perforated 14" noninsulated flex duct. Includes end cap and gable mounting flange. The automatic system operates on temperature and humidity settings for year round automatic ventilation of the attic. The manual system allows for user supplied controls.

Manufacturers and Suppliers of Solar-Powered Attic Vent Fans and Solar Panels

ALTERNATIVE ENERGY ENGINEERING, PO Box 339, Redway, CA 95560 - (800) 777-6609 (707) 923-3009

<u>model</u>	<u>size of fan</u>	<u>maximum cfm</u>
"12" Solar Fan Kit" <u>solar panel output</u> - 10 watts	- 12 inch <u>type</u> - remote	- 550 cfm
"16" Solar Fan Kit" <u>solar panel output</u> - 20 watts	- 16 inch <u>type</u> - remote	- 1000 cfm
"Solar Roof Vent" <u>solar panel output</u> - 10 watts	- 12 inch <u>type</u> - self contained	- 800 cfm
"Solarvent" <u>solar panel output</u> - 1 watt	- approx. 3 inch <u>type</u> - self contained	- 50 cfm

    <u>solar panels</u> - various sizes and watts available
    <u>features</u> - A fan, solar module and 20 feet of two conductor wire are included with the 12" and 16" solar fan kits. By reversing the wire at the motor, fan can be used for intake or exhaust. Flat base of self contained unit designed to be inserted under shingles on pitched roof. Equipped with heavy gauge screen to prevent insects entering when fan not running. "Solarvent" requires a 4 1/2" hole for mounting, compact unit with an overall diameter of 8 1/2". Available with a plastic or stainless cover.

ALTERNATIVE ENERGY SYSTEMS CO. OF MISSISSIPPI, 22 Dillard Road, Poplarville, MS 39470 - (601) 772-9966

<u>model</u>	<u>size of fan</u>	<u>maximum cfm</u>
"12" Solar Fan Kit" <u>solar panel output</u> - 110 watts	- 12 inch <u>type</u> - remote	- 550 cfm
"16" Solar Fan Kit" <u>solar panel output</u> - 22 watts	- 16 inch <u>type</u> - remote	- 1000 cfm

    <u>features</u> - You can purchase heavy venturi frame fans or ring frame fans. Panels sold separately. 11-watt panel can power one 12" fan and 22-watt panel can power two 12" fans or one 16" fan. Panels have a 10-year warranty. The fans use DC motors.

ALTERNATIVE POWER RENEWABLE ENERGY CENTER, 104 N. Main, Viroqua, WI 54665 - (608) 637-2722

model - "12" Solar Fan Kit"	size of fan - 12 inch	maximum cfm - 550 cfm
solar panel output - 10 watts	type - remote	
model - "16" Solar Fan Kit"	size of fan - 16 inch	maximum cfm - 1000 cfm
solar panel output - 20 watts	type - remote	
model - "Solar Roof Vent"	size of fan - 12 inch	maximum cfm - 800 cfm
solar panel output - 10 watts	type - self contained	
model - "Solarvent"	size of fan - approx. 3 inch	maximum cfm - 50 cfm
solar panel output - 1 watt	type - self contained	

solar panels - various sizes and watts available

features - The 12" and 16" solar fan kits include the fan, solar module and 20 feet of two conductor wire. The fan can be used for intake or exhaust by reversing the wire at the motor. The self contained unit has a flat base that is designed to be inserted under shingles on a pitched roof. It has a screen so insects cannot enter when the fan is not running. The "Solarvent" is compact with an overall diameter of 8 1/2", requiring a 4 1/2" hole for mounting. It is available with a plastic or stainless cover.

INTERNATIONAL ENERGY SYSTEMS, PO Box 588, Barrington, IL 60011 - (800) 927-0419 (847) 381-0203

model - "Sun Vent"	size of fan - 12 inch	maximum cfm - 850 cfm
solar panel output - 11 watts	type - self contained	

features - The "Sun Vent" has a solar panel that is non-breakable, shade tolerant and will even operate on low light overcast days. It is available for flat, tiled or sloped mount installations. The top cover and base units are molded with UV protected ABS plastic. The molded top has a shingle appearance so it blends in with the roof. There is a metal screen that prevents insects or small animals from entering the attic. There is a locating arrow on the bottom part of the unit to show the up or North installation — however, the fan will operate in any horizontal or vertical position as long as sunlight reaches the panel. There is a 12-inch cord included to provide for an on/off switch or additional solar panel connections if desired. The aluminum fan has five blades. The DC motor includes external brush holders so it can be checked or changed easily. Three-year limited warranty. A gable vent fan and solar panels are available.

SIEMENS SOLAR INDUSTRIES, PO Box 6032, Camarillo, CA 93011 - (805) 482-6800

solar panels - various sizes and watts available

SOLAR DYNAMICS, INC., PO Box 651, Ottumwa, IA 52501 - (800) 775-2134 (515) 683-1834

model - "SDF series"	size of fan - 12 inch	maximum cfm - 800 cfm
solar panel output - 10 watts	type - self contained	

features - Two models available — for pitched roof installation with a flat base that can be inserted under shingles or flat roof installation, a mounting frame needs to be constructed. Three-year limited warranty. Options available — rain/snow deflector device to be used when roof pitches are greater than 12 pitch and a day/night switch. There is screening attached so insects and small animals cannot enter the attic area. The housing and base is made of UV protected ABS plastic.

SOLAREX, 630 Solarex Ct., Frederick, MD 21701 - (301) 698-4200

solar panels - various sizes and watts available

SUN TUNNEL SKYLIGHTS, 786 McGlincey Lane, Campbell, CA 95008 - (800) 369-3664 (408) 369-7447

model - "Fan-Attic"	size of fan - 12 inch	maximum cfm - 800 cfm
solar panel output - 11 watts	type - self contained	

features - The circular flashing design installs just like the pipe flashings you have on your roof and installation consists of mounting the flashing base over a 12" diameter hole. The roof flashing base is 26 gauge and it has a weather resistant ABS cover.

SUNELCO - THE SUN ELECTRIC CO., PO Box 787, Hamilton, MT 59840 - (800) 338-6844 (406) 363-6924

model - "12" Solar Fan Kit"	size of fan - 12 inch	maximum cfm - 970 cfm
solar panel output - 10 watts	type - remote	
model - "16" Solar Fan Kit"	size of fan - 16 inch	maximum cfm - 1200 cfm
solar panel output - 20 watts	type - remote	
model - "Fan System"	size of fan - 12 inch	maximum cfm - 800 cfm
solar panel output - 10 watts	type - self contained	
model - "Sunvent"	size of fan - approx. 3 inch	maximum cfm - 680 cfm
solar panel output - 1 watt	type - self contained	

solar panel - various sizes available

features - The 12" and 16" solar fan kits include the fan assembly, solar panel and 20 feet of outdoor rated cable. The "Fan System" requires a 14" hole in the roof and sealant for the base. It is a complete unit that incorporates the module into a fan shroud and weatherproof housing. The "Sunvent Fan" is designed to keep water and back drafts out. It is made of high impact polypropylene and it is easy to mount. Great for RVs, hot tub rooms, lofts, stables, boats, greenhouses or farm buildings.

SUNIX, PO Box 3889, San Rafael, CA 94912 - (800) 807-8649 (510) 215-3333

model - "Solar Fan/Panel Kit"	size of fan - 12 inch	maximum cfm - 1000 cfm
solar panel output - 25 watts	type - remote	
model - "Solar SunVent"	size of fan - approx. 3 inch	maximum cfm - 50 cfm
solar panel output - 1 watt	type - self contained	

features - The solar panel has an aluminum frame and weighs only 8 1/2" pounds. The vent fan is hand built with three blades. It has a one-year warranty. Units come complete with all the hardware.

SDF by Solar Dynamics, Inc.

"SDF10" is designed for shingled pitched roof installations. Its base is flat, which will allow it to be inserted under the shingles. "SDF10FR" is designed for flat roof installations. A mounting frame of 19½" x 16¾" x 8" will need to be constructed. The fans will fit over the frame and eight No. 8x2" wood screws will secure the fan base to the frame.

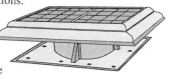

Specifications

Solar panels — 10 watts
Fan blade — 5 blades
Motor — Special design
Screen — Heavy gauge

Housing — ABS UV stable plastic
Color — black
P.V. panels — black
CFM — 600 to 800

SR Series Solar Module by Siemens Solar Industries

SR90

Typical operating specification (12V/6V) under standard test conditions

Rated power — 90 Watts

Current (A) @ Load: 5.4 / 10.8

Voltage (V) @ Load: 17.0 / 8.5

Limited warranty — 25 years

Large area single-crystal solar cells

Large enough to power many fans

Number of Fans Required per Square Foot of Attic

	Attic Width in Feet								
	20	24	28	32	36	40	44	48	52
20	400	480	560	640	720	800	880	960	1040
24	480	576	672	768	864	960	1056	1152	1248
28	560	672	784	896	1008	1120	1232	1344	1456
32	640	768	896	1024	1152	1280	1408	1536	1664
36	720	864	998	1152	1286	1440	1584	1728	1872
40	800	960	1120	1280	1440	1600	1760	1920	2080
44	880	1056	1232	1408	1584	1760	1936	2112	2288
48	960	1152	1344	1536	1728	1920	2112	2304	2496
52	1040	1248	1456	1664	1872	2080	2288	2496	2704
56	1120	1344	1568	1792	2016	2240	2464	2688	2912
60	1200	1440	1680	1920	2160	2400	2640	2880	3120
64	1280	1536	1792	2048	2304	2560	2816	3072	3328
68	1360	1632	1904	2176	2448	2720	2992	3264	3536

(Attic Length in Feet on the vertical column; overlaid diagonal labels: 1 fan, 2 fans, 3 fans)

To determine the number of fans required to cool your attic, find the length of your attic on the vertical column and the width of your attic on the horizontal column. Where the two intersect you find the total square feet.

Solar Panel
• 25 watt
• 12 volts, 18 volt peak
• 1.4 amps
• Weather resistant
• Impact resistant
• 35 cells in series
• 24" x 24" dimension
• 2" deep, 8.5 pounds

Vent Fan
• Hand built 12" fan
• Welded steel frame
• 12 volt ball bearing motor
• 13" diameter/3" depth fan
• 3 12" aluminum fan blades
• 3 point mounts
• CFM of 1000
• 1 year warranty on motor

Solar Powered Attic Fan by Sunix

Sun Vent by International Energy Systems Corp.

• Panel — 11 watts; multiple stacked cell, nonbreakable (shadow and shade tolerant

• Motor — one 38 volt; Direct Current (high efficiency) with external brush assembly

• Height — 6" above roof surface

• Top base — 20½" x 31" ABS UV stabilized with KORAD (acrylic) 22" x 24" FP model • 18" x 20" model

• Air Flow — Up to 850 cfm (dependent on location, direction, & solar insolation). Additional volume with supplemental panel

• Hardware — All components are stainless steel, aluminum or painted galvanized metal

• Screen — Coated metal screen (¼") provides protection from insects or animals and still provides good air flow

• Cord — extra cord length (12") is included to provide for on/off switches or additional solar panel connection

Generators are good backup power

Q: We often have electric power outages. To keep my furnace, sump pump, refrigerator, lights, security system, etc., running, I would like a whole-house emergency generator. What types are available?

A: Electric utility power outages can be a real problem. Even if you have a gas or oil-fired furnace, without electricity for the blower and controls, there is no heat. Extended power outages can allow frozen foods to thaw and spoil. Home security systems often stop functioning.

Eight to 10 kilowatt (KW) emergency standby generators are an adequate size for most homes. These provide enough electricity so that there is minimal disruption to your everyday activities at home during a power outage.

The generator unit is located outside your house and looks like an outdoor central air-conditioner unit. Systems as large as 20 KW are available. The most convenient emergency generators include an automatic transfer switch (ATS) located indoors near your existing circuit breaker panel. Electronic circuitry senses when the utility's power goes off or the voltage is too low.

Should a power outage or brown-out occur, the ATS automatically starts the generator engine and switches your house power from the utility lines to your own generator. Within seconds, you have electricity again.

The controls also start (exercise) the generator for a short period each week to make sure it is operating properly. Manual transfer switches, which require you to throw the switch during a power outage, are also available.

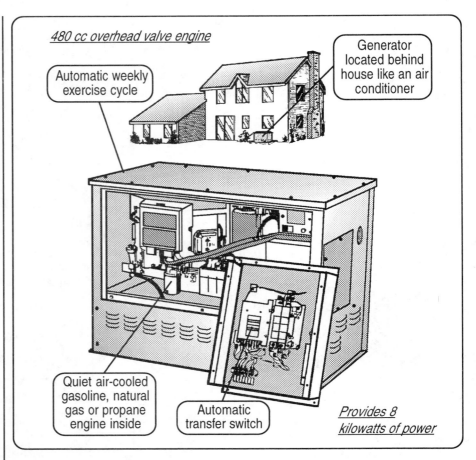

480 cc overhead valve engine

Automatic weekly exercise cycle

Generator located behind house like an air conditioner

Quiet air-cooled gasoline, natural gas or propane engine inside

Automatic transfer switch

Provides 8 kilowatts of power

Most whole-house 8 to 10 KW systems use small air or water-cooled engines. These are similar to motorcycle engines. They are designed to operate on natural gas, propane, diesel or gasoline.

Home-sized emergency generators are efficient. When powered on natural gas, the fuel cost is equivalent to about 12 cents per kilowatt-hour of electricity produced. The only additional operating cost is generally changing the engine oil once a year.

The small gas and propane-powered engines are practically maintenance-free and quiet. They operate very cleanly. For extra reliability, the engines are protected by automatic low oil pressure and high temperature monitors.

In order to determine the size of the emergency generator that you need, add up the watts used by the appliances and lights you want to keep running during a power outage. Wattages are usually listed somewhere on the products' nameplates.

Q: I heard that saving $500 annually on my utility bills from investing in home efficiency improvements is better than making $500 interest on a financial investment. Why is this true?

A: The return from energy-saving improvements is better because it is after-tax money. For example, if you invest $1,000 in bonds and make $50 interest, you have to pay tax on it. This leaves you with only $36.

If a $1,000 energy-saving improvement yields $50 in savings, this is after-tax money. You get to keep all $50 in your pocket. A more efficient house also puts less wear and tear on your heating and cooling systems.

Whole-house standby generators, with an automatic transfer switch, automatically start as soon as there is a power outage. The automatic transfer switch disconnects your house from the utility grid so that utility workers are not electrocuted by your system as they repair lines. An 8-kw generator system is adequate to supply enough electricity for a typical home. Use the charts on page 32 to estimate what your electricity generation requirements would be.

You have several fuel options to power the generator. If you have natural gas available, it is the preferred fuel because it burns cleanly with little maintenance. Propane units are as maintenance-free, but the fuel is more expensive. You can compare the costs to operate various manufacturers' generators by their fuel consumption rates and your local costs for various fuels. The cheapest source of electricity is still your utility company and it is not cost effective to use these generators on a continuous basis for electricity.

Another option for emergency backup electricity is a solar cells battery set. See suppliers list below. The output of these systems is limited, but they can power a refrigerator, lights, radio or TV during a power outage. They are also pollution-free.

Installation

Installation of a home standby system is not a "do it yourself" project. Only qualified electricians or contractors should attempt such installations, which must comply strictly with applicable codes, standards and regulations.

Before Installation

Before installing this equipment, check the ratings of both the generator and the transfer switch. Read "Emergency Isolation Method" and "Total Circuit Isolation Method" carefully. The generator's rated wattage/amperage capacity must be adequate to handle all electrical loads that the unit will power. You may have to group the critical (essential electrical) loads together and wire them into a separate "emergency distribution panel".

Emergency Circuit Isolation Method

One effective way of preventing the generator from being overloaded is to use the "emergency circuit isolation method". Essential electrical loads are grouped together and wired into a separate emergency distribution panel. Load circuits fed by the emergency distribution panel must be within the unit's rated wattage capacity. The following apply to this type of isolation system:
- The transfer switch is installed between the main and the emergency distribution panels as shown.
- The transfer switch must have an ampere rating equal to the ampere rating of the emergency circuit.

Total Circuit Isolation Method

If essential loads cannot be grouped together and wired into an emergency distribution panel, the user will have to select load circuits that will be powered by the generator during a utility power outage.
Be careful to avoid overloading the generator. The following apply to the total circuit isolation method:
- The transfer switch is installed between the utility service entrance and the distribution panel.
- The transfer switch ampere rating must be equal to the main electrical service entrance rating.

Typical Home Standby System

from Generac Corp.

Operation

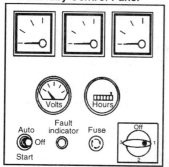

Air-Cooled Home Standby Control Panel

Water-Cooled Home Standby Control Panel

Using the Manual-Off-Auto Switch
1. "Manual" or "Start" Position
- Set the switch to "Manual" to crank and start the engine.
- Transfer to standby power will not occur after any manual start.
2. "Auto" Position
- Provides fully automatic system operation.
- Selecting this switch position allows you to start and exercise the engine every 7 days.
3. "Off" Position
- Shuts down the engine
- Prevents automatic operation

To Select Automatic Transfer Operation
1. Make sure the transfer switch main contacts are actuated to their UTILITY position, i.e., load connected to utility power source side.
2. Be sure normal utility power source voltage is available to transfer switch terminal lugs N1 and N2.
3. Set generator's Manual-Off-Auto switch to AUTO.
4. Actuate the generator main circuit breaker to its ON or CLOSED position.
With the preceding steps completed, the generator will start automatically when utility source voltage drops below a preset level. After the unit starts, loads are transferred to the standby power source. Refer to "Sequence of Automatic Operation".

Manual Operation
To start the generator and actuate the transfer switch manually, refer to the Owner's Manual of your generator or the manual of your particular transfer switch.
Re-transfer back to Utility Power Source: When utility power has been restored, you will want to re-transfer back to that source and shut down the generator. This can be accomplished as follows:
1. Actuate the main circuit breaker to OFF or OPEN.
2. Let the engine run for a minute or two at no-load to stabilize the internal temperatures.
3. Set the generator's Manual-Off-Auto switch to OFF. The engine should shut down.
4. Check that power supply to transfer switch is turned OFF.
5. Manually actuate transfer switch main contacts back to UTILITY position, i.e., loads connected to utility power supply. Refer to Owner's Manual of your generator for transfer switch operation.
6. Turn ON the utility power supply to the transfer switch, using whatever means provided.
7. Set the system to automatic operation as outlined in "To Select Automatic Operation".

DO NOT ATTEMPT TO ACTUATE TRANSFER SWITCH MANUALLY UNTIL AFTER ALL POWER VOLTAGE SUPPLIES TO SWITCH HAVE BEEN POSITIVELY TURNED OFF.

ALTURDYNE, 8050 Armour St., San Diego, CA 92111 - (619) 565-2131

model - "G2.8FGH3PP"	kilowatts - 2.8 kw	fuel - gasoline	fuel consumption - 0.40 gal./hr.
model - "G4.5FGB3EPP"	kilowatts - 4.5 kw	fuel - gasoline	fuel consumption - 0.70 gal./hr.
model - "G6FGB3EPP"	kilowatts - 6.0 kw	fuel - gasoline	fuel consumption - 0.90 gal./hr.
model - "G7.5FGV3EPP"	kilowatts - 7.5 kw	fuel - gasoline	fuel consumption - 0.80 gal./hr.
model - "G9FGV3EPP"	kilowatts - 9.0 kw	fuel - gasoline	fuel consumption - 0.90 gal./hr.
model - "G10.5FGV3EPP"	kilowatts - 4.5 kw	fuel - gasoline	fuel consumption - 1.25 gal./hr.
model - "ARD 005 - 060 HGE"	kilowatts - 5.0 kw	fuel - diesel	fuel consumption - 0.40 gal./hr.
model - "ARD 007 - 060 HGE"	kilowatts - 7.5 kw	fuel - diesel	fuel consumption - 0.50 gal./hr.
model - "ARD 010 - 060 HGE"	kilowatts - 10.0 kw	fuel - diesel	fuel consumption - 1.00 gal./hr.
model - "ARD 008 - 060 HGO"	kilowatts - 8.0 kw	fuel - diesel	fuel consumption - 0.50 gal./hr.
model - "ARD 012 - 060 HGO"	kilowatts - 12.0 kw	fuel - diesel	fuel consumption - 1.00 gal./hr.

features - These systems are available with weather resistant, soundproof and thermal-insulated housing enclosures. Some of them also offer an automatic transfer switch so the unit comes on in case of an emergency. The gasoline units are portable. The "G" series models 7.5 kw and above are available with propane and natural gas.

GENERAC CORP., Highway 59 & Hillside Rd., Waukesha, WI 53187 - (414) 544-4811

model - "EPS-8D"	kilowatts - 8.0 kw	fuel - diesel	fuel consumption - 0.88 gal./hr.
model - "EPS-8-AC"	kilowatts - 8.0 kw	fuel - propane	fuel consumption - 67 cu. ft./hr.
model - "EPS-12"	kilowatts - 11.0 kw	fuel - propane	fuel consumption - 71 cu. ft./hr.
model - "EPS-8-AC"	kilowatts - 8.0 kw	fuel - natural gas	fuel consumption - 145 cu. ft./hr.
model - "EPS-12"	kilowatts - 10.0 kw	fuel - natural gas	fuel consumption - 178 cu. ft./hr.

features - There is an automatic 7-day exerciser that is always checking the system to be sure that it is ready for any emergency. These units have an automatic transfer switch so there is no need to go outside to start the unit in case of an emergency. There is a battery charger that keeps the engine starting circuit ready. The generators are protected by low oil pressure and high temperature shutdowns. Other models available for recreational vehicles (RV) models — see specifications on page 108.

JOHN DEERE CONSUMER PRODUCTS, PO Box 7047, Charlotte, NC 28241 - (704) 588-3200

model - "LRIE5500"	kilowatts - 5.5 kw	fuel - gasoline	fuel consumption - 1.00 gal./hr.
model - "LRE5500"	kilowatts - 5.5 kw	fuel - gasoline	fuel consumption - 1.00 gal./hr.
model - "CG4800"	kilowatts - 4.8 kw	fuel - gasoline	fuel consumption - 0.68 gal./hr.
model - "CG5200"	kilowatts - 5.2 kw	fuel - gasoline	fuel consumption - 0.75 gal./hr.
model - "CGE6300"	kilowatts - 6.3 kw	fuel - gasoline	fuel consumption - 0.83 gal./hr.

features - All of these units are portable. The LRI includes a super lo-tone muffler for quiet operation and it offers a GFCI-protected receptacle for added safety. They have heavy duty air filters, low oil shut off and automatic idle control.

KOHLER POWER SYSTEMS, 444 Highland Dr., Kohler, WI 53044 - (800) 544-2444 (920) 457-4441

model - "5RMY"	kilowatts - 5.0 kw	fuel - gasoline	fuel consumption - 1.10 gal./hr.
model - "6.5RMY"	kilowatts - 6.5 kw	fuel - gasoline	fuel consumption - 1.27 gal./hr.
model - "10RY"	kilowatts - 10.0 kw	fuel - gasoline	fuel consumption - 1.50 gal./hr.
model - "12RY"	kilowatts - 12.0 kw	fuel - gasoline	fuel consumption - 1.80 gal./hr.
model - "6ROY"	kilowatts - 6.0 kw	fuel - diesel	fuel consumption - 0.61 gal./hr.
model - "10ROY"	kilowatts - 10.0 kw	fuel - diesel	fuel consumption - 1.10 gal./hr.
model - "5RMY"	kilowatts - 5.0 kw	fuel - propane	fuel consumption - 58 cu. ft./hr.
model - "6.5RMY"	kilowatts - 6.5 kw	fuel - propane	fuel consumption - 53 cu. ft./hr.
model - "10RY"	kilowatts - 10.0 kw	fuel - propane	fuel consumption - 68 cu. ft./hr.
model - "12RY"	kilowatts - 12.0 kw	fuel - propane	fuel consumption - 75 cu. ft./hr.
model - "5RMY"	kilowatts - 4.5 kw	fuel - natural gas	fuel consumption - 126 cu. ft./hr.
model - "6.5RMY"	kilowatts - 5.3 kw	fuel - natural gas	fuel consumption - 110 cu. ft./hr.
model - "10RY"	kilowatts - 8.0 kw	fuel - natural gas	fuel consumption - 122 cu. ft./hr.
model - "12RY"	kilowatts - 9.0 kw	fuel - natural gas	fuel consumption - 166 cu. ft./hr.

features - These units are equipped with Power Boost™ regulator which responds quickly and with less fluctuation. It allows lights and appliances to switch over without any interruption or flickering. There is a ±2% voltage regulation and a ±1% frequency regulation because of the electronic governing on the "10RY" and "12RY" models. There is an automatic transfer switch that continually monitors the flow of electricity. If the power does go out, the switch starts and brings the generator on-line until normal electrical service returns. Several of the models feature a weatherproof molded fiberglass housing to block the noise level of the unit. There is an enclosed exhaust silencer. It is available in cream beige or forest green.

ONAN CORP., 1400 73rd Ave., NE, Minneapolis, MN 55432 - (800) 888-6626 (612) 574-5000

model - "4.5BDG-FB"	kilowatts - 4.5 kw	fuel - gasoline	fuel consumption - 1.10 gal./hr.
model - "6.5NHE"	kilowatts - 6.5 kw	fuel - gasoline	fuel consumption - 1.30 gal./hr.
model - "7.5KDK"	kilowatts - 7.5 kw	fuel - diesel	fuel consumption - 0.90 gal./hr.

ONAN CORP. - cont'd

model - "10.0KKG"	kilowatts - 10.0 kw	fuel - diesel	fuel consumption - 1.04 gal./hr.
model - "6.5NHE"	kilowatts - 6.5 kw	fuel - propane	fuel consumption - 63 cu. ft./hr.
model - "7.0NHm"	kilowatts - 7.0 kw	fuel - propane	fuel consumption - 73 cu. ft./hr.
model - "6.5NHE"	kilowatts - 6.5 kw	fuel - natural gas	fuel consumption - 93 cu. ft./hr.
model - "7.0NHM"	kilowatts - 7.0 kw	fuel - natural gas	fuel consumption - 100 cu. ft./hr.

features - The units are available with an automatic transfer switch which brings the generator on when the utility power fails. A weatherproof and soundproof housing is available. There are vibration isolators that protect the control panel from any vibration.

Generac Mobile Generator Specifications

Series Number	NP30G	NP40G	NP50G	NP66G	Q55G	Q70G
Watts	3200	4000	5000	6600	5500	7000
Engine RPM	variable	variable	2700	2700	2500	2500
Engine	GN-190 cc	GN-220 cc	GN-360 cc	GN-480 cc	GN-480 cc	GN-570 cc
Amps	26.6	33.3	41.6	55	45.8	58.3
Voltage	120 V Single Phase		120 V (reconnectable to 240 V*) Single Phase			
Hertz	60	60	60	60	60	60
Fuel Consumption (gal. per KW hr.)	0.13	0.13	0.16	0.15	0.15	0.15
Dimensions Inches (L×W×H)	15.5 × 15.93 × 14.42		25 × 18.5 × 15.75			
Weight (lbs.)	86	88	207	213	215	222

Air Cooled RV Generators

Alternator Features: NP-30G and NP-40G

• Permanent magnet design • Microprocessor controlled output • Class F insulation • Large forced air cooling fan • Overload and overspeed shutdown • 12V battery charging

Alternator Features: all others

• 2 pole revolving field design • V/F voltage regulation • Displaced phase excitation • Skewed stator • Class F insulation system • Large forced air cooling fan • 12 volt battery charging

All specifications are subject to change without notice.

Control Features:

• Automatic starter lockout • Remote panel connector • Over voltage protection • Main line circuit breakers

Accessories:

• Muffler kites • Remote on/off switch with plate • Wiring harness with remote plug • Mounting kits • LPG conversion kits

Approximate Wattage Requirements for Home Appliances

Appliance	Wattage	Appliance	Wattage
Air Conditioner	2000 - 3000	Heater (Portable)	1300
Blanket	150	Hot Plate	1250
Broiler	1400	Humidifier	200
Clothes Dryer (Electric)	5000 - 10,000	Light Bulb	60 - 150
Clothes Dryer (Gas)	400	Microwave Oven	800
Coffee Maker	850	Refrigerator/Freezer	600 - 2000
Computer Equipment	600	Security System	250
Dehumidifier	300	Sump Pump	400 - 3000
Dishwasher	1500 - 2500	Television (Color)	100 - 300
Electric Skillet	1250	Toaster	1100 - 1700
Fan (Attic)	375	Washing Machine	500
Fan (Furnace)	800 - 1200	Water Heater	3000 - 4500
Food Freezer	300 - 500	Water Pump	1000 - 3000

Approximate Wattages for Portable Electric Tools

Equipment	Wattage	Equipment	Wattage
Blowers, Electric	370 - 2250	Routers	900 - 1100
Compressors	190 - 2250	Saws, Chain	800 - 1500
Drain Cleaners	250	Saws, Circular 6"	1000 - 2500
Drills 1/4"	250 - 600	Saws, Cutoff	2500
Drills 3/8"	300 - 600	Saws, Jig	200 - 800
Drills 1/2"	350 -1200	Saws, Masonry	1500 - 3750
Drills 1"	1000	Saws, Table	750 - 2250
Grinders, Bench	190 - 750	Saws, Radial Arm	750 - 3750
Grinders, Portable	1000 - 2500	Screw Drivers	550
Hammers, Demolition	1260	Shears, Metal-Cutting	750
Hammers, Rotary	1200	Sanders, Belt	600 -1500
Impact Wrenches 1/2"	600	Sanders, Disc.	1200
Impact Wrenches 1"	1200	Sanders, Orbital	250

Solar cells generate good results

Q: I want to use high-efficiency solar cell panels to produce free electricity. I have heard that electric utility companies buy any excess electricity I generate. What type of system is available for home use and which is best for me?

A: Electricity-generating solar cells (called photovoltaics or PV systems) naturally produce electricity when the sun shines on them. There is no sound, pollution or waste produced. With no moving parts a solar cell panel is nearly maintenance free.

There is a wide range of sizes and complexity of PV systems for homes. Small systems provide enough electricity for a light, a radio, and a power tool in a backyard shed or cabin. Small, lightweight PV systems are also effective on campers and boats for lighting and a radio or TV. Very tiny solar cell panels can be used to keep car and truck batteries at peak charge.

Large whole-house systems can handle most of your electrical needs, except for high consumption appliances like an electric water heater or air conditioner. Most often, it is best to stay connected to your electric utility service lines.

When the solar cells are producing more electricity than needed, your utility company may buy the excess electricity. The amount that they buy is deducted from your monthly electric bill. Special switches and meters are used to control the switching and to record electricity output.

To improve the electricity output by up to 25 percent, mount the PV panels on a sun-tracking rack. The sun-tracking rack follows the sun throughout the day to keep the panels facing it. One simple design,

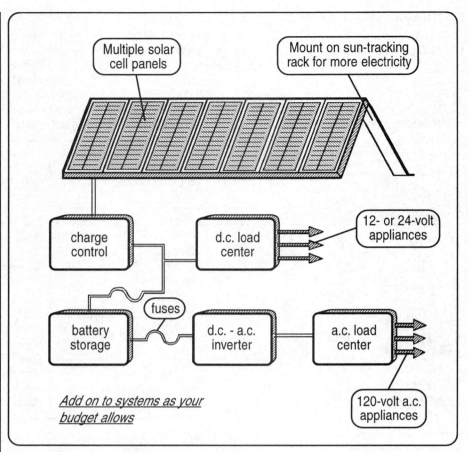

Multiple solar cell panels

Mount on sun-tracking rack for more electricity

charge control

d.c. load center

12- or 24-volt appliances

battery storage

fuses

d.c. - a.c. inverter

a.c. load center

120-volt a.c. appliances

Add on to systems as your budget allows

made by Zomeworks, uses the sun's heat to expand fluids that rotate the rack. No electric motors are needed.

A PV system is simple. Many tiny solar cells are wired together in durable panels. The output is in direct current (d.c.). This can be transformed, with an inverter, into 120-volt alternating current to operate standard home appliances. Excess electricity output is usually stored in batteries. The batteries can also be used as an emergency backup system for power outages.

You can buy special tools, refrigerators, lights, etc., that operate on the lower-voltage direct current coming from the PV panels or batteries. This eliminates the need for an expensive inverter; however, it will not operate your standard 120-volt appliances.

Always do cost payback analysis before investing in a PV system.

Major PV suppliers, like Siemens Solar and Photocomm, can assist you with this.

Q: I am doing some repair work to my windows and storm windows. The storms do not seal well. Should I caulk and weatherstrip them tightly?

A: No. You should not caulk your storm windows or seal them with a gasket. The primary purpose of storm windows is to protect your primary windows from the direct force of the wind and bad weather. If they are tightly sealed, moisture gets trapped in between them causing fogging.

You may notice small holes at the bottom of the storms windows. These are called weep holes and they should not be sealed. Any moisture that condenses during colder weather will dissipate through these holes. A small, but necessary, amount of air circulates through them.

Using solar cell photovoltaic systems for producing electricity from the sun is an effective, pollution-free method to generate electricity. Before you purchase any photovoltaic system, carefully analyze the payback from installing a system as compared to using electricity from your utility company. Environmentally, photovoltaic-generated electricity is almost totally clean and this may also figure into your decision of whether to install a PV system.

Several suppliers of photovoltaic solar cell systems are listed below. There are additional local smaller retailers that purchase solar cell panels from these major manufacturers and assemble and market photovoltaic systems for home, trailer, and recreational use. Systems for recreational vehicles are very effective because of the large flat roofs.

Pages 35 and 36 show detailed specifications on several typical residential size systems (specs. for Photocomm). Also

listed below are manufacturers of special support racks used for mounting the solar cell panels. These are designed to automatically track the sun's position throughout the day to provide the maximum amount of electricity from a photovoltaic system. These also can improve the long-term payback of the entire system. The chart below shows several cities and the total number of hours of sunshine per year. Also shown are descriptions and prices of several typical d.c. voltage appliances.

Suppliers of Photovoltaic (PV) Solar Cell Systems

KYOCERA AMERICA, 8611 Balboa Ave., San Diego, CA 92123 - (619) 576-2600

NORTHERN POWER SYSTEMS, 1 N. Wind Rd., Waitsfield, VT 05673 - (802) 496-2955

PHOTOCOMM, 7812 Acoma Dr.,, Scottsdale, AZ 85260 - (800) 544-6466 (602) 948-8003

SIEMENS SOLAR, 4650 Adohr Ln., Camarillo, CA 93012 - (805) 482-6800

SOLAREX, 630 Solarex Ct., Frederick, MD 21701 - (800) 521-7652 (301) 698-4200

SOLARMETRICS, 3160 Fort Denaud Rd., LaBelle, FL 33935 - (800) 356-4751 (941) 674-1901

SUNNYSIDE SOLAR, 1014 Green River Rd. - Gilford, Brattleboro, VT 05301 - (802) 257-1482

TIDELAND SIGNAL, PO Box 52430, Houston, TX 77052 - (800) 231-2778 (713) 681-6101

WINDSTREAM POWER SYSTEMS, PO Box 1604, Burlington, VT 05402 - (802) 658-0075

Manufacturers of Sun-Tracking Racks for Solar Cell Panels

AMERICAN SUNCO, PO Box 789, Blue Hill, ME 04614 - (207) 374-5700

ARRAY TECHNOLOGIES, 3402 Stanford NE, Albuquerque, NM 87107 - (505) 881-7567

ZOMEWORKS CORP., PO Box 25805, Albuquerque, NM 87125 - (505) 242-5354

Mean Number of Hours of Sunshine

STATE AND CITY	ANNUAL	STATE AND CITY	ANNUAL	STATE AND CITY	ANNUAL
AL BIRMINGHAM	2662	LA SHREVEPORT	3015	ND FARGO	2586
AK ANCHORAGE	1992	ME PORTLAND	2653	OH CINCINNATI	2574
AZ PHOENIX	3832	MD BALTIMORE	2653	CLEVELAND	2352
TUCSON	3829	MA BOSTON	2615	OK OKLAHOMA CITY	3048
AR LITTLE ROCK	2840	MI DETROIT	2375	TULSA	2783
CA LOS ANGELES	3284	LANSING	2378	OR PORTLAND	2122
SAN FRANCISCO	2959	MN DULUTH	2475	PA PHILADELPHIA	2564
CO DENVER	3033	MINNEAPOLIS	2607	PITTSBURGH	2202
CT HARTFORD	2541	MS JACKSON	2646	RI PROVIDENCE	2589
DC WASHINGTON	2576	MO ST. LOUIS	2694	SC CHARLESTON	2993
FL JACKSONVILLE	2713	SPRINGFIELD	2820	COLUMBIA	2914
TAMPA	3001	MT BILLINGS	2762	SD RAPID CITY	2858
HI HONOLULU	3041	GREAT FALLS	2884	TN MEMPHIS	2808
GA ATLANTA	2821	NB LINCOLN	2907	NASHVILLE	2634
SAVANNAH	2752	OMAHA	2997	TX DALLAS	2911
ID BOISE	3006	NV LAS VEGAS	3838	HOUSTON	2633
IL CHICAGO	2611	RENO	3483	UT SALT LAKE CITY	3059
SPRINGFIELD	2702	NH CONCORD	2354	VT BURLINGTON	2178
IN FT. WAYNE	2570	NJ ATLANTIC CITY	2683	VA NORFOLK	2803
INDIANAPOLIS	2668	TRENTON	2653	RICHMOND	2663
IA DES MOINES	2770	NM ALBUQUERQUE	3418	WA SEATTLE	2019
KS TOPEKA	2702	NY BUFFALO	2458	SPOKANE	2605
KY LOUISVILLE	2601	NEW YORK	2677	W VA PARKERSBURG	2265
LA NEW ORLEANS	2744	NC CHARLOTTE	2891	WI MILWAUKEE	2510
		RALEIGH	2680	WY CHEYENNE	2900

Solar Electric Components (by Photocomm) - 12 volts or 24 volts d.c.

P-16 Solar-Powered Refrigerator/Freezer - This is a 16 cubic foot refrigerator including a 4.5 cubic foot freezer. It has two doors with deep interior shelves and compartments. The one-drawer. The compressor is on the top so refrigerator. Door seals are air tight is approximately 800 watt hours per piece liner is easy to clean and there is a large fresh food and vegetable the heat generated from operation escapes harmlessly without warming the with extra insulation throughout. The average daily power comsumption day. See diagram #1.

New Breeze Solar-Powered Cooler - a refreshing indoor climate. It improves are 17 1/2" x 22 1/4" x 20".

Classic Ceiling Fan - The paddle-type duty motor housing and wood-style energy and draws less than 25 watts.

The evaporative cooler adds moisture to hot, dry air, converting the air into breathing air by filtering out dust and pollutants. The overall dimensions

fan helps conserve energy by improving air circulation. It features a heavy-blades which reverse direction for seasonal change. It helps conserve

figure #1

Outdoor Light 162 - The amber lens on this 16-watt weatherproof outdoor light will not attract mosquitoes or other insects. It is made of long-lasting aluminum for maximum durability.

Omegalux 1200 Series Outdoor Lighting - These are floodlights with a high-tech stylized housing with PL/DULUX fluorescent lamps for energy savings. Excellent in landscapes, for security lighting or as a controlled general purpose illumination. Suitable for use in wet locations and for mounting within 3' of the ground. All metal cast and extruded hous-ing in baked enamel finish. Available from 5 to 40 watts.

Solar Lantern - This solar lantern is lightweight, portable, and rugged enough for outdoor use. The light source provides 360 degrees of illumination with three illumination levels - 4 hours on high; 7 hours on medium; 10 hours on low. See diagram #3.

diagram #2

Thin-Lite® Fluorescent Fixtures - Anodized aluminum hous-ings and clear acrylic diffuser lenses provide high light output on 3 sides. Designed for use in remote areas in conjunction with alternative sources of energy. Available in three styles - circular ceiling, standard rectangular 115 and 116 fixtures.

diagram #3

Photocomm Home Solar Electric Systems

You should be able to choose the correct key components to build a power system that satisfies your electrical requirements or you can buy complete systems.

The following five systems are complete home power systems. These systems are made of the highest quality matched components; ready to ship, complete.

All systems feature the Kyocera 51 watt, LA51, solar electric module which carries a 12-year warranty. If you find the cost of these systems does not fit your budget, Photocomm offers custom components.

A Photocomm sales technician or authorized dealer can help you choose the appropriate equipment. All systems include all parts necessary for complete installation.

System 200 — Remote Cabin, RV or Boat Basic System

Typical System Power Output: approximately 1200 watt hours per day

This is a very comfortable cabin or weekend vacation home system which can be used as a starter system for a full time residence. Everything that is needed for complete installation is provided. Sealed batteries and controller with full metering allow for low maintenance. A fuse box is provided for easy hook-up to home wiring. Choice between small and large inverter offered as an option to take care of air-conditioning needs.

System 200 Components

4 - 51 watt Kyocera LA51 solar electric modules
1 - 4 module metal roof or ground mount
1 - 15 amp controller with meters
4 - 200 amp hour, 6-volt sealed, 5-year warranty deep-cycle batteries
battery interconnects/#4 wire
module interconnects
25' lead wire/#8-2
1 - 9 circuit fuse box
instructions and warranties
options — 4 module tracker - for up to 35% increase in array power
600 watt inverter & cables
2500 watt inverter & cables
controller upgrade to 30 amp with meters so more modules can be added

System 400 — High Power AC/DC Remote Home System

Typical System Power Output: approximately 2.4 kW hours per day

A real AC/DC home power system. More than a thousand-plus amp hours of battery storage gives the home owner assurance of power during cloudy or stormy weather. The powerful inverter will run up to 1/2 HP well pumps and motors as well as kitchen, lighting and entertainment equipment. The high-quality PCU controller comes in a waterproof enclosure and has three meters for system monitoring.

System 400 Components

8 - 51 watt Kyocera LA51 solar electric modules
1 - 8 module metal roof or ground mount
1 - PCU 30 amp/12 volt - 3 meters, central wiring, temperature compensation in waterproof enclosure
6 - L16 350 amp hour/6-volt heavy duty, deep-cycle batteries
battery interconnects/#4 wire
module interconnects
25' lead wire/#8 wire
1 - 2500 watt inverter
1 set inverter interconnects
instructions and warranties
options — 8 panel tracker for up to 35% more power, battery upgrade: 2-volt industrial, deep-cycle batteries, 5 year warranty

System 600 — High Power AC/DC Home Power System

Typical System Power Output: approximately 5000 watt hours per day

A powerful home electric system which should take care of the energy needs of most families. The passive tracker maximizes solar module daily output and the 5000 watt inverter can run up to a 1 1/2 HP pump or motor. The inverter is very efficient and will provide enough power for a home and workshop. This 24-volt system includes high performance PCU controller with 3 system meters, waterproof enclosure and temperature compensation. A system for those who want electrical independence and enough power to live in comfort. This system can be turned into an unlimited power, solar GenSet system by using the options offered.

System 600 Components

12 - 51 watt Kyocera LA51 solar electric modules
12 - L16 350 amp hour, 6-volt deep-cycle batteries
12 - module tracker
 1 - PCU 24-volt 30 amp - 3 meters, central wiring, temperature compensation
battery interconnects
module interconnects
50' lead wire/#6
5000 watt 24-volt inverter
1 set inverter interconnects
instructions and warranties
options — industrial cells
battery upgrade: 12 - 1000 AH/2-volt
Honda Generator 6000 watts
24-volt/100 AH battery charger - heavy duty
Transfer Switch
Auto Gen Starter

System 100 — Remote Cabin, RV or Boat Mini System

Typical System Power Output: approximately 600 watt hours per day

This is a basic cabin system which will allow for the addition of two more modules (or doubling system size) without changing controller or mounting structure.

It is designed for the weekend cabin or vacation home, System 100 will provide enough power for lights and entertainment. With the addition of a 250-watt inverter (system option), TV, VCR, computer and printer or hand power tools can be used. Sealed batteries and controller with meter allow for low maintenance.

System 100 Components

2 - 51 watt Kyocera LA51 solar electric modules
1 - 4 module metal roof or ground mount
1 - 15 amp controller with meters
2 - 100 amp hour, sealed 5-year warranty, deep-cycle batteries
battery interconnects/#4 wire
module interconnects
25' lead wire/#10-2
1 - 6 circuit fuse box
instructions and warranties
options — 250 watt inverter

System 1400 — Solar Genset Advanced Home Power System

Typical System Power Output: approximately 10,000 watt hours per day plus

TRACK RACK™
TWIST-PLATE Components For Passive Solar Tracking

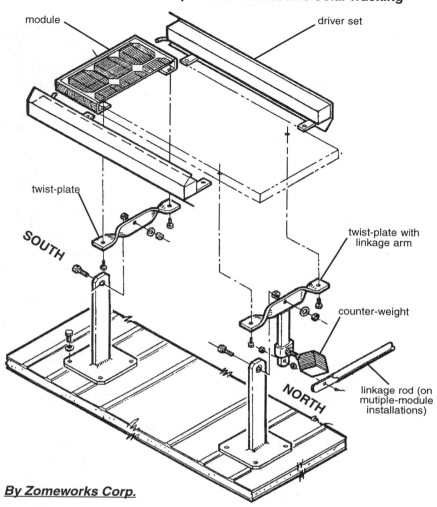

By Zomeworks Corp.

Twist-Plate components are designed to allow each photovoltaic module to rotate. (On ARCO modules they bolt to the intermediate holes of the modules.) The components are classified as "driver" and "slave" sets. The driver set includes refrigerant-charged canisters in addition to the Twist-Plates, stands and counterweights. Each driver tracks one module. An additional one to three modules, each with a slave set, may be linked to a single driver. The driver follows the sun; linked slaves follow the driver.

there is also unlimited generator back-up power.

This gives you virtually unlimited electrical power without utility hook-ups. This solar GenSet system incorporates the latest advances in solar electricity with the highest quality, automatic generator back-up system. System is composed of top-of-the-line equipment. Two-volt industrial cells are energized by a large tracker-held solar electric system and industrial battery charger attached to a superior propane powered generator. All electronic controlling, metering and switching equipment is housed in an easy-to-use, state-of-the-art Photocomm integrated power board. This system is truly a personal power company.

System 1400 Components

24 - 51 watt Kyocera LA51 solar electric modules
lead wire/#6
Photocomm Ultra Power Center with built-in controller 45 amp, digital meters, centralized input transfer switch
2 - 12 module trackers
12 - 1400 AH/2-volt cells deep-cycle industrial batteries
heavy duty battery charger 24-volt 125 amp
Honda Generator 6000 watts
7500 watt inverter
Auto Gen Starter
inverter, battery and module interconnects
instructions & warranty information
options — Utility Interconnect System

Inexpensive solar heater easy to build

Q: I would like to build a simple and inexpensive solar heater myself. My materials budget is limited to $100 and I want it to be able to heat one large room. What design do you recommend?

A: In order to stay under $100 in materials, a simple thermosiphoning design is best. As the sun heats the air inside the solar heater, it becomes less dense and naturally flows up and out into your room. It self regulates the temperature as more air volume flows through it.

Cool room air is continuously drawn in the bottom inlet creating a steady flow. On a sunny day, it should easily heat one room. As your budget allows, add a circulation fan to increase the heated air output.

This simple air-type solar heater can be mounted flat against a south-facing wall. As long as the wall is oriented within 15 degrees of true south, it will be effective.

This design concept uses a perforated metal collector sheet (painted black) inside a shallow insulated box. The sun shines on the collector sheet and heats it.

Slant the perforated sheet inside the solar box. This forces the cool room air to pass through the openings in the sun-heated metal sheet as it circulates from the bottom inlet to the top outlet opening.

If you install an electric blower, a small 100-cubic feet per minute (cfm) blower should be adequate for a 4 by 8 foot solar heater. This also allows it to be tilted more directly toward the sun for the greatest efficiency.

For the most inexpensive design, build a shallow box with 1/2-inch plywood. Make it 4 feet by 8

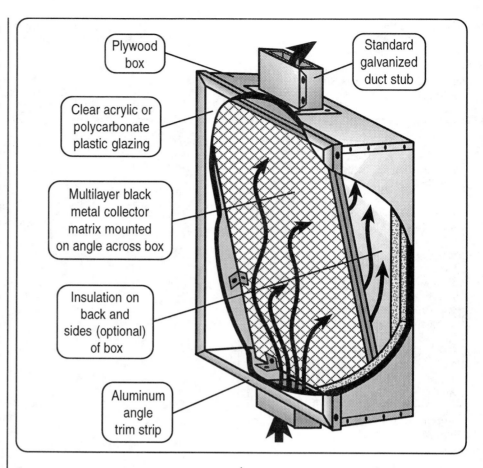

feet to use standard size lumber. Leave the top of the box open. Later the top will be covered with a glass or clear acrylic plastic sheet. Acrylic is inexpensive, durable and easy to cut.

Standard expanded metal sheeting is easiest to use for the metal absorber sheet. Lath can also be used. Wire three or four layers of it together, staggering each one a little to offset the openings.

In this way, the sun shines on most of the metal of each layer. This still allows the room air to easily flow through. Punching or drilling holes in aluminum sheets or old printing plates and spacing them slightly apart is also effective. Saw an inlet and an outlet opening in the ends of the box.

Lay foil-backed fiberglass wall insulation (painted black) in the bot-

tom and sides. Rigid foam insulation, covered with foil will work too. Slant the metal absorber plate above the insulation and attach the clear top.

Q: What is the cause of an ice dam on a roof? Is it a sign of good attic insulation and energy efficiency since the roof stays so cold?

A: An ice dam is a sign of energy inefficiency. It forms when heat, escaping from the ceiling into the attic, causes snow to melt on the roof. At night, the water refreezes and forms the dam. This blocks drainage off of the roof and the water can back up under the shingles and cause a lot of damage.

The best way to stop formation of damaging ice dams is to properly insulate your attic. Also, increase the attic ventilation to make sure the roof stays cold enough and any moisture does not condense in the attic.

1) Cut the 2×8 lumber for the frame. It is a good idea to use pressure-treated lumber for the structural components. Size the frame so that the outside dimensions are exactly 4 ft. by 8 ft. This is a convenient size so that you can use a standard 4 ft. by 8 ft. sheet of plywood for the back. Also, most of the other materials are also commonly available in 4 ft. and 8 ft. sizes.

2) Saw rectangular holes for the metal duct stubs (available at furnace contractors) in the 4-ft. long 2×8 end pieces. 2-inch high duct stubs are the best height to use so they fit nicely in the frame above the insulation. If you are not using a blower, get the widest duct stubs to minimize resistance to the air flow. Locate the 2-inch high rectangular holes 1 inch from the top edge of the 2×8 lumber. Attach the duct stubs to these holes in the frame.

3) Assemble the frame using screws — not glue. With changes in temperature and moisture of the collector lumber from day to night and throughout the year, screws will resist the stresses from shrinkage and growth of the lumber.

4) Screw the plywood cover on the bottom of the 2×8 frame lumber to form the collector box. Caulk all the joints in the box with silicone caulk.

5) Cut the foil-faced fiberglass insulation to a size 4 inches larger than the size of the inside dimensions of the collector box. Carefully cut off 2 inches of insulation around the perimeter, leaving the foil facing extending out 2 inches. This will be used for stapling the insulation in place.

6) If you can't find foil-faced insulation, use unfaced insulation, cover it with a layer of attic-type reflective foil. Do not use kraft paper-faced insulation.

7) Lay foil-faced fiberglass insulation in the bottom of the box with the foil side facing up. Staple the foil to the sides of the box to secure the insulation in place. Paint the foil surface flat black.

8) Cut a support piece from 2×4 lumber to fit the interior length dimension (a few inches less than 8 ft.) inside of the box. Screw it in place so it is flush with the open top of the collector box. This will support the clear top and the collector matrix panel.

9) Make the two collector matrix panels using expanded sheet metal or lath. Aluminum is best, steel works fine too. You will need two panels, one on each side of the center 2×4 support piece which you already installed in the box. First measure the diagonal length from the top surface of the insulation on one end to just below top edge of box on the other end. Since the collector panel will be slanted upward, it will be slightly longer than the flat horizontal inside dimension of the box.

10) Carefully cut enough pieces of the expanded metal to make the two panels of either four or five layers each. Stack the layers so that the openings are offset. This maximizes the amount of the sun's rays that strike the collector panel. Use wire to tie the layers together in many spots to form a rigid four or five layer matrix. An optional method is to use thin aluminum sheets. You can buy them at most hardware stores. Drill, saw, or punch many small holes in the aluminum sheets. Wire several of them together spacing them apart with thick washers. Stagger them so the holes are offset on each layer.

11) Cut ¾ × ¾ wood collector matrix support pieces. These will be attached in a slanted position from the top of the insulation to 1 inch below top surface of box. You will need eight pieces total. Cut four pieces to fit between center 2×4 support and inside surfaces of box. (These will be a few inches less than 2 ft., depending on the actual width of the lumber used.)

12) Attach one piece between each side of the box and the center support directly on top of the insulation. These will support the lower edge of the collector panels. Attach the other two pieces on the other end of the box up near the top edge of the box. These will support the upper edge of the collector panels. Position these two pieces far enough down from the edge so that there is about ½ inch clearance from the top edge when the collector panels are set on top of them.

13) Using the ¾ × ¾ lumber, cut four collector panel side support pieces. These will be attached on an angle along the inside of the box from the lower to the upper supports. Therefore, all the edges of the collector panels will be supported by the ¾ × ¾ lumber pieces. Nail or screw the collector panels to its support pieces.

14) Cut the 1½ in. aluminum angle to fit around perimeter of the top of box. This holds the clear cover in place.

15) Make the clear cover about 1 inch smaller than the top of the box to allow for expansion and contraction. You might find it easier to make two pieces and join them over the 2×4 center support. Clear plastic is much easier and safer to work with than glass. If you do use glass, contact a glass delaer or expert to determine the best type of glass for this application. These are large pieces of glass and tehy can be hazardous to handle and dangerous if they break. Some types of clear plastics good for solar collectors are — acrylic, polycarbonate, or fiberglass-reinforced polyester.

16) When using a clear plastic cover, lay the clear cover over the top of the box and lay the aluminum angle over that. Drill holes through both the angle and the clear plastic. The holes should be about $^1/_8$ inch larger in diameter than the size of the nails or screws. This allows for expansion and contraction of both the angle and the plastic cover.

Required Materials for Solar Heater	
expanded metal lath or aluminum sheet with perforations	2×16 metal duct stubs
½-inch plywood	1½-inch aluminum angle
2×8 lumber	metal wire
2×4 lumber	metal and rubber washers
¾×¾ lumber	nails and screws
clear plastic or glass sheets	stapler
foil-faced batt insulation	silicone caulking
small electric blower	hinge for cooling door
thermostat	foam weatherstripping
	small door latches

Remove the cover and lay a beam of silicone caulk on the top edge of the box. Lay clear plastic cover over the bead of caulk. Put rubber washers over holes and lay the angle over that. Then nail or screw the angle down to the box. Don't tighten it down too much to squeeze out the caulk. A thicker bead of caulk will handle more expansion and contraction.

17) If you use a glass cover, attach aluminum angle on the sides of box instead of the top. By doing this, you will not have to make holes in the glass itself. Use the caulk under the top edge.

18) You should make doors or covers for the inlet and outlet opening of the ducts into your room. Once the sun goes down, the air flow will naturally reverse in the solar heater and it will actually begin to cool off your room. Hinged covers similar to the ones described below will work well. A piece of 1½ or 1-inch rigid foam insulation is also effective. It is easy to cut with a knife. Cut it about ¼ inch smaller than the duct opening. Attach foam weatherstripping to the edge and push it into the duct openings. Screw a small drawer knob onto it so you can easily pull it out each day.

19) If you use a small blower, mount it on the lower inlet opening. This will create a positive pressure inside solar heater and eliminate air leaks. A small squirrel cage blower is most effective and quiet, but an inexpensive small fan-type blower will also work. To be most efficient, you can install a small photovoltaic panel (electric solar cells) to operate a 12-volt d.c. blower or fan. It will produce electricity only when sun shines, which makes it a perfect fit with solar heating.

20) If you use your solar heater for summer cooling, saw two square vent openings in the top (warm air outlet side) 2×8 on each side of the stringer support. Make two doors from the ½-inch plywood to fit in the openings. Nail a ½-inch square wood strip ¾ inch down from the outside. Attach ³/₈-inch thick foam weatherstripping on top of this strip. Attach the two doors over the openings with hinges. Attach latches to keep them closed. When they are closed and latched, the weatherstripping should be compressed to form a tight seal. On cool days when you are not air-conditioning, open the vents and some windows for natural ventilation.

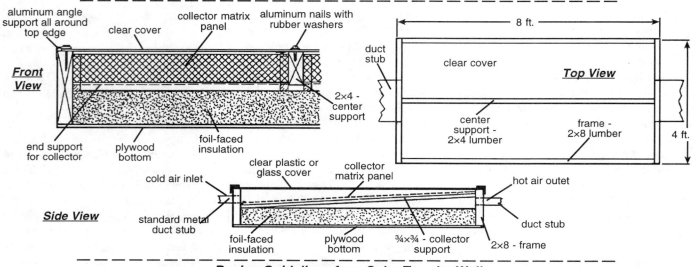

Design Guidelines for a Solar Trombe Wall

It is easy to build a solar Trombe wall. The actual design and dimensions are not critical to its performance. Following the basic design features for climate zones (shown on the following page) is most important.

The diagram on page 40 shows a modified Trombe wall built under a window. This looks "more-normal" from the outside of your house. You can use the window (a double-hung is best) for the upper vent holes.

If you plan to use a single-glazed window for the glass covering, you can probably make a simple wood frame. Use 1×2 or 2×2 lumber. Silicone caulk around the glass is the longest-lasting type. If necessary, due to climate zone or problems with condensation, use double pane insulated glass. You should have the window made by a replacement window manufacturer. It is difficult to handle the desiccant and seal the glass well enough to avoid fogging in between the glass panes.

A rule of thumb is that the wall should be from 8 to 16 inches thick if made of concrete. You can use the chart to determine the equivalent thickness for the same heat capacities for other wall materials. For example, you will need slightly more brick and the actual amount of stone will

Thermal Mass Heat Storage Capacities			
Material	**Specific Heat Btu/lb** X	**Density lb/ft³** =	**Heat Capacity Btu/ft³/°F, no voids**
Water	1.00	62.4	62.4
Concrete	0.22	140	30.8
Stone	0.21	90 to 170	18 to 36
Brick	0.21	130	27.3
Stucco	0.22	116	25.5
Drywall	0.26	50	13.0
Dry Soil	0.21	105	22.0
Wet Soil	0.44	125	55.0
Wood, hardwood	0.30	45	13.5

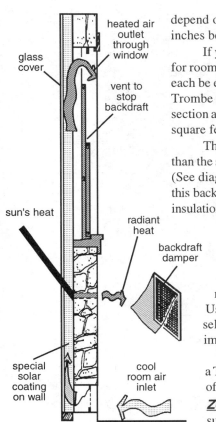

glass cover

heated air outlet through window

vent to stop backdraft

sun's heat

radiant heat

backdraft damper

special solar coating on wall

cool room air inlet

depend on the density of the particular type of stone you use. Leave a gap of approximately 3 to 4 inches between the glass and the wall.

If you are seeking daytime heating also, you will need upper and lower vents through the wall for room air circulation. A rule of thumb is that both the top (outlet) and bottom (inlet) vents should each be equal to one half the area of the horizontal cross section of the collector. For example, if the Trombe wall is 10 feet wide and the air gap between the glass and wall is 4 inches, the collector cross section area is 3.33 square feet. Therefore, the size of the upper vents (and lower vents) should be 1.67 square feet.

The easiest way to make a backdraft damper is to make a light wood frame just slightly smaller than the size of each vent opening. First staple a piece of thin plastic film to the top edge of the frame. (See diagram). Then staple hardware wire over the frame on the same side as the plastic film. Recess this back several inches into the vent opening and caulk around it. This will allow room for a piece of insulation to cover the vent openings at night.

Special Design Features for Trombe Walls in Various Climates

Zone 1 — The severe climate in this zone calls for special design features. The most effective Trombe walls are those with a selective absorber surface, night insulation, and single glazing. This combination yields good daytime performance and nighttime heat retention. If the Trombe wall is freestanding, single glazing can cause condensation problems. Using double insulated glazing can reduce the condensation problem. A Trombe wall with a selective coating and insulation is fairly expensive, but the additional cost is generally offset by improved performance.

If the initial cost of this type of wall is too great for your budget, the next best option is a Trombe wall with a combination of triple glazing and night insulation. In this zone, other types of design will generally result in a net energy loss throughout the year.

Zone 2 — The only Trombe walls that perform well in this zone are those that use a selective surface or night insulation. A combination of both is best. Single glazing will work well and can reduce the total cost of the project.

Another option for this zone is a Trombe wall with a selective surface, double insulated glazing, and no night insulation. Also, a wall with night insulation, triple glazing, and no selective surface is workable. Trombe walls without either a selective surface or night insulation will be net energy losers throughout the entire year.

Zone 3 — A Trombe wall is a good fit with this zone's relatively mild climate. Although a Trombe wall with a selective surface and night insulation is most effective, the increased cost may not be justified. Generally, a wall with triple glazing and night insulation is best. Another option is double glazing and a selective surface. It is only slightly less effective than the first option. Since summertime heat gain can be a problem with a Trombe wall in this zone, it should have summer shading and be vented. A large roof overhang or deciduous trees are good shading devices.

Zone 4 — You have many options for the design of a Trombe wall in this zone. The only wall that will be a net energy loser is just a plain wall (no selective surface or night insulation) and single glazing. Any combination of one or more of the other wall design options will be effective. You will definitely need summertime shading and ventilation in this zone to avoid overheating.

Zone 5 — In this zone, the thermal performance is not with the selective surfaces and night insulation will be effective. Since this climate is so mild, the payback from using selective surfaces and night insulation is not generally worth the added expense.

Summertime overheating is probably your greatest problem. In Zone 5A, the humidity is relatively low, so a simple roof overhang can provide effective shading. In Zone 5B, the high level of humidity can diffuse and scatter the sunlight. Therefore, a simple roof overhang may not block enough of the heat. Exterior shading devices that actually cover the glass are the best option. In both zones, venting of the Trombe wall will reduce the heat buildup.

Zone 6 — In this zone, any design works well. Summertime overheating can be a significant problem. You should contact a local solar designer to give you some advice about the feasibility and payback of installing a Trombe wall.

important. Any design from a plain wall to a more high-tech one

Trombe Wall Climate Zones

Zone 3 Zone 2 Zone 1

Zone 4

Zone 5 A B

Zone 6

Solar window heater easy to make

Q: The sun shines in a small window in my kitchen, but it's still the chilliest room. What type of inexpensive solar device can I build myself to capture more of the sun's heat through this window?

A: A small do-it-yourself solar window heater can produce enough free solar heat to keep your kitchen comfortably warm all day. Using just hand tools and about $50 in materials, I built a simple thermosiphoning (no fan needed) heater for my own home.

On a bright sunny winter day, I have measured the solar heated air output as high as 110 degrees. By installing a small fan or blower, the total heat output and air volume can be increased.

There are several design variations for small do-it-yourself solar heaters. The simplest and cheapest design mounts in your window and angles downward outdoors. The window closes down against the shallow (less than one foot high) air inlet and outlet openings. It is barely noticeable from indoors.

This do-it-yourself solar heater design utilizes a shallow plywood box with a clear top. An old storm door or window works well for the top. Split box horizontally inside with a collector divider panel (painted black). This creates two shallow chambers, one over the other.

The divider panel should be several inches shorter than the box leaving a gap at the bottom which connects the upper and lower chambers. Clear acrylic or polycarbonate plastic are durable alternatives to a glass top.

As the sun shines through the top on to the divider panel, it heats the air in the upper chamber. This

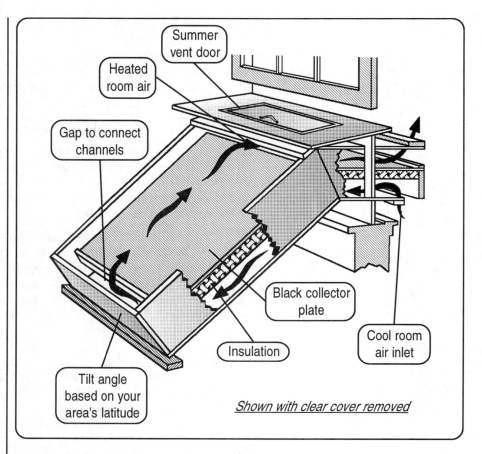

Heated room air

Summer vent door

Gap to connect channels

Black collector plate

Insulation

Cool room air inlet

Tilt angle based on your area's latitude

Shown with clear cover removed

hot air naturally rises (the box is tilted upward to your window) and flows out into your room. Cool room air is then drawn into the lower chamber for continuous natural circulation.

Insulating the sides and bottom increases efficiency, temperature and air flow volume. Since the solar heater does not get very hot, use easy-to-attach rigid foam insulation panels.

A plywood sheet with rigid insulation attached to the bottom makes a simple divider panel. Another option is to lay fiberglass insulation over the wood and paint the vapor barrier black. Scrap corrugated metal roofing is also effective. The corrugations increase surface area and air turbulence.

When air-conditioning in the summer, you can easily remove the solar heater and close the window as always. For natural ventilation,

add a vent door in the top of the outdoor portion of the heater. Opening this vent makes the solar heater operate as an exhaust fan by drawing hot air out of your home.

Q: I have a one-year-old high efficiency refrigerator which I plan to move to a new apartment. I heard that it will be damaged or its efficiency reduced if it is laid flat. Is this true?

A: New refrigerators, made within the past five years, should not be damaged if they are laid flat for transportation. Many are shipped this way to the retailer. If it has the coils on the back, don't risk damaging the coils by laying it down.

Once you move your refrigerator to the new location, place it upright at room temperature for several hours before turning it on. This allows the compressor oil to drain back to its proper location.

You can make a simple solar window heater yourself. I built one for my own home using about $50 worth of old materials. I used two sheets of clear acrylic glazing to form an insulated top. Acrylic is much lighter, safer, and easier to work with than glass. I lined the entire inside of the box with 1-inch thick rigid foam insulation. On a sunny day, it produces a lot of heated air.

There are three different designs shown on the following pages. They are all equally effective. The materials list to the right is for design #1. You can substitute any similar materials that you may have on hand. The inside of these solar heaters does not get extremely hot.

When you support the solar heater outside your window, especially a second-floor window, allow for thermal expansion and contraction. Make the attachment holes or clips large enough to accommodate the size changes.

Do-It-Yourself Solar Window Heater Designs

Design #1

This solar window heater is basically a wooden box with a glass top that collects heat from the sun. As the air inside gets hot, it flows out into your room drawing in more cool room air to be heated. Before you begin this project, make sure you wear adequate safety clothing and safety glasses. You will be handling glass, so be careful. Also, if you are going to use spray paint, use it outdoors and do not smoke while you spray it.

These are general instructions. Since everyone's application and design will be a little different, modify it for your specific home. Other than the 3" and 4" dimensions shown in the diagram, the rest of the dimensions are not extremely critical to its effectiveness.

1) You will first have to determine the proper size of the box for your specific window. It should be slightly narrower than your window so it fits through the window and snugly against the sides of the window frame. You will use foam weatherstripping to seal it.

2) Once you have determined the basic dimensions for the solar window heater, begin to build the plywood box. You can use 2×2's or 2×4's to make the basic frame, and then cover it with $3/8$ inch plywood. Remember that the width will be $3/4$ of an inch wider after the plywood sides are added, so make the frame small enough to fit into the window. Screws will hold up better than nails since it will get warm in the sun. Use silicone caulking to seal all the joints in the box.

3) Leave the top of box open for the piece of glass. It is a good idea to build a two-inch wide plywood lip around the open top. This will add rigidity to the box, and provide support for the glass, without blocking much of the sun's heat.

4) For the most effective operation, you should insulate the inside of the box with rigid foam board insulation. This will reduce the heat loss from the cool room air in the lower portion and from the solar heated air in the upper portion.

5) Make the plywood divider piece to fit as shown on page 43 and 44. Attach foam insulation board to the underside of it and paint the top flat black. Mount the divider as shown in the diagram. Seal all around it with silicone caulking. It is very important that the air is forced to flow down around the end of the divider and back up under the glass.

6) Cut an opening in the horizontal top piece by your window. This will be the location of the outdoor vent. Cut carefully so you can use this piece for the flap door itself. Otherwise, cut another piece for door. Attach that piece with hinges to use as vent door. Use foam weatherstripping around the edge to seal it when it is closed.

7) Make another flap door to mount on the inside opening from the upper chamber into your room. Mount it with hinges and use weatherstripping again to seal it. You should close it when the sun goes down and in the summertime. You can also add a small plywood apron where the bottom section comes into your window.

8) The next step is to add the glass cover. *Wear safety glasses*. It may be easier and cheaper to use two or three pieces of glass instead of one. Have the glass cut to fit the finished box. Unless you're an accomplished cabinetmaker, the finished box will not end up exactly the same size as you planned.

Required Materials for Window Mounted Solar Room Heater

lumber - 2 x 2's or 2 x 4's (quantity needed depends on size of window)
$3/8$" plywood
rigid foam board insulation with
$1/2$" gypsum per local fire codes
glass, clear acrylic or polycarbonate plastic
scrap corrugated metal roofing
hinges
duct tape
handle
aluminum angle
wood screws or nails
rubber washers
steel washers
glazier points for locating glass cover
silicone caulking
foam weatherstripping
black paint
optional fan or blower
optional old storm door or window

9) Place the glass on the box and hold it in place with glazier points. Don't putty the glass in place. That won't hold up to the temperature changes of the box. Instead, use duct tape stapled to the sides of the box, or caulk the glass all the way around the edges so you get a good seal.

10) Paint the wood box with house paint before you put it into your window. Seal it against the window frame with adhesive foam weatherstripping.

11) In the winter, close off the indoor top flap at night to minimize heat loss. During the summer, you can store the solar window heater in your garage or basement. Or, close the top flap inside the house and open the outdoor top flap. Open the window on the other side of your room for cross-ventilation. Select a shady window for the coolest air to be drawn in.

Design #2

1) Actual dimensions vary depending on your window size. The basic relationship of dimensions shown on page 16 provide efficient operation. Before you begin to assemble the collector, paint both sides of all wood parts with two coats of outdoor paint. First make a box by sawing 1×4's at an angle forming a hockey stick shape by attaching the two pieces with a sheet metal strip. Add a top lip and nail on the bottom sheet plus the end piece.

2) Make another assembly like the first. When the two assemblies are piggybacked and fastened together, the two air-circulation channels will be created. This puts the heat-absorbing surface on a $1/8$" hardboard sheet that is fixed 1¾" over the hardboard bottom. This creates the lower cold-air channel. (See illustrations on page 44.)

3) Use a 23"-wide section of 2¾"-thick fiberglass insulation batt with kraft-paper or foil backing painted black. Secure the batt at each end with screen mold and small nails. You can also cover the insulation batt with a thin sheet of metal (aluminum is easy to cut and work with) and paint it black. Complete the assembly as shown in the illustration. Seal all the edges between the hardboard and the screen stock with duct tape on the outside.

4) You can use glass (an old storm door), clear rigid acrylic, or 5 to 10-mil acetate for the clear top. The flexible acetate is easiest to use. You can either tack or staple it down and trim off the excess around the edges.

5) When you install the collector in your window, the hot-air outlet to the room must be either horizontal or pitched upward slightly. This allows for proper air flow. Add a rain cover and seal any gaps between the collector and the window frame with insulation and duct tape.

6) To prevent reverse convection at night or on cloudy days, make two snug fitting wood doors to plug up the intake and outlet openings. If you plan to mount the collector on a roof under a window, bolt it with angle braces. You can remove it in the summer.

Illustrations for Making Design #1

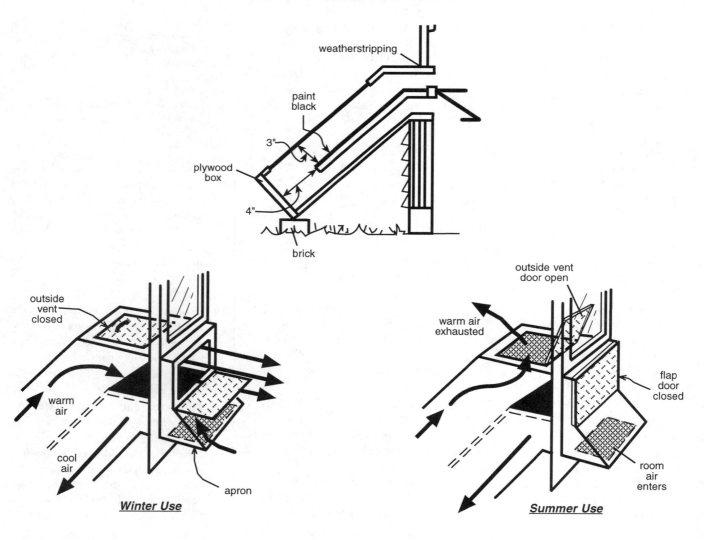

Winter Use

Summer Use

Design #2

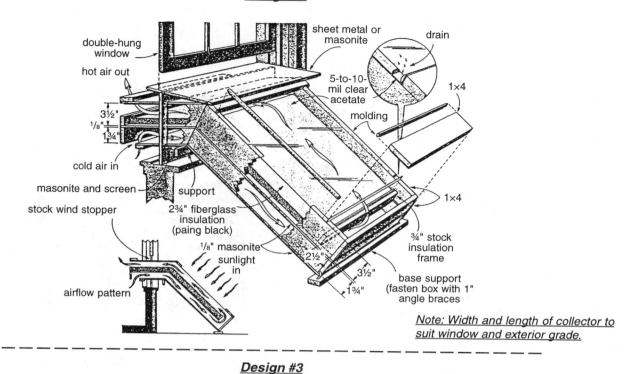

double-hung window

hot air out

3½"
⅛"
1¾"

cold air in

masonite and screen

stock wind stopper

support

2¾" fiberglass insulation (paing black)

⅛" masonite

sunlight in

airflow pattern

sheet metal or masonite

drain

5-to-10-mil clear acetate

molding

1×4

1×4

¾" stock insulation frame

2½"

3½"

1¾"

base support (fasten box with 1" angle braces

Note: Width and length of collector to suit window and exterior grade.

Design #3

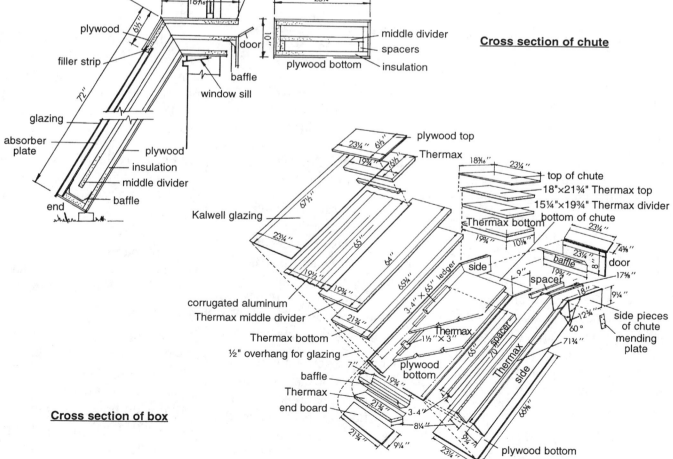

60°

window plywood

18 ³⁄₁₆"

plywood

6½"

filler strip

72"

glazing

absorber plate

plywood

insulation

middle divider

baffle

end

door

baffle

window sill

23¼"

10"

middle divider

spacers

plywood bottom

insulation

Cross section of chute

plywood top

Thermax

23¼" 6½"

19¾" 6½"

18 ³⁄₁₆" 23¼"

top of chute

18"×21¾" Thermax top

15¼"×19¾" Thermax divider

bottom of chute

Thermax bottom

19¾" 10⅛"

Kalwell glazing

67½"

23¼"

65"

64"

65¾"

19½"

19¾"

3-4" × 65" ledger

side

21¾"

corrugated aluminum

Thermax middle divider

Thermax bottom

½" overhang for glazing

Thermax

1½"×3"

plywood bottom

7"

baffle

Thermax

end board

19¾"

21¾"

21¾"

8¼"

9¼"

9¼"

23¼"

spacer

Thermax

Thermax

65"

spacer

70"

side

71¾"

60°

12¾"

9¼"

65¾"

baffle

23¼"

8"

door

17⅝"

18"

9¼"

4³⁄₁₆"

side pieces of chute

mending plate

3-4"

plywood bottom

Cross section of box

44

Easily constructed inexpensive solar heater

Q: Will you describe how to build a solar heater (not a big ugly one on my roof) that can heat one or two rooms? I'm on a limited budget, so I want to use as many low-cost and scrap materials as possible.

A: A flat (only 5 inches deep) wall-mounted solar collector is the least expensive and easiest to build. Since it mounts vertically against a wall, it is not unattractive. It looks like a large window from outdoors, but can easily heat two rooms on a sunny day.

It is designed to use many scrap materials to keep the costs low. Old corrugated metal roofing, scrap printing plates, or sheet metal makes an efficient solar absorber. Second-hand window glass or inexpensive clear plastic sheet or film makes an effective cover for the solar heater.

Since standard size lumber is most reasonably priced, a 4 x 8 foot solar heater is a good size. If you have an old glass storm window or door, make it that size to avoid having to buy new clear glazing.

This solar heater design is basically a shallow plywood box with a metal solar absorber laying flat inside. Corrugated roofing, that is painted flat black, is good because the corrugations cause turbulence in the air flow. This increases the heat transfer to the air and it will boost its efficiency.

Room air enters one opening and circulates underneath the solar-heated absorber plate. After picking up the solar heat from the absorber, the heated air then blows back out into your room through an outlet register.

Use thin plywood for the solar heater back (if you mount it directly

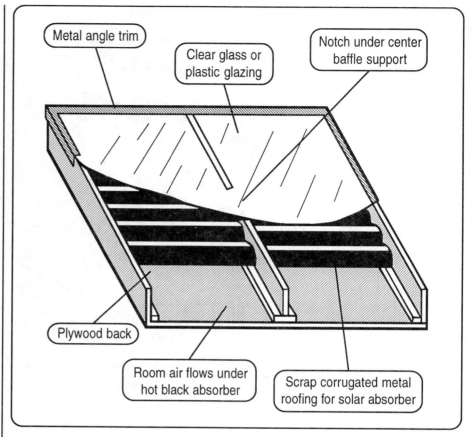

Metal angle trim

Clear glass or plastic glazing

Notch under center baffle support

Plywood back

Room air flows under hot black absorber

Scrap corrugated metal roofing for solar absorber

against your house) and 1 x 4's for the box framing. The wall of your house provides the rigidity to the solar heater.

Split the box lengthwise with a 1 x 4 center baffle with a shallow notch cut out one-third of the way up its length. This forms two long cavities connected by the notch under the center baffle.

Nail the corrugated roofing absorbers into the box covering each cavity. This design forces the cool room air to circulate from the bottom inlet opening, across the hot absorber, up through the baffle notch, and back down the other side to the hot air outlet register.

Cover the entire box with the clear glazing. You can use glass or plastic. This creates a dead air space above the hot absorber to reduce the heat loss back outdoors. You should attach a small blower for increased

heat output into your home.

Q: I have a brick fireplace that I cannot use because smoke always comes out into the room. The fireplace opening is 36 x 36 inches. How can I improve the draft and stop the smoke?

A: First, you should have the chimney inspected to make sure that it is not blocked. The chimney top should be at least 2 feet above the roof peak or 3 feet above a flat roof for proper draw. If your house is very airtight, you may have to open a window a little to provide combustion air.

The height of the top of the fireplace opening is important. If it is too high above the burning logs, the draft may be insufficient. Use a grate to raise logs from the floor. Try adding a few bricks under the legs of the grate. If this helps, build up the entire hearth floor with fire bricks.

The solar air heater is a simple device for catching some of the sun's energy to help heat your home. Basically, it is a shallow box, covered with glass or plastic glazing to trap solar energy. The box also contains a black metal absorber plate for changing the sun's radiant energy into heat energy. Between the glazing and the absorber is a dead air space that helps keep captured heat from escaping to the outside air. Behind the absorber is an air chamber through which cool air from the house circulates. This house air passes through an opening behind the solar panel where it is heated as it comes in contact with the absorber plate. The heated air is then returned to the house through another opening in the panel.

The panel can be mounted in a vertical or horizontal position on the south wall of a house. Mounting the collector there will allow it to catch most of the winter sunlight. The only alteration that will have to be made to the house is the addition of two vents to allow for the opening in the panel. During the winter, the panel should not be shaded by trees or bushes. In the summer, the sun is higher in the sky, so most of the sunlight will bounce off the top of the glazing which will prevent overheating.

This solar heater uses some electricity to power a fan that moves air through the panel. It is also possible to build a solar heater that does not use any outside energy. These thermosiphoning systems require larger openings. They also move less heated air as a result of slower natural air circulation. The solar air heater described here performs more efficiently than the thermosiphoning model. The cost of the electricity is offset by the increased heat output of the design with a fan.

Construction Procedure

1) Assemble all materials before starting. Read all instructions and be sure you understand each step. A materials list is shown below.

2) Cut 1×4 lumber to length. Notch center baffle and attach metal ledger to notch with ¾" nails. Use aluminum ledger and aluminum nails if you use an aluminum absorber. Mixing galvanized materials with aluminum will cause electrolysis and corrosion.

3) Cut out a 2" diameter hot air vent into dead air space on upper side panel. Install screens and "temperature-vents" over the holes on the inside of the frames. This type of vent opens automatically to ventilate the dead air space when its temperature reaches 150°F. It opens to prevent overheating in summer and will remain closed during winter operation. As a substitute for "temperature-vents," you can cover the holes with small corks or wood during the winter and remove them during the summer. Locate the hot air vent on the side of the panel to prevent rain from entering the opening.

4) Glue and nail the 1×4 frame and baffle to the plywood back. Be sure the baffle is centered properly. Caulk with latex caulking where the 1x4 meets the plywood on the inside to form a weathertight joint.

5) Cut, glue, and nail the 1×2 lip to the frame. Note: Vent openings should be in the dead air space only. Drill a series of ¼" vent holes through the center 1×4 baffle in the dead air space and install one "temp-vent."

6) Cut the absorber metal to size. Use an aluminum ledger and aluminum nails if you use an aluminum absorber. Clean any grease or oil from the metal with detergent or solvents and wash thoroughly. Etch the metal with vinegar or muriatic acid so that the paint will adhere to the metal. Again, wash the metal to remove the etching solution.

7) Fasten the absorber to 1×2 lip with ¾" galvanized roofing nails every 3". Note: Apply a thick bead of silicone caulking onto the metal ledger before laying down the absorber. This creates a formed-in-place gasket between the metal ledger and the absorber. To keep

Required Materials for Solar Heater

1 each 4' × 8' × ⅜" CD exterior plywood or substitute with masonite
4 each 1" × 4" × 8' pieces of lumber
5 each 1" × 2" × 8' pieces of lumber
wood glue
1 lb. galvanized nails (4D to 6D)
2 each 2' × 8' sheet galvanized steel corrugated roofing or corrugated aluminum or offset printing plates or aluminum flashing. If you use a non-corrugated sheet, add baffles to cause turbulence in the air flow.
1 small bottle of vinegar, muriatic acid, or metal etcher
1 pint flat black paint (any moderate-temperature paint will work)
1 lb. ¾" galvanized roofing nails or aluminum nails
4 tubes black silicone caulking
2 tubes of latex caulking
1 each 3" × 24" pieces of metal (to support absorber at center bar opening)
1 each 4' × 8' piece of flat icy clear fiberglass, Kalwall, or glass
3 each 8' long 90-degree angle aluminum, for holding down glazing
    (¾" × ¾" aluminum angle works well)
1 each 8' × ¾" flat pieces of aluminum
75 each #7 × ¾" wood screws
1 each 200 cfm squirrel cage blower
1 each thermostat (on between 90° to 155° F - off under 90° F)
1 length 2/12 UG wire (to reach from electric outlet to blower)
1 each electric plug
1 each Temp-Vent for summer ventilation
1 qt. exterior grade latex paint
assorted lumber, duct tape and insulation for ducting cold and hot registers

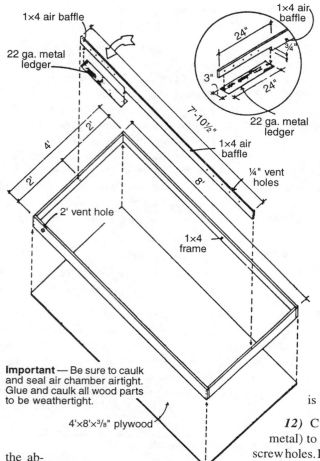

Important — Be sure to caulk and seal air chamber airtight. Glue and caulk all wood parts to be weathertight.

the ab-sorber embedded in the bead of caulking, drive small nails into the 1×4 air baffle to hold the absorber down to the ledger. Be sure to put the absorber in the frame so that the corrugations in the metal are perpendicular to the air flow. This will cause the air flowing over the absorber to be turbulent and increases the heat transfer to the air.

8) Paint the absorber and the inside of the wooden frame with one coat of flat black paint and let dry thoroughly.

9) Carefully caulk (with silicone caulking) the entire edge of the absorber where it meets the wood to form an airtight seal between the wood and the metal. Also use silicone caulking on the nail heads to seal the holes.

10) Touch up any scratches with the flat black paint. Turn the frame over and paint the back of the plywood and the outside of the 1×4's with exterior house paint to seal the lumber.

11) Cut the plastic or glass glazing to size. Run a bead of caulking on the panel 1×4's and lay the glazing onto the panel. If you are using plastic with an ultraviolet coating, make sure the coating is on the outside.

12) Cut edging (wood or metal) to length and predrill the screw holes. Lay the edging onto the glazing and drill through the plastic glazing. If you are using glass, make the size of the glass slightly smaller so the drill will miss the edge of the glass, yet still screw into the frame. Fasten the 4 ft. edge first, the center strip next, then the sides, and finally fasten the end. Be sure glazing does not extend beyond the outer edge of the frame to prevent ripples in the glazing.

Installation Instructions

This typical installation is for a wood framed home with wood siding. By using lumber, ducts can be made at the house site. For homes with stucco siding, use a masonry blade in your circular saw to cut duct openings. For a brick or concrete block house, use a hammer drill (available at most tool rental shops) or hammer and cold chisel the duct openings.

1) Decide where to locate the solar panel. Check inside walls for electrical outlets and obstructions. Note the floor level inside the home and its position in relation to the outside wall siding. This is to ensure that the duct comes above the inside floor height and not into floor list area. Locate the wall framing to place the duct openings between the studs.

2) Mark openings for the ducts on the outside wall. Duct openings in the solar panel should be as close to the panel edge as possible. (For a 4" × 12" floor register, the openings should be 5¾" × 13¾".) Cut rough openings into the outside wall only. Do not cut the inside paneling or drywall at this time.

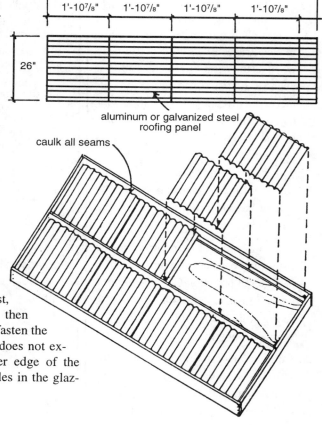

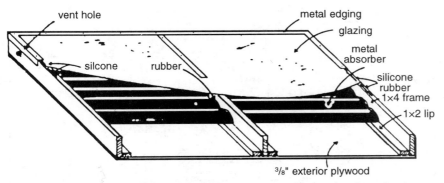

Labels for image: vent hole, metal edging, glazing, metal absorber, silcone, rubber, silicone rubber, 1×4 frame, 1×2 lip, ³/₈" exterior plywood

3) Measure the duct length, which is the distance from the extreme outside wall surface to the back of the the interior paneling or drywall. This measurement is the length of the wall ducts. Rip a piece of 1" lumber to the duct length size. Then cut the duct lumber to size and build the ducts, gluing and nailing them together.

4) Insert the ducts into the wall openings and mark the inside dimensions on the inside wall surface through the duct. Remove the ducts and cut the inside wall openings. By using this method, the interior wall surface will cover the duct edge and no interior trim will be needed.

5) Run a 3 ft. length of wire (No. 2 conductor exterior grade) through the wall from the cool air opening to the hot air opening for later thermostat connection. Drill a hole into the ducts to run the wire from one duct to the other. Also drill through any studs for the wire run.

6) Latex caulk the inside edge of the ducts liberally and insert the ducts into place, running the wires into the holes drilled in the ducts. Fasten the ducts into the siding or nearby framing.

7) Caulk the rough openings around the ducts to seal openings from the weather. At this point, the wall ducts are in place and the thermostat wire is installed.

8) Next, hold the panel up against the wall and mark the openings for the ducts on the back of the panel by reaching through the ducts from the inside of the house. This method will insure proper panel-to-duct alignment. Be sure to hold the panel straight so that it will look plumb and square once it is fastened to the building. Also, mark the location of the panel on the wall.

9) Lower the panel and cut the duct openings into the back of the panel. Take care not to damage the absorber by cutting or drilling too deep into the panel back. Use a circular saw, set to a shallow cut, or a short saber saw blade. Now the panel is ready to be mounted on the wall.

10) Latex caulk the outside edge of the ducts and lift the panel into place, aligning the panel openings to the ducts. Fasten the panel to the wall with corner braces or angles and screws. Use two corner braces or angles at the top, sides, and bottom of the panel to fasten it securely to the wall. Latex caulk the top and sides of the panel where it meets the wall to prevent moisture from getting between the panel and the wall. Paint the wood edge of the panel with white exterior house paint or a color to match your house. At this point, the panel is mounted.

11) Inside your home, install the thermostat and blower. Drill a small hole into the absorber in the hot air opening for the self-tapping screw which holds the thermostat in place. Be sure to put the thermostat in the hot air opening so that the thermostat rests

securely on the absorber to sense the absorber temperature properly. Connect the two wires to the thermostat connector screws.

12) Latex caulk all seams and joints in the hot air duct to insure an airtight seal and place the register into the duct. This completes the hot air duct installation.

13) Now latex caulk the cool air duct seams and joints. Caulk the lip of the blower opening. Fasten the blower in place over the cool air opening with the blower intake facing away from the hot air register.

14) Connect one wire from the thermostat to the blower using electrical tape. Connect the other blower wire and the other thermostat wire to an electrical plug. Be sure all wire connections are clean, tight, and safe.

The solar heater is now installed and ready for operation. Plug the solar heater into an electrical outlet and adjust the thermostat so the blower will come on at a temperature which is reached at about 9 a.m. on a sunny day.

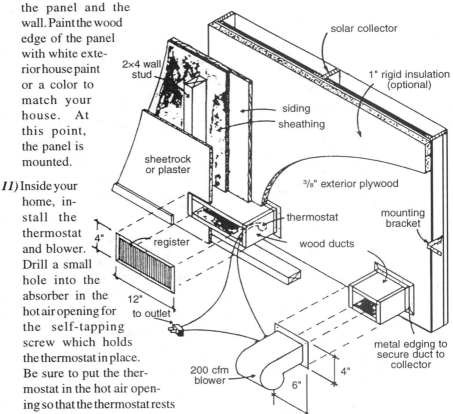

Labels for image: 2×4 wall stud, sheetrock or plaster, register, 4", 12" to outlet, 200 cfm blower, 6", 4", solar collector, 1" rigid insulation (optional), siding, sheathing, ³/₈" exterior plywood, thermostat, wood ducts, mounting bracket, metal edging to secure duct to collector

Warm floor radiant heat is very comfortable

Q: I was recently in a house with "warm feet" radiant floor heat and it was extremely comfortable. Can I install this type of heating system in just several rooms of my house and is it efficient?

A: "Warm feet" radiant floor heat is the most comfortable system available. It is ideal in all climates for its comfort, good indoor air quality and low utility bills. You can use your existing duct system for central air-conditioning or install ductless central air.

Imagine getting out of your bed in the morning and putting your feet on a warm floor. The heat radiates up from the floor producing the same feeling as sitting in the sun by a window on a winter day. The heat will come up right through your existing carpeting.

Unlike forced-air or radiator systems where the warmest air stagnates at the ceiling, the warmest temperature is much lower with a radiant floor system. These systems are noiseless with minimal temperature variations. With no registers, you have total freedom in furniture placement and interior design.

A typical radiant floor system uses your standard water heater or a boiler for the heat source. Thin flexible water tubing is attached under the floor between the joists or in a concrete slab (new construction).

There are many types of tubing used by various manufacturers. The most commonly used is PEX (cross-linked polyethylene) and some manufacturers offer a lifetime warranty. The actual life is projected to be more than 100 years, so there is little chance of leaks.

A radiant floor system is easy

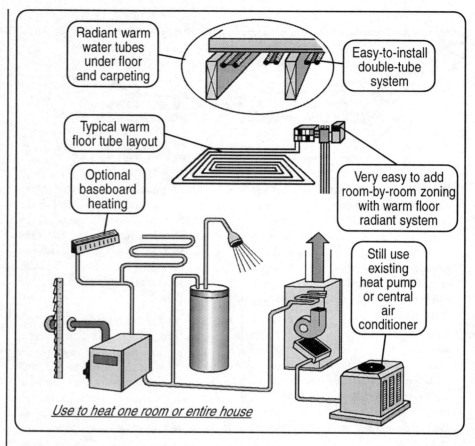

Radiant warm water tubes under floor and carpeting

Easy-to-install double-tube system

Typical warm floor tube layout

Optional baseboard heating

Very easy to add room-by-room zoning with warm floor radiant system

Still use existing heat pump or central air conditioner

Use to heat one room or entire house

to install in just one room or in your entire house. It can be a fairly simple do-it-yourself job. Many of the manufacturers offer installation kits (Vari-Takk or Radiant-Trak) to provide the proper tubing spacing and attachment under the floor.

For a second-story room, place the tubing on the floor and spread a thin layer of special cement over it or add another false floor. You'll just have to trim the door a little. This also helps block noise through the floor.

The key efficiency feature of a radiant floor is its unusual comfort. This allows you to save by setting the thermostat lower without feeling chilly. Also, room air is not excessively dried out as with forced-air systems.

Efficient zoning is simple with a radiant floor system. A central command unit controls the warm

water flow to each of the room floors. You can literally set each room to a different temperature so your kids won't have to fight anymore over the thermostat setting.

Q: I am remodeling my bathroom and adding a large super efficient R-8 casement window. I am having trouble removing the old tile adhesive from the walls so I can paint them. What do you recommend?

A: Old tile adhesive can get rock-hard. You will need a hammer and a scraper to get some of it off. Do not worry about gouging the wall surface. You'll have to skim coat the wall anyway before painting.

Another method is to remove the old adhesive covered drywall and replace it with new drywall. It's not a lot more work and you'll have access to the wall cavity. Fill gaps with insulation where it has settled.

Manufacturers of Warm Water Radiant Floor Heating Systems

BURNHAM RADIANT HEATING CO., PO Box 3079, Lancaster, PA 17604 - (888) 581-2742 (717) 481-8400
  type of tubing - cross-linked polyethylene with and without oxygen barrier
  diameter sizes - 1/2" • 3/4" • 1"   zoning available - yes — individual room/zone
  features - Tubing covered with 25-year limited warranty. Brass or copper manifolds available. Brass manifolds will accept only 1/2" tubing and has 2, 3 or 4 circuit configurations that can be connected to allow different manifold sizes. Copper manifolds available as buildable units or long sections that need to be cut to correct size. Plastic bend supports, pipe fasteners and anchor clips available, will not damage pipe during installation. Boilers available with lifetime limited warranty.

EHT SIEGMUND INC., 14771 Myford Rd., Suite E, Tustin, CA 92680 - (714) 731-4143
  type of tubing - polyethylene with an inner core of aluminum • cross-linked polyethylene with oxygen diffusion barrier
  diameter sizes - 3/8" • 1/2" • 3/4" • 1"   zoning available - yes — up to twelve zones
  features - Three system configurations available. "Vari-Takk" system (five different varieties) is primarily for new construction with high-density polyurethane foam plate affixed to flooring. Has an aluminum laminate fused to it which serves as template for laying tubing. "Vari-Plan" system is suited for older buildings. Consists of foam-laminated plastic sheets with evenly spaced notched protrusions. These serve as a template for tubing to run through. In the "Air-Con" system, warm or cool air is radiated evenly from piping matrix imbedded in the "Air-Con" subfloor. Air is circulated through air spaces where it is either heated or cooled by absorbing residual warm or cold temperatures given off by the flow of water through the tubing. These modular sheets provide noise reduction, prevent heat loss, provide a moisture barrier, and serve as the base for easy installation of the heating pipe without the use of tools. Manifolds are extruded of solid brass.

EMBASSY INDUSTRIES, INC., 300 Smith St., Farmingdale, NY 11735 - (516) 694-1800
  type of tubing - cross-linked polyethylene with and without oxygen barrier
  diameter sizes - 3/8" • 1/2" • 5/8" • 3/4"   zoning available - yes — up to four zones with three zone extensions
  features - The manifold is modular, you can add a section to the manifold if needed. The manifold has a flow-rate indicator so it is easy to adjust the flow-rate to each zone. Accessories available — aluminum snap plate (tubing snaps into groove), fasten between joists below the floor, in the ceiling or on plywood floors • double groove aluminum snap plates for floor, wall or ceiling • plastic tube support channel that holds tubing in place in 8' lengths • bend support that allows 90° angle bends • baseboards, finned tube, kick space heaters and unit heaters.

HEATLINK USA, INC., 89 54th St. S. W., Grand Rapids, MI 49548 - (800) 968-8905 (616) 532-4266
  type of tubing - cross-linked polyethylene with and without oxygen barrier
  diameter sizes - 3/8" • 1/2" • 5/8" • 20×2 • 3/4" • 1"   zoning available - yes — up to ten zones
  features - A "TwistSeal" manifold can be connected together and locked in place with a 360° rotation, providing a positive leak tight seal. There is pipe tracking that can accept 3 different sizes on the same length and maintain from 12" to 3" spacing for high heat load areas. It is available in 5' lengths. There are heat transfer plates for tubing installed between joists. "StatLink" is a modular control system that allows multiple room thermostats to control different heating zones — maintaining temperatures within 1/4 of one degree.

HEATWAY, 3131 W. Chestnut Expressway, Springfield, MO 65802 - (800) 255-1996 (417) 864-6108
  type of tubing - synthetic rubber with an aluminum oxygen barrier and braided fiber reinforcing • cross-linked polyethylene with and without oxygen barrier
  diameter sizes - 3/8" • 1/2" • 5/8" • 3/4" • 1"   zoning available - yes — up to sixteen zones
  features - Tubing has a limited lifetime warranty for residential applications and a 20-year warranty for snow melting applications. "HydroControl" panels (pumps, controls, valves and gauges) are custom built for your application and comes with a one-year parts and labor warranty. The standard manifold is all brass, the swedged manifold (2-, 3- and 4-branch that can be connected to one another) is 1" copper and the "CustomCut" manifold is 4' long with fittings spaced 3" apart.

MAXXON CORP. - INFLOOR HEATING, 920 Hamel Rd., Hamel, MN 55340 - (800) 588-4470 (612) 478-9600
  type of tubing - cross-linked polyethylene with and without oxygen barrier
  diameter sizes - 3/8" • 1/2" • 5/8"   zoning available - yes — up to nine zones
  features - Tubes are embedded directly in a concrete slab or covered with 1 1/4" of "Therma-Floor" underlayment. This is a pourable floor underlayment. It is crack-resistant, noncombustible and transfers heat from the tubes to the room. It eliminates hot and cold spots, squeaky floors and helps stop noise between living areas. The floor temperature can be thermostatically controlled through a heat sensor inside the "Therma-Floor" or through an air-sensing thermostat. There is a 25-year warranty on the tubing and a 1 year warranty on mechanicals.

RADIANT TECHNOLOGY, 11A Farber Dr., Bellport, NY 11713 - (800) 784-0234 (516) 286-0900
  type of tubing - cross-linked polyethylene with an oxygen diffusion barrier
  diameter sizes - 3/8" • 1/2" • 5/8" • 3/4"   zoning available - yes — up to ten zones
  features - Other products available — "RadiantPanel", aluminum, white baseboard panel with quick connect fittings to 3/8" tubing • "Radiant-Rack" is a wall mount radiator/towel heater that includes mounting hardware and air vent, available in a white finish • "Radiant-Rail" is 6 1/2 feet long and provides even pipe spacing with notches to place the tubing in • "Radiant-Trak" is an aluminum heating track panel with preformed channel to hold tubing to use in floors, walls and ceilings.

RADIANTEC, PO Box 1111, Lyndonville, VT 05851 - (800) 451-7593 (802) 626-5564
  type of tubing - partially cross-linked polyethylene • cross-linked polyethylene
  diameter sizes - 3/8" • 1/2" • 7/8"   zoning available - yes — up to five — prefers to use individual pumps
  features - There are complete solar systems available. Free design assistance is offered and a design and construction manual is available. A complete system can be designed for you or you can get individual components.

REHAU INC., PO Box 1706, Leesburg, VA 22075 - (800) 247-9445 (703) 777-5255

  type of tubing - cross-linked polyethylene with an oxygen diffusion barrier
  diameter sizes -1/2" • 3/4" • 1"   zoning available - yes — individual room/zone
  features - An outdoor sensor signals a weather compensating control to adjust supply water temp. as outdoor temp. fluctuates. Brass compression sleeve fittings can be used as a repair coupling or to join lengths of tubing to help reduce waste. One method of installation is a joint spacer with conductive plates that holds the tubing in place and is used to install tubing under the floor when poured thermal mass is not practical.

SLANT/FIN CORP., 100 Forest Dr., Greenvale, NY 11548 - (516) 484-2600

  type of tubing - cross-linked polyethylene with an oxygen diffusion barrier
  diameter sizes - 1/2" • 3/4" • 1"   zoning available - yes — up to fourteen zones
  features - "Terra Therma" radiant heating system is baseboard compatible and has adapters for connecting the tubing to baseboard heating. The manifold is modular and allows for easy expansion of zones. It has a built-in balancing valve and is made of fiberglass reinforced nylon, injection molded parts. There are pipe tracking systems — grooved channels for wet installation or conductive plates that holds the tubing in place for dry installation for underfloor jobs.

STADLER CORP., 3 Alfred Circle, Bedford, MA 01730 - (617) 275-3122

  type of tubing - cross-linked polyethylene with oxygen diffusion barrier
  diameter sizes - 1/2" • 3/4" • 1"   zoning available - yes — individual room/zone
  special features - The "Climate Panel", an underlayment system is made for wood-frame construction. The panels are 7" or 10" wide by 48" long and allow the tubing to snap into place and stay there. You simply walk the tubing into the panels. There are special U-Turn panels when the tubing needs to be curved. The panels can be installed either above or below the subfloor or on top of existing concrete slabs. It can be screwed down from above or below the subfloor. The preassembled panel consists of two pieces of floor underlayment bonded to an aluminum heat transfer sheet to form one panel unit. The tubing has a 30-year warranty. See page 3 for an illustration of the "Climate Panel".

THERMAL EASE, 20714 State Highway 305, Suite 3C, Poulsbo, WA 98370 - (360) 779-1960

  type of tubing - cross-linked polyethylene with and without oxygen barrier
  diameter sizes - 3/8" • 1/2" • 5/8" • 3/4" • 1"   zoning available - yes — up to six zones
  features - Tubing carries a 25-year warranty. Computerized design assistance available for a system installed in an existing home or for new construction. Two manifolds available — an adjustable brass manifold or a copper line "Easy Mod" manifold.

VANGUARD, 831 Vanguard St., McPherson, KS 67460 - (800) 775-5039 (316) 241-6369

  type of tubing - cross-linked polyethylene with and without oxygen diffusion barrier
  diameter sizes - 3/8" • 1/2" • 3/4" • 1"   zoning available - yes — up to nine zones
  features - There are footage markers every two feet for measuring and cutting the tubing for each circuit loop. A modular manifold plumbing control unit, "Manabloc" is available. Each appliance or fixture is fed by a dedicated distribution line.

WIRSBO COMPANY, 5925 - 148th St. W., Apple Valley, MN 55124 - (800) 321-4739 (612) 891-2000

  type of tubing - cross-linked polyethylene with and without oxygen diffusion barrier
  diameter sizes - 3/8" • 1/2" • 5/8" • 3/4" • 1"   zoning available - yes — up to ten zones
  features - Heat transfer plates are available where the tubing is placed in the plates for use on suspended floors. There are also heat emission plates that can be attached to the ceiling joists or sheetrock. These methods are a good choice for remodeling projects or new room additions. There is a baseboard and radiator supply system, "Rapidex", available.

Floor Heating System Configurations by eht-Siegmund, Inc.

Vari-Takk Floor Heating System

Designed for installation in new construction. Low-profile, high-density polyurethane foam plates are affixed to the slab, sub-flooring or flooring. Each plate has an aluminum laminate fused to it, and is factory printed with a quadrille pattern of raised protrusions which serve as a template for laying the heating pipes. The plates are notched to permit overlapping which precludes temperature loss and lessens sound. Pipes are laid out evenly on the foam template.

Vari-Plan Floor Heating System

This is a low-profile, light-weight system which is suited for installation in older, existing buildings. It can be rapidly and easily installed on any surface, and requires no structural modifications.

The system consists of a foam-laminated plastic sheets with evenly spaced, notched protrusions. The protrusions serve as a template for heating pipe installation. These sheets also help control temperature and lessen sound. The concrete overlay can then be applied either conventionally or by a dry pack method.

Air-Con Heating and Cooling

Warm or cool air is radiated evenly from the piping matrix imbedded in the Air-Con subfloor. Air is circulated through the air spaces created by the Air-Con subfloor where the air is either heated or cooled by absorbing the residual warm or cold temperatures generated by the flow of warm or cold water through the piping system. The warm or cold air is dispensed into the room through floor vents and returned to the air handling system via adjustable return air grills located near the ceiling.

The Stadler Climate Panel System

Consists of two pieces of floor underlayment bonded to an aluminum heat transfer sheet to form one panel unit. Can be screwed down from above or below the subfloor. Sshallow design of panel system results in a maximum of only ½" buildup. 7" width allows two panels to be installed under subfloor between joists. Can react to temperature changes within minutes (rather than hours, which is characteristic of concrete systems) a feature extremely important to woodframe buildings.

By using this system, tubing remains exposed while nailing finish floors. Low weight panels eliminate special structural reinforcements normally needed for wet concrete floor heating systems.

½" plywood

close tolerance groove to lock tubing in place

heat transfer sheeting

Installation Methods Recommended by Wirsbo

Single Concrete Pour Over Slab Insulation Using Copper Coated Wire Ties

1) Lay out the recommended type high density insulation over the base material.
2) Lay out the wire mesh or rebar.
3) Connect one end of the loop to the supply manifold using only compression fittings.
4) Secure the tubing to the wire mesh or rebar.
5) Tie the tubing to the wire mesh or rebar using copper coated wire ties and wire twister. Secure the tubing to the wire mesh or rebar every four feet along straight runs. At the 180° turns tie the tubing at the top of the arc and once on each side, 12" from the top of the arc, to prevent it from dislodging and/or floating up into the pour.
6) Once the complete loop has been laid out, connect the end of the loop to the return manifold. Complete the tubing installation.
7) Securely fasten, as necessary, the wire mesh or rebar to the insulation.
8) Pressure test the system in accordance with local building codes.
9) Apply a suitable concrete mixture over the tubing.

Poured Floor Underlayment on a Suspended Wood Floor

1) Connect one end of the loop to the supply manifold.
2) Make sure the wood stapler head is securely fastened to the stapler and the stapler is loaded with 1¼" staples. Staple the tubing to the wood subfloor.
3) Staple the tubing as necessary along the straight runs to ensure it will stay in place (additional staples will be added later). At the 180° turns, secure one staple at the top of the arc and two staples, one on each side, 12" below the top of the arc.
4) Once the complete loop has been laid out, connect the end of the tubing to the return manifold.
5) Attach the walking stick to the stapler and fasten the tubing to the subfloor every two feet or as necessary to prevent it from dislodging and/or floating up into the pour. Complete the tubing installation.
6) Pressure test the system in accordance with local building codes.
7) Apply a suitable concrete mixture over the tubing.

Single Concrete Pour Over a Sand Bed Encasing the Tubing

1) Lay out the wire mesh or rebar over the base material.
2) Connect the loop to the supply manifold.
3) Secure the tubing to the wire mesh or rebar.
4) Secure the tubing every four feet along straight runs. At the 180° turns, tie the tubing once at the top of the arc and once on each side, 12" from the top of the arc, to prevent it from dislodging and/or floating up into the pour.
5) Once the complete loop has been laid out, connect the end of the loop to the return manifold. Complete the installation.
6) Pressure test the system in accordance with local building codes.
7) Apply sand over the tubing.
8) Apply a suitable concrete mixture over the sand.

On a Suspended Wood Floor Using Aluminum Heat Emission Plates

1) Mark the approximate location of the tubing on the subfloor.
2) Starting at the area farthest from the manifold, glue and nail a 1×6 furring strip to the subfloor along the exterior wall.
3) Using a heat emission plate as a guide, nail and glue another 1×6 furring strip parallel to the first. Be sure to leave a 1" space between furring strips for the groove of the heat emission plate.
4) Staple the heat emission plates to the furring strips on one side of the tubing only. This will allow the plates to expand as the subfloor or finish flooring is nailed down. Leave a small gap between plates.
5) Connect one end of the loop to the supply manifold.
6) Following the tubing layout pattern, snap the tubing into the heat emission plate.
7) Connect the other end to the return manifold. Complete the tubing installation.
8) Pressure test the system in accordance with local building codes.
9) Apply a suitable construction adhesive to the furring strips where exposed between the heat emission plates.
10) Apply a suitable subfloor or finish flooring over the tubing.
11) Install suitable insulation below the floor to limit downward loss.

Poured Floor Underlayment on a Suspended Wood Floor Using a Rail System

1) Lay out rails parallel with floor joists (perpendicular to tubing layout direction). Space the rails 12" from the edge of each wall, and 3' on center thereafter.
2) Fasten rails to subfloor using 1" wood screws.
3) Connect one end of the loop to the supply manifold.
4) Snap the tubing into each rail at the recommended spacing. The tubing will be installed in a single wall serpentine layout pattern.
5) Once the complete loop has been laid out, connect the end of the tubing to the return manifold.
6) Pressure test the system in accordance with local building codes.
7) Apply a concrete mixture over the tubing.

Under a Suspended Wood Floor Using Aluminum Heat Emission Plates

1) Connect the loop to the supply manifold.
2) Snap the tubing into the heat emission plates, and following the tubing layout plan, staple the heat emission plates to the under side of the subfloor. Leave a small gap between each plate. Place two staples on each end between the tubing, and two in the center between the tubing.
   Note — Be sure to use only ⅝" staples. Longer staples may pass through the subfloor and floor covering above.
3) During installation, it will become necessary to loop the tubing from one joist cavity to another. This is achieved by looping the tubing below the joist dividing the two cavities. This presents problems if the underside of the floor is finished. It will then be necessary to either lower the ceiling to accommodate the thickness of the tubing, or drill a hole through the floor joist and run the tubing through the joist.
4) Connect the end of the loop to the return manifold. Complete the installation.
5) Pressure test the system in accordance with local building codes.
6) Install suitable insulation below the plates to limit downward loss.

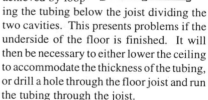

Using solar energy to cool, heat house

Q: I would like to use free solar energy to help cool my house in the summer without sacrificing solar gain in the winter. Are there any do-it-yourself solar-cooling projects?

A: You can use free solar energy to help cool your home in the summer. Building a solar ventilation chimney is an effective and simple project. With the proper use of solar heat mass storage, you can have cooling well into the evening hours too.

First, you should make some simple do-it-yourself improvements. Extend the roof overhang on the south and west sides of your house. This blocks the summer sun which is high in the sky. The winter sun, which is lower in the sky, still shines under the large overhang, on to your walls and in windows for solar heating.

It is not a difficult task to increase the overhang. Just remove the soffit sheathing and extend the roof rafters or joist. Cover this with roof sheathing and match the old shingle color. Cover soffit area again and add inlet air vents to the attic.

A do-it-yourself solar chimney is basically a natural whole-house exhaust vent from the ceiling in your home up through the roof. As the portion of the solar chimney extending up past the roof gets warm from the sun, the hot air inside it naturally flows upward and out.

This draws hot air out of your home and pulls cooler air indoors. The air inlet can be from a cool well-ventilated crawl space or through windows or vents near the floor. Install screens on both inlet and outlet openings.

A solar chimney has clear glazing (acrylic plastic, glass, etc.) on the south and west sides. A two-foot-square size is ideal because

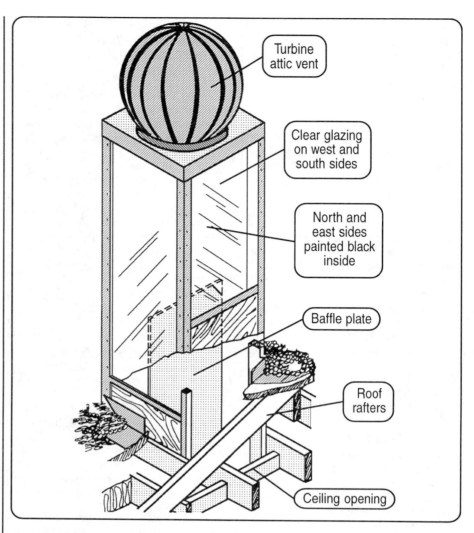

Turbine attic vent

Clear glazing on west and south sides

North and east sides painted black inside

Baffle plate

Roof rafters

Ceiling opening

there is less material waste when using inexpensive standard 4 foot by 8 foot lumber and other materials. Seven feet high is a typical size.

Install clear glazing on only the top half of the south side. Otherwise, since the sun is so high at noon, it will shine down into your room below and actually heat it. Glaze the entire west side of the solar chimney.

Install foil-faced rigid insulation board on the inside of the plywood north and east sides of the solar chimney. Paint foil flat black so it becomes an effective solar heat collector when the sun shines in the glazed west or south sides. You can also install an 18-inch turbine attic vent on top of the chimney to improve the draw in windy weather.

Q: I have a problem with rusty water coming out of my hot water faucets. My electric water heater is only a couple of years old. What is the source of the rust and how can I get it out?

A: Since your water heater is fairly new and it is glass-lined, it probably is not the source of the rust. The most likely source is one or more of the hot water supply pipes between the water heater and faucets.

Try flushing the pipes to remove the rust. First turn off the power to your water heater. Open all the hot water faucets and allow the water to run for 15 minutes. If this doesn't help, contact your plumber for a more thorough analysis of the problem.

Building a solar chimney can be a very effective method to ventilate your house. It also adds natural lighting like a skylight without the direct sun's heat getting in. Not only does it operate for free, but it does not contribute to air pollution and global warming as electric fans do. Be sure to keep your windows tightly closed so that the cooler air is drawn in crawl spaces, basement windows or vents. If you are allergic to molds and mildew and live in a humid climate, the air from a crawl space or basement may aggravate your allergy. In this case, open windows on the ground level floor of your home.

Installing an optional turbine vent on top of the chimney helps to increase the vertical draft when it is breezy outdoors during the day. An 18-inch turbine vent is a good size to use on top of a 2 ft. by 2 ft. solar chimney. In the winter, you can close the insulated hinged plywood 2 ft. by 2 ft. door in the ceiling. Also close it when you run your air conditioner.

You can make the solar chimney any size you want. The bigger it is, the more ventilation it will create. If you make it too big, it may detract from the exterior appearance of your house. A height of seven feet above your roof is a good initial target height. A steeper pitched roof, as in the northern climates, can accommodate a taller solar chimney.

Check the location of trees around your roof to find a location for the solar chimney that is not shaded. Keep in mind that neighbors' trees will grow and you probably will not be able to prune them. Consider the orientation of your roof to the south and west. If possible, locate it near an outside wall where the roof slopes downward. This makes the lightwell channel shorter between the roof and the ceiling. Also, the solar chimney will be less obvious sticking up from your roof. To be effective, it must be in the sun from late morning to early evening.

You should be able to find most of the materials at a home center or building supply outlet. There are several options for the clear glazing on the south and west sides of the solar chimney. Clear acrylic plastic (Plexiglas) sheet is easy to work with. Fiberglass reinforced polyester is another durable option. Clear polycarbonate (Lexan) is unbreakable, but it is more expensive. Always wear appropriate safety equipment and eye protection. I would avoid using ordinary window glass because it can break during installation or from the impact from a bird, hail, or baseball. Most local plastic supply outlets carry these types of plastic sheeting.

Do-It-Yourself Instuctions for Building a Solar Chimney

1) To keep costs down and simplify the availability of materials, build the solar chimney with standard size building materials. Make it a size that divides evenly into 4×8 sheets (both glazing and plywood) to minimize waste.

2) Go up into your attic and find the exact location where you plan to cut through the ceiling. Cut the 2-foot square hole in the ceiling. Frame the hole with double 2×4's. Make sure to keep the blocking plumb because you will cover it with plywood to connect the hole in the ceiling to the hole in the roof. This will create the lightwell channel for the breeze and provide natural lighting.

3) Using a plumb line, find the locations for the four corners of the hole in roof directly above the hole in the ceiling. Drill small holes through these four spots in the roof. These will mark the desired location of the opening in roof.

4) Go up on your roof and carefully remove the shingles surrounding the four locator holes. Saw through the roof sheathing at the holes to make the square roof opening. Frame the opening with 2×4's, making sure to keep them plumb for when you nail on the vertical 2×4's to form the lightwell channel between the ceiling and the roof.

5) Cut and nail vertical 2×4's to the inside of the openings to form the lightwell channel from the roof to the ceiling. These should then be recessed so the inside surface is flush with the very edge of the hole in the ceiling. You will nail the uprights for the chimney portion to these 2×4's in the lightwell. You will then later cover the inside of these 2×4's with plywood so they will enclose and finish the lightwell.

6) For three of the corners, between east and south, east and north, and north and west, you will nail other vertical chimney 2×4 uprights to the ones below. Attach these in a suitable manner for adequate support. These 2×4's will form the corners of the solar chimney above the roof. Use a 2×2 on the south and west corner so that less of the glazed area is blocked. Nail horizontal 2×4's between the uprights at the top to support the uprights and provide a mounting surface for the top cover and turbine vent.

7) If you have a very short lightwell, the sun at high noon may shine down into your room through the lightwell. If you find that this happens in your area, secure a horizontal 2×4 across the east to west side at the top of the lightwell. Cut and nail a plywood baffle to the 2×4 and to the plywood on the sides. This baffle will block any sun from shining directly down into your room below.

8) Cut foil-faced rigid foam insulation board to cover all the inside unglazed surfaces in the chimney. Paint the foil surface flat black and glue and nail it to the plywood surfaces with the black foil facing inward. This black surface will become the solar absorber to capture the sun's heat.

9) Use some type of clear plastic sheets for the south and west sides. The various types of materials are listed in the materials list. Glaze only the upper half of the south side to avoid direct sunlight from shining in your room around noontime.

Required Materials for a Solar Chimney

clear acrylic, polycarbonate sheet glazing
2×2, 2×4 lumber
½x½- inch wood strip, ½-inch plywood
roofing flashing
aluminum angle trim
aluminum sheet metal for top
silicon caulking
adhesive-backed foam weatherstripping
nails, hinges, wood and sheet metal screws
paint — exterior house and flat black
18-inch turbine vent
foil-faced rigid foam insulation board

10) Lay a bead of silicon caulking on the 2×4 and 2×2 uprights and place the sheets against the uprights. Cut four lengths of the aluminum angle trim and drill holes in it every one foot. Place a bead of caulking under each leg and screw these in place through the glazing sheets along the exterior corners to finish them.

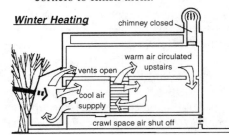

Winter Heating
chimney closed
warm air circulated upstairs
vents open
cool air suppply
crawl space air shut off

11) You can either have a 2-foot square sheet metal top made to cover the chimney and mount the turbine vent or you can make a plywood top. If you make a plywood top, use the aluminum angle to finish the edges. Use silicon caulking under the top.

12) Paint all the unglazed exterior surfaces with house paint to match your house or roof. Attach flashing around the chimney and replace the shingles. Finish the inside of the lightwell with plywood or drywall.

13) Make a plywood door to fit the opening in your ceiling. Attach a ½×½ strip around the inside of the opening about ¾ of an inch above the

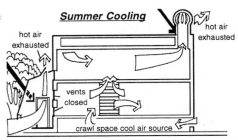

Summer Cooling
hot air exhausted
hot air exhausted
vents closed
crawl space cool air source

opening. Stick adhesive-backed foam weatherstripping against the strip. Attach the door with hinges and attach a latch to hold it closed when you are air-conditioning or in the winter. Glue several inches of foam insulation board on top of it to block heat flow when it's closed.

Manufacturers of Whole-House Ventilation Fans

BROAN, PO Box 140, Hartford, WI 53027 - (800) 548-0790 (414) 673-4340

model - 2220 • 2224 • 2230	blade diameter - 20 inch • 24 inch • 30 inch	maximum air flow - 3300 • 3600 • 5100
rpm - 1060/650 • 825/525 • 700/400	drive type - direct-drive	motor - n/a
speed control - two-speed	amperage - 4.5 amps • 4.5 amps • 5.0 amps	wattage - 400 • 460 • 490
model - 2236	blade diameter - 36 inch	maximum air flow - 6850 cfm
rpm - 440	drive type - belt-drive	motor - n/a
speed control - single-speed	amperage - 5.5 amps	wattage - 500

KOOL-O-MATIC CORP., 1831 Terminal Rd., Niles, MI 49120 - (616) 683-2600

model - 360 and 360T	blade diameter - 36 inch	maximum air flow - 7320/5400 cfm
rpm - 380/200	drive type - direct-drive	motor - 1/3 hp
speed control - variable-speed	amperage - 4.5/5.2 amps	wattage - 450/420

LESLIE-LOCKE, 4501 Circle 75 Parkway, Suite C-3250, Atlanta, GA 30339 - (800) 755-9392 (770) 953-6366

model - Pace Setter	blade diameter - 30 inch • 36 inch	maximum air flow - 5800 cfm • 8800 cfm
rpm - 825/725 • 1725/1160	drive type - belt-drive	motor - 1/4 hp • 1/3 hp
speed control - two-speed	amperage - 6.8 amps • 6.8 amps	wattage - 500 • 500

LOMANCO, PO Box 519, Jacksonville, AR 72076 - (800) 643-5596 (501) 982-6511

model - 2480 • 3082	blade diameter - 24 inch • 30 inch	maximum air flow - 3700 cfm • 5900 cfm
rpm - n/a	drive type - direct-drive	motor - 1/4 hp • 1/2 hp
speed control - variable-speed	amperage - 4.7 amps • 8.0 amps	wattage - 564 • 960

NUTONE INC., Madison & Red Bank Rds., Cincinnati, OH 45227 - (800) 543-8687 (513) 527-5100

model - WHV20	blade diameter - 24 inch	maximum air flow - 3200 cfm
rpm - 1050 • 800	drive type - direct-drive	motor - 1/4 hp
speed control - single-speed	amperage - 8.0 amps	wattage - 550
model - WHV24DD • WHV30-02	blade diameter - 24 inch • 30 inch	maximum air flow - 2800 cfm • 4800 cfm
rpm - 800 • 850	drive type - direct-drive	motor - 1/5 hp • 1/4 hp
speed control - two-speed	amperage - 3.6 amps • 5.0 amps	wattage - 340 • 480
model - WHV30BD • WHV36BD	blade diameter - 30 inch • 36 inch	maximum air flow - 5600 cfm • 6800 cfm
rpm - 1725 • 1725	drive type - belt-drive	motor - 1/3 hp • 1/3 hp
speed control - two-speed	amperage - 6.5 amps • 6.5 amps	wattage - 545 • 615

PATTON & FASCO, 800 E. 101 Terrace, Suite 100, Kansas City, MO - (800) 334-4126 (919) 483-0421

model - A20DD • A24DD • B30DD	blade diameter - 20 inch • 24 inch • 30 inch	maximum air flow - 3600 • 5500 • 6900
rpm - 1050 • 1065 • 625	drive type - direct-drive	motor - n/a
speed control - three-speed	amperage - 3.0 amps • 5.2 amps • 5.5 amps	wattage - 360 • 624 • 660
model - UF22 • UF30	blade diameter - 22 inch • 30 inch	maximum air flow - 3600 cfm • 6950 cfm
rpm - 1120/965 • 695/575	drive type - direct-drive	motor - 1/4 hp 1/3 hp
speed control - two-speed	amperage - 3.1 amps • 6.5 amps	wattage - 372 • 780
model - 2438 • 3038 • 3638	blade diameter - 24 inch • 30 inch • 36 inch	maximum air flow - 3900 • 5500 • 7100
rpm - 745 • 545 • 430	drive type - belt-drive	motor - n/a
speed control - three-speed	amperage - 5.7 amps • 5.5 amps • 7.2 amps	wattage - 684 • 660 • 864

1) Positioning the Whole-House Fan — Drive a nail through the center of the ceiling in the hallway location selected. In the attic, remove the insulation from the area selected, and locate the nail driven through the ceiling. The long dimension of the ceiling shutter 48½" is designed to fit between 16" or 24" on center ceiling joist construction with the joist located in the shutter opening removed as required. From each side of the locator nail select a ceiling joist with a total measurement of 46½" between the joists as the two ventilator/shutter mounting joists. Drill a ¼" hole flush to the inside edge of each joist. Electrical or plumbing lines located between the drilled holes should be moved clear of the opening. From below, position the template on the ceiling between the two outside drilled holes, and, with the template on the ceiling between the two outside drilled holes, and, with the template sides parallel to the hallway walls, tack it into place. Then draw a line around the template, as shown in diagram #1. This marked opening will measure 46½"×33⅝".

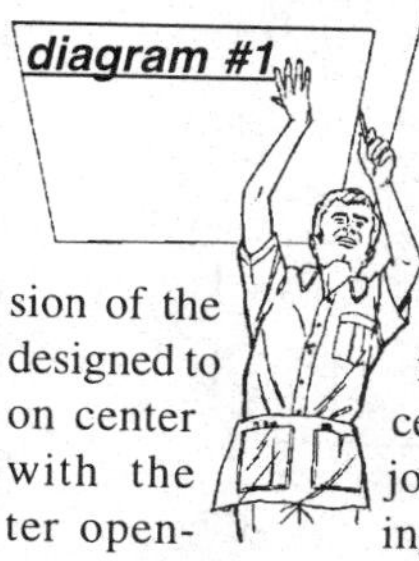

2) Cutting the Opening — Drill four ¼" holes in the corners of the marked-off ceiling opening. Using a keyhole or sabre saw, cut the ceiling board along the inside edge of the template marked "opening", skipping the joist areas, until the entire marked outline has been cut, as shown in diagram #2. Score the uncut segments of the marked outline at the joist areas with a utility knife. Break out the ceiling board within the marked opening with a hammer, and remove the ceiling board. Working in the attic, remove the ceiling joist within the opening. Cut the joist perpendicular to the ceiling 1½" in from the outside edges of the opening. See diagram #3. For the final cut to the ceiling surface, use a keyhole saw with the handle reversed to avoid damaging the ceiling below. On truss type construction, plywood reinforcement gussett plates should be nailed and glued to both sides of the truss being cut. See diagram #4. These gussets should be installed before cutting the joist from the opening. Do not stand on the cut joists until the framing headers are installed.

3) Framing the Opening — The distance between the uncut joists flanking the opening should measure 46½". Cut two 2"×6" headers to this length. Place the headers at the edges of the opening, and nail them to the sides of the

uncut joists and the ends of the cut joists. See diagram #5. If the joists are 2"×4" construction, as used in truss type roof construction nail 2"×2" wood strips on the joists to complete a 2"×6" framed opening for the shutter. Since the shutter opening is rectangular and the fan panel is square, it will be necessary to construct a platform plate on which to mount the whole-house fan. Using 1"×4" and 1"×6" lumber, construct a platform to the joist and headers, remove the ventilator assembly from its carton and install the self-adhesive rubber gasket around the mounting flange. Carefully lift the ventilator assembly into the attic through the opening, placing it on hoist adjacent to the opening. After the ventilator is inside the attic the platform can be nailed to the joist and headers.

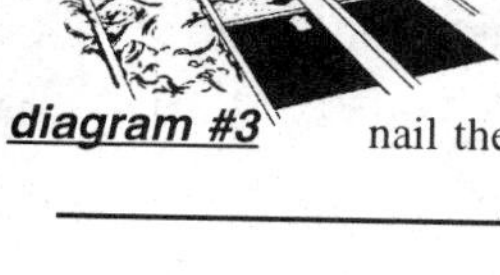

4) Installing the Fan Assembly — Using a marking pen, mark the sides of the platform at 44" centered. Set the whole-house fan assembly onto the platform motor side on one of the 1"×4" boards with the outside edges of the mounting flange at the 44" centering mark. Place (8) nails in the center of the flange mounting holes, tapping them through the rubber gasket into the platform. These nails should not be set tight as they are intended only to keep the fan assembly from shifting, as shown in diagram #7. Check all bolts and nuts on the whole-house fan to make sure they are tight and have not loosened in transit handling. Hand turn the fan assembly to make sure it turns freely and that it clears the mounting platform and the end of the motor by ½" on all blades. Proper belt tension should allow the belt to be hand pressed together approximately ½" on each side. Excessive belt tension will result in stalled or slow starting of fan. On ceilings with extra thick loose insulation which extends above the ventilator, it may be necessary to install an retainer wall.

5) Installing the Ceiling Shutter — Remove the shutter from the carton and lay it flat

on the floor. Lift the tension spring post and snap-lock it into position on the edge of the shutter frame. With shutter blades open, connect the spring and adjustment link to the tie-rod as shown in diagram #8. Adjust the spring tension by moving the hook link from one hole to another in the tie-rod until the blades of the shutter just close. In most cases this will be seven holes from the end. This balancing adjustment is important. Check the ceiling on both sides of the opening to see that it is level. If the ceiling is not level, install the shutter with the blade pivots towards the high side.

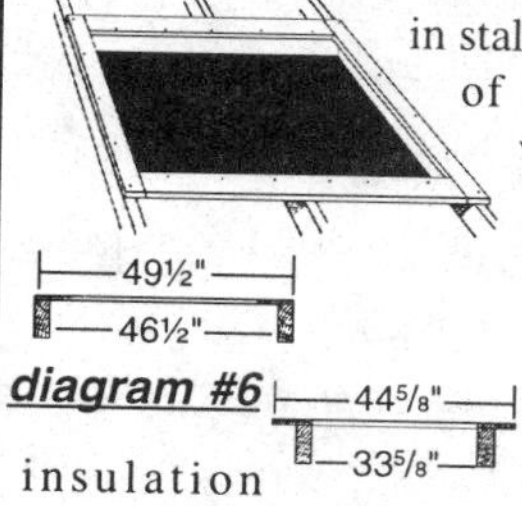

With a helper, lift the shutter into the ceiling opening, centering the shutter within the opening. Mark four corner mounting holes in the shutter on the ceiling.

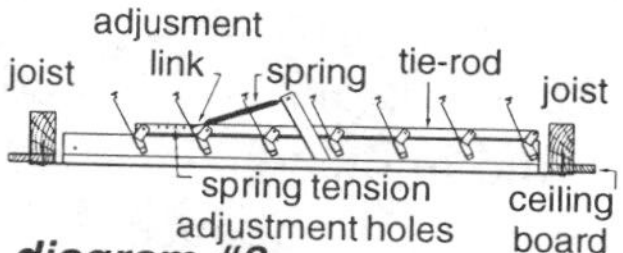

diagram #8

Remove the shutter and pilot drill for No. 8 screws at these four marked mounting holes. With a helper, again lift the shutter into the ceiling opening and secure the shutter through the ceiling material into the joist frame above, using No. 8×1½" long round head wood screws. Do not force the shutter into the opening as the blades will not operate freely. In cases of uneven mounting surfaces, leave the mounting screws slightly loose to avoid putting a twist in the shutter frame. Drill pilot holes and insert 1½" screws into the joist/headers at the 10 remaining shutter mounting holes. The shutter may be painted to match the ceiling, if desired. You may spray the shutter before installation or spray the shutter mounted in the ceiling at the time the hallway is being repainted. See diagram #9.

6) Wiring the Whole-House Fan — The whole-house fan's speed control should be mounted at a convenient location in the living area. The easiest method is to use an existing circuit. However, your area electrical code or existing circuit load may require a separate circuit. For existing circuit connection it is suggested that the hall light switch be used. In the attic, attach with screws an electrical junction box to the rafter next to the motor. Run the lead wires from the motor into the junction box and fasten the flexible electrical conduit to the box using the ⅜" flexible cable connect furnished with the fan.

diagram #1

diagram #2

diagram #3

Kingpost Truss
Whole-house fans cannot be installed on homes if Kingpost type roof trusses as shown are used through-   out attic.

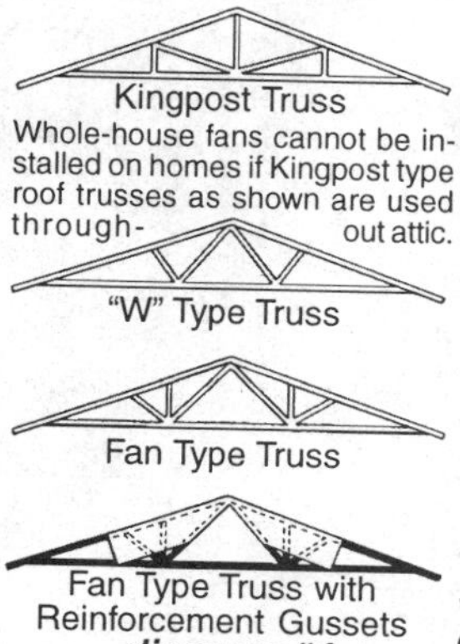

"W" Type Truss

Fan Type Truss

Fan Type Truss with Reinforcement Gussets
diagram #4

diagram #5

diagram #6

49½"
46½"
44⅝"
33⅝"
insulation

diagram #7

diagram #9

Block summer sun and cold winter winds

Q: I cannot afford a new patio door, but I need to find a low-cost method to block the sun in the summer and cold drafts in the winter. What is the best do-it-yourself way to do this?

A: An old leaky patio door is about the greatest single year-round energy waster in most homes. It also makes you uncomfortable and allows dust, allergens, humidity, fading rays and noise into your house.

Building a simple low-cost sun/wind shield is one of the simplest and best methods to reduce energy losses and discomfort near an old patio door. In the summer, the sun's intense fading rays will be totally blocked. By deflecting the cold wind in the winter, sweating on the glass is also reduced.

A sun/wind shield can be attractive. It also provides an excellent location for hanging plants, a covered area for kids' muddy shoes, privacy from neighbors and allows you to open the door when it rains.

Depending on how you plan your sun/wind shield, you can make its top large enough to place chairs under. The larger the top, the more months of shading and fading protection it provides in fall and spring too.

Before starting this project, it is important to make any needed repairs (caulking, weatherstripping and latch adjustments) to your patio door. This project consists basically of 2x4 framed sides and top that are covered with plywood siding. If your budget is not too limited, use pressure treated lumber for all the pieces that touch the patio.

Plan the slope of the top so that it is consistent with the slope of the house roof. This gives it a more professional look. Decorative plywood

2x4 framing around glass patio door

Three hinged and insulated panels on each side

Rigid foam insulation blocks heat, cold and outdoor noise

Extend top to provide more room for hanging plants

Slope top at same angle as house roof

Window or shutter on side for cool breezes in the evening

Make sides deeper for more privacy

siding prices vary, so you must compromise between appearance and cost.

For natural ventilation in the evenings, install a simple hinged plywood shutter or window into the southwest or west side of the sun/wind shield. This helps catch cool prevailing evening breezes. Building a flowerbox/sun shield for smaller windows also provides ventilation and shade.

Another do-it-yourself option is an insulated interior patio door shutter. It has three hinged panels on each side and opens accordion style. It can be finished with paneling or covered with decorative fabrics.

Make a frame around the door with 2x4's. Next make six frames using 1x2's and cover one side with the paneling and plywood. Cut and lay a piece of one-inch thick rigid

foam insulation in each frame and cover the other side. Hinge each set of three panels together and attach them to the frame.

Q: During the summer, our refrigerator seems to run almost constantly. It is noisy and I am afraid that it will wear out prematurely. Is this normal and what should I do about it?

A: Your refrigerator compressor should not run almost continuously. This not only wears it out and wastes electricity, but it creates excess heat indoors which makes your air conditioner run longer too.

Refrigerators are often placed tight against a wall, under cabinets or in a corner. Pull it out a couple of inches, especially in the summer, to allow more air flow through the coils. Vacuum condenser coils regularly.

Instructions for Making a Patio Door Sun/Wind Shield

1) Before starting to build this shield, plan the size and slope of roof that you want. It will depend on the size and style of your house. Also consider the orientation

diagram #1

to the sun. A door facing toward the east or west will require a deeper shield to block the sun. (The sun is lower in the sky in the morning and afternoon.) Determine the type of plywood siding that will look best. It may be desirable to use pressure treated plywood (CCA), except the additional cost must be considered. When handling or sawing pressure treated lumber, follow recommended safety procedures. Cedar siding is also an option.

2) You should determine if you want a window or shutter in one of the sides of the shield. Depending on your house orientation, it may allow for more natural ventilation in the summer.

3) First assemble the frames for the side walls of the shield. It is usually easiest to assemble these flat on the ground. Make sure the frame is square. Cut the vertical pieces (1) (see diagram #1) from the 2x4 lumber (pressure treated lumber is recommended) to a length to give adequate headroom under the shield. Cut the horizontal pieces (2,3) to provide the depth of shield you want.

4) Nail the horizontal and vertical pieces together to form two side walls. Use #16 penny nails (3 1/2" long), either cement coated or galvanized type. If you plan to add a window or shutter, cut and nail

the header supports in the side wall for it.

5) Cut vertical door opening pieces (4) and the cross piece (5) from the 2x4 lumber. Nail these to the house around the sliding glass door opening. These will be used to attach the shield to the house.

6) Nail the side wall frames to the door opening pieces (4,5). Temporary diagonal wood bracing (light scrap wood) may be used to ensure the unit is true square, plumb, level and perpendicular. Remove bracing as permanent outer siding is installed.

7) Cut a piece of 2x4 lumber for the front roof support (6) and nail it to the top of the side wall frames. This will tie the ends together. Add two cross supports (7) from the top piece (6) to piece (5).

8) After you have determined the pitch of the roof that you want, cut and nail the horizontal roof support (8) to the house. Locate the wall studs before you drive in the nails.

9) Cut the roof rafters (9) and nail them securely to the roof support (8) and to the front support (6). You may want to bevel the ends of the rafters to the angle of the roof.

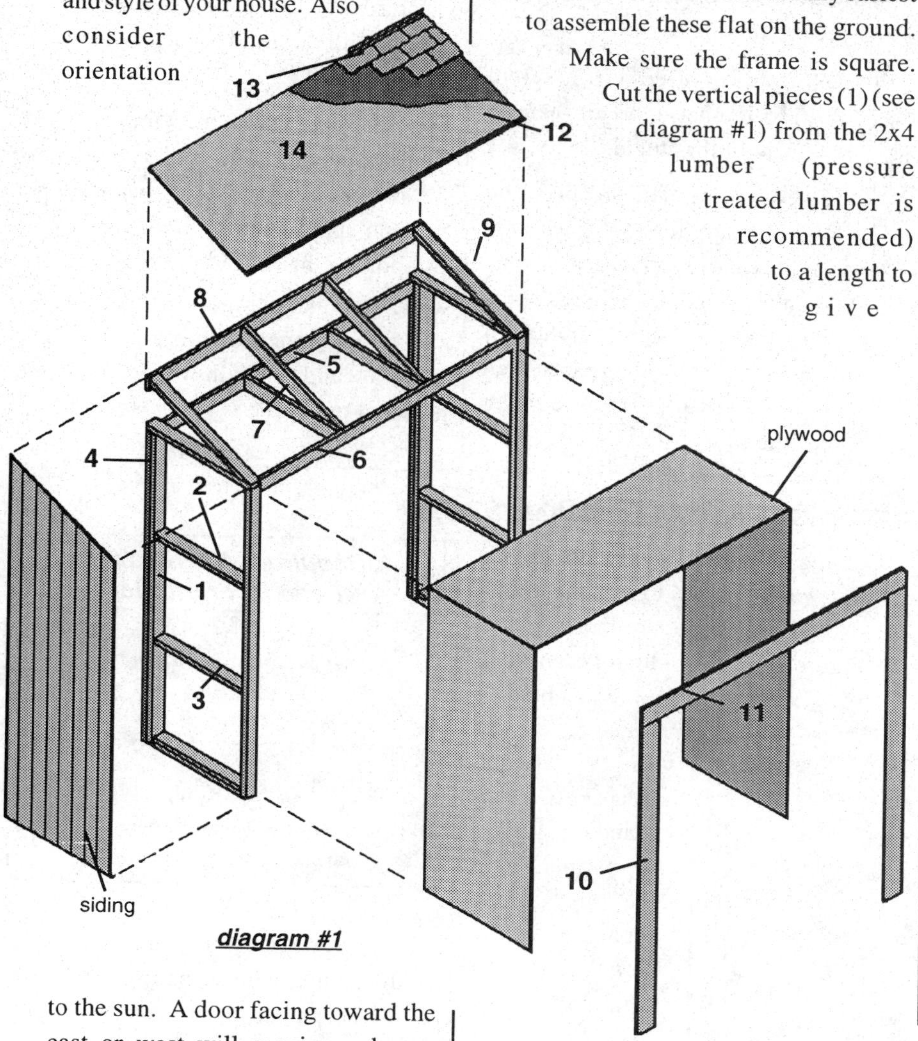

Required Materials for Patio Door Shelter

lumber - 2"x4" — 10 pieces pressure treated for framing
lumber - 1"x6" — 3 pieces cedar or redwood for trim
plywood - 3/8"x4" — 2 sheets exterior grade
plywood siding - 5/8"x4" — 1 sheet
galvanized metal flashing - 2"x3"x16' (45° angle type)
narrow metal strip
caulking sealant cartridge type — 1 or 2 cartridges
building paper (dimensions same as size of roof sheathing)
#8 penny nails — 1 pound cement coated or galvanized
#16 penny nails — 1 pound cement coated or galvanized
3/4" length galvanized roofing nails — 1 pound
roof shingles
galvanized lag bolts required only if attachment is needed at masonry or cement surfaces
exterior grade latex paint for prime and finish coats
optional - exterior grade stain, varnish or polyurethane
Note — Material list based on door shelter of 2' maximum depth and overall length of not more than 8'. Material list adjustment required for deeper or longer shelter.

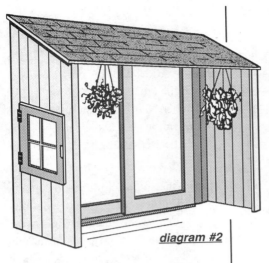

diagram #2

10) Cut the ⁵/₈" siding to make the covers for the side walls. Nail these covers to the side wall frames.

11) Cut the ³/₈" plywood for the inside surface of the side walls and underneath the roof. Nail these pieces into place.

12) Cut trim pieces (10,11) from the 1x6 lumber and nail them to the front of the shield.

13) Cut a piece of the ³/₈" plywood (14) to use for the roof sheathing. Nail it in place over the roof frame. #8 galvanized nails will resist the dampness the best. Cover the roof sheathing with building paper. Nail a metal drip strip (12) to the lower end of the roof.

14) Cover the roof with shingles using ³/₄" length galvanized roofing nails. Lighter-colored shingles will not get as hot in the summer. Nail metal flashing (13) against the house. Seal it with a good quality caulking sealant.

15) You should paint the completed unit both inside and out with several coats of good quality exterior paint or stain and apply exterior grade varnish or polyurethane.

Note: Optional storage compartment may also be incorporated into a longer door shield as conditions allow or for your own personal preference.

Instructions for Making a Patio Door Shutter

1) Before starting to build this sliding glass patio door shutter, be sure to have very accurate measurements. The tighter fitting

diagram #3

the panels are, more energy will be saved.

2) Measure the height and width of your sliding glass patio door. Include the casing around the doorway. Divide the width by six to get the rough overall size for one shutter panel. Figure the exact width for each panel by subtracting the amount of space used by hinges between the panels. You can get a tighter fit by recessing the hinges. The shutters need to be as tall as the top of the door casing.

3) Make a frame for each shutter using 1×2's (1, 2). Cut rabbets in the 1×2's, see the door panel detail in diagram #4. Glue and nail the frame pieces together, using butt joints.

4) Cut a piece of ¼-inch plywood (3) for the back of each panel. Glue and nail into place. Fit a piece of rigid foam insulation (4) inside the frame. Face the panel with another piece of ¼-inch plywood (3). Glue and nail into place. Countersink the nailheads and fill them

Required Materials for Patio Door Shutter
lumber — 2"×4", 1"×4", 1"×2" lumber — ¼" plywood 2"×2" metal angles nails and screws handles hinges glue and wood putty 1" foam insulation sheets stain or paint

with wood putty. If you plan to cover the shutters with decorative fabric, you need to put the material on before putting the panels together.

5) Stain or paint the shutters as desired and let them dry thoroughly.

6) Next you will construct the surround. First, build a header (5, 6, 7) as shown in diagram #5 for the header detail. Remember when you are cutting the pieces for the header that the outside dimension of the surround will be 7 inches wider than the outside dimension of the sliding door's trim.

7) This step requires a helper to lift the finished header assembly into position above the sliding glass patio door casing. Screw 2×2-inch metal angles to the header and to the wall studs.

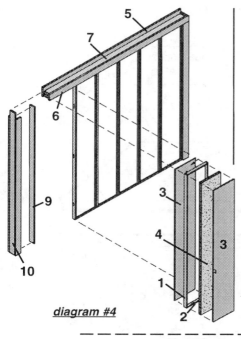

diagram #4

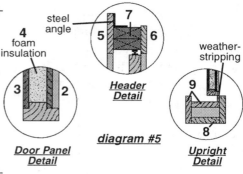

Door Panel Detail — foam insulation, steel angle, **Header Detail**, weatherstripping, **Upright Detail**, *diagram #5*

This will secure the header assembly. See header detail in diagram #5.

8) Build the surround's uprights (8,9) as shown in the detail in the illustration. The end member (8) is 3½ inches taller than the three other members (9) Position the uprights and nail them into the header's 2×4's and anchor at the bottom with metal angles fastened to the floor. Countersink the nailheads and fill them with wood putty.

9) Finish the frame to your personal preference.

10) Hinge each trio of panels together, using three hinges between each adjoining panel. Fasten a length of folding door track to the header. Attach heavy-duty folding door hardware, simply follow the instructions on the package. Lift the panels into position. If there are any air gaps you can seal them with foam weather stripping.

Manufacturers of Super-Efficient Sliding Glass Patio Doors

AMERICAN WEATHER SEAL, 324 Wooster Rd., N., Barberton, OH 44203 - (800) 358-2954 (330) 745-1661
type of door - standard sliding • French slider
frame color - white, sandalwood, brown
frame material - aluminum-clad wood • wood — pine
height - 6'8", 8'0"

ANDERSEN WINDOWS, 100 4th Ave. N., Bayport, MN 55003 - (888) 888-7020 (612) 439-5150
type of door - standard sliding • French sliding
frame color - white, sandtone (beige), Terratone® (brown)
frame material - vinyl-clad wood — pine
height - 6'8", 6'11", 8'0"

CARADCO, 201 Evans Rd., Rantoul, IL 61866 - (800) 238-1866
type of door - standard sliding • French slider
frame color - white, sandstone, hartford green, slate blue
frame material - alum.-clad wood • wood — pine
height - 6'8", 8'0"

CERTAINTEED CORP., PO Box 860, Valley Forge, PA 19482 - (800) 233-8990
type of door - standard sliding
frame color - white, tan, brown
frame material - vinyl
height - 6'8", 8'0"

COMFORT LINE, 5500 Enterprise Blvd., Toledo, OH 43612 - (419) 729-8520
type of door - standard sliding • French sliding
frame color - white, almond, cobblestone (beige), dark brown
frame material - fiberglass • fiberglass-clad oak veneer
height - 6'8", 8'0"

EAGLE WINDOW, PO Box 1072, Dubuque, IA 52004 - (800) 453-3633 (319) 556-2270
type of door - standard sliding • French sliding
frame color - white, sierra bronze, pebble tan, forest green
frame material - alum.-clad wood • wood - pine or oak
height - 6'8", 8'0"

KOLBE & KOLBE MILLWORK CO., 1323 S. 11th Ave., Wausau, WI 54401 - (715) 842-5666
type of door - standard sliding • French sliding
frame color - white, sand, beige, rustic, hartford green
frame material - aluminum-wood clad • wood
height - 6'8", 6'10", 6'11"

MARVIN WINDOWS & DOORS, PO Box 100, Warroad, MN 56763 - (800) 346-5128
type of door - standard sliding • French sliding
frame color - white, brown, pebble gray, bronze, evergreen
frame material - aluminum-wood clad • wood — pine
height - 6'5", 6'8", 6'11", 8'0", 8'3"

OWENS CORNING, One Owens Corning Parkway, Toledo, OH 43659 - (419) 248-8000
type of door - standard sliding (insulated)
frame color - white, almond, beige
frame material - fiberglass • vinyl
height - 6'8"

PEACHTREE (CARADON DOORS), 435 Peachtree Industrial Blvd., Norcross, GA 30071 - (888) 888-3814
type of door - standard sliding • French sliding (insulated)
frame color - colonial white, driftwood
frame material - alum.-clad fiberglass • fiberglass • steel
height - 6'8", 8'0"

POZZI WOOD WINDOWS (JELD-WEN), PO Box 5249, Bend, OR 97708 - (800) 257-9663
type of door - standard sliding • French sliding
frame color - white, bronze, champagne, hunter green
frame material - aluminum-clad wood • wood — pine
height - 6'8", 6'11", 7'3", 8'3"

WEATHER SHIELD, PO Box 309, Medford, WI 54451 - (800) 477-6808 (715) 748-2100
type of door - standard sliding • French sliding
frame color - white, western adobe (brown), desert tan, hartford green, sunbeam yellow, boysenberry (reddish), mist grey, obsidian (black), meridian blue, turquoise
frame material - aluminum-clad • vinyl-clad • wood
height - 6'8", 6'10", 8'0"

Solar tile stores a.m. heat for p.m. storage

Q: The sun shines in my kitchen in the morning and in the dining room in the afternoon. It feels great. How can I save some of this free heat for the evening in the winter without overheating in the summer?

A: Installing solar tile on your floor or the lower part of the walls is effective, durable, and attractive. It collects the sun's warmth during the day and slowly releases it in the evening. In the summer, the thermal mass of the tile and floor actually help reduce overheating.

Traditionally, certain types and colors of ceramic tile have been used for this purpose. These have the natural ability to efficiently conduct, store, and reradiate the solar heat at night. Installing ceramic tile properly for passive solar heat is a simple do-it-yourself project.

For existing homes, you can lay it directly over your standard floor. Pouring a thin layer of cement first raises your floor only a little, but it greatly improves efficiency. For the highest efficiency, you should put the solar tile over a heavier masonry floor. This is ideal for new construction.

Today there are some new attractive earth-friendly tile alternatives to traditional ceramic tile. These products use recycled or cement-based materials to produce tile with good passive solar qualities and durability. They are also available in many different varieties, including many with several types of finishes and colors.

The wide variety of shapes and sizes available in ceramic tile offer many design possibilities. For south-facing rooms especially, one alternative is to install tile on the walls as well as the floor. This increases the

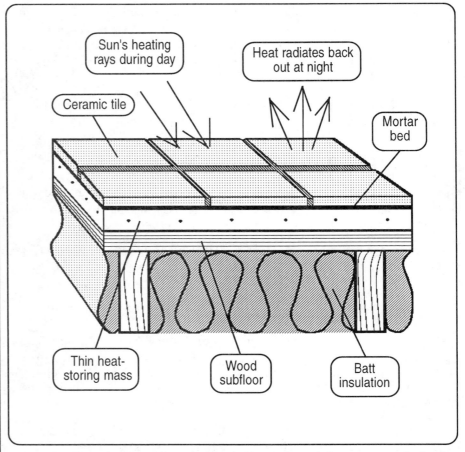

passive solar area as well as being very attractive.

When you select the tile, it is important to consider several solar energy properties of the specific tile and color: solar absorptance, emittance, and thermal diffusivity and conductivity.

Absorptance refers to the percentage of the sun's heat the material absorbs. I installed a special dark brown tile in the entryway of my home. It has a higher solar absorbance than other tiles would.

Emittance refers to the tile's ability to release its stored heat back out into the room at night (when the temperature drops). Many materials readily absorb and store heat, but they don't emit it well.

Thermal diffusivity and conductivity both relate to the speed at which solar heat passes through the

tile to the subfloor material. It also affects how fast the tile gives off the heat at night to warm your feet.

Q: I recently added a new deeper carpeting in my bedroom and hallway. I have to shorten a hollow core door to clear the carpeting and then I plan to add retractable weatherstripping. What is the best way to shorten the door?

A: Shortening a hollow core door can be a little tricky to get a nice, clean appearance. Remove the door from frame and mark a cut line for the amount to be removed. Saw slightly below line and finish file it to the line.

Using a chisel, drive the cardboard core up inside the door. Peel the plywood veneer from the sides of the old bottom block in the cutoff piece. Put glue on the bottom block and insert it back up into the door. Put the door back on the frame.

The natural thermal properties of ceramic tile are ideal for passive solar heating. Ceramic tile readily absorbs the sun's heat and transmits it through to the thermal mass below. At night, it reradiates the stored solar heat back out into your home. Although ceramic tile is somewhat effective for passive solar heating when it is laid directly over a wood floor, it is most effective over a concrete, brick, or stone floor.

If you have ever been in a sun room with inadequate thermal mass in the floors and walls during the winter, it overheats very quickly in the sun. With the proper amount of thermal mass, the room heats up slowly and does not get too hot. In the summer, the thermal mass (shaded with a roof overhang or window shades) tends to moderate temperature changes throughout the day inside your home. This delays the indoor temperature rise and makes you more comfortable. You can often set your air conditioner thermostat several degrees higher and save electricity.

Several ceramic tile floor and wall installation methods are shown on pages 63 and 64. Each diagram lists the thermal capacity of the complete floor and wall structure. A higher thermal capacity indicates that more solar heat can be stored for each degree increase in its temperature. This improves efficiency and the length of time in the evening that heat reradiates out into your home.

Depending on the amount of glass area, the orientation to the sun, and your climate, there is an optimum total thermal capacity value. Although most homes generally have little thermal capacity, you can actually have too much thermal capacity in the walls and floor. When this occurs, the floor or walls do not get warm enough throughout the day to properly reradiate the heat back out at night. As a result, you will not feel as comfortably warm as you should. The solar thermal properties of different colors and types of ceramic tile varies. The properties of several common tiles are shown on page 63.

Manufacturers of Solar Ceramic Tiles

AMERICAN MARAZZI TILE, 359 Clay Rd., Sunnyvalle, TX 75182 - (972) 226-0110

AMERICAN OLEAN TILE, 1000 Cannon Ave., Lansdale, PA 19446 - (215) 855-1111

CONGOLEUM CORP., PO Box 3127, Mercerville, NJ 08619 - (800) 934-3567 (609) 584-3601

EPRO INC., 156 E. Broadway, Westerville, OH 43081 - (614) 882-6990

FLORIDA TILE, P.O. Box 447, Lakeland, FL 33802 - (800) 789-8453

CROSSVILLE CERAMICS, PO Box 1168, Crossville, TN 38557 - (615) 484-2110

INTERCERAMIC, 2333 S. Jupiter Rd., Garland, TX 75041 - (800) 496-8453

KPT INC., P.O. Box 468, Bloomfield, IN 47424 - (800) 444-5784 (812) 384-3563

LAUFEN INTERNATIONAL, 6531 N. Laufen Dr., Tulsa, OK 74117 - (800) 331-3651 (918) 428-3851

LONE STAR CERAMICS CO., PO Box 810215, Dallas, TX 75381 - (800) 256-5248

METROPOLITAN CERAMICS, P.O. Box 9240, Canton, OH 44711 - (330) 484-4876

MONARCH CERAMIC TILE, 834 Rockwood Rd., Florence, AL 35630 - (800) 289-8453 (205) 764-6181

QUARRY TILE, 6328 Utah Ave., Spokane, WA 99212 - (800) 423-2608

RO-TILE INC., 1615 S. Stockton, Lodi, CA 95240 - (800) 688-1380 (209) 334-3136

SUMMITVILLE TILES, PO Box 73, Summitville, OH 43962 - (330) 223-1511

TERRA-GREEN TECH., 1650 Progress Dr., Richmond, IN 47374 - (765) 935-4760

TILE CERA, 300 Arcata Blvd., Clarksville, TN 37040 - (800) 782-8453 (615) 645-5100

Ceramic tile works very well with the heat storage system in the living area and complements the appearance of the room. Carpets, cushioned vinyl flooring and finished wood floors are heat insulators so do not readily conduct the absorbed heat into the storage system. Dark colors, both glazed and unglazed, absorb more heat than light colors. However some medium shades are reasonably efficient for passive solar walls and floors and should not be overlooked.

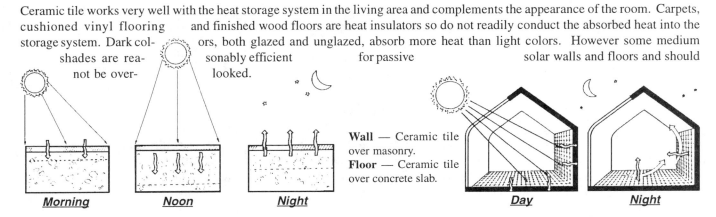

Wall — Ceramic tile over masonry.
Floor — Ceramic tile over concrete slab.

Morning   *Noon*   *Night*   *Day*   *Night*

Typical Ceramic Tile Solar Properties (shown for American Olean tiles)

AO Crystalline® Tile

	Absorptance
362 Cr. Charcoal	0.8
345 Cr. Cobalt	0.7
Specific Heat	0.18 Btu/lb., F
Specific Heat	0.53 Btu/sq. ft., F
Emittance	0.81
Diffusivity	0.00102 in²/sec.
Thermal Conductivity	6.0 Btu/hr., ft², in., F
Thermal Expansion	4.3×10^{-6} in/in, F

AO Ceramic Mosaic Tile

	Absorptance
A42 Cinnabar	0.7
A49 Sepia	0.7
Specific Heat	0.19 Btu/lb., F
Specific Heat	0.40 Btu/sq. ft., F
Emittance	0.82
Diffusivity	0.00135 in²/sec.
Thermal Conductivity	10.1 Btu/hr., ft², in., F
Thermal Expansion	3.3×10^{-6} in/in, F

AO Quarry Tile

	Absorptance
Q07 Umber	0.8
Q02 Ember Flash	0.8
Q01 Canyon Red	0.7
Q04 Sand Flash	0.7
Q06 Fawn Gray	0.7
Q16 Gray Flash	0.7
Q03 Sahara	0.7
Specific Heat	0.18 Btu/lb., F
Specific Heat	1.08 Btu/sq. ft., F
Emittance	0.82
Diffusivity	0.00128 in²/sec.
Thermal Conductivity	9.5 Btu/hr., ft², in., F
Thermal Expansion	3.4×10^{-6} in/in, F

AO Quarry Naturals® Tile

	Absorptance
N07 Timber Brown	0.8
N02 Fire Flash	0.8
N22 Burnt Sequoia	0.8
N01 Lava Red	0.7
N16 Stone Flash	0.7
N06 Stone Gray	0.7
N04 Prairie Flash	0.7
N24 Burnt Adobe	0.7
Specific Heat	0.18 Btu/lb., F
Specific Heat	0.96 Btu/sq. ft., F
Emittance	0.82
Diffusivity	0.00128 in²/sec.
Thermal Conductivity	9.5 Btu/hr., ft², in., F
Thermal Expansion	3.2×10^{-6} in/in, F

- -

Ceramic Tile Installation Methods on Walls

Cement Mortar on 8" Hollow Concrete Block

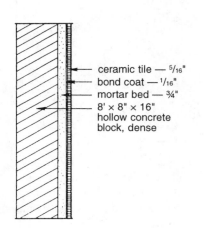

ceramic tile — ⁵/₁₆"
bond coat — ¹/₁₆"
mortar bed — ¾"
8' × 8" × 16" hollow concrete block, dense

Thermal Capacity

10.8 Btu's per sq. ft. of wall surface per degree F temperature rise when American Olean glazed wall tile are used.

Thermal diffusivity for the AO ceramic tile is 0.00102 in² per second. Average diffusivity for this wall is 0.00211.

Dry-Set Mortar on 4" Grouted Concrete Block

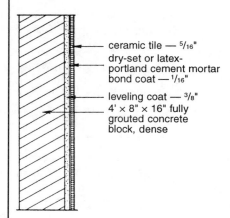

ceramic tile — ⁵/₁₆"
dry-set or latex-portland cement mortar bond coat — ¹/₁₆"
leveling coat — ³/₈"
4' × 8" × 16" fully grouted concrete block, dense

Thermal Capacity

9.4 Btu's per sq. ft. of wall surface per degree F temperature rise when American Olean glazed wall tile are used.

Thermal diffusivity for the AO ceramic tile is 0.00102 in² per second. Average diffusivity for this wall is 0.00124.

Cement Mortar on Wood Studs

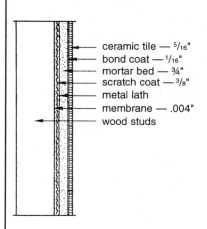

ceramic tile — ⁵/₁₆"
bond coat — ¹/₁₆"
mortar bed — ¾"
scratch coat — ³/₈"
metal lath
membrane — .004"
wood studs

Thermal Capacity

2.9 Btu's per sq. ft. of wall surface per degree F temperature rise when American Olean glazed wall tile are used.

Thermal diffusivity for the AO ceramic tile is 0.00102 in² per second. Average diffusivity for this wall is 0.00122.

Ceramic Tile Installation Methods on Floors

Epoxy Grout and Mortar on Cement Mortar, 4" Concrete Slab

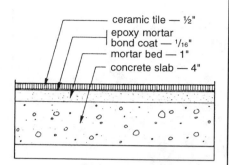

ceramic tile — ½"
epoxy mortar bond coat — ¹/₁₆"
mortar bed — 1"
concrete slab — 4"

Thermal Capacity

12.5 Btu's per sq. ft. of floor surface per degree F temperature rise when American Olean quarry tile, Quarry Naturals tile or Primitive tile are used.

Thermal diffusivity for the AO ceramic tile is 0.00128 in² per second. Average diffusivity for this floor is 0.00110.

Cement Mortar on Wood Sub Floor

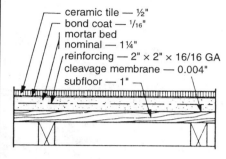

ceramic tile — ½"
bond coat — ¹/₁₆"
mortar bed nominal — 1¼"
reinforcing — 2" × 2" × 16/16 GA
cleavage membrane — 0.004"
subfloor — 1"

Thermal Capacity

4.2 Btu's per sq. ft. of floor surface per degree F temperature rise when American Olean quarry tile, Quarry Naturals tile or Primitive tile are used.

Thermal diffusivity for the AO ceramic tile is 0.00128 in² per second. Average diffusivity for this floor is 0.00128.

Dry-Set Mortar on Cement Board and Wood Floor

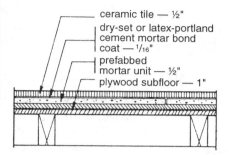

ceramic tile — ½"
dry-set or latex-portland cement mortar bond coat — ¹/₁₆"
prefabbed mortar unit — ½"
plywood subfloor — 1"

Thermal Capacity

2.4 Btu's per sq. ft. of floor surface per degree F temperature rise when American Olean quarry tile, Quarry Naturals tile or Primitive tile are used.

Thermal diffusivity for the AO ceramic tile is 0.00128 in² per second. Average diffusivity for this floor is 0.00117.

- -

Cement Mortar Bonded

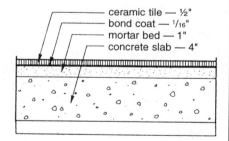

ceramic tile — ½"
bond coat — ¹/₁₆"
mortar bed — 1"
concrete slab — 4"

Thermal Capacity

12.5 Btu's per sq. ft. of floor surface per degree F temperature rise when American Olean quarry tile, Quarry Naturals tile or Primitive tile are used.

Thermal diffusivity for the AO ceramic tile is 0.00128 in² per second. Average diffusivity for this floor is 0.00110.

Dry-Set Mortar Bonded

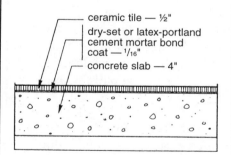

ceramic tile — ½"
dry-set or latex-portland cement mortar bond coat — ¹/₁₆"
concrete slab — 4"

Thermal Capacity

10.5 Btu's per sq. ft. of floor surface per degree F temperature rise when American Olean quarry tile, Quarry Naturals tile or Primitive tile are used.

Thermal diffusivity for the AO ceramic tile is 0.00128 in² per second. Average diffusivity for this floor is 0.00109.

Epoxy Grout and Mortar Bonded

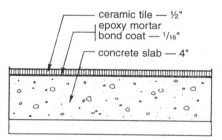

ceramic tile — ½"
epoxy mortar bond coat — ¹/₁₆"
concrete slab — 4"

Thermal Capacity

10.5 Btu's per sq. ft. of floor surface per degree F temperature rise when American Olean quarry tile, Quarry Naturals tile or Primitive tile are used.

Thermal diffusivity for the AO ceramic tile is 0.00128 in² per second. Average diffusivity for this floor is 0.00108.

Adding attic foil and vents keeps house cool

Q: From afternoon well into the evening, I can feel heat blasting down from the ceiling into the house. Our air-conditioning bills are becoming very outrageous. On a limited budget, do you have any suggestions of what I can do to stop the heat?

A: A hot roof literally becomes a blast furnace, making you uncomfortable, pushing up your electric bills and wearing out your air conditioner. A typical dark roof can reach 150 degrees in the afternoon and it holds this heat well into the evening.

Adding more attic insulation will not help. It may actually make the problem worse by absorbing and holding the heat longer.

Installing do-it-yourself radiant barrier attic foil or special new water-based reflective paint on the underside of the roof is effective. Foil blocks 95 percent of the radiant heat from the hot roof. I installed radiant foil in my attic and it dropped my bedroom temperature by as much as 10 degrees.

Attic radiant barrier foil is basically the same type of aluminum foil that you use in your kitchen. For durability and easy installation, attic foil is thicker and reinforced with nylon mesh or kraft paper.

Attic foil is very easy to install. Simply staple it to the underside of the roof rafters. The neatness of the job is not important for it to be effective. It took me about two hours to do a 30 ft. by 50 ft. attic. You should install the foil barrier in the evening or in the early morning when it is cooler.

The lightweight aluminum foil is often available in four-foot wide rolls from 50 to 100 feet long. Start stapling at one end near the roof

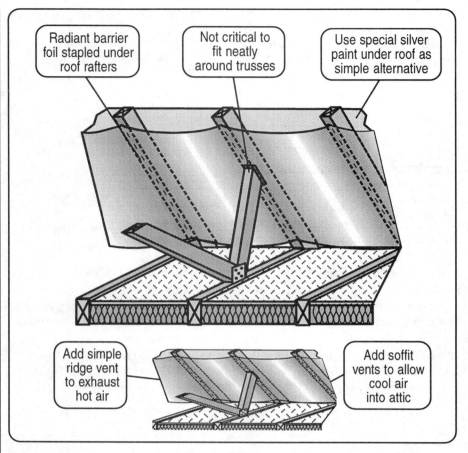

Radiant barrier foil stapled under roof rafters

Not critical to fit neatly around trusses

Use special silver paint under roof as simple alternative

Add simple ridge vent to exhaust hot air

Add soffit vents to allow cool air into attic

peak and work your way down with each successive strip.

Overlap each strip several inches. Stop several inches above the attic insulation. This gap is important to allow air in the attic to be drawn up between the underside of the roof and the top of the foil.

Heat reflective silver paint, Lomit-II, has many of the heat-rejection properties of aluminum foil. It is sprayed, brushed or rolled onto the underside of the roof sheathing. It is quick to apply since it is not important how neat the job looks.

For the foil or paint to be most effective, install vents near the peak of the roof to exhaust this hot air. Because this air is hot and less dense, it naturally flows upward and ventilates your attic.

If you do not have vents near the roof peak, install do-it-yourself

ridge vents. Many ridge vent kits are available in rolls or strips and are only several inches high, barely noticeable from the ground.

Q: Even though it wastes water, I rinse my dishes first because my dishwasher does not clean as well as it used to. What are the possible causes of this problem and how can I fix it?

A: Two likely causes of poor cleaning are clogged spray holes or a cracked spray arm. Over time, small particles can build up and totally clog some of the holes. Inspect the spray holes and clean them out with a safety pin.

A cracked spray arm lets water leak out the side of the arm instead of spraying on the dishes. First, try repairing it with high temperature epoxy glue. If it leaks again, the arm will have to be replaced.

Using attic radiant barrier foil and increasing attic ventilation will help to block the summer sun's heat. These summer improvements will not have a negative impact in the winter. With adequate attic insulation, increased attic ventilation in the winter will not increase heat loss. Since there is very little heat gain from a hot room in the winter, the foil is not a problem either.

There are many types of radiant barrier foils available and all are about equally effective. Base your buying decision on the price and a size that will fit your roof best without excessive waste. The chart below shows how much foil is needed for various size attics at various slopes. If you use lower cost single sided foil, staple it to the rafters with the shiny side down.

To be most effective, you should in-crease the attic ventilation if you install radiant barrier foil or paint. The increased ventilation will help remove the hot air and also keep the roof cooler for longer shingle life. The most effective combination is a continuous ridge vent, see page 18, along with many soffit vents. This produces an excellent air flow pattern inside the attic. It will also carry away excess moisture in the winter.

Safety Tips for Installing an Attic Radiant Barrier System

• If you use a ladder for access to the attic, make sure it is stable and tall enough for easy entry and exit.
• Work in the attic only when temperatures are reasonable. Attic daytime temperatures can rise far above 100° during much of the year in many areas. Install your radiant barrier system early in the morning, or wait until cool weather sets in. • Work with a partner. Not only does it make the job go faster, it also means that you will have help should a problem occur. • Watch where you walk and use a movable support surface. Step only on the attic trusses or rafters and your working surface. Never step on the attic insulation or the ceiling drywall below it. • Step and stand only on the center of your movable working surface. Don't step on the edge; it can cause the surface to tip. • Watch your head. In most attics, roofing nails penetrate through the underside of the roof. If you bump your head, it can cause a serious cut or puncture. If your skin is punctured by a nail, an up-to-date tetanus vaccination is a must. Avoid potential problems by wearing a hard hat. • Be especially careful around electrical wiring, particularly around junction boxes and older wiring. Never staple through or over electrical wiring. • Make sure that the attic space is well ventilated and well lighted. Bring in fans and extra work lights if necessary. • If your attic has blown-in insulation, direct fans upward, away from the insulation. • Avoid exposure to mineral fiber insulation. Wear goggles, long pants, a long-sleeved shirt, and a particle mask or kerchief over your nose and mouth. Wear gloves if you are particularly sensitive to fiberglass. • Wear a tool belt/utility apron to carry staples, staple gun, scissors, measuring tape, etc. • Take frequent breaks • Pace yourself. It's better to get the job done over a longer period than to risk an accident due to fatigue or to end up with a poor-quality installation.

See table below

Area of Foil Needed for Various Size Houses

House Size in ft	Slope of Roof — Rise Over Run of 12						
a, b	2	3	4	5	6	7	8
20, 30	609	619	633	650	672	695	722
20, 40	811	824	843	866	894	926	961
20, 50	1014	1031	1054	1083	1118	1157	1202
30, 30	913	928	949	975	1007	1042	1082
30, 40	1217	1237	1265	1300	1342	1389	1442
30, 50	1521	1546	1581	1625	1677	1736	1803
30, 60	1826	1856	1898	1950	2013	2084	2164
40, 30	1217	1237	1265	1300	1342	1389	1442
40, 40	1623	1650	1687	1734	1790	1852	1924
40, 50	2028	2061	2108	2166	2236	2316	2404
40, 60	2434	2474	2530	2600	2684	2778	2885

Typical Valeron Radiant Barrier Applications by Van Leer

roof decking
ventilation space
radiant barrier (alum-side down)
rafter
joist
insulation

radiant barrier (aluminum side up)
plywood
roof tiles
radiant barrier (alum-side facing siding)
interior wall framing
battens
siding
roof felt

Recommended Net-Free Vent Area for Attic — sq. in.

		Attic Width in Feet										
		20	22	24	26	28	30	32	34	36	38	40
Attic Length in Feet	20	192	211	230	269	288	307	326	348	365	384	403
	24	230	253	276	300	323	346	369	392	415	438	481
	28	269	296	323	349	376	403	430	484	511	538	564
	32	307	338	369	399	430	461	492	522	553	584	614
	36	346	380	415	449	484	518	553	588	622	657	691
	40	384	422	461	499	538	576	614	653	691	730	768
	44	422	465	507	549	591	634	676	718	760	803	845
	48	461	507	553	599	645	691	737	783	829	876	922
	52	499	549	599	649	699	749	799	848	898	948	998
	56	538	591	645	699	753	807	860	914	967	1021	1075
	60	576	634	691	749	807	864	922	979	1037	1094	1152

Manufacturers of Do-it-Yourself Attic Foil, Roof Decking and Paint

AMOCO FOAM PRODUCTS, 2907-T Log Cabin Dr., Smyrna, GA 30080 - (800) 241-4402
 <u>type</u> - Amocor® — FP14/FP38 is a residing underlayment made from extruded polystyrene foam with one aluminized reflective surface. The sheets are installed over old siding and attached with standard roofing nails or staples. A utility knife can be used to trim around window and door openings. It is available in 1/4" and 3/8" board thicknesses. It is lightweight and comes in 4 foot high by 50 foot long fanfold sheets.

FI-FOIL CO., INC., 612 Bridgers Ave., W., Auburndale, FL 33823 - (800) 448-3401 (941) 965-1846
 <u>type</u> - single-sided foil bonded to kraft paper with a fire retardant adhesive and reinforced with scrim • double-layer of aluminum foil laminated to natural kraft, fire retardant paper with scrim reinforcement • two layers of aluminum bonded to 26 lb. medium paper with a polypropylene reinforcement and a flame retardant adhesive

HORIZON ENERGY SYSTEMS INC., 1233 E. Bell Rd., Phoenix, AZ 85022 - (602) 867-3176
 <u>type</u> - "EcoGuard Radiant Barrier Chip" is made from metalized film which reflects 95% of infrared heat. The chips are blown in over existing attic insulation.

INNOVATIVE ENERGY, INC., 10653 W. 181st Ave., Lowell, IN 46356 - (800) 776-3645 (219) 696-3639
 <u>type</u> - reinforced polymer film sandwiched between two layers of aluminum foil

INNOVATIVE INSULATION INC., 6200 W. Pioneer Pkwy., Arlington, TX 76013 - (800) 825-0123 (817) 446-6200
 <u>type</u> - two-sided aluminum foil with reinforced scrim • two-sided aluminum foil with poly fabric • two-sided aluminum foil with woven polyolefin • two-sided metalized film • two-sided aluminum foil with nylon single or double air bubble insert

KOOL PLY, 9905 Woodlake Cove, Austin, TX 78733 - (512) 443-4747
 <u>type</u> - This is roof decking for remodeling or new construction. It is a laminated radiant barrier applied to 1/2" CDX plywood, 7/16" OSB or 5/8" CDX plywood — special orders are available.

PLYCO CORP., PO Box Q, Elkhart Lake, WI 53020 - (800) 558-5895
 <u>type</u> - two-sided foil, fiberglass scrim with flame retardant poly insert • bubble laminate between two sheets of aluminum foil

POLYAIR INSULATION, 195 Rexdale Blvd., Toronto, Ontario M9W 1P7 - (416) 740-2687
 <u>type</u> - two layers of bubble laminate sandwiched together, heat-sealed and encased by an aluminum outer surface
RABAR PRODUCTS, INC., 11 Hurwood Ave., Merritt Island, FL 32953 - (407) 453-8562
 <u>type</u> - layer of foil laminated with fire resistant adhesives to white polypropylene, reinforced by bi-directional fiberglass webbing

REFLECTIX, INC., PO Box 108, Markleville, IN 46056 - (800) 879-3645 (765) 533-4332
 <u>type</u> - two outer layers of foil bonded to a layer of polyethylene, two inner layers of bubblepack, center layer of polyethylene

SEALED AIR CORP., Park 80 East, Saddle Brook, NJ 07663 - (201) 791-7600
 <u>type</u> - one layer specially formulated bubble material or bubble film laminated between two layers of foil • two layers of specially formulated bubble material or bubble film laminated between two layers of foil

SIMPLEX PRODUCTS, PO Box 10, Adrian, MI 49221 - (800) 545-6555 (517) 263-8881
 <u>type</u> - double-faced with poly mesh backing

SOLAR SHIELD INC., 1264 Old Alpharetta Rd., Alpharetta, GA 30005 - (800) 654-3645 (770) 343-8091
 <u>type</u> - foil with polyethylene sheet in center and flame retardant — reinforced with mylar scrim and backed with kraft paper

SOLEC, 129 South Walter Avenue, Trenton, NJ 08609 - (609) 883-7700
 <u>type</u> - Lomit-I and Lomit-II are silver colored, low-emissivity coatings that can be sprayed, brushed or rolled onto the underside of the roof sheathing as a radiant barrier. Lomit-II is a water-based radiant barrier.

VAN LEER, 9505 Bamboo Rd., Houston, TX 77041 - (800) 825-3766 (713) 690-2746
 <u>type</u> - single or double-sided multi-layered cross-laminated high density polyethylene and aluminized film

Installation Methods of Radiant Barrier Foil

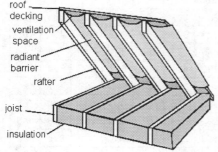

The radiant barrier may be draped over top chord of the rafters before the upper deck is installed.

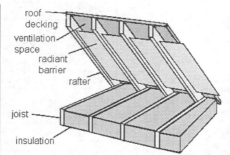

The radiant barrier may span between the top chords of the rafters and be stapled to each side.

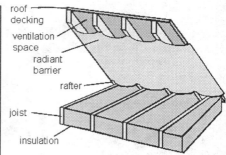

The radiant barrier may be stapled to the bottom surface of the top chord of the rafter.

Installation Instructions for a Radiant Barrier

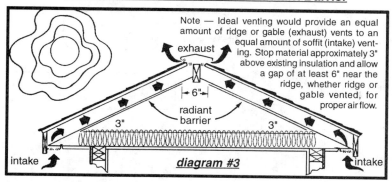

Note — Ideal venting would provide an equal amount of ridge or gable (exhaust) vents to an equal amount of soffit (intake) venting. Stop material approximately 3" above existing insulation and allow a gap of at least 6" near the ridge, whether ridge or gable vented, for proper air flow.

exhaust

6"

radiant barrier

3"   3"

intake   *diagram #3*   intake

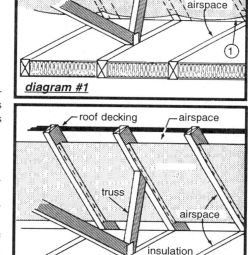

roof decking   airspace   ①

③   ②

truss

airspace

①

diagram #1

roof decking   airspace

truss

airspace

insulation

diagram #2   1A
                        end view

Tools and materials needed to install a radiant barrier include — Enough radiant barrier material to cover the underside of the roof • Measuring tape and flashlight • Heavy-duty scissors or utility knife • Staple guns and heavy-duty staples • Two movable support surfaces such as 3×2-foot sheets of one-inch plywood or three-foot lengths of 1×12 board

Bottom of Truss Application — diagram #1

Measure, roll out and cut material in lengths best handled by two people.

1) Whether you start at the bottom (nearest soffit vent) or at peak (nearest ridge), leave spacing as shown in diagram #3.

2) Slit or trim the radiant barrier at uprights or obstructions as necessary. It is not necessary to have a tight fit.

3) Staple the radiant barrier to truss face approximately 6" on center the entire width of the product. Suggested staple size is a corrosive resistant type with a $^9/_{16}$" crown and a $^5/_{16}$" leg.

Between Truss Alternate — diagram #2

Lay pre-scored piece of the radiant barrier flat and bend each edge as shown in diagram #2 — 1A and place between trusses. Position material and space as shown in diagram #3. Flush left side bottom edge of the radiant barrier with bottom edge of truss and staple entire length. Repeat stapling on right side bottom edge.

Ventilation — diagram #3

Because ventilation can greatly enhance the radiant barrier performance, it is important to consider the following:

1) Where no existing ridge or gable vents exist, you should install one system or the other. Consult manufacturers for instructions and proper location and installation.

2) Where no soffit vents exist, be sure ridge, pan or gable end vents are of adequate size to properly ventilate area.

LOMIT-II — Radiant Barrier Coating

LOMIT-II is a silver colored, non-thickness dependent, low emissivity water borne emulsion coating. Its superb ability to reflect both heat (infrared radiation) and light make it an excellent substitute for metallic foils or metallized plastic films. Absence of combustible solvents eliminates flammability hazards and allows application in enclosed areas.

Optical Characteristics — Laboratory application of LOMIT-II on glass substrates has produced emissivities of .22-.25 and a diffuse reflectivity of 81%-85%

Viscosity — 29 seconds #1 Zahn's cup

Hardness — Extremely durable 3H hardness when heat cured 20 minutes at 450°F. Ambient cure hardness increases with time. Extremely flexible, cured.

Degradation — Unaffected by UV or elevated temperatures. Thermally tolerant to 1000°F.

Coverage — 250-800 square feet/gallon, depending on surface and application method.

ASTM Standard — LOMIT-II conforms to a standard presently being promulgated for Interior Radiation Control Coating (IRCC),

ASTM Subcommittee C16.21

Mixing — Coating is supplied ready for use. No thinning is required or suggested. Mix well for at least two minutes before use. Do not allow the pigments to settle and mix often during use.

Surface Preparation — Normally, adhesion is the only factor affected by surfaces preparation. Optical properties will remain constant except on very porous surfaces. Appropriate primers may be used on porous surfaces to increase smoothness and coverage, such as cold rolled or galvanized steel may require primers to prevent future corrosion. Rusted surfaces should be wire brushed and primed before applying LOMIT-II. Plastic surfaces may require surface treatment to increase adhesion. Most building materials require no surface preparation except that they be grease and dust free. Masonry surfaces should be allowed to cure to a minimum of one month.

Application — LOMIT-II may be applied using: air atomization (gun pressure of 25-35 PSI), remote paint supply pots (should be equipped with an air drive agitator — pot pres-

sure of 4-7 PSI), airless spray (using low pressure and a #613 self cleaning tip), low nap roller or fine bristle brush. Coverage will lessen when using brush or roller. Apply to dry surfaces at a temperature above 40°F. *Note:* Good ventilation is necessary for operator safety, drying and curing.

Clean Up — Clean spray equipment with a 50% solution of isopropyl alcohol and water. Brushes and rollers may be cleaned with soap and water.

Drying and Curing — Coating will cure slowly at temperatures of 50-100°F. Curing can be accelerated by application of heat up to 500°F for 4 to 30 minutes.

Storage — Do not store below 35°F or above 80°F. Keep out of direct sunlight to avoid pressure increase in container. Do not freeze.

First Aid — EYE CONTACT: Flush eyes with plenty of water. • SKIN CONTACT: Launder contaminated clothing before reuse. Clean exposed area with isopropyl alcohol, soap and water • INHALATION: Remove victim to fresh air. • INGESTION: Get medical attention. **DO NOT** induce vomiting.

New wood furnaces are efficient and convenient to use

Q: I have thought about using a central wood furnace to heat my home. I know that wood is a cheap, renewable fuel. How is the comfort from these furnaces and are they convenient to use?

A: Using a new wood, corn or pellet central furnace is about as convenient as any gas or oil furnace. They look similar to a regular furnace, have a wall thermostat and heat your house through a duct system.

The most convenient-to-use wood furnaces have built-in backup gas or oil burners or electric resistance heat. When the wood burns down, the backup units come on automatically. There is no more getting up at night to add more wood. If your existing furnace works, use it as the backup heat.

Heating your home with firewood is generally the least expensive source of heat. Unlike fossil fuels (oil and gas), burning wood produces no "net" additional carbon dioxide (global warming gas). It just gives off the same amount of carbon dioxide that was consumed as the tree grew.

Most wood furnaces have large fireboxes that accept logs up to 24" long. On some models, you just switch on the gas or oil backup burner for 15 minutes first to get the logs started. A wood furnace can produce just a little heat for mild climates or up to 150,000 Btu for frigid areas.

There are many designs of wood furnaces available. Some have the backup gas or oil burner attached directly to the wood furnace. Other designs include a conventional super condensing gas furnace attached to it. Many models include coils to also heat your domestic water.

One unique design doubles as a fireplace. One side of the furnace, with folding glass doors, is built into a living room wall and looks like a typical

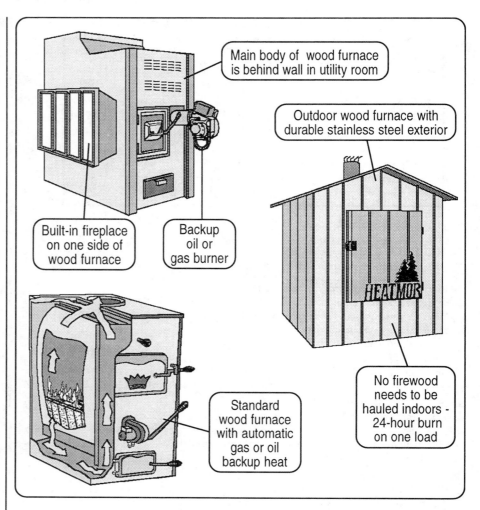

Main body of wood furnace is behind wall in utility room

Outdoor wood furnace with durable stainless steel exterior

Built-in fireplace on one side of wood furnace

Backup oil or gas burner

HEATMOR

Standard wood furnace with automatic gas or oil backup heat

No firewood needs to be hauled indoors - 24-hour burn on one load

fireplace. The furnace body with the door for adding wood is in an adjacent room. When not viewing the fire, you close safe metal covers.

Another convenient system is an outdoor wood furnace. The entire furnace is located in an outdoor unit that resembles a small storage shed. It can be located from 20 to 150 feet from your house. This eliminates fire hazards and you never have to haul messy wood indoors.

Most outdoor wood furnaces heat water to about 180 degrees. It flows through small insulated pipes to a heat exchanger in your existing furnace blower unit or to a "warm feet" floor radiant system.

There are special furnaces to burn corn. Corn, available in bags at feed stores, is inexpensive, clean to handle and is a renewable fuel. It burns hotter than wood and produces very little pollution.

Q: I found some one-year-old latex caulk in my garage and my windows need to be caulked. I am hesitant to use it because I do not want to do the job over if it is too old. Will it still work?

A: One year should not be too long to store a sealed tube of latex caulk. Your main concern should be whether your garage has ever gotten below freezing. Latex caulk will be ruined if it freezes solid.

Most water-based products, like latex paint, spackling compound, carpenter's glue, etc., are ruined by freezing. Since these products are so thick, the temperature must stay well below 32 degrees to freeze them solid.

Manufacturers of Wood, Coal or Multi-Fuel Boilers/Furnaces

CENTRAL BOILER, Route 1, Box 220, Greenbush, MN 56726 - (800) 248-4681 (218) 782-2575
model - 2 Classic models - outdoor   fuel - wood   Btuh output - 250,000 • 500,000
firebox capacity - 26.25 cu. ft. • 54 cu. ft.   log length - 72"   water capacity - 170 gal. • 400 gal.
features - The boiler is available in a variety of colors and it is designed to look like a storage building. There is urethane foam surrounding the water jacket. The cast iron door has a lifetime warranty that it won't warp. There is a night light on the unit. A domestic water-to-water heat exchanger can be added to heat all your hot water. There are larger models available.

HARDY MFG. CO., Rt. 4, Box 156, Philadelphia, MS 39350 - (800) 542-7395 (601) 656-6948
model - The Hardy - outdoor   fuel - wood   Btuh output - 180,000
firebox capacity - 15 cu. ft.   log length - 30"   water capacity - 100 gal.
features - The unit is stainless steel construction inside and out. There are several heating coils available to heat hot water for household use or to heat your swimming pool. There is a 10 year warranty on the unit.

HEATMOR, INC., Hwy. 11 E., Box 787, Warroad, MN 56763 - (800) 834-7552 (218) 386-2769
model - 3 models - outdoor   fuel - wood   Btuh output - 175,000 • 200,000 • 400,000
firebox capacity - n/a   log length - 36" • 54"   water capacity - 129 gal. • 150 gal. • 169 gal.
features - The units have 10" fiberglass insulation. The firebox is lined with fire brick. There is a water temperature gauge and the water temperature is adjustable. There is an outside door lock and an inner door safety latch. Accessories available — water to water or water to air heat exchangers, and circulation pumps. These are stainless steel units with a 10-year warranty.

HORTSMAN IND., INC., 301 2nd St., Elroy, WI 53929 - (608) 462-8431
model - 3 Royall models - indoor   fuel - wood or coal   Btuh output - 130,000 • 150,000 • 250,000
firebox capacity - 6.25 cu. ft. to 17.7 cu. ft.   log length - 25" • 43"   water capacity - 23 gal. • 35 gal. • 84 gal.
model - 3 Royall models - outdoor   fuel - wood or coal   Btuh output - 200,000 • 300,000 • 490,000
firebox capacity - 13.0 cu. ft. to 50.0 cu. ft.   log length - 32" • 40" • 56"   water capacity - 60 gal. • 84 gal. • 135 gal.
features - The boilers have a cast iron rocker grate system. The firebox is lined with fire brick. The ash door and ash pan allows for easy ash removal. Accessories available — water to air heat exchanger, domestic water coils and circulation pumps. The outdoor boiler has an automatic air float on the top to release air. The exterior door is insulated and has a lockable door handle for safety. They have 6" insulation on top and 4" surrounding the boiler. There is a 5 year limited warranty on the boiler.

HS TARM, PO Box 285, Lyme, NH 03768 - (800) 782-9927
model - 2 Excel 2000 models - indoor   fuel - wood / gas or oil   Btuh output - 140,000 • 180,000
firebox capacity - 4.0 cu. ft. • 6.6 cu. ft.   log length - 20"   water capacity - 64 gal. • 72 gal.
model - 2 Tarm 2000 models - indoor   fuel - wood / electric   Btuh output - 112,000 • 140,000
firebox capacity - 4.0 cu. ft. • 5.3 cu. ft.   log length - 20"   water capacity - 48 gal. • 62 gal.
features - The boilers are constructed of ¼ inch thick steel plate. The doors are cast iron. There are fully automatic controls that automatically switch from wood to gas/oil whenever the wood fire burns out. A domestic hot water coil for household water can be used year round. There are ceramic bricks in the combustion chamber that have air injection slots built into them to provide the oxygen needed for complete combustion. There is a 20-year limited warranty. There are add-on models available.

TAYLOR MFG., PO Box 518, Elizabethtown, NC 28337 - (800) 545-2293 (919) 862-2576
model - 5 Streamheat models - outdoor   fuel - wood or coal   Btuh output - 115,000 • 165,000
firebox capacity - n/a   log length - 36"   water capacity - 360 gal. • 600 gal.
features - There are two different designs available — the original "workhorse" design and the storage shelter look. The carbon steel door is heavily insulated. Options and accessories available include — heat exchange cabinet, hydronic baseboard heater, heat exchanger coil, circulator pump and additional coils are available for swimming pools, hot tubs or other applications. The units are covered by a 6-year warranty.

— —

Manufacturers of Wood, Coal or Multi-Fuel Furnaces (not boilers)

ALPHA AMERICAN CO., PO Box 20, Palisade, MN 56469 - (800) 358-0060 (218) 845-2224
model - Eagle I • Eagle II   fuel - wood or coal / gas or oil   Btuh output - 112,000 • 151,000
blower cfm - 800 to 1400 • 1200 to 1800   firebox capacity - 4.0 & 4.5 cu. ft.   log length - 24"
model - Eagle III   fuel - wood or coal / electric   Btuh output - 68,000
blower cfm - 800 to 1400   firebox capacity - 4.0 cu. ft.   log length - 24"
features - There is a 2-stage thermostat which shows which fuel is being used. It controls both combustion chambers at separate temperature settings. The oil/gas fire comes on automatically if the wood fire dies down or does not maintain the temperature you set. (Electric model not self-igniting.) You can also ignite the fire with kindling. The furnaces are lined with two inch thick fire brick, 18" high. There are optional cast iron shaker grates for coal usage. The handle design keeps the door lock always in the closed position. The heat exchanger is made of stainless steel. The furnaces have a 20-year limited warranty. There is a wood only unit available.

AMERICAN ENERGY SYSTEMS, 50 Academy Lane, Hutchinson, MN 55350 - (800) 495-3196 (320) 587-6565

model - Magnum 400   fuel - wood or coal / oil   Btuh output - 135,000

blower cfm - 1780   firebox capacity - 6.0 cu. ft.   log length - 16"

features - The cabinet is fully insulated so it is cool to the touch. The firebox is lined with firebrick. There are cast iron grates and a scoop type ash drawer. There are wood only units available.

CHARMASTER, 2307 Highway No. 2 West, Grand Rapids, MN 55744 - (218) 326-6786

model - 3 Chalet oil or gas models   fuel - wood / gas or oil   Btuh output - 105,000 • 125,000

blower cfm - 1780 or 2500   firebox capacity - n/a   log length - 24"

model - 4 Charmaster models   fuel - wood / gas or oil   Btuh output - 125,000 • 170,000

blower cfm - 1780 or 2500   firebox capacity - n/a   log length - 30"

model - 3 Charmaster II oil or gas models   fuel - wood / gas or oil   Btuh output - 125,000 • 170,000

blower cfm - 1780 or 2500   firebox capacity - n/a   log length - 30"

features - The "Charmaster II" is a wood/oil or gas combination furnace/fireplace. It has full brass-bound bi-fold doors with heat resistant glass. There is a steel door that contains the logs and fire when the fireplace is not used. The fireplace extension bolts on. You have your own choice of fireplace materials — brick, stone, etc. to blend into your home's decor.

DAKA CORP., Route 3, Box 65F, Pine City, MN 55063 - (800) 884-3252 (320) 629-6737

model - 6 Deluxe models   fuel - wood or coal   Btuh output - 25,000 to 105,000

blower cfm - 500 or 1580   firebox capacity - 80 to 110 pounds   log length - 20" • 22" • 24" • 25"

model - 2 Super Line models   fuel - wood   Btuh output - 50,000 to 140,000

blower cfm - 1200   firebox capacity - 100 • 140 pounds   log length - 24" • 33"

features - Several of the "Deluxe" models have a built-in washable air filter. A shaker grate kit is available to allow burning of coal. A "Hot-Tube" domestic hot water preheater kit that connects to the hot water tank is available. The firebox in the "Super Line" models has an angled fire brick lining. There are external heat fins and a double-back design for greater heat transfer. There is a 5 year warranty for the combustion chamber, all other components are covered by a period of 1 year.

DECTON IRON WORKS, INC., 5200 N. 124th St., Milwaukee, WI 53225 - (414) 462-5200

model - 2 Russell models   fuel - wood or coal   Btuh output - 100,000 to 150,000

blower cfm - 1000 to 1300   firebox capacity - 4.5 & 7.0 cu. ft.   log length - 18" • 27"

features - The firebox is completely lined with fire brick. Standard features include — automatic safety shutdown, cast iron grate system with external access to the grate shaker, cast iron doors and door frames, ash scoop, door interlock system and an interior view window to check on the operation. A remote wall-mounted thermostat for heat regulation is provided with the units. It automatically reduces the burn rate to prevent overheating. There is an optional water loop to heat all household hot water needs. There is a 5 year limited warranty.

DORNBACK, 9545 Granger Rd., Garfield Heights, OH 44125 - (216) 662-1600

model - 6 CWOG models   fuel - wood or coal / gas or oil   Btuh output - 70,000 • 120,000 • 140,000 blower cfm - 800 to 1600   firebox capacity - 2.5 cu. ft.   log length - 12"

features - The units are completely automatic — thermostat controlled. There is a cast iron feed door, ash door, ash drawer and a grate with a shaker handle. The firebox is lined with fire brick. The heat exchanger for the wood/coal unit is 12 gauge steel and for the gas/oil unit it is 16 gauge steel.

HAHSA CO., R. D. #1, Box 311, Falls, PA 18615 - (717) 388-6172

features - This is a "plans only" package to build a do-it-yourself outdoor wood furnace with easy to follow step-by-step instructions. The unit can be built completely from locally-purchased materials. The unit is approximately 8'x10' and is designed to heat the average-size home (less than 2500 sq. ft.) and supply the domestic hot water.

HORTSMAN IND., INC., 301 2nd St., Elroy, WI 53929 - (608) 462-8431

model - 3 Royall models   fuel - wood or coal   Btuh output - 95,000 to 150,000

blower cfm - 1500 to 1900   firebox capacity - 5.6 & 7.4 cu ft.   log length - 25"

features - The furnaces have a prorated 5 year limited warranty. There is a cast iron rocker type shaker grate that allows complete burn. There is a removable ash pan and the ash door has a positive seal for safety. The lower part of the firebox is lined with firebrick to increase heat storage and protect the steel sides.

L. B. BRUNK & SONS, INC., 10460 State Route 45., Salem, OH 44460 - (330) 332-0359

model - 4 Brunco models   fuel - wood or coal   Btuh output - 90,000 to 190,000

blower cfm - 495 • 1300 • 1500   firebox capacity - 4.1 to 6.3 cu. ft.   log length - 22" • 25" • 30"

features - The firebox has shakable grates, a cast iron rear brick and it is lined with high temperature 1½ inch fire brick. The furnace has a wall thermostat control that maintains the heat output you desire. The baffle system is adjustable to help burn extra gasses and to reduce heat loss up the chimney.

SURE-FLAME MFG., 245 Erie St., Huntington, IN 46750 - (219) 356-1905

model - 1 model S-F 6000 - outdoor unit   fuel - wood or coal   Btuh output - 160,000 to 200,000

blower cfm - 1900   firebox capacity - 16 cu. ft.   log length - 30"

features - The firebox has a 5-year warranty. The fire is laid directly on the fire brick hearth. The ashes are removed easily through the loading doors. Depending on the type of fuel, you could get 12 hours or longer burn time. There is 5" fiberglass insulation inside the furnace. The fuel door ash has a safety shield and a 2-stage safety latch for security.

Wood Heat Evaluation Worksheet	
1. Heating fuel you now use	
2. Fuel unit (gal., cu. ft., etc.)	
3. Number of Btu's per fuel unit - see Chart A	
4. Number of fuel units you used last year	
5. Money that you spent for this fuel	
6. Potential Btu's you actually received (#3 × #4)	
7. Efficiency of your heating system - see Chart B	
8. Btu's you actually recieved (#6 × #7)	
9. Percentage of the heat load you want from wood	
10. Convert to percentage (#9 ÷ 100)	
11. Type of wood you will burn	
12. Cost of one cord of wood	
13. Potential heat content in cord of wood - see Chart A	
14. Number of cords containing enough heat to heat your home (#8 ÷ #13)	
15. Number of cords to supply the heat you need (#14 × #10)	
16. Type of wood-burning device you install	
17. Efficiency rating of device - see Chart B	
18. Number of cords you will need to buy (#15 ÷ #17)	
19. Money you will spend on wood (#18 × #12)	
20. Proportional cost of heat (#5 × #10)	
21. Annual savings from burning wood (#20 − #19)	

Heat Value Per Cord in Btu per Cord*

High	Medium	Low
24-31	20-24	16-20
Live oak	Holly	Black spruce
Shagbark	Pond pine	Blue spruce
Black locust	Nut pine	Hemlock
Dogwood	Loblolly pine	Catalpa
Slash pine	Tamarack	Red sider
Hop hornbeam	Shortleaf pine	Tulip poplar
Persimmon	Western larch	Red fir
Shadbush	Juniper	Sitka spruce
Apple	Paper birch	Black willow
White oak	Red maple	Large-tooth aspen
Black birch	Am. elm	Butternut
Yew	Black gum	Noble fir
Blue beech	Sycamore	Redwood
Red oak	Gray birch	Quaking aspen
Rock elm	Douglas-fir	Sugar pine
Sugar maple	Pitch pine	White pine
Am. beech	Sassafras	Balsam fir
Yellow birch	Magnolia	Cottonwood
Longleaf pine	Red cedar	Basswood
White ash	Norway pine	Western red cedar
Oregon ash	Bald cypress	Balsam poplar
Black walnut	Chestnut	White spruce

*Assume 80 cubic feet of solid wood per cord and 8600 Btu/lb. of oven dry wood.

Heat Content per Fuel Unit - Chart A

Fuel	Unit	Btu/Unit
Oil	gallon	138,700
Kerosene	gallon	138,500
Natural Gas	therm	100,000
	cu. ft.	1,025
Electricity	kwh	3,414
Hardwood	cord	19,000,000
Mixed Woods	cord	17,000,000
Soft Woods	cord	15,000,000
Propane	cu. ft.	2,500
	gallon	91,000
	pound	21,500
Coal	ton	27,000,000

Heating System Efficiency - Chart B

Fuel	Heating Device	Efficiency
Oil or Kerosene	New high efficiency	.85
	Recently tuned with flue damper	.70
	Without flue damper	.60
	Average untuned	.50
Electricity	Resistance type	.95
	Heat pump	1.75
Natural Gas or Propane	New high efficiency	.94
	Good condition with stack damper	.80
	Average condition	.70
	Untuned	.60
Coal	New high efficiency	.70
	Good with flue damper	.60
	Without flue damper	.55
Wood	High efficiency wood stove or furnace	.74
	Standard wood stove	.50

Royall Wood/Coal Burning Furnace by Hortsman Ind.

Parallel Backup Installation

This is the most common installation, utilizing the energy efficient blower and filter box furnished.

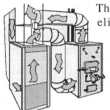

Series Backup Installation

This installation eliminates the Royall blower and utilizes the blower on the existing furnace.

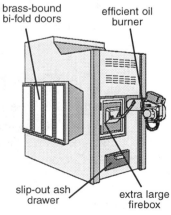

- Eight to twelve hour burn time per filling
- Wide rocker type shaker grate eliminates wood hang-up and assures complete burn with wood or coal
- Two-speed blower — 1500/1900 cfm
- Log Length — 25"
- Door Size — 10" x 14"
- Prorated 5-year limited warranty

Charmaster II Wood/ Oil Burning Furnace/Fireplace

brass-bound bi-fold doors

efficient oil burner

slip-out ash drawer

extra large firebox

Get several months more use from your deck or patio

Q: We like to use our deck on fall evenings, but it gets chilly. We tried an electric heater, but it didn't help much and used too much electricity. Are there any wood or gas deck heaters that cost less to use?

A: There are many sizes and designs of deck and patio heaters ideal for any home or climate. Often, just a slight amount of heat is needed to extend the deck usage by a month or more.

Gas (either natural gas or propane) and wood-powered deck/patio heaters cost much less to operate than an electric heater. They are also much safer to use outdoors because they are not a hazard in wet conditions.

A portable propane powered deck/patio heater is the most convenient to use. Most use standard 20-pound propane tanks (like in a barbecue grill) hidden inside the base. Just push a button and it automatically lights.

A typical propane heater, set on high, can comfortably heat a 30 ft. by 30 ft. deck and burns for 10 hours on one tank. On lower heat settings, the time can be doubled or tripled. Hooking it to a natural gas line cuts the operating cost substantially 50 percent over using propane tanks.

These heaters produce radiant heat. When turned on, it feels as if the sun came out. Radiant heat is the only effective outdoor heating method. Heated air from a regular electric convection heater would just blow away outdoors.

There are several styles available. To heat an entire deck or patio, select a tall umbrella-style heater. The radiant burner is positioned on an eight-foot high post with a three-foot diameter heat reflector umbrella.

These units are attractive and are available in white, stainless steel

Multi-level heat outputs

Reflective umbrella distributes heat evenly

Heats up to 30 ft. diameter

Tank hidden under decorative cover

Standard 20-pound propane tank

Unidirectional propane heater for smaller area

Radiant wood-burning heater made of pottery

or custom colors. The sturdy decorative base, which houses and hides the propane tank, is mounted on wheels for easy mobility. If the patio has a roof, hanging models which eliminate the post are available.

Small unidirectional propane heaters are ideal for smaller decks or to heat just a specific area where several people are sitting. Some have the radiant burner mounted directly on the tank. These are lightweight and easily moved.

Specially-designed wood radiant heaters are the least expensive to use and the scent and sound of the fire is pleasant. One model, Chimenea, is a unique small pot-bellied heater hand made of terra cotta pottery.

Another easy-to-use wood heater, Firepit, is mounted on wheels. With its circular shape, heat radiates out in all directions through screened sides. To quickly extinguish the fire when you go indoors, lift out the three screen sections and place the cover over the fire to smother it.

Q: My ten-year-old gas water heater makes a lot of noise. The noise starts soon after the hot water faucet is turned on and continues after the water is turned off. What causes this?

A: The most likely cause of the noise is scale and sediment buildup in the bottom of the water heater tank. The noise is the expansions and contractions as the burners come on.

Drain several gallons of water out of the bottom of the tank each month to remove the sediment. This is also important to keep efficiency high. The sediment acts as an energy-robbing insulator between the burner and water.

Manufacturers of Natural Gas, Propane and Wood Deck/Patio Heaters

AEI CORP., PO Box 16097, Irvine, CA 92713 - (714) 474-3070

model - "Sunglo" location - outdoor

description - These umbrella infrared heaters are available for either natural or propane gas. The heater heats a 15-foot diameter heating area. The reflector is 34½" and the height is 93". There are four different styles to choose from. The in-ground model, the freestanding and the hanging heater have a 50,000 Btuh rating. The freestanding portable model has a 40,000 Btuh rating. The units are available in either a powdercoat finish or shining stainless steel. Stainless steel models include a spark ignition system that lights the pilot by the touch of a button. They are equipped with 100% safety shutoff controls. See page 76 for illustrations.

model - "Sunpak" location - indoor or outdoor

description -The "Sunpak" is a ceiling or wall mounted infrared heater with an optional mounting kit available. It is available for either natural or propane gas. You can choose either a 25,000 Btuh model that covers a 10' × 10' area or a 34,000 Btuh model that covers 12' × 12' area. It has a direct spark ignition and 100% safety shutoff. The heaters carry a 1-year limited factory warranty.

BERKELEY PRODUCTS INC., 14680 Alondra Blvd., La Mirada, CA 90638 - (714) 228-0688

model - "Sunrise 2000" location - outdoor

description - This portable umbrella infrared heater is available for either natural or propane gas. The reflector is 35" and the height is 99". The unit has a 40,000 Btuh rating.

DECKPLACES, INC., PO Box 54179, Cincinnati, OH 45245 - (513) 474-7369

model - "The Chimenea" location - outdoor

description - The "Chimenea" is a pot-bellied portable woodburning heater. It may be used on patio surfaces as well as wooden decks. Three stout legs make it stable on any surface and act as a barrier for heat. It is made from a natural terra cotta pottery, measuring 50 inches tall and 24 inches wide with only two sections. It weighs about 60 lbs. The top cone can be personalized with a textured design, name, monogram, log or emblem. See page 76 for the care and use of the "Chimenea".

DESA INTERNATIONAL, 2701 Industrial Dr., Bowling Green, KY 42101 - (502) 781-9600

model - "Heat Demon HD24" location - outdoor

description - This is a tank top infrared heater that operates on 20 lb. or larger propane cylinders. It has two burners and they both can swivel 180° so you can direct the heat where it is desired. The heat output is 8,000 to 24,000 Btuh. There are other models available.

model - "Hot Spot" location - outdoor

description - A portable convection heater that is ideal for workshops, patios and recreational activities. It uses a 20 lb. propane cylinder with push-button matchless ignition. It weighs 4.7 lbs. A 10-foot hose allows the propane cylinder to be placed outside when the heater is inside. It has an adjustable regulator for heat output of 15,000, 20,000 or 25,000 Btuh.

DYNAMIC COOKING SYSTEMS INC., 10850 Portal Dr., Los Alamitos, CA 90720 - (714) 220-9505

model - "The Phoenix" location - indoor or outdoor

description - The "Phoenix" umbrella infrared heater is available as a portable freestanding model or a built-in model with configurations for use with natural or LP/propane gases. It has an efficient 40,000 Btuh burner system with 100% safety shutoff, piezo electric ignition and an adjustable heat control knob. The reflector is 34½" and the height is 92". It has a circle of heat up to 20 feet. The freestanding model has a weighted base that houses a 20 lb. LP/propane tank that will last for approximately 10 hours when the heater is on high. It is constructed of polished stainless steel and is covered by a 5-year limited warranty on the stainless steel components and a 1-year limited warranty on parts and labor.

INFRARED DYNAMICS, 1040 W. Seventeenth St., Costa Mesa, CA 92627 - (714) 548-2244

model - "Sunglo" location - outdoor

description - The "Sunglo" umbrella infrared heater is available for either natural or propane gas. The heater will cover a 15 foot diameter heating area. The reflector is 34½" and the height is 93". There are four different styles to choose from. The freestanding portable model has a 40,000 Btuh rating. The in-ground model, the freestanding and the hanging heater have a 50,000 Btuh rating. The units are available in a shining stainless steel or powdercoat finish. The stainless steel models include a spark ignition system. They are equipped with a safety shutoff control.

model - "Sunpak" location - indoor or outdoor

description - This is a wall or ceiling mounted infrared heater that is available for either natural or propane gas. An optional mounting kit is available. You can choose either a 25,000 Btuh model that covers a 10' × 10' area or a 34,000 Btuh model that covers 12' × 12' area. It has a direct spark ignition and 100% safety shutoff. The heaters carry a 1-year limited warranty.

MARTIN FIREPLACES, PO Box 128, Florence, AL 35631 - (205) 767-0330

model - "Martin Freedom" location - indoor

description - This is a freestanding vent-free gas fireplace heater. It is 99.9% efficient and is available in LP or natural gas. There is a piezo ignition with an on/off modulating thermostat. It has an automatic two-speed blower with the Btu's per hour — 40,000 high and 24,000 low, hidden controls and an attractive screen. There are six refractory logs including split wood twigs with realistic wood features and glowing embers. There are two colors to choose from — duotone taupe or charcoal gray. There is a 10-year limited warranty on the dual steel burners and a 2-year limited warranty on the other components. The dimensions are 27⁵/₁₆" high × 31½" wide × 19" deep and the unit weighs 135 lbs. Needs to be protected from the weather.

MINNESOTA HEARTH PRODUCTS INC., 110 S. Main, Lakefield, MN 56150 - (507) 662-5757

model - "Patio Fireplace"   location - indoor or outdoor

description - This is a portable vent-free fireplace mounted on four wheels to enjoy outdoors that can add up to 34,000 Btuh's near your hot tub or swimming pool or on your patio or deck. See specifications below.

MR. HEATER CORP., 2685 East 79th St., Cleveland, OH 44104 - (800) 321-0552 (216) 881-5500

model - "Mr. Double Heater"   location - outdoor

description - A tank top infrared heater that operates on 20 lb. cylinder. It has a variable output of 8, 12, 14, 16, 24 and 28,000 Btuh. You can run one burner or two. It will heat for approximately 15 hours using both burners. It has a 1-year warranty. There are other models available.

NATIONAL-RIVERSIDE CO., PO Box 5050, Upland, CA 91785 - (909) 981-0861

model - "Model 36-AP"   location - outdoor

description - This is a three burner infrared heater that includes a stainless steel reflector, ceramic burners, breeze deflector and a piezo ignitor. It has adjustable height and a directional stand with a stability base including a 20 lb. tank mount. It operates approximately 11 hours from a 20 lb. propane tank and the output rating is 33,000 Btuh. There are other models available.

PERFECTION SCHWANK, PO Box 749, Waynesboro, GA 38030 - (800) 776-8459 (706) 554-2101

model - "Hot-Tot" or "Handi-Heater"   location - outdoor

description - These are both portable infrared heaters that are available in natural and LP gas models. They are equipped with a tip over switch that shuts the heater off if it is knocked over. The "Hot-Tot" has a Btuh input of 90,000 and weighs 28 lbs. The "Handi-Heater" has a Btuh input of 13,600 and weighs 6 lbs. It will run for approximately 31.7 hours on a 20 lb. LP cylinder. The aluminized steel reflector shade is movable so you can direct the heat where desired.

model - "Elite"   location - indoor

description - This is a vent-free infrared unit available in two models — 17,000 Btuh or 24,000 Btuh. It is equipped with an electronic ignition and thermostatic controls that constantly monitor the room conditions. The auto sensor fan adjusts its speed so that it runs faster when the heat is higher. When less heat is required the fan automatically adjusts itself to low speed saving 30% on electricity. It has an oxygen depletion sensor that automatically turns off the gas supply if the levels become inadequate. There are built-in handles and a wall mount. The heater is available as propane or natural gas. Needs to be protected from the weather on a covered or screened porch.

SEA & STREAM PRODUCTS, PO Box 8432, San Diego, CA 92138 - (360) 659-4205

model - "Warm-Glo"   location - outdoor

description - The "Warm-Glo" umbrella infrared heater warms a 12' to 20' area and can be adjusted to your own comfort level. It is available as a portable freestanding model, in-ground post model, portable patio base or a heater hanger. It is rated at 48,000 Btuh and a 5 gallon LP tank operates for 10 to 12 hours. There is a matchless ignition with no electrical connections and it has 100% safety control. The reflector is 34.8" diameter and the height is 92".

TEMCO FIREPLACE PRODUCTS, 301 S. Perimeter Park Dr., Suite 227, Nashville, TN 37211 - (615) 831-9393

model - "American Dream ADSB"   location - indoor

description - This is a freestanding vent-free gas fireplace heater. It is available in two sizes — 28¼" high × 28" wide × 16" deep and 34¼" high × 36" wide × 22" deep and you can choose either black or almond baked-enamel finish with brass trim. It needs no noncombustible stove board. It requires only 1" clearance to combustible walls from back and sides and zero floor clearance.

WHALEN MFG. CO., 1270 E. Murray St., Macomb, IL 61455 - (800) 225-1438

model - "FirePit" and "FirePit Jr."   location - outdoor

description - This is a portable outdoor fireplace for use on the patio, deck, campsite or in your own backyard. The bottom bowl, surrounding three screens and lid radiate heat in all directions, feeding the fire slowly so it lasts longer. Two wheels and a pull handle make the "FirePit" easy to transport and empty. It is made of durable heavy-gauge steel with a baked porcelain enamel finish in black, red and forest green. It is available in two sizes — 20" diameter × 40" high, 45 lbs. and 28" diameter × 45" high, 50 lbs. The "FirePit Jr." is sealed with baked black porcelain enamel finish to prevent rusting, staining and burning. It has a 20" diameter × 33" high. It weighs approximately 39 lbs.

The Patio Fireplace by Minnesota Hearth Products

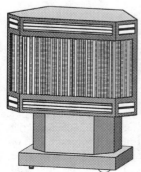

Standard Features
- 99.9% efficient
- 34,000 Btuh high setting
- 18,000 Btuh low setting
- O.D.S. System Incorporated
- Black anodized screen
- Soft golden reflective plate
- Brass grills
- Yellow dancing flames
- Four glowing light-weight fiber logs
- Bay window design

- Manual modulating valve
- Five year limited warranty
- 20 lb. cylinder bracket
- Pedestal with four wheels
- Four exterior paint colors— green, ivory, red, black

Specifications
- Height (including wheels)   38"
- Width (bay)   32¼"
- Depth (pedestal)   16¼"
- Depth (unit)   16¼"

Optional Features
- Available in natural gas or propane
- Pedestal can support a 5, 11 or 20 lb. LP tank (Portable for outdoors)
- Vinyl protective cover
- Quick connect gas outlet connection
- Automatic fan with variable speed

Safety Features
- Tested to ANSI safety requirements for indoor and outdoor applications
- Certified by Warnock Hersey
- Fireplace screen

Care & Use of the Chimenea by DeckPlaces, Inc.

1) Maintain a supply of dry seasoned firewood. Dry seasoned wood burns the cleanest. "Green" wood may produce unwanted smoke, ashes and embers.

2) Use an even layer of play sand to line the inside bottom of the "Chimenea". Small bags of play sand are available in most hardware stores. About 2" of sand will allow for an even disbursement of heat and will minimize the heat that radiates downward.

3) The first fire should be of moderate heat and flame to temper the inside pottery surfaces. Each "Chimenea" has been kiln fired to cure the clay. This final tempering (approximately 1 to 2 hours) will add strength and maximize the usefulness of the product.

4) When lighting the "Chimenea", always begin with a small fire to allow the pottery to gradually adjust to the drastic changes in temperature. This is especially important when burning during extreme cold weather. Always light and use outdoors. Never use gasoline, lighter fluid or other fuels to light or propel a fire.

5) Extra care should be given when using processed fire logs. They artificially produce and emit extreme heat. Use smaller size logs (2 to 3 lbs.) or use one section cut from a large log. A 5 lb. log may be easily cut into 3 or 4 sections.

6) The "Chimenea" is made of natural terra cotta pottery. Each unit is hand finished and unique, as with all pottery, minor "hairline" cracks may appear on the surface. A minimal amount of these lines are to be expected. A hairline crack is such that it will not effect the physical integrity of the piece or allow light, smoke or ashes to escape.

7) For thirty days after purchase, the "Chimenea" will be replaced with any damage caused by defective materials or processing.

8) Terra cotta pottery should not be exposed to moisture and extreme temperatures at the same time. Applying water to extinguish a warm fireplace will result in severe cracks. Freezing temperatures will cause any absorbed moisture in a unit to expand also causing scaling and cracking. This damage will not be covered under a limited warranty.

General Rules for Locating Heaters — It is much easier to maintain a comfort level in weather protected areas than in areas completely exposed to the elements. Weather and wind protection allows the surrounding air to be warmed and used to enhance direct-radiant warming effects. When adding heaters to existing construction, consideration should be given to locating heaters as near as possible to a gas supply line. Patio heaters warming areas subject to prevailing wind may be offset slightly to the windward side of the heated area to allow the wind to carry warmed air into the desired area. Always locate heaters so specified clearances to combustible materials are maintained.

Clearance from top of reflector — 18"
Clearance from sides of reflector — 24"

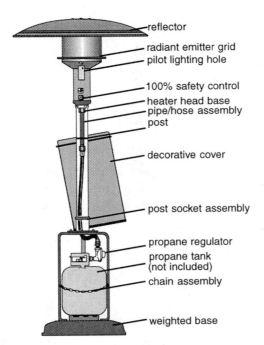

— reflector
— radiant emitter grid
— pilot lighting hole
— 100% safety control
— heater head base
— pipe/hose assembly
— post
— decorative cover
— post socket assembly
— propane regulator
— propane tank (not included)
— chain assembly
— weighted base

Sunglo by Infrared Dynamics or AEI Corp.

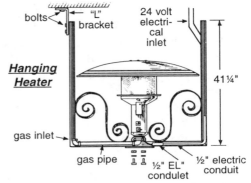

Hanging Heater

bolts — "L" bracket — 24 volt electrical inlet — 41¼" — gas inlet — gas pipe — ½" EL" condulet — ½" electric conduit

Placement and Area of Warmth

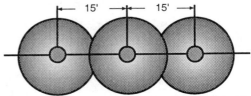

15'   15'

Spacing for — *Well Protected Areas* and mild climatic conditions.

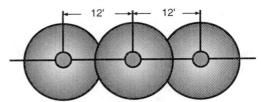

12'   12'

Spacing for — *Semi-Exposed Areas* with average weather conditions.

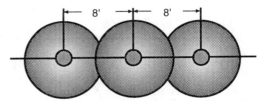

8'   8'

Spacing for — *Completely Exposed Areas* with severe weather conditions.

Pellet stoves are convenient and clean to use

Q: Our home center store sells attractive pellet stoves (some with large glass doors) and bags of pellets. Are these heaters efficient and do I need to build a chimney to use one?

A: Pellet stoves are good for your wallet and for the environment. I have tested several designs of pellet stoves in my own home for the past five years. They are efficient, quiet, clean and convenient to use. Bags of pellets are often available in hardware, feed and some discount stores.

Most pellets are made from compressed waste sawdust from lumber mills. Depending on the area of the country, waste peanut shells, cherry pits, etc. are also used. Using this homegrown fuel not only reduces landfill waste, but it keeps jobs and energy dollars in the United States.

Most pellet stoves are about the same size as a small wood-burning stove and are very decorative. The large glass door allows you to watch the flames. Being highly efficient, the exhaust gases are not very hot and can be vented outdoors horizontally with a 4-inch pipe - no chimney needed. I installed mine in about an hour. Fireplace insert models are also available.

To operate a pellet stove, dump a bag of pellets into the hopper and push a button to light it. An auger slowly feeds the pellets into the firepot. The heat output is controlled by adjusting the pellet feed rate or connecting it to a wall thermostat.

On the medium heat setting, a bag of pellets will last about one day. On the high setting, some pellet stoves can heat up to a 2,500 square foot efficient house. Variable-speed blower controls allow you to control the heated air flow. Some models also have adjustable directional louvers.

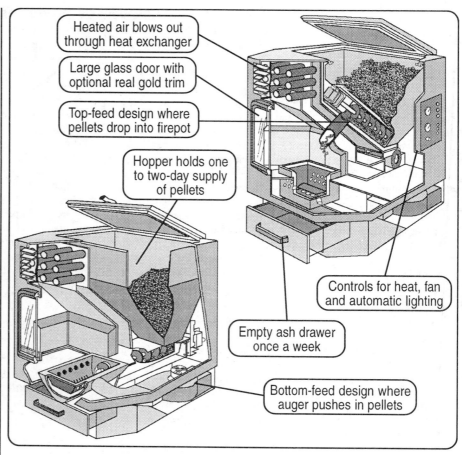

Heated air blows out through heat exchanger

Large glass door with optional real gold trim

Top-feed design where pellets drop into firepot

Hopper holds one to two-day supply of pellets

Controls for heat, fan and automatic lighting

Empty ash drawer once a week

Bottom-feed design where auger pushes in pellets

The built-in hoppers hold up to three bags. Since pellets burn completely and contain only about one percent ash, the ash drawer needs to be emptied only once a week. There is no need to put out the fire to empty the drawer.

There are two basic designs of pellet stoves - an auger feed from the top or the bottom. The top-feed system burns slightly more efficiently, but it requires premium, low ash pellets. This is the type that I use in my home.

A bottom-feed design can use regular-quality pellets with higher ash content. These can also burn hard corn. If you live in the grain belt, unusable waste feed corn can be an extremely cheap source of clean heat.

If you have frequent power outages, select a model with a battery backup. This keeps the auger and exhaust blower running. Some designs come with a solar panel for electrical power and to keep the battery charged.

Q: I am remodeling my kitchen. People have recommended using indirect lighting instead of recessed lighting. Exactly what is the difference and which type of lighting is most efficient?

A: Your advisors are comparing apples and oranges. Indirect lighting usually refers to lights directed toward the ceiling or the walls. It provides good background light, but is not always the most efficient choice.

Recessed lighting refers to a type of light fixture. It can be used as general lighting or specific task lighting. Recessed task lights, directly over a counter, for example, are a very efficient light source.

Manufacturers of Pellet Stoves and Room Heaters

ALADDIN STEEL PRODUCTS, 401 N. Wynne St., Colville, WA 99114 - (800) 234-2508 (509) 684-3745

body material - steel plate	type - freestanding and inserts	Btu output - 28,000 to 40,000
hopper capacity - 45 to 70 lbs.	heating capacity* - 2,000 to 2,500 sq. ft.	burn time** - 40 hours
vent - top or rear	auger/feed design - top	

features - The units have an automatic self-ignition system, turning itself on and off by responding to the thermostat setting. They have self-cleaning glass and "easy clean" aluminum heat exchangers. There is optional 24 karat gold-plated accents or an optional log set. Safety features include — pressure sensitive switches • electronic thermometers • high-temperature glass • heat activated shutdown switches.

AMERICAN ENERGY SYSTEMS, 50 Academy Lane, Hutchinson, MN 55350 - (800) 495-3196 (320) 587-6565

body material - steel plate	type - freestanding and inserts	Btu output - 15,000 to 45,000
hopper capacity - 75 lbs	heating capacity - 2,000 sq. ft.	burn time - 40 hours
vent - rear	auger/feed design - bottom	

features - This is a multifuel stove that can even burn corn. The fuel feed shuts off automatically if the fire goes out. It is available with 24 karat gold-plated doors and trim. There is a draft knob for fine tuning the fire efficiency and the air directional system lets you direct the heated air where you want it. An optional thermostat is available.

COUNTRY FLAME, PO Box 151, Mt. Vernon, MO 65712 - (417) 466-7161

body material - steel plate	type - freestanding and inserts	Btu output - 8,400 to 42,000
hopper capacity - 55 lbs	heating capacity - 2,000 sq. ft.	burn time - 40 hours
vent - rear	auger/feed design - bottom	

features - There is a variable speed auger to regulate the fire. A solid brass door or decorative brass trim is available.

EARTH STOVE, INC., 10595 SW Manhasset St., Tualatin, OR 97062 - (503) 692-3991

body material - steel plate or cast iron	type - freestanding and inserts	Btu output - 8,500 to 50,000
hopper capacity - 35 to 55 lbs	heating capacity - 1,500 to 1,800 sq. ft.	burn time - 60 hours
vent - top or rear	auger/feed design - bottom	

features - The "RP45" can be ordered with a built-in battery backup system to keep things warm in the event of a power failure. The stoves are equipped with "NaturalFire" — a burn system that has the look of a realistic fire. It includes a stainless steel, self-cleaning flame-spread firepot and a four piece split wood refractory log set. Optional no-polish gold or marble accents are available. These stoves are designed to burn a variety of fuel, including corn.

HARMAN STOVE CO., 352 Mountain House Rd., Halifax, PA 17032 - (717) 362-9080

body material - cast iron	type - freestanding and inserts	Btu output - 7,000 to 55,000
hopper capacity - 40 to 65 lbs	heating capacity - 1,700 to 1,800 sq. ft.	burn time - 50 hours
vent - rear	auger/feed design - bottom	

features - The "Exhaust Sensing Probe (ESP) Control" lets you manage the heat output two ways — room temperature mode lets you install a small sensing probe in the room to maintain a constant temperature without installing a wall thermostat • stove temperature mode gives you constant heat output. The insert has "EasyTrack" installation — place the stove on the track (after installing the shell), slide it into position and secure the latches. The "Pellet Pro II" has an optional decorative ceramic tile inset.

HI-TECK STOVES, INC. (JAMESTOWN), 560 S. Main St., Clearfield, UT 84015 - (800) 456-8606 (801) 773-8607

body material - steel plate	type - freestanding and inserts	Btu output - 6,000 to 55,000
hopper capacity - 37 to 110 lbs	heating capacity - 500 to 3,500 sq. ft.	burn time - 70 hours
vent - rear	auger/feed design - top	

features - Custom colors are available to match your decor — 2 and 3 tone paint finishes, pin stripes or you can choose brass or gold trim. Another decorative option is etched glass doors with custom etching available. There is an air wash system, a self-ignitor and thermostatic control.

NATIONAL STEELCRAFTERS OF OREGON, PO Box 24910, Eugene, OR 97402 - (541) 683-3210

body material - steel plate	type - freestanding and inserts	Btu output - 7,000 to 40,000
hopper capacity - 60 to 70 lbs	heating capacity - 2,250 sq. ft.	burn time - 70 hours
vent - top or rear	auger/feed design - top	

features - An optional ceramic log set or a remote thermostat is available. It is equipped with the "Hot Rod" push-button, automatic fire lighter. The units are available with 24 karat gold-plated doors, cowls and window frames.

NU-TEC INC., PO Box 908, E. Greenwich, RI 02818 - (800) 822-0600 (401) 738-2915

body material - cast iron	type - freestanding	Btu output - 5,000 to 30,000
hopper capacity - 75 lbs	heating capacity - 800 to 2,000 sq. ft.	burn time - 12 to 50 hours
vent - top	auger/feed design - bottom	

features - The "Upland" series has realistic ceramic logs. There are optional gold-plated doors or a thermostatic control is available. There is a large stay-clean window.

PYRO INDUSTRIES (WHITFIELD), 695 Pease Rd., Burlington, WA 98233 - (800) 610-0468 (360) 757-9728

body material - steel plate	type - freestanding and inserts	Btu output - 5,500 to 37,000
hopper capacity - 40 to 60 lbs	heating capacity - 800 to 2,000 sq. ft.	burn time - 40 to 60 hours
vent - rear	auger/feed design - top	

features - The patented "Ultra Grate" achieves almost 100% combustion efficiency. The air wash system helps prevent ash buildup on the viewing glass. There is an optional thermostat and the "Fastfire" self-igniter makes starting the fire easy with a push of a button. There are five heat output levels and a multiple speed convection blower.

RELIANT INDUSTRIES INC., 333-3 Industrial Dr., Placerville, CA 95667 - (800) 729-4769 (530) 622-5887

body material - steel plate	type - freestanding and inserts	Btu output - 5,500 to 37,000
hopper capacity - 30 to 80 lbs	heating capacity - 200 to 2,000 sq. ft.	burn time - 40 to 60 hours
vent - top or rear	auger/feed design - top	

features - The stoves can be run on a 12 volt backup battery which is kept fully charged by an automatic built-in trickle charger. As an optional feature, the stove can be powered by a solar panel during the day and by battery-stored energy at night. There is an optional 24 karat gold-plated door, gold legs or a gold grill available. The "Energy Miser" uses only 24 watts of power consumption. There are optional black and gold trivets for cooking.

SNOW-FLAME INC., 5 Piney Dr., Arden, NC 28704 - (828) 684-4444

body material - steel plate	type - freestanding and inserts	Btu output - 8,000 to 40,000
hopper capacity - 60 to 85 lbs	heating capacity - 800 to 2,000 sq. ft.	burn time - 48 hours
vent - rear	auger/feed design - bottom	

features - This stove burns shelled corn. No chimney is required, vent through an exterior wall with zero-clearance, dryer-type vent or as an insert that is vented directly into an existing chimney. It circulates room air through a 7-layer filter system.

THELIN CO., 12400 Loma Rica Dr., Grass Valley, CA 95945 - (800) 949-5048

body material - steel plate	type - freestanding and inserts	Btu output - 21,600 to 40,000
hopper capacity - 28 to 43 lbs	heating capacity - 500 to 2,500 sq. ft.	burn time - 20 hours
vent - rear	auger/feed design - top	

features - There is a 12 volt battery backup if the power fails and the stove will run for 12 to 18 hours. Safety features include — automatic shut down in case of blocked flue or high temperature condition • automatic shut down when the heater runs out of pellets or the fire goes out for any reason. It is available with a chrome or gold finish.

TRAVIS INDUSTRIES, 10850 117th Place NE, Kirkland, WA 98033 - (425) 827-9505

body material - steel plate	type - freestanding and inserts	Btu output - 8,700 to 40,000
hopper capacity - 40 to 65 lbs	heating capacity - 800 to 2,000 sq. ft.	burn time - 30 to 40 hours
vent - rear	auger/feed design - top	

features - The "Avalon 900" and the "Lopi" stoves have an automatic push-button electronic ignition. It comes with a log set and an optional pedestal of cast black or brass legs. Also available is a solid brass door or nature-inspired etched glass. There is an optional battery backup pedestal that can be added to the pellet stove for continuous operation during power outages. The firepot is manufactured from stainless steel.

UNITED STATES STOVE CO., PO Box 151, S. Pittsburgh, TN 37380 - (423) 837-2100

body material - steel plate	type - freestanding and inserts	Btu output - 6,500 to 41,300
hopper capacity - 65 to 70 lbs	heating capacity - 1,800 sq. ft.	burn time - 50 hours
vent - rear	auger/feed design - top	

features - The "Paragon" requires only 24 watts for operation. In the event of a power outage, the stove will run for 24 to 48 hours on a 12 volt DC automotive type battery that can be left permanently wired to the stove. It will remain fully charged, as the system includes a built-in trickle charger to maintain battery performance. Solar power is optional. Safety features include — low pressure switch • high-temperature shut-off sensor. An optional hopper is available with a capacity of 100 lbs. It has a cast iron firepot and a 4-position switch.

WATERFORD IRISH STOVES, 20 Airpark Rd., W. Lebanon, NH 03784 - (800) 828-5781 (603) 298-5030

body material - cast iron	type - freestanding	Btu output - 5,000 to 30,000
hopper capacity - 43 lbs	heating capacity - 1,500 sq. ft.	burn time - 50 hours
vent - top or rear	auger/feed design - top	

features - The glass air wash system gives a full view of the flame. An optional thermostat hookup is available for automatic operation. It is available in porcelain enamel colors of flat black, majolica brown, blushstone or blue.

WINRICH INTERNATIONAL, PO Box 51, Bristol, WI 53104 - (800) 755-8403 (414) 857-7800

body material - steel plate	type - freestanding and inserts	Btu output - 8,000 to 40,000
hopper capacity - 60 lbs.	heating capacity - 2,000 sq. ft.	burn time - 40 hours
vent - top or rear	auger/feed design - top	

features - There is a top and bottom air wash that eliminates the need to clean the glass daily. During a power failure an electromagnetic shut-off device prevents smoke and backdraft from entering your home. There is a choice of 8 door and louver colors or an optional 24 karat gold-plated finish.

Residential Fuel Cost Comparisons

Fuel	Price	Cost per Million Btu of Usable Heat*	Fuel	Price	Cost per Million Btu of Usable Heat*
#2 OIL	Per Gal	Per MM Btu	WOOD PELLETS**	Per Ton	Per MM Btu
	$1.10	$9.98		$130	$9.79
	$1.20	$10.88	bagged low ash 8,200	$140	$10.54
138,000 Btu/Gal	$1.30	$11.79	Btu/lb	$150	$11.30
	$1.40	$12.68		$160	$12.05
80% Eff.	$1.50	$13.59	80% Eff.	$170	$12.80
	$1.60	$14.49		$180	$13.55
PROPANE	Per Gal	Per MM Btu	AG RESIDUE PELLETS***	Per Ton	Per MM Btu
	$0.70	$9.91		$80	$6.41
	$0.80	$11.32		$90	$7.21
90,000 Btu/Gal	$0.90	$12.42	bagged 3% ash	$100	$8.01
	$1.00	$13.80	8,000 Btu/lb	$110	$8.81
80% Eff.	$1.10	$15.18	78% Eff.	$120	$9.61
ELECTRIC	Per KWH	Per MM Btu	CORN	Per Bushel	Per MM Btu
	.045	$13.87		$3.50	$9.76
	.055	$16.96	8,000 Btu/lb	$4.00	$11.16
3,415 Btu/KWH	.065	$20.05	56 lbs/bushel	$4.50	$12.55
	.075	$23.11		$5.00	$13.94
95% Eff.	.085	$26.20	80% Eff.	$5.50	$15.34
NATURAL GAS	Per MCF	Per MM Btu	WOOD BRIQUETTES	Per Ton	Per MM Btu
	$5.50	$6.88		$140	$11.38
	$6.00	$7.50		$150	$12.20
1 MM Btu/MCF	$6.50	$8.13	3" dia., bagged	$160	$13.01
	$7.00	$8.75	8,200 Btu/lb	$170	$13.82
80% Eff.	$8.00	$10.00	80% Eff.	$180	$14.63
COAL	Per Ton	Per MM Btu	FIREWOOD	Per Cord	Per MM Btu
	$150	$8.33		$90	$6.92
	$170	$9.44	air dried	$110	$8.46
12,000 Btu/lb	$190	$10.55	20MM Btu/cord	$130	$10.00
	$210	$11.66		$150	$11.53
75% Eff.	$230	$12.77	65% Eff.	$170	$13.08

* Usable heat costs are comparable. Each fuel has been adjusted for gross cost (per gal., ton, cord), Btu value, and firing efficiency.
** Includes wood, cardboard, and certain types of papers and ag residues. This premium fuel category has under 2% ash.
*** Includes peanut hulls, sunflower hulls, and oat hulls. Ash contents are greater than 3%

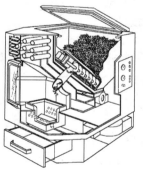

Top Feed — The auger moves pellets up an inclined tube or chute where they drop into the burn pot above the fire. These stoves may have some advantage in overall heating efficiency since pellets remain in the burn pot until they are completely burned, and exhaust gases tend to move slower, allowing improved heat transfer.

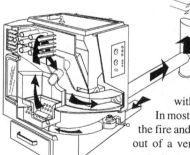

Combustion Air/Exhaust System — The amount of air needed for optimum combustion efficiency is delivered automatically or with minor manual adjustments. In most designs, a fan delivers air to the fire and blows exhaust by-products out of a vent pipe that is smaller and typically less expensive than a chimney.

Freestanding pellet stoves offer greater flexibility in installation choices. Supported by a pedestal or legs, they are designed to be installed in almost any living area of the home (restrictions may apply to sleeping areas). Freestanding stoves are placed on a non-combustible floor protector. They are installed a specified distance from combustible surfaces that is usually smaller than that required for comparable cordwood appliances.

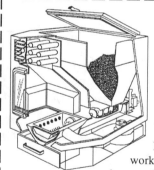

Bottom Feed — The auger pushes the pellets directly into the burn pot. These tend to perform better with the wider range of ash content in standard grade fuel because the feeding action moves ash and clinkers away from the burn area. This action helps keep air inlets open and thereby reduces the frequency of cleaning the burn pot.

Fireplace inserts are installed in existing, working fireplaces. A decorative panel covers the space between the insert and the fireplace opening. Some pellet inserts are approved only for use in masonry fireplaces, while others can also be installed in approved factory-built metal fireplaces.

EasyTrack Installation

With the EasyTrack installation system, the Invincible Insert is a snap to install. Just place the stove on the track (after installing the shell), slide it into position, secure the latches, and you're ready to go. Plus, when it comes time to clean your stove, you can just slide it out for easy access.

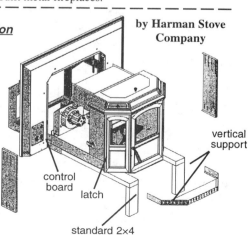

by Harman Stove Company

control board
latch
standard 2×4
vertical support

Large European fireplace can heat entire house

Q: When I visited Europe, our entire house was comfortably heated with just one decorative fireplace. We needed only one 30-minute fire each day. Can these fireplaces be used in the U.S.? Are they efficient?

A: These are true masonry fireplaces and have been used as far back as the Roman Empire and are used to a great extent in Europe today. They provide gentle radiant warmth, like sitting in the sun, for your entire house. Various designs are applicable for mild southern to frigid northern climates.

These European-design (Finnish, Swedish, Russian etc.) fireplaces are truly beautiful works of art. The exterior is hand built from decorative tiles, brick, stone or stucco. Many have built-in shelves, storage areas, even cushioned seats for relaxing.

In recent years, true masonry fireplace kits have become available. These have tongue-and-groove blocks for simple assembly. Some of the kits literally assemble like a large Lego's set. You can try to build it yourself and have almost any local mason decoratively finish it for you.

True masonry fireplaces operate on the principle of a short intense, high-temperature burn. At this high temperature, wood burns completely and efficiently with almost no pollution. The fire generally lasts no more than 30 minutes. You never need to have a fire going while you sleep.

Inside the masonry fireplace, hot flue gases are channeled through many feet of maze-like flues. By the time the flue gases leave the chimney, nearly all of the heat has been absorbed by the heavy masonry walls. Some designs have efficiencies of 90%, as high as today's hi-tech furnaces.

Shape, colors and materials are designed for your house

Stucco exterior with built-in benches and seats

Attractive tile exterior - pre-formed block/ brick interior

Flue gas paths in Finnish contraflow design

Oven for baking breads

Small firebox for quick hot fire only once or twice a day

The masonry fireplace slowly radiates this heat into your house. The outside never gets above a safe, comfortable 140 degrees. You can also order masonry fireplace kits with an optional baking oven (imagine the aroma of bread baking).

Your climate, the efficiency and size of your house determine the best design. A Russian design is massive and is good for cold climates. By the design of the gas paths inside, it is ideal for a room divider.

A Finnish fireplace typically uses a "contraflow" vertical flue gas flow design. It is tall and requires less floor space. A German design, Kachelofen, uses horizontal flow inside. It can be designed with light, medium or heavy construction depending on your climate.

A typical house can be heated with a surprisingly small amount of firewood per day. The wood is cut into small, easy-to-handle pieces so that it burns rapidly.

Q: My old electric garage door opener has a built-in light that stays on whenever the door opens. I rebuild cars so the door is open a lot. How can I get the light to stay on for only two minutes?

A: Always check your local electrical codes before attempting any wiring. One simple method is to remove the light bulb from the opener and screw in a plug adapter. Purchase a standard trouble light with a long cord.

Plug the trouble light into the plug adapter in the opener. When it is in the on position, it will operate automatically like the light does now. When you do not want it on, just switch it off at the trouble light.

Manufacturers and Builders of Masonry and Soapstone Heaters

AMERICAN ENERGY SYSTEMS INC., 50 Academy Lane, Hutchinson, MN 55350 - (612) 587-6565
    <u>description</u> - seven different models to choose from • arched series in either one-sided or see-through models • two-sided see-through model • tri-view with large glass door and 18" x 58" viewing area • damper and combustion controls on one rod • preheated air wash glass system to keep glass clean for clear fire viewing • high-temperature ceramic glass • ½" solid heavy door latches keep the doors shut under all operating conditions • gas log lighter access — optional gas log lighter or installation of a gas log set • optional 24 karat gold-trimmed doors • 25 year warranty

BIOFIRE INC., 3220 Melbourne, Salt Lake City, UT 84106 - (801) 486-0266
    <u>description</u> - masonry stove custom designed, sized and engineered • designs vary and heat 350 sq. ft. to 2,000 sq. ft. • modular bricks made of ceramic material has 25% more surface area extracting more heat from the exhaust gases • fit together with tongue and groove • components come with a three dimensional model and complete installation instructions • baking and warming ovens • stucco or tile finish — many colors, shapes, dimensions to choose from • hand-painted tiles with flowers, animals and folk designs (see page 4) • several door options — black, arch, glass, gold trim • fuel load door can be located anywhere on the four sides • custom heated benches

BOHEMIA INTN'L, 18875 S. W. 220 St., Miami, FL 33170 - (305) 246-5414
    <u>description</u> - ceramic tiled woodstoves and heated benches (Kachelofen) • hand made and decorated tiles by Czech artists • custom made • average stove has approximately 60 pieces of tile • average tile weighs 6 pounds • will give estimate to build stove to completion if you do not have an installer

BRICK STOVE WORKS, 15 Nelson Ridge South, Washington, ME 04574 - (207) 845-2440
    <u>description</u> - masonry heater, bake and cooking oven construction • custom designs

CROSS-FIRE, 12159 Brawn Rd., Wainfleet, Ontario, Canada L0S 1V0 - (905) 899-2432
    <u>description</u> - modular precast refractory blocks • may be finished in brick, stucco, stone, marble, tile or soapstone • optional bake oven • doors are available in all black, all brass or a combination of both, equipped with ceramic glass • air wash system built into the door frames for clear fire viewing

DWS, INC., — ENVIROTECH, PO Box 323, Vashon Island, WA 98070 - (800) 325-3629 (206) 463-3722
    <u>description</u> - modular heater core kits • tongue and groove firebrick pieces that are numbered for installation • precast sections and step by step instruction manual reduce construction time • may be finished in brick, stone stucco or tile • arched door is cast iron and ceramic glass • air wash to keep glass clean for viewing • bake oven option on front or rear of unit with cast iron door • see-through unit with two loading doors • standard size heats 2,000 sq. ft. to 3,500 sq. ft., compact size heats 1,000 sq. ft. to 2,000 sq. ft.

EARTHCORE IND. — ISOKERN, 8917 Western Way, # 120, Jacksonville, FL 32256 - (800) 642-2920 (904) 363-3417
    <u>description</u> - pre-engineered masonry fireplace and chimney system made of recycled volcanic stone • interlocking modular components with an R-30 insulation value • will accept facings of brick, marble, stone or tile • opening can be customized to match any interior and can be arched • in three sizes — 36", 42" and 46" width • see-through systems • unvented gas log heater for areas where a chimney is not feasible

FIRESPACES, INC., 921 S. W. Morrison St., Suite 440, Portland, OR 97205 - (503) 227-0547
    <u>description</u> - pre-engineered 9-course block core system (see page 4) • capable of heating over 1,000 sq. ft. • 42" wide firebox • rectangular or arched glass doors with concealed air wash system • accepts any style or finish material — brick, stone, tile, etc. • wood mantels and sheetrock walls can be placed 46" above the hearth • small brass knob on face controls bypass damper • manually controlled dampers with optional metal handle finishes • heavy cast iron grate • tubular gas line access built in both sides for optional gas log set or gas fire starting • other products available — soapstone heaters and ovens, tile or stucco Swedish heaters

KENT VALLEY MASONRY, PO Box 1290, Maple Valley, WA 98030 - (206) 432-0134
    <u>description</u> - masonry fireplace and bake or warming oven construction • specializes in Grundofen which is basically a custom unit • unit consists of refractory pieces and firebrick • exterior is a personal choice, usually brick, stone or tile • hot water coils are optional • work area is the Pacific Northwest • sell and install contraflow and soapstone heaters

LOPEZ QUARRIES MASONRY HEATERS, 111 Barbara Lane, Everett, WA 98203 - (425) 353-8963
    <u>description</u> - Frisch-Rosin fireplace/heater with a large double glass viewing door — 27" x 36" • longer burn time — 4 hours total every 24 hours • can use standard cord wood — 5" to 6" diameter • bake oven • based on Swedish style with a top exit • optional heated bench • can be faced with any masonry material — brick, stone, stucco, tile, marble or granite • retrofit liner is for use in an existing masonry fireplace • sell and install most heater types — Russian heater or stove, Finnish style (contraflow) masonry heater, soapstone heaters, Swedish heater, cooktops • hot water heating available with stainless steel coils

MAINE WOOD HEAT CO., INC., RFD 1, Box 640, Norridgewock, ME 04957 - (207) 696-5442
    <u>description</u> - masonry fireplace and bake oven construction • specializes in custom designs

MASONRY HEATER ASSOC., 11490 Commerce Park Dr., Reston, VA 22091 - (703) 620-3171
    <u>description</u> - association with list of masons and builders of masonry heaters and fireplaces

MASONRY STOVE BUILDERS, RR 5, Shawville, Quebec, Canada J0X 2Y0 - (613) 722-6261

    <u>description</u> - HeatKit contraflow heater core — complete system includes a foundation, heater, which consists of a core and a facing, and chimney • detailed brick-by-brick assembly instructions are available for all models • bake oven option with cast iron door with glass • cast iron and ceramic glass doors • customized cores — see-through, curved or angled side walls, extra height, etc. • heated benches • domestic hot water by using a heat exchanger of one or more loops of stainless steel boiler tubing is located against the back of the firebox, heat transfer occurs by thermosyphoning with natural convection or by means of a small circulation pump, safety devices are required

NEW ENGLAND HEARTH & SOAPSTONE LLC, 127 North St., Goshen, CT 06756 - (860) 491-3091

    <u>description</u> - custom designed masonry heater, bake oven and cooktop construction • specializes in soapstone

OVENCRAFTERS, 5600 Marshall-Petaluma Rd., Petaluma, CA 94952 - (415) 663-90140

    <u>description</u> - bread and pizza oven plans with building instructions • five different plan packages to choose from • ovens designed for wood firing but are suitable with either natural gas or propane • construction of masonry bake oven — usually the central core is constructed while local contractors build the foundation, base, housing, flue or chimney, etc.

TEMP-CAST ENVIROHEAT, PO Box 94059, Toronto, Ontario, Canada M4N 3R1 - (800) 561-8594 (416) 322-6084

    <u>description</u> - fully modular heater core kits — wood fired heater kit with corner, bake and see-through options or a direct vent gas fired heater kit • interlocking pieces that are precisely keyed to fit the next piece preventing any leakage of air through the parts • design flexibility — bricks, natural stone, fieldstone, soapstone, concrete blocks covered with tile, marble or stucco • standard fireplace is 36" wide, corner model is 46" wide" • cast iron arched door option with a viewing area of 18" wide by 16" high, optional 24 karat gold plating • stainless steel hot water coil can be installed to provide hot water for a family of four • other options — electric fresh air dampers, insulating boards, roof top dampers, soot clean-out door or an air supply door

TULIKIVI, PO Box 7825, Charlottesville, VA 22906 - (800) 843-3473 (804) 977-5500

    <u>description</u> - soapstone heaters and cooking systems — contraflow design • many basic models to choose from, when combined with extras over thirty variations can be created • standard options include mantelpieces, benches, bake ovens, and decorative serpentine veneer or roughface stone • custom models are available • interior and exterior are built of solid soapstone blocks fitted with mortar, pins and clips to allow for expansion and contraction with heating and cooling cycles • heating capacity ranges from 750 sq. ft. to 1,550 sq. ft. • temperature gauge located on the exterior to monitor bake oven temperature • air washed airtight doors • air adjustment on the ash box or the bake oven door • corner units • cast iron cooktop/bake oven combination units

VESTA MASONRY STOVE, 373 Old Seven Mile Ridge Rd., Burnsville, NC 28714 - (800) 473-5240 (704) 675-5666

    <u>description</u> - masonry fireplace and bake oven construction • custom designs • some prefabricated pieces available

WILKENING FIREPLACE CO., HCR 73 Box 625, Walker, MN 56484 - (800) 367-7976 (218) 547-3393

    <u>description</u> - Intens-A-Fyre — masonry enclosed fireplace ducted for outside air • closed door operation with self cleaning glass • dual control operation — chimney damper and air control • special refractory liner to direct radiant heat back into the fire to efficiently burn large wood • two sizes — 20" wood length, 6-8 hour burn time, 1,600 sq. ft. heating capacity, 429 sq. inches viewing area or 27" wood length, 8-10 hour burn time, 2,400 sq. ft. heating capacity, 561 sq. inches viewing area • multiple door options including — standard black rectangular, arched glass, 24 karat gold finish • optional features — polished brass finished vents, air tight ash dumps or a 220 cfm blower

---

Firewood Tips from The Chimney Safety Institute of America

Seasoned Wood — All firewood contains water. Freshly cut wood can be up to 45% water, while well seasoned firewood generally has a 20-25% moisture content. Well seasoned firewood is easier to start, produces more heat, and burns cleaner. It is important that the water is gone before the wood will burn. If your wood is cut 6 months to a year in advance and properly stored, the sun and wind will do the job for free. Splitting the wood helps too by exposing more surface area to the sun and wind, but cutting the wood to shorter lengths is of primary importance.

Well seasoned firewood generally has darkened ends with cracks or splits radiating out from the center. The bark comes off easily. It is lightweight and produces a clear ring when two pieces are hit together. Green wood will give a dull thud when struck, it is very heavy, the ends look moist and fresh. The best way to be sure you have good wood when you need it, is to buy your wood the spring before you intend to burn it and store it properly.

Storing Firewood — Wood should be stored off the ground if possible. A wood shed, where there is a roof but open or loose sides for plenty of air circulation to promote drying, is an ideal site. Next best is to keep the wood pile in a sunny location and cover it on rainy or snowy days, being sure to remove the covering during fair weather to allow air movement and to avoid trapping ground moisture under the covering.

Don't forget that your woodpile also looks like heaven to termites, so it's best to only keep a week or so worth of wood near the house. With proper storage you can turn even the greenest wood into firewood in 6 months or a year, and it can be expected to last 3 or 4 years if necessary.

Buying Firewood — Firewood is generally sold by volume, the most common measure being the cord. A standard cord of firewood is 128 cubic feet of wood, generally measured as a pile 8 feet long by 4 feet tall by 4 feet deep. A face cord of firewood is also 8 feet long by 4 feet tall, but it is only as deep as the wood is cut, so a face cord of 16" wood actually is only 1/3 of a cord, 24" wood yields 1/2 of a cord, and so on.

It is best to have your wood storage area set up in standard 4 or 8 foot increments, pay the wood seller the extra dollars often charged to stack the wood, pay only when the wood actually measures up to an agreed upon amount.

**Stucco-finish heater
by Biofire**

**Heater with bake oven
by New England Hearth**

The MRC — Masonry Refractory Core preengineered 9-course block system is the heart of the fireplace. Capable of heating over 1,000 square feet for up to 12 hours after the fire is out.

Moberg MRC by Firespaces

Hardwood Fuel Values				
Species	**Energy Content**	**Moisture Content**		**Average Density**
	(millions Btu/cord	**Heartwood**	**Sapwood**	**lb/cord @ 20% moisture**
White Oak	29.1	39	44	4400
Sugar Maple	27.0	39	42	4100
American Beech	27.4	35	42	4000
Red Oak	27.6	38	42	3900
Yellow Birch	26.6	43	42	3800
White Ash	25.7	32	31	3700
American Elm	23.8	49	48	3400
Red Maple	23.8	38	49	3400
White Birch	23.6	47	42	3400
Black Cherry	21.4	37	52	3300
Douglas Fir	20.6	27	53	2900
White Pine	15.8	35	55	2200
Eastern Hemlock	17.1	49	54	2200

A heater with a simple design that should be located in a central part of the home, often built as a room divider. It can be faced with brick, stone, stucco, soapstone, tile granite or marble.

1) Capping slab
2) Chimney
3) Clean-out
4) Combustion air
5) Downdraft channel
6) Exhaust gas
7) Exterior wall
8) Firebox
9) Firebox door
10) Heat exchange area
11) Shut-off damper
12) Updraft channel
13) Expansion joint

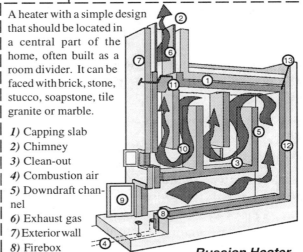

Russian Heater

Typically a Russian heater has three to five flue passages — vertical or horizontal.

**Decorative Tiles
by Biofire**

Finnish — Contraflow Heater

1) Insulating base with slab with outside air damper
2) Combustion air inlet
3) Ash drop
4) Firebox lintel with heat shield
5) Bake oven floor heat bypass
6) Exhaust gas (to chimney)
7) Chimney damper
8) Hi-temperature insulating board
9) Refractory capping slab
10) Insulating concrete

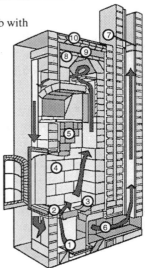

Store bought logs are great for quick fires

Q: On occasion, I use fireplace logs instead of wood for a fast-starting couple-of-hour-long fire. Do they burn as hot as real wood? How do I select the best types of real firewood to buy?

A: Fireplace logs, that you buy at your grocery store, are ideal for the quick evening fire. Depending on the brand, they produce more than twice as much heat per pound as real firewood and burn for more than three hours.

In addition to the ease of handling and lighting, fireplace logs are friendly to the environment. They burn much cleaner than real wood - 80% less carbon monoxide, 50% less smoke, 78% less creosote, 69% less particulate matter, and 50% less ash.

Fireplace logs are made of waste sawdust and a low-grade paraffin wax to bind it together. Before fireplace logs were developed, all of this sawdust ended up in landfills.

To get the maximum heat output from your fireplace, real wood is the best choice. It is important to buy the proper type of firewood for a long hot fire without building up chimney creosote or polluting the air.

When you select firewood, the most important factors to consider are its heat content and burning qualities. Also, the aroma given off as it burns, is important. Many of the fruit, nut, and cedar woods give off pleasant scents.

Heat content of wood depends primarily on the weight of the wood. Most firewoods produce about 7,000 Btu of heat per pound. Resinous woods produce a little more heat, but they produce more chimney creosote.

1. Moisture in wood boils off

2. Pyrolysis breaks wood into coals and gasses

3. Coals and gasses burn

Grate provides path for air

Seasoned wood has cracks and checks in end

The weight of woods varies from about 25 to 70 pounds per cubic foot. Figure on about 90 cubic feet of usable wood per cord (depending on how tightly it is stacked).

Firewood is generally classified as hardwood or softwood. Deciduous trees are typically denser hardwoods and conifers are less-dense softwoods.

Don't just select all dense hardwoods to get the longest burning, cleanest fire. Resinous softwood is easier to light and is excellent for starting the fire. You can then add the denser hardwood heat content logs.

To make sure the wood is well-seasoned, look for cracks and checks in the ends of the logs. Knock two logs together. Well-seasoned logs make a sharp ringing sound, not a dull thud.

Q: I plan to install ceramic tile on my foyer floor to capture solar heat. How rigid must the flooring be to keep the tiles from cracking?

A: The Tile Council of America specifies a deflection no greater than 1/360 of the span for the floors that will be covered with ceramic tile. This means a ten foot long floor should not deflect more than 1/3 of an inch. Remember, the tile and thin set are additional weight.

If your floor deflects too much, you should contact a structural engineer. The engineer will recommend the best method to support it for better rigidity.

If you are tiling over two different surfaces, wood flooring and a concrete slab, you need to lay down tar paper or plastic film. Float mortar reinforced with galvanized mesh under the tile.

Fireplace logs burn cleaner than real wood, as shown below. They are safer because less carbon monoxide and chimney creosote are produced. (See manufacturers list and specifications. "*n/a*" means specs. are not available.) Also, fireplace logs are made from low-grade wax and sawdust that would otherwise end up in a landfill.

A typical 5-lb. fireplace log burns for about 3 hours and a 3-lb. log burns for about 2 to 2-1/2 hours. It takes about 15 minutes for one to reach "full flame". These logs are ideal for a short evening fire when you plan to go to bed in several hours. Even though they burn down quickly without hot coals like real wood, follow standard safety precautions as if you are burning real wood.

Pine Mountain logs are uniquely shaped like a quarter of a log with two flat sides. This reduces the possibility of their accidentally rolling out of the fireplace. Duraflame logs are the largest, at 6 lb., so they burn longer and provide more heat per log. I sometimes use a fireplace log to start my wood fire when I run out of kindling. The 3-lb. logs or several even smaller "starter logs" work well.

Pages 86, 87 and 88 list many common types of firewood, the densities, and general burning characteristics. The heat content of wood is generally a function of the density of the wood. Hardwoods are usually the heaviest so they produce more heat. The densities are listed in lbs. per cubic foot for each type of wood. For seasoned firewood, there are approximately 7,000 Btu of heat per lb. of wood. Resinous wood has a slightly higher heat content than other wood of equivalent density. The resinous wood also lights easily, but it burns dirtier and can create more chimney creosote deposits.

Starting a fire with some soft resinous wood followed by denser hardwoods is a good fire building technique. Diagram #1 shows several methods for laying a fire. The top method is commonly used in England. The bottom method, teepee method, creates many narrow vertical paths to promote better draft between the logs. Place a layer of crumpled newspapers on top of the logs to warm the chimney and create a quick draft.

diagram #1

Manufacturers of Fireplace Logs

DURAFLAME, INC., PO Box 1230, Stockton, CA 95201 - (209) 461-6600

name - "Duraflame"	heat content - 15,000 Btu/lb.	particulate - 69% less	carbon monoxide - 880% less
ash - 90% less	creosote - 78% less	smoke - 87% less	weight - 3 lb., 5 lb., 6 lb. logs

FOREST TECH. CORP., 299 N. Arlington St., Akron, OH 44305 - (800) 833-2262

name - "HearthLogg"	heat content - 15,000 Btu/lb.	particulate - 66% less	carbon monoxide -78% less
ash - n/a	creosote - 66% less	smoke - 57% less	weight - 3.2 lb., 5 lb., 6 lb. logs

KROGER COMPANY, 1014 Vine St., Cincinnati, OH 45202 - (513) 762-4000

name - "Firelog or Northern"	heat content - 15,000 Btu/lb.	particulate - n/a	carbon monoxide - n/a
ash - 92% less	creosote - 75% less	smoke - n/a	weight - 3 lb. and 5 lb. logs

PINE MOUNTAIN, 1375 Grand Ave., Piedmont, CA 94610 - (510) 654-7880

name - "Pine Mountain"	heat content - 15,000 Btu/lb.	particulate - 66% less	carbon monoxide - 78% less
ash - 50% less	creosote - 66% less	smoke - 57% less	weight - 3 lb. and 5 lb. logs

---

Type of Tree	Density	General burning characterisitcs
Eastern Trees		
AMERICAN BEECH	52	Hard to split, slow burning
AMERICAN LINDEN	30	Very soft, poor flue
ARBORVITAE	23	Easy to split, aromatic
BIG RHODODENDRON	47	No need to split, good fuel
BLACK ASH	47	Easy to split, good fuel
BLACK CHERRY	42	Expensive, easy to split, good fuel
BLACK GUM	47	Can't split, fair fuel
BLACK HAW	62	No need to split, good fuel
BLACK LOCUST	58	Easy to split, good fuel
BLACK OAK	51	Easy to split, good fuel
BLACK WALNUT	47	Easy to split, fair fuel
BLUE ASH	54	Easy to split, good fuel
BOX ELDER	32	Easy to split, fair fuel
BROOM HICKORY	65	Hard to split, good fuel, slow burning
BUR OAK	55	Hard to split, good fuel
BUTTERNUT	30	Easy to split, fast burning
CANADA PLUM	51	Easy to split, good fuel

Type of Tree	Density	General burning characterisitcs
CHERRY BIRCH	51	Difficult to split, good fuel
CHINKAPIN OAK	64	Difficult to split, excellent fuel
COMMON JUNIPER	31	Aromatic, resinous, fast burning
COTTONWOOD	32	Easy to split, fast burning, poor fuel
EASTERN HEMLOCK	30	Easy to split, resinous, fast burning
EASTERN IRONWOOD	60	No need to split, slow burning
EASTERN RED CEDAR	36	Easy to split, resinous, fast burning
EASTERN WHITE OAK	57	Easy to split, slow burning, good fuel
FLOWERING DOGWOOD	60	No need to split, excellent fuel
FRINGE TREE	48	No need to split, good fuel
HACKBERRY	41	Easy to split, good fuel
HONEY LOCUST	52	Slow burning, excellent fuel
JACK PINE	35	Easy to split, resinous, fast burning
MAGNOLIA	40	Easy to split, fair fuel
NORTHERN BALSAM	31	Easy to split, resinous, fast burning
NORTHERN RED OAK	50	Difficult to split, good fuel
OHIO BUCKEYE	33	Easy to split, fair fuel
PAPER BIRCH	47	Easy to split, bark is good starter
PECAN	54	Aromatic, difficult to split
PERSIMMON	62	No need to split, excellent fuel
PIN OAK	51	Excellent fuel, slow burning
PIN CHERRY	37	Aromatic, fair fuel, easy to split
PITCH PINE	41	Easy to split, resinous, fast burning
RED ASH	47	Easy to split, good fuel
REDBUD	46	Easy to split, slow burning
RED HAW	60	No need to split, excellent fuel
RED MAPLE	45	Easy to split, good fuel
RED SPRUCE	32	Easy to split, resinous, fast burning
RIVER BIRCH	32	Easy to split, resinous, fast burning
SASSAFRAS	38	Easy to split, fair fuel
SCARLET OAK	50	Easy to split, excellent fuel
SHADBUSH	60	Easy to split, excellent fuel
SHAGBARK HICKORY	63	Difficult to split, slow burning
SILVER MAPLE	39	Easy to split, fair fuel
SLIPPERY ELM	52	Difficult to split, good fuel
SOURWOOD	55	Difficult to split, excellent fuel
SOUTHERN BALSAM	32	Easy to split, resinous, fast burning
SUGARBERRY	44	Easy to split, good fuel
SWAMP CEDAR	24	Easy to split, resinous, fast burning
STAGHORN SUMAC	32	Easy to split, poor fuel
SUGAR MAPLE	52	Easy to split, excellent firewood
SWAMP WHITE OAK	56	Easy to split, slow burning
SWEET BUCKEYE	30	Difficult to split, poor fuel
SWEET GUM	43	Easy to split, resinous, poor fuel
SYCAMORE	42	Slow burning, good fuel
TAMARACK	45	Easy to split, resinous, fast burning
TULIP TREE	33	Easy to split, fair fuel
WATER LOCUST	53	Slow burning, excellent fuel
WHITE ASH	48	Easy to split, good fuel
WHITE BASSWOOD	31	Poor fuel
WHITE ELM	42	Difficult to split, fast burning
WHITE PINE	30	Easy to split, resinous, fast burning
SWEET CRABAPPLE	52	Aromatic, easy to split
WITCH HAZEL	42	Aromatic, No need to split
YELLOW BIRCH	51	Difficult to split, good fuel

Western Trees

Type of Tree	Density	General burning characterisitcs
ALPINE FIR	26	Easy to split, resinous, poor fuel
ARIZONA CYPRESS	36	Aromatic, easy to split, resinous
BALSAM POPLAR	26	Easy to split, poor fuel
BIGLEAF MAPLE	36	Easy to split, fair fuel
BITTER CHERRY	33	Easy to split, fair fuel

Type of Tree	Density	General burning characterisitcs
BLACK COTTONWOOD	29	*Easy to split, fair fuel*
BLACK SPRUCE	39	*Easy to split, resinous, poor fuel*
BLUEBERRY ELDER	37	*Easy to split, fair fuel*
BUE OAK	66	*Slow burning, excellent fuel*
BLUE SPRUCE	28	*Easy to split, resinous, poor fuel*
BROWN BIRCH	45	*Easy to split, good fuel*
BUR OAK	54	*Difficult to split, excellent fuel*
CALIFORNIA BUCKEYE	37	*Easy to split, fair fuel*
CANOE CEDAR	28	*Easy to split, resinous, fair fuel*
CASCARA BUCKTHORN	44	*Easy to split, good fuel*
CHITTAWOOD	49	*Easy to split, poor fuel*
COAST REDWOOD	30	*Easy to split, poor fuel*
DESERT CATALPA	44	*Good fuel*
DESERT IRONWOOD	79	*Very hard to cut, excellent fuel*
DESERT SMOKETREE	41	*No need to split, fair fuel*
DOUGLAS FIR	38	*Easy to split, resinous, fair fuel*
DWARF MAPLE	45	*Easy to split, good fuel*
ELEPHANT TREE	46	*Aromatic, resinous*
ENGELMANN SPRUCE	26	*Easy to split, poor fuel*
FIRE CHERRY	37	*Aromatic, easy to split, fair fuel*
GAMBEL OAK	63	*Excellent fuel*
GRAND FIR	26	*Easy to split, resinous, poor fuel*
INCENSE CEDAR	30	*Aromatic, easy to split, resinous*
MACNAB CYPRESS	41	*Aromatic, easy to split, resinous*
MOUNTAIN ALDER	36	*No need to split, good fuel*
MOUNTAIN ASH	41	*Easy to split, fair fuel*
MOUNTAIN HEMLOCK	33	*Easy to split, resinous, poor fuel*
BLACK COTTONWOOD	29	*Easy to split, poor fuel*
NETLEAF HACKBERRY	27	*No need to split, good fuel*
NEW MEXICAN LOCUST	60	*No need to split, excellent fuel*
NOBLE FIR	34	*Easy to split, resinous, poor fuel*
OREGON ALDER	36	*Easy to split, good fuel*
OREGON ASH	42	*Easy to split, good fuel*
OREGON CRAB APPLE	61	*Easy to split, good fuel*
OREGON WHITE OAK	55	*Excellent fuel*
PACIFIC DOGWOOD	56	*Excellent fuel*
PACIFIC PLUM	48	*Aromatic, good fuel*
PORT OXFORD CEDAR	34	*Aromatic, easy to split, resinous*
SILVER FIR	32	*Easy to split, resinous, poor fuel*
SITKA SPRUCE	31	*Easy to split, resinous, poor fuel*
SUGAR PINE	26	*Easy to split, poor fuel*
TAN OAK	51	*Easy to split, excellent fuel*
TREMBLING ASPEN	30	*Easy to split, fair fuel*
TRUE MESQUITE	57	*Aromatic, excellent fuel*
UTAH JUNIPER	41	*Aromatic, resinous*
VALLEY OAK	55	*Easy to split, excellent fuel*
VELVET ASH	50	*Easy to split, excellent fuel*
VINE MAPLE	50	*Easy to split, excellent fuel*
WESTERN CHINQUAPIN	41	*Easy to split, good fuel*
WESTERN HEMLOCK	38	*Easy to split, resinous, fair fuel*
WESTERN LARCH	55	*Easy to split, good fuel*
WESTERN MULBERRY	57	*Difficult to split, excellent fuel*
WESTERN SOAPBERRY	64	*Easy to split, excellent fuel*
WESTERN SUGAR MAPLE	55	*Easy to split, excellent fuel*
WESTERN SYCAMORE	36	*Difficult to split, fair fuel*
WHITEBARK PINE	31	*Easy to split, resinous, poor fuel*
WHITE FIR	27	*Easy to split, resinous, poor fuel*
WHITE PINE	33	*Easy to split, resinous, poor fuel*
WILD RED PLUM	47	*Aromatic, easy to split, good fuel*
WILLOWS	40	*No need to split, fair fuel*
YELLOW OAK	64	*Easy to split, excellent fuel*
YELLOW PINE	35	*Easy to split, resinous, fair fuel*

It is easy to improve the comfort and efficiency of your fireplace

Q: We love to use our fireplace, but the room often gets smoky and the furnace seems to run nonstop. What can we do to make the fireplace heat better without smoke, yet still watch the dancing flames?

A: Unfortunately, the typical open wood-burning fireplace is one of the major energy wasters in a home. You feel toasty warm in front of it, but it literally sucks all the heated air out of the rest of your house. This is why your furnace runs so much while the fire is raging.

Fortunately, there are several simple do-it-yourself fireplace improvements to increase overall heat output and eliminate the smoke. These also improve the appearance of your fireplace and can make it a real focal point.

The four best fireplace improvements are 1) an add-on heat circulating grate, 2) special fireplace glass doors, 3) a heat radiating fireback, 4) a chimney sealing device (when the fire is out).

A heat circulating grate has a small built-in blower. The quiet blower (only 24 dB) draws in cool room air. This air is heated as it circulates through the tubular grate and then blows back out into the room.

The unit fits inside the fireplace. A shallow (less than 1.5 inches high) air inlet/outlet grille is all that is exposed under the fireplace doors. Heat output can be as high as 40,000 Btu. This can easily heat several rooms without your furnace ever coming on.

Select a grate with a built-in thermostat and variable-speed blower. This lets you control heat output and sound level. For a decorative look, select one with an add-on satin brass or antique copper grille.

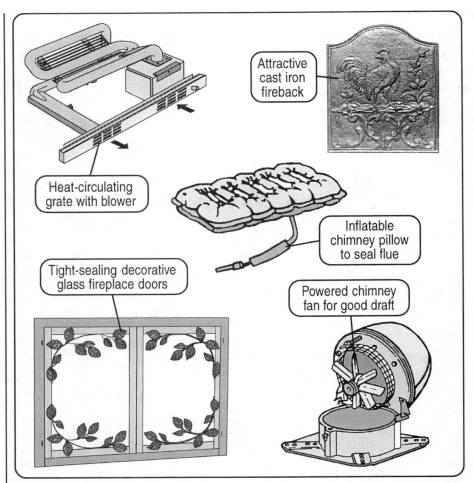

Heat-circulating grate with blower

Attractive cast iron fireback

Tight-sealing decorative glass fireplace doors

Inflatable chimney pillow to seal flue

Powered chimney fan for good draft

Tight-fitting glass fireplace doors are a must. The range of styles is nearly endless. Some have special high-temperature silicon gaskets for an excellent seal. If you are like I am and like to poke at the logs, select doors with easy-to-open graphite impregnated or teflon screen slide rods.

A fireback is an age-old technique used often in Europe. A heavy cast iron plate, often with decorative patterns, is set up in the back of the fireplace. This fireback gets very hot and radiates more warmth into the room.

Most fireplace dampers do not seal well and lose room air year-round when there is no fire. Try a low-cost inflatable chimney pillow. Push the pillow slightly up into the chimney and blow it up. It is durable and seals well.

Installing a chimney fan/screen unit on top of the chimney is the easiest method to improve the draft and eliminate smoke in the room. It takes about 15 minutes to install and has adjustable speeds to fine tune the draft.

Q: I like to restore antique cars and do woodworking. I was wondering whether electric or pneumatic (air) tools are more efficient to use? Electric tools are much less expensive.

A: If you consider the overall electricity usage, electric tools are probably more efficient. Unfortunately, electric tools cannot supply as much instantaneous power, without tripping a circuit breaker, as air tools.

A compressor stores energy in the compressed air in the tank. It may run for 60 seconds to fill the tank. Your air tool may use all that air in a 15-second burst, so the air tool's peak power is several times higher.

Manufacturers of Energy Efficient Heat-Circulating Grates

CUSTOM FIRESCREEN, 108 Jefferson, Des Moines, IA 50314 - (800) 284-1517 (515) 243-3942
> <u>type</u> - "Gas Log Hearth Heater"   <u>heat output</u> - 26,000 Btuh   <u>size</u> - 24" w x 20" d • 19½" w x 17½" d
> <u>type</u> - "Emberaire"   <u>heat output</u> - 31,000 Btuh   <u>size</u> - 24" w x 20¼" d • 20" w x 18¼" d
> <u>features</u> - The heater will handle 15" to 30" logs. The 40 watt blower provides 60 cfm of hot air to your living area. The tubular exchanger is manufactured of 12 gauge steel. A ceramic sensor will turn the blower motor on and off automatically. Equipped with a variable speed fan control. Vent bars for most every door type available in custom or stock lengths in antique brass, polished brass, satin brass, smoked chrome, polished chrome, brushed nickel, polished copper, antique copper and velvet black. Three year limited warranty. Requires only 1-3/8" clearance under the glass door. The "Emberaire" is quiet with a maximum decibel level of 24 dB. It can also be used as a gas log insert.

DIAMOND W PRODUCTS, 30 Railroad Ave., Albany, NY 12205 - (518) 459-6775
> <u>type</u> - "Gas Log Heater"   <u>heat output</u> - 25,000 Btuh   <u>size</u> - 24" w x 21" d • 21" w x 17½" d
> <u>type</u> - "Hearth Heater"   <u>heat output</u> - 40,000 Btuh   <u>size</u> - 24" w x 21" d • 21" w x 17" d
> <u>features</u> - The heater is manufactured of 1/8" welded steel pipes. The electrical components are UL approved. The variable speed motor (100 cfm) is equipped with a thermostat control that turns on automatically at 110°F and off at 90°F. The motor box can be easily removed for any maintenance of the motor or thermostat without having to remove the entire heater from the fireplace. All units come with a brass-colored grille which is 1-3/8" high and 29" to 48" wide, simply trim to fit fireplace opening. Custom-sized heater can be made to fit all shapes or sizes of fireplaces including see-through and corner models. The wood heater has 3-legged cradle design for easy cleaning and ash removal. The wood heaters are designed with a removable grate for easy replacement.

HEAT-N-GLO, 6665 W. Highway 13, Savage, MN 55378 - (612) 890-8367
> <u>type</u> - "Gas Log Heater"   <u>heat output</u> - 25,000 Btuh   <u>size</u> - 24" w x 20" d • 20" w x 17" d
> <u>type</u> - "Grate Heater"   <u>heat output</u> - 40,000 Btuh   <u>size</u> - 24" w x 22" d • 22" w x 20" d • 20" w x 17" d
> <u>features</u> - The concealed blower is 60 cfm on the gas unit and 100 cfm on the grate heater. Equipped with a thermostat control that turns on automatically at 110°F and off at 90°F. It is manufactured of heavy 12 gauge steel. All units come with a black grille which is 1-3/8" high and 29-1/4" to 48" wide, simply trim to fit fireplace opening. Custom heaters can be ordered to fit any fireplace including see-through and corner units. Special finish grilles available in antique brass, polished brass, polished chrome, satin brass and antique copper. This grille slides over the existing black front grille and can be bent around the corners to give a finished look. There is one intake and one floor level outlet to provide rapid heat circulation. All electrical components are UL approved. The gas heater holds 16" to 30" gas logs.

THERMO-RITE, P.O. Box 1108, Akron, OH 44309 - (330) 633-8680
> <u>type</u> - "Gas Log Heater"   <u>heat output</u> - 25,000 Btuh   <u>size</u> - 24" w × 20" d • 20" w × 17" d
> <u>type</u> - "Cozy Grate Heater" <u>heat output</u> - 40,000 Btuh   <u>size</u> - 24" w × 22" d • 20" w × 22" d
> <u>features</u> - The heater has a variable-speed blower of 100 cfm on the grate heater and 60 cfm for the gas log heater. Equipped with a thermostat control that turns on automatically at 110°F and off at 90°F. It is manufactured of 12-gauge steel. The heater comes with a front grille 1-3/8" high and wide enough to fit any standard or custom enclosure. Special finish trim bars are available to match your enclosure finish. The gas heater holds 16" to 30" gas logs. The electrical components are UL approved. Custom heaters can be ordered to fit any fireplace including see-through and corner units. Finishes available — antique brass, polished brass or black.

Manufacturers of Energy Efficient Fireplace Improvements

ADAMS CO., P.O. Box 268, Dubuque, IA 52004 - (800) 553-3012 (319) 583-3591
> <u>product</u> - heat radiating fireback — Antique French-design cast iron firebacks in several sizes and shapes. Other accessories available are decorative toolsets, folding screens, fire screens, very decorative and beautiful wrought iron screens and baskets, log carriers and andirons.

BENSON ENERGY, 2940 East 4430 South, Salt Lake City, UT 84124 - (801) 273-1800
> <u>product</u> - "All Season Control Cover" — A damper replacement system for woodburning masonry fireplaces. Also for new construction. It is fully assembled and comes with a complete installation kit. It installs with clamp-on mounting brackets that slip over a flue tile. It opens approximately 85° and is powered by a torsion spring.

BYERS PORTLAND WILLAMETTE, 6800 NE 59th Place, Portland, OR 97218 - (800) 288-7511 (503) 288-7511
> <u>product</u> - glass fireplace doors — Rectangle, arch, corner, multisided or unusual shapes available. Some of the glass doors have a top and bottom damper. Glass tints — clear, smoke, bronze, brass, mirror or black. All available plain or with beveled vertical edges. Door and trim finishes — satin black, antique copper, polished copper, brushed nickel, polished nickel, polished brass, satin brass or antique brass. The finishes can be mixed. Door options — cabinet doors open 180° for full access, full-fold doors open 180° for access and cleaning or bifold, in-track doors open to a 90° angle and are easily removed for cleaning. Available with a mesh curtain. The curtain rods are graphite impregnated for smooth operation of the mesh screen. There are several styles of decorative filigree patterns to choose. The "Illusions" series is available with several different marble finishes, leaf and floral designs or leaf and rope trim options. Other accessories available are decorative hand polished metal and marble panels with trim, folding screens, attached screens, standing screens, decorative toolsets, andirons, fenders, woodholders and firelighters.

COUNTRY IRON FOUNDRY, 800 Laurel Oak Dr., Suite 200, Naples, FL 34108 - (800) 233-9945

product - heat radiating fireback — Design and manufacture a line of firebacks made specifically to fit into prefabricated fireplaces. The antique replicas are primarily of American and French firebacks and stove plates. A collection of antique firebacks and stove plates are used. Each replica is hand cast in sand molds with patterns made directly from the originals. They are all authentic replicas; non is a copy of a reproduction. Over 30 different styles of firebacks and stove plates with a wide range of images and sizes.

Use with a safety support systems — supports keep the fireback from falling forward • allow a fireback to slant with the back wall if necessary • will raise the fireback 2-1/2 inches which make the fireback more visible • slots (not visible) in the supports that can be used to insert the legs of a grate or andirons.

DIAMOND W PRODUCTS, 30 Railroad Ave., Albany, NY 12205 - (518) 459-6775

product - glass fireplace doors — The custom designed door frames are welded and will not twist or bend. Complete with heat-resistant gray fiberglass insulation for a complete seal. The inner screen safety doors have 1/8" opening in the mesh to keep sparks inside. The doors swing freely on double hinges and fold back 180° and lift off for cleaning or storage. The doors can be equipped with keyed locks to provide safety and security if there are small children around. Several styles available are standard straight for rectangular fireplaces, arch top for rectangular or arch top fireplaces and a bowed unit for a bay look for rectangular fireplaces. Choose twin or bifold doors in either full view or with decorative handles. Door and frame finishes — flat black, gloss black lacquer, polished copper, polished brass, polished chrome, pewter, gun metal gray, satin brass, stucco, old English brass, satin chrome, antique copper, antique brass, darkened natural steel, hammered finishes or ancient age.

ENVIRO/ENERGY TECH., 126-16 Midlake Blvd. SE, Calgary, AB T2X 2X7 - (800) 263-3674

product - "DraftStopper" — An easy to install inflatable pillow for chimney openings to save energy and stop backdrafting. The pillow is made of polyurethane and measures 20-3/4" x 43-1/2". It comes with an optional adjustable Tee device to help fit the pillow in the firebox. The Tee has a locking positioning wedge to allow the Tee to fit your firebox. If the Tee is too long, simply cut the sliding tube with a saw for the correct height. Maximum firebox size for standard installation is 20" wide by 40" long.

EXHAUSTO, INC., P.O. Box 720651, Atlanta, GA 30358 - (800) 255-2923

product - "RS Chimney Fan" — A residential type chimney top mounted fan (cast aluminum construction) to be used in conjunction with wood, gas, oil and coal fired appliances. Can be used with fireplaces, fireplace inserts, stoves, ovens, BBQ's and more. Used for draft problems and mounts outside, atop the chimney, where it sucks the smoke from the flue. It can be installed on any type chimney system (steel, masonry or cast material — installation on prefabricated chimneys requires a special adapter). The variable speed motor assures the fan will never overdraft the appliance. The speed can be adjusted to provide a perfect draft. Top of fan is hinged and can be opened for cleaning. Designed for minimum energy consumption, using about as much energy as a regular light bulb. 2-year factory warranty, 10-year corrosion perforation warranty and 6-months performance guarantee. Standard equipment includes — fan, mounting brackets, gasket, 5 amp fan speed control and a weathertight junction box. Four models — RS9, 450 cfm • RS12, 950 cfm • RS14, 1400 cfm • RS16, 1800 cfm.

HEAT-N-GLO, 6665 W. Highway 13, Savage, MN 55378 - (612) 890-8367

product - glass fireplace doors — "Seal Tight Glass Doors" with "Aluma-Seal" technology uses a high temperature silicone gasketing that minimizes heat loss while extending the burn time. Options available — ceramic glass, full frame glass doors for an uninterrupted view of the fire, air control, grate heater or sliding mesh. The extruded aluminum frame is available in eight standard sizes with finishes of polished brass, satin brass, antique brass or black.

LYEMANCE INTN'L, P.O. Box 505, Jeffersonville, IN 47131 - (812) 288-9953

product - "Lyemance Original Damper" — Top sealing fireplace damper can be installed on chimney tops in minutes, used with new or existing fireplace. No special tools required. Available in sizes to fit most standard flue liners, including round. The lid on the damper is spring loaded in the normally open position. It is shut with a stainless-steel cable that extends through the cable guide then down the flue to firebox, where it is held to a bracket fastened into a forward part of the side fireplace wall. Dampers completely assembled with a 32' cable and a tube of silicone sealant to bond the damper to flue tile. The "OPC" includes damper, chimney cap and screens.

PENNSYLVANIA FIREBACKS, INC., 2237 Bethel Rd., Landsdale, PA 19446 - (215) 699-0805

product - heat radiating fireback — Cast iron fireback can be supported with a pair of 3" or 4" Safe-T-Boot supports. They have a step design so the fireback can be held at an angle against the back wall. They can be used with any iron grate, log dogs, andirons or gas log system. Many decorative styles and shapes to choose including reproductions from the renowned Winterthur Museum in Delaware that has a collection of American antiques and decorative objects.

VIRGINIA METALCRAFTERS, P.O. Box 1068, Waynesboro, VA 22980 - (540) 949-9403

product - heat radiating fireback — Decorative cast iron firebacks in several sizes and shapes.

WILKENING FIREPLACE CO., HCR 73, Box 625, Walker, MN 56484 - (800) 367-7976

product - glass fireplace doors — The "Ultimate Seal" door is a 1/4" constructed steel door with a dual gasket system. The cam activated latch mechanisms assure a locked fit and will keep the door closed even when a heavy log rolls against the glass. Standard features — rectangular flush mount frame, heat resistant black finish, 1/4" tempered safety glass, heat resistant gasket seals and all mounting hardware.

The DraftStopper by Enviro/Energy Technologies

The Tee device is used to provide a quick and clean installation of the DraftStopper. Because the firebox heights vary, the Tee is adjustable and has a locking positioning wedge to allow the Tee to fit your firebox. If the Tee is too long for your firebox, cut the sliding tube with a saw to desired height.

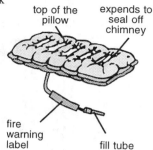

top of the pillow
expends to seal off chimney
rest
fixed tube
sliding tube to set tee height in the fireplace
fire warning label
fill tube

Firebox Preparation for First Time Installation Only

Check for anything that could puncture the DraftStopper pillow. Puncture points could be metal spurs on the damper, damper hinge, damper retaining brackets or angle iron lintel. Any rough-finished mortar should be chipped away and flattened with a hammer. If you have glass doors, bolt ends may need to be filed smooth or removed.

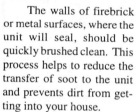

The walls of firebrick or metal surfaces, where the unit will seal, should be quickly brushed clean. This process helps to reduce the transfer of soot to the unit and prevents dirt from getting into your house.

Next, take a look at your damper handle. If the handle is on either end of the firebox, the DraftStopper will mold around it for a good seal. If the handle passes through the center of the firebox, remove the handle if you can.

If the handle cannot be removed easily, there are five places where you can cut a slit for your damper. Decide which slit you will use and with a sharp knife make an incision in the middle area slightly smaller than the handle. This is done to reduce air leakage. If the hole is too big, fill it with a piece of foam rubber insulation or paper towel.

Installation

1) Place the DraftStopper Tee onto the floor of the firebox and raise up until it reaches 1" below the damper. Lock into place. Check the walls of the firebox to be sure that there are no metal protrusions.
2) Place the DraftStopper on the Tee. Partially inflate, put into position, then complete inflation.
3) Wrap the inflation tube around the Tee and tuck into orange warning sleeve.

The All Season Contol Cover by Benson Energy

Damper replacement system for masonry fireplaces
Contents — 1 All Season Control Cover • 30 feet of stainless steel cable • 2 cable ties • 10 links of chain • 1 spring • 1 o-ring • 1 tube of silicone • 1 locking bracket • 2 anchor bolts

Flue sizes available — 9 x 9 • 9 x 13 • 9 x 17 • 13 x 13 • 13 x 17
- Functions like an insert
- Preserves chimney life
- Fully assembled, with complete installation kit
- Does not obstruct air flow
- Does not interfere with cleaning operation
- Installs simply with clamp-on mounting brackets
- Will mount to oval or round shaped flue tile
- Will not freeze when c__ed
- Will not allow any debris to enter fireplace when _____ opened
- Full year limited warranty on all parts

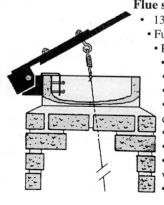

Chimney Fan by Exhausto

Installation on a Brick Chimney — If a flue tile sticks up, cut it back so it is flush with the chimney crown. Place the fiber mat on the top of the flue. Install the mounting brackets on the fan base. Mount the fan on the mat and adjust the mounting brackets, so they almost touch the flue wall.

Features
- Used with oil, gas, wood and coal.
- Energy efficient motor is standard.
- Cast aluminum construction.
- Low silhouette and low weight.
- Quiet operation.
- Variable speed.
- Fan opens for easy cleaning.
- Easy to install.
- 2-year factory warranty.
- 10-year corrosion perforation warranty.
- 6-month performance guarantee.

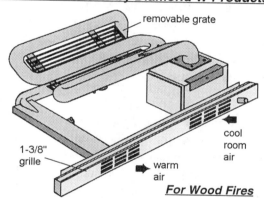

The Hearth Heater by Diamond W Products

removable grate
1-3/8" grille
cool room air
warm air

For Wood Fires

- Simple, removable motor box means easy maintenance of the motor or thermostat without having to remove the entire heater from the firechamber.
- Wood model has 3-legged wood cradle design for easy cleaning and ash removal. Designed with a removable grate for easy replacement.
- Thermostat automatically turns the heater on at 110° and off at 90°. Variable speed control for comfort.
- Curved grate design exposes more surface area of the heat exchanger to the heat of the fire for best heat absorption and transfer.
- One intake and one heater duct — all air passes through the entire length of tubing for maximum heating power.
- Custom Hearth Heaters can be made to fit all shapes and sizes of fireplaces including see-through and corner models.
- Made to fit most mfgs. models of fireplace glass doors.
- Made with heavy, 1/8" welded, steel pipe construction, has a three-year warranty.
- Electrical components including the blower are UL approved and carry a one-year warranty.

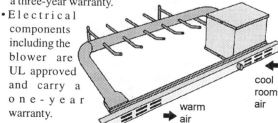

cool room air
warm air

Heat-circulating fireplace can easily heat several rooms

Q: I want to add a regular-looking fireplace to my living room. I want it to produce heat, but not look like an insert stove with tiny glass doors. What types of attractive, efficient fireplaces are available?

A: Adding a wood-burning fireplace, or replacing an old inefficient one, is one of the best home improvement investments possible. It often increases resale value of the house more than the cost of the fireplace. A new efficient fireplace helps lower utility bills.

For low-cost do-it-yourself installation, a zero-clearance heat circulating fireplace is best. A typical model with large glass doors can warm a 2,000 square foot area. Some models have extra ducts to heat adjacent rooms.

The walls of a zero-clearance fireplace can rest directly against the framing lumber for simple installation. These fireplaces are designed with either triple-wall or insulated double-wall construction.

There are many new unique styles available including, traditional flat or arched top single-opening, contemporary see-through (two glass sides), peninsula (three glass sides) and island (glass on all sides). Attractive options like solid brass or 24-karat gold-plated door trim are available.

For the convenience of a gas fireplace and the attractiveness of real wood flames, Kozy Heat makes a bi-fuel design. Simply by flipping a switch, it converts from gas to wood burning.

When comparing new efficient fireplaces, check for tight-fitting doors, a convenient damper control lever and provisions for outdoor combustion air. These features reduce the amount of heated room air lost up the chimney.

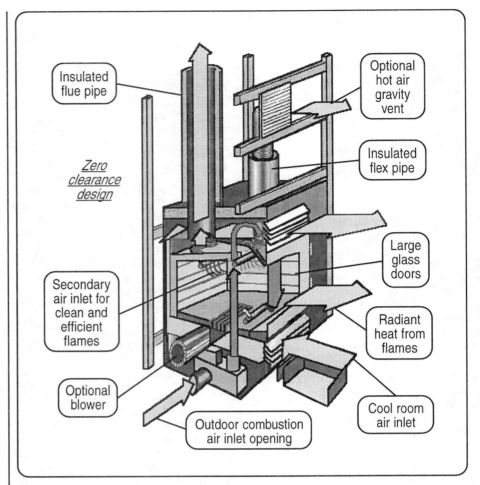

Zero clearance design

- Insulated flue pipe
- Optional hot air gravity vent
- Insulated flex pipe
- Large glass doors
- Radiant heat from flames
- Cool room air inlet
- Outdoor combustion air inlet opening
- Optional blower
- Secondary air inlet for clean and efficient flames

If you plan to use your fireplace often, select one with a thermostatically controlled blower. As the room warms up, the blower speed is automatically reduced to maintain an even temperature. One model by Heat-N-Glo even has a built-in filter to clean the air in the room.

For the best view of the flames, choose a model with an air wash door feature. This minimizes creosote and soot buildup on the glass. Preheated air is directed over the inside glass surface before it enters the fire. New fireplaces burn cleanly and meet the EPA's clean air standards. Efficiencies range from 60 to 70 percent - higher than most older furnaces.

To realize the maximum heat output and enjoyment from your fireplace, burn only well-seasoned wood. With a lower moisture content, seasoned wood starts easier and burns hotter. Harder types of wood tend to burn cleaner.

Q: I live in an older house. The water pressure has gradually decreased over the years. It is especially low in one bathroom. What is causing this and what can I do to improve it?

A: Gradually decreasing water pressure often results from mineral deposit buildup in water lines over many years. This is a particularly common problem in areas with very hard water.

Turn off water at main shutoff valve. Open a faucet that is far away from the main shutoff valve. When the valve is opened again, the water rushing through the pipes often dislodges some of the deposits.

Manufacturers of Radiant and Heat-Circulating Fireplaces

COUNTRY FLAME, PO Box 151, Mt. Vernon, MO 65712 - (417) 466-7161

sizes - 18¾" • 22" viewing area — 30½" • 33¼" • 35¾"   design - bay: Model B • Model BBF • E Series • Model O-2
features - These are fireplace inserts that are available all cast, with a brass trim option or with a brass package option. They are equipped with a door glass airwash system that reduces the accumulation of soot and creosote to give you a nice view of the fire. They have Neoceram® glass installed in the doors and they have brass cool-touch handles. The "BBF • B • E1" have a 600 cfm blower. The blower is thermostatically controlled. The are equipped with the "High Performance Package" that consists of a honeycomb catalytic combustor, cast iron holder, 8" probe thermometer and a stainless steel protective plate. For greater efficiency, the smoke and gases released during normal combustion are reburned within this package. The "BBF" will heat up to 3,000 square feet, the firebox is 3.9 cubic ft. an holds 29" logs.

FIREPLACE MFGS. INC., 2701 S. Harbor Blvd., Santa Ana, CA 92704 - (714) 549-7782

sizes - 36" • 42" • 43½"   design - corner: Enticer • Inglenook — peninsula: Monterey
— see-through: Windsor — standard: Regency • Bel Air • El Toro • La Fiama II • La Costa • Eliminator • Equalizer • Baja
features - Some of the units have an outside air kits and "Full-View™" glass door styles. There are decorator hoods, louvered facings and other trims available in polished brass, antique brass or polished chrome. The heat circulating models have the option of adding the "Deluxe 3-Fan System". The "Windsor" has a mesh screen with brass pulls with an optional feature that includes a decorative gas log set. It is available as an insulated fireplace for cold weather climates and it is recommended for mobile homes. The "Inglenook" will accommodate a 200 cfm blower to provide improved heat circulation.

FUEGO FLAME, PO Box 807, Burlington, IA 52601 - (800) 444-8759 (319) 752-2781

sizes - 40" • 48"   design - see-through: AZS Series — standard: AZ • BZ Series
features - The units are available with an optional 24 karat gold strip or decorative surrounds. The fireplaces come with 1,400°F safe ceramic glass doors • grate • temperature gauge • safety strip • fingertip damper control • a can of touch up paint and a natural convection blower. The 40" units hold 18" logs and the 48" units hold 20" logs. When the damper is at 95% closed, the fireplace can deliver up to 50,000 Btuh.

HEATILATOR, 1915 W. Saunders St., Mt. Pleasant, IA 52641 - (800) 843-2848

sizes - 36" • 40" • 42" • 48"   design - bay: SF48A — corner: CL/CR Series — island:
HA112 — peninsula: FL92 — see-through: ST36D • ST42A — standard: E/EC Series • T Series • HB Series
features - The units are available as radiant and heat-circulating fireplaces. Optional fans can be added to the heat-circulating fireplaces to provide additional air movement. Accessories include — brass trim kits • glass doors • outside combustion air kit • gas log sets for converting a woodburning fireplace into a gas appliance.

HEAT-N-GLO, 6665 W. Hwy 13, Minneapolis, MN 55378 - (888) 743-2887

sizes - 31½" • 35½" • 36" • 42"   design - arch: Royal Arch — island: Oasis — peninsula:
Bay • Pier — see-through: HST Series — standard: Energy Master Series • Clean Burn System • Royal Hearth • Grate Heater
features - These units have optional outside air combustion kits and several door finishes to choose from — polished brass • polished chrome • antique brass or black. The "Energy Master" features up to 60,000 Btuh with optional airtight ceramic doors and an optional blower. They have fully insulated fireboxes. Other options include — Aire-Supreme blower system that includes magnetic blower mount, thermal sensor switch that automatically turns blower on and off, variable speed control designed to be installed in the bottom of the unit or on a wall • Clean Air Filtering System is a cartridge that will clean room air when fireplace is operating.

KOZY HEAT (HUSSONG MFG. CO.), PO Box 577, Lakefield, MN 56150 - (800) 253-4904

sizes - 26" • 32" • 34" • 36" • 41" • 60"   design - arch: Two In One 231ZC • AuraFlame — bay:
Model 432 — standard: Model 232 • Model 234 — see-through: Model 332 • Model 336
features - The "231ZC" can be converted to a wood or gas fireplace by flicking a wall switch or a remote control. It can accommodate 22" logs and it has an air wash system that maintains clear glass in the wood burning mode. The doors are available in black cast iron or an optional gold plate. It has an insulated convection cabinet and ceramic glass doors. A remote heat outlet option allows ducting to adjacent rooms. Fan kits are available for all models and a variable speed control is included.

MAJESTIC PRODUCTS CO., 1000 E. Market St., Huntington, IN 46750 - (800) 525-1898

sizes - 30" • 36" • 42" • 48"   design - corner: Open-End Series — island: Island Series
— peninsula: Bay Series • Cove Series — see-through: See-Through Series — standard: Builder-Tech Series • MBU Series
• R/MR Series • SuperHEARTH® Series • WarmMajic® Series • PureEnergy™ Balance-Flue
features - There are several natural stone surround facings to choose from — black slate • polished limestone • white marble • gray marble • beige marble • green marble. Mantelpieces are available as full mantels, trim kits or mantel shelves in red oak, northern sugarberry and paint-grade hardwoods. Optional outside combustion air kits and glass doors are available in radiant or heat-circulating models.

MARCO FIREPLACES, 2520 Industry Way, Lynwood, CA 90262 - (800) 232-1221 (213) 564-3201

sizes - 36" • 41" • 46"   design - standard: Builder • Designer • Architect
features - The "Designer Door System" has the option of polished brass, polished chrome or a black finish. The screens retract into hidden side pockets. The refractory is available in standard or herringbone design. The grilles are hand-welded on the heat circulating models. The optional grille and edge trim on the heat circulating models are available in polished brass or chrome. The heat circulating models have an optional fan kit available. You can get an insulated firebox and a cold climate kit for draft protection.

MARTIN FIREPLACES, 301 E. Tennesse St., Florence, AL 35631 - (800) 227-5248 (205) 767-0330

sizes - 36" • 39" • 42" • 48" • 54"   design - bay: SB3D — corner: B36 Series — island: MI200 — peninsula: MPL • MB200 — see-through: SST — standard: BE42 • S Series • SB Series • SA39 • M Series • LF Series

features - The units have an optional outside air kit. An adjustable, easy-to-install "Flex-I-Mantel" is available that adjusts to fit most of the 36", 39" and 42" units. It is made of stain-grade poplar that also can be painted. The "S Series" is available with a 200 cfm blower and the "LF Series" has an optional 300 cfm fan. The "SST" has been approved for mobile homes. The "BE42" has an optional insulation blanket for cold climates.

NAPOLEON FIREPLACES (WOLF STEEL), RR 1 (Hwys. 11 & 93) Barrie, ON L4M, 4Y8, Canada - (800) 461-5581

sizes - 38¾"   design - standard : Prestige - Model NZ25

features - The "Prestige" is available with a black or gold-plated door. The grate is made of cast iron, it has a self-closing ash dump and has a 600 cu. inch capacity with convenient handles and tri-fold lid. A variable speed switch and heat sensor for the blower are factory pre-installed. It has an air wash system that maintains an extremely clean viewing glass. Additional accessories available — blower kit • electric wall thermostat to control burn rate • hot air gravity vent system • central heating system • outside combustion air kit • hot air vent louvre in polished brass or black. The burn time on a low fire is approximately 8 hours. The maximum log size is 18 inches.

SUPERIOR FIREPLACE CO., 4325 Artesia Ave., Fullerton, CA 92633 - (800) 731-8101 (714) 521-7302

sizes - 33" • 35" • 38" • 40" • 43" • 45" • 48"   design - corner: CC • CR — peninsula: CPF • PR — see through: CST — standard: EST • TMC • LBC • FP • HCE-A • HC-A

features - Some units have a brass trim option and an outside combustion air kit. Many of the units have recessed screen pockets, an integrated ash lip and either a heavy steel grate or an iron grate. The "TMC" is a heat-circulating unit with a variable speed control that provides up to 10,000 additional Btuh of output. It has clear or smoked ALL-GLASS™ bi-fold doors. The "CST" has more than 1400 square inches of viewing area, while the "CPF" has 1800 square inches. The "CC - Corneramic" features an exclusive curved class design. The viewing area 26"×57". The "HCE-A" has a choice of metallic trim kits such as jet black, polished brass, antique brass and brass filigree in multiple combinations.

TEMCO FIREPLACE PRODUCTS, 301 S. Perimeter Park Dr., Suite 227, Nashville, TN 37211 - (615) 831-9393

sizes - 36" • 39" • 41" • 42" • 44"   design - corner: TFRC — standard: TFC • TLC • TCH

features - The fireplace units are available with outside air combustion kits. They are equipped with a spring-loaded damper mechanism for tight closure and easy operation. The doors are available either full frame bi-fold in polished brass finish or clear view bi-fold doors with a polished brass finished trim. The "TLC" units are louvered heat circulating fireplaces with a blower kit option. The "TCH" fireplaces have recessed screen pockets that hide the screen for an unobstructed view.

VERMONT CASTINGS, Route 104 Box 501, Bethel, VT 05032 - (800) 227-8683

sizes - 39½" • 41" • 44"   design - standard: Wood FP • WinterWarm System • WinterWarm Insert

features - The "Wood FP" has optional trackless bi-fold glass doors, a 270 cfm plug-in fan with rheostat and an outside air kit. The "WinterWarm System" features a heat output up to 50,000 Btuh with thermostatic control. It has twin fans with a rheostat for heat circulation. It is constructed of solid cast iron with solid brass trim around the door. An optional cabinet fan will increase the heating power. It will hold logs up to 24". The "WinterWarm" units are available in two porcelain enamel color choices — sand or midnight. They are available with optional outside air kits.

WILKENING FIREPLACE CO., HCR 73, Box 625, Walker, MN 56484 - (800) 367-7976

sizes - 28" • 36" • 42"   design - arch: Magna-Fyre • Intens-A-Fyre — standard: Intens-A-Fyre

features - These units have an air wash system that provides an ample flow of incoming air to continually sweep the glass clean for viewing enjoyment. They use outside air for combustion. The doors are available with 24 karat gold finishes to complement your decor. Optional features include — designer series vents with polished brass finish • air tight ash dumps • 220 cfm blower.

— —

Options for Auraflame Fireplace Heating System from Kozy Heat

A. Ash Chute — Allows easy ash disposal.

B. Outside clean-out doors for the ash dump.

C. Outside Air Vent Closure With Choke Cable — Prevents cold air transfer in heat chamber when not using fireplace.

D. Fan Kits — Available for all models. Variable speed control is included.

• Polished brass trim kits — available for doors and face.

• Gold plated doors, Tempax™ glass.

May be easily converted to a gas burning unit with the Kozy Heat 45 KLS gas log conversion system.

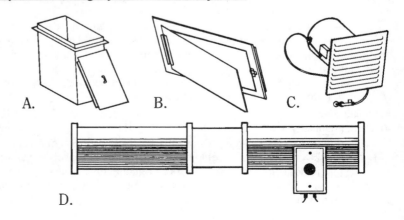

Installation Instructions for a Zero-Clearance Fireplace by Fuego Flame

WARNING: *Safety Notice* - If this fireplace is not properly installed, a house fire may result. For your safety, follow the installation instructions. Contact local building inspector about restrictions and installation inspection in your area.

IMPORTANT: These units are tested and listed for installation with any 8 inch U. L. approved factory built insulated class "A" chimney. The use of aluminum type "B" gas vent for solid fuels is unsafe and prohibited by the National Fire Protection Association Code.

Be sure to use the chimney manufacturer's recommended installation instruction for the type of pipe you select, as special methods are used in passing through the ceiling and roof.

IMPORTANT: These zero-clearance fireplaces are for use with solid fuel only, and the chimney must be vented out-of-doors.

The manufacturer is not responsible for installation, down drafting or negative pressure created by the home.

IMPORTANT: The minimum area covered by the hearth should extend 16 inches in front of the doors and 48 inches wide for A size units, and 40 inches wide for B size units. The minimum distance between the hearth pad and the mantel must be 48 inches. Refer to label on the inside of the firebox for clearance to combustibles. This fireplace has not been tested for use in mobile homes.

Step 1 — Check Contents — Remove the zero-clearance fireplace and parts from the cardboard shipping container. You should have the following items: zero-clearance fireplace • baffle plate • safety strip • grate • set of ceramic glass doors • temperature gauge • can of touch-up paint.

Step 2 — Installing the Zero-Clearance Fireplace — The fireplace can be placed with no clearance to combustible materials on the bottom, back, sides and top of stand-offs. The base must be flat, hard and have sufficient area to support the entire fireplace uniformly. NOTE: Be sure that the face of the fireplace cabinet is plumbed level. If a combustible wall facing is to be used, keep the facing flush with the face of the fireplace cabinet and use ceramic tile, brick, marble or the optional metal decorative surround to finish from the decorative screening to the wall facing. If a non-combustible wall facing is to be used, it may cover the cabinet up to the decorative screen. All combustible materials must be kept flush with fireplace cabinet. Do not put combustible material on top of heat deflector.

IMPORTANT: Under no circumstances is any of the decorative screen to be blocked on the bottom sides or top.

NOTE: Use metal safety strip under bottom front of fireplace cabi-

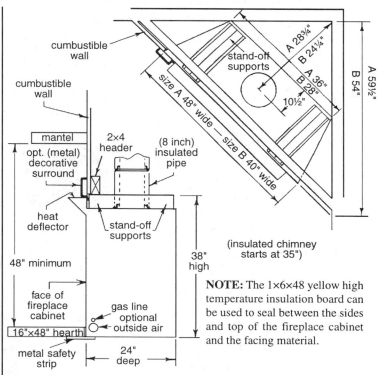

NOTE: The 1×6×48 yellow high temperature insulation board can be used to seal between the sides and top of the fireplace cabinet and the facing material.

net. See detailed diagram, and also refer to tag on inside of firebox for other minimum clearances to combustibles.

Step 3 — Installing Chimney — Refer to chimney manufacturer's installation instructions for proper clearance and termination.

Step 4 — Finishing Installation

4A. Place baffle plate on the two pins in the back of the firebox and push it all the way down behind the brackets at the bottom.

4B. Position grate on its four legs toward the back of the firebox with the higher end facing towards the front.

4C. Install doors by putting the longest pin into the upper hole of the firebox frame. This will allow the short lower pin to drop into the lower firebox hole.

NOTE: If doors need to be adjusted, the pins can be bent slightly.

4D. Install temperature gauge in center of top screening.

Step 5 — Operation of the Unit — Refer to owner's manual for instructions.

Versatile Installations for the Prestige - Model NZ25 by Napoleon Fireplaces

Install as a zero clearance fireplace with factory-built chimney or as a masonry fireplace using an existing or new masonry chimney.

Four different heating usage options:

1) Standard installation heats through natural convection.

2) Gravity, hot air vent system to heat adjoining rooms.

3) Central system with thermostatic control for multi room heating.

4) Thermostatically controlled system connects to existing duct work.

Note: Masonry remote venting options dome off the side instead of the top.

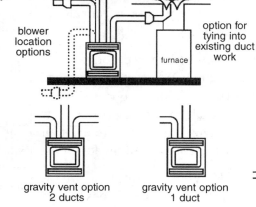

Hot Air Venting Options

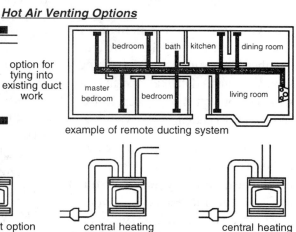

example of remote ducting system

no ducting

gravity vent option
2 ducts

gravity vent option
1 duct

central heating
& gravity vent option

central heating

Do-it-yourself solar dryer for firewood or starting plants

Q: I have a good wood-burning fireplace with tight glass doors like you recommended. I had two trees taken down recently, so the wood is green. How can I season the wood quickly so I can burn it soon?

A: The best method to season wood (reduce the moisture content) is to build a simple do-it-yourself solar wood dryer. It needn't be fancy to be effective. Once the wood is seasoned, you can use the dryer as a mini-greenhouse for starting plants in early spring.

Whatever you do, do not burn much green wood. Not only will it be hard to start, but it is inefficient and will smoke out the neighbors. Much of the heat of combustion is wasted just boiling the water out of the wood as it burns.

An even more serious problem is a possible chimney fire. The damp inefficient fire, from burning green wood, allows the unburnt gases to condense as creosote inside the chimney. Later in the winter, when you burn a good hot fire, the creosote can ignite and cause a house fire.

You can safely burn a ratio of one green log to three seasoned logs. The seasoned logs burn hot enough to dry out the green log and minimize creosote formation.

Generally, you can identify seasoned wood by knocking two logs together. They should make a ringing sound, not just a dull thud. The ends of seasoned logs often have deep checks and cracks depending on the type.

A traditional Virginian design is the easiest solar wood dryer/mini-greenhouse to make yourself. To utilize standard lumber and plywood most effectively to minimize scrap, size it in increments of four feet.

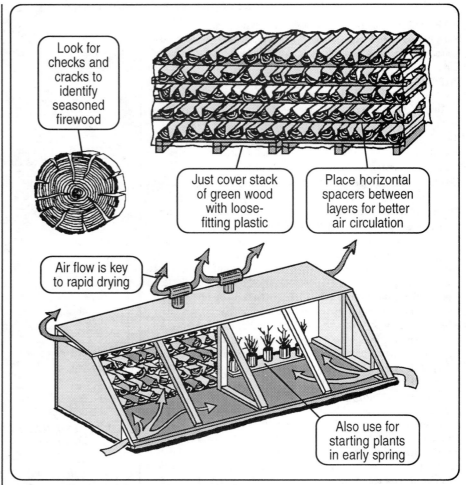

Look for checks and cracks to identify seasoned firewood

Just cover stack of green wood with loose-fitting plastic

Place horizontal spacers between layers for better air circulation

Air flow is key to rapid drying

Also use for starting plants in early spring

Make the top narrower than the bottom so that the front slopes back and cover it with a clear material. Clear plastic film, an old storm door or rigid fiber-reinforced plastic (FRP) are excellent, low-cost covers.

The key to effective drying is adequate air flow. Add several air outlet vents to the plywood top section and in the top of the sides near the back. Standard roof vents work well or make your own from aluminum flashing.

Build two large doors in the back panel. When stacking wood inside, place long wood strips between each layer of logs to separate them. This provides more even air circulation around all the logs.

If you are not a do-it-yourselfer, just stack the logs loosely with spacers between each layer. Place them with the bark side down for faster drying. Cover it with a clear plastic film to keep the rain off.

Q: Even though the thermostat is set high enough, I always feel chilly in our living room at night. I live in an older house with little, if any, wall insulation. What can I do inexpensively?

A: The basic problem is that your underinsulated walls get cold. Just like your body draws (radiant) heat from the hot sun outdoors on a cold day, a cold living room wall draws heat from your body even in a warm room.

You need to block the direct path from yourself to the cold outside wall. Hang curtains or paintings on the wall to create a buffer. If you have any high back chairs or cabinets, place them along the cold wall.

It is important to use well-seasoned (low-moisture content) firewood in your fireplace. It will not only be much easier to start and burn with less smoke, but it is much safer and produces more heat.

Burning unseasoned (green) wood can create creosote buildup in your chimney. Before any log can burn, it must reach a certain temperature to ignite. If the log is green (has a high moisture content) the heat from the rest of the burning logs, newspaper or starter logs, is used to boil off the water in the green log. It takes a long while for the green log to get to the necessary combustion temperature. This also wastes heat from the other logs in the fire.

Although the green log starts to burn, the fire is still not hot enough to burn the volatile combustible gases that are given off. These gases start up the chimney and then condense on the chimney walls as creosote. This creosote can build up and when you build a very hot fire, this layer of creosote inside the chimney can ignite. This is a common cause of house fires and fire-related deaths.

The time required to dry wood depends on the size of the logs, the air temperature and the air flow rate through them. The Virginian solar firewood dryer, that I have described below, is an excellent method to dry wood quickly. In early spring, you can also use it as a mini-greenhouse to start your flowers and vegetables.

- -

Instructions for Making a Virginian Solar Firewood Dryer/Mini-Greenhouse

1) Measure and cut 12 2×4's (see figure #2). Be sure to rip-cut pieces 7, 9 and 10 into equal halves as shown. Caution: Use the saber saw, or a table saw if available, to rip-cut the 2×4's. Make 45° cuts (see figure #3). Cut all lath strips to size for glazing battens, door stops, and latches as shown in figure #4. Make all cuts on the 4 ft. × 8 ft. plywood sheets as shown in figure #5. For the door openings, drill a hole large enough for your saber saw to fit. Insert saber saw and cut along line to next hole. For

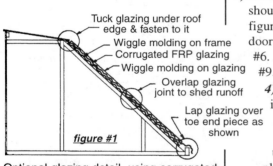

Tuck glazing under roof edge & fasten to it
Wiggle molding on frame
Corrugated FRP glazing
Wiggle molding on glazing
Overlap glazing joint to shed runoff
Lap glazing over toe end piece as shown

figure #1

Optional glazing detail, using corrugated fiber-reinforced plastic (FRP)

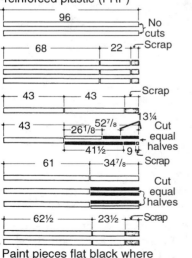

Paint pieces flat black where shown in black. *figure #2*

the vent cap openings, drill a hole large enough for the saber saw and follow line around the vent cap opening.

2) Prime all wood surfaces with a good quality primer to protect wood from the elements. Be sure to apply the primer according to the mfg's. instructions. Paint interior pieces of wood and both sides of dryer's roof black as shown in figures #2 and #5. Paint the exterior pieces of the wood the color of your personal preference.

3) Attach lath around door openings. Lath should overlap openings by ½-inch (see figures #6 and #9). Drill holes for the door latches as shown in figures #4 and #6. Attach the latches, shown in figure #9.

4) Assemble the vent caps as shown in figure #7. Spray paint the completed vents flat black.

5) Lay plywood flat, black side up, and mark and drill holes in plywood (see figure #6). Screw middle nailer to one half of back as shown in figure #10. This will be used to assemble two back halves on site. Attach other nailers as shown.

6) Fit vent camps into the openings in roof piece (see figure #9). The vent cap should face into the prevailing winds. Then fasten them to the roof. Screw nailer to one half of roof. This will be used to assemble the two roof halves on site.

7) Drill two nail holes in each 45° end of 2×4's (see figure #3). These holes will reduce the chance of splitting while nailing. Assemble the support frame pieces using 12-penny nails as shown in figure #8. It is easier to do if you work with the pieces flat on the floor or on a table.

8) Pick a shade-free, level site, and remove any rocks or debris that could puncture the black plastic bottom.

9) Use scrap 2×4's to support the plywood back or get assistance from one or two helpers to hold the plywood back flush with the support framing until you have the first end frame attached. Then screw two halves of dryer back together at the nailer. Nail all the glazing support frames to the back. Nail the two toe pieces to the front of the glazing support frames.

10) You now need to assemble the roof. Screw two roof halves together at the

Materials for Solar Firewood Dryer/Mini-Greenhouse

(3) 4 ft. × 8 ft. CDX ⅜ in. plywood
(16) 8 ft. 2×4 studs
(9) 8 ft. #3 1×4's
18 ft.- 4 ft. wide black screen
16 ft. 10 ft. wide plastic — black
16 ft. 10 ft. wide plastic — clear
100 ft. ⅜ in. × 1½ in. lath
1 box 1¼ in. #6 galvanized screws
½ lb. 1¼ in. galvanized nails
1 lb. 3½ in. galvanized nails
1 quart flat black paint
1 quart exterior paint or stain
1 gallon primer
(2) 3 lb. coffee cans
24 in. × 12 in. wide sheet metal
3½ ft. thin wire
(20) #8 ¾ in. panhead screws
1 can flat black spray paint
caulking
(8) #8 washers

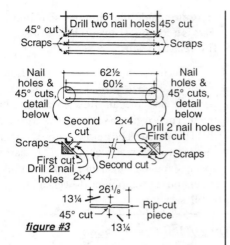

figure #3

11) Cut plastic to 16 ft. 4 in. × 6 ft. 2 in. for the floor. Tip dryer on its back. Staple the plastic to the dryer bottom leaving a 2-inch flap all around the dryer. Return the dryer to the normal position. Staple 2-inch flap to the dryer.

12) Cut screen to fit upper and lower vents and staple to openings. **DO NOT** staple screen to plywood roof yet!

13) Cut clear plastic to 5 ft. 10 in. × 16 ft. 4 in. Remove the six screws securing the front side of the roof. Position the plastic about 2 inches under the plywood roof, making sure it's centered. Climb inside the dryer and staple the plastic to the roof. Start in the middle and work to the ends. Pull plastic down snugly

across the dryer face. You may need someone to help you stretch the plastic over the dryer's front. Staple plastic to middle glazing support and attach lath. Repeat for mid-support frames, and then end supports. Fold under any excess plastic, staple to the face of the toe piece, and attach lath. Replace screws in plywood roof. Staple upper vent screens to roof.

14) Climb inside the dryer

Door Latch Detail

figure #4

and staple screen to the roof and the middle and end frame supports. Screen should hang approximately 6 inches from the floor.

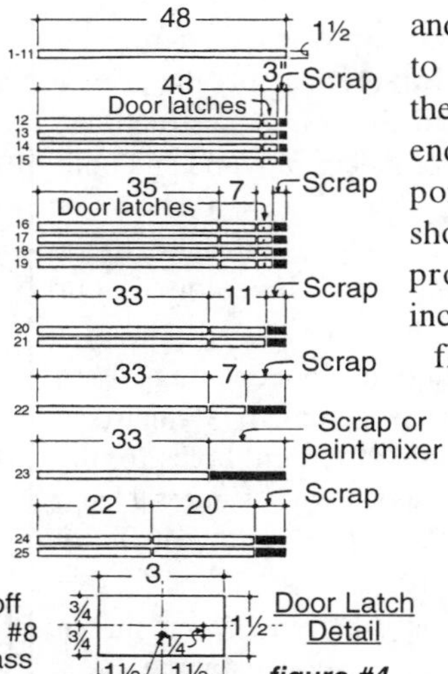

15) Cut and assemble wood to make four pallets. Place the pallets on the dryer floor 4 inches from the dryer back as shown in figure #8.

16) Cut the plastic for side glazing. Staple the plastic into place, wrapping excess around dryer's back and front. Be sure vent openings are not covered with plastic.

17) Using stickers between the layers, stack your split firewood on the pallets bark side down with the ends of the logs facing north and south. At each end of the pile the logs can be alternated for added support. Be sure to maintain 4 inches between the wood pile and

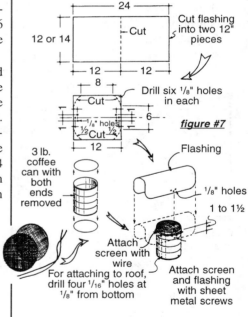

figure #6

figure #7

the back and top of the dryer to ensure adequate air circulation. The dryer is designed to hold approximately three-quarters of a cord of wood. Do not overload the dryer or it will take longer for your wood to dry.

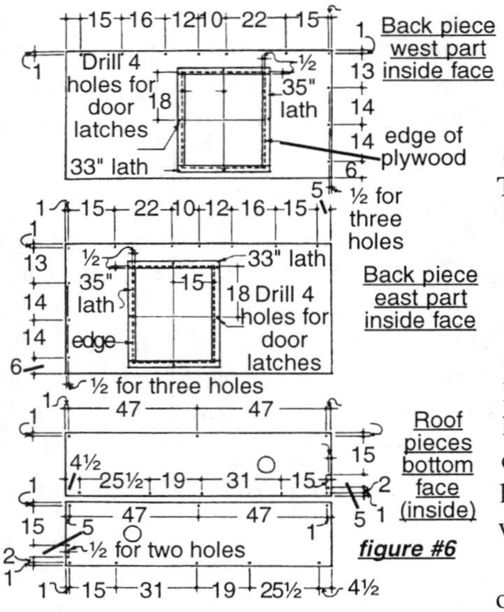

For ease of construction the glazing angle has been set at 45 degrees. However, the amount of sunlight entering the dryer can be increased by adjusting the glazing angle to better match the angle of the sun. For best year-round

nailer. Screw the roof to dryer framing. The six screws on the dryer's front will be unscrewed later.

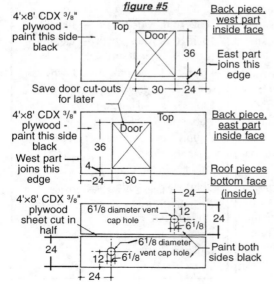

figure #5

figure #8

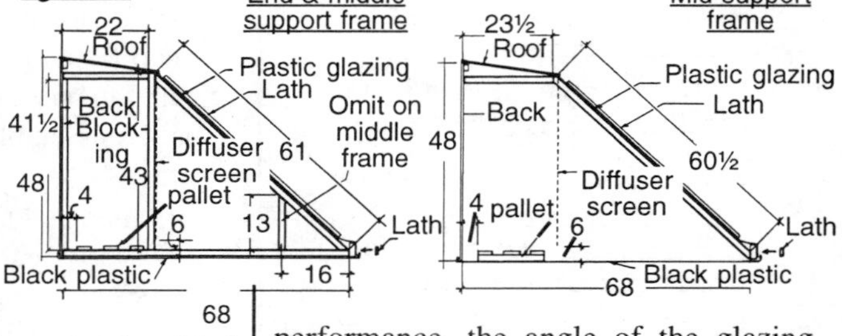

performance, the angle of the glazing should be equal to the latitude where the dryer is located. For the best wintertime drying, the glazing angle should be equal to the latitude plus 10 degrees.

For example, a dryer constructed in Philadelphia should have a glazing angle of 40 degrees for the best year-round performance or 50 degrees for the most efficient drying in the winter months. Obviously, in Philadelphia, a 45 degree angle is a perfectly acceptable compromise. And a 45 degree angle is definitely the simplest to construct.

If you should decide to alter the glazing angle, be sure to alter the glazing support cuts accordingly.

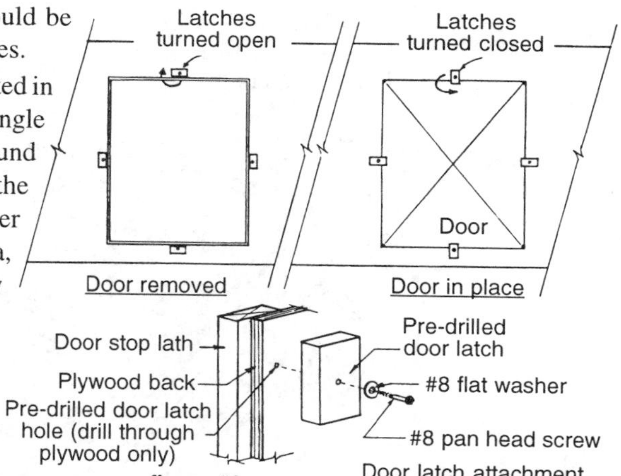

To keep bees and other pests out of your wood dryer, be sure to keep your vent screens in good repair.

Safe Wood Burning Checklist

- Open damper wide — always make sure it is open enough to ensure an adequate oxygen supply to the fire. Build a small, hot fire first to preheat the firebox and chimney. This helps the flue establish a good draft.
- Leave a thin layer of ash for insulation.
- Crumple a few sheets of uncolored newspaper and add some small pieces of kindling (small twigs, pine needles, pine cones), then light. Add bigger kindling (large twigs, small branches, small splits of wood anywhere from 1/4" to 1" in thickness) as fire grows. When hot coals are visible, add 2 or 3 logs close enough together to keep hot, but far enough apart to let sufficient air move between them.
- Burn only seasoned firewood. "Seasoned" firewood contains little moisture and creates less polluting smoke when burned. It should be dried for 6 to 12 months minimum.
- When buying seasoned wood look for the following — wood should have dark colored, cracked ends, with cracks radiating from the center like bicycle spokes. Wood should be light in weight with little moisture left. Hardwood logs are heavier than softwood. Pay attention to the sound of wood when two logs are hit together. Dry wood sounds like a bat hitting a ball. Wet wood makes a dull "thud" sound. Peel back bark and make sure no green is showing under the bark. Burn a mixture of hardwoods and softwoods.

- Start your fire with softwood kindling like pine or fir. It ignites easily, burns fast and hot and will heat the firebox and flue quickly. Then burn hardwoods (eucalyptus, almond, apple, cherry, etc.). Hardwoods are denser and take longer to ignite, but burn slower and more evenly, producing less smoke. They also provide more heat energy than softwood logs the same size.
- Light and refuel your fire quickly and carefully. Smoldering fires cause as much as six times more pollution than hot, clean fires.
- Maintain your fire properly. Look for a thin stream of white smoke coming from your chimney. If you see billows of dark smoke, you are causing pollution! Adjust fire to burn cleaner.
- Make sure that the door latch closes properly.
- Clean and inspect fireplaces and chimneys before the heating season begins.
- Fireplaces should be equipped with a tight fitting spark screen or enclosed with glass doors to stop sparks from landing on carpet or other nearby combustibles.
- Special retaining screens can also keep children at a safe distance from the fire

Figure #9 labels:
Latches turned open — Door removed
Latches turned closed — Door in place — Door
Door stop lath
Plywood back
Pre-drilled door latch hole (drill through plywood only)
Pre-drilled door latch
#8 flat washer
#8 pan head screw
Door latch attachment

figure #9

Exploded View of the Virginian Solar Firewood Dryer/Mini-Greenhouse

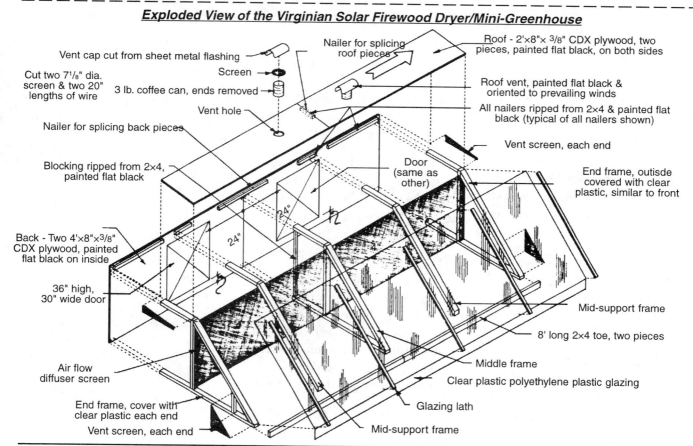

Vent cap cut from sheet metal flashing
Nailer for splicing roof pieces
Roof - 2'×8"× 3/8" CDX plywood, two pieces, painted flat black, on both sides
Cut two 7 1/8" dia. screen & two 20" lengths of wire
Screen
3 lb. coffee can, ends removed
Vent hole
Nailer for splicing back pieces
Blocking ripped from 2×4, painted flat black
Back - Two 4'×8"×3/8" CDX plywood, painted flat black on inside
36" high, 30" wide door
Air flow diffuser screen
End frame, cover with clear plastic each end
Vent screen, each end
Door (same as other)
24"
24"
Roof vent, painted flat black & oriented to prevailing winds
All nailers ripped from 2×4 & painted flat black (typical of all nailers shown)
Vent screen, each end
End frame, outside covered with clear plastic, similar to front
Mid-support frame
8' long 2×4 toe, two pieces
Middle frame
Clear plastic polyethylene plastic glazing
Glazing lath
Mid-support frame

Solar food dryer inexpensive, easy to construct

Q: I want to protect the environment and do things naturally. With fruits and vegetable on sale now and the surplus from my own garden, I would like to dry them naturally without chemicals. How can I make a "low-cost" solar dryer myself?

A: Drying fruits and vegetables in a solar dryer is an excellent no-chemical food preservative method. You should be able to build a solar food dryer yourself for less than $50 using old scrap materials around your house.

Solar food drying and cooking are not only good for the environment, but they are good for your budget. No electricity is used, so your utility bills are much lower. By not creating excess heat in the kitchen, air-conditioning costs are lower and indoor humidity levels stay low for comfort.

Drying your excess fruits and vegetables is a perfect fit with solar energy. Properly dried food takes up very little space and the dried food lasts a long time. The savings from buying larger quantities of fruits and vegetables on sale should easily pay back the material costs in one summer alone.

For the solar food dryer to work properly, the temperature inside the dryer should be about 110 degrees. There must also be adequate warm air circulation around the foods to draw out the moisture.

Fruit is easier to dry than vegetables. Since fruit has higher natural acidity than vegetables, less moisture must be removed for full preservation.

The least expensive do-it-yourself design is a simple plywood box covered with a solar absorber top. The sun should not shine directly on the

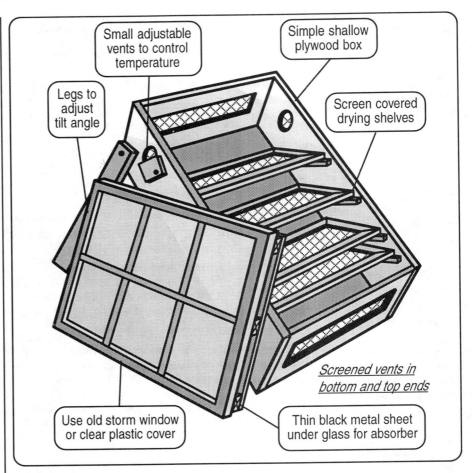

Small adjustable vents to control temperature

Legs to adjust tilt angle

Simple shallow plywood box

Screen covered drying shelves

Screened vents in bottom and top ends

Use old storm window or clear plastic cover

Thin black metal sheet under glass for absorber

foods or it will diminish nutrition, color and flavor.

For the absorber top, use an old storm window with a piece of sheet metal collector (painted black) beneath it. This black collector absorbs the sun's heat, yet blocks the direct rays from striking the food.

The plywood box should have screen-covered vent openings in the top and the bottom ends. Cool dry air enters the bottom vent (the box is tilted up when drying). Hot moist air naturally exhausts out the top vent.

Using a hole saw, make a couple of extra adjustable vent openings in the sides near the top. Screw on a small piece of plywood (just one screw) next to each hole so they can be rotated to cover the holes. These allow the air flow and temperature to be fine tuned.

Attach legs to tilt the box toward the sun. Tilt the back up at an angle equal to your area's latitude minus five degrees. Make screen covered drying shelves to allow free air flow all around the foods.

Q: I have noticed that the toilet is loose on the floor. I have tightened the nuts as tight as possible, but it is still loose. What would cause this and will it leak and waste water?

A: Your toilet may be leaking now but you do not notice it. This leak will not waste water like a leaky flapper, but it can destroy the floor. Most likely, the flange is rusted out or the wax ring is overly compressed.

First turn off the water valve and flush the toilet. Using a sponge, dip out any remaining water. Remove the nuts and the toilet and inspect it. Replace the wax ring or flange if necessary. Check the subfloor for rot.

The easiest fruits to dry are apples, apricots, cherries, dates, nectarines, peaches, pears and plums. The easiest vegetables are beans, carrots, corn and peas. You can make fruit strips by mixing the fruits in a blender and then spreading the mixture on wax paper. Place it on the drying trays. You can also make pasta and dry breakfast cereals in the solar dryer.

A solar food dryer is basically a plywood box that gets hot in the sun. The heat does two things — 1) it warms the air to speed the drying of your foods, and 2) the warm air creates a natural air flow over the foods to be dried. Since warm air is less dense than cool air, the solar heated and moist air flows out the top vent while cooler dry air is pulled in the bottom. There is a metal solar collector sheet under the storm window glass top. This sheet absorbs the solar heat, yet blocks the sun's rays from striking the food directly. The screen-covered drying shelves hold the pieces of foods. The ideal interior dryer temperature is 110°. It will take about two sunny days to dry most foods. Vegetables must be drier than fruits because of their lower acid content.

In the following do-it-yourself design, the drying shelves are staggered - alternate ones are toward the front or back. This causes the air to wind around all the shelves somewhat as it rises from the lower inlet vent to upper outlet vent.

Do-It-Yourself Instructions for Solar Food Dryer

1) Construct the box

a. Measure the outside dimensions of your storm window. This will be used for the top of your dryer. If you do not have a storm window and must make the clear top, make it to a size that will divide easily into 4 × 8 sheets of lumber and glazing.

b. Cut the back of your box from the 3/4" plywood. Make the back the same length as the length of your window, but decrease the width by 2".

c. Also from the plywood, cut the side panels of the box. The left and right side panels should be cut the same length as the length of the window and 15" wide. The upper panel should be cut to the same width as the back piece and 14 1/4" high. The lower panel should be cut to the width of the back and 17" high. Cutting the bottom side higher than the top side creates a ledge for the storm window to rest on when the box is tilted toward the sun.

2) Locate the shelf supports

a. Choose and label the "inside" and "outside" of each side piece. Starting with the inside of the left side panel, measure 4" from the top and make a mark at the right edge. From this mark measure in 4" intervals down the rest of the side, marking each at the right edge. Use these marks to draw angle lines (see diagram #3 for the proper angle) down from the right to the left. Repeat this procedure with the right side piece, marking the left edge and drawing the angle lines down from the left to the right. When facing together, the lines on both side pieces should match up exactly.

b. To make the supports for the shelf trays, cut as many 1"x1"x15" slats of wood as you have angle lines. Attach these with glue and screws, staggering their placement. That is, the first support on each side should be positioned 1" from the back edge, the second support 1" from the front edge, the third support 1" from the back edge, etc. This provides for more efficient air circulation.

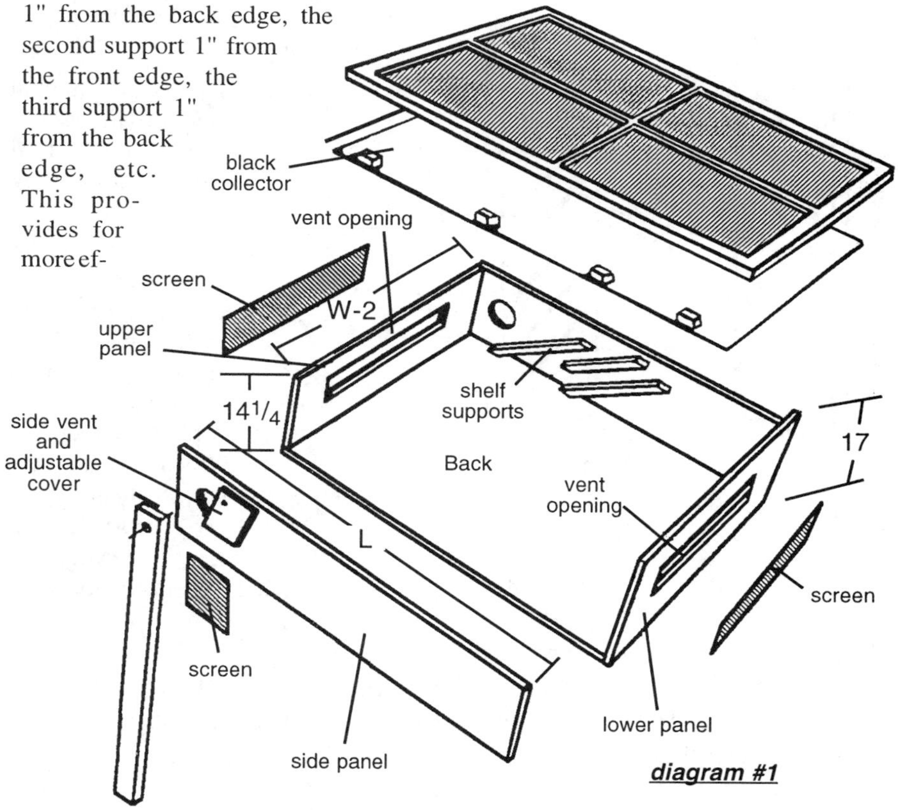

3) Make the vents

a. At the top of each side panel in the 4" area before the first support strip, locate the center and cut a hole 3" to 4" in diameter. Take care to avoid cutting the shelf support pieces.

b. The vent holes in the upper and lower panels should be no more than 20% of the surface area of each panel. For instance, if your lower panel is 24" wide and 18" high, cut a rectangular vent approximately 4" high and 18" wide in the center of the board.

c. Cut pieces of nylon screening material about 1" larger than the four vent openings and staple to the inside of the plywood.

d. Using plastic from an old flat waste basket, cut round or square flaps, big enough to cover the side vent holes. Screw them to the side panels with one

diagram #1

Labels in diagram: black collector, vent opening, screen, upper panel, W-2, side vent and adjustable cover, screen, 14 1/4, L, side panel, shelf supports, Back, vent opening, 17, screen, lower panel screw above the vent holes, so that you can rotate them to adjust the open area of the vent holes.

4) Assemble the box

a. With a helper, pre-assemble the box, as shown in the diagram, to make sure all the pieces fit together properly.

b. Since the box will be exposed to the weather, you should use both waterproof glue and screws to assemble it. Countersink the screw holes for a finished appearance.

c. Starting with the upper panel, attach it with glue and screws to the back piece. Attach each side panel in the same way. The support pieces should be angled down and out. Finally, attach

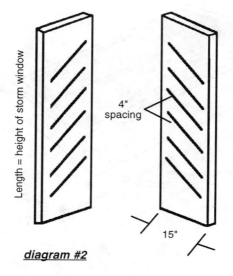

Length = height of storm window

4" spacing

15"

diagram #2

the lower panel to the back and side panels.

d. Spray the outside of the box with a flat black paint. Spray paint the inside of the box with shiny aluminum paint.

e. Let it get hot in the sun for several days before you use it. This makes sure that the solvents have baked out of the paint.

5) Make the dryer shelves

a. You should make the shelves from 1" × 2" lumber. These shelves will sit on the angled shelf supports mounted on the inside of the side panels of the box.

b. Build a rectangular frame that is slightly narrower than the inside of the box and

the same length as the shelf support pieces. Construct the frames with glue and screws and paint them a flat black.

c. Once you have made the shelf frames, cover them with screening. Wrap the screening tightly around the back of the shelf frame and staple it to the shelf frame.

6) Make the top and collector sheet

a. Size the collector sheet about 2" smaller than the storm window you are using. Use an old aluminum printing plate from a print shop or any other piece of thin aluminum sheet. Clean the plate with steel wool and wipe it with solvents.

b. Spray paint the aluminum plate and the frame of the storm window with flat black paint. This improves the solar heat absorption.

c. Cut eight spacers from the 1" × 2" lumber, each 3" long. Mount these, four on each side, between the aluminum plate and the inside of the storm window, centering the plate over the window frame. When the top is set on the box, the spacers should fit just inside the sides, so that the aluminum plate slips down inside the box. This will position the storm window top on the box.

Angle shelf supports so the shelves are level when the box is tilted up toward the sun - see instructions for proper tilt angle

7) Position the dryer

a. You will have to experiment with tilt angle and the opening of the vents to get the desired temperature and air

flow for proper food drying. During the summer, you will get the greatest amount of solar heat by tilting it up at your area's latitude angle minus ten degrees. Since the summer is the hottest season, you will generally tilt it higher or lower to avoid overheating, even with the vents open.

b. During fall and spring, tilting it at the latitude angle absorbs the greatest amount of solar heat. With the cooler weather, you may have to close the side vents or even block the upper and lower vents a little to maintain the proper temperature.

c. It is a good idea to install a bulb-type outdoor thermometer in the dryer. As the sun moves throughout the day, you may want to check the thermometer and change the tilt angle several times.

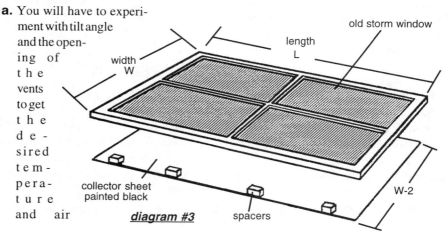

old storm window

length L

width W

W-2

collector sheet painted black

diagram #3

spacers

Suggestions for Successful Drying

- Select fruits and vegetables that are ripe. It is better to err of the under-ripe than the overripe condition. Wash and dry the foods thoroughly. Cut the food into as small a pieces as you can and still be able to handle them easily when they are dried. They will shrink in size considerably. Pieces that are about 3/8" in thickness are best.

- Vegetables have a lower acid content than fruits, so vegetables must be made drier to preserve them. Therefore, cut vegetables in very thin pieces. Remember, the faster the food dries, the better it will taste and the more nutrition ity will retain.

- Do not remove the skins from the foods. Especially with vegetables, much of the nutritional content is in the skin and immediately below it. Vegetables and fruit with strong tasting skins will taste fine after drying. The drying process reduces the strong, sometimes unpleasant, flavors of many vegetable skins.

- If you are concerned about the appearance of the dried foods, dip it in lemon or lime juice before drying. This will help to retain the color.

- You may blanch the sliced foods first in 180° scalding water to sterilize it. This stops the natural ripening process and helps to retain the color. The food should also dry more quickly because the cell walls will be more permeable to water as ithe food dries.

- Wait until the weather prediction is for at least two sunny days in a row before drying the food. Low humidity should also be in the forecast.

- Choose a location that is free of dust, smog or other pollutants.

- Under normal conditions, it should take about two days at the target 110° dryer temperature to dry most fruits. Certain vegetables may take a little longer. Put the sliced fresh food in the dryer in the morning as early as you can.

- Check the temperature periodically throughout the day and adjust the angle and vent openings to maintain the proper temperature. Once you are familiar with your dryer, you will probably have to adjust it only two to three times a day.

- You should stir the pieces of food twice a day. This means just moving them around on the drying shelves to make sure all surfaces are exposed to the drying air for even drying. Temperatures are 4 degrees higher in the top of the dryer than in the lower part. Uneven drying can result in the food not becoming thoroughly preserved and spoilage can occur.

- At night, do not remove the food. Just lay a blanket over the dryer to block the air flow through the vents. The evening and early morning air is usually very humid. If this circulates through the dryer, it can rehydrate the food and make the drying process take longer than the two days.

- If the sun is hot enough and the humidity is low, food will generally dry in two days. However, drying times can take up to three days depending on the weather conditions. If it is cloudy on the second day of drying and the next day is bright and sunny the food will be fine. If it is rainy or cloudy for several days you will need to bring the food indoors and oven dry it.

- You may need to regulate the temperatures on cool or windy days. Partially close the vents.

- When you test fruits for dryness there should be no moisture when a piece is cut. If you press several pieces together they should not stick together and fall apart when the pressure is released.

- Slices will be leathery but will also be pliable. Be sure not to overdry to hardness. Vegetables are dry when they are brittle, they will snap like a chip.

- You can weigh produce before and during the drying process — when half the original weight is gone, the food will be two-thirds dried.

- Be sure to store your dried foods in sealed containers that are safe from insects or animals. Do not store in paper or plastic bags — a coffee can works fine.

- Keep dried foods in a cool and dark place. Light will cause the food to lose flavor, color and vitamins. The cooler the storage, the better.

Advantages of Solar Dried Foods

- A simple, safe, healthy and natural way of food preservation.

- Absolutely free operating costs — freezing and canning are complicated and can have potentially dangerous procedures.

- Freezing and canning use energy for the processing — stoves, pressure cookers, freezers, etc.

- Canning and freezing involve a loss of vitamins.

- The taste is close to fresh — nutrient and flavor retention is very high.

- Canning has the increased danger of bacterial growth.

- Great emergency food.

- Provides healthy snacks.

- Many flavors (especially herbs, spices and mushrooms) improve with dehydration.

- Dried food is an ideal compact food supply for an outdoor type person — hiker, fisherman, camper, biker, etc.

- Good type of food storage where electricity is unavailable or infrequently used.

- Solar dried foods will keep indefinitely with airtight packing.

- If the food is properly stored it has a longer shelf life than foods preserved by other methods.

- You can reduce storage space by at least 25 percent.

- You can store food in small quantities.

- You can be sure there are no chemical preservatives as in commercially dried foods.

- You can take advantage of an overabundance of food and special sales at the supermarket or road side stands.

Solar cooking for home or camping

Q: Our kitchen gets awfully hot. Is it possible to purchase an outdoor solar cooker kit or build one inexpensively myself? It must get hot enough to roast meats and bake breads.

A: There are several inexpensive ready-to-use solar cooker kits available starting at about $45. You can also make one yourself using scrap lumber or old cardboard boxes for only about $10 in materials.

A solar cooker can easily reach 400 degrees for baking breads and cakes. Meats can be roasted or slow cooked at 300 degrees. Using a solar cooker cools your kitchen and reduces your electric bills and air pollution.

Most ready-to-use kits are collapsible for quick easy storage. This also makes them ideal for fishing, camping or backpacking. For most cooking or baking, just face the cooker toward the sun. Even on partially cloudy days, it can get hot enough to slow cook meats and make stews and soups.

The Solar Chef has a tubular frame with attached wheels so it can be moved easily to a sunny location. You point the cooker at the sun and adjust the rack. Place your pan inside the cooking chamber. Close the large clear dome and watch your dinner cook.

Another more traditional design uses a one-piece insulated fiberglass box with a clear top. It uses hi-tech insulation and seals for efficiency.

A built-in levelator food tray keeps pots level no matter what angle the cooker is tilted toward the sun. When done cooking, reflective side panels with a handle fold over the glass top to form a carrying case.

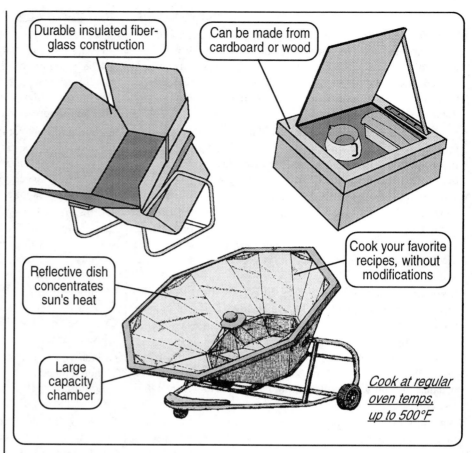

Durable insulated fiberglass construction

Can be made from cardboard or wood

Reflective dish concentrates sun's heat

Cook your favorite recipes, without modifications

Large capacity chamber

Cook at regular oven temps, up to 500°F

It is easy to build a small plywood solar cooker in a couple of hours. It has a glass front, a door on the back and a rack inside to hold the cooking pots. Line it with rigid duct insulation and paint it black to absorb heat.

A common size is roughly an 18 to 24-inch cube. Make it slightly larger than you need and put a few bricks inside to hold heat. Saw vent holes in the side to control the heat. Cover them with adjustable flaps.

You can increase the effectiveness of the solar oven by adding cardboard reflectors that are covered with aluminum foil or reflective mylar. These catch more of the sun's heat and provide a longer cooking day.

The least expensive design (about $10) is made from old cardboard boxes, newspaper, aluminum foil and window glass. Make two open-top cardboard boxes (one small and one large). Line the boxes with aluminum foil. Set one box inside the other and use the newspaper to separate and insulate them.

Q: Our garage is attached to the house with two common walls. The garage stays fairly warm in the winter and gets very hot in the summer. Do you think it would help if I put insulation in the garage attic?

A: It probably does not make sense to spend several hundred dollars on insulation for the garage attic. Since it is not heated directly in the winter, it would stay only a couple of degrees warmer if insulated.

In the summer, attic insulation does not do a lot to block the radiant heat from a hot roof. Installing more vents in the garage roof will do more than adding insulation.

You can easily build your own solar cooker or buy a ready-to-use cooker or kit. Using a solar cooker not only cuts your energy usage for cooking, but it reduces the load on your air conditioner. It also reduces the overall peak usage for your electric company. This helps to reduce future utility rate increases and pollution.

To get the maximum heat in your solar cooker, it should face the sun directly. In summer, angle the back up 15° (from horizontal) lower than your area's latitude angle. In fall and spring, angle it up at your latitude angle. In winter, angle it about 15° higher than your latitude angle.

Many of the ready-to-use cookers and kits listed below use special efficient lens and concentrating collectors to intensify the heat. These require fewer angle adjustments than a simple build-it-yourself cooker. You will have to experiment to get the correct angles for

Manufacturers of Solar Cookers and Kits

KERR-COLE ENTERPRISES, INC., 331 E. 14th St., Tempe, AZ 85285 - (602) 968-3068
type - box cooker constructed of durable cardboard with glass lid

SMOKELESS COOKING PRODUCTS, 420 N. Basque Ave., Fullerton, CA 92633 - (714) 780-8446
type - backpack cooker, box cooker, BBQ grill

SOLAR CHEF INTN'L, LLC,14012 FM 1730, Lubbock, TX 79424 - (806) 794-2150
type - ½" plywood shell covered with ⅛" silvered glass mirrors for reflectors — the removable dome is ⅛" window glass set in silicone — tubular steel frame with three wheels for easy moving

SOLAR COOKERS INTNL., 1919 21st St., Suite 101, Sacramento, CA 95814 - (916) 455-4499
type - box cooker constructed of foiled cardboard with polyester window

SUN OVENS INTN'L, 39 W. Midon Dr., Elburn, IL 60119 - (800) 408-7919 (630) 208-7273
type - box cooker constructed with a fiberglass case and tempered glass door

SUNDYNE CO., 988 Blvd. of the Arts, #212, Sarasota, FL 34236 - (941) 954-6562
type - 48" diameter reflective dish with a Fresnel reflecting lens in the center

Instructions for Making a Plywood Solar Cooker

1) Cut two side pieces from the plywood to the dimensions shown on page 2. Cut two small circular vent holes in one of the pieces to control the heat. You will cover them with adjustable and rotating flaps made from scrap pieces.

2) Cut a plywood rectangle 17½" × 23" for the bottom of the box. Bevel one of the 23" sides, this will match the slope of the sides.

3) Cut a piece of plywood to 4" × 24" for the top of the oven. Bevel one of the longer edges to match the slope of the sides.

4) Cut a plywood rectangle 18" × 23" for the back of the oven. Cut a 9" × 13" door into this. Mark dimensions so the door will be 3½" up from the bottom edge and centered.

5) Use the rest of the plywood and cut two strips that measure ¾" × 17". The glass window will rest on these ledger strips. Place each ledger strip along the sloped edge about 4" up from the bottom front corner and 3/16" in from the edge on the right and left sides of the oven. Drill two holes through the

ledger and into the side panel about 6" apart. Put wood glue on each side piece and on the ledgers. Clamp the ledgers into place and screw them to the side panels.

6) Line up the back edge of the oven bottom with the edge of the oven back. Be sure that it forms a right angle, then drill holes every 6". Spread the glue along the surfaces and screw the two pieces together. Check to be sure the surfaces are square.

7) Now you can screw the bottom and back together. Drill the holes, then glue and screw. Again check to make sure all surfaces are square.

8) You can screw the top into the back and sides. Again drill two holes every 6" along the back. Do not glue or screw the top into place yet.

9) Use silicone rubber caulking and caulk all the inside joints.

10) It is best to use pressed fiberglass ductboard. It helps the cooker to retain the heat. The aluminum side should always be facing into the cooker. The back piece should be cut to 17½" × 21". Center this cut piece on the back

and mark the 9" × 13" door opening. Cut out the opening for the door and save the scrap piece to be used later.

11) See the diagram on page 106 for the dimensions of the insulation for the sides. Cut out for the ledger strips. You need to measure 3" up from the bottom front corner of the insulation side piece. Remove a strip ½" × ¾" xx 17".

12) The bottom insulation should be cut to 16⅛" × 21". Bevel the front edge to match the slope of the sides. Cut a 2¼" × 21" piece for the top. You need to bevel one of the longer edges to match the slope of the sides.

13) Glue the ductboard pieces to the plywood with adhesive. Seal all seams with aluminum foil duct tape. Glue the scrap piece to the inside of the door and let it dry with the door closed. Glue the ductboard to the top, making sure it is placed 1½" in from the back and sides. Screw the top into place.

14) Cut a piece of molding or ¾" plywood 24". Tack the molding into place with brads making sure it is flush with the bottom of the oven. Now cut two pieces to 21⅛". Tack these pieces ¾"

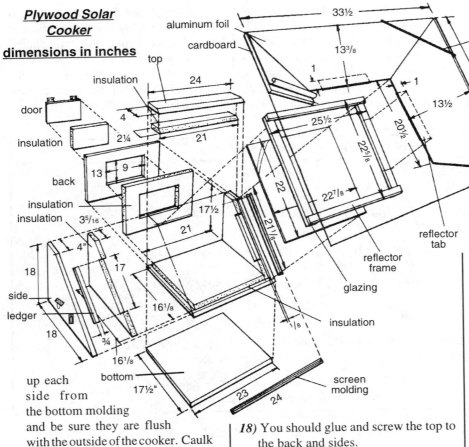

Plywood Solar Cooker

dimensions in inches

14) up each side from the bottom molding and be sure they are flush with the outside of the cooker. Caulk along the outside of the molding and plywood for a tight seal.

15) You need a piece of glass that is 22" × 22⅞". (Always wear gloves when handling glass.) Slowly slide the glass into place. You should not force it. It will rest on the ledgers and beneath the molding. If any of the brads are in the way of the glass, remove and retack them. Now you need to remove the glass.

16) Paint the inside and outside of the oven with flat black paint. Make sure that the paint you use is non-toxic. Let the paint dry for 24 hours.

17) Clean the glass with water and slide it into place between the ledgers and moldings. Screw the top to the sides. Place the oven outdoors with the window facing the sun. The black paint might give off fumes that will show up as a film on the inside of the glass. Wipe off the film until the glass stays clear. Caulk behind the bottom strip of molding, then slide the glass between the ledgers and side molding. Be sure the glass sets in the caulking so that it forms an airtight seal.

18) You should glue and screw the top to the back and sides.

19) Caulk the sides of glass and the joint between the top and the glass.

20) You need to make reflectors which can be made inexpensively of cardboard and aluminum foil. You need to cut two pieces of plywood ¾" × 22½" and two pieces ¾" × 22⅝" for the frame. Drill and screw the pieces of the frame together. The frame rests between the bottom and side molding. If you are going to paint the frame, you should do that now.

21) Now you need to cut four reflectors from cardboard. See the dimensions in the diagram. To make it more rigid you can use a double thickness of cardboard glued together (exclude the tabs on the second piece). Cut strips of heavy duty, double strength aluminum foil to cover each reflector. Spread the glue thinly and evenly on the cardboard surfaces.

22) Attach foil to a dowel with scotch tape and roll tightly around the dowel. Make sure that when you unroll the foil the shiny side will be up. Slowly unroll the foil onto the glued cardboard surface making sure the foil lies flat. (If

you need to use more than one strip of foil, be sure to leave a 2" overlap.) Cover the cardboard reflector, excluding the tab. If any bubbles have appeared you can prick them with a pin and flatten them with a clean, dry cloth.

23) Use a sharp knife or scissors to trim the foil. You can place the reflectors under a heavy object until the glue dries to prevent the cardboard from curling. After the glue dries you can attach the reflectors to the frame. Bend the tabs for the bottom and top reflectors. Center the tab on the face of the bottom and top of the frame. Staple the tabs to the frame.

24) You will need supports for the corners. Use four pieces of wire 10" long. At either end, bend the last 2" of wire 90° with pliers.

25) Slide the frame around the oven window. You can slip the tabs of the side reflectors between the plywood and the frame.

26) Push one end of the wire into the corrugations of the cardboard near the corner of one reflector. The other end should reach across the diagonal to a second reflector to hold the proper angle, and slide in between corrugations. This will secure the corners. Do this to all the corners. The reflectors should be at an angle of 120° from the oven window.

Required Materials for Plywood Solar Cooker
1 sheet exterior plywood
1 tube silicone caulking
1 roll aluminum foil duct tape
foamboard and panel adhesive
ductboard
clear glass
optional screen molding
screws and brads
hinges and staples
non-toxic flat black paint
double strength aluminum foil
cardboard
wood and white glue
wire

Instructions for Making Cardboard Solar Cooker

1) Glue foil thoroughly to toppers and reflector flap to withstand wear and tear. Use a 50-50 mixture of glue (water-based white glue or carpenter's glue) and water. On the other pieces, foil can be wrapped, taped, or spot-glued. Put shiny side out, and overlap foil edges slightly.

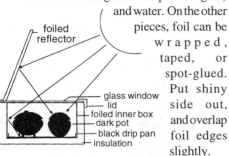

2) The inner box is foiled on both sides. Size is important. If the box is too small, it won't collect enough solar energy to get hot enough to cook reasonable quantities of foods. Start with a box that is 19" × 23" × 8½" or proportionally bigger. Cover any holes with cardboard patches, then cover both sides with foil. You can make a box from flat cardboard. It is easier to glue aluminum foil onto both sides after making creases for the folds, but before actually folding the box. Fold the box and use full-strength glue or tape to make the box.

3) The outer box is foiled on the inside only. Use a 24" × 28" × 10" box or larger. It needs to be bigger than the inside box so that there is about 2½" space between all four sides of the two boxes and 1" between bottoms. The outer box can be made of material other than cardboard, like plywood.

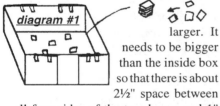

4) Glue or tape small stacks of 2" cardboard squares to make 8 supports in the bottom of the outer box, see diagram #1. Fill the rest of the bottom with small balls of newspaper or other insulation material. Place the inner box so that there is 2½" space between the two boxes on all sides.

5) There are many ways to insulate the boxes. Crumpling newspaper is one way. A little crumpled newspaper with four foiled insulators is better. The bottom of each insulator piece is against the outside box, and the top is against the inner box, with crumpled newspaper in the spaces. Other clean dry materials may be used such as wool, straw, or rice hulls. For a hotter box, add foiled layers in the insulation. While cooking, a well-insulated cooker should not feel hot on the outside except the glass.

6) When all the insulation is installed, seal the top spaces between the boxes with 4 cardboard toppers, see diagram #2. The two short and two long toppers are foiled on both sides just to the outside fold. The four toppers fold to cover both the inside of the inner box and the outer side of the outer box. Glue the toppers in place with full-strength glue, see diagram #3.

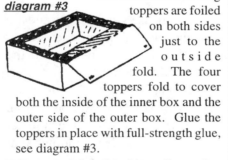

7) You can make a lid with a reflector flap in several ways, but you must provide a snug-fitting seal. After a basic lid is made, cut three sides of an opening that

Required Materials for Cardboard Solar Cooker

- corrugated cardboard
- clear glass pane
- white or wood glue
- aluminum foil
- insulation - crumpled newspapers
- large thin metal tray
- non-toxic black paint
- stick or wire
- silicone caulk or papier mache

will frame the glass window. Fold back the flap created from the 3 cuts and cover its inside surface with foil to make a reflector, see diagram #4. Put silicone caulk or papier mache around the edge of the glass on one side. Then press the glass into the inside of the lid so that there is a seal all the way around.

8) You can prop up the reflector flap to reflect sunlight into the box. Take a pointed stick, tie it to the flap and its free end is set in one of the holes in a stick glued to the lid. Hold the flap in position against the stick with a string looped from the flap to a hole in the lid. A simpler prop can be made by notching a stick at both ends and tying with strings, or stiff wire can be used.

9) On the bottom of the inner box, place a thin metal tray painted black. It catches spills and also draws heat to the cooking pots. A cardboard piece covered with aluminum foil and painted black will work.

10) Let the solar cooker heat empty in the sun for several hours to be sure all paint and glue is dry and won't give off fumes.

Instructions for Making a Hot Dog Cooker

1) Cut the top and front out of one cardboard box to make a frame for your solar cooker.

2) Cut four parabolic cross sections from the other cardboard box. Glue 2 pieces together to make 1 that is twice as heavy.

3) Glue a smooth piece of aluminum foil to one side of the poster board. Tape the poster board to the two curved pieces. Attach the cooker to the frame using nuts and bolts.

4) Adjust the cooker so that you can see the sun's rays cross on the focal points.

Required Materials for Hot Dog Cooker

- 1 hot dog
- 2 carboard boxes
- 2 small nuts & 2 bolts
- aluminum foil
- coat hanger (unpainted)
- scissors
- rubber cement
- black foil
- poster board

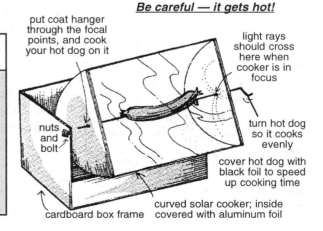

Be careful — it gets hot!

Efficient garden window kits add openness to room

Q: I cannot afford a sunspace or large bay window so I am considering installing a mini-garden window kit over my kitchen window. I want to grow some plants and get more natural light. What is available?

A: There are many new designs of garden window kits available with nearly every option and design variation imaginable. If you are handy with tools, it is not difficult to install a kit yourself.

If your window needs to be replaced anyway, a garden window kit is an excellent choice. Installing one can make a room appear more spacious and open. Some models use special curved insulated glass to eliminate the center frame member for a more contemporary open appearance.

Garden windows are constructed to be energy efficient. With the bottom seat and shelf designed to hold a planter or flowerpots, they must be insulated well to maintain a fairly even year-round temperature for healthy plants. Since garden windows extend out from the exterior wall, they catch even slight breezes in the summer for effective natural cooling. In the winter, the super-efficient glass options and airtight seals minimize heat loss.

Side opening casement window configurations are often used. These can have the hinge side near the house or away. They also have double lock latches on each side for security and an airtight seal when they are closed. Other window options are a front awning (hinges at top and swings out) and a top venting (hinged at the top near the house). These configurations are ideal in rainy areas so the window can be kept slightly open.

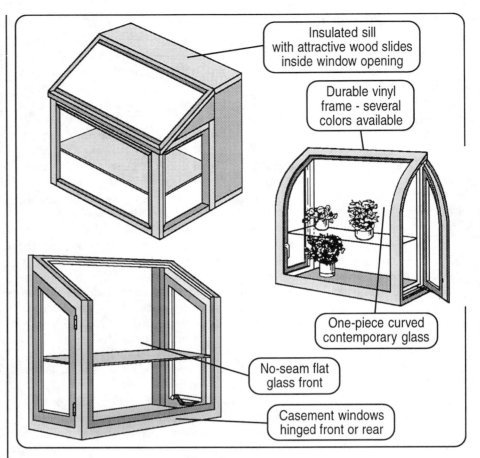

Insulated sill with attractive wood slides inside window opening

Durable vinyl frame - several colors available

One-piece curved contemporary glass

No-seam flat glass front

Casement windows hinged front or rear

Many use vinyl frames and are available in white, tan and brown. Vinyl is maintenance-free and the channels inside the frame improve insulation. Some vinyl frames are filled with foam for extra insulation. There are also attractive natural wood frame garden windows that can be stained or painted.

If the plants you select are very sensitive to cold, choose a garden window with a special insulated seat (also called muffler) and sides. A layer of rigid foam insulation is sandwiched in the seat and sides.

If your budget is limited, build a do-it-yourself garden window. Since it uses single pane glass or easy-to-work-with clear acrylic plastic sheets, leave your existing window sashes in place for winter efficiency.

To reduce summer heat gain, make a slanted clear roof covered with 1x4 lumber slats mounted on edge and spaced about five inches apart. The slats allow diffused light to enter from above, but block the sun's direct rays.

Q: Whenever I take a shower and someone flushes a toilet or turns on cold water, I nearly get scalded. I keep my water heater set at 120 degrees to save energy. Should I set it even lower?

A: Lowering the water heater temperature will not help much. Your problem is caused by a pressure imbalance when cold water is being used elsewhere.

Your best solution is to install a new pressure-balancing, anti-scald shower valve. It senses a pressure drop when another faucet is opened and automatically compensates to reduce the hot water pressure too.

Manufacturers of Garden Windows

CERTAINTEED CORP., PO Box 860, Valley Forge, PA 19482 - (800) 233-8990
frame material - vinyl   *color of frame* - white, tan   *style* - casement
type of glass - $^7/_8$" insulating, Thermaflect™ — low-e argon, tempered roof
features - The windows are constructed with a special honeycomb frame and sash adding to the insulating properties. There is also a 2-inch thick insulated birchwood seatboard that you can paint or stain. The foam core retards moisture and improves the thermal performance. Full screens protect against insect invasion. The hardware consists of a multi-point locking system for added security. There are adjustable tempered glass shelves.

FEN-TECH, 1510 North 5th St., Superior, WI 54880 - (715) 392-9500
frame material - thermoplastic composite   *color of frame* - white, beige, brown, sierratone   *style* - slider
type of glass - HP-4 glass — low-e argon with edgetech super spacer and "MagiClean" exterior glass coating
features - The thermocomposite framing is made of a modern GE Plastics Cycolac/Geloy, making it easy to clean and never needing paint. The shelf is $^3/_8$" thick plate glass with polished edges. The support braces are decorative scroll "Load Bear™" supports that adjustable and accent the underside supports. The windows open up to 90° for ventilation. The seatboard is finished with an oak veneer and will accommodate wall thicknesses to 5$^1/_8$". For thicker walls an 8" projected seatboard extension is optional. Underside insulation provides R-13 value and is protected by aluminum cladding. One style features a unique curved frame and glass for an uninterrupted view.

GEORGIA PACIFIC, PO Box 105605, Atlanta, GA 30348 - (404) 652-4000
frame material - vinyl   *color of frame* - white • beige   *style* - casement
type of glass - $^7/_8$" insulating, low-e argon
features - There is a multipoint locking system that locks the unit along the full length of the window jamb. There is a special weatherstrip around the casements for maximum insulation and to stop air infiltration. An optional polyurethane insulated seat is available. The window shelf is tempered glass.

GREAT LAKES WINDOW, INC., PO Box 1896, Toledo, OH 43603 - (800) 666-0000 (419) 666-5555
frame material - aluminum   *color of frame* - white, camel, earthtone   *style* - casement
type of glass - dual insulating, Hi R+Plus™ — soft coat low-e argon, Easy-Clean Glass ™ — a higher quality of glass that makes frequent and strenuous glass cleaning obsolete, designer glass — decorative designs etched in glass
features - The frames are insulated with a patented R-Core® insulation for more energy efficiency with an R factor of 13. The window is equipped with a multi-point lock system for added security. The full-length trapezoid windows open a full 90°. It has a tempered glass interior shelf. The seat is 1¼" birch or oak which can stained or painted. An optional inside set of DuPont Corian® that is a low maintenance and durable surface is available. An optional polyurethane insulated seat will add energy efficiency. The "Architectural" series features a single, continuous piece of insulated bent glass extending outward from the top panel to the base of the front panel, eliminating the need for a crossbar. The windows are custom made to fit your home's existing opening. There is a limited lifetime-plus warranty that covers the basic window unit, all moving parts and screens. It is transferable to a new owner if you sell your home.

KENSINGTON WINDOWS, RD #1, Vandegrift, PA 15690 - (800) 444-4972
frame material - vinyl   *color of frame* - white, brown   *style* - casement
type of glass - dual insulating low-e argon, Heat Mirror™
features - The vinyl window frame is filled with foam insulation for added efficiency. The interior is oak that you can either stain or paint.

KOLBE & KOLBE MILLWORK CO., 1323 S. 11th Ave., Wausau, WI 54401 - (800) 477-8656 (715) 842-5666
frame material - wood   *color of frame* - unfinished Douglas fir   *style* - top vent
type of glass - $^7/_8$" double glazed H°K, low-e, bottom sash is ½" H°K, low-e tempered glass
features - The interior wood options for the "Sundance" include Douglas fir and red oak. Flowing curves and an angled glass bottom panel eliminates need for additional support and adds another dimension to your view. Optional shelves of wood slats or wood-framed glass can be used for your displays. A sturdy aluminum-framed (optional wood-framed), charcoal-colored fiberglass mesh screen will keep insects out. The hardware for the top venting sash uses a chain drive mechanism with stainless steel hinges. An optional vent crank extension handle is available.

NAPCO, 300 N. Pike Rd., Sarvar, PA 16055 - (724) 353-3511
frame material - vinyl   *color of frame* - white, brown   *style* - casement
type of glass - dual insulating low-e argon, solar bronze, obscure glass
features - The roof is sloped for good drainage. There is adjustable shelf hardware so you can position the shelf in any position that you desire.

REPUBLIC ALUMINUM, INC., 1930 Evergreen Ave., Chicago, IL 60622 - (800) 248-1775 (312) 932-8000
frame material - aluminum   *color of frame* - white   *style* - casement
type of glass - dual insulating, Super G® with low-e argon, v-groove
features - The window is equipped with dual compression seals for air and water tightness. There is a multi-point locking system and the hinges are tamper resistant. The shelf is available as a vinyl-coated wire shelf or a tempered glass shelf.

THERMAL INDUSTRIES, INC., 4884 Duff Dr., Cincinnati, OH 45246 - (800) 445-0758 (513) 874-0501

frame material - vinyl   color of frame - white or earthtone color   style - casement

type of glass - ³/₁₆" dual insulating, low-e argon, low-e krypton, tinted, safety laminated glass roof, designer glass — beveled leaded • decra-led • jewel cut • etched • brass came

features - Colonial, diamond or prairie maintenance free grids are available. An optional lightweight Exolite shelf is available in bronze or clear for displaying your plants. The bulb seal weather-stripping eliminates any air or water infiltration. The hinges are of heavy-duty construction with concealed hinge hardware. The interior is specially treated birch or an optional oak veneer wood that is sanded to a high quality furniture finish. A sill muffler can be added for comfort and insulation. The windows are equipped with fiberglass screens for ventilation and to keep insects and dust from entering your home. The "Designer 290" has a multiple-point locking system.

VIKING INDUSTRIES, PO Box 20518, Portland, OR 97294 - (503) 667-6030

frame material - vinyl   color of frame - white, almond   style - slider

type of glass - ¾" insulating, low-e, argon gas, shading co-efficient glass

features - The bottom shelf is an insulated foam panel covered with prefinished aluminum. The window has a warm edge spacer and poly-pile weatherstripping to help with energy savings. A full nailing fin around the interior window frame saves energy with a weather-tight seal. A setting lip allows the window to bet on the sill and rotated into position. The windows are equipped with screens so hot air can escape. There is an adjustable wire shelve that offers natural airflow. The window has a lifetime warranty for defects in material and workmanship.

VINYL MAX, 114 17 Lippleman Rd., Cincinnati, OH 45246 - (800) 837-9103 (513) 772-2247

frame material - vinyl   color of frame - white, desert sand, autumn bronze   style - casement

type of glass - dual insulating, low-e, tempered glass roof

features -The 30° roof slope lets in light and allows proper water drainage. The window is equipped with multi-point locks. The hinges are stainless steel and tamper proof. There are dual weather seals for air and water tightness. The casement can be hinged to open toward or away from the house. The oak seat and side jambs can be stained or painted to match your decor. An optional insulated seat is available. The shelf is full width and is constructed of white coated wire.

WEATHER SHIELD, PO Box 309, Medford, WI 54451 - (800) 477-6808 (715) 748-2100

frame material - vinyl   color of frame - white, tan   style - casement

type of glass - Value R10 — three panes glass, two low-e squared surfaces and krypton gas between both airspaces, Value R6 — three panes with two argon-only filled airspaces and two low-e surfaces, Value R5 — one argon/krypton-filled airspace and two low-e surfaces, Value R4 — one argon-filled airspace and two low-e surfaces, Insul — single airspace with low-e surface

features - The "Visions 2000" has interior head/seatboard and jamb returns that are vinyl-laminated wood with the option of upgrading to True Oak™, Cherrywood™ or clear pine. A multi-point lock mechanism operates from a single sash lock that is mounted low on the frame. This locking system secures the window at the top and bottom of the frame for a safe and energy efficient seal. An optional plant shelf is available. Optional white or tan finished metal grilles for the airspace of insulating units is available. The aluminum framed screens are available in a white or tan finish.

Garden Window by Vinyl Max

The vinyl garden window is designed to be the perfect showplace for your plants and collectibles. Trim frame and sash profiles and a straight-through view create a maximized glass area. Operating windows on both sides allow fresh ventilation.

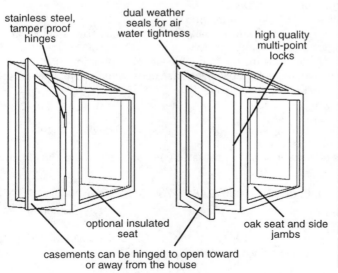

stainless steel, tamper proof hinges

dual weather seals for air water tightness

high quality multi-point locks

optional insulated seat

oak seat and side jambs

casements can be hinged to open toward or away from the house

Garden Window by Great Lakes

available with Hi R+ Plus™ low-e glass with argon gas

Traditional Series

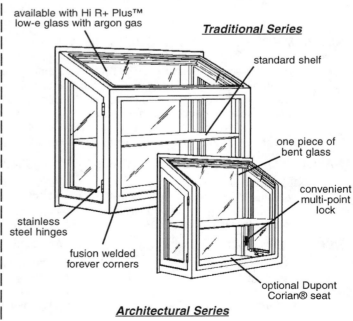

standard shelf

one piece of bent glass

convenient multi-point lock

stainless steel hinges

fusion welded forever corners

optional Dupont Corian® seat

Architectural Series

Fast, Simple Installation for Fen-Tech Windows

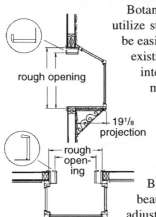

rough opening

19¹/₈ projection

rough opening

Botanica II™ Traditional style windows utilize standard window framing and can be easily and quickly installed in new or existing openings. In existing openings, interior wall is not disturbed and trim may be reapplied if desired. Botanica II™ Windows are available in custom sizes.

All Botanica II™ garden windows require underside support These decorative "Load Bear™" supports will accent and beautify underside supports. They are adjustable.

Botanica by Fen-Tech

- Curved profile adds attractive dimension to home exterior.
- Energy efficient — high performance, insulated glass with argon gas.
- MagiClean™ Glass — protective coating repels dirt and dust.
- Totally maintenance free, inside and out.
- Available in 4 colors — white • beige • brown • sierratone.
- Available in 4 sizes
- Maximum ventilation — side window sash opens to full 90°.

Do-it-Yourself Instructions for making a Garden Window

1) Plan the dimensions of this unit carefully before beginning construction. Allow enough space in the vertical measurements to accommodate the back-to-front slope of the slatted roof. Plan the width of the boxlike base so that your plants will be easy for you to tend.

2) Build the base first. Start by rabbeting the plant box 1×8's (*A,B*) to accommodate the plywood bottom to be attached later. Then glue and nail the 1×8's together, using butt joints.

3) Cut the bottom of the plant box (*C*) from ¾-inch exterior plywood. Size it to fit flush with the bottom of the 1×8's. Drill ½-inch drain holes in the plywood. Treat it and the inside of the 1×8's with wood preservative to prevent rot. Let dry. Nail the bottom piece to the 1×8's.

4) Cut two 1×4 verticals for the front of the greenhouse (*D*) and two longer ones for the back (*E*). Miter the tops of the verticals to the appropriate angle. Notch the longer verticals (*E*) to accept the 1×4 roof slat that will butt against and attach to the sidewalls of your house.

5) Fasten the verticals to the plant box as shown in the sketch. Use glue and screws.

6) Construct 1×6 "rafters" (*F*) as shown in the sketch. You'll need to angle-cut each end of the rafters and notch the back end to accommodate the roof slat closest to the house. Then cut the notches for the roof slats. Cut both

boards at the same time to ensure matching notches. Fasten the rafters to the uprights with glue and screws.

7) Cut 1×4 slats (*G*) to fit into the notches in the rafters. Cut small notches in the bottoms of the slats for drainage. Nail the slats to the rafters.

8) Build a frame for the front "window" of the unit from mitered 1×2's (*H,I*) and a 1×4 top piece (*J*). Notch the ends of the 1×2's as shown so that the 1×4 top piece will fit around the 1×6 rafters. Using glue and nails, fasten the frame members together.

9) Paint or stain the unit inside and out. Let dry.

10) Have pieces of ¹/₈-inch clear acrylic sheet cut to fit the top, sides, and front of the unit. Drill holes in the acrylic

(drill slowly to avoid cracks) and screw the top and side sheets to the inside of the greenhouse as shown. Attach the remaining piece of acrylic to the window frame, then screw the entire frame to the rest of the unit.

11) Fasten the greenhouse securely to the wall studs of the house, using lag screws driven through the rear 1×8 box member and the rear 1×4 roof slat.

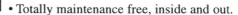

1×4 — G
drainage notch
1×4
¹/₈" acrylic sheet
1×2
F
1×6
1×4 E
D
B
1×8
H I
C
¾" exterior plywood

Passive solar home looks conventional

Q: I want to build a conventional-looking house that uses solar heating and cooling without the big solar roof collectors. I would like a spacious open floor plan. What solar features are best?

A: What you want to build is called a passive solar house. Passive solar means that there are no solar collectors, pumps, water tanks, etc. The house itself captures and stores the sun's heat in the winter and naturally stays cool in the summer.

A spacious open floor plan with many windows, lofts, cathedral ceilings, and sunrooms is a natural fit with passive solar heating and cooling. This allows the sun's warmth to naturally circulate throughout the house.

In most climates, it is possible to build a 100-percent solar house that looks conventional. Several companies now sell do-it-yourself passive solar home kits up to 4,000 square feet in size.

The keys to an effective passive solar house are high insulation, much south-facing glass and thermal mass built into the floors and walls. Having the proper ratio of glass area to thermal mass is important.

In the summer, a passive solar house stays comfortable without air-conditioning. The thermal mass absorbs excess heat in the daytime to keep the house cooler. Building a simple solar ventilation chimney creates a natural breeze throughout the house to cool it all day.

Four basic passive solar design features to use are direct gain windows, solar walls, sunrooms and solar roofs. To attain nearly 100-percent solar, a combination of all these features is needed. You'll still prob-

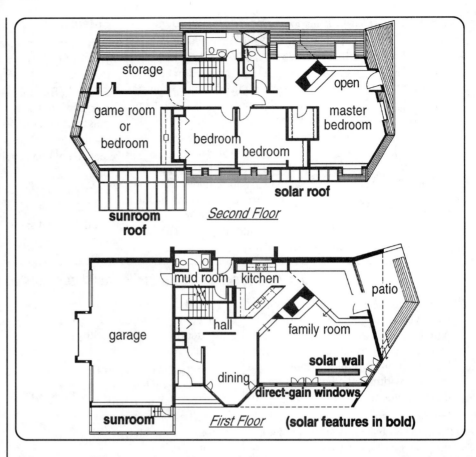

ably want a fireplace or small space heater for the coldest winter nights.

Direct solar gain with large south-facing windows is most effective for capturing the sunlight. Typically, a thick concrete floor covered with decorative ceramic tile is in front of the window to store the sun's heat. At night, ceramic tile is effective at slowly reradiating the heat out into your house.

A solar wall is a masonry or decorative stone wall (for thermal mass) built just inside a large south-facing window. A sunroom is effectively a giant solar collector. Its floors and walls store some of the solar heat for the night. The remainder of the heat circulates throughout the house in the day.

For summer comfort, the house should have large roof overhangs. These are attractive and block the summer sun which is high in the sky.

If you want to run a small window air-conditioner, the thermal mass stores the "coolth" and allows you to run it at lower off-peak nighttime electric rates.

Q: I want to place my new clothes dryer on an inside wall. It would be easiest to vent it upward through the roof. What is the best and most efficient way to vent it?

A: You must vent a dryer properly through the roof or it will constantly suck heated air out of your house. Use a special vent cover made just for roof venting. It seals very well when the dryer is not running. Twenty feet is about the maximum duct length or the air resistance may become too great.

Insulate the duct in the unheated attic area. Even in a mild climate, the moisture laden air inside the duct can sometimes condense and drip down.

You can use passive solar energy to heat and cool a house. Passive solar energy means that there are no roof collectors or mechanical systems (other than perhaps an indoor fan) to store and circulate the heat throughout the house. The walls and floor of the house itself store the solar heat.

Page 115 shows typical floor plan layouts of how several common passive solar features are incorporated in a house. The solar features are in bold italic type. Most of the features shown are for heating the house in the winter.

For summer cooling, a large roof overhang on the south and west sides is critical. Since the sun is higher in the sky in the summer than in the winter, the overhang will block the summer and let the winter sun shine in under it. Also for cooling, a whole-house fan is often used. This draws in cool air at night which cools the thermal mass in the walls and floor. The cool floors and walls moderate the daytime temperature increases. A small window air conditioner is also sometimes used. Operate it at lower nighttime off-peak electric rate.

One of the most important features of a passive solar house is adequate thermal mass in the walls and floors. See the chart above. Contact a local solar expert for guidelines for the relationship of thermal mass to glass area for your climate.

Thermal Storage Capacity

Material	Specific Heat Constant	Density	Total Heat Storage
	Btu/lb. °F	lb./ft.³	Btu/ft.³/°F
Adobe	0.22	90	20
Brick	0.20	120	24
Concrete	0.23	150	34.5
Earth	0.21	95	20
Sand	0.20	110	22
Steel	0.12	490	59
Stone	0.21	165	34.6
Water	1.00	62.5	62.5
Wood	0.33	32	10.6

Manufacturers of Kit Homes

AMOS WINTER HOMES, RR 5, Box 168B, Brattleboro, VT 05301 - (802) 254-3435 - panelized
DECK HOUSE (ACORN STRUCTURES), 930 Main St., Acton, MA 01720 - (800) 727-3325 - post and beam
DELTEC, PO Box 6279, Asheville, NC 28816 - (800) 642-2508 (704) 253-0483 - circular
ENERCEPT INC., 3100 Ninth Ave. SE, Watertown, SD 57201 - (605) 882-2222 - panelized
HELIKON DESIGN CORP., PO Box 48, Cavetown, MD 21720 - (800) 323-7863 (301) 824-2254 - circular
LINDAL CEDAR HOMES, PO Box 24426, Seattle, WA 98124 - (800) 426-0536 - cedar
N. AMERICAN HOUSE, PO Box 145, Point of Rocks, MD 21777 - (301) 694-9100 - modular
PAN ABODE, 4350 Lake Washington Blvd., N., Renton, WA 98056 - (800) 782-2633 - cedar
REAL LOG HOMES, PO Box 202, Hartland, VT 05048 - (800) 732-5564 - log
TIMBERLINE GEODESICS, 2015 Blake St., Berkeley, CA 94704 - (800) 366-3466 - dome
TRI-STEEL, 5400 S Stemmons, Denton, TX 76205 - (940) 497-7070 - steel
WILDERNESS LOG HOMES, PO Box 902, Plymouth, WI 53073 - (800) 237-8564 - log
WISCONSIN LOG HOMES, PO Box 11005, Green Bay, WI 54307 - (800) 678-9107 - log
YANKEE BARN HOMES, 131 Yankee Barn Rd., Grantham, NH 03753 - (800) 258-9786 - panelized

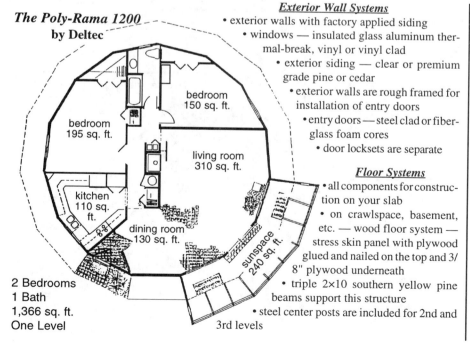

The Poly-Rama 1200
by Deltec

bedroom 150 sq. ft.
bedroom 195 sq. ft.
living room 310 sq. ft.
kitchen 110 sq. ft.
dining room 130 sq. ft.
sunspace 240 sq. ft.

2 Bedrooms
1 Bath
1,366 sq. ft.
One Level

Exterior Wall Systems
• exterior walls with factory applied siding
• windows — insulated glass aluminum thermal-break, vinyl or vinyl clad
• exterior siding — clear or premium grade pine or cedar
• exterior walls are rough framed for installation of entry doors
• entry doors — steel clad or fiberglass foam cores
• door locksets are separate

Floor Systems
• all components for construction on your slab
• on crawlspace, basement, etc. — wood floor system — stress skin panel with plywood glued and nailed on the top and 3/8" plywood underneath
• triple 2×10 southern yellow pine beams support this structure
• steel center posts are included for 2nd and 3rd levels

Roof Systems
• half scissor trusses of southern yellow pine bear against a center steel compression ring
• double 2×10 headers of southern yellow pine are built into all exterior wall panels resulting in roof loading capacity of over 45 lbs. per square foot
• all roof framing materials included—trusses, roof decking, felt, nails, truss anchor straps, panel jointing plates, roof hardware
• fascia/sub-fascia/soffits with factory applied vents
• optional ceiling insulation (R-19 or R-30)

Other Available Options
• decks — pressure treated lumber
• deluxe energy package R-19/R-30
• deluxe overhang
• pine or cedar lap siding over CDX plywood
• clear grade cedar RB and B
• fiberglass shingles
• 2×6 wall construction
• 9' and 10' wall heights
• hurricane (high wind load) strapping

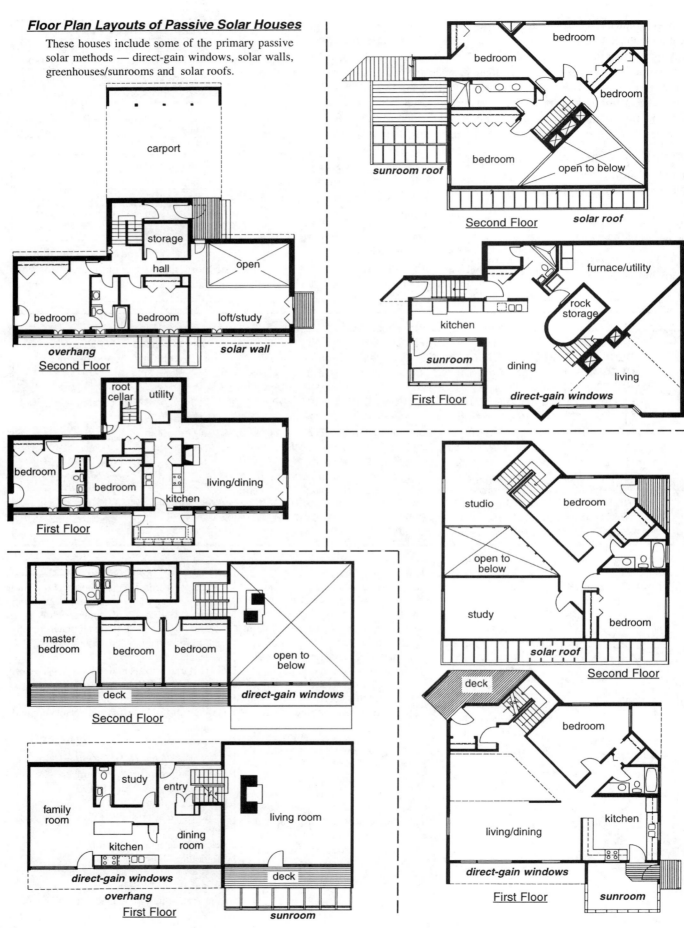

Floor Plan Layouts of Passive Solar Houses

These houses include some of the primary passive solar methods — direct-gain windows, solar walls, greenhouses/sunrooms and solar roofs.

carport

storage

hall

open

bedroom

bedroom

loft/study

overhang

Second Floor

solar wall

root cellar

utility

bedroom

bedroom

kitchen

living/dining

First Floor

bedroom

bedroom

sunroom roof

bedroom

bedroom

open to below

Second Floor

solar roof

furnace/utility

rock storage

kitchen

sunroom

dining

living

First Floor

direct-gain windows

master bedroom

bedroom

bedroom

deck

open to below

direct-gain windows

Second Floor

family room

study

entry

kitchen

dining room

living room

direct-gain windows

overhang

deck

First Floor

sunroom

studio

bedroom

open to below

study

bedroom

solar roof

Second Floor

deck

bedroom

living/dining

kitchen

direct-gain windows

First Floor

sunroom

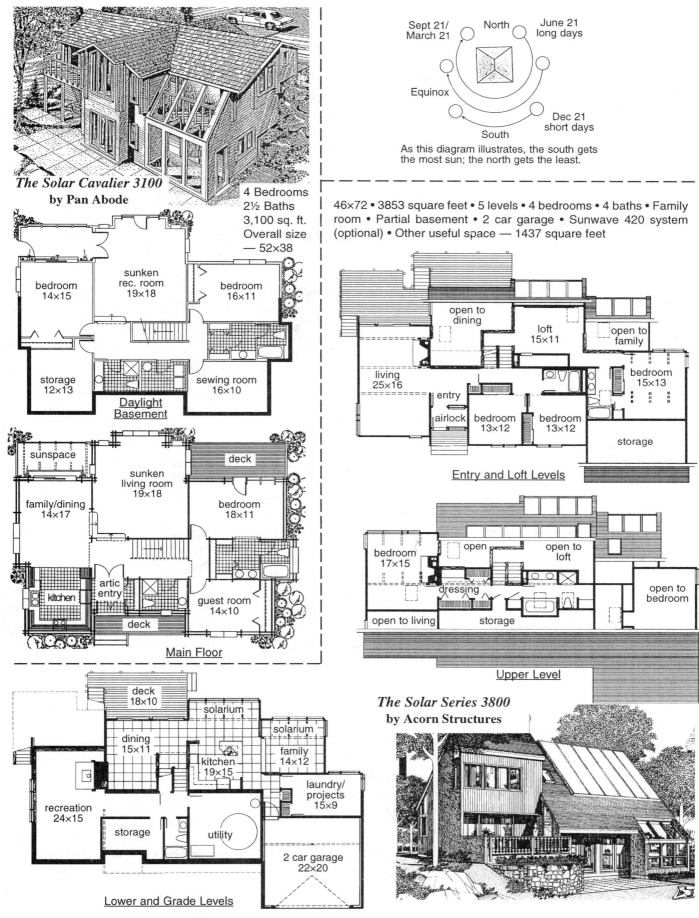

The Solar Cavalier 3100
by Pan Abode

4 Bedrooms
2½ Baths
3,100 sq. ft.
Overall size
— 52×38

Daylight Basement

bedroom
14×15

sunken
rec. room
19×18

bedroom
16×11

storage
12×13

sewing room
16×10

Main Floor

sunspace

family/dining
14×17

sunken
living room
19×18

deck

bedroom
18×11

kitchen

artic
entry

deck

guest room
14×10

Lower and Grade Levels

deck
18×10

solarium

dining
15×11

solarium

kitchen
19×15

family
14×12

recreation
24×15

storage

utility

laundry/
projects
15×9

2 car garage
22×20

Sept 21/
March 21

North

June 21
long days

Equinox

Dec 21
short days

South

As this diagram illustrates, the south gets
the most sun; the north gets the least.

46×72 • 3853 square feet • 5 levels • 4 bedrooms • 4 baths • Family
room • Partial basement • 2 car garage • Sunwave 420 system
(optional) • Other useful space — 1437 square feet

Entry and Loft Levels

open to
dining

loft
15×11

open to
family

living
25×16

entry

airlock

bedroom
13×12

bedroom
13×12

bedroom
15×13

storage

Upper Level

bedroom
17×15

open

open to
loft

dressing

open to
bedroom

open to living

storage

The Solar Series 3800
by Acorn Structures

116

New efficient easy-to-build sunspace kits

Q: I hate feeling like a mole each winter, so I'd like to add an efficient bright sunroom. My budget is tight, so I plan to install it myself. Are professionally-looking do-it-yourself kits available?

A: You are in luck. There are many new designs of reasonably-priced do-it-yourself sunroom kits ideal for your needs. If you install one on the south side, it may even provide some extra free heat for your home this winter.

With new computer-aided design methods, sunroom manufacturers have produced very efficient, durable kits. They use the newest technology in high-tech glass and clear plastics, shading methods and ventilation systems. Some manufacturers have over 100 sizes and shapes of sunroom kits to choose from.

Even the easiest-to-install kits, that literally bolt together like huge erector sets, have professionally-installed appearances. This is particularly true of models with real curved front glass. There is even a new mini-office sunroom kit complete with a desk, cabinets, drawers and computer wiring.

On most kits using aluminum or vinyl frames, all the structural members are precut, predrilled and color-coded for easy assembly. They also include all the required screws (rustproof stainless steel), seals, etc. You and a couple of friends can easily build a kit over a weekend.

Although more expensive, sunrooms with gently curved real wood frames are beautiful. If you like natural wood, but want low maintenance, select a kit with an aluminum-clad exterior. It never needs painting and is strong.

There are several important design and comfort features to consider when selecting your kit. If you

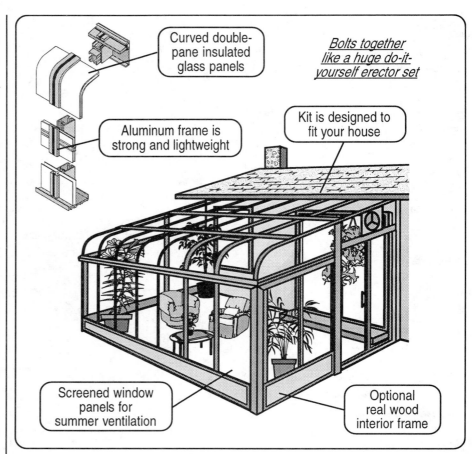

Curved double-pane insulated glass panels

Bolts together like a huge do-it-yourself erector set

Aluminum frame is strong and lightweight

Kit is designed to fit your house

Screened window panels for summer ventilation

Optional real wood interior frame

plan to get an aluminum-framed model for reasonable cost and easy assembly, select one with a thermally-broken frame. This frame design is efficient and minimizes condensation.

Even in cool climates, a sunroom can overheat in the afternoon summer sun. If you plan to use it throughout the day, select a kit with good ventilation and an easy-to-operate shading system. A kit with built-in channels for electric remote control or automatic shades and vents is most convenient.

One unique convertible sunroom kit has quick-change window panels that snap out. This exposes screens to create a summer porch. Another unique kit (Sun Crescent) has a semicircular design. It is actually five-sided, assembles easily and adds openness to any room.

The type of glazing is important for a year-round efficient and comfortable sunroom. Clear or tinted double-pane, low-e argon or Heat Mirror glass is most efficient. Double-pane clear acrylic, although it requires more gentle care than glass, is less expensive and assembles easily.

Q: I have wood siding on my older house and it is splitting in several spots. Is this a problem that should be fixed so that cold air does not leak into my house? How should I fix it?

A: It is not uncommon for siding to split due to repeated expansion/contraction cycles over the years. Although the air leakage through just a few cracks is not great, repair the cracks anyway.

If the cracks are longer than two feet, replace the entire piece. To repair shorter cracks, pry them open a little with a screwdriver. Squirt in waterproof exterior glue. Force the crack closed and nail it in place.

Manufacturers of Highest-Quality Sunrooms and Kits

BRADY ROOMS INC., 10A New Bond St., Worcester, MA 01603 - (800) 882-7239

glazing option - standard tempered and low-e glass

style - curved eave • straight eave

shading system - exterior solar screen system consisting of fiberglass mesh material mounted in aluminum frames

frame material - southern yellow pine wood interior with a clear polyurethane finish, aluminum exterior in dark bronze or white

ventilation - double vent awning or sliding windows • sliding doors • screens

features - Assembled in factory, delivered in one piece. All wood beams are curved eave in the interior. For a work-at home professional, the "Office Alcove" is delivered fully assembled, ready to use and attaches to your home in hours. Interior has been ergonomically designed for comfort and efficiency. Equipped with built-in oak cabinetry, 20 electrical outlets, 4 phone lines, 1 ISDN line, 2 cable outlets, slat walls for shelving flexibility, track lighting and many other features.

Conservatory

FLORIAN GREENHOUSE, 64 Airport Rd., W. Milford, NJ 07480 - (800) 356-7426 (973) 728-7800

glazing option - Heat Shield R-2.3 has 7/8" tempered over tempered double-sealed insulated glass with argon gas fill and is standard • Heat Shield Premium R-4.0 double sealed insulated with low-e coating and argon gas • Heat Shield Ultra R-4.8 with Heat Mirror XUV film with argon and barrier edge tape • Heat Shield Ultra Premium R-6.3 with Heat Mirror XUV film and krypton gas fill • Heat Shield Ultra Plus R-10.0 with Heat Mirror XUV film, krypton gas and low-e and barrier edge tape • all available in clear, bronze tint or Azurlite

style - curved eave • straight eave

shading system - exterior and interior roll-up shades, manual or motorized in a variety of materials

frame material - "Sierra" is aluminum with bronze or white baked-on enamel, dark bronze or clear anodized aluminum with thermal break • "Woodhaven" is laminated southern yellow pine or laminated knotty western red cedar interior with a painted bronze or white aluminum-clad exterior

ventilation - built-in vent with adjustable baffle for regulating airflow • single or triple-lite awning window with screens • optional intake louver and exhaust fan • doors — thermally broken wood or aluminum patio slider, single swing style or double swing style with tempered insulated glass

features - Heat Shield glass has lifetime warranty. Panic and handicap hardware available for doors. "Woodhaven" has thermally broken wood frame that is precut, predrilled and ready to assemble.

FOUR SEASONS SUNROOMS, 5005 Veterans Memorial Hwy., Holbrook, NY 11741 - (800) 368-7732 (516) 563-4000

glazing option - MC2 Wonderglass is tempered, double glazed with argon gas fill • MC3 Wonderglass is tempered, triple glazed with krypton gas fill • Heat Mirror with film and argon gas fill • polycarbonate • clear, solar bronze tint or Azurlite

style - curved eave • straight eave • conservatory

shading system - duet, pleated and window quilts • "Patio Sun 'N Shade Room" has built-in track shades

frame material - thermally-broken aluminum frames in bronze, white or sandtone finish • white pine or oak laminated beams with built-in shade tracks, aluminum-clad exterior in white or bronze

ventilation - roof vent • electrical fans • sliding, awning or casement windows with insect screens • sliding or swinging doors • French inswing or outswing doors • roof skylight vent with screens, manual or motorized

features - Wonderglass has lifetime limited warranty with 10 years full product replacement coverage. Grilles available for wood-clad casement windows. "SmartDeck" insulated flooring system available with optional aluminum underskin, for installations close to ground level, R-28 insulation value. Can be finished with carpet, tile or most other flooring types.

Straight Eave

LINDAL CEDAR SUNROOMS, PO Box 24426, Seattle, WA 98124 - (800) 426-0536

glazing option - standard clear tempered insulated glass • Heat Mirror • Heat Mirror Plus • low-e with argon gas fill • bronze tint

style - curved eave in aluminum frame only • straight eave • conservatory

shading system - exterior woven vinyl screens for solid-cedar sunrooms only that block 70 percent of the sun's heat

frame material - solid western red cedar • baked-on enamel finished white or bronze aluminum with thermal break

ventilation - cedar awning or casement windows with thermal glass, weatherstripping, fiberglass screens and bronze hardware • aluminum awning or sliding windows in white or bronze frames with screens • fullview glass panel swinging door, wood-framed for cedar rooms and metal-framed for aluminum rooms • wood or aluminum sliding glass door with sliding screen • fixed and opening wood-framed or aluminum-framed skylight • 9" or 12" Vent Axia exhaust fan with three-speed control and thermostat

features - Optional base or knee walls (solid cedar, 12" or 31" • aluminum, 11-1/2" or 21-1/2") available for furniture placement and electrical outlets. Cedar-framed sunroom mullions use bird's mouth joints for air and watertight connections. "Sun Crescent" is a semicircular sunroom design which is five-sided. "SunCorner" has two sides and is V-shaped with a unique hip roof. 10-year limited warranty.

OMEGA SUNSPACES, 3852 Hawkins NE, Albuquerque, NM 87109 - (800) 753-3034 (505) 344-0333

glazing option - Lexan XL transparent polycarbonate sheet with bronze tint • Lexan Thermoclear translucent polycarbonate sheet with an air space and a bronze tint or a pre-glazed insulated panel for the roof and curve

style - curved eave • straight eave

shading system - interior insulated roman pleat shades with metal mylar center layer, easily adjusted with a manual control wand, 100 percent light blockage, nylon guides slide easily in tracks, several decorative colors and patterns available, Add-A-Trak feature allows installation of the shade system either at time of construction or a later date • aluminum clad, insulated roof on some models

frame material - electrostatically applied bronze or white finished aluminum

ventilation - horizontal single or double pane regular or tempered sliding windows with screens and night locks, optional bronze tint • custom specialty glass windows available upon request • sliding patio or fullview swing doors with tempered safety glass • three-speeds (500, 750, 1000 cfm) and thermostatically controlled exhaust fan with rain sensor

features - An insulated (2" laminated panel) kneewall is standard. It has 1/8" hardboard siding (can be painted) in and out or can be finished in aluminum. Five colors/textures or aluminum to match your room. Electrical raceways in kneewall. Limited 5-year warranty.

SKYTECH SYSTEMS, 7030 New Berwick Hwy., Bloomsburg, PA 17815 - (800) 437-5795 (717) 752-1111

glazing option - dual insulated $7/8$" clear and bronze tint tempered glass is standard • $7/8$" tempered over laminated available for slopes • $7/8$" tempered over tempered • low-e • Heat Mirror • argon fill

style - curved eave • straight eave

shading system - interior track guided roman fold shades in several colors and fabrics, motorized or manual

frame material - thermally broken aluminum with a baked-on finish in Quaker bronze or white • wood in unfinished poplar, pine or cedar

ventilation - awning windows with screen • sliding glass door with screen and keyed lock • outswing door • approximately 960 cfm roof exhaust fan • "Intelligent Skylight" — thermostatically controlled and fully automatic ridge sash vent complete with rain sensor and screens, available in 3 foot panels up to 5 bays long (15 foot)

features - Also available is the "Mirage" system — this is an aluminum-and-glass window and wall folding system. The aluminum frames are available with a white or a Quaker bronze finish. The system comes complete with clear or bronze, low-e double insulated and safety tempered glass, dual weather seals and a thermally broken frame. The hardware is flush and it locks at the top and the bottom for maximum security. The trolley system only takes less than 12 pounds of force to open an average system. Maximum ventilation, over 92% opening. The systems can be manufactured up to 70 feet long with screens included. "Mirage 2" is a folding screen system, can be used with the folding wall or independently. See page 120 for more information and an illustration. Limited 5-year warranty.

Curved Eave

SOLAR INNOVATIONS, INC., 60 S. Prospect St., Hellam, PA 17406 - (800) 618-0669

glazing option - bronze tint low-e is the most popular • insulated tempered glass • clear, blue-green, bronze or gray tint • clear or solar cool reflective • low-e • argon fill • tempered over laminated • will work with you to get whatever you specify

style - curved eave • straight eave • conservatory

shading system - exterior solar shade screens

frame material - solid, hollow and thermally broken aluminum extrusions in sapphire blue, bronze, white, Caribbean blue, forest green, gray, lava black, natural clay, sandstone, terra cotta, terratone, wedgewood or any custom color can be matched • anodized finished can be ordered • clear, straight eave grained mahogany or other hardwoods available

ventilation - roof exhaust fan with approximately 800 cfm • sliding, single swing, Atrium or French doors • custom windows

features - The nits are made and put together to insure a proper fit. The sunrooms are then taken apart and finished, and all gaskets, foam and tape are installed prior to packaging. The glass/panels are structurally installed using double sided, sticky, closed cell, foam tapes which eliminates the need for heavy caulking.

SUN ROOM DESIGNS, Depot & First Sts., Youngwood, PA 15697 - (800) 621-1110 (724) 925-1100

glazing option - single or double insulated glass • low-e • tempered • frosted • bronze tint • Heat Mirror • argon fill • laminated • reflective • solar cool bronze and clear

style - curved eave • straight eave

shading system - quilted insulated fabric shades in decorator colors and patterns, with light blocking or light diffusing thermal/vapor barrier, manual or motorized models available • Llumar roof shades • Sunblocker panels for roof and knee walls glazed in like regular glass, wood interior with bronze or white exterior

frame material - red oak, cedar, poplar or mahogany wood clad aluminum, the wood and aluminum are interlocking without laminating, bonds or fasteners (see diagram) • baked enamel and electrostatically applied in bronze or white • aluminum frame also available with thermal break

ventilation - aluminum sliding doors, thermally broken with insulated glass panel • wood clad hinged door • swing door with deadbolt and key throw bolt • insulated or uninsulated sliding window • wood or aluminum awning style window • gable end exhaust fans with thermostatic control • roof exhaust fans • aluminum skylight

Main support bar assembly
Wood clad aluminum

features - The "SunBlocker" room has a wood interior ceiling and skylights but still has sides and curved eave areas of glass to give you a nice view. There is a patented variable pitch option — it adjusts slope to give a custom look to any installation. It is a good choice for low overhangs.

SUNSHINE ROOMS, 3333 N. Mead, Wichita, KS 67204 - (800) 222-1598 (316) 838-0033

glazing option - single pane where insulated glass not required • dual pane • dual pane laminated blocks up to 99 percent of ultraviolet radiation • dual pane Heat Mirror with a clear film suspended between panes and low-e coating • all available in clear, $3/16$" bronze tint, $3/16$" solar cool reflective bronze tint or low-e coating

style - curved eave • straight eave

shading system - interior insulated fabric that is moistureproof, mildew and fade-resistant, gravity-fed or motorized metal batten roll on nylon gliders with the ComfortGlide built-in shade tracks • interior roman shades available in 58 colors • exterior fixed or roll-drop shades available in 10 colors

frame material - electrostatically applied, baked-on bronze or white aluminum with thermal break • red oak, American ash, mahogany or walnut with exterior aluminum

ventilation - roof-mounted fan with thermostat and motor-operated damper • awning or sliding window with screen • foam-filled steel frame and insulated glass hinged door with keyed lock and deadbolt • thermally broken sliding insulated glass door with screen and keyed lock • double-insulated, tempered glass skylight with several options

features - The sunrooms are vailable with detailed do-it-yourself instructions and a videotape to help you with construction of the unit. Most components are precut, predrilled and prepunched for quick and accurate assembly. The "Tearduct Weepage Control" helps prevent moisture problems by draining moisture down dual hidden channels to sloped sills where it is forced outside. Stainless steel screws are used throughout to prevent rust. Custom sunrooms are available for applications where a standard model does not meet your needs.

TEXAS ALUMINUM INDUSTRIES, INC., 2900 Patio Dr., Houston, TX 77017 - (800) 231-4009 (713) 946-9000

<u>glazing option</u> - curved eave glass is 3/16" tempered over 3/16" clear with 1/4" bronze spacer • clear or insulated glass standard • bronze tint as option • tinted lexan

<u>style</u> - curved eave

<u>shading system</u> - The "DayStar Sunroom" has a 3-1/2" insulated R-23 roof system ("Starlight" with 3" roof of R-21) with a white or eggshell factory painted finish that meets the curved eave glass.

<u>frame material</u> - white or bronze aluminum frame, thermally broken

<u>ventilation</u> - horizontal sliding windows • sliding door with lockset • fullview steel clad security door with lockset and deadbolt • skylights

<u>features</u> - Hidden fan beams are optional in the roof system for enclosed wiring. Hidden electrical raceways and floor channels hide wiring and conduit.

VEGETABLE FACTORY, 495 Post Rd. East, Westport, CT 06880 - (800) 221-2550 (203) 454-0040

<u>glazing option</u> - GE Lexan polycarbonate roof • double pane Plexiglas DR acrylic sides in clear or bronze

<u>style</u> - straight eave

<u>shading system</u> - exterior slide-in aluminum-framed fiberglass mesh fabric screens for summer use, hinged in 3'×3' sections, blocks up to 75% • interior blankets for winter use are rigid polypropylene double-wall sections

<u>frame material</u> - baked-on bronze or white enamel finished aluminum

<u>ventilation</u> - self-storing windows with screens • top ridge screened vents • left or right-hinged storm/screen combination door with insulated panel • exhaust fan (760, 1,250 or 3,000 cfm) and motorized intake

<u>features</u> - The sunroom can be converted quickly to a screen room by flipping the latch and removing the panels.

WINDSOR VINYL, 3913 Todd Ln., Austin, TX 78744 - (888) 727-4464

<u>glazing option</u> - triple wall polycarbonate roof • clear, solar cool or bronze gray • low-e • High Performance southern low-e

<u>style</u> - conservatory

<u>shading system</u> - A 3" insulated roof is available on the "SunRoom" model.

<u>frame material</u> - multichambered vinyl extrusions are metal reinforced for strength in white, bronze (brown) or oak woodgrain

<u>ventilation</u> - dual pane, insulated awning, casement, fixed, horizontal or tilt-n-turn windows with screens • swing or French doors • doors and windows have multi-point locking systems • skylights • operable roof vents • solar-powered exhaust roof fan

<u>features</u> - Custom built to meet your requirements and preconstructed for easier installation. Insulated walls are available for above and below the windows. Stained glass and brass handles available. 10-year guarantee on all materials. pitch option — it adjusts slope to give a custom look to any installation. It is a good choice for low overhangs.

- -

Mirage — Folding Glass Walls and Windows by Skytech

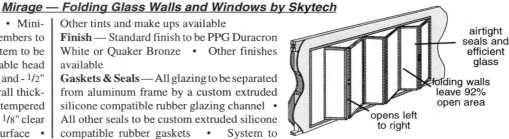

Framing — All aluminum 6063-T6 • Minimum wall thickness .080 • Sill members to have positive water control • System to be 100% thermally broken • Adjustable head can accommodate tolerance of + 1/4" and - 1/2"

Glazing — All glass to be 7/8" overall thickness • 1/8" clear/bronze tinted safety tempered • 5/8" black air spacer, dual sealed • 1/8" clear safety tempered with low-e on #3 surface •

Other tints and make ups available

Finish — Standard finish to be PPG Duracron White or Quaker Bronze • Other finishes available

Gaskets & Seals — All glazing to be separated from aluminum frame by a custom extruded silicone compatible rubber glazing channel • All other seals to be custom extruded silicone compatible rubber gaskets • System to

airtight seals and efficient glass

folding walls leave 92% open area

opens left to right

- -

The Intelligent Skylight by Skytech

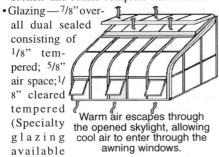

- All aluminum skylight is 100% thermally-broken and comes complete with screens
- Glazing — 7/8" overall dual sealed consisting of 1/8" tempered; 5/8" air space; 1/8" cleared tempered (Specialty glazing available — tints, low-e or Heat Mirror.)

Warm air escapes through the opened skylight, allowing cool air to enter through the awning windows.

- When temp. reaches the thermostat control setting, the skylight opens allowing the warm air to escape through the vent. Closed it forms a weather tight seal.
- Comes with a rain sensor
- Color options of white or quaker bronze Duracron acrylic baked enamel
- Fully automatic ridge sash vent

How to convert your sunroom to a heat-producing sunspace

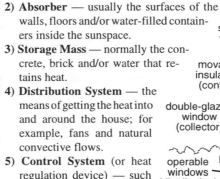

1) **Collector** — such as the double layer of greenhouse window glazing.
2) **Absorber** — usually the surfaces of the walls, floors and/or water-filled containers inside the sunspace.
3) **Storage Mass** — normally the concrete, brick and/or water that retains heat.
4) **Distribution System** — the means of getting the heat into and around the house; for example, fans and natural convective flows.
5) **Control System** (or heat regulation device) — such as movable insulation used to prevent heat loss from the sunspace at night, roof overhangs that block the summer sun, thermostats that activate fans, vents for summer ventilation, doors and operable windows for heat transfer to adjoining rooms.

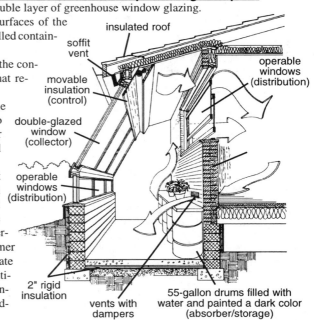

insulated roof

soffit vent

operable windows (distribution)

movable insulation (control)

double-glazed window (collector)

operable windows (distribution)

2" rigid insulation

vents with dampers

55-gallon drums filled with water and painted a dark color (absorber/storage)

Do-it-yourself sunroom is inexpensive and easy to build

Q: I want an attached sunroom, but my budget won't allow a fancy do-it-yourself kit. How can I design and build an inexpensive one myself? I want to use it for living space, growing plants and passive solar heating

A: You have several sunroom options if you are on a limited budget. There are low-cost do-it-yourself starter sunroom kits available that offer add-on sections as your budget allows. Look for ones with simple lightweight aluminum framing and clear acrylic plastic windows.

The least expensive do-it-yourself sunroom option is to build one from scratch. If you are handy with tools, you should be able to build an attractive and efficient 8x12-foot sunroom for less than $500.

For the lowest cost, size the sunroom in multiples of four feet to minimize waste. If you plan future improvements or expansion as your budget allows, initially design and size the framing and window/door placement accordingly.

The best design depends on how you plan to use your sunroom. For use primarily for living space and a few plants, a vertical front wall design is best. This provides more headroom and simplifies the installation of doors. A partial solid roof provides afternoon shade to minimize overheating.

A slanted front design is simpler to build and reduces material costs, especially the roofing. This design is ideal for a greenhouse that is used primarily for gardening and solar heating. For just starting plants, a simple solar cold frame is an inexpensive option.

True solar south is the best orientation of the sunroom. Check with

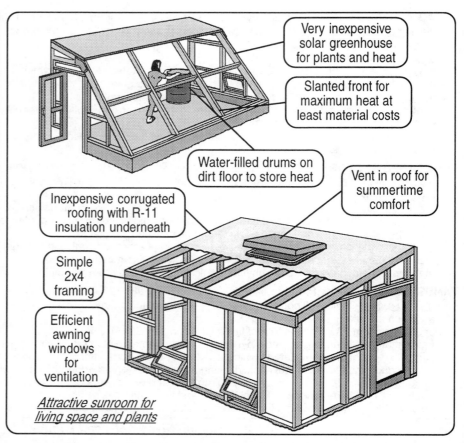

- Very inexpensive solar greenhouse for plants and heat
- Slanted front for maximum heat at least material costs
- Water-filled drums on dirt floor to store heat
- Vent in roof for summertime comfort
- Inexpensive corrugated roofing with R-11 insulation underneath
- Simple 2x4 framing
- Efficient awning windows for ventilation

Attractive sunroom for living space and plants

your local weather service because it varies from compass south. Very few houses face directly south. Within 30 degrees to either side is acceptable. Note nearby trees and try to anticipate the shade patterns.

Use 2x4 studs for the basic sunroom framing. Clear acrylic plastic, available at home centers, is inexpensive, lightweight, easy to cut and maintains it clarity. Temporary use of thick translucent plastic film is a very low-cost option for the sides.

Although it is more work, make separate weatherstripped frames for the windows so that they can be replaced by screens in the summer. Screen Tight and Snapscreen make simple screening attachment kits. One strip is nailed to the window frame and a finishing trim strip snaps in trapping the screen.

To maintain an even sunroom temperature and provide winter heating for your house, some type of thermal storage mass is needed. Brick or concrete flooring is effective. Also, using bricks or concrete blocks to support tables or planting trays adds thermal mass.

Q: I am planning to install an efficient range hood as you recommended last year, but I am having difficulty sizing it properly. I do not understand why the instructions limit the number of duct bends to two?

A: The proper size range hood (measured in cubic feet per minute of air flow - cfm) is based on the size, shape and height above your range. The range hood salesman can help you determine the cfm required.

As bends and length are added to the duct, there is more air flow resistance which reduces the actual cfm of the range hood. If you need more than the two bend limit, buy a higher-cfm rated range hood.

Footings

A footing in the ground is intended to make sure that the weight of the sunroom, along with any superimposed

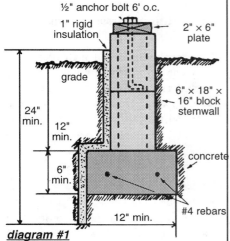

½" anchor bolt 6' o.c.

1" rigid insulation

2" × 6" plate

grade

24" min.

12" min.

6" × 18" × 16" block stemwall

6" min.

concrete

12" min.

#4 rebars

diagram #1

weight load, such as snow or wind, is evenly distributed. A typical solar sunroom weighs very little. However, wind could be troublesome when it is an upward force that could conceivably shake your sunroom loose if you leave the door open. Anchoring in a good solid footing will prevent both the problems of weight distribution and the vagaries of the wind. Moreover, a good footing below the frost line will prevent winter frost from heaving the structure.

You can use a wooden footing if you desire, as long as it is anchored securely in the ground. Why not use concrete? Build your sunroom to last, and leave something for archeologists to ponder 500 years from now. Here is one footing option: Diagram #1 depicts a conventional footing that conforms to the Uniform Building Code. The footing and stem wall insulation should extend at least 24 inches below the ground on the outside of the masonry. This assures that the heat transmitted through the glazing is soaked up in the floor and not lost to the ground outside.

Framing

Methods of framing a solar sunroom vary, depending on the type of glazing you plan to use, the weather in your area, and the way in which the sunroom will communicate with your house. The type of glazing you choose will determine the frame spacing you will need to construct; refer to the section on glazing for the choices available.

A sunroom that has a vertical south face will be cooler in the summer. A vertical wall will collect 25 percent less solar energy from October through April than a wall built at a 60° angle, but the same wall will conduct only half as much heat energy in the summer months. A vertical wall also allows for more interior space, and is easier to insulate against nighttime heat loss.

You will have to make some compromises when deciding upon the right design for your location and purposes. You may want maximum winter performance, which means an angled south wall. In this case, the summer heat can be reduced by an additional investment in some kind of shades, vents or electric or solar powered-exhaust fan.

Good ventilation is extremely important for proper temperature control. A vent should promote the natural flow of air from a low entry to a high exit across the sunroom. The vent placement should be such that the prevailing summer breeze pushes right through the vents. When you design the vents, try to recall the direction the summer wind comes from most of the time in your location. The low vent should face the prevailing wind.

Diagrams #3, #4, #5, and #6 illustrate framing designs you might consider. Use these designs as guides. Select the best features of each, and then make a sketch of your own personal design to be sure you don't forget anything. Use cross-hatched graph paper and an architectural scale with a straightedge to draw where each board, door, window, etc., will be placed. Remember, a 2×4 is really 1½ inches x 3½ inches; a 2×6 is really 1½ inches x 5½ inches, and so on.

A word about finishing: paint all components that will be in contact with water or soil with copper naphthenate; paint all framing a light color before the glazing is applied. Use latex base paint.

Glazing

No glazing material is best. Every product has advantages and disadvantages. The type you choose is determined by appearance, cost, and how you intend to use your sunroom. An optically clear

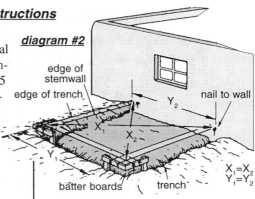

diagram #2

edge of stemwall

edge of trench

nail to wall

Y_2

X_1

X_2

Y_1

batter boards

trench

$X_1 = X_2$
$Y_1 = Y_2$

product like glass will let direct rays through, while a plastic like fiberglass will scatter the rays into what is known as a diffuse pattern. Diffuse lighting is preferable for plant growth.

Glass is optically clear, can withstand high temperatures, and can be heat-treated to withstand impact. If you choose to use glass, one convenient technique is to design your framing for double glazed patio door replacement panels. They come in 28-inch × 76-inch, 34-inch × 76-inch, 46-inch × 76-inch, 34-inch × 92-inch, 46-inch × 92-inch, and other sizes. Check your glass supplier for prices and availability. Be sure to pinch off the vent in the panel before installation since this stabilizes the air pressure. Use a generous amount of silicone sealant around all sides of the window.

There is fairly clear, .007-inch laminated plastic film available which is very tough and has been successfully tested for long-term weatherability. It comes in a 4-foot-wide roll. Clear polycarbonate (Lexan) and acrylic (Plexiglas) are other easy-to-work with options. Most other plastics, like fiberglass, are translucent — they let the light in, but you can't see through them. If you prefer plastic, be sure the product you choose transmits at least 85 percent of the solar spectrum and is ultraviolet stabilized. A sunroom dealer can help you with this.

A very convenient but expensive material is Thermoclear polycarbonate which comes in a very strong, lightweight, and double-glazed 4-foot-wide sheet. You can nail it with self-sealing nails after you thoroughly seal the cells with silicone. Use nothing but silicone and be sure that penetration is at least one-half-inch on all cells. The most important aspect of the glazing process is to be sure to seal every

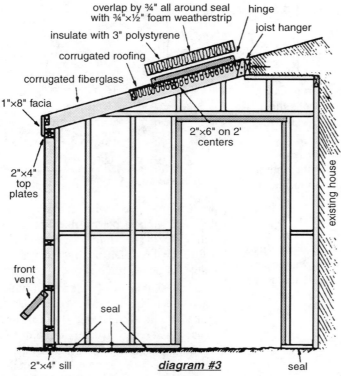

overlap by ¾" all around seal
with ¾"×½" foam weatherstrip

hinge

insulate with 3" polystyrene

joist hanger

corrugated roofing

corrugated fiberglass

1"×8" facia

2"×6" on 2'
centers

2"×4"
top
plates

existing house

front
vent

seal

2"×4" sill

diagram #3

seal

joint. Your sunroom must be airtight. Use good quality sealant — at least a polymer and preferably silicone.

Heat Storage

Without a lot of dense materials (such as adobe, concrete block, water containers, etc.), the air temperature inside your sunroom could vary considerably from day to night. The addition of thermal mass will stabilize sunroom temperatures. When you have completed your sunroom, one option is to install some dark-colored (black, brown, or green) 55-gallon drums

diagram #4

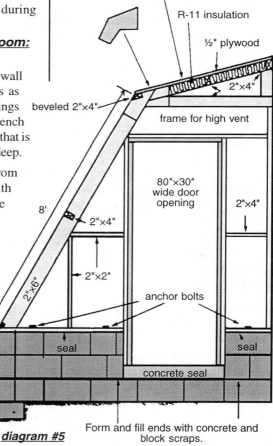

jamb

vent

4'

in the sunroom. Fill them with water, add one-fourth cup of sodium dichromate as a corrosion inhibitor in each drum, cover them, and use them as supports for the benches you will construct on which you will place planting boxes for vegetables, flowers, and so on. Although not quite as effective, use concrete blocks or, better yet, solid bricks, as supports. The growing beds, insulated floor, massive north wall, and water-filled drums should provide the heat storage you need. To make sure the heat stored in the sunroom is transferred to your house, install a thermostatically-controlled fan to blow warm air into the house during the winter.

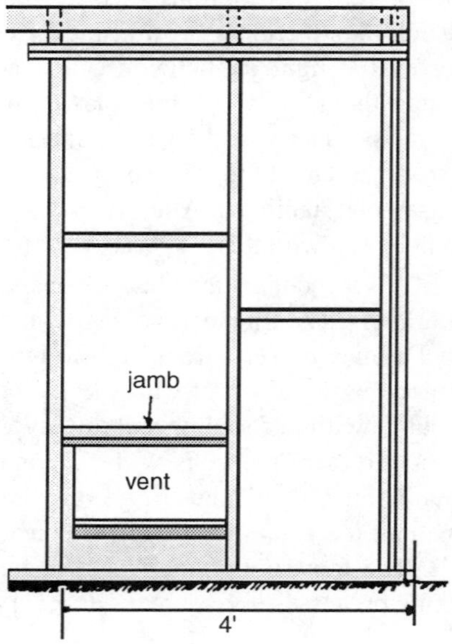

Building a Typical Solar Sunroom: Step-by-Step Instructions

1) Lay out the footing and stem wall using batter boards and strings as shown in diagram #2. The strings define the edge of the footing trench and the stem wall. Dig a trench that is 12 inches wide and 18 inches deep.

2) Place ½ inch rebar 3 inches from the bottom. Block it in place with flat stones or stakes with the rebar wired onto the stakes. Pour concrete into the trench at least 6 inches deep. Use a level and trowel to form a smooth level top surface.

3) When the footing is firm, lay the stem wall, using mortar mix for the joints. Stagger the vertical joints.

4) Every 4 feet, fill the core with concrete or mortar mix. Fill the other cores with vermiculite insulation or tamped dirt if most of the stem is below grade. Leave 4 inches of each core unfilled and then pour in concrete or mortar. Don't forget to install the anchor bolts for the sill plate.

5) Place a minimum of 1-inch thick polystyrene bead board 24 inches into the ground on the outside of the stem wall and footing. This assures that the heat transmitted through the glazing is soaked up in the floor and not lost to the ground outside. The foundation and stem wall should now be complete.

6) Place the front sill plate in position by indenting each anchor bolt location and drilling holes to slide the plate in place. Using the sill plate as the first member, lay out the south face on level spot and nail the sill, studs, and headers with 16-penny nails, as shown in diagram #7.

7) Place the front face in position with

shingles, corrugated roofing, etc.

R-11 insulation

½" plywood

beveled 2"×4"

2"×4"

frame for high vent

8'

2"×4"

2"×6"

80"×30"
wide door
opening

2"×4"

2"×2"

anchor bolts

2"×2"

6"×8"×16"
blocks

seal

concrete seal

seal

Form and fill ends with concrete and block scraps.

diagram #5

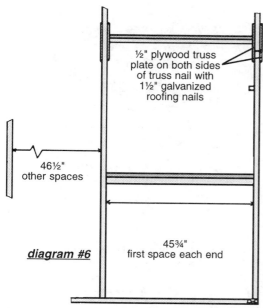

½" plywood truss plate on both sides of truss nail with 1½" galvanized roofing nails

46½" other spaces

45¾" first space each end

diagram #6

strips of insulation, weatherstripping or caulk between the sill and stem wall to cut off possible air leaks. Brace to the desired upright angle.

8) Cut the side sills, permanently seal, and put into position.

9) Affix a 2×6 ledger on the house. You can nail through the existing siding into the house studs; use lead anchors and lag screws; or whatever means are appropriate for your house (see diagram #3).

10) Place roof joist hangers on the ledger in their proper locations.

11) Cut and nail 2×6 roof joists to fit the angle of the roof, the joist hanger, and the front face. If the house and south face are not parallel, custom-fit each joist.

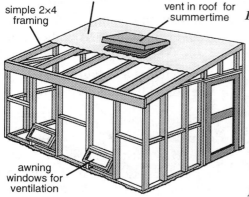

Simple sunroom with vertical front for living space and growiug some plants

12) Cut the end members to fit the roof and front face contour, door, and vents. The framing is now complete.

13) Let's assume that the roof is made of corrugated steel. The safest method for avoiding roof air leaks is to caulk all seams and pop-rivet the sections into a continuous strip. You can also use an abundance of lead-headed roofing nails to put the roof in place.

14) Insulate between the joists with roll fiberglass insulation (6-inch fiberglass has a heat resistance rating of R-19), stapled in place with no folds or tucks.

15) Finish the interior ceiling with masonite,

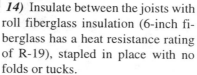

corners

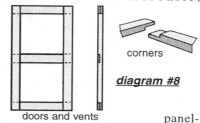

diagram #8

doors and vents

paneling, or green waterproof sheetrock. Seal and nail rigid corrugated fiberglass to roof portions that are not opaque. (A polyethylene vapor barrier could be installed if desired.) Add the front fascia plate when the roof is completely built. Paint the entire frame with an exterior latex-base house paint.

17) Glazing is next. Nail acrylic, polycarbonate, or Tedlar-coated rigid fiberglass on the inside and outside of the studs. Be sure to generously apply caulking to the studs before attaching each sheet. Finish the inside and outside seams with trim made of prepainted batten strips. Don't skimp on the nails for these operations.

18) Construct the vents and doors to fit the openings you provided. The main key is the provision of

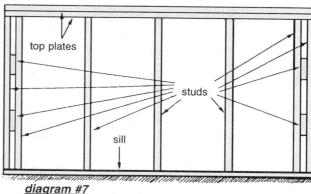

top plates

studs

sill

diagram #7

strong corners. Test the hinges by simulating the movement of the device before notching or attaching hinges. Weatherstrip all moving joints.

19) Place dark-colored 55-gallon drums inside the sunroom (as discussed in Heat Storage). If you can comfortably fit more than five storage drums inside the sunroom, add as many as you desire. It is difficult to get too much thermal storage mass. Also use concrete blocks and bricks wherever possible.

20) Get a fan and 110-volt thermostat that can be set at 90°F. Wire the thermostat into the lead and plug into a socket. The fan will blow hot air into your house when the sunroom reaches 90°F during the winter. You should also get a mini/max thermometer which will tell you the temperature swings in the sunroom. Adjust the house blower so the sunroom temperature does not rise above 95°F and harm your plants. Each installation requires experimentation to achieve optimum results

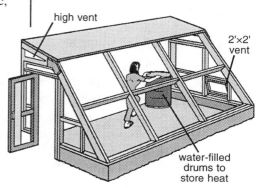

Very low-cost simple sunroom with slanted front used just for solar heat gain and starting plants

Use natural copper and silver ions to purify pool

Q: The chlorine chemicals for my swimming pool and hot tub water are expensive and irritate my eyes and skin. Are ionization (no-chemical) purifiers effective and expensive to operate?

A: Natural ionization water purification (copper and silver ions) has been used for centuries. The settlers in the 1800's tossed silver and copper coins in their water barrels. Notice how wishing wells are crystal clear due to the pennies and dimes.

Harsh purification chemicals, often chlorine and bromine, are an irritant to many people - stinging eyes, dry skin and hair, bleached bathing suits and that medicinal smell.

Using an electric or solar-powered ionization purifier can reduce the chlorine chemical usage by up to 80%. Many systems have been tested and are now approved by the National Sanitation Foundation (NSF).

Solar-powered models operate for free. Electric (120-volt) ion purifiers use only about 20 watts - about as much electricity as a small night light.

An ionizer produces very low levels of copper and silver ions in the water. These low ion levels (0.2 parts copper per million parts of water) are safe for people and animals, but are lethal to algae, bacteria and viruses.

The simplest ionizer, Floatron, is a solar-powered model. It is one-foot in diameter and floats on the water. A built-in solar panel on the top converts the sun's rays into a low-voltage electric charge to power it.

Another solar-powered model, Solarcide, mounts on the side of the pool. It uses a small solar panel and the purifying electrode hangs in the

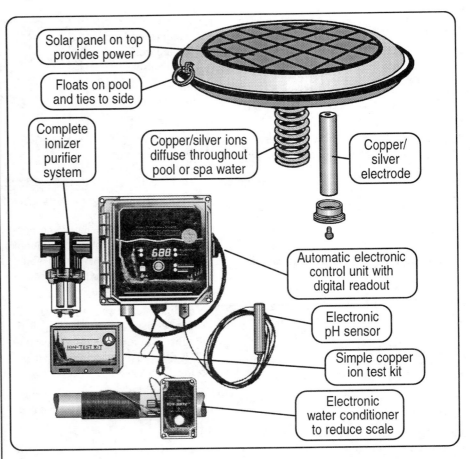

Solar panel on top provides power

Floats on pool and ties to side

Complete ionizer purifier system

Copper/silver ions diffuse throughout pool or spa water

Copper/silver electrode

Automatic electronic control unit with digital readout

Electronic pH sensor

Simple copper ion test kit

Electronic water conditioner to reduce scale

strainer. As the water flows through the copper/silver electrode, ions are given off.

The electric-powered models create a safe low voltage between two copper/silver electrodes. The electrodes are mounted in the filter plumbing where the water picks up the ions and carries them into the pool or spa.

New electronic models are simple to install and use. Some have a digital readout to indicate how fast ions are being produced. Other options include a pH sensor/readout and electronic water conditioners.

Unlike chlorine or bromine which evaporates relatively fast, copper and silver ions tend to maintain a safe residual purifying level in the water.

Using a simple test kit, the copper ion level is checked frequently at first until it reaches the proper level. Then the electronic control is set to maintain that level automatically with less frequent checks.

Q: The window in our oven is so dirty that we have to open the door to see how the foods are baking and this wastes heat. What is the best way to thoroughly clean an oven window?

A: You should be able to clean the window with common spray oven cleaner just like the rest of the oven interior. Although I do not bake a lot, I use oven cleaner on my glass fireplace doors. It cuts the soot fast.

If you want to clean the interior glass surfaces (all are double pane) you must remove the oven door and disassemble it. Be sure to mark the inside and outside glass panes. They are made of different types of glass.

Manufacturers of Ionization Swimming Pool and Spa Purification Systems

CARDINAL CONTROLS, INC., 570 North St., Longwood, FL 32750 - (407) 260-6301

power - 120 volts   capacity - pools — up to 50,000 gallons

features - The "Sterling 4000" is easy to use…the controller buttons allow a quick adjustment to correct the levels of ion.

CAREFREE CLEARWATER LTD., PO Box 204, Cornelia, GA 30531 - (800) 364-5710 (706) 778-9416

power - 120 volts • 220 volts   capacity - Model 1100 — spas/pools up to 25,000 gallons • Model 1000-S — spas/pools up to 25,000 gallons. • Model 1200-R — pools 15,000 to 45,000 gallons

features - These units come with a lifetime warranty. Model "1100" has a variable power output for spas and pools. Model "1000-S" has an LED display for switchable power settings for pool or spa operation. It has a clear acrylic view cover that is tamper proof. The enclosures are watertight and weatherproof.

CARIBBEAN CLEAR, PO Box 539, Batesburg, SC 29006 - (800) 431-4854

power - 120 volts • 220 volts   capacity - Model SPA-II — up to 1,000 gallons • Model 15-R — spas/pools up to 15,000 gallons • Model 25-R — spas/pools up to 25,000 gallons • Model 50-R — pools up to 50,000 gallons

features - "Model 50R" has a digital display of both the water temperature and the ion current. The other models have a performance indicator to advise the user of proper operation.

CLEARWATER ENVIRO TECHNOLOGIES, INC., 1054 Kapp Dr., Clearwater, FL 34625 - (813) 562-5186

power - 120 volts   capacity - spas/pools — up to 2,000 gallons • pools — up to 50,000 gallons

features - The "Galaxy" (see page 4) is a complete package and includes — the micro-processor control box in a durable weatherproof box • the "Ion-Mate", an electronic water conditioner and descaler • pH probe, plugs into the control box and gives a digital readout of the pools pH level.

CRYSTAL KING, G-5254 S. Saginaw St., Flint, MI 48507 - (800) 243-5464 (810) 694-3300

power - 120 volts • 240 volts   capacity - spas/pools — up to 50,000 gallons

features - These units are portable or available as in-line applications. The electronics are housed in a plastic weatherproof box for outdoor installation. The panel has three lights to indicate the operating condition. The electrodes are housed in a clear plastic housing for visual verification of their condition.

CRYSTAL POOL TECHOLOGIES, INC., 1301 S. Genesee Ave., Los Angeles, CA 90019 - (213) 965-1901

power - n/a   capacity - Model 100-A for in-ground pools • Model 2001-A for spas and on-ground pools

features - The "Algae Inhibitor" is an in-line water treatment system. It is a sealed cylinder with a series of zinc plates on the inside. Each plate has staggered kidney-shaped openings that generate internal eddies and channels as water flows through the device. This hydraulic action causes the plates to erode slowly, adding tiny amounts of zinc to the water. Half of it becomes zinc ions — attacks the non-chlorophyllous algae, the other half zinc oxide — fights chlorophyllous algae.

ECOSMARTE, 730 West 78th St., Richfield, MN 55423 - (800) 466-7946

power - 120 volts • 240 volts   capacity - spas — 1,000 to 10,000 gallons • pools — up to 50,000 gallons

features - The "Excalibar" has a two-stage process — the catadyne process that is similar to ionization (100% pure copper with coating electrode) and the anadyne process with chemical-free oxidation (proprietary titanium composite material electrode). You select "ionize" or "oxidize" on the control panel. The titanium electrode is used 4 to 6 hours per day in pools, and only when you use the spa. The copper electrode is used once a week.

ENVIRONMENTAL WATER PRODUCTS, 9316 Deering Ave., Chatsworth, CA 91311 - (818) 718-1795

power - 120 volts • 240 volts   capacity - SBX-65 — pools up to 20,000 gallons • SBX-75A — pools up to 23,000 gallons • SBX-75A with pool + option — pools up to 50,000 gallons

features - The power consumption for these units is only 20 watts. The "SBX-65" has a heavy duty indoor/outdoor UL approved plastic enclosure. The "SBX-75A" includes a state-of-the-art output indicator and an all metal enclosure.

FLOATRON, PO Box 51000, Phoenix, AZ 85076 - (602) 345-2222

power - solar   capacity - spas/pools — up to 50,000 gallons

features - The "Floatron" is backed by a 2-year warranty against defects in materials and workmanship. It is 12 inches in diameter and weighs 4½ pounds. It can be used with pool covers by folding back a corner. The average electrode life is 1 to 3 years, depending on conditions.

HERCULES PRODUCTS, 2928 Nationwide Pkwy., Brunswick, OH 44212 - (800) 359-7727

power - 120 volts   capacity - pools — up to 50,000 gallons

features - The "Power Ionizer" is equipped with a green "Power On" light that lets you know your system is operating correctly. A red "Service" light alerts you when it's time to replace the chamber. There is fingertip adjustability to help lengthen the chamber life.

LIFEGUARD PURIFICATION SYSTEMS, 4306 W. Osborne Ave., Tampa, FL 33614 - (800) 678-7439 (813) 875-7777

power - 120 volts   capacity - spas (hang-in, with transformer) — up to 5,000 gallons • above ground (hang-in) — up to 12,000 gallons • above ground (in-line) — up to 15,000 gallons • residential pools (in-line) — up to 40,000 gallons.

features - "Mineralizer" for spas is portable, battery powered or an optional plug-in power supply available. The in-line model has the printed circuit board sealed in a wall-mounted plastic box that protects the electronics from moisture and corrosion.

LIQUITECH, INC., 649 Executive Dr., Willowbrook, IL 60521 - (800) 635-7873 (630) 655-0331

power - 120 volts   capacity - spas and pools — up to 50,000 gallons

features - Shipments are made within 24 hours via UPS. A typical installation can be completed in 20 minutes by the homeowner with simple hand tools by following the instructions that are enclosed with the unit.

MILLER TECHNOLOGY INC., PO Box 1651, Manchester, MO 63011 - (314) 825-2841

power - solar   capacity - hot tubs/pools — up to 15,000 gallons • pools up to 35,000 gallons

features - All models of the "Solarcide" include solar panel(s), purification cell, brackets and hardware, copper ion test kit, brush, instructions, wire connectors and backed by a full one year warranty.

OXYPURE, 8229 Melrose Dr., Lenexa, KS 66214 - (913) 894-2828

power - 120 volts • 240 volts   capacity - spas/pools — up to 25,000 gallons

features - "PureWater Ionizer" is 9" × 6" × 4", weighs approximately 4 pounds. The maximum power consumption is 70 watts.

PRECISION POOL ELECTRONICS, INC., PO Box 12544, Scottsdale, AZ 85260 - (800) 844-8514 (602) 443-0481

power - 120 volts • 240 volts   capacity - pools — up to 50,000 gallons

features - The "Challenger 3000" has a lifetime limited product warranty and two years on the electrode. The components consist of — weatherproof plastic control enclosure (5" × 9.75" × 3.5") • 3" PVC chamber and conditioning probe. Copper electrode only (no silver content) - must maintain 0.4 ppm of chlorine for effective purification

SUPERIOR AQUA ENTERPRISES, INC., 2140 Bispham Rd., Sarasota, FL 34231 - (941) 923-2221

power - 120 volts • 240 volts   capacity - spas/pools — up to 6,000 gallons • pools — 10,000 to 40,000 gallons

features - The "HealthCare" system weighs only 20 pounds. The "Ion Perfector" and the "HealthCare" are easily installed onto an existing filtration system.

WITHERS MILLS CO., PO 347, Hannibal, MO 63401 - (800) 223-0858 (573) 221-4747

power - solar   capacity - spas — up to 15,000 gallons • pools up to 35,000 gallons

features - The "Solarcide" solar panel measurements are — 5¼" × 5¼" • 14⅝" × 8⅛" • 14⅝" × 16¼". The purification cell is 7" long × 2¼" diameter.

- -

Floatron Start-up Instructions

Getting Started

1) Begin with normally chlorinated water, approx. 1.0 ppm (parts per million) chlorine, and a normal pH of 7.2 - 7.4. Use regular chlorine test kit.
2) Place your Floatron in the water in bright sunlight.
3) Keep circulation pump on when ionizing, i.e., sunlight hours.
4) Read and understand the copper test kit instructions and test water for copper content. It should read 0 ppm at this beginning point. If you have a positive reading at this point, consult the factory.

The First Few Weeks

1) Float daily.
2) Maintain normal chlorine level and pH.
3) Inspect spring electrode for accumulation of white, scaly deposits. Scaling is more rapid in hard water. Clean per electrode instructions.
4) Test copper level every few days. Normal range is .20 - .40 ppm copper.

Upon Reaching Copper Level (.20 - .40 ppm)

1) Allow chlorine to fall to approximately .20 - .40 ppm over the next few days. This is a trace amount and is all that is normally necessary.
Note — Hard or hot water conditions or high swimmer load requires a greater amount of chlorine.
2) If copper ion reading exceeds .40 ppm, remove unit from water.

Routine Care

1) Test copper level once a week, more often if water is added.
2) When copper level falls off to low range reading, replace Floatron into water until .20 - .40 ppm is reestablished.
3) Keep electrodes clean. **This is very important.**
4) Maintain approx. .20 - .40 ppm chlorine.
5) Maintain pH at 7.2 - 7.4 in normal manner.

Electrode Cleaning and Maintenance

1) Rest the Floatron on top of a quart size jar filled with approximately ½ water and ½ muriatic or hydrochloric acid; all buildup will dissolve quickly and easily from the spring.
2) After removing from acid dip, use a high pressure nozzle on a hose to blast away scale from center electrode.
3) Use wire brush to clean center electrode by inserting bristles between spring and copper element. Rinse with hose blast.
4) Copper electrode can be unscrewed and removed for cleaning if preferred.

Electrode Removal and Replacement

1) To remove the center electrode, unscrew the black thumbscrew counterclockwise, and remove the plastic end cap. While depressing spring electrode with one hand, unscrew the center electrode counterclockwise and remove.
Note — Spring electrode does not unscrew. Do not attempt removal. Do not twist spring.
2) While reinstalling the electrode, hand tighten to be snug against rubber base. Do not overtighten.
3) Replace copper alloy electrode when reduced to a short stub.

Seasonal Closing and Reopening

1) Ensure copper level at .40 ppm.
2) Follow normal procedure, but do not use any chemicals.
3) When opening, top-off and reionize to normal concentration.
4) If water is cloudy, apply mild superchlorination (oxidizer).

Caution

- Do not drop your Floatron
- Do not jump or dive onto device while it is floating.
- Do not lay solar panel face down on any hard surfaces.
- Avoid freezing temperatures; store indoors during off season.
- Do not overionize your water. Maintain normal range of .20 - .40 ppm copper. More does not mean better. 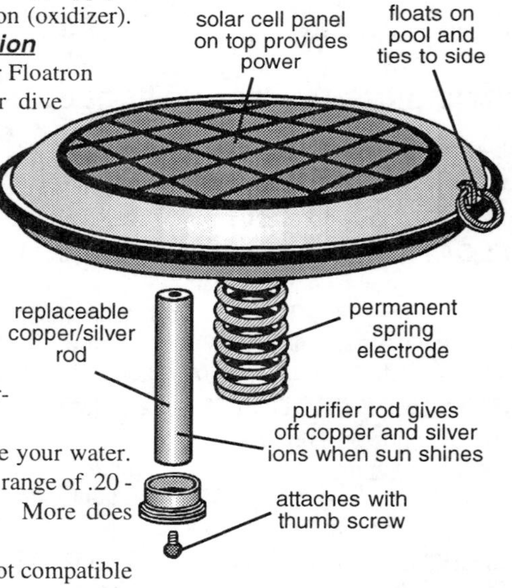
- The Floatron is not compatible with Baquacil brand chemicals. Pool water must be changed first; otherwise, oxidize all Baquacil by superoxidizing. Consult you Baquacil dealer as to how.
- Do not use the Floatron in conjunction with an ozone system.
- Do not use any algaecides as they are unnecessary.
- Avoid floating for extended periods in very shallow areas, such as around pool steps, where water circulation is insufficient.

solar cell panel on top provides power

floats on pool and ties to side

replaceable copper/silver rod

permanent spring electrode

purifier rod gives off copper and silver ions when sun shines

attaches with thumb screw

Instructions on Using the Solarcide System for Swimming Pools and Spas by Withers Mill Company

Swimming Pools

1) Proceed with Solarcide installation as outlined in the owners manual.

2) Continue with your normal pool chemical maintenance, while monitoring for increasing copper levels with your copper test kit. Optimum copper level is 0.4 ppm.

3) When copper level reaches the 0.3-0.4 range, chlorine level can be reduced and maintained in the range of: 0.2-0.4 ppm (the lowest lever on your tester).

Occasional shock treatments may be necessary if water becomes cloudy.

Recommended Treatment

• Keep pump and filter running while shocking (about 8 hours).

• Add 2 to 4 quarts of liquid household bleach per 10,000 gallons of pool water. **OR**

• Add 1 lb. of non-chlorine oxidizer per 10,000 gallons pool water. (Pool chlorine level should reach an approximate and temporary high of only 1.5 ppm.)

By following the recommendations, clear, healthy water can be maintained while reducing costs and exposure by at least 80%. The copper/silver electrode (mineral cell) will eventually be used up, requiring replacement in 1-2 seasons. Installation of a new electrode takes about one minute.

• There are no moving parts.

• Estimated service life is 10 years or more.

• Solarcide (including all components) is manufactured in the United States.

Spas

• Ionizing a spa with the Solarcide system only takes a few hours.

• Check the copper level frequently until the optimum level has been reached — 0.4 ppm.

• The water is now ionized, discontinue standard chlorination.

Maintenance — The only treatment that is needed is a small amount of oxidizer at the end of a days use, with nothing remaining but clear, pure mineral water. During periods of non-use, the water will still remain ionized and clear.

Recommended Treatment (only after a days use)

• ½ to 1 cup of household bleach per 200 to 300 gallon spa (2 cups at most, for the largest spa). **OR** • ¼ ounce non-chlorine oxidizer (oxygen-based) per 200 to 300 gallon spa.

Ionizing a spa (replacing mineral ions) will only be necessary about every 4 to 6 weeks. Monitor copper level once a week.

Installation Options

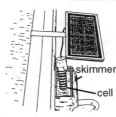

The same installation can be used for in ground pools by installing the solar panel in an optimum location and placing the purification cell in the skimmer.

cell

In Ground Pool

The Solarcide unit can be installed for an above ground pool by mounting the solar panel in an optimum location and placing the purification cell in the skimmer.

skimmer
cell

Above Ground Pools

Installation of the Solarcide purification cell can also be made permanent by use of the optional in-line equipment.

In-Line Options

Pool Balance Information

Adjustment of your pool water to the following specifications before installation is essential to the proper operation of your "Crystal King" unit. Using the Hamilton Index below, test for hardness and balance the alkalinity and pH as indicated.

NOTE — Do not use excessive amounts of chemicals to accomplish this. Adjust alkalinity first, then pH. All adjusting should be done gradually. Maintain chlorine levels until pool is balanced, then install your unit. Do not hurry, the results will be realized after you do it right.

Hamilton Index for Pool and Spa Chemistry

Order of Importance — 1) Alkalinity • 2) Hardness • 3) pH
Run at pH 7.8 to 8.2

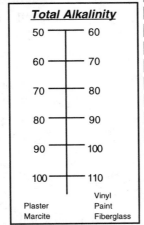

Total Hardness	
1500	
1000	
750	Recommend draining the pool water.
500	
300	
250	
	Ideal Hardness Range
150	
100	

Total Alkalinity	
50	60
60	70
70	80
80	90
90	100
100	110
Plaster Marcite	Vinyl Paint Fiberglass

Example: If 100 ppm hardness, keep alkalinity at 100 ppm. If 500 ppm hardness, keep alkalinity at 70 ppm. TDS (total dissolved solids) has no diagnostic value.

To lower alkalinity, add acid in a 2 to 3 foot circle away from return lines and skimmer.

C. JOCK HAMILTON 1988

Model 50-R by Caribbean Clear

Includes a compact computer control module which regulates amount of electrical current that is transferred to the electrodes. Electrodes are composed of copper and silver, and wear down as copper and silver ions are added to the pool water. Over time these electrodes will gradually decrease in size and will need to be replaced. Electrodes are located in a PVC tee which is installed in the pool plumbing, either before or after the filter. The system is usually wired directly to the pump timer control. The system should operate only when the pool circulating system is running.

filter
optional location
electrode chamber
timer or switch
control box
pump

The Challenger 3000 by Precision Pool Electronics

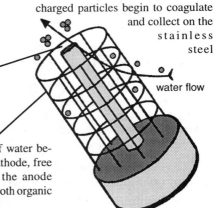

These particles are periodically released on the microprocessor's command and sent to the filter to be removed from the water.

The 100% copper anode/stainless steel cathode imparts copper ions in the recirculating water.

Through electrolysis of water between the anode and cathode, free oxygen is formed on the anode which helps to oxidize both organic and inorganic particles.

As the water passes through the cage, charged particles begin to coagulate and collect on the stainless steel

water flow

Heating swimming pool with solar is simple

Q: Our swimming pool water is too chilly to use in early spring, I cannot afford the gas bills of a pool heater. By summer, the water gets too warm. Is a solar pool heater kit the answer?

A: Yes! Installing a do-it-yourself solar pool heating kit provides several months additional pool use. Imagine doing laps in your 80-degree pool water when it's only 60 degrees outdoors on a sunny crisp fall or spring day. Don't forget a heavy robe when you get out - brrrr!

The beauty of low-cost solar swimming pool kits is their simplicity and high efficiency (up to 80%). Many kits use lightweight flexible collectors that are delivered to your house in a roll. These collectors can be mounted on the roof, a rack or even laid on the ground by the pool.

The kits include every part you need. Just roll the collector out on your roof (or on your driveway first), attach the headers and run the hoses or standard two-inch PVC pipe to your pool.

Some systems are glued (withstands 120-mph winds) on the roof so no holes are required. The thin collectors can barely be seen from the ground.

Your existing filter pump is used to move the pool water through the collector. The better models have automatic temperature sensors. These divert the pool water to the collector only when the collector is warmer than the pool water. You can override the sensor with a manual switch.

If your pool water gets too warm in the summer, operate the pump at night to naturally cool the water. Instead of absorbing heat, the pool water flowing through the collector gives

Pool water flows through radiator in the attic

Solar deck kit heats the water as it keeps the deck comfortable

Uses the entire roof to capture the sun's heat - cools attic too

Flexible tubing collector kits are simple to assemble and install

Unique curved web design traps and absorbs the sun's heat

off heat to the clear night sky.

Heating swimming pool water is the most cost effective use of solar heat. As compared to using a gas or oil pool heater, a low-cost do-it-yourself solar pool kit can pay back its cost in just a few years.

Several unique solar kits do not require collectors on your roof. One design, Solar Attic, uses a small fan and radiator inside your attic. By lowering the attic temperature, it may reduce your air-conditioning load too.

Whenever your attic temperature is eight degrees warmer than the pool water, the fan runs to draw the hot attic air through the radiator which heats the pool water. In effect, it uses your entire roof as a giant solar collector.

In another unique kit, the pool water flows through special hollow

pool decking. The plastic deck transfers the sun's heat to the water. This also keeps the decking comfortably cool to walk and lie on. Entire aboveground solar pool kits are available too.

Q: Our gas range is fairly old and the oven does not seem to hold its temperature as steady as it once did. Do you think that replacing the oven gasket will help?

A: The gasket or the thermostat are the most likely culprits and both can be repaired. If the oven door is not snug when it is closed or you see any sign of gasket deterioration, replace the gasket.

Even if your oven temperature is not a problem, inspect the oven door gasket regularly. Especially with a gas range, the excess waste heat and humidity from a bad gasket can push up your air-conditioning bills.

Manufacturers of Solar Swimming Pool Heating Systems

FAFCO, INC., 9690 Middlefield Rd., Redwood City, CA 94063 - (650) 363-2690

model/type - "SunSaver" — flexible for above ground, in-ground pools and spas • "Revolution" — flexible for in-ground pools

installation - deck mounted • ground mounted • rack mounted • roof mounted

material - ultraviolet stabilized polypropylene

collector size - 4' x 8' • 4' x 10' • 4' x 12'

features - "SunSaver" includes a Velcro® carry strap so the collector can be rolled up, stored during winter. "Revolution" solar panel has dimples in tubes that directs pool water into a spiral flow, thoroughly mixing, revolving and exposing all the water molecules to the sun's warmth. Automatic microprocessor-driven system with easy-to-use set it and forget it programming for desired temperature available. It controls pool pump and filtering operations for efficiency and reduced energy consumption. Can be linked to a gas or back-up heating system to meet heating needs. Can also purify pool water, reducing chemicals. In limited sunshine, sensor triggers controller to shut system off, draining water from panels automatically.

HARTER INDUSTRIES, INC., PO Box 502, Holmdel, NJ 07733 - (800) 566-7770 (908) 566-7055

model/type - "EZ Heat" and "EZ Heat Deluxe" — flexible for above ground pools and smaller in-ground pools and spas • "Hi-Tec" — flexible for above ground and in-ground pools and spas to be mounted on a roof or a rack • "Hi-Temp" — flexible for in-ground pools and spas

installation - deck mounted • ground mounted • rack mounted • roof mounted

material - "EZ Heat" and "EZ Heat Deluxe" — EPDM (synthetic rubber) • "Hi-Tec" — polypropylene with ultraviolet screen • "Hi-Temp" — EPDM (synthetic rubber)

collector size - "EZ Heat" — 4' x 12' • 4' x 20' • 4' x 25' / "Hi-Tec" — 4' x 10' • 4' x 12' / "Hi-Temp" — 4' x 15' • 4' x 20' • 4' x 25' • 4' x 30' • 4' x 35' • 4' x 40' • custom collectors that are field assembled in any length

features - "EZ Heat" and "EZ Heat Deluxe" are complete assembled systems. "EZ Heat" has a built-in 3-port control valve, you can turn it off when the pool is warm enough. Optional automatic electronic control. Set desired temperature on control panel and system does the rest. When solar sensor finds that there is enough solar energy and the pool water is too cool, it automatically sends water through the solar collectors to warm the swimming pool. In hot weather it can cool an overheated pool. "Hi-Tec" heating system has imited lifetime warranty. "Hi-Temp" can be ordered in custom sizes that can be assembled on site in any length to fit your application. The "Hi-Temp" collectors will conform to irregular surfaces and are freeze-damage resistant when used on flat ground or a flat roof. The collectors can be run horizontally or vertically up a sloping roof. The solar collectors have a tube-on-fin design that captures more of the indirect sunlight and is effective on cloudy or windy days. There is an optional gapless system that eliminates spaces between the collectors.

HELIOCOL, 927 Fern St., Suite 200, Altamonte Springs, FL 32701 - (407) 831-1941

model/type - "Heliocol" — flexible for above ground and in-ground pools and spas

installation - deck mounted • ground mounted • rack mounted • roof mounted

material - ultraviolet stabilized polypropylene

collector size - 1' x 10' • 1' x 12' • 4' x 8' • 4' x 10' • 4' x 12'

features - Individual "over-molded" tube design eliminates all welds, allows for expansion and contraction of each tube reducing cracks and leaks. Individual tubes also prevent moisture from being trapped under collector. This helps eliminate roof deterioration. Designed to withstand 180 mph wind load. 10-year warranty includes labor and freeze protection.

ISLAND FANTA-SEA POOLS, 1865 Grand Island Blvd., Grand Island, NY 14072 - (800) 356-3025 (716) 773-7500

model/type - "Solar Mark VI" and "Solar Sea Lion" — above ground pools with solar decks / "Add-A-Deck" — customize your existing pool deck or design your own deck with a solar deck

material - molded walnut-colored polyelfin (to attract heat) decking • 25 mil vinyl beaded print track liner • polyolefin and pressure treated structural components • polyolefin safety ladder • stainless steel in-pool ladder • steel joists and channels • 3/4" poly-vinyl laminated 7-ply waterwalls

swim size - 12' x 20' • 12' x 24' • 16' x 24' • 16' x 32' • 20' x 40' • custom sizes available • standard 4' depth with optional 5 1/2" or 7 1/2" deep ends • conditioning lap pool in 8' or 12' widths, up to 40' long

features - A built-in system of solar deck panels automatically heats or cools the pool water. The sun heats the pool water as it passes through collectors in the pools decking. Heating process has the reverse effect on the surface of the decks, transferring the heat to the water and keeping the surface cool to the touch. There is a self-latching and swing-up safety ladder. Modular construction allows for do-it-yourself installation. It also provides flexibility in installation, when moving or if repairs need to be made parts are easy to replace. Built-in fence with interlocking insert panels on "Mark VI" and the "Sea Lion" for privacy, wind break and safety. Comes with a dual suction filtration system and a top load auto skimmer.

PROFESSIONAL SOLAR PRODUCTS, 4630 Calle Quetzal, Camarillo, CA 93012 - (805) 383-7171

model/type - "Pro Panel" — rigid for above ground and in-ground pools and spas

installation - deck mounted • ground mounted • rack mounted • roof mounted • trellis mounted

material - all-metal, extruded aluminum with copper waterways

collector size - 44" x 94 7/8" • 44" x 118 7/8" • 44" x 142 7/8"

features - "Pro Panel" is self-supporting, does not require a substrate for support. Each panel interlocks into the next giving appearance of one continuous panel. Can be installed for trellis covers or patio roofs. Special mounting systems available. "Tile Trac" mounting system for installing to any kind of tile roof. "Pro Rack" mounting system for mounting on flat roofs. "Ground Pro" mounting system for mounting on hillside or flat ground. All-metal construction makes the system completely fireproof. The panels are painted on both sides with a polyester flat black paint that is electrostatically applied.

SEALED AIR CORP., 3433 Arden Rd., Hayward, CA 94545 - (510) 887-8090
model/type - for pools and spas: "FP series" — flexible frameless collector • "FS series" — rigid standard framed collector • "FW series" — rigid collector has windscreen mounted directly above absorber panel for areas with cooler climates and prevailing winds
installation - deck mounted • groundmounted • rack mounted • roof mounted
material - ultraviolet stabilized polypropylene
collector size - 4' x 8' • 4' x 10' • 4' x 12'
features - Panel is extruded in a single monolithic four-foot width and designed to enhance optimum heat collection by providing maximum contact between the sun and water. Material is not affected by scaling or strong chemicals. Each framed panel is framed with 16 gauge galvanized steel. Every panel is backed by a polyester substrate to shield bottom side of collector from wind and weather, also protects roof. Automatic control turns system on and off depending on weather conditions and pool water temp. desired. Sensor activates automatic control when there is enough solar energy to heat the pool.

SOLAR ATTIC INC., 15548 95th Circle NE, Elk River, MN 55330 - (612) 441-3440
model/type - "PCS1 (Pool Convection System One)" for above ground and in-ground pools and spas
installation - attic mounted
attic space required - 3 ft. minimum height to peak; and sq. ft. of attic equal to or greater than pool sq. ft.; minimum attic opening recommended is 21" x 31"
size - 33" w x 30" h x 20" d, weight 135 pounds — fits through standard 24" o.c. trusses
features - When sun shines, roof acts as a large solar collector. Heat accumulates inside attic. "PCS1" heater acts as an exchanger, safely uses attic heat to warm pool and cool attic. Can cool down overheated pools in evening hours with a manual control that will send hot pool water to attic where cooler attic air is drawn across heat exchanger. Equipped with manual off/on or automatic heat when used with solar controller. Automatic control will automatically turn on when heat is available to meet desired water temp. of pool. Will work for pools up to 1000 square feet or 35,000 gallons. Up to 70,000 gallons with "FlowReversal" valves. These valves take water off of the top of pool and return it to the bottom of the pool.

SOLAR IND. (AQUATHERM), 1940 Rutgers University Blvd., Lakewood, NJ 08701 - (800) 227-7657 (732) 905-0440
model/type - "SI" — flexible for spas, above ground and in-ground pools
installation - deck mounted • ground mounted • rack mounted • roof mounted
material - ultraviolet stabilized polypropylene
collector size - 4' x 8' • 4' x 10' • 4' x 12' • smaller sizes on request
features - A unique patented tube and curved web heat trap design (104 individual tubes per collector) exposes more surface area directly to the sun so the collectors can face in directions other than due south. The collector is backed by a lifetime warranty. It is made with all welded construction for a seamless weld between the collector's body and header for strength and durability. The mounting hardware is stainless steel.

SOLAR SPECIALISTS, INC., 6825 Mercedes Ave., Citrus Heights, CA 95621 - (916) 969-2018
model/type - "Solapool" — rigid for spas, above ground and in-ground pools
installation - deck mounted • ground mounted • rack mounted • roof mounted • trellis mounted
material - black ABS plastic pipes (specially compounded with ultraviolet stabilizers)
collector size - 20 foot length pipes, standard 1 1/2" diameter — cuts and configures to any space — custom sizes
features - Mounting structure attaches only to the eaves of the roof so there are no holes over the living area of your house. Mounting system design lets air circulate beneath the system, preventing moisture from rotting the roof. Pipes hold a large capacity of hot water in the collector and when it is full of hot water a switch can be flipped to fill spa instantly with hot water (takes approximately two to three minutes). Since the pipes are round, sunlight can hit the pipe at a 90 degree angle during most of the day. Even on cloudy days, it absorbs heat because more surface area is exposed. Sunlight can even warm pipe water from underneath. Extremely flexible — it cuts and configures to any space — goes around anything (antennas, chimneys, etc.) Can also be mounted on a flat roof or as a trellis cover to shade garden plants.

SUNTREK IND., 26081 Merit Circle, #103, Laguna Hills, CA 92653 - (800) 292-7648 (714) 348-9276
model/type - "Solar In A Box" — flexible for above ground pools • "Suntrek" — flexible for above ground and in-ground pools, spas
installation - deck mounted • ground mounted • rack mounted • roof mounted
material - "Solar In A Box" and "Suntrek" — ultraviolet stabilized EPDM (synthetic rubber — ozone and chemical resistant)
collector size - "Solar In A Box" — 4' x 16' / "Suntrek" — roll is 200' long x 6" wide • 2' x 20' • 2' x 25' • 2' x 30' • 2' x 35'
features - "Solar In A Box" available with full automatic control that will turn system on and off to keep your pool at a desired preset temp. "Suntrek" solar collectors are custom cut to needed length, then solar tubes (72 water channels) are slid over barbs on polypropylene manifold. (Factory assembled panels available.) Solar heater is secured with provided straps and clamps. A check valve, solar valve and return line Tee are included, should be installed at pool pump/filter. Adjustable thermostat control can be added so you can set temp. to your preference. If you have a spa on the same pool plumbing system, you can heat it with a "Suntrek" heater by turning the valves to draw and return water to the spa.

TECHNO-SOLIS INC., 12929 44th St. N, Clearwater, FL 34622 - (813) 573-2881
model/type - "TS" Series — flexible for spas, above ground, in-ground pools, heat supplementation for indoor pools, spas, hot tubs
installation - deck mounted • ground mounted • rack mounted • roof mounted
material - ultraviolet stabilized polypropylene
collector size - 4' x 8' • 4' x 10' • 4' x 12'
features - Controller can be set to automatically keep the pool temperature anywhere from 65 to 100 degrees. When the system controller senses that the collectors are warmer than the pool water, it opens a valve diverting water from the pool circulator through the collectors and then back into the pool.

Sea-Lion Solar Pool by Island Fanta Sea

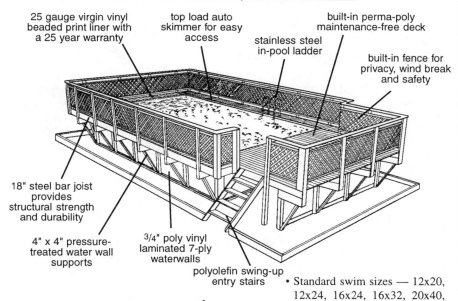

25 gauge virgin vinyl beaded print liner with a 25 year warranty

top load auto skimmer for easy access

stainless steel in-pool ladder

built-in perma-poly maintenance-free deck

built-in fence for privacy, wind break and safety

18" steel bar joist provides structural strength and durability

4" x 4" pressure-treated water wall supports

3/4" poly vinyl laminated 7-ply waterwalls

polyolefin swing-up entry stairs

Water flows from filter, through the decking and then back to the pool, transferring the sun's heat to your pool.

- Standard swim sizes — 12x20, 12x24, 16x24, 16x32, 20x40, custom sizes
- Standard 4' depth with optional 5$^{1/2}$" or 7$^{1/2}$" deep ends
- Conditioning lap pools in 8' or 12' widths, up to 40' long
- Modular construction allows for self installation or installation by factory trained crews

Benefits of Collector Materials

EPDM (synthetic rubber) is preferred for above-ground pools. It is resistant to freezing. It is very flexible, rolls up easily and will withstand a lot of abuse. Because of the great flexibility, it will conform to an irregular surface. It works well on flat surfaces and can be run horizontally or vertically up a sloping roof. Can be cemented down eliminating nail holes. Can be run in longer sections.

Polypropylene is the preferred choice for in-ground pools where the collector will be mounted on a roof or a rack. It is best to place the collector at an angle rather than flat. It is extremely efficient with thinner walls. It is noncorrosive and resistant to freezing. It is flexible, rolls up but not as tightly as rubber. It needs to be placed in the sun for a period before it is pliable.

Copper panels are completely fireproof. Nearby fires or sparks from chimneys will not burn through the panels. They are architecturally pleasing. The rigidity of the panels make them a good choice for trellis cover, patio roof or ground-mounted systems.

ABS plastic panels are very tough, the only way to damage the pipe is to break it by impact. Repair is easy and inexpensive. Cuts and configures to any space. A good choice for flat roof, pitched roof or trellis-mount systems.

The PSC1 Solar Attic Pool Heater

Description of Operation — Solar radiation bombards the house's roof structure throughout the day. The roof functions as a massive solar collector. Solar radiation reaches the attic through a process called conduction. The attic functions as a storage and heat transfer area. The PCS1 is physically located inside the attic and then transfers this solar radiation from the attic air into the swimming pool's water through a process called forced air convection.

Full Automatic Operation — Is achieved with the optional LX220 control. When the attic is eight degrees hotter than the pool and the pool needs heat, the LX220 automatically routes water up to the PCS1 and turns it on. It can even synchronize the pool's pump by turning it on at the same time. Temperature sensors sense the pool and attic temperatures. Maximum heat is then extracted automatically. The pool owner simply sets the desired thermostat setting on the LX220. Flow reversal can substantially reduce the pool's heat demand by allowing the heat to rise from the main drain. (These valves take the water off of the top of the pool and return it to the bottom of the pool.) A pool blanket can be used when the pool is not in use thereby minimizing heat losses caused by evaporation (60%).

Specifications —
- Pool Sizes — Up to 1,000 sq. ft. or 35,000 gal.
- Up to 70,000 gallons with Flow Reversal

valves
- Nominal Btu Rating — 60,000 Btu per hour at 32° F (at pool temp of 72°F and attic temp of 104°F)
- Btu Transfer Range — 20,000 to 150,000 Btu's per hour
- Attic Space Required — 3 ft. minimum height to peak; and, sq. ft. of attic equal to or greater than pool sq. ft.
- Fits through standard 24" o.c. trusses
- Min. attic opening recommended — 21" x 31"
- Disassembles for smaller attic openings
- Size — 33"w x 30"h x 20"d
- Weight — 135 pounds
- Power — 220 vac 1.8 amps @ Full load
- Operating Cost — $5 to $11 per month @ 9¢ per kwh
- U.L. Listed — Coil, motor and other components
- Plumbing — 1$^{1/2}$" or 2" PVC typical
- Pressure Drop — 4 to 6 psi

typical
- Water Flow Rate — Range of 15 to 80 gpm
- Optimal Water Flow Rate — Range of 45 to 55 gpm
- Fan Air Flow Rate — 2500 scfm
- Operation Modes — Manual off, manual on
- Optional Automatic Operation — LX220 control

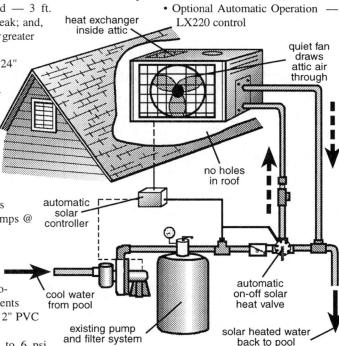

heat exchanger inside attic

quiet fan draws attic air through

no holes in roof

automatic solar controller

cool water from pool

existing pump and filter system

automatic on-off solar heat valve

solar heated water back to pool

Attractive retaining walls are easy to build

Q: I want to build up the ground a little, with a retaining wall, around the south and north sides of my house. I plan to plant flowers and ornamental shrubs. Will this lower or increase my utility bills?

A: Adding a low earth berm around your house is one of the most energy efficient improvements you can make to your house. The flowers and shrubs will also be an attractive and value enhancing improvement.

The earth itself will create a natural insulating and air-sealing barrier to the extremes of winter cold and summer heat. The top edge of the foundation is the area of greatest air leakage into most homes. Your earth berm should seal this completely.

In the summer, you will really notice a difference. The heavy thermal mass of the earth and the retaining wall will moderate the typical mid-afternoon temperature rise. Having the plants close to the house will also lower the air temperature near the house.

The easiest way to do this project is with a mortarless do-it-yourself retaining wall kit. These are very attractive, strong and easy for anyone to install. You just stack up the blocks. The hardest part is carrying them from the driveway to the house.

There are many shapes, sizes and textures of retaining wall blocks to choose from. Most are designed with tapered sides so that they can be easily arranged into nearly any curve, inside and outside corners, even built-in steps.

Depending on the look that you want or the strength of your back, you can select blocks from 30 pounds to more than 100 pounds.

Attractive wall has built-in planter sections

Beveled blocks form an attractive, simple texture

Adhesive is used to fix the finishing cap in place

Pins align and stabilize the wall

Blocks are designed to interlock and produce the proper setback

Larger blocks are often more stable and allow you to build a higher wall without reinforcement.

Most blocks have alignment holes and pins to make assembly easy. The placement of the pins determine the setback for each successive coarse. You can build a flat wall with no setback, but it is often less stable. The top of the wall is finished with cap sections glued into place.

Keystone makes a very attractive planter retaining wall system. Some of the blocks are designed with cutouts to be used as planters in the retaining wall. The Ashlar Blend uses a combination of three different sized blocks to simulate an old style handmade stone wall.

If you would like to highlight your other landscaping or a walkway near the retaining wall, install Pisa Lights. These lights are designed to fit perfectly in Pisa II retaining wall blocks. The lens of the 110 or 12-volt lights have a concrete texture so that they blend in.

Q: I plan to build some storage area in my kitchen. I will put it on an outside wall for insulation like you suggested. When I buy the plywood, what do all the AA, CD, etc. mean and which should I use?

A: The letter designations from A through D refer to the surface quality. An A-rated surface is best and is free from knots and blemishes. A D-rated surface is roughest and can have open knot holes.

Since a piece of plywood is laminated from many plies, each side can have a different rating. If only one side will show, an AD piece is fine. For your storage area, which will be opened at times, an AA or AB grade is best.

ALLAN BLOCK RETAINING WALL SYSTEMS, 7400 Metro Blvd., Suite 185, Edina, MN 55439 - (612) 835-5309

unit - AB Stones	dimensions* - 8 x 18 x 12	weight - 75 lbs.	exposed face area - 1.0 sq. ft.
unit - AB Three	dimensions - 8 x 18 x 12	weight - 75 lbs.	exposed face area - 1.0 sq. ft.
unit - AB Rocks	dimensions - 8 x 18 x 12	weight - 70 lbs.	exposed face area - 1.0 sq. ft.
unit - AB Lite Stones	dimensions - 4 x 18 x 12	weight - 35 lbs.	exposed face area - .50 sq. ft.
unit - AB Lite Rocks	dimensions - 4 x 18 x 12	weight - 35 lbs.	exposed face area - .50 sq. ft.
unit - AB Junior	dimensions - 6 x 8 x 8	weight - 20 lbs.	exposed face area - .33 sq. ft.

features - There is a raised front lip and a notched bottom on each block providing an interlocking surface between blocks for a tight wall. The notched bottoms provide an automatic built-in setback. The hollow-core blocks provide water drainage within the wall and reduce the amount of drainage material needed behind the wall. There are straight-faced or beveled blocks so you can build straight walls, curves or steps. There are caps and corner units available to finish off the block wall. There is a special blend — "Ashlar Blend" — that combines three different sizes of blocks and colors to give the appearance of an old style hand laid stone wall. There are standard colors, blends and optional colors to choose from. The blocks are environmentally friendly.

ANCHOR WALL SYSTEMS, 6101 Baker Rd., Suite 201, Minnetonka, MN 55345 - (800) 473-4452 (612) 933-8855

unit - Vertica Pro	dimensions - 8 x 18 x 22-1/2	weight - 115 lbs.	exposed face area - 1.0 sq. ft.
unit - Vertica	dimensions - 8 x 18 x 11	weight - 86 lbs.	exposed face area - 1.0 sq. ft.
unit - Diamond	dimensions - 6 x 15-7/8 x 12	weight - 68 lbs.	exposed face area - .67 sq. ft.
unit - Windsor	dimensions - 4 x 8 x 11-5/8	weight - 24 lbs.	exposed face area - .33 sq. ft.
unit - Sahara	dimensions - 4 x 8 x 8-3/4	weight - 19 lbs.	exposed face area - .25 sq. ft.
unit - Border	dimensions - 4 x 8-1/2 x 5-1/2	weight - 19 lbs.	exposed face area - .25 sq. ft.

features - The blocks have a beveled, three-way face so you can build inside curves, outside curves and straight walls. There are integral lips or built-in locators molded into every block making installation of the wall fast and easy. The blocks are automatically guided into each new course with proper alignment and setback with an integral rear lip that is molded into each block. They are available in earth tones with a natural rock-like texture. The "Diamond" unit is a straight-face or a beveled unit and the "Sahara" has a straight face. The blocks are environmentally safe, nonpolluting and will not deteriorate. There are corner, step and cap units available.

ICD CORP., 3934 N. Ridgefield Circle, Milwaukee, WI 53211 - (800) 394-4066 (414) 962-4065

| unit - StoneWall Select | dimensions - 8 x 16 x 12 | weight - 65 lbs. | exposed face area - 1.13 sq. ft. |

features - You can design walls with curves, steps and 90 degree corners to fit any contour. The "StoneWall Select" blocks have a textured, split face that simulates real rock. There are two interlocking clips that fit into the precut grooves on the top of each unit's back. The units in the next course are stacked in half bond to overlap the units in the course below, then slid forward and snugged up against the interlock clips. The interlock clips and the tapered cores of the blocks provide an automatic setback. There is an electrical cable slot cast into each block, so you can easily add lighting to your retaining wall. The blocks are hollow so they can be filled with gravel for drainage. There is a cap unit available to finish the top of the wall. A corner unit is also available as is an optional straight face block. "Selectedge" is 3-5/8 x 3-5/8 x 4 and can be used for garden edging, tree rings, planting beds or pavement borders. With flush installation in the ground, grass trimming is eliminated, the mower wheel rolls across the block. A smaller block is available — "StoneRidge", for small landscape walls of 2 feet or less. The colors available are natural gray, buff or brown — they vary by region. Custom colors are available by special order.

KEYSTONE RETAINING WALL SYSTEMS, 4444 W. 78th St., Minneapolis, MN 55435 - (800) 747-8971

unit - Standard	dimensions - 8 x 18 x 21-1/2	weight - 95 lbs.	exposed face area - 1.0 sq. ft.
unit - Compac	dimensions - 8 x 18 x 12-1/4	weight - 85 lbs.	exposed face area - 1.0 sq. ft.
unit - Mini/Cap	dimensions - 4 x 8 x 10-1/2	weight - 45 lbs.	exposed face area - .50 sq. ft.
unit - Intermediate	dimensions - 7-1/4 x 17 x 11	weight - 77 lbs.	exposed face area - .85 sq. ft.
unit - Garden Wall	dimensions - 4 x 12 x 9	weight - 27 lbs.	exposed face area - .33 sq. ft.
unit - Regal Stone	dimensions - 4 x 12 x 8	weight - 23 lbs.	exposed face area - .33 sq. ft.
unit - Arbor Stone	dimensions - 4 x 12 x 8	weight - 23 lbs.	exposed face area - .33 sq. ft.
unit - Arbor Stone Planter	dimensions - 4 x 12 x 9	weight - 14 lbs.	exposed face area - .33 sq. ft.

features - These blocks can be used for building straight walls, curves, steps or 90 degree corners. The "Standard", "Compac" and "Mini/Cap" system uses reinforced fiberglass pins placed in paired holes in the blocks to join the units together. The pins create an automatic setback for each additional course. The setback can be adjusted by inserting the pins in different holes. There are optional straight face pattern blocks available. The cap unit is available with straight sides to eliminate the triangular space between cap units on straight walls and concave curves or with angular sides for convex curves. The other blocks are designed with a segmented rear lip to handle curves and to maintain a consistent setback. The "Arbor Stone Planter" unit can be used to build a two foot high planter wall or can be incorporated into a retaining wall. The "Edge Rock" unit is for edging around plantings or other areas in the landscape. It is placed in the ground, will handle curves and corners and the unique shape locks each unit into place. The "Edge Rock" dimensions are 3-1/2 x 4 x 6, weight is 4 lbs. and the exposed face area is 1/2 lineal ft.

RISI STONE SYSTEMS, 8500 Leslie St., Suite 390, Thornhill, Ontario, Canada L3T 7P1 - (905) 882-5898

unit - PISA II Standard	dimensions - 6 x 8 x 12	weight - 45 lbs.	exposed face area - .38 sq. ft.
unit - PISA II Tapered	dimensions - 6 x 6-7/8 x 12	weight - 43 lbs.	exposed face area - .38 sq. ft.
unit - PISA Lite	dimensions - 6 x 8 x 12	weight - 3 lbs.	exposed face area - .38 sq. ft.
unit - PISA Sounds	dimensions - 6 x 8 x 12	weight - 5 lbs.	exposed face area - .38 sq. ft.
unit - Roman Pisa	dimensions - 6 x 8 x 12	weight - 45 lbs.	exposed face area - .38 sq. ft.
unit - Garden Stone	dimensions - 4-1/2 x 8 x 8	weight - 24 lbs.	exposed face area - .33 sq. ft.
unit - Split 'N Stack	dimensions - 4 x 8 x 8	weight - 18 lbs.	exposed face area - .33 sq. ft.

features - All of the blocks are solid and they are self sloping and self aligning using an interlocking system molded into each unit. The units have a cast tongue and groove interlock. The "Pisa Lite" and "Pisa Sounds" unit are fiberglass enclosures for incorporating lights or speakers into the wall. The lens have a concrete-like texture so they blend in. The "Pisa Lites" are available for 110V and 12V applications. The "Pisa Sounds" are preassembled and only require connection to the audio source. (See page 4 for more information.) There are 90 degree corner and cap stones available. The "Roman Pisa" is a tumbled block that has rounded corners and edges that gives the wall a worn cobble appearance. These units look like real stone as opposed to concrete blocks. Both sides of the "Split 'N Stack" stone are rock faced so the freestanding wall is attractive from any angle. It is a tapered garden stone and the maximum height for this system is 2 feet. The blocks are available in various earth tone colors.

ROCKWOOD RETAINING WALLS, INC., 7200 N. Hwy. 63, Rochester, MN 55906 - (800) 535-2375

unit - 8" Classic	dimensions - 8 x 18 x 12	weight - 78 lbs.	exposed face area - 1.0 sq. ft.
unit - 6" Classic	dimensions - 6 x 18 x 12	weight - 56 lbs.	exposed face area - .75 sq. ft.
unit - 8" Classic Half	dimensions - 8 x 9 x 12	weight - 39 lbs.	exposed face area - .50 sq. ft.
unit - 6" Classic Half	dimensions - 6 x 9 x 12	weight - 28 lbs.	exposed face area - .38 sq. ft.
unit - E-Z Wall Standard	dimensions - 6-3/8 x 10 x 10	weight - 49 lbs.	exposed face area - .50 sq. ft.
unit - E-Z Wall Mini	dimensions - 4-1/2 x 8 x 8-3/4	weight - 25 lbs.	exposed face area - .33 sq. ft.
unit - Cottage Stone	dimensions - 4 x 12 x 8-1/2	weight - 26.5 lbs.	exposed face area - .33 sq. ft.
unit - Stonehedge	dimensions - 4 x 12 x 8	weight - 18 lbs.	exposed face area - .33 sq. ft.
unit - Legend	dimensions - 8 x 18 x 22	weight - 110 lbs.	exposed face area - 1.0 sq. ft.
unit - Supreme	dimensions - 8x24 /27x27	weight - n/a	exposed face area - 1.5 sq. ft.

features - The blocks allow construction of straight walls, inside curves, outside curves, serpentine curves and an unlimited variety of corners and steps. The "Classic" has two face options — beveled or straight splitface. It has an interlocking design that allows for automatic setback and perfect alignment. The "Stonehedge" is straight split on both sides. There is an anchor bar on the bottom that vertically centers the blocks while building the wall. The "Cottage Stone" is available in straight or wedge-shaped units for easy curves. It has an interlocking rear lip as does the "E-Z Wall" stone. The "Supreme" system consists of a stone face, anchor, rod and u-clip — the blocks are hollow for drainage. The blocks are available in a variety of earth tone colors. There is a stone available — "Classic Edge" that is used for edging flower beds, walkways, shrubs and trees. It has a ball/socket configuration and a T-Lock base design that anchors the system in place. Pavers, soil, decorative stone or patio blocks can be placed directly on the T-Lock. It allows curves and short radius turns.

VERSA-LOK RETAINING WALL, 6348 Hwy. 36, Suite 1, Oakdale, MN 55128 - (800) 770-4525 (612) 770-3166

| unit - Mini | dimensions - 4 x 12 x 8-3/4 | weight - 32 lbs. | exposed face area - .33 sq. ft. |
| unit - Standard | dimensions - 6 x 16 x 12 | weight - 82 lbs. | exposed face area - .67 sq. ft. |

features - The concrete blocks have a natural splitface texture. The units are made from high-strength, low-absorption concrete on standard block machines. The blocks are environmentally safe. The blocks are solid making them resistant to damage in all climates. Holes and slots are molded into the blocks that will hold fiberglass pins. As wall courses are installed, pins are inserted through holes in uppermost course units and are received in slots of adjacent lower course units. Pins interlock units and help provide alignment. The trapezoidal shape of the block allows construction of straight walls, inside curves, outside curves, serpentine curves and an unlimited variety of corners and steps. There are two different matching concrete caps available for the "Standard" units to finish the wall. They are 3-5/8" tall and 14" wide at the face with tapered sides that are different. One unit is for outside curves, while the other unit is for inside curves. They are alternated on straight walls. Maximum height for an unreinforced wall is four feet for the "Standard" unit and three feet for the "Mini" unit.

Versa-Lok Retaining Walls

Pins connect units to one another

AB Stones by Allan Block

Interlocking raised front lip and notched bottom

Classic by Rockwood

Anchor bar locks into unit below

Interlocking anchor bar

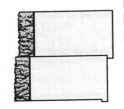

Anchor Windsor Stone

Built-in rear lip molded into each block

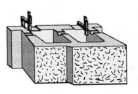

StoneWall Select by ICD

Hollow core system uses interlock clips

Installation Procedure for PISA II by Risi Stone Systems

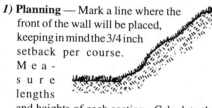

1) Planning — Mark a line where the front of the wall will be placed, keeping in mind the 3/4 inch setback per course. Measure lengths and heights of each section. Calculate the amount of material needed. If necessary, contact local utility companies for the location and depth of buried services.

2) Excavate — Remove soil to create a trench that is a minimum of 12 inches deep and 24 inches wide. Remove sod, roots, rocks and organic materials. Shape slope to allow for 12 inches of drainage material behind the wall.

3) Prepare Base — Ensure native soil is stable and compact

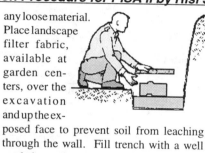

any loose material. Place landscape filter fabric, available at garden centers, over the excavation and up the exposed face to prevent soil from leaching through the wall. Fill trench with a well graded angular gravel and compact to a depth of 6 inches. A small amount of sand can be used for final leveling.

4) First Course — Split units apart using a chisel and hammer, if not already presplit. Position a level string line to mark the location of the first course. Place the first course of units on the prepared base and ensure that the unit is level front to back and left to right.

5) Stack Units — Sweep the top of the units. Place

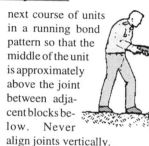

next course of units in a running bond pattern so that the middle of the unit is approximately above the joint between adjacent blocks below. Never align joints vertically.

6) Backfill — Place a drain tile behind the first course of units and fill behind the wall with a free draining granular soil. Compact this soil in 6 inch lifts. Place soil in front of the wall to ensure that one course is completely buried. Stack more units and backfill until the desired height is achieved, 4 foot maximum.

7) Secure Coping — On the last course of wall units place a line of adhesive on both sides of the tongue. Place the coping unit on top and apply pressure to secure.

8) Finish Grading — Pull filter cloth towards wall and place 8 inches of soil on top. Slope the soil above and below the wall to ensure water will flow away from and not accumulate near the wall units.

PISA Lite

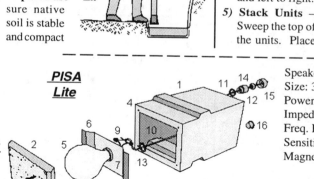

Speaker Specifications
Size: 3.5" dual cone
Power handling: 30 watts
Impedance: 4 ohm
Freq. Response: 80 - 18K Hz
Sensitivity: 90dB
Magnet weight: 4.3 oz.

PISA Sounds

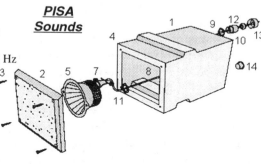

by Risi Stone Systems

1. Fiberglass PISA Lite enclosure
2. Lens with concrete-like texture
3. Screws (4)
4. Water resistant seal
5. Bulb (not included)
6. Socket plate holder
7. Light socket
8. Ridge for socket holder (not shown)

9. Wire connector
10. External wire (not included)
11. Rubber 'O' ring
12. Conduit adapter
13. Metal nut
14. Grommet (to suit wiring)
15. Grommet cover
16. Opening plug

1. Fiberglass PISA Sounds enclosure
2. Lens with concrete-like texture
3. Screws (4)
4. Water resistant seal
5. Speaker
6. Speaker mount nuts (not shown)
7. Wire connector

8. External audio wire
9. Rubber 'O' ring
10. Conduit adapter
11. Metal nut
12. Grommet (to suit wiring)
13. Grommet cover
14. Opening plug

Installation Instructions for a Single PISA Sounds

1) Remove the four screws from the lens of the enclosure.

2) Remove mounting accessories from enclosure.

3) Place 'O' ring on conduit adapter, and secure through opening in the back of the enclosure using the metal nut.

4) Run external audio wire through grommet cover, the appropriate grommet, through the conduit adapter and into the enclosure.

5) Connect speaker wires to the exterior wires using wire connectors.

6) Tighten the grommet cover, ensuring that some slack is left in the wiring inside the

enclosure.

7) Close extra opening at the rear of the enclosure with the plug.

8) Replace lens using screws and position enclosure in wall.

9) Connect external wiring to audio source.

Decorative paver patios are simple to make yourself

Q: I plan to build a decorative concrete walkway and small patio along the south side of our house. Will this concrete patio capture the sun's heat in the winter and do you have any building tips?

A: Your concrete walkway/patio idea is a good one and very simple to build yourself. With the high heat capacity of concrete, it can capture a lot of free heat from the winter sun. This creates a warm air buffer near the wall and reduces heat loss even late into the evening.

The south side is the best location for your solar patio. First, it is easy to shade the south side of your house in the summer with deciduous trees or do-it-yourself awning kits because the sun is so high in the sky.

Also, the prevailing summer winds are from the southwest, so warm air by the patio will blow away. The winter prevailing winds are often from the northwest, so the warm air from the patio will stay near your house.

For the first-time do-it-yourselfer to the professional, using precast concrete pavers on a sand bed is a good, cost effective method. There are many unique shapes and colors of concrete pavers. Some even are shaped like lizards and frogs that interlock perfectly.

Hundreds of decorative paver patterns are possible by using various sizes, shapes and colors. Several companies make safe, easy-to-install decorative border treatments and paver lights. The low-voltage (only 12 volts) lights are efficient and you won't have the expense of hiring an electrician.

By doing the work yourself, you should be able to build an attractive patio or walkway for about

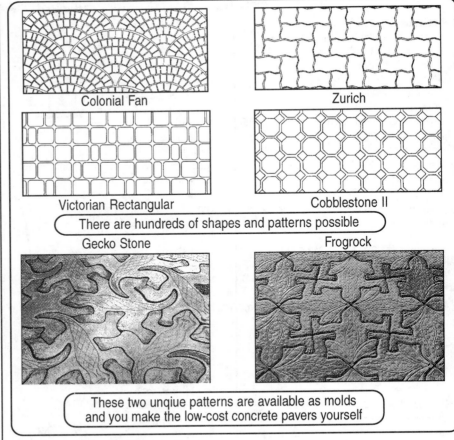

Colonial Fan

Zurich

Victorian Rectangular

Cobblestone II

There are hundreds of shapes and patterns possible

Gecko Stone

Frogrock

These two unqiue patterns are available as molds and you make the low-cost concrete pavers yourself

half the cost of a professional installation. Also, the free solar heat buffer it creates will lower your utility bills.

To save even more money, make your own pavers with reusable molds. Molds for the Gecko Stone and Frogrock (sounds strange, but they are attractive), and other conventional shapes are available. This takes more time, but you can get creative with unique color patterns.

The key to building a concrete paver patio is proper planning and ground preparation. Generally, about four inches of 2A quarry stone is used as the base. This is covered with about one to two inches of sharp coarse sand. The sand is leveled and the pavers are placed on the smooth sand bed.

Some pavers are cast with separator spacers. If you purchase ones without spacers, space them no more than one-eighth inch apart. If

you are really unsure of your skills, use a Patio Pal layout guide on the sand first. This positions the pavers perfectly and stops future weed growth between them.

Q: I argue with my husband about which corn popping method uses less electricity. He likes the greasy microwave method (his waistline shows it), but I like it air popped. What method uses the least energy?

A: Unfortunately for your husband's waistline, using a microwave oven consumes less energy than air popping. I still always use an air popper myself to avoid that greasy smell every time I use the microwave afterwards.

If you are energy and waistline conscious, definitely avoid popping corn in a pot on the range. These electric heating elements or gas burners are large and it takes time and energy just to get the metal pot hot.

Associations and Manufacturers of Unique Paving Products

ARGEE CORP., 9550 Pathway St., Santee CA 92071 - (619) 449-5050

product description - "Patio Pal" — brick and block laying plastic guide that holds bricks in place. Assures alignment of brick or block rows. Blocks out weed growth. Holes allow for drainage. Each package covers approximately 20 sq. ft. Three sizes — fits bricks 3-5/8" x 7-5/8" • fits bricks 4" x 8" • fits blocks (patio pavers) 8" x 16".

product description - "Lets Edge It" — plastic brick edging with or without built-in lights. Bricks and mortar connectors snap together and are pressed into the ground. Mortar connectors swivel for either curves or straight runs. The plastic bricks have the color and texture of real bricks. Spikes under the bricks hold them in place. Lens lifts off the light bricks so you can easily replace the bulb. A low voltage timer/transformer with a 24-hour on-off timer available in 50 or 80 watts.

BRICK INDUSTRY ASSOCIATION, 11490 Commerce Park Dr., Reston, VA 22091 - (703) 620-0010

description - Offers publications on brick paving for the do-it-yourselfer. Will send a free catalogue of publications available by phoning the number above and requesting extension 310.

CONCRETE PAVER & CONCRETE MASONRY ASSOC., 2302 Horsepen Rd., Herndon, VA 22071 - (703) 713-1900

description - Offers publications and pamphlets for a fee on paving walkways, patios and drives for the do-it-yourselfer.

DAVIS COLORS, 3700 E. Olympic Blvd., Los Angeles, CA 90023 - (800) 356-4848 • East (800) 638-4444

product description - powdered pigments for mixing with cement

DIMEX CORP., Route 1, Box 140G, Marietta, OH 45750 - (800) 334-3776

product description - "EdgePro Paver Restraint" — heavy-duty PVC edging for interlocking concrete or brick pavers. Can be used for walkway, patio or driveway installations. Designed for straight and radius installation without snipping or cutting. Will not rot, crack or deteriorate. L-shape design eliminates turf brownout by allowing maximum backfill against pavers. 7-1/2 foot length. Can be anchored with standard 3/8 x 12 inch landscape spikes or 9 inch landscape stakes. "EdgePro Rigid" is for straight installations.

INTERLOCKING CONCRETE PAVEMENT INST., 1444 I St. NW, Suite 700, Washington, DC 20005 - (800) 241-3652

description - Self-governed, self-funded, association representing the interlocking concrete pavement industry. Offers publications and videos for a fee relating to interlocking pavers.

INVISIBLE STRUCTURES, INC., 14704-D East 33rd Place, Aurora, CO 80011 - (800) 233-1510 (303) 373-1234

product description - "Grasspave²" — porous paving system made from 100% post-consumer recycled plastics (film canisters, soda bottles, bread tray, etc.). Thin-walled independent plastic rings connected by an interlocking geogrid structure, which, because it is installed below the surface, is invisible in the completed project. While the rings are rigid, the grid itself is flexible, which makes it easy to install on uneven grades, and reduces usual cut and fill requirements. The plastic rings and spaces between them are filled with a soil/sand mix and planted with grass. Rings prevent compacting of the soil. Great installed along a driveway, as additional parking or as a pathway.

product description - "Gravelpave²" — decorative gravel porous paving system for reinforcing drives, paths and walkways. 100% recycled plastic rings are molded onto non-woven geotextile filter fabric. The rings become invisible or camouflaged by the decorative gravel which is contained for a smooth, well-dressed finish. Settling of fill gravel can be done by either compacting with a roller or irrigating with water.

GECKO STONE, PO Box 521, Kula, HI 96790 - (888) 876-1190

product description - Polyurethane unbreakable molds to make your own interlocking concrete pavers that form a mosaic pattern. Surface details are in the molds. Each mold comes with complete instructions on mixing concrete, coloring, casting, curing and installation. Four designs available — "Gecko Stone" shaped liked a lizard, based on a hexagonal grid, Surface area: 1 square foot, Thickness: 2 inches, Volume: 0.16 cubic feet, Paver weight: 22 lb., Mold weight: 7 lb. • "Frogrock" shaped like a frog, based on a square grid, Surface area: 0.66 square feet, Thickness: 2.5 inches, Volume: 0.14 cubic feet, Paver weight: 20 lb., Mold weight: 4.3 lb. • "Hexacon Interplexus" based on a hexagonal grid, designed for high traffic areas, looks like an interlocking puzzle piece with a triangular pattern and intertwining circles, Surface area: .5 square feet, Thickness: 2.5 inches, Volume: 0.10 cubic feet, Paver weight: 14 lb., Mold weight: 3.3 lb. • "Hexacon Concentrex" based on a hexagonal grid, designed for high traffic areas, looks like an interlocking puzzle piece with a hexagon pattern throughout the stone, Surface area: 0.5 square feet, Thickness: 2.5 inches, Volume: 0.10 cubic feet, Paver weight: 14 lb., Mold weight: 3.3 lb. Paver weights approximate, varies depending on type of concrete mix used.

KERR LIGHTING, 185 Andrews Ave., Smiths Falls, Ontario, Canada K7A 4R9 - (800) 884-8657

product description - "Paver Light" — 12 volt lighting brick system that can be used in driveways, pathways, walkways, around pools and patios, anywhere interlocking pavers are used. Paver Light is available for installation into preexisting, and new asphalt and concrete driveways. The 4 x 8 Paver Light is made of durable plastics, which can be driven on by cars and trucks. Top lens is made of a durable shatter-proof plastic. Two year warranty on the brick. Brick comes with a 7 watt wedge base bulb that has an average life expectancy of 2000 hours. Also available are — 4 x 8 Deck Light, 4 x 4 Dock Light, 4½ x 7 Casino Light, 4½ x 9 BC Light.

MASTER MARK, PO Box 662, Albany, MN 56307 - (800) 535-4838 (320) 845-2111

product description - "Pavemaster" — edging for interlocking concrete or brick pavers available in 8 foot or 6 foot sections. Each retainer is made from heavy gauge HDPE. The unique design allows each retainer to be used for straight or curved areas. Held in place with "Pavemaster Stakes".

PORTLAND CEMENT ASSOCIATION, 5420 Old Orchard Rd., Skokie, IL 60077 - (800) 868-6733 (847) 966-6200

<u>description</u> - Since 1916, PCA has conducted market development, research, education, and public affairs work on behalf of its members — cement companies in the United States and Canada. Offers a book (small fee), "The Homeowner's Guide to Building with Concrete, Brick & Stone" — practical guide for the residential contractor and do-it-yourselfer. Photos, illustrations, and step-by-step instructions explain the most common household jobs: sidewalks, steps, walls, driveways, and patios.

QUIKRETE COMPANIES, 2987 Clairmont Rd., Suite 500, Atlanta, GA 30329 - (404) 634-9100

<u>product description</u> - "WalkMaker Mold" — reusable plastic mold for creating walkways or patios. Resembles running bond brick, cobblestone or a European block design. The mold can be placed on any relatively flat surface. The mold will configure the concrete to the existing base. You may also remove one inch of top soil and level the mold before filling with concrete. You will need a wheelbarrow or mixer, trowel and shovel. Mix concrete, fill the mold with concrete, smooth the surface and remove the mold. Place mold adjacent to completed section and continue the process. Liquid cement color in red, brown, buff or charcoal can be added. You can add wood chips, pebbles, play sand, etc. for texture approximately one hour after concrete has been placed. Sand or mortar mix can be applied dry to the hardened concrete to fill the joints.

VALLEY VIEW INDUSTRIES, 13834 S. Kostner Ave., Crestwood, IL 60445 - (800) 323-9369 (708) 597-0885

<u>product description</u> - "Diamond-Lok Paver Edging" — durable and weather resistant polyurethane edging for interlocking concrete or brick pavers. Designed for easy installation, creates permanent edge restraint. Available in 6 and 15-foot lengths, flexible and rigid configurations, and "T" and "L" designs, can fit any application you need to fill.

Interlocking Concrete Pavement Installation from EP Henry Corp.

Interlocking concrete pavements can be installed by a do-it-yourselfer. While not overly difficult, the job is hard work, primarily because the materials are heavy. You will probably have to rent some tools that the average homeowner does not have. If you take your time and pay close attention to the base preparation, you will be quite pleased with the results.

Materials Required

Stone Base — should be 3/4-inch modified stone, also known as 2A, or 3/4-inch quarry blend. A 1" depth of compacted base weighs approximately 1,200 lbs. per 100 sq. ft. Always add 5 to 10% for edges and miscellaneous areas.

A notched 2x4 can be used as a drag board for sand fill.

Bedding Sand — Coarse concrete sand is recommended. At a depth of 1", this weighs approximately 900 lbs. per 100 sq. ft.. Figure an extra 5% for jointing sand.

Pavers — Are typically sold by the square foot. Calculate the square footage needed for your project and add 5 to 10% for overage, cuts, waste, etc.

Edge Restraint — All exposed edges must be restrained.

Separation Fabric — Recommended for all installations and always where clay type soils are present. This will help maintain the integrity of the base.

Tools Required

Wooden stakes • 6 to 8 ft. 2x4 or 2x6 • Stiff bristle street broom • 3 to 5 pound hammer • 4 ft. level • Flat shovel • Diamond blade wet saw • 3 to 5 hp vibrating plate compactor • Wire cutters (for cutting bands on pavers) • 1" diameter sand screed guides (galvanized steel or PVC) • Wide blade masons chisel • Masons string (twine) • Small pry bar • Hard garden rake • 25 ft. tape measure • Wheelbarrow • Chalkline • Safety glasses • Work gloves

Layout and Preparation

Measure the area you intend to pave. Determine square footage (length x width = square feet) adding 5% for cuts and extra pavers that might be needed later. Measure the lineal feet of all edges, those not up against a permanent structure such as a house, etc., to determine the amount of edge restraint needed.

Draw a plan on a piece of paper showing all important dimensions. Take this plan to an authorized dealer so they can

help you determine the amount of materials needed to complete your project. Mark the outline of your project with stakes every 4 to 6 feet and at each corner. These stakes should be 8" outside of the planned edge of the finished pavement.

Excavation

NOTE: Before digging, always call your local utility companies to locate any underground line.

In general terms, a minimum of 4" of compacted aggregate base is recommended for patios and walkways, and 8" for residential driveways where freeze/thaw conditions exist. Add 3" for the depth of the bedding sand and the paver thickness to determine the total depth to excavate. Excavation should be 6" wider than the finished pavement's dimensions on sides where edge restraint is to be used.

Slope and grade are important to ensure proper runoff. It is best to plan at least a 1/4" per foot drop, but try not to exceed 1/2" per foot.

Level the job as you progress with it.

Base Preparation

As with any building project, the finished pavement will only be as good as the construction of the base. For this reason, this is the most important part of the installation process.

First, run your plate

compactor over the excavated soil, making sure no soil gets stuck to the bottom of the plate tamper. Each pass should overlap the previous one by about 4". It is suggested that a separation fabric, such as Mirafi 500 X, be laid down over the compacted subgrade.

bevel toward waste

To custom fit, cut to desired size with chisel and mallet.

scored line

Now spread your stone base material out evenly in a 2" layer. If material is dry and dusty use a garden hose to thoroughly wet it down; this helps make the gravel faster to compact and easier to rake. Starting around the outer perimeter, use the plate compactor to pack together the base, again overlapping each pass about 4" and working towards the center. You should make at least two complete passes for each layer. Repeat this process for each subsequent layer of base material until the final thickness is achieved.

When finished with the base it should be very smooth and flat and reflect the final grade of your project, less the thickness of the bedding sand and pavers. If you were to put a straight edge flat on the surface there should be no more than 1/4" gap at any point along the straight edge.

Sand Setting Bed
NOTE: It is important to keep your sand dry. Always keep your sand covered in case of rain. It is suggested that you only screed sand for areas where you will be laying pavers that same day. Do not attempt to level any area or surface irregularities with the sand. This will result in an uneven surface and unwanted settling.

Lay the screed guides (1" outside diameter electrical conduit, strips of wood or other suitable rigid material) on top of the compacted base material 4' to 6' apart and parallel. Evenly distribute a quantity of bedding sand between the guides and drag the 6 to 8 ft. 2x4 or 2x6 over the guides to create a smooth even layer of sand, striking off any excess. Do not walk on or work from your screed sand. Fill voids left by the screed guides with sand and trowel them smooth as you are laying the pavers.

Laying the Pavers
NOTE: All projects must start at a perfect 90 degree angle. Use the 3 - 4 - 5 triangle method to establish this. For an even mix of pavers, draw from several cubes at a time when installing them. Starting from a permanent edge such as a house, driveway or even a piece of rigid PVC edge restraint, lay your first paver starting from either side. (As you start laying pavers, work from right to left, then left to right and so on, one row of pavers at a time.) Set the pavers lightly onto the sand; never press or hammer them in. Every 4 feet or so, run a string across the front of the laying edge to maintain straight lines. If you are doing the project over a couple of days, cover the entire area with plastic over-

Sprinkle sand over pavers when finished. With a broom, work the sand into all the joints.

night if rain is expected.

Cutting the Pavers
Mark any stones to be cut with a wax crayon and use either a diamond blade wet saw (recommended), a paver splitter or a hammer and chisel. Try and keep cut pieces along the edges to a size at least that of one half paver. Always wear safety glasses.

Installation of Edge Restraint
Restrain all edges not up against a permanent structure with an appropriate product. Any restraint material should rest entirely on the compacted aggregate base.

Seat the Installed Paver in the Bedding Sand
Sweep off debris that may be on the pavers and scatter a thin layer of dry joint sand over the surface. Starting around the perimeter and working inward, make at least two passes over the pavers with a vibratory plate compactor, overlapping each pass 2 to 4 inches. Make the 2nd pass at a 45-degree angle to your first. This step will level the pavers, compact the bedding sand, and fill the joints with sand from above and below.

Finish Filling Joints with Sand
Spread more jointing sand over the surface. Use a stiff bristle street broom and sweep back and forth over the entire pavement until all joints are filled to the top with sand.

Sweep off all excess sand and backfill edges with top soil and sod or seed. (Water freshly seeded or sodded areas regularly.)

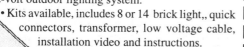
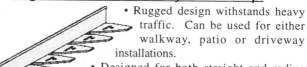

Keep your cool with flowering vines

Q: The afternoon heat from the south and west bakes us. The walls stay hot all evening. Is planting flowering climbing vines on a trellis an effective shading method? Which vines are best?

A: Growing flowering or nonflowering climbing vines is an effective natural method to cool your home. Every imaginable color of flower or bright berry is available. Several vines also have attractive foliage with unique shapes and colors.

In addition to just providing shade for your house, vines cool by a natural process called transpiration. As they give off moisture, the air is cooled, like when you perspire. Vines planted several feet from your wall can lower the air temperature near the wall by as much as 10 degrees or more.

Plant deciduous vines on the south and west exposures so the winter sun can shine through for free solar heat. You should select ones with an open vine pattern. Even without leaves, a heavy vine pattern blocks much of the winter sun.

The simpler the trellis design, the better. Some very ornate trellises look great, but they can block too much of the winter sun. A simple rectangular trellis built with lightweight lumber is very effective and easy to make.

When selecting climbing vines, check the weather "hardiness zone" of each variety. Not all varieties can survive severe winter temperatures or harsh summer conditions. Also consider the maximum length of the vine to be sure it will cover the trellis that you build.

Two excellent groups of shading vines are ones that attach themselves with tendrils and ones that twine. Avoid vines that attach directly to a wall because they may hold in moisture and may damage the wall over time.

Twining vines are my favorite type for growing on a trellis. A simple copper wire trellis works well with a twining vine. They quickly twist around it. Copper weathers to a green patina, so it blends with the vines.

Ask your nurseryman which way each twining vine typically twists, clockwise or counterclockwise. Most varieties twist one way or the other. It helps to know this to twist them the proper way when you plant them.

To shade a glass patio door or picture window, select a vine that naturally grows horizontally, too. Make a copper wire trellis that runs vertically up the west side of the window and horizontally along the top to form an overhead awning.

Climbing vines are good for the environment. They consume carbon dioxide and produce oxygen, thus improving the environment and reducing the harmful greenhouse effect. They do not harm the ozone layer like air conditioners.

Q: In the winter it makes sense to lower the thermostat setting whenever I am away. Is the same true in the summer? Should I raise it or does it just use more electricity to cool it down again when I arrive home?

A: The only difference between summer and winter is that the heat flows in instead of out. The rules for setting the thermostat are the same for both seasons. Setting the thermostat higher makes good sense if you are gone for several hours.

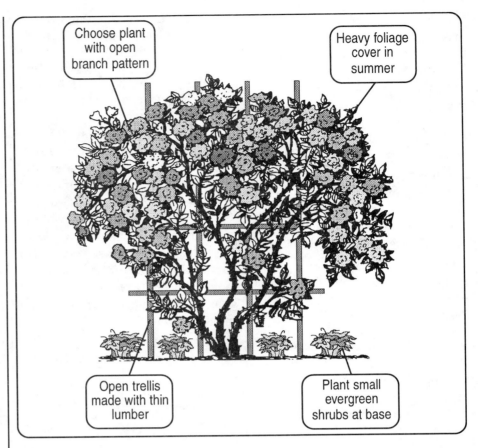

Choose plant with open branch pattern

Heavy foliage cover in summer

Open trellis made with thin lumber

Plant small evergreen shrubs at base

Vines offer a natural way to reduce energy bills. During the summer months vines shade and cool the walls of your house. They help keep the surface temperatures down and reduce the amount of heat entering the house. In the winter the vines can be trimmed back to allow the sun to shine through. This will let in extra light and heat during the winter months.

Vines climb in several ways so it is important to know the climbing methods. Below is a description of the growth patterns of vines. Vines which climb and cling by roots or tendrils with discs, support themselves. They should only be used on walls or buildings of stone or masonry. They cannot be easily removed and may damage the surface. They keep the wood moist and tend to cause rot. It is also a good idea to keep vines away from gutters and drainpipes. You can disentangle and remove the vine but with age some vine stems can grow to 6 inches in diameter. This can easily force a drainpipe away from the wall if it grows behind it.

Wooden structures or walls are best covered by vines that are separated from the walls by a trellis or some other structure. The trellis should stand a few feet from the surface. This allows easy maintenance for the wall and good air flow for the growing vines. You should choose a twining or tendril climber that will cling to the trellis.

You can make a simple trellis using copper or galvanized wire strung over a wooden frame. Start screws in the top and bottom horizontal pieces allowing them to stick out about one-half inch. Wrap the wire around each one from top to bottom. Space the screws depending on how dense you want the shading to be. Uncoated copper wire quickly weathers to a natural green color. Once it turns green, the corrosion stops and it will last may years.

Types and Growth Patterns of Vines

Twining vines — climb by winding themselves around their support as they grow. They need a vertical support to wrap around — string, wire or a trellis. You may need to tie the vine to its support at first, but as it grows the vine will climb on its own. Wrap it around the support in the direction it naturally grows.

Tendril climbers — clings to supports by means of tendrils that are like threadlike fingers which grow from the stem opposite the leaves. These vines can be trained to grow vertically or horizontally if they have a small support (wire, lattice, stakes, string, even other plants) for the tendrils to wrap around.

Clinging or rooting vines — adhere to their support by means of small aerial roots that attach to any flat or solid surface. These vines do not need any type of trellis, they grip with their adhesive roots on rough vertical surfaces.

Morning Glory   *Sweet Pea*   *English Ivy*

Twining Vine   *Tendril Climber*   *Rooting Vine*

Flowering Climbing Vines

Actinidia chinensis — Chinese Actinidia
climbing method - twining   bloom - early summer
length - 25 feet   colors - white to yellow
growth rate - fast   exposure* - S, PS
zones - 7 to 9   soil - any
characteristics - Young shoots are the most colorful covered with red hairs giving it a velvety effect.

Actinidia kolomikta — Kolomikta Actinidia
climbing method - twining   bloom - early summer
length - 20 feet   colors - white
growth rate - fast   exposure - S, PS
zones - 4 to 9   soil - any
characteristics - Fragrant flowers on a vine with large (4" to 5") variegated leaves.

Actinidia polygama — Silvervine
climbing method - twining   bloom - early summer
length - 15 feet   colors - white
growth rate - fast   exposure - S, PS
zones - 4 to 9   soil - any
characteristics - Fragrant flowers. Partially variegated leaves. Favorite of cats!

Akebia quinata — Five-leaf Akebia
climbing method - twining   bloom - early summer
length - 35 feet   colors - purple
growth rate - fast   exposure - S, PS
zones - 4 to 9   soil - any
characteristics - Semi-evergreen. Fragrant flowers. Trained and maintained as a climber, it is one of the best.

Aristolochia durior — Dutchman's Pipe
climbing method - twining   bloom - early summer
length - 20 feet   colors - yellow
growth rate - moderate   exposure - PS, FS
zones - 4 to 9   soil - well-drained
characteristics - Deciduous with very large, heart-shaped leaves. Unusual, yellow-brown flowers. Dense growth for screening.

Bignonia capreolata — Crossvine
climbing method - tendrils   bloom - late spring
length - 40 feet   colors - orange-red
growth rate - fast   exposure - FS, PS
zones - 6 to 10   soil - moist
characteristics - Evergreen vine. In the fall, foliage color changes to reddish green. Excellent for screen planting.

Bougainvillea — Bougainvillea
climbing method - twining   bloom - all year
length - 40 feet   colors - various
growth rate - moderate   exposure - FS
zones - 9 to 10   soil - well-drained
characteristics - Ornamental evergreen. Cling with hooked spines. Flowerlike bracts surround tiny inconspicuous fragrant flowers.

Campsis grandiflora — Chinese Trumpet Vine
climbing method - rooting   bloom - mid summer
length - 20 feet   colors - orange-red
growth rate - fast   exposure - FS
zones - 5 to 9   soil - any
characteristics - Showiest Campsis with 3" diameter funnel-shaped flowers. Needs assistance with climbing.

Campsis x tagliabuana — Madame Galen
climbing method - rooting   bloom - mid summer
length - 25 feet   colors - salmon-red
growth rate - fast   exposure - FS
zones - 4 to 9   soil - any
characteristics - Heavy vine needs support or is susceptible to severe weather. Attracts hummingbirds.

Clematis armandii — Armand Clematis
climbing method - twining   bloom - spring
length - 15 feet   colors - white
growth rate - fast   exposure - PS
zone - 7 to 9   soil - moist
characteristics - Evergreen vine. Clusters of fragrant, starlike, 2½" flowers. Thrives in northwest. Prune after flowering.

Clematis jackmanni — Jackman Clematis
climbing method - twining   bloom - summer
length - 12 feet   colors - purple
growth rate - fast   exposure - PS
zones - 5 to 9   soil - moist,
characteristics - Showy hybrid with 5" diameter flowers. Late bloomer, should be pruned heavily in spring.

Clematis maximowicziana — Sweet Autumn Clematis length - 30 feet growth rate - fast zones - 5 to 9
  climbing method - twining bloom - late summer colors - white exposure - PS soil - moist
  characteristics - One of the best clematis for screening purposes. Masses of fragrant flowers followed by fluffy silver seedheads.

Clematis montana rubens — Oriental Clematis length - 20 feet growth rate - fast zones - 6 to 9
  climbing method - twining bloom - summer colors - pink, white exposure - PS soil - moist
  characteristics - Young leaves are tinged with a bronze to purple color.

Dicentra scandens — Yellow Bleeding Heart length - 10 feet growth rate - fast zones - 6 to 9
  climbing method - tendrils bloom - summer colors - yellow exposure - S, PS soil - moist
  characteristics - Delicate, divided foliage. Best in morning sun with afternoon shade. Excellent for trellises or arbors.

Dioscorea batatas — Cinnamon Vine length - 10 feet growth rate - fast zones - 5 to 10
  climbing method - twining bloom - late summer colors - white exposure - FS, PS soil - moist
  characteristics - Cinnamon-scented flowers. Needs support.

Distictis lactiflora — Vanilla Distictus length - 20 feet growth rate - fast zones - 9 to 10
  climbing method - tendrils bloom - summer to fall colors - purple, white exposure - S, PS soil - moist
  characteristics - Ornamental vine. Morning glory-shaped flowers.

Gelsemium sempervirens — Carolina Jasmine length - 20 feet growth rate - fast zones - 7 to 9
  climbing method - twining bloom - spring to summer colors - yellow exposure - S, PS soil - moist
  characteristics - Evergreen vine with fragrant, tubular 1½" flowers in early spring.

Hydrangea anomala petiolaris — Climbing Hydrangea length - 75 feet growth rate - moderate zones - 4 to 9
  climbing method - rooting bloom - midsummer colors - white exposure - FS, PS soil - any
  characteristics - Serrated leaves and large 6" flat flowers in clusters. Red bark is a winter feature. Grow slow at first.

Jasminum mesnyi — Primrose Jasmine length - 10 feet growth rate - moderate zones - 8 to 9
  climbing method - climbing bloom - spring to summer colors - yellow exposure - FS, PS soil - well-drained
  characteristics - Very beautiful but relatively fragile jasmine. Single flowers are over 1" in diameter.

Jasminum nudiflorum — Winter Jasmine length - 15 feet growth rate - moderate zones - 5 to 9
  climbing method - climbing** bloom - spring to summer colors - yellow exposure - FS, PS soil - well-drained
  characteristics - Early blooming vine is most hardy jasmine. Flowers can also be forced into bloom indoors.

Jasminum officinale — Common White Jasmine length - 30 feet growth rate - moderate zones - 8 to 10
  climbing method - climbing bloom - spring to summer colors - white exposure - FS, PS soil - well-drained
  characteristics - Widely found in the south covering arbors/trellises. Semi-evergreen. Fragrant flowers. Requires little attention.

Kadsura japonica — Scarlet Kadsura length - 12 feet growth rate - moderate zones - 5 to 7
  climbing method - twining bloom - summer to fall colors - yellowish white exposure - FS, PS soil - well-drained
  characteristics - Evergreen. Vine turns reddish green in fall with clusters of scarlet berries.

Lonicera heckrottis — Everblooming Honeysuckle length - 20 feet growth rate - slow zones - 5 to 9
  climbing method - twining bloom - summer colors - yellow, red exposure - FS, PS soil - well-drained
  characteristics - Very fragrant flowers. Considered one of the best.

Lonicera japonica — Hall's Honeysuckle length - 25 feet growth rate - slow zones - 5 to 9
  climbing method - tendrils bloom - summer to fall colors - white exposure - FS, PS soil - well-drained
  characteristics - Largely evergreen. Sweet fragrant flowers. Flowers turn to soft yellow as they age.

Lonicera sempervirens — Trumpet Honeysuckle length - 20 feet growth rate - fast zones - 4 to 9
  climbing method - twining bloom - summer to fall colors - orange-scarlet exposure - FS, PS soil - well-drained
  characteristics - Deciduous (semi-evergreen where warm). Trumpet-shaped flowers, scarlet berrylike fruit. Attracts hummingbirds.

Mandevilla laxa — Chiliean Jasmine length - 15 feet growth rate - fast zones - 8 to 10
  climbing method - twining bloom - midsummer colors - various exposure - FS, PS soil - well-drained
  characteristics - Good trained on a trellis. It is a very good container plant. Can bring indoors for the winter

Passiflora x alatocaerulea — Passionflower length - 25 feet growth rate - fast zones - 8 to 10
  climbing method - tendrils bloom - summer colors - red, purple, blue exposure - FS soil - well-drained
  characteristics - Tender vine with fragrant flowers. Good container plant. Flowers open in a.m., close by noon.

Pileostegia viburnoides — Tanglehead length - 15 feet growth rate - slow zones - 7 to 10
  climbing method - rooting bloom - summer to fall colors - white exposure - FS, PS, Sh soil - moist
  characteristics - Evergreen with panicles of flowers that hang profusely among dark-green leaves. Good against a north wall.

Polygonum aubertii — Silverlace or Fleecevine length - 25 feet growth rate - fast zones - 4 to 8
  climbing method - twining bloom - late summer colors - white exposure - FS soil - average
  characteristics - Dense green foliage. Clusters of small, fragrant flowers. Attracts bees. Tolerates dryness. Good on chain-link fence.

Pueraria lobata — Kudza Vine length - 75 feet growth rate - fast zones - 6 to 9
  climbing method - twining bloom - summer colors - violet-purple exposure - FS soil - average
  characteristics - Requires careful pruning. Flowers hidden by large leaves. Best covering a large area in a short amount of time.

Rosa x Rambler — Roses length - 14 feet growth rate - fast zones - 5 to 9
  climbing method - climbing bloom - summer colors - various exposure - FS soil - well-drained
  characteristics - Not a true vine. Must be tied to its support. Requires pruning to encourage blooming, but blooms profusely.

Solandra grandiflora — Chalice Vine length - 20 feet growth rate - fast zones - 9 to 11
  climbing method - twining bloom - spring to summer colors - yellow exposure - FS, PS soil - well-drained
  characteristics - Evergreen vine. Red berries after blooms.

Trachelospermum jasminoides — Confederate Jasmine length - 20 feet growth rate - fast zones - 9 to 11
  climbing method - twining bloom - early summer colors - white exposure - PS, Sh soil - well-drained
  characteristics - Evergreen vine forms thick screens with fragrant flowers. Prune annually. Excellent greenhouse plant.

Tripterygium regelii — Regel's Threewingnut length - 8 feet growth rate - fast zones - 4 to 9
  climbing method - twining bloom - early summer colors - white exposure - FS, PS soil - well-drained
  characteristics - Unique vine with large 8-10" clusters of flowers. Needs some support in order to grow as a vine.

Wisteria floribunda — Japanese Wisteria   length - 24 feet   growth rate - moderate   zones - 4 to 9
climbing method - twining   bloom - summer   colors - various   exposure - FS   soil - well-drained
characteristics - Right to left twining vine with small leaves and very large, fragrant flower clusters. Leaves turn yellow in fall.

Wisteria sinensis — Chinese Wisteria   length - 25 feet   growth rate - moderate   zones - 5 to 9
climbing method - twining   bloom - late spring   colors - blue, violet, white   exposure - FS   soil - well-drained
characteristics - Short pea-shaped flower clusters. Lightly fragrant blooms. Needs sturdy arbor, trellis or wall support.

* Exposure: FS — Full Sun, PS — Part Shade, Sh — Full Shade   ** Requires mechanical support to trellis

Annual Flowering Climbing Vines

Asarina scandens — Snapdragon Vine   length - 10 feet   growth rate - fast   zones - any
climbing method - tendrils   bloom - summer to fall   colors - pink, purple, white   exposure - FS, PS   soil - well-drained

Cardiospermum halicacabum — Balloon Vine   length - 20 feet   growth rate - fast   zones - any
climbing method - tendrils   bloom - summer to fall   colors - white   exposure - FS   soil - well-drained

Cobaea scandens — Cathedral Bells   length - 25 feet   growth rate - fast   zones - any
climbing method - tendrils   bloom - summer to fall   colors - lavender, purple   exposure - FS   soil - well-drained

Dolichos lablab — Hyacinth Bean   length - 20 feet   growth rate - fast   zones - any
climbing method - twining   bloom - summer   colors - white, pink, purple   exposure - FS   soil - well-drained

Hummulus japonicus — Japanese Hop Vine   length - 25 feet   growth rate - fast   zones - any
climbing method - twining   bloom - summer   colors - pink   exposure - FS, PS   soil - average

Ipomea alba — Moonflower or Moonvine   length - 30 feet   growth rate - fast   zones - any
climbing method - twine/tendrils   bloom - midsummer   colors - white   exposure - FS, PS   soil - humus-rich

Impomea x multifida — Cardinal Climber   length - 20 feet   growth rate - fast   zones - any
climbing method - twine/tendrils   bloom - summer to fall   colors - red   exposure - FS, PS   soil - well-drained

Impomea species — Morning Glory   length - 20 feet   growth rate - fast   zones - any
climbing method - twine/tendrils   bloom - summer to fall   colors - various   exposure - FS, PS   soil - humus-rich

Lathyrus odoratus — Sweet Pea   length - 20 feet   growth rate - fast   zones - any
climbing method - tendrils   bloom - early spring   colors - various   exposure - FS, PS   soil - humus-rich

Mandevilla x amabilis — Mandevilla   length - 20 feet   growth rate - fast   zones - any
climbing method - twining   bloom - spring to fall   colors - pink   exposure - FS, PS   soil - humus-rich

Mina lobata — Exotic Love   length - 10 feet   growth rate - fast   zones - any
climbing method - twining   bloom - summer to fall   colors - red-orange-yellow   exposure - FS, PS   soil - humus-rich

Thunbergia alata — Black-eyed Susan Vine   length - 10 feet   growth rate - fast   zones - any
climbing method - tendrils   bloom - summer to fall   colors - orange   exposure - FS, PS   soil - well-drained

Tropaeolum peregrinum — Canary-bird Vine   length - 20 feet   growth rate - fast   zones - any
climbing method - tendrils   bloom - summer to fall   colors - yellow   exposure - FS, PS   soil - well-drained

Tropaeolum majus — Nasturtium   length - 20 feet   growth rate - fast   zones - any
climbing method - tendrils   bloom - summer to fall   colors - various   exposure - FS, PS   soil - well-drained

Non-Flowering Climbing Vines

Ampelopsis megalophyllas — Spikenard Ampelopsis   length - 30 feet   growth rate - fast   zones - 6 to 8
climbing method - tendrils   exposure - FS, PS   soil - well-drained
characteristics - Extra-large (10-25") leaves provide shade.

Celastrus flagellaris — Korean Bittersweet   length - 24 feet   growth rate - fast   zones - 4 to 8
climbing method - twining   exposure - FS, PS   soil - good
characteristics - Thorny with yellow and red berries. Fall foliage is yellow. Tolerates dryness. Needs support. Invasive

Celastrus scandens — American Bittersweet   length - 20 feet   growth rate - fast   zones - 2 to 8
climbing method - twining   exposure - FS, PS   soil - good
characteristics - Deciduous with yellow-orange fruit capsules bursting to form bright red berries in fall. The fall foliage is yellow.

Euonymus fortunei — Common Winter Creeper   length - 20 feet   growth rate - moderate   zones - 4 to 8
climbing method - rooting   exposure - FS, PS   soil - varied
characteristics - Evergreen vine attaches with aerial holdfasts. Pink fruit pods open in fall to orange berries. Good on masonry.

Hedera helix — English Ivy   length - 90 feet   growth rate - fast   zones - 5 to 8
climbing method - rooting   exposure - PS, FS   soil - varied
characteristics - One of the best clinging evergreen vines. Is easy to cultivate. The dull green leaves have 3 to 5 lobes.

Parthenocissus quinquefolia — Virginia Creeper   length - 50 feet   growth rate - fast   zones - 3 to 9
climbing method - twining   exposure - FS, PS   soil - humus-rich, moist
characteristics - High-climbing vine with small bluish black, slightly bloomy berries. Brilliant red leaves in fall.

Parthenocissus tricuspidata — Boston Ivy   length - 60 feet   growth rate - fast   zones - 4 to 8
climbing method - rootlet   exposure - FS, PS   soil - humus-rich, moist
characteristics - Deciduous to semi-evergreen. Leaves turn orange-red-purple in fall. Blue-black berries. Hardy.

Smilax megalantha — Coral Greenbriar   length - 18 feet   growth rate - fast   zones - 7 to 9
climbing method - twining   exposure - FS, PS   soil - well-drained
characteristics - Evergreen with lustrous foliage and bright red fruits. Not self-pollinating, beautiful even without the fruit.

Vitus coignetiae — Gloryvine   length - 50 feet   growth rate - moderate   zones - 5 to 9
climbing method - rooting   exposure - FS   soil - loam, with peat moss
characteristics - Can grow up to 50 ft. in one summer. 10" diameter leaves turn red in fall. Non-edible fruit. Excellent for screen.

Vitus labrusca — Grape   length - 20 feet   growth rate - moderate   zones - 3 to 9
climbing method - rooting   exposure - FS   soil - loam, with peat moss
characteristics - Deciduous ornamental vines. Colorful fruit is edible. Trunk and branch patterns are an interesting winter design.

Dwarf shrubs can shrink energy bills

Q: I want to landscape my front yard and around my deck with decorative evergreen and flowering dwarf shrubs. What types of shrubs are available and where should I locate them for the greatest energy efficiency?

A: There are hundreds of decorative evergreen and deciduous (drops leaves in fall) dwarf shrubs. Foliage colors, flowers, berries and shapes vary considerably. By planting a variety of dwarf shrubs, the attractive colors and textures change throughout the seasons.

Dwarf shrubs are ideal for energy-efficient landscaping because they remain small at maturity (2 to 3 feet high). Plant some near the house foundation and some farther away for windbreak ramps. Since they stay small, they require little care.

Many dwarf shrubs have flowers, small fruits for wildlife and beautiful autumn coloration. Some deciduous varieties also have ornamental bark or branching habits that are attractive in the winter too.

Dwarf shrubs can cut your utility bills year-round. The sillplate on the foundation is the area of greatest air leakage into most homes. Planting dwarf shrubs near the house, especially evergreen varieties, can block the force of the cold winter winds and reduce this leakage.

As a windbreak ramp, dwarf shrubs can be planted to the northwest side of taller shrubs and trees. These begin directing the cold winds upward toward the taller trees. The upward wind path continues over the top of your home.

In the summer, dwarf shrubs cool the air near your house with shade and by a process called transpiration. As plants give off moisture to the air, the air cools. This is a similar process to the way perspiring cools you. The air temperature can be as much as 10 degrees cooler by the shrubs.

Several types of flowereng dwarf shrubs

Potentilla   Barberry   Mockorange   Azalea

Dwarf shrubs behind trees as windbreak ramp

Shrubs seal air leaks at foundation

Shrubs stay low for use under windows

Flowering shrubs in planter to block heat from sidewalk

Dense-foliage deciduous dwarf shrubs are ideal for summer heat control. Plant an area of dwarf shrubs near your house on the south and west sides to create a cooling buffer. This buffer blocks the indirect heat radiating from hot patios, sidewalks and driveways.

Dwarf shrubs are often more expensive than other types of common fast-growing larger shrubs. However, since the shrubs maintain their initial size, you will not have to relandscape every several years. Cheaper common shrubs look great when they are small, but can quickly outgrow the space.

When selecting dwarf shrubs, always consider the "hardiness zone" of each shrub. Hardiness relates to the coldest winter temperature which it can withstand and other area-specific conditions.

Q: I unfortunately had to cut down several large trees this year. I plan to use it for firewood. How can I make a low-cost adjustable cover to keep the wood pile dry so the wood seasons well?

A: Generally, cut the logs to about an 18-inch length for easy handling and burning. Buy a two-foot wide (any length you need) sheet of fiberglass corrugated roofing. Saw a hole in each corner 18 inches from one long edge.

Drive two tall poles in the ground 16 inches from your house wall. When the roofing is slipped over the poles and the wood pile, it rests against the wall and slopes down. As more wood is added, just slide up the roofing.

You can landscape your home for efficiency with dwarf shrubs. The following pages list dwarf shrubs and information about each type. A map of hardiness zones is shown on page 151. Because some areas have very unique microclimates, check with a local nurseryman before buying. Three general types of dwarf shrubs are listed. Deciduous shrubs can be effective foundation windbreaks in the winter, too. Choose ones with a coarse texture and heavy branch patterns.

There are several techniques for using dwarf shrubs to landscape efficiently. A windbreak ramp refers to using progressively larger plants nearer your house on the north and northwest sides. This gently guides the cold winter winds up and over your house. If you just plant some large trees without the dwarf shrub ramp, much air turbulence is created at the tree line. This causes more air movement around your house and defeats the purpose of a windbreak in the winter.

Deciduous Dwarf Shrubs

Abelia x grandiflora — Glossy Abelia
size* - 3 to 6 by 3 to 6   rate** - medium   texture - medium-fine   hardiness - zone 6 to 9
habit - spreading, dense, rounded, multistemmed, arching branches

Abeliophyllum distichum — White Forsythia
size - 3 to 5 by 3 to 4   rate - medium   texture - medium   hardiness - zone 5 to 8
habit - rounded and multistemmed developing arching branches

Berberis thunbergii var. **atropurpurea 'Crimson Pygmy'** — Barbery
size - 1½ to 2 by 3   rate - medium   texture - medium-fine   hardiness - zone 4 to 8
habit - dense rounded shrub, much branched

Callicarpa dichotoma — Purple Beautyberry
size - 3 to 4 by 3 to 5   rate - fast   texture - medium-fine   hardiness - zone 5 to 8
habit - long slender branches arch and touch ground at their tips

Caryopteris x clandonesis — Blue-mist Shrub
size -1½ to 3 by 2 to 4   rate - fast   texture - medium   hardiness - zone 6 to 9
habit - low, mounded and arching

Ceanothus ovatus — Mountain Sweet
size - 2 to 3 by 3 to 5   rate - medium   texture - medium   hardiness - zone 4 to 8
habit - low, broad, compact, rounded top, slender upright branches

Chaenomeles japonico — Japanese Flowering Quince
size - 2 to 4 by 2 to 4   rate - medium   texture - medium-fine   hardiness - zone 5 to 8
habit - upright shrub with glossy green foliage

Clethera hummingbird — Summersweet
size -1 to 2 by 2 to 3   rate - medium   texture - medium   hardiness - zone 3 to 8
habit - compact, rounded form

Comptonia peregrina — Sweetfern
size - 2 to 4 by 4 to 8   rate - slow   texture - medium-fine   hardiness - zone 2 to 5
habit - slender erect branches, flat-topped to rounded outline

Cornus canadensis — Bunchberry
size - 3 to 9 in. - spread   rate - slow   texture - medium-fine   hardiness - zone 2 to 6
habit - forms carpet-like mat, used as ground cover

Cornus serica 'Keleyi' — Kelsey Redosier Dogwood
size - 2 to 3 by 2 to 4   rate -fast   texture - medium   hardiness - zone 2 to 8
habit - rounded, compact form, multistemmed shrub

Cotoneaster apiculatus — Cranberry Cotoneaster
size - 2 to 3 by 3 to 6   rate -slow   texture - fine   hardiness - zone 4 to 7
habit - low, wide spreading with stiff branching pattern

Cotoneaster horizontalis — Rockspray
size - 2 to 3 by 5 to 8   rate - slow   texture - fine   hardiness - zone 5 to 7
habit - low, flat, dense shrub with branches spreading horizontally

Cytisus decumbens — Prostrate Broom
size - 6 to 8 in. - spread   rate - fast   texture - fine   hardiness - zone 5 to 8
habit - low ground cover

Daphne x burkwoodii 'Somerset' — Somerset Burkwood Daphne
size - 3 to 4 by 3 to 4   rate - slow   texture - medium   hardiness - zone 4 to 8
habit - rounded form

Daphne giraldii — Giraldi Daphne
size - 2 to 3 by 2 to 4   rate - medium   texture - medium   hardiness - zone 4 to 8
habit - bushy and high

Deutzia gracilis — Slender Deutzia
size - 2 to 4 by 3 to 4   rate - slow   texture - medium-fine   hardiness - zone 4 to 8
habit - low, broad mound, graceful with slender ascending branches

Euonymus alatus 'Compactus' — Burning Bush
size - 2 to 3 by 2 to 3   rate - slow   texture - medium   hardiness - zone 3 to 8
habit - mounded to horizontal, spreading, flat-topped

Forsythia viridissima 'Bronsensis' — Bronx Greenstem Forsythia
size - 6 to 12 in. by 2   rate - slow   texture - medium   hardiness - zone 5 to 8
habit -stiff and upright, flat-topped

Fothergilla gardenii — Dwarf Fothergilla
size - 2 to 3 by 2 to 3   rate - slow   texture - medium   hardiness - zone 5 to 8
habit - slender, crooked, spreading branches, rounded dense mound

Genista tinctoria — Dyer's Greenwood
size - 2 to 3 by 2 to 3   rate - slow   texture - fine   hardiness - zone 4 to 7
habit - vertical, slender, spiky and twiggy

Hydrangea arborescens 'Annabelle' — Smooth Hydrangea
size - 2 to 4 by 3 to 5   rate - fast   texture - coarse   hardiness - zone 4 to 9
habit -low growing, clumpy, rounded shrub

Hydrangea macrophylla 'Pia' — Bigleaf Hydrangea
size - 1 to 2 by 1 to 2   rate - medium   texture - medium   hardiness - zone 6 to 9
habit - rounded with erect thick stems

Hypericum calycinum — Aaronsbeard St. Johnswort
size - 12 to 18 in. by 24 in.   rate - slow   texture - medium   hardiness - zone 5 to 8
habit - ascending stems

Hypericum frondosum 'Sunburst' — Golden St. Johnswort
size - 3 to 4 by 3 to 4   rate - slow   texture - medium   hardiness - zone 5 to 8
habit - upright shrub with stout branches

Jasminum nudiflorum — Winter Jasmine
size - 3 to 4 by 4 to 7   rate - fast   texture - fine   hardiness - zone 6 to 8
habit - broad spreading mounded mass of trailing branches

Ligustrum vulgare 'Lodense' — Lodense European Privet
size - 2 to 4½ by 2 to 3   rate - fast   texture - medium   hardiness - zone 4 to 7
habit - low, dense, compact form

* Size in feet unless otherwise noted — width (spread) by height.
** Rate of growth refers to vertical increase and is influenced by many variables such as soil, water, drainage, fertility, light, exposure, etc. Slow means the plant grows 12" or less per year; medium means the plant grows 13" to 24" per year; and fast means the plant grows to 25" or more.

***Lonicera xylosteum* 'Emerald Mound'** — Fly Honeysuckle <u>habit</u> - low growing and mounded
<u>size</u> - 2 to 3 by 4½ to 6 <u>rate</u> - fast   <u>texture</u> - medium   <u>hardiness</u> - zone 4 to 6

***Philadelphus* 'Silver Showers'** — Sweet Mockorange   <u>habit</u> - rounded with stiff, straight, ascending branches that arch
<u>size</u> - 2 to 3 by 3 to 6 <u>rate</u> - fast   <u>texture</u> - coarse   <u>hardiness</u> - zone 4 to 8

Potentilla fruticosa — Bush Cinquefoil   <u>habit</u> - bushy with upright slender stems forming a low, rounded outline
<u>size</u> - 1 to 4 by 2 to 4 <u>rate</u> - slow   <u>texture</u> - fine   <u>hardiness</u> - zone 2 to 7

***Rhus aromatica* 'Gro-Low'** — Gro-Low Fragrant Sumac <u>habit</u> - low, irregular spreading shrub, lower branches turn up at tips
<u>size</u> - 2 to 5 by 6 to 10 <u>rate</u> - slow   <u>texture</u> - medium   <u>hardiness</u> - zone 3 to 9

***Ribes alpinum* 'Green Mound'** — Dwarf Alpine Currant <u>habit</u> - densely twiggy, rounded, stiff, upright stems, spreading branches
<u>size</u> - 2 to 3 by 2 to 3 <u>rate</u> - medium   <u>texture</u> - medium-fine <u>hardiness</u> - zone 2 to 7

***Spiraea x bumalda* 'Anthony Waterer'** — Anthony Waterer Spirea   <u>habit</u> - broad, flat-topped, densely twiggy, erect branches
<u>size</u> - 2 to 3 by 3 to 5 <u>rate</u> - fast   <u>texture</u> - medium-fine <u>hardiness</u> - zone 3 to 8

***Spiraea x bumalda* 'Crispa'** — Crisped-leaved Spirea   <u>habit</u> - broad and flat-topped
<u>size</u> - 2 to 4 by 4 to 5 <u>rate</u> - fast   <u>texture</u> - fine   <u>hardiness</u> - zone 3 to 8

***Stephandra incisa* 'Crispa'** — Crisped Stephanandra   <u>habit</u> - low, thick tangle of stems
<u>size</u> - 1½ to 3 by 4 to 5 <u>rate</u> - fast   <u>texture</u> - medium   <u>hardiness</u> - zone 3 to 8

***Syringa patula* 'Miss Kim'** — Dwarf Korean Lilac   <u>habit</u> - stiff, spreading branches
<u>size</u> - 2 to 3 by 4 to 5 <u>rate</u> - slow   <u>texture</u> - medium   <u>hardiness</u> - zone 5 to 9

***Viburnum carlesii* 'Compactum'** — Koreanspice Viburnum <u>habit</u> - rounded, dense shrub with stiff, upright spreading branches
<u>size</u> - 2½ to 3½ to 2 to 4 <u>rate</u> - slow   <u>texture</u> - medium   <u>hardiness</u> - zone 4 to 9

***Viburnum opolus* 'Nanum'** — Dwarf European Cranberrybush   <u>habit</u> - much branched and dense
<u>size</u> - 1½ to 2 by 2 to 4 <u>rate</u> - medium   <u>texture</u> - medium   <u>hardiness</u> - zone 3 to 8

***Weigela florida* 'Minuet'** — Old Fashioned Weigela   <u>habit</u> - spreading, dense, rounded shrub with coarse branches
<u>size</u> - 2 to 3 by 2 to 5 <u>rate</u> - medium   <u>texture</u> - medium   <u>hardiness</u> - zone 4 to 9

Xanthorhiza simplicissima — Yellowroot   <u>habit</u> - flat-topped with erect stems
<u>size</u> - 2 to 3 - spread   <u>rate</u> - medium   <u>texture</u> - medium   <u>hardiness</u> - zone 3 to 9

Broad Leaf Evergreen Dwarf Shrubs

Arctostaphylos uva-ursi — Bearberry   <u>habit</u> - low growing, glossy ground cover forms broad, thick mats
<u>size</u> - 6 to 12 in. by 2 to 4 <u>rate</u> - slow   <u>texture</u> - fine   <u>hardiness</u> - zone 2 to 5

Ardisia japonica — Japanese Ardisia   <u>habit</u> - solid ground cover with dark green leathery leaves
<u>size</u> - 8 to 12 in. by 2 to 4 <u>rate</u> - fast   <u>texture</u> - medium-fine <u>hardiness</u> - zone 8 and 9

Aspidistra elatior — Cast-iron Plant   <u>habit</u> - upright clumps that develop from rhizomes
<u>size</u> - 1½ to 2 by 2 to 3 <u>rate</u> - slow   <u>texture</u> - coarse   <u>hardiness</u> - zone 7 to 9

Berberis candidula — Paleleaf Barberry   <u>habit</u> - dense, branches rigidly arching with three-prong spines
<u>size</u> - 2 to 4 by 2 to 5 <u>rate</u> - slow   <u>texture</u> - medium-fine <u>hardiness</u> - zone 5 to 8

***Buxus microphylla* 'Compacta'** — Compact Littleleaf Box <u>habit</u> - small, dense with dark green foliage
<u>size</u> - ½ in. to 1 by 1 to 4 <u>rate</u> - slow   <u>texture</u> - medium-fine <u>hardiness</u> - zone 5 to 9

***Buxus sempervirens* 'Suffruticosa'** — Common Box   <u>habit</u> - dense, compact and ideal for edging
<u>size</u> - 1 to 3 by 2 to 4 <u>rate</u> - slow   <u>texture</u> - medium-fine <u>hardiness</u> - zone 5 to 8

Calluna vulgaris — Scotch Heather   <u>habit</u> - upright branch, dense, ascending branches forming thick mats
<u>size</u> - 1 to 2 by ½ in. to 2 <u>rate</u> - slow   <u>texture</u> - fine   <u>hardiness</u> - zone 4 to 6

Cotoneaster dammeri — Bearberry Cotoneaster   <u>habit</u> - slender-creeping stems, roots when in contact with soil
<u>size</u> - 1 to 1½ by 3 to 6 <u>rate</u> - fast   <u>texture</u> - fine   <u>hardiness</u> - zone 5 to 8

Cyrtomium falcatum — Japanese Holly-fern   <u>habit</u> - holly-like with prominent serrations
<u>size</u> - 1 to 2 by 1 to 2 <u>rate</u> - slow   <u>texture</u> - fine   <u>hardiness</u> - zone 8 to 10

Daphne cneorum — Rose Daphne   <u>habit</u> - long, trailing and ascending branches formis low, loose masses
<u>size</u> - 6 to 12 in. by 1 to 2 <u>rate</u> - slow   <u>texture</u> - fine   <u>hardiness</u> - zone 4 to 7

Euonymus fortunei — Wintercreeper Euonymus   <u>habit</u> - ground cover, mature types make mounding woody shrubs
<u>size</u> - 4 to 6 in. - spread <u>rate</u> - fast   <u>texture</u> - medium-fine <u>hardiness</u> - zone 4 to 9

Gardenia jasminoides — Cape Jasmine   <u>habit</u> - dense, rounded
<u>size</u> - 3 to 4 by 4 to 6 <u>rate</u> - medium   <u>texture</u> - medium   <u>hardiness</u> - zone 8 to 10

Gaultheria procumbens — Creeping Wintergreen   <u>habit</u> - low growing, creeping can be used as ground cover
<u>size</u> - 6 in. - spread   <u>rate</u> - medium   <u>texture</u> - medium   <u>hardiness</u> - zone 3 to 7

***Ilex crenata* 'Helleri'** or **'Repandens'** — Japanese Holly   <u>habit</u> - mounded, compact form
<u>size</u> - 2 to 4 by 3 to 5 <u>rate</u> - slow   <u>texture</u> - medium-fine <u>hardiness</u> - zone 5 to 8

***Ilex glabra* 'Nordic'** — Inkberry   <u>habit</u> - compact rounded form
<u>size</u> - 3 to 4 by 3 to 4 <u>rate</u> - slow   <u>texture</u> - medium   <u>hardiness</u> - zone 4 to 9

***Kalmia latifolia* 'Tiddlywinks'** — Mountain Laurel   <u>habit</u> - multiple-branching
<u>size</u> - 12 to 24 in. by 30 in. <u>rate</u> - slow   <u>texture</u> - medium   <u>hardiness</u> - zone 4 to 9

Ledum groenlandicum — Labrador Tea   <u>habit</u> - erect branches forming a rounded mass
<u>size</u> - 2 to 4 by 2 to 4 <u>rate</u> - slow   <u>texture</u> - medium-fine <u>hardiness</u> - zone 2 to 5

***Leucothoe fontanesiana* 'Scarletta'** — Fetterbush   <u>habit</u> - mounded with dense foliage
<u>size</u> - 1 to 2 by 2 to 3½ <u>rate</u> - slow   <u>texture</u> - medium   <u>hardiness</u> - zone 5 to 8

***Mahonia aquifolium* 'Compactum'** — Oregon Grapeholly <u>habit</u> - upright, heavy stems, dense and rounded
<u>size</u> - 2 to 3 by 2 to 3 <u>rate</u> - slow   <u>texture</u> - medium   <u>hardiness</u> - zone 5 to 8

***Pieris japonica* 'Compacta'** — Japanese Andromeda   <u>habit</u> - upright stiff, spreading branches and dense rosette-like foliage
<u>size</u> - 2 to 4 by 3 to 6 <u>rate</u> - slow   <u>texture</u> - medium   <u>hardiness</u> - zone 5 to 8

Raphiolepis umbellata — Indian Hawthorn
    size - 4 to 6 by 4 to 6   rate - medium   texture - medium   habit - dense, mounded, rounded leaves clustered at end of branches
    hardiness - zone 8 to 10

Rhododendron 'Herbert' or 'P.J.M.' — Herbert's or P.J.M. Azalea
    size - 3 to 4 by 3 to 4   rate - slow   texture - medium   habit - dense and rounded
    hardiness - zone 5 to 8

Rhododendron 'Purple Gem' — Purple Gem Rhododendron
    size - 1 to 2 by 1 to 2   rate - slow   texture - fine   habit - rounded and dwarf
    hardiness - zone 5 to 8

Rhododendron yakusimanum — Yak Rhododendron
    size - 2 to 3 by 2 to 3   rate - slow   texture - medium   habit - dense and mounded
    hardiness - zone 4 to 8

Sarcococca hookeriana humilis — Sweetbox
    size - 1 to 1½ by 1 to 2   rate - slow   texture - medium-fine   habit - dense, forming a mounded outline
    hardiness - zone 6 to 9

Skimmia japonica — Japanese Skimmia
    size - 3 to 4 by 3 to 4   rate - slow   texture - medium   habit - rounded to dome-shaped
    hardiness - zone 7 to 9

Needle Evergreen Dwarf Shrubs

Abies balsamea 'Nana' — Dwarf Conifer
    size - 6 to 12 in. by 24 in.   rate - slow   texture - medium-fine   habit - irregular branching, tidy mound
    hardiness - zone 3 to 6

Abies concolor compacta — Compact White Fir
    size - 1 to 2 by 2 to 3   rate - slow   texture - medium   habit - low, conical and branched to base
    hardiness - zone 4 to 7

Abies koreana 'Compact Dwarf' — Dwarf Korean Fir
    size - 2 to 4 by 2 to 4   rate - slow   texture - medium   habit - irregular branching with the needles curling up
    hardiness - zone 5 to 7

Chamaecyparis obtusa 'Kosteri' — Koster's Hinoki False Cypress
    size - 2 to 3 by 2 to 4   rate - medium   texture - medium   habit - drooping frond-like and spreading branches
    hardiness - zone 5 to 6

Chamaecyparis obtusa 'Nana' — Hinoki Cypress
    size - 2 to 3 by 2 to 4   rate - slow   texture - medium   habit - spreading and drooping branches
    hardiness - zone 4 to 8

Juniperus chinensis var. *sargentii* — Sargent Chinese Juniper
    size - 18 in. to 2 by 9   rate - slow   texture - medium   habit - wide spreading branchlets
    hardiness - zone 3 to 9

Juniperus conferta — Shore Juniper
    size - 1 to 1½ by 6 to 9   rate - slow   texture - medium   habit - dense and bushy
    hardiness - zone 6 to 9

Juniperus horizontalis 'Bar Harbor' — Bar Harbor Juniper   habit - low growing with long, trailing branches forming large mats
    size - 1 to 2 by 6 to 8   rate - slow   texture - medium-fine   hardiness - zone 3 to 9

Juniperus horizontalis 'Mother Lode' — Mother Lode Juniper
    size - 1 to 3 in. by 1 to 3   rate - slow   texture - medium   habit - rich gold coloration, very low and compact
    hardiness - zone 4 to 9

Juniperus horizontalis 'Wiltonii' — Wilton's Creeping Juniper
    size - 4 to 6 in. by 6 to 8   rate - slow   texture - medium-fine   habit - very flat with trailing branches
    hardiness - zone 3 to 9

Juniperus procumbens 'Nana' — Dwarf Japgarden Juniper
    size - 8 to 24 in. by 12 in.   rate - slow   texture - medium   habit - forms a compact mat with branches on top of the other
    hardiness - zone 4 to 9

Microbiota decussata — Siberian Carpet Cypress
    size - 6 to 12 in. by 15   rate - slow   texture - fine   habit - lacy-plumed branches
    hardiness - zone 2 to 8

Picea abies 'Little Gem' or 'Maxwellii' — Norway Spruce
    size - 12 in. by 12 in.   rate - medium   texture - medium   habit - dwarf and dense
    hardiness - zone 4 to 8

Picea glauca 'Conica' — Dwarf Alberta White Spruce
    size - 1 to 2 by 1 to 2   rate - slow   texture - medium   habit - broad, dense pyramid with ascending branches
    hardiness - zone 2 to 6

Picea mariana 'Nana' — Dwarf Black Spruce
    size - 1½ to 2 by 1 to 3   rate - slow   texture - medium   habit - dense mound of dull gray-green needles
    hardiness - zone 2 to 5

Picea omorika 'Nana' — Dwarf Serbian Spruce
    size - 8 to 10 by 2 to 4   rate - slow   texture - medium   habit - conical form with irregular outline, needles closely set
    hardiness - zone 4 to 7

Picea pungens 'Glauca Globosa' — Globe Colorado Spruce
    size - 2 to 3 by 4 to 6   rate - slow   texture - medium   habit - compact, rounded, flat-topped
    hardiness - zone 2 to 7

Pinus densiflora 'Prostrata' — Prostrate Japanese Red Pine
    size - ½ to 1 by 2 to 5   rate - slow   texture - medium   habit - dwarf, broad-rounded top
    hardiness - zone 3 to 7

Pinus mugo 'Compacta' — Hill's Mugo Pine
    size - 2 to 4 by 3 to 5   rate - slow   texture - medium   habit - dense with a rounded shape
    hardiness - zone 2 to 7

Pinus nigra 'Hornibrookiana' — Hornibrook Austrian Pine   habit - very compact, shrubby and rounded
    size - 1 to 2 by 2 to 6   rate - slow   texture - medium   hardiness - zone 4 to 7

Pinus strobus 'Nana' — Dwarf Eastern White Pine
    size - 2 to 3 by 2 to 3   rate - slow   texture - medium-fine   habit - dense, rounded form
    hardiness - zone 3 to 8

Pinus sylvestris 'Beuvronensis' — Dwarf Scotch Pine
    size - 1 to 3 by 1 to 3   rate - very slow   texture - medium   habit - broad low bushy form with bluish green needles
    hardiness - zone 2 to 8

Pseudotsuga menziesii 'Fletcheri' — Fletcher's Douglasfir   habit - spreading, flat-topped and compact form
    size - 2 to 2½ by 3   rate - slow   texture - medium   hardiness - zone 4 to 6

Taxus x media 'Chadwickii' — Anglojap Yew
    size - 2 to 4 by 4 to 6   rate - slow   texture - medium   habit - compact spreader
    hardiness - zone 4 to 7

Thuja occidentalis 'Hetz Midget' — Eastern Arborvitae
    size - 3 to 4 by 3 to 4   rate - slow   texture - medium-fine   habit - dense, globe-shaped form
    hardiness - zone 2 to 8

Thuja occidentalis 'Holstrup' — Eastern Arborvitae
    size - 2 to 5 by 1 by 2   rate - slow   texture - medium-fine   habit - compact, pyramidal form
    hardiness - zone 2 to 8

Tsuga canadensis 'Jeddoloh' — Weeping Canadian Hemlock   habit - arching branches, weeping tips, cascading effect
    size - 1 to 2 by 2 to 3   rate - slow   texture - fine   hardiness - zone 2 to 7

Trees can branch out into savings and comfort

Q: I want to landscape my house to cool it with less electricity, but I do not want to block the winter sun. Will trees help much, and if so, where should I locate them and what types are best?

A: By planting the proper types of trees in the proper locations in your yard, you can cut your air-conditioning costs by 25% or more. By shading your walls, your house stays cooler and you feel more comfortable. You can feel the difference when sitting indoors near a shaded wall.

Trees are nature's air conditioners. A single large tree can produce as much actual cooling in a single day as running a large room air conditioner. When you include the benefit from the shade that it provides, the combined cooling effect from just one tree is significant.

Trees cool the air by a natural process called transpiration. The tree continually draws water from its roots which eventually evaporates from its leaves. This evaporation process cools the tree and the air around it just like when you perspire. The air near a tree can be 10 degrees cooler.

On a grand scale, planting trees reduces global warming. Trees consume carbon dioxide (greenhouse gas) and produce oxygen. By reducing electricity usage, less carbon dioxide is emitted from power plants.

To landscape efficiently with trees, the basic goal is to block the cold winter winds and the intense summer sun while letting the beneficial winter sun and summer breezes through.

This typically includes a row of deciduous trees (ones that lose their leaves in the winter) from the

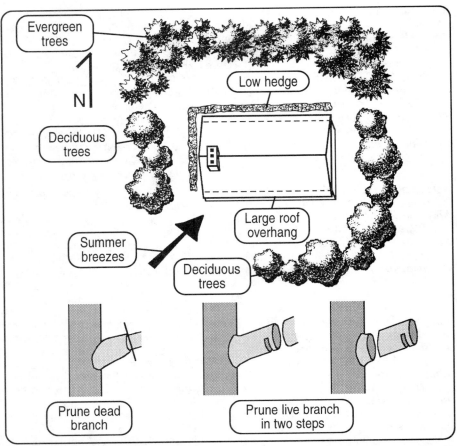

southeast to the southwest sides of your house. Plant evergreens to the north. In most climates, leave a small gap on the southwest side to allow the prevailing evening breezes through.

When selecting trees, consider the height and shape of the tree as it matures. This allows you to determine how many to plant and how far to locate them from your house for shading. Growth rates and winter hardiness are also important selection criteria.

The branch pattern of some trees is too dense to be used on the south side. They are great for blocking the summer sun, but they also block too much of the winter sun's free heat. Check out varieties with a local landscaper.

When making your tree selection, keep in mind that some fast-growing trees also are short-lived and you may have an expensive tree

removal job ahead. For the most efficient use of trees, you will have to do some pruning. Remember to make a small bottom cut first so the bark does not tear.

Q: I installed a whole-house fan in our hall ceiling last fall. I know it saves electricity as compared to air-conditioning, but how do I know when to turn it on?

A: Running a whole-house fan, especially the new small twin-fan models, is much less expensive than running a central air conditioner.

If you feel comfortable with the fan on, it probably is the proper time to use it. As a rule of thumb, in dry climates, turn it on when the outdoor temperature drops to the same as indoors. In humid climates, use it only when the outdoor temperature is at least 10 degrees cooler than indoors.

The chart below shows information about many types of trees. The information is presented in the following order - "name of tree", "hardiness zone rating" (the minimum temperature it can survive), "type of tree" (deciduous or evergreen), "shape of tree for shading", "height at maturity", and "growth rate". Keep in mind that fast-growing trees are often short-lived.

You can select a tree with a hardiness zone rating less than your area because it will handle your milder winters. If you choose one with a hardiness rating several points lower, it may have difficulty surviving the summer heat.

Description of Common Trees for Landscaping

AFRICAN TULIP TREE 10, evergreen, irregular, 70 feet, fast
AILANTHUS 5, deciduous, round, 70 feet, fast
APRICOT 6, deciduous, round, 30 feet, fast
ARBORVITAE, GIANT 6, evergreen,, irregular, 180 feet, fast
ARBORVITAE, ORIENTAL 6, evergreen, pyramidal, 50 feet, moderate
ASH, GREEN 2, deciduous, pyramidal/round, 60 feet, moderately fast
ASH, WHITE 3, deciduous, irregular, 120 feet, fast
ASPEN, EUROPEAN 2, deciduous, oval/round, 50 feet, fast
ASPEN, QUAKING 1, deciduous, oval/round, 90 feet, fast
BALDCYPRESS 5, deciduous, pyramidal, 150 feet, moderate
BEECH, AMERICAN 3, deciduous, conical, 90 feet, moderate
BEECH, EUROPEAN 5, deciduous, pyramidal, 90 feet, moderate
BIRCH, PAPER 2, deciduous, pyramidal, 90 feet, fast
BOX ELDER 2, deciduous, round, 60 feet, fast
BO TREE 10, deciduous, irregular, 75 feet, slow
BUCKTHORN, DAHURIAN 2, evergreen, irregular, 30 feet, fast
CAMELLIA, COMMON 7, evergreen, round, 45 feet, moderate
CAMPHOR TREE 9, evergreen, irregular, 40 feet, slow
CATALPA, NORTHERN 5, deciduous, round, 75 feet, fast
CATALPA, SOUTHERN 5, deciduous, round, 45 feet, fast
CEDAR, ATLAS 6, evergreen, irregular, 120 feet, moderately fast
CEDAR, EASTERN RED 2, evergreen, conical, 90 feet, slow
CEDAR, INCENSE 6, evergreen, conical, 135 feet, moderate
CEDAR OF LEBANON 6, evergreen, conical, 120 feet, moderate
CEDAR, WHITE 2, evergreen, pyramidal, 60 feet, slow
CHERRY, BLACK 3, deciduous, round, 90 feet, moderately fast
CHERRY, ORIENTAL 6, deciduous, pyramidal, 30 feet, fast
CHERRY, WILD, RED 2, deciduous, round, 35 feet, fast
CHESTNUT, CHINESE 5, deciduous, round, 60 feet, moderate
CHINABERRY 7, deciduous, round, 45 feet, fast
CHINESE TALLOW TREE 9, deciduous, irregular, 40 feet, moderate
CORK TREE, AMUR 3, deciduous, round, 30 feet, moderately fast
COTTONWOOD 2, deciduous, round, 90 feet, fast
CRABAPPLE 2, deciduous, round, 30 feet, fast
CRAPE MYRTLE 7, deciduous, round, 21 feet, moderate
CRYTOMERIA 6, evergreen, pyramidal, 150 feet, fast
CUCUMBER TREE 5, deciduous, oval, 90 feet, moderately fast
CYPRESS, ARIZONA 7, evergreen, pyramidal, 50 feet, fast
CYPRESS, ITALIAN 7, evergreen, conical, 75 feet, fast
DAWN REDWOOD 6, deciduous, columnar, 100 feet, very fast
DOGWOOD, GIANT 6, deciduous, irregular, 60 feet, slow
DOGWOOD, PACIFIC 7, deciduous, pyramidal, 75 feet, slow
DOUGLAS FIR 5, evergreen, conical, 300 feet, fast
ELM, AMERICAN 2, deciduous, irregular, 120 feet, fast
ELM, CHINESE 6, deciduous, wide, 50 feet, fast
ELM, ENGLISH 6, deciduous, oval, 120 feet, moderately fast
ELM, EUROPEAN FIELD 5, deciduous, oval, 90 feet, moderately fast
ELM, SIBERIAN 5, deciduous, round, 75 feet, fast
FIG, BENJAMIN 10, deciduous, oval, 50 feet, fast
FIR, BALSAM 3, evergreen, oval, 75 feet, fast
FIR, SILVER 5, evergreen, conical, 150 feet, slow
GINKGO 5, deciduous, irregular, 120 feet, moderate
GOLDENRAIN TREE 6, deciduous, round, 30 feet, moderate

HACKBERRY, EAST 3, deciduous, round, 90 feet, moderate
HACKBERRY, EUROPE 6, deciduous, round, 75 feet, moderate
HEMLOCK, CANADIAN 3, evergreen, conical, 90 feet, slow
HEMLOCK, CAROLINA 5, evergreen, pyramidal, 75 feet, slow
HICKORY, BITTERNUT 5, deciduous, round, 90 feet, moderate
HOLLY, AMERICAN 6, evergreen, pyramidal, 45 feet, slow
HOLLY, ENGLISH 6, evergreen, conical, 70 feet, moderate
HORNBEAM AMERICAN 2, deciduous, oval, 36 feet, moderate
HORNBEAM, HOP 5, deciduous, pyramidal, 60 feet, slow
HORSECHESTNUT 3, deciduous, oval, 75 feet, moderate
HORSECHESTNUT, RED 3, deciduous, round, 75 feet, fast
KALOPANAX 5, deciduous, wide, 90 feet, moderate
KATSURA TREE 5, deciduous, wide, 80 feet, fast
LARCH, EASTERN 1, deciduous, columnar, 60 feet, moderate
LARCH, EUROPEAN 2, deciduous, pyramidal, 100 feet, fast
LINDEN, AMERICAN 2, deciduous, columnar, 120 feet, fast
LINDEN, SILVER 5, deciduous, pyramidal, 90 feet, moderate
MAGNOLIA, SOUTHERN 7, evergreen, wide, 90 feet, moderate
MAPLE, BIGLEAF 6, deciduous, round, 90 feet, fast
MAPLE, NORWAY 3, deciduous, round, 90 feet, moderate
MAPLE, SUGAR 3, deciduous, oval, 120 feet, moderate
MESQUITE 9, deciduous, wide, 50 feet, moderate
MIMOSA 7, deciduous, wide, 36 feet, fast
MULBERRY, RUSSIAN 5, deciduous, round, 45 feet, fast
OAK, BURR 3, deciduous, round, 85 feet, slow
OAK, ENGLISH 6, deciduous, round, 120 feet, slow
OAK, HOLLY 9, evergreen, round, 60 feet, slow
OAK, PIN 5, deciduous, pyramidal, 75 feet, fast
OAK, WATER 6, deciduous, round, 75 feet, fast
OAK, WHITE 5, deciduous, wide, 90 feet, slow
OLIVE, RUSSIAN 2, evergreen, wide, 20 feet, slow
PEAR, CALLERY 5, deciduous, pyramidal, 30 feet, fast
PECAN 6, deciduous, round, 150 feet, fast
PERSIMMON 5, deciduous, columnar, 75 feet, moderate
PINE AUSTRIAN 5, evergreen, pyramidal, 90 feet, fast
PINE, CANARY ISLAND 8, evergreen, pyramidal, 80 feet, fast
PINE, WHITE 3, evergreen, pyramidal, 125 feet, moderate
PINE, PONDEROSA 6, evergreen, conical, 150 feet, fast
PINE, NORWAY 2, evergreen, pyramidal, 75 feet, moderate
PISTACHE, CHINESE 6, deciduous, round, 50 feet, slow
PLANETREE, AMERICAN 6, deciduous, wide, 120 feet, fast
PLANETREE, LONDON 6, deciduous, wide, 100 feet, fast
POPLAR, BOLLEANA 3, deciduous, irregular, 90 feet, fast
REDBUD, EASTERN 5, deciduous, irregular, 36 feet, moderate
ROYAL POINCIANA 9, evergreen, wide, 50 feet, fast
SASSAFRAS 5, deciduous, irregular, 60 feet, moderate
SPRUCE, COLORADO 2, evergreen, pyramidal, 100 feet, slow
SPRUCE, WHITE 2, evergreen, pyramidal, 90 feet, slow
SWEETGUM 6, deciduous, pyramidal, 125 feet, fast
TANOAK 7, evergreen, pyramidal, 75 feet, slow
TULIP TREE 5, deciduous, pyramidal, 150 feet, fast
WAX-MYRTLE 9, evergreen, irregular, 36 feet, fast
YELLOWWOOD 3, deciduous, round, 50 feet, fast

Zones of Plant Hardiness

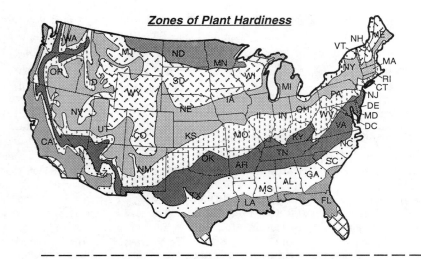

Approximate Range of Average Annual Minimum Temperatures for Each Zone

Zone 1	Below -50°F	
Zone 2	-50° to -40°F	
Zone 3	-40° to -30°F	
Zone 4	-30° to -20°F	
Zone 5	-20° to -10°F	
Zone 6	-10° to 0°F	
Zone 7	0° to 10°F	
Zone 8	10° to 20°F	
Zone 9	20° to 30°F	
Zone 10	30° to 40°F	

The main objective in this region is to minimize the heat and humidity. Landscape designs should channel breezes while blocking out the sun. Good planning is very important. Overabundant planting will compound the problem by creating more humidity. Avoid using water in the landscape design when possible for the same reason. The ideal structure has a two-stage or vented roof (a roof that has vents or openings that allow air to circulate), minimal interior walls, elongated shapes with high surface areas (i.e., ranch-style houses), and raised floors. This design allows maximum air movement within the structure. Trees need to be tall enough to shade during the warm seasons (late spring to early fall) without blocking the winter sun. Palm trees are well suited for this purpose. Optimum shade is created by planting shorter trees and shrubs along the east and west, with taller trees along the south. Plants with light, smooth leaves reflect better than those with dark, coarse leaves. Canopies of trees work best when they block the sunlight overhead by reflecting it, which decreases the amount of radiation that reaches your home. Conversely, ground covers should absorb the radiation instead of reflecting it back up into your home. Breezes can be channeled and heightened with walls and fences, which will decrease the need for hedges. This will help cut down on the humidity because there are less moisture-producing plants. Landscaping design in this area can take advantage of beautiful, lush, indigenous flora.

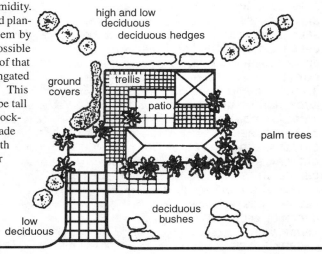

Hot/Humid Climate

This region is known for its extreme daily temperatures. Landscaping designs should attempt to stabilize temperatures and create moisture and evaporation. The ideal house forms a hollow square, with doors and windows that open onto an interior courtyard. This creates a sheltered microclimate within the four walls, making it easier to retain moisture by blocking out the hot desert sun. Plant for shade and moisture. A good design controls the sun during warmer periods (late spring to early fall). Tall, high-crowned palm trees, live oaks and other native trees will block the sun while allowing breezes to circulate underneath their canopy. Bushes and shrubs planted 10 or more feet from the house reduce heat and glare. Trellises along the walls prevent the sun from penetrating your home. Use non-reflective ground covers such as wood chips or gravel in the garden. Remember to plant vegetation that thrives with little moisture. Cacti and other succulents can make dramatic landscapes. Place pools, ponds and fountains upwind so breezes will carry cooling moisture into your home. Shade trees will reduce evaporation from the water sources. Houseplants improve the air inside your home by adding humidity, so allow for a variety of them.

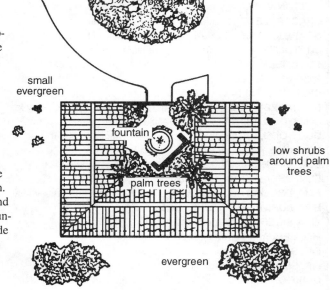

Hot/Arid Climate

The main objectives of a landscape design in this region are to insulate, deflect cold northern winds, and collect solar radiation. Cape Cod or slatbox structures (square, solid squat buildings with sloped roofs) are most suitable for this area. The majority of windows should face southeast to southwest for maximum solar exposure. In the winter, 85 percent of the sun's heat is collected between 9 a.m. and 3 p.m., so avoid obstructing southern windows during this time. Deciduous trees should be planted at a distance three times their expected height from the building. (For example, a tree expected to grow to a height of 30 feet should be planted 90 feet away from the house.) This will allow maximum sun in the winter, yet will provide you with some shade in the summer. Driveways or parking spaces with dark pavement absorb and reradiate heat during cold winter days as well. You may want to shade these areas in the summer. Large bodies of water also store and reradiate heat, but small bodies of water lose their heat quickly, so you may want to screen ponds with a row of trees or shrubs to deflect cold wind and glare emanating from them. Earthberms cool. Hedges planted close to the walls of the building will create dead air space, providing insulation. Dark walls are best for absorbing solar radiation.

Windbreaks are necessary in this region. Ideally, a windbreak is a row of trees wider than it is tall, planted perpendicular to the wind. A tight barrier should be planted at a distance from the building two to five times the expected height of the trees. These barriers are most effective when planted along the northwestern face of your home, where they will block the winter wind. Loose windbreaks should be planted farther from the house along the southern face, where they will not obstruct the sun. A combination of deciduous and coniferous trees. These trees are much denser, creating a more solid block. Earthberms are also a good means of deflecting wind. They channel winds over the roof if placed correctly beside or against the building. Hedges deflect winds away from doors and garages. With a little planning, these deflected winds can be used to blow snow away from these areas too.

This region consists of contrasting seasons. The main objectives when landscaping in this region are to capture sun in the winter and block the wind, and to funnel breezes in the summer while blocking the sun. Compact building designs that allow solar gain work best. To the east and northeast, plant low density, low-crowned trees. This filters the sun without blocking the light. High-crowned, tall deciduous trees along the southern face create shade in the summer without obstructing the sun in winter. They also allow breezes to pass under their canopy in the summer. Western exposures generally overheat in summer, and in winter the glare can be excessive. Short coniferous and deciduous trees and shrubs planted along the northern and northwestern face will alleviate these problems. Shrubs, vines and groundcovers will also reduce reflection, draw heat away from buildings, and provide shade and insulation.

Hedges can be used to channel summer breezes by means of the Venturi effect. The Venturi effect can be used to alter the windstream. It occurs at breaks in wind barriers. Wind pressure is built up along the barrier until it reaches a break, where it is released with increased velocity.

Abundant planting decreases erosion caused by heavy precipitation. Minimal use of water in the landscape design is recommended for the high humidity areas to this region. In more arid areas, water should be incorporated into the design. Shade any pavement, rock gardens and dark surfaces in the summer.

Ventilated panels make cathedral ceilings simple

Q: I want to build a family room addition with a cathedral ceiling and skylights. What is the best and easiest-to-build method for this type of ceiling? I would like to convert my bedroom ceiling too.

A: You are in luck. Vented nail-based roofing panels are both the easiest-to-install and the most efficient cathedral ceiling option. Installing skylights in these roof panels is a breeze. A cathedral ceiling and skylights make even small rooms seem open and spacious.

Vented roofing panels are ideal for converting your flat bedroom ceiling to an attractive cathedral ceiling. Another excellent panel application is to provide insulation when converting an attic to living space.

Most vented insulated roofing panels are made of thick isocyanurate foam insulation (up to R-40). Air gap spacers are bonded to the top foam surface and oriented strand board (OSB) is attached to the spacers. The OSB provides an excellent nailing surface for shingles or any type of roofing.

Another unique vented design, AirFlo, uses lower-cost expanded polystyrene (EPS) foam insulation without spacers. Grooves are cut into the foam before the top OSB sheet is attached. These groove allow for the air flow. You can also use a standard foam panel and attach your own venting layer.

It is critical to provide ventilation under the roof. Many shingle manufacturers will not warrant their shingles without adequate ventilation because of excessive heat buildup. Using vented panels with a continuous ridge vent can really reduce your summer air-conditioning bills.

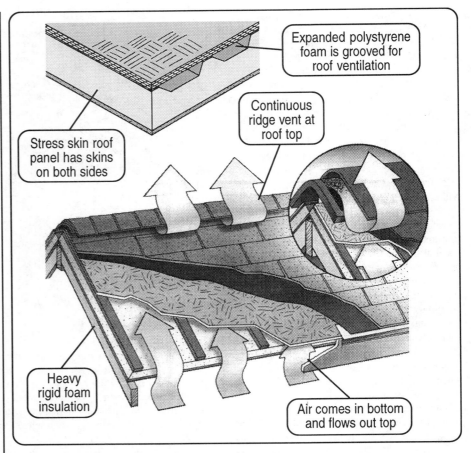

Expanded polystyrene foam is grooved for roof ventilation

Continuous ridge vent at roof top

Stress skin roof panel has skins on both sides

Heavy rigid foam insulation

Air comes in bottom and flows out top

Several of these vented panels are designed with shiplap joints or splines to create an airtight roofing system. Even with a skylight, the overall efficiency can be greater than a conventional insulated flat ceiling/attic design.

Most vented panels need to be installed over roof sheathing for support. If you plan to have exposed wood ceiling beams, use stress skin vented panels.

These strong stress skin panels have drywall or wood paneling already attached to the bottom for quick and simple do-it-yourself installation. To cover extra large ceiling beam spacing, up to 6 feet, choose structural stress skin panels. These have an extra thick OSB skins.

Another construction method is to use insulation on top of the cathedral ceiling. Install special foil-backed insulation shields one inch under the roof decking. These hold blow-in insulation in place and create an air gap for ventilation. The reflective surface blocks the summer sun's heat.

Q: I recently bought a new flapper valve for the toilet tank because the old one did not seal. Now I have to hold the flush lever for a while to make it flush properly. What did I do wrong?

A: You may have done nothing wrong. You probably purchased a water-saving flapper valve (fits in the bottom of the tank). These require more careful adjustment and may always require a slightly longer hold.

First, make sure that the chain or strap connecting the flush lever to the flapper does not have excessive slack and adjust it if necessary. Check to see if the flapper has adjustable hole sizes and try different settings.

Manufacturers of Roof Insulation Panels

AFM CORP., 24000 W. Highway 7, Box 246, Excelsior, MN 55331 - (800) 255-0176 (612) 474-0809
<u>roof insulation</u> - "R-Control"   <u>type of insulation</u> - expanded polystyrene   <u>size of panel</u> - 4' x 8' to 8' x 24'
<u>thickness inches / R-value</u> - 5 sizes — 4.5 / R-14.8 •   6.5 / R-22.5 •   8.25 / R-29.3 •   10.25 / R-37.0 •   12.25 / R-44.7
<u>description</u> - The structural panel consists of a rigid foam core welded between an inner and outer sheathing of 7/16" OSB*. The foam core is treated (built-in) with a natural mineral for insect resistance. It is approved by the EPA and non-corrosive and non-toxic. It has been tested against termites and carpenter ants. "SpecLam" is a nailbase panel that consists of a foam core with an exterior of 7/16" OSB sheathing. It is available with an optional spline joint of OSB that connects the panels together.

APACHE PRODUCTS CO., PO Box 5287, Anderson, SC 29623 - (864) 224-0900
<u>roof insulation</u> - "Nail-Line V" — venting   <u>type of insulation</u> - polyisocyanurate   <u>size of panel</u> - 4' x 8'
<u>thickness inches / R-value</u> - 14 sizes — 2.2 / R-6.0 •   2.5 / R-8.3 •   2.7 / R-10.0 •   2.8 / R-11.1 •   3.0 / R-12.5 •   3.2 / R-14.3 •   3.3 / R-15.0 •   3.5 / R-16.7 •   3.7 / R-18.2 •   3.9 / R-20.0 •   4.2 / R-22.0 •   4.6 / R-25.0 •   5.0 / R-28.1 •   5.2 / R-30.0
<u>description</u> - This venting nailbase roof insulation consists of a rigid foam base panel, ¾" OSB or wood runners (furring strips), and a 7/16" OSB laminated to the top and a facer on the other side. It provides airflow channels above the foam insulating layer but below the shingle deck and shingles. Requires 15 lb. felt or 1 layer of shingle underlayment to the deck.

ATLAS ROOFING CORP., 1303 Orchard Hill Rd., LaGrange, GA 30240 - (800) 955-1476 (706) 882-9355
<u>roof insulation</u> - "Vented-R" — venting   <u>type of insulation</u> - polyisocyanurate   <u>size of panel</u> - 4' x 8'
<u>thickness inches / R-value</u> - 8 sizes with ½" airspace — 2.0 / R-7.1 •   2.2 / R-8.6 •   2.5 / R-11.1 •   3.0 / R-15.4 •   3.5 / R-19.1 •   4.0 / R-23.1 •   4.5 / R-27.1 •   5.0 / R-31.1 •   7 sizes with ¾" airspace — 2.2 / R-7.4 •   2.5 / R-9.7 •   3.0 / R-13.9 •   3.5 / R-18.1 •   4.0 / R-22.1 •   4.5 / R-25.8 •   5.0 / R-29.4
<u>description</u> - This venting nailbase insulation consists of an insulation board with ½" or ¾" insulating vent strips separating 7/16" OSB. Minimum 15 lb. roofing felt is required. Custom sizes are available on special order.

BRANCH RIVER FOAM PLASTICS, INC., 15 Thurber Blvd., Smithfield, RI 02917 - (401) 232-0270
<u>roof insulation</u> - "Air-Flo" — venting   <u>type of insulation</u> - expanded polystyrene   <u>size of panel</u> - 4' x 8'
<u>thickness inches / R-value</u> - 5 sizes — 4.5 / R-14.8 •   6.5 / R-22.5 •   8.25 / R-29.3 •   10.25 / R-37.0 •   12.25 / R-44.7
<u>description</u> - The insulating and venting panel system consists of a top layer of 7/16" OSB pressure-laminated to a bottom layer of grooved EPS foam in any density or configuration to meet your insulation specifications. Must be installed with soffit and ridge vents. The panels are available in lengths up to 16 feet. Three types of panels are available. The "Air-Flo Panel" is designed for installation over exposed wood decking and has a standard, reinforced-aluminum foil vapor barrier. "Air-Flo Stress Skin Panel" is designed for installation over structurally framed systems with interior gypsum exposed with maximum 4' on center spanability. The "Air-Flo Structural Stress Skin Panel" is for 6' on center spanability and a gypsum interior. It has a thicker layer of foam.

CELOTEX CORP., PO Box 31602, Tampa, FL 33631- (813) 873-1700
<u>roof insulation</u> - "Celo-Vent" — venting   <u>type of insulation</u> - polyisocyanurate   <u>size of panel</u> - 4' x 8'
<u>thickness inches / R-value</u> - 5 sizes — 2.5 / R-6.0 •   3.5 / R-14.3 •   4.5 / R-21.7 •   5.0 / R-25.8 •   5.5 / R-30.2
<u>description</u> - The ventilated nailbase roof insulation system consists of a roof insulation board, and 7/16" OSB, with 2" shiplap, separated by 1" x 3" wide fiberboard strips, set 16" on center Requires two layers of 15 lb. asphalt felt plain or one layer of shingle underlayment.

CORNELL CORP., PO Box 338, Cornell, WI 54732 - (715) 239-6411
<u>roof insulation</u> - "ThermaCal" — venting   <u>type of insulation</u> - isocyanurate   <u>size of panel</u> - 4' x 8'
<u>thickness inches / R-value</u> - 7 sizes with one layer of OSB — 2.25 / R-8.0 •   2.75 / R-12.0 •   3.25 / R-16.0 •   3.75 / R-20.0 •   4.25 / R-24.0 •   4.75 / 28.0 •   5.25 / R-32.0 •   6 sizes with two layers of OSB — 2.75 / R-9.0 •   3.25 / R-13.0 •   3.75 / R-17.0 •   4.25 / R-21.0 •   4.75 / 25.0 •   5.25 / R-29.0
<u>description</u> - This is a ventilated nailbase roof insulation that combines OSB sheathing and isocyanurate foam with a built-in ventilated air space. "Vent-Top ThermaCal 1" has one layer of 7/16" OSB and "Vent-Top ThermaCal 2" has two layers of 7/16" OSB. 5/8" OSB is available for special applications. The panels have a non-slip upper surface for roof applications. The vent space is 7/8" deep and is maintained by solid wood spacers. The spacers are less than 12" apart to reduce deflection of top sheathing. "Vent-Top ThermaCal" can be modified for special applications such as different surfaces, and special eaves pieces to support sheathing over the overhang.

ENERCEPT, INC., 3100 9th Ave. SE, Watertown, SD 57201 - (800) 658-3303 (605) 882-2222
<u>roof insulation</u> - "Superinsulated Panel"   <u>type of insulation</u> - expanded polystyrene   <u>size of panel</u> - 4' x 8' to 4' x 28'
<u>thickness inches / R-value</u> - 3 sizes — 8.25 / R-32.0 •   10.25 / R-40.0 •   12.5 / R-48.0
<u>description</u> - The core of this structural panel is foam laminated between an interior and exterior 7/16" OSB sheathing. The panels are interconnected with factory installed 2" x 8" lumber. The panels can be custom cut to include skylight or gable windows.

FIRESTONE BUILDING PRODUCTS, 525 Congressional Blvd., Carmel, IN 46032 - (800) 428-4442 (317) 575-7000
<u>roof insulation</u> - "Nail Base"   <u>type of insulation</u> - polyisocyanurate   <u>size of panel</u> - 4' x 8'
<u>thickness inches / R-value</u> - 6 sizes — 1.5 / R-6.9 •   2.0 / R-11.3 •   2.5 / R-15.4 •   3.0 / R-18.5 •   3.5 / R-22.2 •   4.0 / 26.7
<u>description</u> - The nailbase insulation panel consists of a foam core with a facing of 7/16" OSB on one side and a black glass reinforced mat facer on the other. It is also available in board sizes of 4' x 4'. Other sizes and thicknesses may be special ordered with a minimum order required.

FISCHERSIPS INC., 1843 Northwestern Pkwy., Louisville, KY 40203 - (502) 778-5577 (800) 792-7477

roof insulation - "FischerSips"   type of insulation - expanded polystyrene   size of panel - 4' x 8' to 8' x 24'

thickness inches / R-value - 3 sizes — 3.625 / R-17.0 • 5.625 / R-25.0 • 7.625 / R-36.0

description - There are several different panels to choose from. The nailbase panel consists of ³/₈" OSB and foam. The structural panel consists of ³/₈" OSB, foam and ³/₈" OSB. The pine T1-11 panel consists of ³/₈" OSB, foam and ⁵/₈" pine. The tongue and groove panel consists of ³/₈" OSB, foam, ³/₈" OSB and 1" x 8" tongue and groove pine. The panels carry a limited lifetime warranty.

GAF MATERIALS CORP., 1361 Alps Rd., Wayne, NJ 07470 - (800) 700-3411

roof insulation - "Insul-Air" — venting   type of insulation - polyisocyanurate   size of panel - 4' x 8'

thickness inches / R-value - 5 sizes — 2.5 / R-14.0 • 3.0 / R-18.6 • 3.25 / R-20.0 • 3.5 / R-22.3 • 4.0 / 25.7

description - This is a foam insulation panel that has moisture resistant glass reinforced facer bonded to both sides. It has a flat bottom side and has formed channels on the top side which provide a ventilated air space when covered by a rigid nailable surface of either plywood or OSB — supplied by others.

GREAT LAKES INSULSPAN, P.O. Box 38, Blissfield, MI 49228 - (517) 486-4844

roof insulation - "Insulspan"   type of insulation - expanded polystyrene   size of panel - 4' x 8' to 8' x 24'

thickness inches / R-value - 4 sizes nailbase — 3.625 / R-14.0 • 5.625 / R-22.0 • 7.375 / R-30.0 • 9.375 / R-37.0 • 4 sizes structural — 3.625 / R-16.0 • 5.625 / R-24.0 • 7.375 / R-30.0 • 9.375 / R-38.0 • 4 sizes drywall-clad — 3.625 / R-16.0 • 5.625 / R-23.0 • 7.375 / R-30.0 • 9.375 / R-38.0 • 4 sizes wood-finished structural — 3.625 / R-17.0 • 5.625 / R-24.0 • 7.375 / R-31.0 • 9.375 / R-39.0

description - There are four different styles available. There are nailbase roof panels that consists of an EPS (expanded polystyrene) core bonded to OSB with an inner face of foil available. The structural panel has an EPS core bonded between two outer layers of OSB. The drywall-clad panel has an EPS core bonded between an outer layer of OSB and an inner layer of drywall. The wood-finished structural panel consists of a structural panel faced on one side with solid, ¾" tongue and groove white pine or red cedar. The OSB skins are ⁷/₁₆" standard with ³/₈" and ⁵/₈" available on request.

HOMASOTE CO., PO Box 7240, W. Trenton, NJ 08628 - (800) 257-9491 (609) 883-3300

roof insulation - "Thermasote"   type of insulation - polyisocyanurate   size of panel - 4' x 8'

thickness inches / R-value - 6 sizes — 1.5 / R-7.2 • 2.0 / R-11.1 • 2.5 / R-14.4 • 3.0 / R-18.2 • 3.5 / R-22.5 • 4.0 / R-27.0

description - This is a nailbase insulation fiberboard that is made from recycled newspapers for application over wood, roof or other structural decking. There is a bottom facer of asphalt-saturated felt, fibrous glass or foil.

INSUL-TRAY INC., E. 1881 Crestview Dr., Shelton, WA 98584 - (360) 427-5930

roof insulation - "Insul-Tray"   type of insulation - n/a   size of panel - 4' x any width

thickness inches / R-value - 2" x 10" cavity / R-31.45 • 2" x 12" cavity / R-38.85

description - This is a water resistant, corrugated cardboard panel that is stapled to the framing boards. It forms cavities that are filled with blown-in cellulose insulation. The panels and cellulose insulation are both made from waster paper. There are also reflective insulation shields available.

J-DECK BUILDING SYSTEMS, 2587 Harrison Rd., Columbus, OH 43204 - (614) 274-7755

roof insulation - "Insulated Roof Deck"   type of insulation - expanded polystyrene   size of panel - 4' x 8', 9' or 10'

thickness inches / R-value - 3 sizes — 3.625 / R-17.0 • 5.625 / R-25.0 • 7.625 / R-36.0

description - The structural panels consist of foam with the skins of ³/₈" plywood on the exterior and ½" plywood on the interior, interior and exterior skins of ³/₈" plywood with ½" gypsum board or interior and exterior skins of ⁷/₁₆" OSB with ½" gypsum board. Optional interior skins are ⁵/₈" T1-11, with grooves 4" on center, or 8" on center in Southern yellow pine, fir or cedar. Also available is an interior skin of 6" on center V-groove knotty pine. The core is recessed around the edge of each panel to allow the panels to be splined with 2" x 4", 2" x 6" or 2" x 8" lumber.

JOHNS MANVILLE, THE ENRGY HOUSE, 27 Pearl St., Portland, ME 04101 - (800) 654-3103

roof insulation - "NailBase"   type of insulation - polyisocyanurate   size of panel - 4' x 8'

thickness inches / R-value - 6 sizes with ⁷/₁₆" OSB — 1.5 / R-7.3 • 2.0 / R-11.4 • 2.5 / R-15.4 • 3.0 / R-20.0 • 3.5 / R-23.1 • 4.0 / R-25.7 • 5 sizes with ⁵/₈" OSB — 2.0 / R-11.1 • 2.5 / R-15.2 • 3.0 / R-19.1 • 3.5 / R-22.4 • 4.0 / R-25.6

description - This is a nailbase rigid insulation panel consisting of a foam core bonded to either a ⁷/₁₆" or ⁵/₈" OSB on one side and a fiber reinforced facer on the other.

roof insulation - "Iso-Vent" — venting   type of insulation - polyisocyanurate   size of panel - 4' x 8'

thickness inches / R-value - 5 sizes — 2.5 / R-14.0 • 3.0 / R-18.6 • 3.25 / R-20.0 • 3.5 / R-22.3 • 4.0 / R-25.7

description - This is a foam insulation panel with a moisture-resistant glass reinforced backer bonded to both sides. It has a flat bottom side and formed channels on the top side which provide a ventilated air space when covered by a rigid nailable surface of either plywood or OSB — supplied by others.

KORWALL INDUSTRIES, INC., 326 N. Bowen Rd., Arlington, TX 76012 - (817) 277-6741

roof insulation - "Kor-Roof"   type of insulation - expanded polystyrene   size of panel - 4' x 8' to 8' x 28'

thickness inches / R-value - 3 sizes — 3.5 / R-19.6 • 5.5 / R-28.0 • 7.5 / R-35.6

description - The panels consist of a foam core sandwiched between ⁷/₁₆" OSB sheathing. The panels are connected to each other along the panel edges by inserting standard lumber — 2" x 4", 2" x 6" or 2" x 8".

MURUS CO., PO Box 220, Mansfield, PA 16933 - (800) 626-8787 (717) 549-2100

<u>roof insulation</u> - "MIPS"   <u>type of insulation</u> - urethane   <u>size of panel</u> - 4' x 8'

<u>thickness inches / R-value</u> - 3 sizes — 4.5/ R-28.0 • 5.5/ R-35.0 • 6.5/ R-43.0

<u>description</u> - This structural panel consists of an exterior skin of ⁷/₁₆" OSB, the urethane foam core and different interior finishes including OSB, ½" gypsum wallboard and tongue and groove paneling (pine, cedar, oak or cherry). The panels have an electrical chase foamed in place. There is a cam-locking system that provide a positive seal between panels.

RMAX, INC., 3811 Turtle Creek Blvd., Suite 900, Dallas, TX 75219 - (800) 527-0890

<u>roof insulation</u> - "Vented Nailable Base" — venting <u>type of insulation</u> - polyisocyanurate <u>size of panel</u> - 4' x 8'

<u>thickness inches / R-value</u> - 7 sizes — 2.0 / R-6.3 • 2.5 / R-10.0 • 3.0 / R-14.36 • 3.5 / R-18.0 • 4.0 / R-22.5 • 4.5 / R-26.3 • 5.0 / R-30.3

<u>description</u> - This vented nailable base insulation has a foam core bonded to ⁷/₁₆" or ½" thick OSB furring strips and a ⁷/₁₆" thick OSB nailing panel on the top surface.

WINTER PANEL CORP., 74 Glen Orne Dr., Battleboro, VT 05301 - (802) 254-3435

<u>roof insulation</u> - "Woodclad"   <u>type of insulation</u> - polyisocyanurate   <u>size of panel</u> - 4' x 8'

<u>thickness inches / R-value</u> - 2 sizes — 4.5 / R-25.0 • 6.5 / R-40.0

<u>description</u> - The structural panel consists of an outer skin of ⁷/₁₆" OSB, the foam core, an inner skin of ⁷/₁₆" OSB with wood cladding of tongue and ¾" groove pine, cedar, oak veneer or cherry veneer laminated to the OSB panel. ⁵/₈" x 3" plywood splines are installed into routed grooves along the panel exterior to reinforce the panel joints. "Structurewall" is available without the wood cladding.

Recommended Installation of Air-Flo Roof Panels by Branch River

1) Before installing the roof panels, snap a chalk line across the roof where the first panel course will be.

2) Before bringing the panels into position,

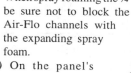

start the nails through the exterior sheathing. Predrilling of nail holes is optional.

3) Nail or screw the panels 6" to 8" o. c. (on center) through the structural decking into the underlying supporting members. Also nail or screw 12" o. c. through the field of the panel. Use galvanized spiral or annular shank spikes or noncorrosive screws with stress plates.

4) Nail or screw 12" from panel's spline edges, so as not to compress spline slots. After splines are installed, nail off the panel edges. If there are no spline slots in panels, disregard nailing 12" away from panel's edges. 1½" minimum penetration on hardwoods. 2" minimum penetration of softwoods. 1" minimum penetration into structural decking.

5) Place and nail panels when aligned with the

chalk line. This will ensure that the eaves and rakes will be straight for the trim.

6) Leave a ¼" gap between non-splined panel joints. Use a wood shim to create the ¼" gap. Fill the ¼" gap with an expanding spray foam after all the panels have been installed. When spray foaming the ¼"gaps, be sure not to block the Air-Flo channels with the expanding spray foam.

7) On the panel's splined edges, apply a bead of sealant before setting the next panel in place.

8) After the first course of panels has been installed, set the first panel of the second course in place. The splines are slid in between the first and second course panels. The second panel of the second course is placed and the splines are slid in between first and second course panels, and so on.

9) After roof splines are installed, screw the splines every 6" to 8" o. c. with 1¼" galvanized drywall type screws and finish nailing of the panel edges.

10) Scoop out the EPS foam with an electric hot wire cutter or a saw to the depth of the framing lumber on the eave and rake edges.

11) Inlet framing lumber at the eave and rake edges.

12) Fasten framing lumber with 8d nails from the outside skin at 6' to 8' o. c. and nail into the structural decking. Note: Skylight and chimney openings

can be cut out before or after panels are installed. Use circular saws or small electric chain saws. If the panel is too thick to cut through with a circular saw, cut the opening from both sides of panel.

13) Skylight and chimney openings — Once the rough openings are cut out from the panel, use an electric hot wire cutter or a saw to scoop out the EPS to the depth of the framing lumber. At Air-Flo channels, scoop EPS back another 1" to 2" beyond the depth of the framing members. This is required so that the constant flow of air remains uninterrupted.

14) The framing lumber is set into the opening's perimeter and fastened with 8d nails from the outside at 6" to 8" o. c. and nailed into the structural decking.

15) After all the roof panels are installed, spray foam the joints between the wall and structural decking on the eave and rake sides of the house, if applicable.

16) After spray foaming of roof panel joints is complete, install roof shingles in accordance with manufacturer's recommendations. If the use of felt paper is recommended under the shingles by the shingle

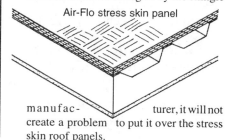

manufacturer, it will not create a problem to put it over the stress skin roof panels.

New fiberglass windows are top quality overall

Q: I want the very best replacement windows and also some for a new room addition. I am willing to pay extra for quality. What is your opinion on maintenance-free fiberglass versus vinyl windows?

A: Although the new designs of vinyl windows are efficient and an excellent efficient choice for the budget-minded homeowner, fiberglass windows are the best available today. Twenty years from now, they will glide open and seal like when they were new. Also, the new glass will reduce curtain and furniture fading.

Even though fiberglass windows cost more initially, their lifetime cost is reasonable. This is because they will never need to be replaced again and seldom caulked or painted. They remain airtight and, with their high insulation value, your utility bills will be lower and your comfort much better.

Fiberglass is the most versatile and functional of all window frame materials. With the extreme strength of fiberglass, the frames can be much narrower. This provides a larger clear view window area than your old windows. This also is a real plus if you want free passive solar heating in the winter.

My favorite fiberglass window designs have natural wood interiors. From indoors, they have a rich elegant look, yet the outdoor fiberglass portion is maintenance-free. The superstrong fiberglass exterior provides the stability and can resist gale-force winds and driving rains.

Fiberglass replacement windows are available in many decorator colors. Since fiberglass resists high temperatures, durable paint can be baked on. Unlike vinyl windows, fiberglass frames can be painted any-

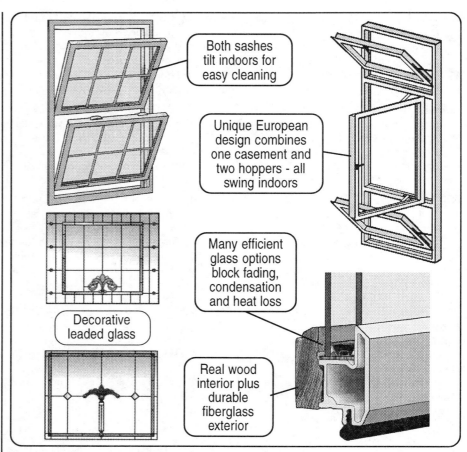

Both sashes tilt indoors for easy cleaning

Unique European design combines one casement and two hoppers - all swing indoors

Many efficient glass options block fading, condensation and heat loss

Decorative leaded glass

Real wood interior plus durable fiberglass exterior

time you decide to change the decor of just one room or your entire house.

Another key advantage of the fiberglass frame material is that it expands with temperature changes at almost the identical rate as the window glass. With nearly identical expansion, the fit stays true and the seals airtight. Vinyl expands about seven times more than glass and aluminum expands about twice as much as glass.

With its superior strength, fiberglass frames offer the possibility of more unique shapes and styles of windows. For example, some of the new sliders also tilt in for easy cleaning. There are also unique combination hopper/casement and tilt-turn windows that are popular in Europe.

Fiberglass windows are tops in energy efficiency. Many of the fiberglass window frames offer optional foam insulation filling (up to R-10). This is more effective than insulated

vinyl frames because the strength of fiberglass does not require all the interior webs in vinyl frames. As with custom-sized vinyl windows, installing fiberglass windows is not difficult for do-it-yourselfers. This can save you a bundle.

Q: I have an extension cord with the big and small slots in the end. It is a hassle trying to plug in my tools, so I ground down the big legs so they fit either way. Does this hurt efficiency?

A: It will not reduce the efficiency of your electric power tools, but it can reduce the efficiency of your heart. That was a very hazardous thing to do and do not use the tools until you install new plug ends.

These plug legs are different sizes so that the hot and neutral wires get attached with the proper polarity. If you reverse the polarity on a lamp, for example, you can be shocked just changing a bulb.

Selected Manufacturers of Efficient Fiberglass Frame Windows

ACCURATE DORWIN CO., 660 Nairn Ave., Winnipeg, Manitoba R2L 0X5 Canada - (888) 982-4640 (204) 982-4640
<u>type</u> - fiberglass • optional oak interior
<u>styles</u> - awning • bay • bow • casement • horizontal slider • picture • single hung
<u>glass options</u> - dual and triple glazing • Low-E • argon gas fill • tinted
<u>frame colors</u> - brown • white • optional custom colors
<u>features</u> - Lifetime warranty on all frames against warping, twisting, rotting, shrinking, denting or bowing. Sealed units are guaranteed for a full 10 years. Lifetime warranty on all hardware. There is tilt and turn hardware on the horizontal slider so the windows can be cleaned easily from indoors. Bottom sash tilts in on single-hung unit for cleaning. Windows feature triple weatherstripping, minimizing air and water infiltration, keeping out air and dust. The outer seal prevents dust, wind and rain from penetrating. The center seal prevents air leakage. The inner seal stops air from circulating into the hardware cavity. The super spacer (warm edge technology) bar is made from extruded silicone and it contributes to the windows' high energy efficiency rating and low condensation levels. Expanded polystyrene foam insulation is inserted into the hollow frames. Sash frames are injection foamed before assembly. An extruded aluminum frame component creates the outer profile of the unit and includes the mounting fin for fastening the unit to the buildings sheathing. It interlocks with the fiberglass frame and recesses the glazing back away from the elements for even lower heat loss. Optional oak interior should be stained and urethaned as soon as possible after installation. Grilles available — aluminum grilles, brass grilles or wood grilles.

ALL WEATHER WIND., 18550 118a Ave. NW, Edmonton, Alberta T5S 2K7 Canada - (800) 638-5709 (403) 451-0670
<u>type</u> - fiberglass — "Infinity"
<u>styles</u> - bay • bow • casement • double hung • horizontal slider • picture • single hung
<u>glass options</u> - dual and triple glazing • "SunStop Solar Control Window System" — allows most natural light to enter freely, but absorbs a significant portion of short wave heat energy. In the long summer, long-wave heat energy, radiating from objects, is reflected back outside, lowering cooling costs. In winter, heat energy is reflected back inside, lowering heating costs, reduction of summer solar heat gain, ultraviolet screening, allows more visible light than any other tinted product, less heat loss in winter • Sungate 100 Low-E • argon gas fill
<u>frame colors</u> - black • brown • forest green • gray • ivory • ivy teal • mist green • pearl gray • rustic red • sandalwood • steel blue • white • custom colors
<u>features</u> - "Super Edge Plus" provides a warmer edge in cold weather, flexibility to withstand all temperature changes, better argon gas retention and a cleaner, better looking sealed units at the edge. The Super Spacer with super adhesive plus a secondary sealant make this 10 year warranty possible. The "Infinity" windows holds its shape and will not warp, twist, rot, shrink or bow. Expanded polystyrene foam insulation is inserted into the hollow frames for energy efficiency. Sash frames are injection foamed before assembly.

ANDERSON WINDOWS, INC., 100 Fourth Ave. No., Bayport, MN 55003 - (612) 439-5150
<u>type</u> - fiberglass exterior with pine wood interior — "FlexiFrame"
<u>styles</u> - all fixed windows, do not open — geometric shapes
<u>glass options</u> - "High-Performance" or "High-Performance Sun" (soft gray tint) solar control insulating glass has a microscopically thin metallic coating bonded to an inner surface of the sealed pane of glass, argon gas is sealed inside the two panes of glass • High-Performance tempered insulating glass
<u>frame colors</u> - white • sandtone • Terratone, dark brown • custom colors
<u>features</u> - There are many standard units or the "FlexiFrame" windows can be custom-made to just about any unique shape you can draw with straight lines and angles. There are decorative glass options with the Art Glass panels collection — available in 11 stained glass designs. The panels are trimmed in maple and have zinc caming (leading). The panels fasten to the inside of the windows and have a special fastening system that provides easy mounting into new or existing Andersen windows. The snap-lock fasteners allow the panels to be removed for cleaning or window maintenance. Prefinished or natural custom divided light interior hardwood grilles are available on special order.

BLOMBERG WINDOW SYSTEMS, PO Box 22485, Sacramento, CA 95822 - (916) 428-8060
<u>type</u> - fiberglass
<u>styles</u> - awning • casement • picture • single hung
<u>glass options</u> - Sungate 300 Low-E • Sungate 500 Low-E
<u>frame colors</u> - standard colors — almond • black walnut • white • Porsche white • custom colors / premium colors — autumn gray • brick red • Canadian white • cypress black • desert tan • eucalyptus • French blue • sea foam green • spruce green • teal green • terra blue / custom colors
<u>features</u> - There are several options for grilles — 1-1/2" applied muntin bar, 1" applied muntin bar or an internal grid. The single-hung window tilts in for easy cleaning. The frames can be painted in the factory with standard of custom colors to match other windows and doors in your home.

COMFORT LINE INC., PO Box 6998, Toledo, OH 43615 - (419) 729-8520
<u>type</u> - fiberglass • optional oak veneer interior — "FiberFrame"
<u>styles</u> - bay • bow • casement • double hung • radius • geometric shapes • custom architectural shapes available
<u>glass options</u> - Low-E • argon gas fill • obscure • tinted
<u>frame colors</u> - almond • brown • cobblestone • dove white • split colors • custom matched to your specifications
<u>features</u> - Available with a veneer of natural oak on the interior that can be stained to match your decor. You can actually feel the grain on the wood veneer. There are two sets of compression weatherstripping to fully seal the perimeter of the sash. There are solid oak colonial grilles with hidden clips so you can remove them in seconds to easily clean the windows. There are also brass internal grilles available. Stainless steel hinges are available for corrosive environments and coastal conditions. Color coordinated screen frame with fiberglass screen wire. Hardware is available in dove white, almond, champagne, classic bronze or optional bright brass. Casement windows over 38" high are fitted with dual locking handles. They open a full 90 degrees so they can be easily cleaned. See page 4 for double-hung style. Tilts in for easy cleaning.

FIBERTEC WINDOW, 157 Rivermede Rd., #2, Concord, Ontario L4K 3M4 Canada - (888) 232-4956 (905) 660-7102
 type - fiberglass • optional oak veneer interior
 styles - awning • bay • bow • casement • double hung • horizontal slider • radius • geometric shapes
 glass options - Low-E • Heat Mirror • argon gas fill
 frame colors - almond • brown • white • can computer match any color to suit your needs
 features - "Portrait Series" combines a real oak interior with a maintenance-free fiberglass exterior. Oak veneer is profile wrapped to side of frame. Oak can be stained any color, finished with an exterior grade varnish. Horizontal slider has a tilt and slide feature — slides easily from end to end, but the sash remains stationary and secure when in a tilt position. Warm edge spacers for efficiency. The windows have a lifetime warranty. Injected foam corners for airtightness and rigidity. The frame cavity is filled with expanded polystyrene (up to R-10) which is laser cut to fit the frame profile for a good energy rating. The frames are treated with an ultraviolet stabilized resin to protect them from sunlight. Grilles available for windows.

INLINE FIBERGLASS LTD., 30 Constellation Ct., Etobicoke, Ontario M9W 1K1 Canada - (416) 679-1171
 type - fiberglass
 styles - awning • bay • bow • casement • double hung • horizontal slider • picture
 glass options - dual and triple glazing • Low-E • argon gas fill
 frame colors - commercial brown • forest green • ivory • sandalwood • white • split colors • custom colors
 features - Colonial and diamond grilles available. Warm edge spacers available. "Series 700" are combination casement and awning that swing in. Horizontal slider has removable panels. A wood jamb extension available for new construction. Double-hungs have tilt-in sashes. Double weatherstripping — interior for air seal and exterior to provide a weather barrier.

MARVIN WINDOWS & DOORS, PO Box 100 Warroad, MN 56763 - (800) 862-7587
 type - fiberglass exterior with pine wood interior — "Integrity"
 styles - awning • bay • bow • casement • double hung • horizontal slider • picture • radius
 glass options - Low-E II with argon gas fill is standard • bronze or gray tint • tempered
 frame colors - pebble gray • white
 features - Interiors are pretreated and ready to be stained or painted. Removable wood interior grilles available. An integral corner key keeps window units square through delivery and installation. Injected with a hot melt adhesive to create corner joints that stay sealed and square. Have warm edge spacers that use low conductive material, reducing temperature transfer. Horizontal slider has a tiltable and removable sash for cleaning. Hardware finished in almond frost finish.

MILGARD WINDOWS, 1010 54th Ave. E., Tacoma, WA 98424 - (800) 645-4273
 type - fiberglass exterior with clear vertical grain Douglas fir wood interior — "WoodClad"
 styles - awning • bay • bow • casement • horizontal slider • picture • single hung • radius • geometric shapes
 glass options - Low-E • tempered • tinted glass in solar bronze, solar gray, Graylite (dark gray, almost black), Solex (green), Evergreen, Azurlite (aquamarine) • reflective tints are Solar Cool Bronze, Solar Cool Gray, Bronze Eclipse, Gray Eclipse, Blue-Green Eclipse • Heat Mirror — specially coated film which is mounted inside insulating glass unit, midway between the panes of glass, combines a Low-E • obscure • heat strengthened • laminated
 frame colors - bronze • hunter green • sand • white
 features - "WoodClad " windows are backed by a lifetime guarantee to original owner. The awning and casement windows have a roto operator and a single-throw multipoint lock system. There are 7/8" wide snap-in wood grids with a full surround frame and hidden attachment clips for the interior of the windows. The "Craftsman" grid system combines 1-1/8" wood applied to interior of the glass with sculptured grids matched to the exterior to give a true divided look appearance. There are sculptured metal internal grids available. Standard grid configurations or will customize a grid to your design. The hardware is available in a standard clay or white or can be upgraded to a brass finish. Screens are color matched to the hardware. The bow and bay windows come with a standard plywood head and seatboard or you can choose a veneer upgrade. The interior is stainable, paintable and can be refinished. The windows are built with precision for the tightest fit and joinery.

PELLA CORP., 102 Main St., Pella, IA 50219 - (800) 547-3552
 type - aluminum-clad exterior sash and fiberglass frame with pine wood interior sash and fiberglass frame — "Precision Fit"
 styles - double hung replacement window only
 glass options - clear insulating glass • InsulShield insulating glass with a multi-layer of Low-E coating and argon gas fill • standard or obscure insulating glass • SmartSash double-glazing system with Low-E, standard or obscure glazing
 frame colors - brown • white
 features - Replacement window slides easily into existing frame of old window from the inside. No need to paint or repaper walls or replace trim after the window is installed. Eliminates the mess and inconvenience of a full tear-out. It is designed to replace older style double-hung windows. Both sash center-pivot and tilt for easy cleaning. Twenty-year warranty on the glass and ten-year warranty on all other components. Fully transferable. Architect Series — look of true divided light, muntin bars are permanently bonded to the interior and exterior surfaces in traditional or prairie patterns. Designer Series SmartSash — between-the-glass blinds and muntin bars. Designer Classic — removable wood muntin bars.

THERMOTECH WINDOWS, 109-42 Antares Dr., Nepean, Ontario K2E 7Y4 Canada - (613) 225-1101
 type - fiberglass
 styles - awning • casement • horizontal slider • picture • single hung • radius • geometric
 glass options - dual and triple glazing • hard coat or soft coat Low-E • argon gas fill • tinted • reflective
 frame colors - brown • white • custom colors
 features - Windows feature "SuperSpacer", an insulating spacer, between glass panes and a nonconductive fiberglass frame. Hollow sections of frame and sash are filled with foam insulation to help decrease heat loss. Dual locks are used on taller casement windows but a single lever multipoint lock is available. Hardware available in either white or bronze. Three seal design weatherstripping — exterior seal prevents dust and rain penetration, center thermoplastic bulb prevent air leakage, inner thermoplastic seal restricts air from circulating into the hardware cavity and condensing on sash and hardware. Unique hardware permits horizontal sliding sash to rotate inward for easy cleaning.

WINDOW PLACE, 2814 A Merrilee Dr., Fairfax, VA 20151 - (703) 641-5400

<u>type</u> - fiberglass • optional oak veneer interior — "Fiber-Last"
<u>styles</u> - casement • double hung
<u>glass options</u> - Low-E • argon gas fill
<u>frame colors</u> - almond • bronze • cobblestone • white • split colors • custom color options and factory prefinished colors
<u>features</u> - All styles either swing out or tilt-in for cleaning from inside home. Window frames available with real oak interior. Stain or finish as you would any oak window. Designed to maximize thermal efficiency utilizing sealed insulating glass, warm edge spacer and two sets of compression weatherstripping. The double-hung windows have tilt-in sashes for easy cleaning. Solid oak grilles in colonial patterns are available to meet the specifications of your own design. Also available are muntin bars in colonial and diamond styles. All operating casement units over 38" high are fitted with dual locks. Stainless steel hinges for corrosive environments and coastal conditions are available. Color-coordinated hardware and screen frames with fiberglass screen wire. Feature a unique installation flange that interlocks with exterior capping material around window opening to create an airtight window sealing system. This design mates window and capping material into one complete unit, relies less on use of caulking material, which can shrink and cause air and water leaks around frame.

Double-Hung Window Installation Instructions from Inline Fiberglass Ltd.

1) Handle carefully — do not distort when handling.

2) Anchors — (2) most common methods to secure window in the opening are "A" by using screws shown on sectional drawing below or "B" by using strap anchor.

3) Common anchor spacing (see below) — anchors should be located at 24" (max.) and 6" from corner and/or mullion centers.

4) Additional anchorage in the inner jamb track — when screw is used in the upper half of window, pull off track cover and use round head screw on the inside area of the balance tube. When screw is used in the bottom half of window, use flat head screw. Drill countersunk holes 3/4" from the inside of window, same as sill dimension.

5) For Maintenance — wash occasionally with nonabrasive detergent, both glass and frames. Annual spray of weather seals with silicone lubricant is also beneficial and revitalizing but not essential.

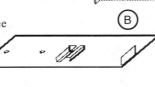

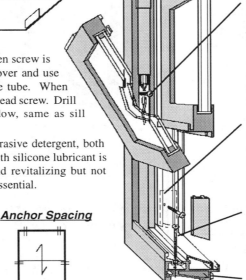

Head Anchor — Drill, tight fit clearance holes, for #8 or #10 round or pan head screw.

If inner track must be used, for screw, pull off cover before.

Muntin Anchor — Drill, tight clearance hole for round head screw, just below the bottom and to the inside of the balance tube.

Always shim each side of window at the center to allow smooth operation of sash and good contact for weatherstrip.

Lower Jamb Anchor — Pull out drop stop from exterior track and drill, tight clearance holes for round head screws as above. Caulk the screw head.

Sill Anchor — Drill 3/8" access hole in cover then tight fitting clearance hole for round head screw - in the frame. Caulk screw under the head, prior to installation.

Always keep weep holes clear of caulking or other obstructions.

Anchor Spacing

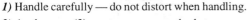

Styles of Windows

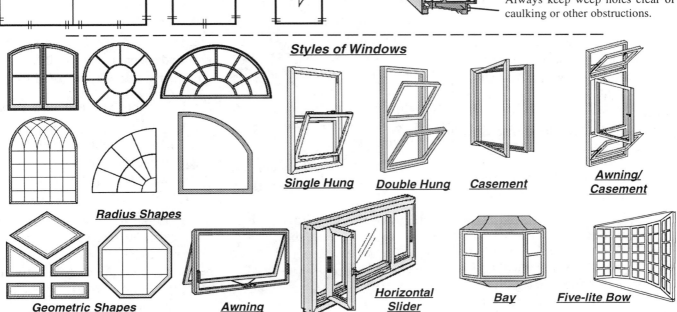

Radius Shapes

Single Hung   **Double Hung**   **Casement**   **Awning/ Casement**

Geometric Shapes   *Awning*   **Horizontal Slider**   **Bay**   **Five-lite Bow**

Many styles of bow and bay replacement windows

Q: I'd love one of the sunspace kits that you recently wrote about, but I cannot afford one. Would adding a bow or bay window be a lower-cost alternative. What design features are best and most efficient?

A: Installing a new efficient bay or bow window is an excellent sunspace alternative at thousands of dollars less. A still lower-cost option is a small V-bay window. The very lowest-cost option for more openness is adding a 90-degree angle or curved glass window.

Bow and bay windows allow you to give a room more space and natural lighting without actually increasing the square footage. They are ideal for creating eating nooks, mini-greenhouses and bathroom windows. You will be surprised at how much larger a room seems with a new bay or bow window.

There have been many improvements in styling and efficiency of bow and bay windows. Contemporary decorative glass (leaded, beveled and tinted) are now available. Some also have snap-out colonial grids for easy cleaning. For privacy with ventilation, select a design with built-in microblinds.

Some of the newest efficient vinyl models (Trawood) have very authentic-looking grained wood interiors without the typical maintenance of real wood. Some of the highest-quality windows offer lifetime warranties.

Other designs combine a super-strong aluminum exterior with an energy efficient, no-maintenance vinyl interior. This design is particularly good for larger windows where efficiency is a primary concern. The aluminum provides the rigidity, the vinyl provides the insulating barrier.

Copper roof

Five-section bow

Casement bow

Casement angle bay

Box bay

Glass top

The basic design styles are angle bays, box bays and bows. The side windows in angle bays are tilted at either 30 or 45 degrees. These typically include double-hung or casement side windows with a center picture window.

For a larger seat (indoor sill), for floor or hanging plants, a 45-degree design provides more depth. A box bay, with side windows perpendicular to the walls, provides the most additional space. A bow window typically consists of three to seven window sections to create a more rounded unit.

The new bay and bow window designs are efficient. Some triple-pane glass options have insulating values up to R-8. In climates where window condensation can be a problem, make sure you get insulated glass with warm-edge spacers. Also, a foam-filled vinyl frame would be a good choice.

For all climates, select a bow or bay window with an insulated seat board. Many use thick rigid foam insulation, as high as R-10, hidden under the seat board. For growing plants, or for just comfort and efficiency, this is a must.

Q: I gave my parents a computer. Their older house has only two-slot electrical outlets. Will using a three-prong adapter plug work well? Is there a right or wrong way to install it?

A: It is important to have a good safety ground on any electronic equipment or appliance. The three-prong adapter plug (which is attached to the faceplate screw) is an accepted fix if there is a true ground inside.

Turn off the electric power and remove the plug faceplate. In order for the screw to be grounded, there must be a metal conduit box and a ground wire must be attached to it. If not, call an electrician to do it correctly.

Selected Manufacturers of Bow and Bay Windows

ANDERSON WINDOWS, INC., 100 Fourth Ave. No., Bayport, MN 55003 - (612) 439-5150

styles - casement, double hung or picture bow (3, 4, 5, 6 or 7-lite units) and angle or box bay (30°, 45°, 90°)

frame -* vinyl-clad wood (pine)   colors - white • sandtone • Terratone, dark brown

warranty - 20-year for glass, 10-year all other parts, even if the owner sells the home

glass options - "High-Performance" or "High-Performance Sun" (soft gray tint) solar control insulating glass has a microscopically thin metallic coating bonded to an inner surface of the sealed pane of glass, argon gas is sealed inside the two panes of glass • High-Performance tempered insulating glass

decorative glass options - Art Glass collection — available in 11 stained glass designs. The panels are trimmed in maple and have zinc caming (leading). The panels fasten to the inside of the windows and have a special fastening system that provides easy mounting into new or existing Andersen windows. The snap-lock fasteners allow the panels to be removed for cleaning or window maintenance.

features - Standard head and seat boards are a natural pine veneer. Oak veneer available as custom design unit. A cable support system provides additional support. Removable glazing panels mounted to exterior are available to provide triple glazing insulation on the casements. Custom maple or oak hardwood grilles available on special order. Simulated grilles, exterior grilles or grilles between the glass are available. There is a low-conductivity spacer made of stainless steel. Its unique shape creates a longer, more difficult path for energy to flow through. The spacer is buried into the sash profile to reduce heat flow around the edges.

CARADCO, 201 Evans Rd., Rantoul, IL 61866 - (800) 238-1866

styles - casement, doublehung or picture bow (4, 5 or 6-lite units) and angle bay (30°, 45°)

frame - solid wood • aluminum-clad wood (pine)

colors - brilliant white • chestnut bronze • dove gray • French vanilla • Hartford green • sandstone

warranty - 20-year against stress cracks and glass seal failures, 1-year limited covering materials and workmanship

glass options - argon-filled LoE2 glass — coated with microscopically thin layers of silver sandwiched between layers of anti-reflective metal oxide coatings. A protective coating layer is then applied to ensure durability and scratch-resistance • clear • bronze or gray tint, regular or reflective • obscure • Solex green • tempered

decorative glass options - There are three decorative glass transom designs available.

features - The assembled units can be furnished without head and seat boards for a full walk-in bay. The head and seat boards are clear pine veneer. There are optional aluminum microblinds available in 18 colors that are installed between the sash and the screen on the casement windows. There are true divided lites available with insulated glass and 1 3/8" wide muntins, or single pane glass with 7/8" or 1 3/8" muntins. Also available are simulated divided lites, removable wood full-surround grilles and flat and profiled grilles between the glass. There are optional handles available for casement windows — a foldable crank handle, a T-handle, a round knob or an easy-to-crank ADA handle for people suffering with arthritis, etc. The center bay window can be either an operating or fixed window.

CERTAINTEED CORP., PO Box 860, Valley Forge, PA 19482 - (800) 233-8990

style - casement, double hung, single hung or picture bow (3, 4, 5 or 6-lite units) and angle bay (30°, 45°)

frame - vinyl   colors - tan • white • oak woodgrain laminate interior

warranty - lifetime limited coverage for original owner, 20 year transferable if you sell your home, SureStart™ protection for 5 years pays cost of materials and labor for repair of replacement of a defective window

glass options - 5/8" or 7/8" double glazing with warm edge low conductance spacer • "Thermaflect" is a low-e glass with two microscopic layers of silver, blocks 84% of ultraviolet radiation • tinted or obscure glass • argon gas fill

features - "CertaLite" interior grids give look of true divided lites. Hidden tabs attach them securely to sash with no gaps, easy to remove for cleaning. Available with grids between glass. Windows have a birch head and seat board which can be painted or stained to match your decor. Insulated with a foam core. Balance system is based on a 3/4" wide stainless steel coil that applies a constant force. Similar to a retractable tape measure, the balance operates easily and exerts a steady pull — making sashes easy to lift and lower.

CRESTLINE WINDOWS & DOORS, PO Box 800, Mosinee, WI 54455 - (715) 693-7000

style - casement, double hung or picture bow (3, 4, 5 or 6-lite units) and angle or box bay (30°, 45°, 90°)

frame - solid wood • aluminum-clad wood (pine) • vinyl • vinyl-clad wood

colors - almond • forest green • pewtertone • sierra brown • white • 12 custom colors available or special custom colors for the window frame — sunshine yellow, maple nut, taupe, clay stone, Williamsburg gold, pebble gray, fuschia rose, country rouge, wedgewood blue, architectural bronze, turquoise, barrel black

warranty - 20-year against seal failure, 2-year on cladding, parts, hardware and materials, transferable, 20-year transferable on vinyl parts

glass options - 3/4" insulated glass is standard • 3/4" SmartR® (northern) or SunPLUS4® (southern) is argon-filled insulated glass • tempered • gray or bronze tint • obscure • high altitude insulated

features - There are 5/8" metal microblinds that fit between the sash and the screen for privacy and ventilation. The blinds are available in 27 colors. Operated from indoors by a tilt-control knob in a copper or white finish. The blinds resists scratches and contains antimicrobial properties to resist bacteria and fungal growth. The center bay unit can be an operating window. Insulated divided lites, removable full-surround wood grilles or grilles in the airspace are available. Custom grille patterns are available. A copper roof is optional. Pine head and seat boards are standard, oak is optional. Wood interiors available in walnut, cherry, red oak or pine.

* Clad means that vinyl (aluminum or fiberglass) wraps around the outdoor portion of the wood frame. The frame is natural wood indoors.

EAGLE WINDOW & DOOR, INC., PO Box 1072, Dubuque, IA 52004 - (800) 453-3633 (319) 556-2270

style - casement, double hung or picture bow (3, 4, 5 or 6-lite units) and angle or box bay (30°, 45°, 90°)

frame - solid wood • aluminum-clad wood (pine)   colors - colony white • green • pebble tan • sierra bronze

warranty - 20-year for failure of the glass seal, 5-year on decorative glass

glass options - Low-E Maximizer Plus — dual, sealed panes filled with argon gas with a low-e coating blocks 84% of the sun's ultraviolet rays • moisture-absorbing beads combine with a low thermal conductance edge seal to help eliminate condensation

decorative glass options - Decorelle glass — includes decorative panels made of leaded, beveled glass, grooved glass, colored glass (clear, medium blue, ruby red or dark green) and a variety of textured glasses. Caming (leading) options include brass, copper and zinc. All decorative glass is encased between two panes of dual-sealed insulated glass for triple-pane insulation, cleaning convenience and protection from dust and damage. Eight different styles to choose from.

features - Head and seat boards offered in either natural birch or oak. Clear natural pine interiors allow you to paint or stain to match decor. Wood windows available primed, unprimed or clear exteriors to allow a variety of finishing options. Blind and shade systems available. One-inch aluminum slat blinds are mounted to frame between sash and screen. Controlled by a knob (white, bronze or tan). Aluminum slat blinds are mounted to a storm panel that is applied to the sash between two panes of glass (available in white or tan.) 1³/8" cellular fabric shades are mounted to a storm panel that is placed between two panes of glass, available in bronze, white or tan. There are 46 designer colors to choose in addition to the standard colors. Custom design divided lites available — simulated grilles, removable wood grilles, between the glass grilles.

GREAT LAKES WINDOWS, PO Box 1896, Toledo, OH 43603 - (800) 666-0000 (419) 666-5555

style - casement, double hung or picture bow (3, 4, 5 or 6-lite units) and angle or box bay (30°, 45°, 90°)

frame - vinyl   colors - camel • earthtone • white • woodgrain

warranty - Lifetime-Plus warranty on the entire window — transferable to a new owner

glass options - Hi-R + Plus with argon gas has soft-coat low-e glass and steel spacer channel system • Easy-Clean glass nonstick coating protects glass from excessive dirt, stains and grime, reduces cleaning frequency. Works like Teflon® coating does on cookware, easier to clean.

decorative glass options - Designer glass panels — hand-cut leaded glass inlays surrounded by genuine brass, lead or antique pewtertone caming, mounted between two continuous sheets of annealed or safety-tempered insulated glass, available in 12 styles and 10 accent colors — ruby red, aqua marine, deep lavender, emerald green, royal blue, lapis blue, sunrise orange, sunflower yellow, champagne pink, mist grey • beveled-leaded glass • v-groove hand-cut glass

features - Vinyl extrusions are filled with R-Core® insulation, same polyurethane used in insulated steel and refrigerator doors, for a high R factor of 13. Woodgrain interiors available are golden oak, natural oak and colonial cherry. Available with furniture-grade 1-1/4" thick head and seat boards in oak or birch. An optional polyurethane insulated seat is available that adds energy efficiency. Optional cable support installation system makes installation easier and stronger. Colonial, diamond or prairie grids available between panes. Custom made to fit your windows. Warm edge technology steel spacer channel is one continuous piece of steel which is formed into a U-shape. Provides warmer indoor glass temperatures and good thermal performance. The casement window has a multi-point locking system to provide security with a single handle.

MARVIN WINDOWS & DOORS, PO Box 100, Warroad, MN 56763 - (800) 346-5128

style - awning, casement, double hung or picture bow (3, 4, 5 or 6-lite units) and angle or box bay (30°, 45°, 90°) • corner window — glass is bent to a 90° angle, no seams or posts to obstruct view • single hung or picture window curved glass • custom made bays with two sides or one side longer than the other

frame - solid wood • aluminum-clad wood • fiberglass-clad wood (pine)   colors - bronze • brown • evergreen • gray • white

warranty - 10-year on materials and workmanship

glass options - High R glazing — three panes of glass, two with low-e coatings, filled with argon or krypton gas • Low E II coating with argon is standard • bronze or gray tint • tempered • single glazing with removable energy panel

features - Have warm edge spacers that use low conductive material, reducing temperature transfer. Electric operator system features a motorized sash, can open and close casements and awnings by wall switch, hand-held remote control or ain sensor. Can control one window, windows in one room or entire house. Preset to partially open for venting. Safety reverse which makes window stop and back up if there's anything in the way as it closes. UL approved motors available in white or bronze. True divided lites available with single glazing or insulating glass. Simulated divided lites and removable grilles available. All of the lites can be custom ordered. Locks on awning and casements concealed so they don't interrupt the smooth wood interior. A crank is offered that has a flip handle, it folds into a flat position so it won't interfere with curtains or blinds. Lever operator available on awning units that has five different lock positions for a range of ventilation openings.

SIMONTON WINDOWS, PO Box 1646, Parkersburg, WV 26102 - (800) 542-9118

style - casement, double hung or picture bow (3, 4 or 5-lite units) and angle bay (30°, 45°)

frame - vinyl   colors - tan • white • woodgrain

warranty - 20-year for glass, lifetime on vinyl

glass options - 3/4" insulated glass • low-e argon gas fill regional packages • tempered • bronze or gray tint • Azurlite® • obscure • laminated • optional 1" insulated glass

features - Head and seat boards available in 1-1/4" thick oak or birch veneer, can be stained or painted. Extra pieces of matching woodgrain veneer provided to cover interior jamb boards. All seat boards insulated with 1-1/2" thick foam. Color-matched knee braces provide added support beneath seat board on exterior of house. Cable support system offers additional support. Woodgrain honey oak or amber oak finish available, interior only. Several different grid options — colonial in flat, sculptured or brass bars, colonial shadow in a bevel-cut glass look, diamond grids in flat or brass bars. Casement windows have multi-point locking system with one handle. Several spacer system available. "Intercept" is standard spacer system, made of tin-plated steel in a U-channel design. Rubberized sealant surrounds spacer to prevent direct metal contact to glass. "Super Spacer" for even greater thermal protection, made of nonmetallic solid silicone foam with millions of small, insulating air pockets.

THERMAL INDUSTRIES, 301 Brushton Ave., Pittsburgh, PA 15221 - (800) 245-1540 (412) 244-6400

style - casement, double hung or picture bow (3, 4 or 5-lite units) and angle bay (30°, 45°) • V-bay — two casement windows that are joined in a "V" to create a unique nook

frame - vinyl   colors - brown • earthtone • white

warranty - 20-year glass seal, lifetime on vinyl

glass options - insulating glass is standard • Peak Performance — soft coat low-e with argon gas fill • Super Peak Performance — triple panes with three layers of soft coat low-e, double layer krypton gas gaps, triple thermal break spacer-edge construction

decorative glass options - "Glamour Glass" — decorative glass available as etched, decra-led, brass can or jewel cut designs

features - Optional EPS foam can be placed around the frame and inside the sash. The "Dreamspace" windows have a smooth, hand-sanded furniture finish of specially treated birch or optional oak veneer. Casements have a dual-action multi-point locking system. Also available is a folding handle that gives more clearance for window shades, etc. Internal muntin bars — colonial wood grille, diamond, prairie or geo designs. The windows have an "Over-The-Edge" maintenance-free design that keeps the windows cleaner by keeping dust, dirt and water from collecting on the outside sill. An optional sill muffler is available to increase the R-value of the sill.

TRACO, 71 Progress Ave., Cranberry Township, PA 16066 - (800) 837-7003

style - casement, double hung or picture bow (4, 5 or 6-lite units) and angle bay (30°, 45°)

frame - vinyl • "Power Two" vinyl interior with aluminum exterior

colors - beige • white • woodgrain — light oak or medium oak interior finish, Trawood® — see description in features • Power Two has 12 possible color combinations — interior colors of white or Trawood® woodgrain with exterior colors of bronze • Hartford green • palace blue • river rouge red • sandstone • white

warranty - limited lifetime

glass options - View-Safe® tempered safety glass is standard — difficult to break, if it does break, it crumbles into harmless pellets with blunt edges and cleans up easily, can withstand impacts up to 24,000 lbs. per-square-inch (12 tons), provides increased protection against high winds due to hurricanes and tornadoes, virtually impossible to cut with a glass cutter, it deters intruders from entering home because it is four times stronger than ordinary glass • Heat Mirror • low-e • argon gas fill

features - Trawood® provides a natural interior woodgrain finish, it has the look and feel of real wood. Provides beauty of wood while protecting natural resources of trees. It is not a laminate. It is a permanent baked-on finish, so it won't peel or scrape off. Because it's not wood, it won't swell. Maintenance commonly associated with wood (scraping, sanding, painting) is eliminated. Internal muntins available in colonial or diamond styles.

Create Your Own Design of Divided Lights by Marvin

Authentic Divided Lites (ADL) — feature separate pieces of single pane or insulating glass that are individually glazed into the muntin bars.

Removable Grilles — provide the illusion of ADLs. Easily removed for glass cleaning. Made from solid pine, designed to fit on interior only.

Simulated Divided Lites (SDL) — Consist of muntins which are permanently attached to the interior and exterior panes of the glass with a durable adhesive. The interior and exterior muntins mirror each other to closely replicate the look of ADLS.

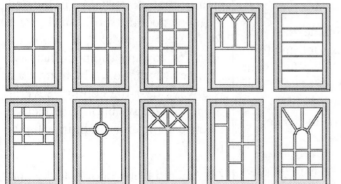

Corner Window by Weather Shield

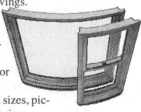

• Alternative to bays or bows.
• Interiors — Pine, oak, cherry, mahogany, maple, white latex, Poly I and primed.
• Energy-efficient Insul glass is standard.
• Interior trim casing styles are available in pine, oak, cherry, mahogany and maple.
• Wood frame is specially treated with water-repellent preservative.
• Several exterior frame finishes available.
• Glass is glazed directly into frame to provide more viewing area.

Curved Window by Marvin Windows

• Alternative to bays or bows.
• Insulating glass standard for energy savings.
• Wood bead glazing stops are removable for repair.
• Weatherstripping at top, middle and bottom minimizes air infiltration.
• Bottom sash tilts in for easy cleaning or can be removed on single-hung unit.
• Single-hungs available in nine standard sizes, picture windows available in ten standard sizes.

Manufacturers of Bay and Bow Roofs and Kits

PROOF IND., 242 Route 110, Farmingdale, NY 11735 - (516) 694-7663

completely preassembled, delivered ready to install with hardware • 5/8" plywood construction • unclad or clad in white or bronze aluminum or 16 oz solid copper • cable support allowance

ZAPPONE, N. 2928 Pittsburgh St., Spokane, WA 99207 - (800) 285-2677

"Copper Accent Bay Window Roof Kit" — all material required is provided — solid copper shingles, trim, counter flashings, nails • tools required — hammer and a pair of snips • standard bay roof can be installed in less than four hours • two standard sizes, six foot bay and eight foot bay, also available for custom-sized windows

Designer Window Glass by Great Lakes Windows

Skylight tube kit brightens room efficiently

Q: My kitchen is dark and needs more natural sunlight. My budget for a skylight is limited. Will a low-cost skylight tube brighten my kitchen?

A: Natural lighting, with its excellent color rendition, is especially appealing in a kitchen. Foods, particularly fresh vegetables and salads, look much more appetizing. Natural light is full-spectrum light which can help alleviate the winter "blues" from being trapped indoors under artificial light all day and night.

There are two basic and attractive options for brightening your kitchen with natural light - a do-it-yourself sunlight tube kit or a small high-efficiency skylight. If your ceiling is flat with an attic area above it, you will have to have a lightwell built to install a skylight.

Skylight tubes are a fairly new natural lighting option which is ideal for kitchens, bedrooms, halls and walk-in closets. There are many innovative designs to meet most house and roof designs. The basic concept is a reflective tube, between 10 and 20 inches in diameter, which runs from the roof to the ceiling. These are easy to install yourself, so the expensive outside labor costs of installing a skylight are eliminated.

On a sunny day, a skylight tube can provide the equivalent lighting of fifteen 100-watt light bulbs. From indoors, it looks just like a bright globe light fixture on the ceiling. The top of the tube, which extends through the ceiling, is covered with a waterproof clear acrylic dome.

The dome shape captures more sunlight and is naturally cleaned whenever it rains. It extends only a few inches above the roof. An optional reflector can increase the brightens. The tube extends up from

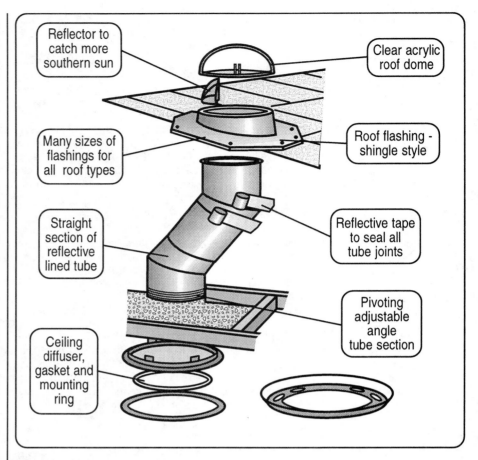

Reflector to catch more southern sun

Clear acrylic roof dome

Many sizes of flashings for all roof types

Roof flashing - shingle style

Straight section of reflective lined tube

Reflective tape to seal all tube joints

Pivoting adjustable angle tube section

Ceiling diffuser, gasket and mounting ring

your ceiling to a few inches above the roof. Since the various tubes are sized to fit nicely between the roof rafters, there is little cutting to do. Installation should take only about two hours.

Some designs use a reflective aluminum surface inside the tube. The sunlight bounces back and forth as it makes its way down into your kitchen, losing very little of its brightness. Other manufacturers use a special super-reflective film bonded to the inside of the tube.

If the attic space above the area where you need light has obstructions, choose a skylight tube made of a flexible corrugated material. This material is very reflective on the inside and can be bent and twisted in any direction. Several of the rigid tube designs have an angle sleeve. This allows the tube to change directions inside the attic and to easily match the slope of any roof or ceiling.

One unique skylight tube kit has an optional built-in vent fan. The air inlet for the vent fan is hidden inside the decorative collar around the ceiling light diffuser. A small quiet exhaust fan is located high up under the roof. This is great for a kitchen to exhaust cooking odors or for any room to increase summer ventilation. The hottest air is always near the ceiling. Several models also have built-in reflective electric lights for nighttime lighting.

Q: My old front door is leaky and I need to replace it. Is it better to buy a separate door, frame and hinges or get a more expansive prehung door?

A: Unless you are a handyman and have replaced doors before, I recommend a prehung door. It can be difficult to line up properly for an airtight seal if you buy the components separately.

ODL INC., 215 E. Roosevelt Ave., Zeeland, MI 49464 - (800) 288-1800 (616) 772-9111
<u>dome</u> - UV (ultraviolet) protected, clear acrylic   <u>light tube</u> - reflective 3M™ Silverlux™ bonded to aluminum
<u>light diffuser</u> - clear acrylic, prismatic design   <u>diameter</u> - 10"   <u>warranty</u> - 5-year
<u>flashing</u> - three types — #1 asphalt, slate and shake shingle • #2 low-profile tile • #3 high-profile tile — polyethylene construction
<u>features</u> - The "Vista EZ Light" has an integral condensation gutter that helps control condesation buildup. The light diffuser twist on/off the ceiling trim ring without additional fasteners. An electric light kit is available that uses a standard 50 watt reflective light bulb.

SOLAR BRIGHT CORP., 3665 E. Bay Dr., Ste. 204-256, Largo, FL 33771 - (800) 780-1759 (813) 581-6063
<u>dome</u> - UV protected, clear acrylic   <u>light tube</u> - reflective 3M™ Silverlux™ bonded to aluminum
<u>light diffuser</u> - translucent   <u>diameter</u> - 10"   <u>warranty</u> - lifetime
<u>flashing</u> - low-profile galvanized steel
<u>features</u> - There is UV protected weatherstirpping around the dome. There are special patented mounting blocks.

SOLATUBE INTN'L, INC., 5825 Avenida Encinas, Ste. 101, Carlsbad, CA 92008 - (800) 966-7652 (619) 929-6060
<u>dome</u> - UV protected, clear acrylic   <u>light tube</u> - anodized aluminum • silver film on aluminum
<u>light diffuser</u> - acrylic prismatic • frosted flush profile <u>diameter</u> - 10"   <u>warranty</u> - 10-year
<u>flashing</u> - one-piece molded in several designs — shingle/shake • cement tile — interlock mechanism, tile thickness 1", not recommended for north slope • flat roof — used for problem drainage areas • S-tile — additional model for Maxtile
<u>features</u> - There are three different dress rings for the light diffuser — gold • silver • white. A dual-glazed diffuser is available for greater insulation from extreme temperatures. A patented reflector on the dome helps to capture the light. A ventilation system is available that helps remove moisture and odors — "VS1000 Ventilated Unit". The fire-rated 6" ductwork is separate from the skylight and is flexible to avoid structural changes. It has a permanently lubricated motor with 200 cfm of ventilation and only 3.0 sones. There is an external damper and rodent screen that prevents backdrafts. An optional electrical light can be added that uses a standard 100 watt incandescent bulb or a 20 watt fluorescent light.

SUN LIGHT SYSTEMS, INC., 21602 N. 2nd Ave., Suite 4, Phoenix, AZ 85027 - (800) 786-7827 (602) 587-7092
<u>dome</u> - UV protected, clear acrylic   <u>light tube</u> - super reflective
<u>light diffuser</u> - white acrylic   <u>diameter</u> - 10", 13" 21"   <u>warranty</u> - n/a
<u>flashing</u> - 26 gauge galvanized heay duty non-corrosive steel
<u>features</u> - The light tube can be angled up to 20° in any direction. The ceiling diffuser is available in 6 designer styles.

SUN TUNNEL SKYLIGHTS, 786 McGlincey Lane, Campbell, CA 95008 - (800) 369-3664 (408) 369-7447
<u>dome</u> - UV protected, clear acrylic   <u>light tube</u> - sola-film is reflective UV proof, 4 layer flexible foil
<u>light diffuser</u> - prismatic acrylic   <u>diameter</u> - 14", 22"   <u>warranty</u> - 7-year
<u>flashing</u> - 26 ga. pre-painted colorbond flat metal • available in pre-bent form to take lead strip for tile roofs
<u>features</u> - A double dome option is available. A series of vent tabs can be used, creating up to 78 square inches of ventable air space. A ventable diffuser panel is available. 0.45 mm mirror finish stainless steel ring is incorporated in the inside of top frame and lower end of the tubing, to catch light from all angles.

SUNPIPE CO., PO Box 2223, Northbrook, IL 60065 - (800) 844-4786 (847 272-6977)
<u>dome</u> - UV protected, clear acrylic   <u>light tube</u> - non-corrosive aluminum with with reflective lining
<u>light diffuser</u> - translucent white acrylic   <u>diameter</u> - 13", 21"   <u>warranty</u> - 10-year
<u>flashing</u> - galvanized steel "B-Vent" with rolled seams — adjustable for roof slopes between flat and 8/12 • optional flashings for roofs exceeding an 8/12 slope
<u>features</u> - An optional SunScoop™ is available. This directs additional sun rays into the tubular skylight increasing light output by 170%+ during the winter solstice and 10%+ during the summer solstice. It attaches to the top dome facing due south. 45 degree and 90 degree elbows are available for unusual offset pipe requirements. There is a variety of optional domes to choose from for cathedral ceilings. A flat or oval light diffuser is available. An unfinished (ready for paint or stain) solid ash trim ring is available.

TUBULAR SKYLIGHT INC., 753 Cattleman Rd., Sarasota, FL 34232 - (800) 315-8823 (941) 378-8823
<u>dome</u> - UV protected, clear acrylic   <u>light tube</u> - reflective surface bonded to aluminum
<u>light diffuser</u> - translucent white acrylic   <u>diameter</u> - 8", 13", 21"   <u>warranty</u> - 10-year
<u>flashing</u> - galvalume — adjustable to fit a variety of pitches • flat to 8/12 pitch — other flashings available for varied roof pitch
<u>features</u> - The insulation rating on the tubular skylight is R-22. There are interior seals and an insulator disk that creates a dead air pocket.

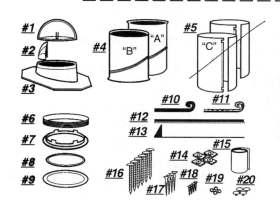

Parts List for Solatube			
Part#	**Description**	**Part#**	**Description**
1	Clear dome	11	Foam seal (white sponge ⁷/₁₆")
2	Curved reflector	12	Pile weather seal (black fur)
3	Roof flashing (shingle style)	13	Zip tie anchors (white)
4	Elbow tubes ("A" & "B" tubes)	14	Ceiling ring anchors (white)
5	Straight tubes ("C" tubes)	15	Foil tape (silver roll)
6	"B" tube seal (white)	16	Flashing screws 2"
7	Ceiling ring (white)	17	Ceiling screws ½"
8	Diffuser	18	Dome screws ½"
9	Dress ring (optional colors)	19	"O" rings (black rubber)
10	Foam seal (black sponge ¾")	20	Ceiling screw caps (white)

Assembly Instructions

Dome

Step 1 — Peel protective film from curved reflector (part 2).

Step 2 — Align the notch on the bottom of the reflector with the mounting lug marked "R" on the inside face of the clear dome (part 1). Slide the reflector onto this mounting lug in the direction shown in diagram #1. For cleanliness, replace dome into bag until installed.

Dome Screws

Slip the rubber "O" rings (part 19) onto the shank of the (4) dome screws (part 18).

Tubes

The elbow tubes, "A" smaller and "B" larger (part 4), and the two straight tubes, "C" (part 5), together extend up to 52" in length. Additional straight tubes are available.

Step 1 — Peel protective film from the inside of all tubes before assembly.

"C" Tubes

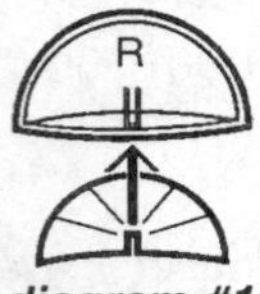

Step 2 — Grasping the notched side, hold "C" tube in front of you with one hand on each open end. Using fingertips or pliers, sharply bend the notched tab at the right end of the tube up 90°. Peel backing paper from the VHB tape on the notched side of the tube, diagram #2-a.

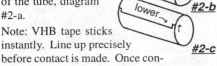

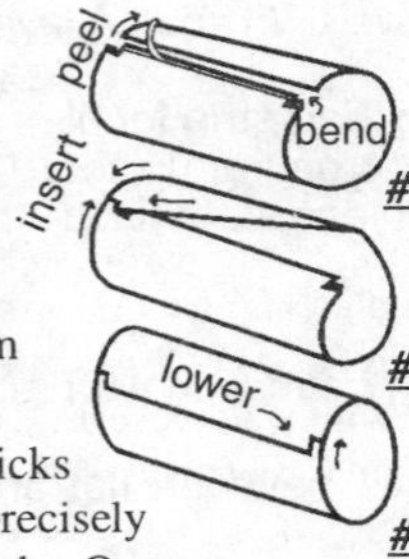

diagram #1

Note: VHB tape sticks instantly. Line up precisely before contact is made. Once contact is made, parts may not be repositioned. Be sure that the tape bonds to clean, bare metal, not to the protective film.

Insert left straight edge under the corresponding notched corner. Push to the bottom of the notch. Keep the right side from contacting. Align left sides. Diagram #2-b. Grip overlap firmly. Lower right corner behind bent tab, diagram #2-c. Rub opposing hands down each side of the tube, very firmly sealing joint. Bend tab back in line, diagram #2-c.

"A" Tube

Step 3 — Remove backing from foam seal (part 10) and adhere to the outer, top flare of tube "A", diagram #3. Cut the seal to create a tight joint.

"B" Tube

Step 4 — Stand the "B" tube with the flange on the upper end. Stretch the "B" tube seal (part 6), with the ribs pointing out and up, over the flanged end of the tube. Adjust the seal up or down to insert the tube flange into the groove circling the inside of the seal, diagram #4.

Roof Flashing

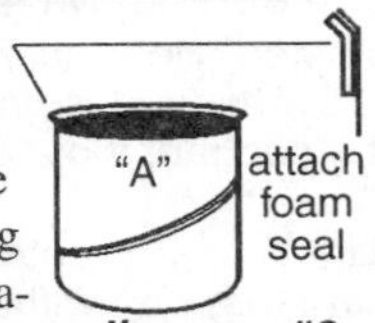

Remove backing from the pile weatherseal (part 12), firmly adhere to the lower edge of the recess circling the roof flashing turret (part 3), diagram #6. Using scissors, cut the seal to, create tight joint.

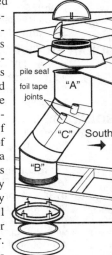

attach foam seal

diagram #3

Ceiling Ring

Step 1 — Place the ceiling ring (part 7) upside down on a work surface so that the "V" shaped groove circling the inner diameter is visible.

Step 2 — Remove backing from the foam seal (part 11) and adhere it in the "V" groove, diagram #5. Cut the seal to create a tight joint.

Required Tools — drill motor • drill bits $^1/_8$", $^3/_{16}$" • keyhole saw • saber or reciprocating saw • #2 phillips screwdriver • hammer • magnetic compass • scissors • chisel • wire stripper • tape measure

Ceiling Location

Step 1 — Identify the desired position on the ceiling. Tap lightly to identify and avoid ceiling joists. Hammer a small nail through the ceiling to mark the approximate position.

Step 2 — In attic, locate the nail. Adjust position to avoid joists or obstacles in the tube's path to the roof (see Step 6) and to ensure clearance for a 10¾" diameter hole at the ceiling.

Ceiling Hole

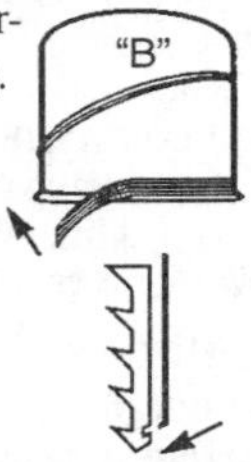

Step 3 — Inside the room, mark a 10¾" diameter circle, centered on the nail. Then cut along line with a keyhole saw. Break off screw caps (part 20) and discard. Break off ceiling ring anchors (part 14). These and the ceiling screws (part 17) are optional fasteners to be used at your discretion.

"B" Tube Ceiling Ring Seal

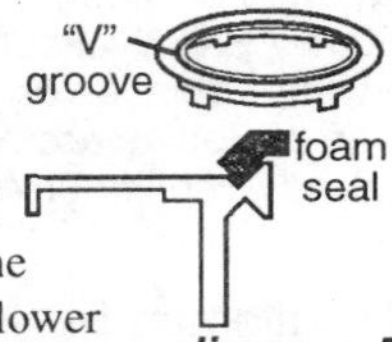

Step 4 — Using gloves, place elbow tube "B" (part 4), with seal assembled on the bottom, into the ceiling ring flange. Gripping the lower wall of the "B" tube between your hands, carefully push tube and seal into the flange. Rotate pressure around perimeter until the tube and seal reach bottom of flange, diagram #7. If needed, moisture wiped on flange will ease resistance. Push the "B" tube through the ceiling hole until flange is flush with ceiling. Adjust the elbow to aim the upper segment toward the roof location (see Step 6). Turn the top of the tube opposite from the bottom of the tube to create the desired angle, diagram #9.

Step 5 — Rotate the ceiling ring to direct the tube accurately toward the roof location. Secure temporarily in place by driving the ceiling screws through the screw holes provided in the flange up into the ceiling.

Roof Location

Step 6 — For the best overall performance of

"B"

diagram 4

"V" groove

foam seal

diagram 5

a Solatube in northern latitudes, the roof hole should be placed slightly south of the ceiling hole, so that the tubing is tilted south when installed, diagram #6. This ensures that the maximum amount of light is captured and reflected down the tubing to the diffuser more efficiently. However, if there is less than 2' of clearance in the attic, a vertical installation is appropriate. You may choose another nearby position if this will simplify installation or reduce shade cover. However, avoid inclining the tube to the north

pile seal

foil tape joints

"A"

"C"   South

"B"

diagram #6

as this may drastically reduce light output. The roof location must provide a minimum clearance of 10¾" diameter between rafters, and be free of other obstacles. Transfer this location onto the roof surface by driving a nail or drilling up through the roof.

Step 7 — Take roof flashing (part 3), "A" elbow tube (part 4), assembled dome/reflector (parts 1 & 2), roof flashing screws (part 16), and dome screws with rubber "O" rings (parts 18 & 19) onto the roof. Center the roof flashing over the nail and mark the inside circle on the shingles with a crayon.

Roof Hole

Step 8 — Using a saber or reciprocating saw, cut through the roof one half inch wider than this circle to provide clearance. The resulting elliptical hole should measure approximately 12 inches by 13 inches, diagram #8.

Flashing

Step 9 — Break seal on shingle tabs with a flat bar, diagram #8. Carefully pry out fastenings on shingles above the mid-to-upper edge of the flashing. Remove enough shingles so that the base felt is exposed at the middle of the flashing. Apply a $^3/_8$" bead of roofing sealant diagram 3# in an inverted "U" pattern around the roof opening. Pre-drill (6) $^3/_{16}$" holes 1" from edge relative to octagon corners as shown. Secure flashing with 2" screws. It is not necessary to fasten screws through heavy framing; however, they must

"B"

diagram #7

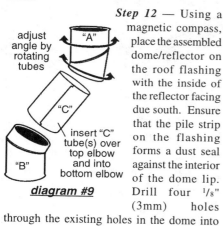

remove and replace shingles

secure with screws

base felt

bead of sealant

shingle tab seals

diagram #8

penetrate the plywood or skip sheathing. As you replace shingles, seal all old fastening holes and new screws with sealant.

Elbow "A" and Seal

Step 10 — Slide elbow tube "A" (part 4) with black foam seal (part 10) attached through the roof flashing into the attic until the seal contacts the top of the flashing turret. Adjust the elbow to aim the lower segment toward the ceiling location. Turn the top of the tube in the opposite direction than the bottom to create the desired angled, diagram #9.

Step 11 — Working your way around the perimeter, push down on the "A" tube until the foam seal enters the flashing turret and the tube flange is flush with the flashing.

Dome

Step 12 — Using a magnetic compass, place the assembled dome/reflector on the roof flashing with the inside of the reflector facing due south. Ensure that the pile strip on the flashing forms a dust seal against the interior of the dome lip. Drill four ¹⁄₈" (3mm) holes through the existing holes in the dome into

adjust angle by rotating tubes

"A"

"C"

insert "C" tube(s) over top elbow and into bottom elbow

"B"

diagram #9

the flashing, diagram #10. Avoid penetrating the elbow tube.

Step 13 — Fasten dome to the flashing using the four dome screws with rubber "O" rings. Tighten only until a seal is made with the "O" ring. Over-tightening may cause the dome or flashing to crack over time.

"C" Tube Assembly

Step 14 — Standing below the ceiling ring, determine the length required for "C" tubes. Measure the distance between the "A&B" tube ends and add 3". If sum is less than 16", it is necessary to trim excess with tin snips. *Note:* "C" tubes are tapered to slide into each other. When the "C" label is upright, the tube is upright. When required to cut, always cut the lower, smaller end.

Step 15 — Assemble "C" tubes with minimum 1½" overlap and join with foil tape to total the length required.

"B" Tube and Seal

Step 16 — Looking at the "A" tube through the ceiling mounted "B" tube, ensure that the elbow is directed precisely at the opposite tube, diagram #9. Remove the ceiling screws, ceiling ring, and "B" tube. Apply and rub out foil tape to seal the elbow joint.

drill through existing holes

south

face reflector south

diagram #10

Step 17 — Assemble the "C" tubes into the "B" tube with an accurate 1½" overlap. *Note:* The "C" label remains upright, diagram #9. Apply foil tape to seal joint. Insert the (4) zip tie anchors (part 13) into the box sockets around the ceiling ring flange, diagram #11, until ¾" of the shank pierces the ceiling ring. Do not push in further as the anchors cannot withdraw.

zip tie anchor

ceiling ring

diagram #11

Step 18 — Insert tube portion of the tube/ring assembly up into the ceiling hole. Twist the anchor heads 90 degrees to the side and insert them one by one through the hole. Direct the "C" tube end over the "A" tube extending down from the roof hole and push the package up while oscillating until the flange is flush to the ceiling. Press the ceiling ring up to the ceiling, while pulling the shank of each zip tie through its socket until resistance of anchor on top of the ceiling feels firm in your grip.

Step 19 — In the attic, seal the last tube overlap and "A" tube angle, using foil tape. *Note:* To prevent bugs and dust from entering the unit, always rub down the foil tape to seal gaps.

zip tie anchor

ceiling

clips

diffuser   dress ring

diagram #12

Diffuser

Step 20 — From inside the house, clean dust from Solatube interior with a lint free cloth. Check the zip ties for final tightening. Then, using a sharp utility knife, flush cut the exposed zip tie shank. With the diffuser (part 8) placed inside the dress ring (part 9), push the two assembled parts over the ceiling ring aligning the clips inside the dress ring's outer edge with the flat sections at the ceiling ring perimeter, diagram #12. Gently twist the unit clockwise until locked into place. Note: If cleaning of tube is required, use only a soft lint free cotton cloth and mild dish soap. Rinse with water • If in an extremely cold climate, or when required to provide dual glazing by the energy department, contact Solatube for dual glazed diffusers.

The Electric Light Kit Manufactured by ODL, Inc.

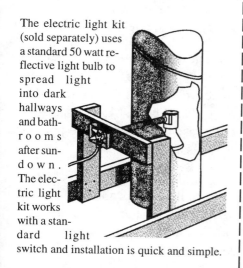

The electric light kit (sold separately) uses a standard 50 watt reflective light bulb to spread light into dark hallways and bathrooms after sundown. The electric light kit works with a standard light switch and installation is quick and simple.

The Sun Tunnel Specifications.

1. Transparent U.V. stabilized grade 1 acrylic dome
2. Dome fixed with 4 non-corrosive screws.
3. Vent tabs, (vented or solid) interchangeable.
4. Luran S KR2854 black skylight base, ASTM tested: D638, D256, D792, D648.5. Base attachment (500-9 screws and 400-6 screws). Two continuous calking beads seal frame to roof flashing base.
5. 26 G. A. pre-painted colorbond flat metal flashing. Available in pre-bent form to take lead strip for tile roofs.
6. Mirror-finish stainless steel ring, 28-gauge with four bendable tabs for tubing attachment.
7. Three continuous wraps of PVC duct tape.
8. Highly reflective, ultraviolet-proof quadruple laminate. It consists of a double outer-layer of metalized polyester film with a double inner-layer of reinforced glass fiber filament. A yarn mesh aluminum foil with coiled-spring wire skeleton is imbedded between the two layers. UL 181 rated.
9. 28-gauge mirror-finish stainless steel ring.
10. Four sheet metal screws attach stainless steel ring to ceiling frame.
11. White ABS injection molded ceiling frame.
12. K-12 prismatic acrylic diffusion panel.
13. Screws attach ring to ceiling with retainer blocks. Screw cover also attaches (500-6 and 400-4).

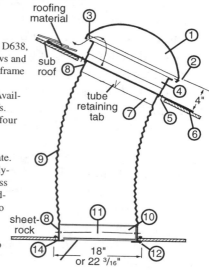

roofing material

sub roof

tube retaining tab

sheet rock

18" or 22 ³⁄₁₆"

4"

Many new and efficient skylight options

Q: My brother just installed a skylight in his living room and it makes the room seem larger and more open. I have seen so many skylight designs at home centers, what are the newest features and what is best?

A: Adding a skylight reduces the need for electric lights while providing summer ventilation and free solar heat in the winter. New low-profile frames provide more glass area, yet still fit neatly between the rafters.

There are many new skylight designs, shapes and features that make them more attractive, efficient and durable. Pyramid, round and multifaceted shapes are unique. By building a simple lightwell from the roof to the ceiling, a skylight can easily be installed in a room with an attic above it.

Although a venting skylight costs about 25 percent more than a fixed design, it is your best option overall. If your budget is very tight, select a fixed design with just a venting edge (only $30 more). A narrow vent is located under the top frame edge. It can be opened even in the rain without leaks.

With hand-held remote controls, new skylights are as easy to operate as TV's. The control operates a small motor to open or close the skylight, shades or mini-venetian blinds below it. Install a rain sensor to automatically close it if it storms while you are away from home.

One new skylight design doubles as a balcony. On steeply pitched roofs, like on a remodeled attic, upper and lower skylight sections pivot out. The lower half is positioned near the floor and it becomes the balcony with a railing. The upper half pivots out from the top and covers it.

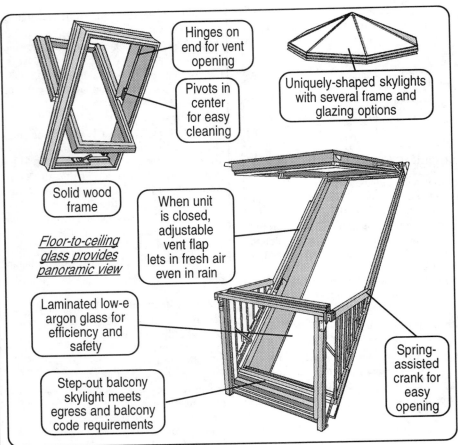

Hinges on end for vent opening

Pivots in center for easy cleaning

Uniquely-shaped skylights with several frame and glazing options

Solid wood frame

Floor-to-ceiling glass provides panoramic view

When unit is closed, adjustable vent flap lets in fresh air even in rain

Laminated low-e argon glass for efficiency and safety

Step-out balcony skylight meets egress and balcony code requirements

Spring-assisted crank for easy opening

Another unique venting skylight opens by sliding back over the roof in tracks. When it is opened, there is a totally unobstructed screened view of the sky. Other designs pivot in the center for easy cleaning from indoors.

It is important to select the proper size for your room. An undersized skylight does not provide enough light and an oversized one may look odd and cause excessive glare. As a rough estimate, divide the room square footage by 23 to get the skylight size in square feet.

Do not just choose the cheapest one on sale. Check the frame design and materials and the quality of the flashing. Copper flashing is attractive and durable.

There are many glazing options that effect the efficiency, the view and block furniture fading. Double pane low-e glass with argon gas is a good overall choice. This is what I have in my family room skylight. For very cold climates choose triple pane or Heat Mirror. Choose tinted glass in hot climates.

Q: I have a fairly new frost-free refrigerator. If I do not use the ice cubes quickly, they disappear. How does the ice evaporate and is there something wrong with the freezer section?

A: The ice does not evaporate. A little of it melts during each self-defrost cycle. Over time the ice cubes melt and are gone. Most people generally use the ice cubes long before they disappear.

If they disappear too fast, it may indicate a problem with the self-defrost system. It may be getting too hot, running too long or often. This wastes electricity. Have it checked by a qualified serviceman.

Manufacturers of High-Efficiency Skylights and Roof Windows

ANDERSEN WINDOWS, 100 4th Ave. North, Bayport, MN 55003 - (888) 888-7020 (612) 439-5150
<u>frame</u> - wood with aluminum or glass-fiber reinforced polymer cladding
<u>shape</u> - rectangular • square
<u>flashing options</u> - shingle flashing kit for low profile shingles or wood shakes • tile flashing kit for tile up to 2" in height or thick wood shakes • incline curb flashing kit to raise the angle of the unit to provide better drainage
<u>glazing options</u> - High-Performance or High-Performance Sun — thin metallic coating bonded to an inner surface of the sealed pane, stainless steel low-conductivity spacer and two panes of gas argon-filled glass • tempered • tempered/laminated
<u>accessories</u> - electric opener with 10' and 20' extension cords • insect screen • adjustable pole that extends from 6' to 10' • pleated shade in antique white with opaque or translucent fabric
<u>features</u> - The wood frame is treated with a water repellent wood preservative.

BRISTOLITE SKYLIGHTS, 401 E. Goetz Ave., Santa Ana, CA 92707 - (800) 854-8618 (714) 540-8950
<u>frame</u> - fiberglass • aluminum • vinyl   <u>shape</u> - circular • dome • pyramid • rectangular • square • multi-faceted
<u>flashing options</u> - self flashing • LF flashing kits for use with asphalt, fiberglass or wooden shingles and shakes • LFH tile flashing kits for various types of tile • gang flashing kits for grouping two or more skylights together in side-by-side groupings with units of identical height or over-and-under groupings with units of identical widths
<u>glazing options</u> - low-e • argon-gas filled • tempered • laminated • bronze tint • acrylic
<u>accessories</u> - almond pleated shades • removable screen • adjustable pole
<u>features</u> - The "Electrolite II" slides completely open to permit an unobstructed view of the sky. It has a cantilever design so there are no tracks on the roof. It is fully assembled and installs easily as a curb-mounted skylight.

CRESTLINE, 888 Southview Dr., Mosinee, WI 54455 - (800) 552-4111 (715) 693-7000
<u>frame</u> - pine with extruded aluminum cladding   <u>shape</u> - dome • rectangular • square
<u>flashing options</u> - self flashing • step flashing kits • copper step flashing kits for coastal areas • low-profile flashing kits for shingles, slate, wood shakes and other flat roofing materials • high-profile flashing kits for barrel/Spanish tile, concrete, flat tiles, corrugated metal roofs
<u>glazing options</u> - SunPLUS4® low-e argon-filled tinted insulating glass • tempered • laminated • polycarbonate
<u>accessories</u> - "Skyline" motorized drive with rain sensor • remote control that operates up to 50' away • "Skyline 2000" motorized drive with wall switch or rain sensor • aluminum extension pole that adjusts from 6' to 10' • translucent pleated shades in six colors • motorized drive for the shades • custom colors

FOX LITE, INC., 8300 Dayton Rd., Fairborn, OH 45324 - (800) 233-3699 (937) 864-1966
<u>frame</u> - wood with aluminum cladding   <u>shape</u> - rectangular • square
<u>flashing options</u> - self flashing • step flashing kits • bronze colored aluminum step flashed • copper-clad flashing
<u>glazing options</u> - low-e • argon-gas filled • triple glaze • tempered • G.E. Lexan polycarbonate

INSULA-DOME SKYLIGHTS, 83 Horseblock Rd., Yaphank, NY 11980 - (800) 551-4786 (516) 924-7890
<u>frame</u> - furniture-grade white birch with extruded aluminum cladding
<u>shape</u> - diamond-shaped • dome • parallelograms • rectangular • square • trapezoids • custom shapes
<u>flashing options</u> - flat roof flashing • lead coated copper step flashing • copper step flashing
<u>glazing options</u> - Heat Mirror™ — film suspended between two panes of clear glass • insulated low-e, argon-gas filled • tempered over laminated safety glass • bronze tint • acrylic
<u>accessories</u> - "Sky Sentry" motorized drive with rain sensor • remote control that operates up to 50' away • "Truth" motorized drive with wall switch • rechargeable motorized pole • aluminum telescopic pole adjusts from 4' to 6' • aluminum telescopic pole adjusts from 6' to 10' • hex ball adapter • eye & hook attachment • pleated sunshades • insect screen • sunscreens
<u>features</u> - There is a quick-release pin that secures the skylight frame to the curb and allows for emergency exits from vented and fixed skylights. It also allows a fixed unit to be converted to a vented unit.

KENERGY SKYLIGHTS, 3647 All American Blvd., Orlando, FL 32810 - (800) 347-9334 (407) 293-3880
<u>frame</u> - pine with extruded aluminum cladding   <u>shape</u> - dome • rectangular • square
<u>flashing options</u> - self flashing • step flashing kits • copper step flashing kits for coastal areas • low-profile flashing kits for shingles, slate, wood shakes and other flat roofing materials • high-profile flashing kits for tile, corrugated metal and high contour roofing materials • clustered flashing kits — allows you to assemble horizontal groupings of skylights with 2½", 4" and 7" spacings or stacked top and bottom with 4" spacing between each unit
<u>glazing options</u> - argon-filled SunPLUS4® low-e glass, in tempered or tempered/laminated • polycarbonate
<u>accessories</u> - "Sky Sentry" motorized drive with rain sensor • remote control that operates up to 50' away • "Sentry 2000" motorized drive with wall switch • aluminum extension pole • hex ball adapter • eye & hook attachment • pleated shades in six colors • motorized drive for the shades • custom color exterior • decorator glass

ODL INC., 215 E. Roosevelt Ave., Zeeland, MI 49464 - (800) 288-1800 (616) 772-9111
<u>frame</u> - hardwood with extruded aluminum cladding • aluminum • vinyl
<u>shape</u> - dome • rectangular • square
<u>flashing options</u> - aluminum self flashing • vinyl self-flashing • bronze colored aluminum flashing kit
<u>glazing options</u> - low-e • argon-gas filled • tempered and laminated glass • bronze tint • polycarbonate • acrylic
<u>accessories</u> - motorized control with rain sensor, wireless remote or wall switch • ivory cloth roller shade with 20" pull cord • off-white aluminum slat mini-blinds • adjustable pole extending 3', 5' and 8' — motorized and hex ball drive handles available

O'KEEFE'S INC., 75 Williams Ave., San Francisco, CA 94124 - (888) 653-3337 (415) 822-4222
<u>frame</u> - aluminum • wood curb   <u>shape</u> - circular • dome • rectangular • square • double-hip domes • pyramid • triangular • multi-faceted • continuous ridge • multiple domes
<u>flashing options</u> - self flashing
<u>glazing options</u> - acrylic • tempered • laminated • low-e argon-gas filled • clear • bronze tinted
<u>accessories</u> - "Sky Sentry" motor with a remote control and rain sensor • steel security grilles • pleated shades • louvered shades • adjustable pole that extends from 3' to 5' with an optional 3' extension • motorized pole handle crank

PELLA CORP., 102 Main St., Pella, IA 50219 - (800) 547-3552 (515) 628-1000
frame - wood with extruded aluminum cladding shape - rectangular • square
flashing options - continuous PVC rubber boot with one-piece molded corners • aluminum step flashing kit
glazing options - InsulShield® argon-gas filled, multi-layer low-e coated insulating glass • tempered • laminated
accessories - telescoping pole that extends from 6' to 10' • aluminum Slimshade® slat blinds with polyester cord ladder and controlled by built-in operating mechanism • polyester pleated shades with vacuum-bonded aluminized backing

ROTO FRANK OF AMERICA, PO Box 599, Chester, CT 06412 - (800) 243-0893 (860) 526-4996
frame - wood with aluminum cladding   shape - rectangular • square
flashing options - step flashing kit • tile flashing kit • built-up (incline curb) flashing kit
glazing options - Allseason-Plus® argon-gas filled, low-e coatings • tempered • laminated
accessories - motorized control with a wall-mounted keypad (also controls shades) and rain sensor • sun screens • beige or blackout pleated shades • 6' to 10' adjustable operating pole • crank handle • roller shades
features - "Vision" series opens two ways — using the top hinges or the pivot position which is tilt and turn so you can clean the glass inside and out easily. There are 5 sash/flashing colors — white • fire red • smoke gray • forest green • terra cotta

SUN-TEK INDUSTRIES, 10303 General Dr., Orlando, FL 32824 - (800) 334-5854 (407) 859-2117
frame - wood with aluminum cladding   shape - dome • rectangular • square
flashing options - step flashing kit • aluminum self flashing • high-profile flashing for shake shingle roofs • tile glass flashing for metal or barrel tile roofs
glazing options - low-e • argon-gas filled • laminated • bronze tint or PPG Azurlite® • G.E. Lexan® polycarbonate
accessories - motorized opener with rain sensor and remote control or wall switches • 10' telescopic pole • pleated shades

THERMO-VU SUNLITE INDUSTRIES, 51 Rodeo Dr., Edgewood, NY 11717 - (800) 883-5483 (516) 243-1000
frame - vinyl • aluminum • wood curb   shape - dome • octagonal • pyramid • rectangular • square • triangular • multi-faceted • ridge • multiple domes • custom shapes
flashing options - vinyl curb and attached flashing • aluminum step flashing • 16 oz. premium full/step copper flashing
glazing options - Heat Mirror™ — film suspended between two panes of clear glass • acrylic • insulated safety glass • low-e • clear and
bronze • clear tempered • bronze tempered • laminated • low-e argon-gas filled
accessories - "Sky Sentry" motor with rain sensor and wall switch or optional remote control • "Sentry 2000" motor with wall switch • telescoping pole and loop adjusts from 6' to 12' • pleated shades • motorized shades with 3' telescopic pole

VELUX-AMERICA INC., PO Box 5001, Greenwood, SC 29648 - (800) 888-3589 (864) 941-4700
frame - wood with aluminum or copper cladding shape - rectangular • square • round top
flashing options - kits available — step flashing for fiberglass shingles, slate, cedar shakes/shingles • high-profile for concrete and Spanish tile • metal roof flashing • prefabricated incline curb flashing for flat or low-slope roofs • combi-flashing — allows side-by-side installations of units of the same height and over-and-under installations of units of the same width
glazing options - Type 48 — two panes of clear tempered safety glass • Type 75 — low-e two panes of tempered glass and argon-gas filled • Comfort Plus — heat strengthened laminated, double layer of low-e coating and argon-gas filled
accessories - electric control system with 3 push-button or remote control (also controls shading devices) • rain sensor • rechargeable, battery-operated pole extending 6' to 10' • telescopic manual rod extending 6' to 10' • 3' rod extension • translucent or opaque beige cotton-polyester fabric shade • silver-gray fabric pleated shade with special coating • translucent black fabric shade for room darkening • eggshell white aluminum venetian blinds • wall mount switch
features - The "Cabrio" balcony roof window (see below) has a two-part opening mechanism — the top sash section opens to provide ventilation, and the bottom sash section opens outward to actually create a step-out roof balcony. The top sash rotates completely inward so you can clean the glass from inside. A ventilation flap allows fresh air circulation when the window is closed. It creates floor-to-ceiling light with a width of 37 inches and height of 100 inches. It features laminated, low-e glass in both the upper and lower sash sections. Argon is injected between the panes for increased energy efficiency. Some of the fixed skylights have ventilation flaps to allow fresh air to enter and the hot, stale air to escape even when it is raining. The flap can be left open year-round.

WASCO, PO Box 351, Sanford, ME 04073 - (800) 388-0293 (207) 324-8060
frame - wood with vinyl cladding
shape - circular • dome • octagonal • pyramid • rectangular • square • hipped end • double pitched • ridge
flashing options - Ultraseal™ system — conforms to roof deck with compliant suction seal • step flashing for thin roofing materials — slate, wood shingles and shakes up to ¾" thick • step flashing for concrete tile or Spanish tile roofs • self flashing • incline curb flashing for flat or low-slope roofs
glazing options - HeatMirror™ — film suspended between two panes of clear glass • Superglass™ — two sheets of Heat Mirror™ suspended between two panes of clear glass • High Performance low-e • argon-gas filled • safety glass • tempered • laminated • clear or bronze tint • acrylic
accessories - motor with rain sensor and optional remote control • motor operated by wall switch • telescopic aluminum pole extends 6'2" to 10'2" in 1" increments • telescopic pole adjusts from 4' to 6' • telescopic pole adjusts from 6'3" to 10'5" • motorized shades • pleated shades made of polyester and antistatic fabric bonded with a micro-thin layer of aluminum

WEATHER SHIELD, PO Box 309, Medford, WI 54451 - (800) 477-6808 (715) 748-2100
frame - wood with aluminum cladding
shape - rectangular • square
flashing options - aluminum self flashing
glazing options - low-e argon-gas filled • Supersmart® triple pane with 2 low-e and 2 argon • laminated
accessories - crank handle • full screen • cover
features - The wood frame is specially treated with a water repellent preservative.

1) Determine the size of the skylight that you need for your room. Select a width that will fit between the roof rafters and attic floor joists. Most skylights are made to fit joists and rafters on 16-inch and 24-inch centers. They will be roughly 1½ inches narrower to allow for the thickness of the 2× lumber.

2) Carefully remove the shingles around the area for the skylight. You will have to replace some of these after the skylight is installed. Saw the hole for the skylight in the roof sheathing. Saw it large enough to allow room for the headers. You may have to saw through a rafter if you selected a wide skylight. Follow the manufacturer's installation instructions very carefully to avoid problems or leaks. Also follow recommended SAFETY GUIDELINES when working on a roof.

3) Get up into your attic and remove the insulation from the location on the floor where you plan to make the lightwell opening. Locate the position of the ceiling opening for the lightwell. Saw the opening in the floor. You may have to saw through some of the floor joists if you selected a wide skylight.

4) Using the same size lumber as used for the rafters and joists, build headers across the openings. (See drawing.) If you had to saw through the rafters and joists, you may want to use a double thickness of headers. Install cripple studs to frame the lightwell opening and to support the cut rafters. Double these in the corners to provide extra support for the roof and rigidity to the lightwell itself.

5) Rigid foam board insulation is the best to use. It forms a natural vapor barrier and has much more insulation value per inch thickness. It is also easy to nail up in the vertical position on the sides of the lightwell frame. If you plan to use this type of insulation, 2×4 lightwell framing lumber is best.

6) If you plan to use fiberglass batt insulation, you should probably use 2×6 or 2×8 lumber to allow adequate space for the thicker insulation. Either use faced insulation or staple polyethylene vapor barrier to the inside of the lightwell opening. Nail the drywall over it when you finish lightwell opening. With faced insulation, the facing should be toward the interior. After you finish the inside of the lightwell, paint it white to reflect as much light as possible.

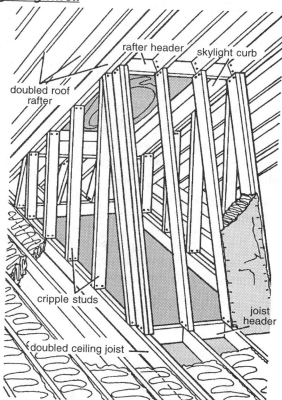

labels: doubled roof rafter · rafter header · skylight curb · cripple studs · joist header · doubled ceiling joist

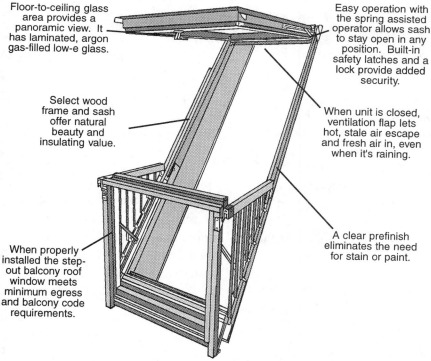

Floor-to-ceiling glass area provides a panoramic view. It has laminated, argon gas-filled low-e glass.

Select wood frame and sash offer natural beauty and insulating value.

When properly installed the step-out balcony roof window meets minimum egress and balcony code requirements.

Easy operation with the spring assisted operator allows sash to stay open in any position. Built-in safety latches and a lock provide added security.

When unit is closed, ventilation flap lets hot, stale air escape and fresh air in, even when it's raining.

A clear prefinish eliminates the need for stain or paint.

Can be installed in roofs with pitches from 35° (8.5/12) to 53° (16/12).

The window pivots completely inward for easy and safe cleaning of the outside glass from inside the room.

Recommended Size of Skylight for Various Room Sizes in Sq. Ft.

Room Size	Skylight Size
80	3.5
100	4.6
140	6.3
160	7.0
225	9.5
340	14.5

Shapes of Skylights

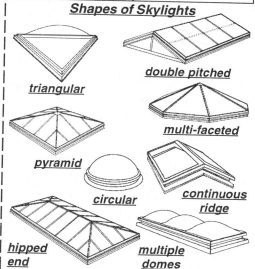

triangular · double pitched · pyramid · multi-faceted · circular · continuous ridge · hipped end · multiple domes

Window film protects furniture, blocks heat

Q: The afternoon sun shining in our windows literally bakes us and is fading our furniture and carpeting. How effective are the new clear do-it-yourself summer/winter window films?

A: Window film is your best solution to block heat and fading, especially if you are on a limited budget. The new summer/winter window films save energy year-round as they extend the life of your furniture and carpeting.

Do-it-yourself year-round window film is simple to install. You just need a sharp knife, a spray bottle, soapy water, a squeegee and about 20 minutes. Window films increase the shatter resistance of glass. In areas prone to tornadoes or hurricanes, this is a real plus. Special extra-heavy clear security films make it difficult for burglars to break through.

Each new generation of window film technology reduces the amount of tint needed and increases the life and performance of the film. Some of the new year-round, anti-fade films are so clear, that it is difficult to notice them. Some window films carry a 10-year durability warranty.

True summer/winter window films have the same type of low-emissivity (low-e) coatings as new expensive high-tech replacement windows. This blocks heat loss through your windows in the winter and heat gain in the summer. As you apply the film yourself, you can feel the heat reduction immediately.

To achieve these super-efficient properties, a microscopically-thin layer of metal atoms is deposited on the polyester film surface. It is far too thin to see and visible light passes right through it. When this film is applied to the window, the view is distortion-free.

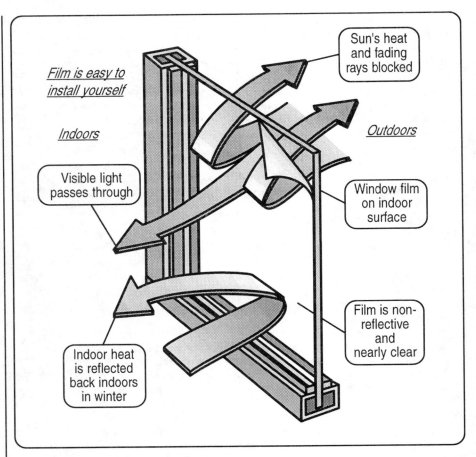

Film is easy to install yourself

Indoors

Visible light passes through

Indoor heat is reflected back indoors in winter

Sun's heat and fading rays blocked

Outdoors

Window film on indoor surface

Film is non-reflective and nearly clear

Although most of the window films look similar in the home center store, there are significant differences among them in the summer heat rejection and the winter heat savings. Do not just buy the least expensive.

It is important to compare performance factors for the different films. All window films block about 99 percent of the ultra-violet (UV) rays. Although UV is commonly thought to cause the majority of fading, it actually accounts for only 40 percent of the fading. Heat and light cause a lot of fading too.

Total solar energy rejection (SER) is important when comparing summer performance. Visible light transmission (VLT) compares the glare from the window. Emissivity effects utility bill savings and comfort in the winter.

To block the southern sun around noon, an awning or large roof overhang is effective. Building a window flowerbox with a shade above is also an attractive option.

Q: I installed a low-flow showerhead last year to save water. It worked well at first, but now the shower flow is not forceful enough. What can I do to fix it or should I buy a new one?

A: Most water-saving low-flow showerheads have very tiny holes in the face. These are small to speed up the reduced water flow to provide a more forceful satisfying shower. The holes are probably clogged with deposits.

Remove the showerhead and take it apart. Clean out any loose deposits. Soak the plate with the tiny holes overnight in white vinegar. If any deposits remain by morning, poke the holes open with a fine wire.

Many of the newer, less tinted do-it-yourself or professionally installed window films save year-round. With an invisible low-emissivity layer on the window film, heat radiation is reduced. This includes heat coming in during the summer and heat going out during the winter months. A lower emissivity specification is better.

All window films block ultraviolet (UV) radiation, one major cause of fading. As the chart below at right indicates, heat and light are also significant factors causing fading. To reduce fading the most, select a film with lower visible light transmission and high solar energy rejection. Always check the specifications listed below when selecting the proper window film for your needs.

See installation instructions on page 176 for do-it-yourself instructions for applying Gila Sunshine Low-e Plus neutral film by Courtaulds. Gila Sunshine films are available in several different sizes of do-it-yourself kits found in home centers. Professionally installed films often have a longer warranty. All films should last many years.

Most films look dark and reflective on the roll. Once they are installed and the entire window is covered, the tint is much less apparent and they are not reflective from indoors. In southern climates, a highly reflective and darkly-tinted film is best for west windows. Shades, awnings, and roof overhangs are best on the south side.

Most of the manufacturers listed make some type of clear heavy-duty film designed to greatly increase the shatter-resistance of window glass. These clear protective films are professionally installed only.

Typical High-Efficiency Window Film Layers Dyed/Reflective/Dyed Scratch Resistant

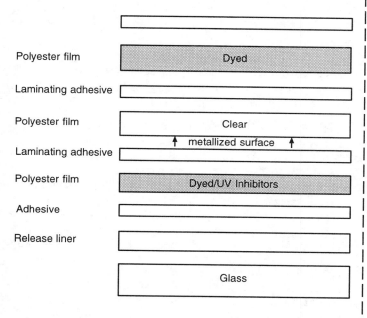

Polyester film — Dyed
Laminating adhesive
Polyester film — Clear / metallized surface
Laminating adhesive
Polyester film — Dyed/UV Inhibitors
Adhesive
Release liner
Glass

Causes of Fading

Generally, four factors cause fabrics to fade from exposure to sunlight.

UV A+B rays = 40%
Solar heat = 25%
Visible light = 25%
Miscellaneous = 10%

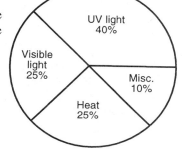

How heat reflective film reduces fabric fading. Shaded area shows reduction with window film installed.

Blocks up to 99% UV light
Blocks 56% of heat gain
Blocks 65% of visible light to reduce harsh glare

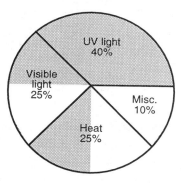

Important Window Film Specifications

Medium Density Film
Parameter

Solar transmittance	22%
Solar reflectance	43%
Solar absorptance	35%
Visible light transmission	28%
Visible light reflectance	44%
U-factor	1.05
Ultra violet transmittance	<1%
Shading coefficient	.36

Total Solar Energy Rejected 68%

film applied to glass surface

glass 35%

incident
reflected
transmitted

43%
+
reradiated outward
25%

22%
+
reradiated inward
10%

= 68% total solar energy rejected

= 32% total solar energy admitted

absorbed

Fabric Fading and Deterioration

Over the months or years, the sun can bleach wood floors and rob the color from carpets, drapes, and wallpaper. And these rays combine with solar heat to rot the fibers in fabrics. Although many people think of fading as a "summer only" problem, UV damage can actually be more intense in the winter when the sun hangs lower in the sky. In fact, the winter "heat" that home owners feel and attribute to sunshine can have the same effect of UV rays destroying the fibers of carpet and upholstery. Overall this is expensive, as it leads to prematurely replacing expensive carpet, drapes and fabrics.

Manufacturers of Window Films for Home Use

COURTAULDS PERFORMANCE FILMS, PO Box 5068, Martinsville, VA 24115 - (540) 627-3000

"Gila Sunshine" — (800) 528-4481 — do-it-yourself from retail outlets

| type - Low-e Plus TPR 90 | color - neutral gray | solar energy transmitted - n/a | visible light transmitted - 47% |
| UV light transmitted - <2% | emissivity - .50 | shading coeeficient - .50 | total solar energy rejected - 52% |

| type - Low-e Ultra TPR 100 | color - platinum gray | solar energy transmitted - n/a | visible light transmitted - 30% |
| UV light transmitted - <2% | emissivity - .42 | shading coeeficient - .38 | total solar energy rejected - 65% |

| type - Optical Grade | color - gray | solar energy transmitted - n/a | visible light transmitted - 38% |
| UV transmitted - <2% | emissivity - .81 | shading coeeficient - .72 | total solar energy rejected - 36% |

| type - Heat Reflective | color - gray & bronze | solar energy transmitted - n/a | visible light transmitted - 27% |
| UV light transmitted - <2% | emissivity - .72 | shading coeeficient - .45 | total solar energy rejected - 58% |

| type - Heat Reflective | color - silver | solar energy transmitted - n/a | visible light transmitted - 35% |
| UV light transmitted - <2% | emissivity - .72 | shading coeeficient - .40 | total solar energy rejected - 65% |

"Vista" — (800) 345-6088 — professionally installed only

| type - Radiance VE-50 | color - gray | solar energy transmitted - 36% | visible light transmitted - 49% |
| UV light transmitted - <1% | emissivity - .36 | shading coeeficient - .49 | total solar energy rejected - 57% |

| type - Soft Horizons V-30 | color - gray | solar energy transmitted - 25% | visible light transmitted - 30% |
| UV light transmitted - <1% | emissivity - .85 | shading coeeficient - .50 | total solar energy rejected - 59% |

| type - Dayview V-45 | color - gray | solar energy transmitted - 43% | visible light transmitted - 45% |
| UV light transmitted - <1% | emissivity - .84 | shading coeeficient - .62 | total solar energy rejected - 46% |

| type - Crystal Elegance V-58 | color - gray | solar energy transmitted - 56% | visible light transmitted - 58% |
| UV light transmitted - <1% | emissivity - .89 | shading coeeficient - .74 | total solar energy rejected - 35% |

"Llumar" — (800) 345-6088 — professionally installed only

| type - E-1220 | color - silver | solar energy transmitted - 14% | visible light transmitted - 17% |
| UV light transmitted - <1% | emissivity - .36 | shading coeeficient - .24 | total solar energy rejected - 79% |

| type - E-1230 | color - silver | solar energy transmitted - 22% | visible light transmitted - 28% |
| UV light transmitted - <1% | emissivity - .54 | shading coeeficient - .37 | total solar energy rejected - 68% |

3M, 3M Center Building 225-4S-08, St. Paul, MN 55144 - (800) 364-3577 (612) 737-6501 — professionally installed only

| type - LE35AMARL | color - amber | solar energy transmitted - 35% | visible light transmitted - 31% |
| UV light transmitted - <1% | emissivity - .34 | shading coeeficient - .29 | total solar energy rejected - 70% |

| type - LE20SIAR | color - silver | solar energy transmitted - 20% | visible light transmitted - 17% |
| UV light transmitted - <3% | emissivity - .45 | shading coeeficient - .25 | total solar energy rejected - 73% |

| type - LE30CUARL | color - copper | solar energy transmitted - 36% | visible light transmitted - 32% |
| UV light transmitted - <2% | emissivity - .39 | shading coeeficient - .34 | total solar energy rejected - 64% |

| type - LE50AMARL | color - amber | solar energy transmitted - 56% | visible light transmitted - 39% |
| UV light transmitted - <3% | emissivity - .35 | shading coeeficient - .42 | total solar energy rejected - 55% |

MADICO INC., 64 Industrial Pky., Woburn, MA 01888 - (800) 225-1926 (781) 935-7850 — professionally installed only

| type - NB-35/NG-35 | color - bronze/gray | solar energy transmitted - 28% | visible light transmitted - 36% |
| UV light transmitted - <4% | emissivity - n/a | shading coeeficient - .45 | total solar energy rejected - 61% |

| type - NB-50 | color - bronze | solar energy transmitted - 42% | visible light transmitted - 48% |
| UV light transmitted - <4% | emissivity - n/a | shading coeeficient - .62 | total solar energy rejected - 46% |

| type - NG-50 | color - gray | solar energy transmitted - 40% | visible light transmitted - 43% |
| UV light transmitted - <4% | emissivity - n/a | shading coeeficient - .60 | total solar energy rejected - 48% |

| type - SB-340 | color - bronze | solar energy transmitted - 25% | visible light transmitted - 40% |
| UV light transmitted - <4% | emissivity - n/a | shading coeeficient - .39 | total solar energy rejected - 66% |

| type - TSG-335 | color - gray | solar energy transmitted - 38% | visible light transmitted - 40% |
| UV light transmitted - <4% | emissivity - n/a | shading coeeficient - .54 | total solar energy rejected - 53% |

METALLIZED PRODUCTS, 2544 Terminal Dr., S., St. Petersburg, FL 33712 - (800) 777-1770 (813) 327-7132

| type - SW 150 S 15 | color - silver | solar energy transmitted - 10% | visible light transmitted - 14% |
| UV light transmitted - <5% | emissivity - .33 | shading coeeficient - .18 | total solar energy rejected - 84% |

| type - SW 150 S 35 | color - silver | solar energy transmitted - 26% | visible light transmitted - 35% |
| UV light transmitted - <5% | emissivity - .47 | shading coeeficient - .40 | total solar energy rejected - 65% |

| type - SW 150 G 30 | color - gray | solar energy transmitted - 28% | visible light transmitted - 27% |
| UV light transmitted - <5% | emissivity - ..56 | shading coeeficient - .46 | total solar energy rejected - 60% |

| type - SW 150 B 30 | color - bronze | solar energy transmitted - 27% | visible light transmitted - 28% |
| UV light transmitted - <5% | emissivity - .57 | shading coeeficient - .45 | total solar energy rejected - 61% |

Tools Required

Pump- or trigger- spray bottle — Squeegee — Single edge razor blade or hobby knife — Distilled water — Joy®, Sunlight® or Clear Ivory® dishwashing liquid (due to their clarity and pH balance) — Ruler — Soft, lint-free cloth

Special Points to Remember

• Handle film very carefully. As with aluminum foil, once creased, the film will remain creased.

• Larger windows (3-4' wide) usually are best tinted by two people working together to remove the liner, install, and trim the film.

• Apply film anytime other than in direct sunlight (film will stick too quickly) or in freezing weather (film will not stick at all). Best temperature is 45-95°F.

• Work in a dust-free area. Turn off fans. Apply film to windows hung vertically; **DO NOT** lay windows down to tint them horizontally, or you will trap air bubbles.

• The adhesive "cures" over a period of several days. Dry, sunny weather speeds curing; wet, cold weather prolongs it.

• Gila Sunshine® films are compatible with standard ⅛" residential windows. Consult the factory before applying film to ¼" plate commercial glass or pretinted windows.

• Film may be removed, but not reused.

Installing the Film

1) Measure the Window — Measure the dimensions of your window carefully before unrolling and cutting the film. Film may be

applied from side to side, or top to bottom from the kit roll. Use the measurement that leaves the least waste. Or you may also choose to pretrim the film to the final dimensions, that is ¹/₁₆" smaller on all sides (see step 8).

2) Clean the Window — Generously spray the window with "The Solution" (1 quart distilled water, ½ teaspoon of Joy®, Clear Ivory® or Sunlight® dishwashing liquid — due to their clarity and pH balance). You will use this "Solution" throughout the installation process. Then use your hand and squeegee to clean the windows thoroughly. Respray the glass, then use a razor blade to remove any caked dirt or paint. Use special care cleaning the corners. Rewet the window, then squeegee downward. Wipe off accumulated dirt from the window gasket with a soft cloth. Repeat process until the glass is clean. If possible, also clean the outside to ensure total clarity. The cleaner the glass, the better the final appearance of the installed film.

3) Cut the Film — Unroll the film on a clean,

flat surface near the window. Use a ruler as a guide and cut the film 1" larger than the dimensions of the window to be sure that the film will fit. Of course, you may wish to use the factory edge of the film for one side of the window.

For windows larger than film size — To cover larger windows, you may need to seam the film as you would seam wallpaper. To obtain a perfect butt seam, vertically overlap two sides of the film, then use a ruler as a straight edge to guide your knife as you cut through both layers of film. After cutting the seam line, peel the loose sheet of film from the top, then lift the edge of the film and slide out the other "waste" piece from underneath the film. Rewet the glass, lay down the film, rewet the top of the film, then squeegee the film from top to bottom in a slow, firm vertical motion. A week after installation, waterproof the seam with a coat of clear fingernail polish.

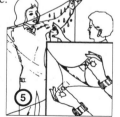

4) Wet the Window Thoroughly — Generously spray "The Solution", which acts as a lubricant, onto the inside surface of the window until beads of the soapy water run down the glass. If the window becomes dry, rewet it completely before applying film.

5) Remove the Clear Film Backing — Take your time with this step: be patient and be careful not to crease the film while removing the clear, protective "liner" from the back (adhesive side) of the film. (NOTE: Usually the liner is on the outside surface of the film roll.) Remove the liner by attaching two 3-4" long pieces of Scotch™ Brand Magic™ transparent tape to the front and back surfaces of a corner of the film so that about 1" of tape is on the film, the rest centered and hanging over the pointed corner of the film. Press the two pieces of tape firmly together, then quickly pull them apart to begin separating the clear liner away from the adhesive side of the film. NOTE: This process may require a quick, snapping pull, much like pressing together and quickly pulling apart of two pieces of Velcro®. As you carefully peel the liner away, be sure to generously spray the soapy solution onto the exposed adhesive. This spray helps break any static cling, reduces contamination, and makes the liner separation easier. Also, wet your hands with "The So-

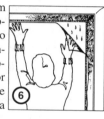

lution" before handling the film to avoid leaving fingerprints on the adhesive. Remove the liner diagonally, from one corner toward the opposing corner. Try to keep the film from touching itself. It is very helpful and recommended for two people to coordinate the liner separation on a large sheet of film.

6) Place the Film on the Window — After completely removing the clear liner from the back of the film and thoroughly wetting the adhesive surface, be sure the window is dripping wet — too much "Solution" is better than not enough. Apply the adhesive side of the film to the wet glass. Start at the top of the window, then allow the film to gently lay down onto the glass. Handle the film carefully at the corners to avoid wrinkles or creases, which cannot be removed. Use your hands to smooth the film onto the glass. Slide the film and position it correctly so long as the window is thoroughly wet. You will be able to evacuate the air and water trapped under the film during the next step.

7) Spray Outside Surface of Film and Squeegee Film Carefully and Firmly — Spray the entire surface of the film facing you with the soapy "Solution" to lubricate its surface. Using a clean squeegee, begin squeegeeing the water and air out from under the film. Start about 2" from the top and from the side and squeegee toward the opposite side. After this, lightly squeegee downward with short (12-18") firm strokes, but leave the 2" perimeter area unsqueegeed. Rewet the top of the film, then you should squeegee again. If the squeegee drags, respray "The Solution" on the top of the film. Press very firmly to remove all the water so that the adhesive can cure clearly. NOTE: Any bubbles that can be removed can be squeegeed out without lifting the film away from the glass.

8) Trim Edges of Film and Squeegee Dry — Use a sharp razor blade or a utility knife and a ¹/₁₆"

wide guide to trim the film around the four perimeter edges. This gap is essential for the proper thermal expansion of the glass and to allow you to completely squeegee the water and air from under the film. Rewet the entire film surface and squeegee again. If "fingers" appear along any edge, squeegee toward the edge of the film and absorb the excess water with a soft cloth.

Mirrored shutter easy to build, saves energy

Q: We leave our window shades open as much as possible to get heat from the sun, but it still doesn't shine very far into our room. Is there any simple way to get more sunshine inside?

A: The sun's rays are most intense near noon, offering the greatest potential for free solar heating at that time. Unfortunately, it is also at its highest point in the sky then, so it often is partially blocked by a roof overhang and it does not shine very far into your room.

For your south-facing windows, you can easily build and install a reflective solar window shutter. It is very effective for directing additional solar heat through your windows into the rooms. It also reduces the need for interior lights, so your electric bills are much lower.

If you make the solar shutter with an insulating material, it will also stop the heat loss back outdoors when it is closed at night. Most windows, without any special covering, lose more heat than they gain over a 24-hour period. An insulating solar shutter can reduce your heating and cooling bills and greatly improve your comfort.

You can easily make an inexpensive insulating solar shutter yourself. You should hinge it at the bottom of the window. Since the position of the sun changes, you can adjust the shutter for the proper open angle depending on the time of day and month of year.

First make a wooden frame of 1 x 2-inch pine, sized to fit snugly inside the exterior window frame opening. Redwood and cedar are more expensive, but they resist the weather better and last a long time. Add gussets to the corners to give it

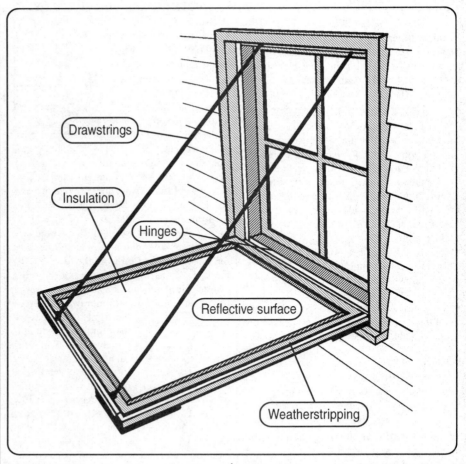

Drawstrings · Insulation · Hinges · Reflective surface · Weatherstripping

more strength. Attach foam weatherstripping around the edge of the frame so it seals snugly against the window frame.

You can use any type of reflective foil-faced insulation board for the body of the shutter. Polyisocyanurate foam has a very high R-value and is durable. Extruded polystyrene is also effective. Apply foil duct tape around the edge of the foam insulation to hold it into the frame, and support it with pipe strapping.

For added convenience, drill two holes through your window frame, opposite each upper corner of the shutter. Attach drawstrings to the shutter so you can adjust it, or close it completely at night, from the inside. Use tight-fitting grommets in the holes to reduce air leakage through them.

Q: We plan to duct the vent from our electric dryer indoors with just a piece of flexible ducting. What would be the best way to make a filter for the duct?

A: Although it saves energy, if you already have excess indoor moisture problems, ducting the dryer indoors may worsen them. Also, check your local building codes about venting a dryer indoors.

You definitely have to add some type of filter. Stretching two layers of nylon stockings over the duct is quite effective. Be sure to clean out both the built-in and stocking filters after each load you dry. You can also run the end of the duct straight down into a very shallow pan of water. As air bubbles through, the water catches the lint. It must be shallow, it can create too much back pressure and cause the dryer to overheat.

Reflective insulating shutters for your windows are easy to make and can increase the solar gain into your windows and reduce the heat loss back outside at night. When making this shutter, it is important that it fits tightly inside and against the sides of the window frame to reduce air leakage when it is closed.

Select straight lumber to start with and measure very carefully. If you want the shutter to cover the entire window, make it several inches larger than the window opening so it rests against the wall surface when it is closed. This makes it more airtight.

These shutters are most effective if you have high-quality airtight windows to start with. This is imperative for an effi-cient passive solar heated house. At the very minimum, you should select low-e argon gas-filled glazing. This has an R-value of about 4. Heat Mirror glass (Insol-8) has an R-value of 8.

Page 180 shows do-it-yourself in-structions for making a sun shade window enclosure and a flowerbox window sun shield.

Do-it-Yourself Instructions for Making a Reflective Shutter

1) Saw the 1" × 2" lumber to make the frame for the shutter. Make them the proper length and height to fit snugly in the window opening.

2) Notch the ends of the pieces of lumber for lap joints when you assemble the frame. This gives strong and smooth corner joints.

3) Assemble the frame using wood screws and waterproof glue. Measure across the diagonals of the frame to make sure that it is square before you drill the holes for the screws. Then clamp the frame assembly and allow it to dry.

4) You can add stiffness to the frame by making triangular gussets for the four corners of the frame assembly. The gussets will also support the reflective foam insulation board. Make them 4" to 5" long on the sides. Drill holes and use glue and screws to secure them to the frame assembly.

5) Paint the frame assembly with good-quality wall paint to match your house. Make sure to get good coverage over all the joints since this will be exposed to the worst winter weather.

6) After the frame has dried, you can cut the reflective foam insulation to fit it. Lay the frame flat with the gussets against the table. Carefully measure the inside dimensions of the frame. You can usually cut the foam insula-tion with a sharp knife. Cut slowly.

7) Lay the piece of insulation into the frame against the gussets.

8) Using the foil duct tape, lay a strip of the tape overlapping the foil and the frame. This will seal the edge of the foam insulation and help to hold it in place in the frame. Use the tape on both sides of the frame and insulation joint for the greatest strength, airtightness, and reflectivity. You can use staples to better secure the tape to the frame and insulation.

9) Cut 2" lengths of the pipe strapping. These will be used to help hold the insulation into the frame. Cut enough to space them about every 2½ ft. around the frame. Mount them so they extend about 1¼" out over the insulation.

10) Stick the adhesive-backed foam weatherstripping around the edge of the frame where it will lay against the window frame. That will produce a good seal when it is closed.

11) Have a helper hold the assembled shutter up against the window where it will be mounted. Mark the loca-tions for the hinges to be attached to the shutter frame and the window frame. It should be hinged at the bottom.

12) If you want to operate the shutter from outdoors (this is the easiest method), attach the boat cleats to the wall above the window.

13) Attach small eyelets to the top of the shutter frame and tie the strings to them. Run the other end of the strings through the cleats above them. You can then adjust the angle that the shut-ter is opened for the maximum heat gain or close it tightly at night.

14) If you plan to operate the shutter from indoors, then you will have to drill two holes through the window frame opposite the eyelets on the top of the shutter frame. Make sure to drill the holes big enough to install plastic grommets for the string to slide through. That will reduce wear on the string and reduce air leakage through the holes.

15) Feed the strings through the grommets into your house. The strings should be about three times the height of the shutter. Tie the indoor ends of the strings to a 1" dowel and glue them so they won't slide around the dowel. You will roll the string up on the dowel to control the position of the shutter on the outside. Hammer a small nail partially into the center of the dowel.

16) Using the pipe strapping, make an upside-down J-hook to mount under your window sill inside your house. You may be able to purchase a strong wire hook at your hardware store. This will hold the dowel. You wind up the strings on the dowel to position the shutter and then hook the nail in the dowel under the pipe strapping J-hook to hold that position.

Required Materials for Reflective Shutter
1" × 2" lumber - carefully select straight pieces
¾" wood screws, staples
1 pair of chrome plated or galvanized hinges
pipe strapping, heavy string
2" wide shiny foil or duct tape
½" plywood - exterior grade
1" thick foil-faced rigid insulation board
closed-cell adhesive-backed foam weatherstripping
spring-loaded cleats from a marine shop

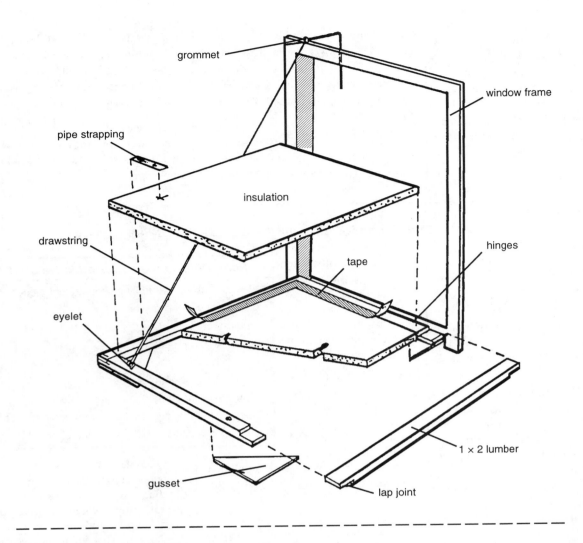

grommet

window frame

pipe strapping

insulation

drawstring

tape

hinges

eyelet

1 × 2 lumber

gusset

lap joint

Manufacturers of High-Efficiency Wood Replacement Windows
ANDERSON WINDOWS, INC., 100 Fourth Ave. No., Bayport, MN 55003 - (612) 439-5150
CARADCO, 201 Evans Rd., Rantoul, IL 61866 - (800) 238-1866
CRESTLINE WINDOWS & DOORS, PO Box 800, Mosinee, WI 54455 - (800) 552-4111 (715) 845-1161
DURATHERM WINDOW CORP., RR #1, Box 945, N. Vassalboro, ME 04962 - (800) 996-5558 (207) 872-5558
EAGLE WINDOW & DOOR, INC., PO Box 1072, Dubuque, IA 52004 - (800) 453-3633 (319) 556-2270
EUROTEC WINDOWS, 1001 E. Kentucky St., Louisville, KY 40204 - (502) 637-6855
H WINDOW CO., 1324 E. Oakwood Dr., Monticello, MN 55362 - (800) 843-4929 (612) 295-5305
HURD MILLWORK CO., 575 South Whelen Ave., Medford, WI 54451 - (715) 748-2011
KOLBE & KOLBE MILLWORK, 1323 S. Eleventh Ave., Wausau, WI 54401 - (715) 842-5666
MARVIN WINDOWS & DOORS, PO Box 100, Warroad, MN 56763 - (800) 346-5128
MW MFGS., PO Box 559, Rocky Mount, VA 241510- (800) 999-8888 (540) 483-0211
OSLO-AMERICA, INC., 2 Vernon St., Suite 153, Framingham, MA 01701 - (508) 875-5514
PELLA CORP., 102 Main St., Pella, IA 50219 - (800) 524-3700
POZZI WOOD WINDOWS, PO Box 5249, Bend, OR 97708 - (800) 257-9663
TISCHLER UND SOHN, 51 Weaver St., Greenwich, CT 06830 - (203) 622-8486
VETTER, PO Box 8007, Wausau, WI 54402 - (800) 552-4111 (715) 845-1161
WEATHER SHIELD WINDOWS & DOORS, PO Box 309, Medford, WI 54451 - (800) 222-2995

Do-It-Yourself Instructions for a Sun Shade Window Enclosure

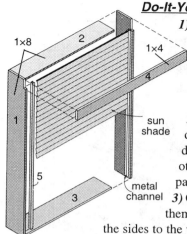

1) Check the frame along the exterior of the window to see if there is enough surface to attach the shade enclosure. If there isn't, you will need to attach it directly to the sidewalls of your house. If any repairs need to be made, this is a good time to do that. Check caulking around edges and the glazing compound holding the window panes in place.

2) Be sure that the enclosure will fit snugly around the window. Select woods that will stand up to the weather — cedar, redwood or pressure-treated wood. If you choose another type of wood, you need to finish it with a good exterior paint or apply a penetrating stain and sealer.

3) Cut two 1×8 boards (1) for the sides of the enclosure. Notch them at the top so a 1×4 facing strip may be applied later. Screw the sides to the window frame or attach them to the side of the house with metal angles and screws. If your house is brick, attach metal angles with screws driven into expansion anchors. Mortar joints are the easiest place to drill holes for the anchors.

4) Rip ¾ inch off the width of a 1×8 to form the top of the enclosure (2). Use screws and glue to attach the enclosure top to the sides (1) and to the top of the window frame.

5) Cut the 1×8 bottom board (3) to size and attach it with glue and screws below the sill of the window. Attach it to the sides as shown.

6) Finish construction of the frame by adding a 1×4 trim strip (4).

7) Fasten a metal channel (5) to the inside of each side of the box. Recess each channel approximately ¾ inch from the outside edge of the frame.

8) Mount a venetian blind to the underside of the box top. When you lower it the edges will fall into the metal channels along the sides. This also keeps the blind from hitting the window when the wind blows.

9) Finish by caulking around the edges of the frame. You can paint or stain the unit if necessary.

Required Materials for Sun Shade Enclosure

lumber - 1×8, 1×4
screws and wood glue
metal channels
venetian blind/wooden shade
optional exterior paint
optional stain and sealer
optional wood preservative
optional metal angles
optional expansion anchors

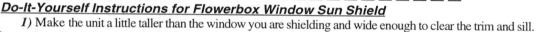

Do-It-Yourself Instructions for Flowerbox Window Sun Shield

1) Make the unit a little taller than the window you are shielding and wide enough to clear the trim and sill.

2) You should use redwood, cedar or pressure-treated lumber to build the flowerbox window unit. If you use any other wood, you need to finish it with a good exterior paint or apply a penetrating stain and sealer.

3) Assemble the flower box from ¾-inch exterior plywood. Butt the sides (1,2) together, and attach the bottom (3) using screws and glue. Drill ½-inch holes in the bottom to help with drainage, and you should treat the inside of the box with a wood preservative to keep it from rotting. Set aside for at least two days to dry.

4) Frame window top and sides with 1×2 strips (4, 5) screwed directly into the wall studs. After the flower box has dried, you should attach it with screws to the wall studs just below the sill.

5) Cut six lengths of 1×6 boards (6) to fit, trimming the tops at a 30° angle. Butt the boards together (if desired leave spaces between each board) and screw them to the flower box. Brace the siding at the top with 1×2 ledgers (7). Cut to fit and attach flush with the top inside edge of the siding boards.

6) Have a piece of ⅛-inch translucent acrylic plastic of correct dimensions formed to match the shape shown in the diagram. Drill holes through the plastic sheet and screw it into the top of the 1×6 boards (6). If it is necessary, you should caulk any areas for a weathertight seal.

Note: Before drilling holes in acrylic, make sure the material is secure so it won't move around. It is a good idea to back plastic with a piece of wood to stop it from chipping when the drill goes through the back of plastic.

Required Materials for Flowerbox Window Sun Shield

lumber - 1×2, 1×6 pressure treated
scrap lumber
exterior plywood
screws
wood glue
optional exterior paint
optional stain and sealer
optional wood preservative
reinforcing rods
acrylic plastic

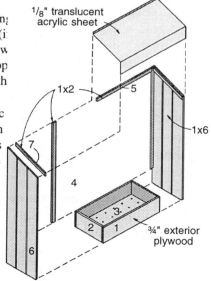

Rolling shutters provide efficiency, security, safety and privacy

Q: In Europe, I saw many homes with attractive rolling shutters for privacy, security and energy savings. When opened, they were totally hidden away. What should I consider when selecting rolling shutters?

A: Energy-efficient exterior rolling shutters are excellent window coverings for security, safety and sun (heat and fading) control. They are available in many colors and double the insulation value of most windows.

In many coastal areas, installation of durable rolling shutters is required by building codes for hurricane protection (withstands 110+ mph winds). They can also be effective in the inland tornado belt or storm-prone regions.

It is very difficult for a burglar to break in through a closed rolling shutter. Even though the shutter is conveniently opened and closed from indoors, some include additional locks for extra security.

Rolling shutters can be operated with an indoor hand crank or an electric motor. Many of the motor-operated models have hand-held, multifunction remote controls, just like your TV. Timers, sun, wind and rain sensors are available to close the shutters automatically when you are gone from home.

An exterior rolling shutter operates similarly to a roll top desk. There are two small channels mounted on either side of the window or patio door. Narrow insulated horizontal slats slide up and down in the side channels.

An attractive box housing is mounted above the window. When the shutter rolls up inside the housing, the view is unobstructed. In many homes, the housing can be

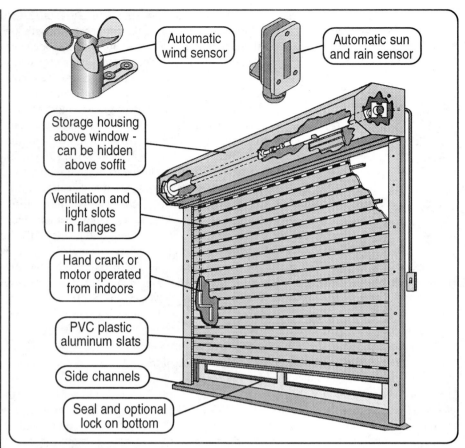

Automatic wind sensor

Automatic sun and rain sensor

Storage housing above window - can be hidden above soffit

Ventilation and light slots in flanges

Hand crank or motor operated from indoors

PVC plastic aluminum slats

Side channels

Seal and optional lock on bottom

mounted above the soffit, so it is totally hidden from view.

The shutter can be adjusted to allow for ventilation and some light when it is down. There are slots cut into the interlocking flange between each horizontal slat. Each slat is about two to three inches high.

Lower the shutter until the bottom just touches the window sill. Even though the window is completely covered, the flange slots between each slat are still exposed for light and air flow. Lower it further and the flanges slide up into the adjacent slats covering the slots. This blocks all light.

The basic slat material options (in increasing cost) are - PVC plastic, rolled aluminum with insulation and extruded aluminum. PVC plastic slats provide the best overall insulation value. This includes the plastic itself and the dead air space

between the shutter and the window or patio door. Insulated rolled aluminum is tougher than PVC for better wind and impact resistance. Extruded aluminum is the strongest material, but it is heavier.

Q: I have to replace my old electric clothes dryer. I was considering replacing it with a natural gas dryer. Is there any advantage of a gas dryer over an electric one?

A: Gas and electric dryers work the same except that the gas dryer is less expensive to operate. The energy cost to dry clothes with gas is typically about half as much as electricity, depending on your local utility rates.

Gas dryers are priced somewhat higher than electric ones. You will also need to run a gas line to the dryer location. Depending on how many loads you do, the savings may or may not pay back the higher cost of a gas model.

Manufacturers of Rolling Shutters

AC ROLLING SHUTTER, 3531 E. 80th St., Cleveland, OH 44105 - (800) 745-5261 (216) 441-9400
<u>material</u> - roll-formed or extruded aluminum • PVC <u>insulation</u> - aluminum — foam • PVC — air space
<u>operation</u> - crank handle • pull strap • electric motor <u>slat width</u> - 1.27" • 2.16"
<u>colors</u> - beige • bronze • cream • ivory • white • woodgrain
<u>features</u> - a combination shutter-window assembly is available by special order — see page 4 for illustration and technical data

AMERICAN ROLL SHUTTER, 12700 Merriman Rd., Livonia, MI 48150 - (800) 442-9646 (734) 422-7110
<u>material</u> - roll-formed or extruded aluminum • PVC <u>insulation</u> - aluminum — foam • PVC — air space
<u>operation</u> - crank handle • pull strap • electric motor <u>slat width</u> - 1.96" • 2.28"
<u>colors</u> - aqua • beige • black • blue • bronze • brown • cream • ivory • red • white
<u>features</u> - can be fitted with special mechanical locking mechanism to prevent shutters from being pushed up from the outside

EUROPEAN ROLLING SHUTTERS, 404 Umbarger Rd., Suites A&B, San Jose, CA 95111 - (800) 794-3740
<u>material</u> - roll-formed aluminum <u>insulation</u> - aluminum — foam
<u>operation</u> - crank handle • pull strap • electric motor <u>slat width</u> - 1.57" • 1.81" • 1.89"
<u>colors</u> - beige • bronze • brown • cream • grey • oak • teak • white
<u>features</u> - double coated for abrasion resistant finish

PIONEER ROLL SHUTTER CO., 155 Glendale Ave., #8, Sparks, NV 89431 - (702) 355-8686
<u>material</u> - roll-formed or extruded aluminum <u>insulation</u> - aluminum — foam
<u>operation</u> - crank handle • pull strap • electric motor <u>slat width</u> - 1.57" • 1.81" • 1.89"
<u>colors</u> - beige • bronze • brown • cream • grey • oak • teak • white
<u>features</u> - available for garden windows • sunrooms and greenhouse • interior and exterior skylights • shutter housing box is available as 5-sided hex or square-shaped

ROLLAC SHUTTER OF TEXAS, INC., 10800 Blackhawk Blvd., Houston, TX 77089 - (888) 276-5522 (713) 485-1911
<u>material</u> - roll-formed or extruded aluminum • PVC • Lexan <u>insulation</u> - aluminum — foam • PVC — air space
<u>operation</u> - crank handle • pull strap • electric motor <u>slat width</u> - 1.30" • 1.57" • 2.01" • 2.16" • 2.30"
<u>colors</u> - beige • bronze • brown • cream • grey • ivory • silver • white
<u>features</u> - shutter housing box is available as 5-sided hex or square-shaped

ROLLADEN ROLLING SHUTTERS, 6168 W. Charleston Blvd., Las Vegas, NV 89146- (702) 878-1072
<u>material</u> - roll-formed aluminum • PVC <u>insulation</u> - aluminum — foam • PVC — air space
<u>operation</u> - crank handle • pull strap • electric motor <u>slat width</u> - 1.50" • 2.00"
<u>colors</u> - beige • bronze • grey • ivory • white
<u>features</u> - available for garden windows • sunrooms and greenhouse • interior and exterior skylights

ROLLAG MFG. CORP., 7401 Pacific Circle, Mississauga, Ontario, Canada L5T 2A4 - (800) 665-5553 (905) 670-1014
<u>material</u> - roll-formed aluminum • PVC <u>insulation</u> - aluminum — foam
<u>operation</u> - crank handle • pull strap • electric motor • winch <u>slat width</u> - 1.50" • 2.00"
<u>colors</u> - beige • brown • cream • grey • teak • white
<u>features</u> - can be equipped with concealed, automatic steel locks • available for garage doors • skylights • curved sunrooms

ROLL-A-SHIELD, 4695 N. Oracle Rd., Tucson, AZ 85705 - (800) 457-8723 (602) 293-0666
<u>material</u> - roll-formed aluminum <u>insulation</u> - aluminum — foam
<u>operation</u> - crank handle • pull strap • electric motor <u>slat width</u> - 1.57" • 1.81" • 2.48"
<u>colors</u> - beige • brown • cream • grey • ivory • white
<u>features</u> - shutter housing box is available as 5-sided hex or square-shaped

ROLL-A-WAY, 10597 Oak St. NE, St. Petersburg, FL 33716 - (800) 683-9505 (813) 576-1143
<u>material</u> - roll-formed or extruded aluminum • PVC • Lexan <u>insulation</u> - aluminum — foam • PVC — air space
<u>operation</u> - crank handle • pull strap • electric motor <u>slat width</u> - 1.25" • 2.16" • 2.48"
<u>colors</u> - beige • bronze • grey • ivory • white • clear anodized
<u>features</u> - shutter housing box is available as 5 & 6-sided hex or square-shaped
<u>related products</u> - Folding accordian shutters — with vertical slats • nylon guide at top and bottom for easy operation • extruded aluminum with strong bar that locks with pin on the bottom • optional keylock / Storm panel system — aluminum in three different gauges

SHUTTERHAUS-NUSASH, 2501 Anvil St. N., St. Petersburg, FL 33710 - (800) 330-7210 (813) 381-6522
<u>material</u> - roll-formed or extruded aluminum • PVC <u>insulation</u> - aluminum — foam • PVC — air space
<u>operation</u> - crank handle • electric motor <u>slat width</u> - 1.50" • 2.00"
<u>colors</u> - bronze • ivory • taupe • white
<u>features</u> - shutter housing box is available as 5 & 6-sided hex or square-shaped • guide channels are lined internally with polypropylene pile, high density weatherstripping
<u>related products</u> - Folding accordian shutters — with vertical slats in 4" and 5" widths — interlocking blades which glide horizontally in a top and bottom guide track • stainless steel wheel carriages and nylon wheels allow smooth operation • 5 point locking system locks in closed position / Panel system — aluminum or Lexan panels are light weight and removable / See thru barriers — heavy duty perforated metal shutter for severe weather protection and security

THERMO ROLLING SHUTTER, 5100 Jackson Rd., Ann Arbor, MI 48103 - (734) 995-0577
<u>material</u> - extruded aluminum • PVC <u>insulation</u> - PVC — air space
<u>operation</u> - crank handle • pull strap • electric motor <u>slat width</u> - 1.62" • 2.47"
<u>colors</u> - beige • bronze • ivory • white
<u>features</u> - lock designs available — sliding bolt latch which fastens the base slat to the side rail • slat lock that operates automatically when the shutters are lowered ¨ remote radio control that can be operated from outdoors

* Extruded aluminum has no insulation but it is very strong. Roll-formed aluminum is injected with foam insulation after it is rolled into shape.

TOP ROLLSHUTTERS., PO Box 3279, Salmon Arm, British Columbia, Canada V1E 4S1 - (800) 665-5550

    material - roll-formed aluminum • PVC   insulation - aluminum — foam • PVC — air space

    operation - crank handle • pull strap • electric motor • winch   slat width - 1.50" • 2.00"

    colors - beige • brown • cream • grey • teak • white

    features - can be equipped with concealed, automatic steel locks • available for skylights • curved sunrooms • garage doors

TUCSON ROLLING SHUTTERS INC., 543 E. 27th St., Tucson, AZ 85713 - (520) 798-1294

    material - roll-formed aluminum   insulation - aluminum — foam

    operation - crank handle • pull strap • crank strap • electric motor slat width - 1.73" • 2.16"

    colors - beige • cream • grey • white • woodgrain

    features - electrostatically baked enamel finish • shutter housing box is available as 5-sided hex or square-shaped

WHEATBELT INC., 300 Industrial Rd., Hillsboro, KS 67063 - (800) 264-5171 (316) 947-2323

    material - extruded aluminum • PVC   insulation - PVC — air space

    operation - crank handle • pull strap • electric motor   slat width - 1.62" • 2.47"

    colors - beige • bronze • ivory • white

    features - bottom slat options — nap pile for energy loss, noise reduction • vinyl seal for rain, moisture / lock designs available — slat lock operates automatically when shutters are lowered • sliding bolt latch which fastens the base slat to the side rail

---

Motors and Electronic Controls for Rolling Shutters

ELERO USA, INC., 10880 Alder Circle, Dallas, TX 75238 - (800) 752-8677 (214) 343-1676

    features - tubular motor with optional compact manual override so the shutter can be raised or lowered with a quick turn of a hand crank in the event of a power failure • Elero-Matic controllers — lowers or raises the shutters if the wind exceeds a preselected speed or when the sun level reaches a preset intensity — up to 16 cycles per day • automatic timer can be set to open and close shutters in daily and weekly cycles — random timing program that provides up to a 30 minute deviation from the preset time • infrared remote system that controls up to 15 individual stations with one button, covers 60 foot radius • decorative rocker switch • Elero-Matic Network — automates all shutters with low voltage system with singular to multiple switch control panels • Automatic Controlling System (ACS) — stops the motor on the way up or down when the bottom slat reaches the housing or when it closes, or if the shutter makes contact with an obstruction such as a child, pet or ice

SIMU U.S. INC., 1405 Poinsettia Dr., Suite 12, Delray Beach, FL 33444 - (561) 274-0111 (800) 822-7468

    features - tubular motor with built-in manual override to control the shutters during power failures • automatic environmental controls — lowers shutters automatically during high winds or from the heat of the sun • remote — two and four channels standard (8, 16 and 100 channels are available), up to 1000 feet • timer to program up to four different up/down operations for a 7-day schedule • IGC operates all motors from one location — one room, one floor or an entire house • designer toggle, rocker and paddle switches • security key switch — recessed or surface mount • low voltage solar kit — 12-volt operator relies on combo battery/solar charger, solar panel, control unit, two-channel radio remote and optional switch

SOMFY SYSTEMS INC., 47 Commerce Dr., Cranbury, NJ 08512 - (609) 395-1300

    features - tubular motor with optional override to control the shutters at all times, even during power failures • digital timer to control shutters on a 24-hour or full 7-day schedule • IGC individual switch controls a single shutter • IGC master switch controls shutters on one floor or the entire household • hand-held remote to control the shutters from anywhere inside or outside of your home • quick release system is a lever handle for immediate opening of shutters in an emergency • storm control monitors — lowers shutters in high winds or the sun's heat • digital keypad programmable outdoor/indoor switch — use your own personal code to control your shutters • decorator toggle or rocker switch • Anti-Blocking System (ABS) — when the downward motion of the shutter is blocked by an obstruction such as a pet, child or toy, the shutter is disengaged from the motor drive to protect it from damage, will reverse only when you press the button to raise the shutter

---

Types of Shutter Operations

A Geared Controller with Crank Handle — No strap is involved. Instead, a metal rod links shutters with gear box affixed to shutter system. Allows you to handle significantly heavier shutters. Gears available in various reductions and materials. One crank can be used for numerous shutters. The crank is removable and can be stored out of sight. Lifting capacity — approximately 88 pounds.

Pull Strap — Raise and lower the shutters manually by pulling a polypropylene strap that is 0.55" wide and 0.05" thick. A strap box mounted on wall or optionally in wall contains spring loaded wheel to take up slack when shutter is raised.

Crank Operated Pull Strap — A reduction gear and crank for the strap allow you to raise and lower heavier shutters. Lifting capacity — approximately 60 pounds. Lifting capacity of the strap box — approximately 25 pounds.

Motorized — Push a button and shutters lift or lower automatically. Motorized control offers the most flexibility. The switches can be operated with keys or numerical keypads. Timers can be set for seven days in advance. Sun and wind sensors can control the shutters. You can even use a computer and modem for control. The shutters can be operated all at once, by zones or individually. Lifting capacity — approximately 350 pounds.

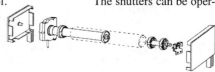

Construction and Operation of AC Rolling Shutters

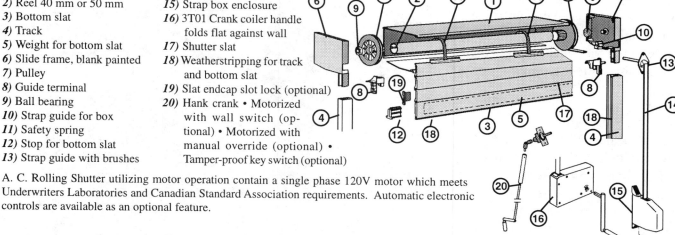

1) Extruded box/hood panels
2) Reel 40 mm or 50 mm
3) Bottom slat
4) Track
5) Weight for bottom slat
6) Slide frame, blank painted
7) Pulley
8) Guide terminal
9) Ball bearing
10) Strap guide for box
11) Safety spring
12) Stop for bottom slat
13) Strap guide with brushes
14) Strap — grey/brown
15) Strap box enclosure
16) 3T01 Crank coiler handle folds flat against wall
17) Shutter slat
18) Weatherstripping for track and bottom slat
19) Slat endcap slot lock (optional)
20) Hank crank • Motorized with wall switch (optional) • Motorized with manual override (optional) • Tamper-proof key switch (optional)

A. C. Rolling Shutter utilizing motor operation contain a single phase 120V motor which meets Underwriters Laboratories and Canadian Standard Association requirements. Automatic electronic controls are available as an optional feature.

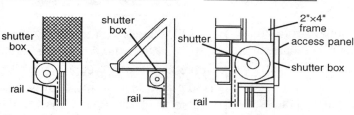

Retrofit

shutter box
shutter box
rail

Surface Mounted

shutter box
rail

Frame Mounted

Above Soffit

shutter box
access panel
rail
rail

shutter box
rail
rail

Below Soffit

New

2"×6" frame
access panel
shutter box
shutter
rail

Frame Construction

2"×4" frame
access panel
shutter box
shutter
rail
rail

Brick/Block Construction

Technical

Radiation Transmittance —White, aluminum, closed = .02
Radiation Transmittance — White, PVC closed = .01
Shading Coefficient — Aluminum = .0596
Shading Coefficient — White, PVC = .0436
U-Value — Foam, aluminum, winter = .51, R = 1.943
U-Value — PVC with air space, winter = .45, R = 2.232
Radiation, conduction, and infiltration are controlled.
Noise Reduction — 85% closed position, 52 vented position.

A. C. Shutter will manufacture a combination shutter-window assembly for special orders. Contact the factory for details. Contact for information concerning special applications requiring additional insulation and security.

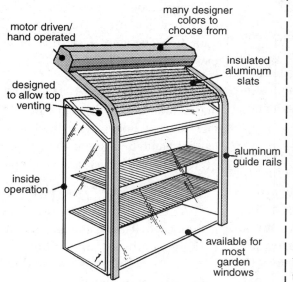

motor driven/
hand operated

many designer colors to choose from

insulated aluminum slats

designed to allow top venting

aluminum guide rails

inside operation

available for most garden windows

"Solar-Flex" Rolling Shutters by Pioneer Roll Shutter Co.

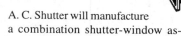

		Winter	Summer
Thermal Properties			
		U-Value (lower number is better)	
A.	single glass	1.13	1.06
	with shutters	.406	.395
	improvement with shutters	64%	63%
B.	double insulated glass	.58	.56
	with shutters	.301	.297
	improvement with shutters	48%	47%
		R-Value (higher number is better)	
A.	single glass	.88	.94
	with shutters	2.47	2.53
	improvement with shutters	64%	63%
B.	double insulated glass	1.72	1.78
	with shutters	3.31	2.60
	improvement with shutters	48%	32%
SC-Value (lower number stops heat)		.04	.04

U-Value — is the BTU heat loss value through any given material. **R-Value** — is the resistance value of heat transfer of any given material. The lower the U-value number or the higher the R-value, the greater the insulating quality of the material. **SC-Value** — or shading coefficient, is the effectiveness of a glass and shade assembly in stopping heat gain from solar radiation. The values range from 0 to 1.

Retractable and butterfly awnings for decks and patios

Q: I saw some retractable patio awnings that attach to the house. I want it to block the rain and the sun's heat on the patio. I want to sit outdoors and have the patio uncovered in the cool evenings. Are these awnings effective?

A: A self-supporting retractable awning is ideal for decks and patios. Strong folding arms, attached to the house, support the entire awning with no other supports. When it is retracted, it is totally hidden in a painted hood cover or under the gutter against the wall.

Extending the awning not only makes your patio more comfortable and allows use in the rain, but it can cut your air-conditioning costs. By blocking the sun's direct rays on the patio or deck and through the patio door, heat gain into your house and carpet fading is significantly reduced.

A self-supporting retractable awning works similarly to your own arms. When it is retracted, it is like having your elbows bent and your arms folded flat against your chest (the house wall).

Retractable awnings range in size from 40 feet wide with a 13-foot projection down to small window-size units. There are many types of awning fabrics available depending on the color, durability, water-resistance, cost, etc. that you need.

The two arms are spring loaded at the elbows with the awning fabric rolled up on a spool. As the spool is unrolled, the spring-loaded arms keep the fabric taut. It can be opened only one foot or fully extended. I use one made by Arbor at my own home to cover my firewood and motorcycle.

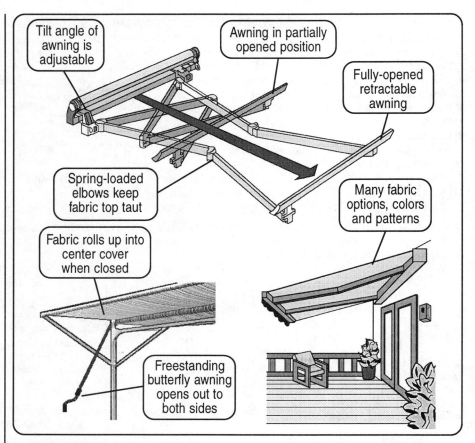

All wall-mounted retractable awnings come with standard hand cranks to open and close them. Optional motorized operators are available to fit most awning manufacturers' products. For unusually windy areas, Regel makes a quick release awning brace for extra support.

For the ultimate convenience, Somfy makes hand-held remote control motorized units. For hi-tech buffs, they also make automatic computerized sun, rain and wind sensors to control when the awning retracts or opens.

There are also several types of freestanding retractable awnings for patios or decks not adjacent to a house wall. Sunesta makes a "butterfly" model that extends out both sides and retracts into a narrow protective hood over the center. The lightweight aluminum frame is easy to move.

FIM makes an attractive contemporary freestanding retractable umbrella. The main support, with the hand crank, is positioned off to one side so the patio or deck is totally unobstructed.

Q: I have several lamps in my home that have halogen bulbs in them. The light they give off is great, but they seem to get very hot. Does this mean that they are inefficient?

A: Halogen light bulbs get hotter than standard incandescent bulbs. In fact, some halogen light bulbs can get hot enough to ignite some types of fabrics that may accidentally touch them.

This higher temperature does not mean that they are inefficient. Halogen bulbs produce about as much light per watt as standard incandescent bulbs, but they last about twice as long.

Manufacturers and Distributors of Retractable and Other Types of Awnings

ALPHA PRODUCTIONS, INC., 10459 Jefferson Blvd., Culver City, CA 90232 - (800) 223-0883 (310) 559-1364
type - retractable patio awning   projection - 5'3" • 7'0" • 8'6" • 10'3" • 11'6" • 13'0"   width - 6' to 40'
type - retractable window awning   projection - 1'6" • 2'0" • 2'6" • 3'0" • 3'6" • 4'0"   width - 3' to 14'
type - retractable solarium awning   projection - 6'0" to 24'0"   width - 6' to 26'
type - retractable vertical awning   projection - window/door up to 14'0"   width - 2' to 20'

AMERICAN BUILDING PRODUCTS (HINDMAN), PO Box 1808, Centralia, IL 62801 - (800) 851-0865
type - retractable patio awning   projection - 5'0" • 6'6" • 8'0" • 10'0" • 12'0" • 13'0"   width - 7' to 35'

ANCHOR INDUSTRIES, PO Box 3477, Evansville, IN 47733 - (800) 255-5552 (812) 867-2421
type - retractable patio awning   projection - 5'3" to 11'6"   width - 6' to 20'
type - awning with frame   projection - 8'0" to 12'0" (3' pitch recommended for 12' proj.)   width - 10' to 25'
type - retractable umbrella   diameter - 12'0" • 20'0"   width - not applicable
description - The "Fiesta Patio Canopy" has a galvanized steel frame and tubing. It is designed with curved uprights so water drains away from the patio. See page 4 for installation instructions. The "Funbrella" has a 4" aluminum center pole and galvanized steel tubing rafters and supports. It has a removable crank handle.

ARBOR AWNING, 5100 Jackson Rd., Ann Arbor, MI 48103 - (313) 995-0838
type - retractable patio awning   projection - 8'0" • 10'0"   width - up to 30'

ASTRUP, 2937 West 25th St., Cleveland, OH 44113 - (800) 786-7616 (216) 696-2820
type - retractable patio awning   projection - 4'2" • 5'7" • 6'11" • 8'7" • 10'2" • 11'6" • 12'6"   width - 10' to 40'
type - retractable wraparound awning   projection - 6'0" • 8'0" • 10'0" • 11'6" • 13'0"   width - 8' to 22'
description - The "Patio Variette" uses heavy-duty wraparound trolleys and works on the principle of gravity to carry the fabric to the desired position on the tracks. The fabric can be extended vertically down the front supports to eliminate morning or late afternoon sun. The framework is available in silver, brown and white powder-coat.

CRAFT-BILT MFG. CO., 53 Souderton-Hatfield Pike, Souderton, PA 18964 - (215) 721-7700
type - retractable patio awning   projection - 4'1" • 5'3" • 6'11" • 8'6" • 9'10" • 11'6"   width - 6' to 35'

DURASOL AWNING, 197 Stone Castle Rd., Rock Tavern, NY 12575 - (800) 556-0025 (914) 778-1000
type - retractable patio awning   projection - 3'6" • 5'0" • 7'0" • 8'6" • 10'0" • 11'6" • 13'0"   width - 5' to 40'
type - retractable window awning   projection - up to 3'0"   width - up to 10'
type - retractable window awning   projection - 2'0" to 5'0"   width - 5' to 34'

EASTERN AWNING SYSTEMS, 843 Echo Lake Rd., Watertown, CT 06795 - (800) 445-4142 (860) 274-9218
type - retractable patio awning   projection - 5'0" • 6'6" • 8'2" • 10'0" • 12'0" • 13'0"   width - 6' to 30'
type - retractable window awning   projection - up to 3'0"   width - up to 10'
type - retractable window awning   projection - 2'0" to 5'0"   width - 2' to 30'

EGE SYSTEMS, 15203 N.E. 95th St., Redmond, WA 98052 - (800) 343-1003
type - retractable patio awning   projection - 4'1" • 5'9" • 6'10" • 8'6" • 10'2" • 12'0"   width - 6' to 40'
type - retractable window awning   projection - 20" • 24" • 28" • 32" • 36" • 40" • 44"   width - up to 12'
type - retractable window awning   projection - 24" • 28" • 32" • 36" • 40" • 44" • 47" • 51" • 55"   width - 7' to 24'

EUROPEAN ROLLING SHUTTERS, 404 Umbarger Rd., San Jose, CA 95111 - (800) 794-3740 (408) 629-3740
type - retractable patio awning   projection - 5'3" • 6'11" • 8'6" • 10'0" • 12'0" • 13'5"   width - up to 28'

FIM MANUFACTURING INC., 12556 Stave Lake Rd., Mission, B.C., V2V 4J1, Canada - (604) 820-5221
type - retractable freestanding   shade dimension - 12'3"×7'5"   outside dimension - 16'4"×9'8"
type - retractable freestanding   shade dimension - 9'4"×9'4" • 14'3"×10'0"   outside dimension - 11'6"×9'4" • 18'7"×10'2"
type - retractable umbrella   diameter - 10'7"   outside dimension - 11'7"×10'7"
description - Side post umbrellas available in ten colors and have a side mount pole. The "Capri" umbrella has an extruded aluminum structure with a tilt device. The "Tuscany" has a solid mahogany pole and ribs. The "Elba" is a rectangular umbrella. The units are easily opened and closed with a crank and can be rotated in position 360°. The "Miami Elite II" and the "California Elite" are freestanding with offset poles and are available in five colors. A tilt device fixes multi-positions of the awning. The poles are either solid mahogany or extruded aluminum. A pulley device opens and closes the awnings.

REGEL ALUMINUM PRODUCTS, 12 Gres Court, Bradford, Ontario, L3Z 2S4, Canada - (905) 775-4125
type - retractable patio awning assist brace   lengths - 4' • 8' • custom
description - This is an anodized aluminum pole that supports retractable awnings. It is easy to install and can be flush mounted in wood or concrete, floor mounted in a wooden deck or side mounted in wood, concrete or steel. There is finger ring control for quick release.

ROLLADEN ROLLING SHUTTERS, 6168 W. Charleston Blvd., Las Vegas, NV 89102 - (702) 878-1072
type - retractable freestanding   shade dimension - 10'0"×10'0"   outside dimension - 10'0"×10'0"
description - This is a square-shaped freestanding awning with the pole on the side so there are no obstruction. It opens from the side for easy operation. There is a vented top that adds more stability and allows air circulation. The entire frame is made of heavy duty aluminum. It can be mounted on a portable concrete base or fastened directly to a solid surface.

SUNESTA PRODUCTS, 11320 Distribution Ave., E., Jacksonville, FL 32256 - (904) 268-8000
type - retractable patio awning   projection - 3'4" • 5'0" • 6'8" • 8'3" • 10'0" • 13'0"   width - 3' to 38'
type - retractable window awning   projection - 24" to 40"   width - 2' to 13'
type - retractable window awning   projection - 28" to 60"   width - 2' to 23'
type - retractable canopy awning   projection - 1'4" to 5'0"   width - 1'6" to 28'
type - retractable freestanding   length - 11'6" • 15'3"   width - 10'
description - The "Butterfly" retractable freestanding awning is made with an aluminum and galvanized steel frame. The 11'6" model covers 115 sq. ft. and the 15'3" model covers 152 sq. ft. It is lightweight, portable and easily assembled and taken apart for winter storage.

UNITEX MIDWEST, 8026 Woodland Dr., Indianapolis, IN 46278 - (800) 843-6236 (317) 876-7017

type - retractable patio awnings	projection - 4'1" • 5'9" • 6'11" • 8'6" • 10'2" • 12'0"	width - 10' to 40'
type - retractable window awning	projection - 2' to 3'	width - 2'6" to 12'
type - retractable window awning	projection - 1' to 6'	width - 4' to 30'

Typical Installation Instructions

1) Attach Mounting Brackets

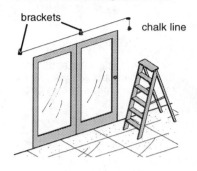

brackets   chalk line

2) Apply Fabric to Awning Roll

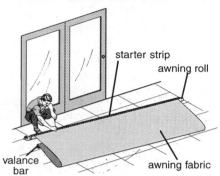

starter strip
awning roll
valance bar
awning fabric

3) Hang Awning on Brackets

torque bar   awning assembly

Important — If optional protective hood cover is used, it is important to refer to the enclosed hood cover instructions first — before continuing with installation.

Mounting

• Decide where awning is to be located and mark center line.
• If door swings out, bottom of bracket must be at least 9" above top of door (diagram #1).

Units with Odd Number of Brackets

• Measure 5' to each side of center line.
• End brackets must attach to torque bar no more than 12" on inside of arm shoulder. Locate on nearest stud or vertical mortar joint (diagram #1).

Unit with Even Number of Brackets

• Measure 7' to each side of center line.
• End brackets must attach to torque bar within arm shoulder and end of torque bar (diagram

#2). This allows approximately 12" to locate a stud or vertical mortar joint.
• Evenly space middle brackets to closest stud or vertical mortar (diagram #2).

Wood-Mounting Installations — All brackets must mount to studs.
• Mount end brackets by drilling ¼" holes and mount using ⁵/₁₆" diameter lagbolts and washers (diagram #4).
• Using a chalk line, snap a line from opposite end brackets. Using chalk line as a guide, mount remaining brackets.

Mortar-Mounted Installations — All bottom bracket holes must line within a horizontal mortar line and top holes within a vertical mortar line.
• Mount brackets by drilling ½" holes and mount using stud bolt, washers and sleeve anchors (diagram #5). Align sleeves so they expand against the brick instead of in the mortar line.

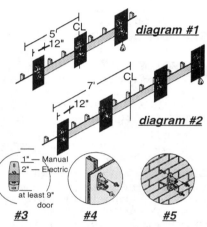

5' CL diagram #1
12"
7' CL
12" diagram #2
1" — Manual
2" — Electric
at least 9" door
#3   #4   #5

Optional Installations — In cases where the awning is being installed on an irregular surface such as aluminum siding, it may be necessary to install a 2"×8"×10'/14' weatherized header to provide a solid support.

Mounting Unit to Brackets

Insert ¼" rod or something similar (not supplied) into mounting bracket as shown. This is an optional step to ease sliding of bar into "U" of bracket. This is not a mandatory step (diagram #6).

Lift awning and hardware assembly onto rods and slide torque bar into "U" of the mounting brackets. (Remove ¼" rod is used.) Secure torque bar with supplied round head bolts and hex nuts. Insert bolts from the bottom. The nuts will lock in top of brackets (diagram #7). At this time tighten all mounting bracket lagbolts securely. Press plastic cover over bolt.

diagram #6
torque bar
¼" rod

hex nut
plastic cover
round head bolts
diagram #7

Awnings by FIM Mfg.

• Freestanding retractable awning
• Open and close quickly by a simple pulley mechanism
• Offset poles in white extruded aluminum
• Complete with base frames and protective covering
• Simple device fixes multi-positions of the awning
• Solid mahogany pole and ribs
• Mahogany ribs easily replaceable
• Unit can be rotated in position 360° on the base

Miami Elite II

Remove red plastic protectors from arms.

Caution — Arms are under tension.

Valance Fabric

Insert aluminum rod into valance fabric loop. (Rod is packed inside of the valance bar.) Slide fabric with rod into bottom opening of the valance bar. Replace end cover on valance bar.

diagram #8
valance end plate
sheet metal screws
valance bar
valance fabric

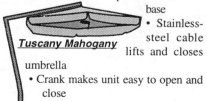

Tuscany Mahogany

• Stainless-steel cable lifts and closes umbrella
• Crank makes unit easy to open and close
• Complete with base frame

wall bracket · center support · wall bracket · gudgeon w. hole · end bracket · end cap · pin · gudgeon with sq. pin · torsion bar · end cap · end bracket · arm retainer · shoulder bracket · gear · crank · arm with built-in spring · arm retainer · elbow · front piece · valance · front profile · end cap · end cap

Custom-Made Awnings by EGE System

- Built-in heavy duty springs for proper fabric tension.
- Hundreds of fabric colors and patterns to choose.
- 100% acrylic fabric awnings can be rolled up when wet.
- 5-year limited warranty on frame and hardware.

Technical Information

- **Width** — 6' to 40' • multiple units to any width.
- **Height of Unit** — 10" to 11", depending on installation.
- **Projection** — Six available: 4'11", 5'9", 6'10", 8'6", 10'2", 12'0".
- **Slope angle** — 0 to 45 degrees.
- **Operation** — Manual gear with hand crank or self-contained electric tubular motor.
- **Hardware and Frame** — 100% maintenance-free, pretreated, polyurethane and powder-coated finishes. Aluminum tubes and arm extrusions. Torsion bar made of galvanized steel or aluminum. White, Bronze, Silver, Custom colors available.
- **Options** — Aluminum hood, retractable valance, electronics and decorator switches, including automatic sun and wind devices, remote controls, digital timers.

Awning Fabric Selector Guide

Generic Classification	Painted Army Duck	Vinyl Coated Cotton	Vinyl Laminated Polyester	Solution Dyed Acrylic	Acrylic Coated Polyester	Vinyl Coated Poly Cotton Blend	Solution Dyed Modacrylic
DESCRIPTION AND TYPICAL WEIGHT	Acrylic-painted cotton duck fabric. Typical weight is 11 oz. per square yard. Resistant to ultraviolet light, mildew and water.	Vinyl coated on cotton duck fabric. Typical weight is 15 oz. per square yard, resistant to ultraviolet light, mildew and water.	Tri-layer fabric; top and bottom layers are vinyl, middle layer is a polyester scrim. Typical weight range is 15 oz. per square yard, resistant to ultraviolet light, mildew and water.	Woven fabric, made of 100% acrylic solution dyed fibers with a fluorocarbon finish. Typical weight is 9.25 oz. per sq. yd. Resistant to ultraviolet and color degradation, also water and mildew.	Acrylic coated on each side of a polyester base fabric. Weights range from 9.5 oz. to 12.5 oz. per square yard. Resistant to ultraviolet light and mildew. Water repellent.	Vinyl coated on each side of a 50% polyester. Weight is 13 oz. per square yard. Resistant to ultraviolet light and mildew. Water repellent.	Woven fabric made of 100% modacrylic solution-dyed fibers with flourocarbon finish. Typical weight is 9.25 oz. per sq. yd. Resistant to ultraviolet and color degradation. Water repellent.
COLORS	Stripes or solids, primary colors, pastels, some earth tones.	Solids or stripes - all colors are available.	Stripes, solids, primaries and pastels.	Wide variety - primaries and earth tones, solids and stripes.	Predominantly solids with some stripes. Same color, both sides.	Solid colors; same color both sides.	Solid colors and tweeds. Same color, both sides.
UNDERSIDE	Pearl gray, green or pearl gray with floral print.	Solid pearl gray.	Linen-like pattern, solid coordinating color to match topside or same color as top.	Same as top surface.	Same as top surface.	Same as top surface.	Same as top surface.
SURFACE	Matte finish, with linen-like visible texture.	Smooth, non-glare surface with little or no texture.	Smooth or matte, with slight woven or linen-like texture.	Woven texture.	Surface is textured, with cloth appearance.	Surface is textured.	Woven texture surface.
TRANSPARENCY LEVEL	Opaque.	Opaque.	Translucent, depending on color.	Translucent, depending on color.	Translucent, depending on color.	Opaque.	Translucent, depending on color.
ABRASION RESISTANCE	Very good.	Very good.	Good. Base fabric is very strong.	Good.	Very good.	Very good.	Good.
DIMENSIONAL STABILTY (Stretch)	Very good.	Very good.	Very good.	Good. Some shrinkage in cold weather, some stretch in hot weather.	Very good.	Very good.	Good.
MILDEW RESISTANCE	Good. Not recommended for areas of constant high humidity.	Good. Not recommended for areas of constant high humidity.	Very good. Recommended for sustained high humidity.	Very good.	Very good.	Very good.	Very good.
DURABILITY/ AVERAGE LIFE SPAN	5-8 years (depends on climate and proper care of fabric)	5-8 years (depends on climate and proper care of fabric)	5-8 years (depends on climate and proper care of fabric)	5-10 years (depends on climate and proper care of fabric)	5-8 years (depends on climate and proper care of fabric)	5-8 years (depends on climate and proper care of fabric)	5-10 years (depends on climate and proper care of fabric)
FLAME RESISTANCE	Some colors are available with flame retardant treatment.	Some colors are available with flame retardant treatment.	All colors are flame resistant.	Non-flame resistant.	All colors are flame resistant.	All colors are flame resistant.	All colors are flame resistant.

Block heat and fading with removeable window film

Q: I get a lot of heat and annoying glare through my windows and it fades the furniture. Is there any inexpensive method to block the sun (not in the winter), yet still have a clear view outdoors?

A: The sun's intense heat through windows is a major contributing factor to high summertime electric bills. The ultraviolet (UV) light not only fades your furniture, but the UV-A rays actually break down the fibers.

Excessive glare is especially annoying when watching TV or using a computer. Often, you end up closing a shade or curtain and switching on a lamp. This wastes even more electricity.

There are three basic summer-only do-it-yourself methods to block the sun's heat without totally blocking the view - static-cling window film, see-through pull-down shades and sun-control fiberglass and polyester screening.

All of these can be easily removed in the winter to take advantage of passive solar heating and re-used again each summer. Another major advantage of these window treatments is more indoor privacy day and night.

Tinted vinyl static-cling window film is available in window-size kits or in bulk on rolls at home center stores. It is easy to install yourself. Some of the kits include a small utility knife and squeegee.

Static-cling window film sticks with static electricity to the indoor window surface. In the fall, peel it off and roll it up for next year. Vinyl film blocks about 80% to 90% of the sun's fading UV rays.

These films are available in various shades of bronze and smoke

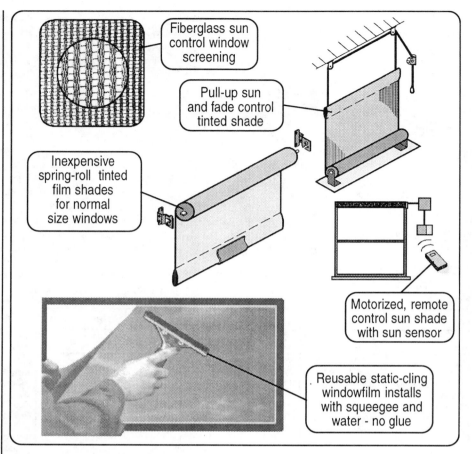

Fiberglass sun control window screening

Pull-up sun and fade control tinted shade

Inexpensive spring-roll tinted film shades for normal size windows

Motorized, remote control sun shade with sun sensor

Reusable static-cling windowfilm installs with squeegee and water - no glue

(dark gray). Although all types look similar on the rolls or in the kits, there are differences in their heat and glare reduction properties.

Visible light transmission ranges from about 20% (greatest glare and heat reduction) to about 50% (lightest tint). Various manufacturers' film thicknesses range from about 6 mils (thousandths of an inch) to 12 mils.

Roll-up see-through tinted window film shades (15 colors) are another option. These use multilayer polyester film with a special invisible heat-reflecting coating on the inner layers. These block more than 99% of the fading UV rays.

For smaller windows, a standard spring roll shade works well. For the most convenience, select motorized shades with hand-held remote controls or automatic sun sensors to open and close them.

Special heavy, close-weave window screening is a third option and allows for ventilation with sun control. Kits are available for easy installation.

Q: We have one room that does not stay cool enough in the afternoon. Does it make more economic sense to add a second zone to our central air conditioner ducts or should we just add a window air conditioner in the room?

A: If you have only one hot room, install a small high-efficiency room air conditioner. Using it will eliminate the need to set the central thermostat lower just to cool that one room adequately.

If you have several rooms that do not cool properly, usually in the same area of the house, consider adding a zoned cooling system with duct dampers.

Manufacturers of Removable Tinted Vinyl Window Films

COURTAULDS PERFORMANCE FILMS, PO Box 5068, Martinsville, VA 24115 - (800) 528-4481 (540) 627-3000

| type - Cling View | VLT - 56% | total UV rejection - 90% | shading coefficient - .78 | color - bronze/grey |
| type - Cling View | VLT - 23% | total UV rejection - 90% | shading coefficient - .56 | color - dark bronze thickness - |

12 mils*   sizes - 36" and 48" widths × 6½" length

METALLIZED PRODUCTS, 2544 Terminal Dr. South, St. Petersburg, FL 33712 - (800) 777-1770 (813) 327-2544

| type - Sun-Gard | VLT - 19.3% | total UV rejection - 93% | shading coefficient - .54 | color - bronze |
| type - Sun-Gard | VLT - 11.7% | total UV rejection - 93% | shading coefficient - .53 | color - grey |

thickness - 9 mils   sizes - rolls of 36" width × 6½" length

SOLAR STAT, 511 N. E. 190th St., Miami, FL 33179 - (800) 783-0454 (305) 652-0454

| type - Solar Stat | VLT - 33.4% | total UV rejection - 93% | shading coefficient - .64 | color - bronze |
| type - Solar Stat | VLT - 27.5% | total UV rejection - 93% | shading coefficient - .67 | color - grey |

thickness - 6.5 mils   sizes - 2, 3 and 4 foot width and 6½, 15, 50 and 100 foot long rolls. Complete do-it-yourself kits are available that include the film, knife and the squeegee.

* One mil is equal to one-thousandth of an inch thick

— —

Manufacturers of Interior and Exterior Shading Systems

CLEAR-VIEW SHADE CO., 6124 N. Broadway, Chicago, IL 60660 - (773) 262-2360

type - KL-1	**VLT - 5%	total UV rejection - 98%	shading coefficient - .29	color - bronze/grey
type - KL-2	VLT - 5%	total UV rejection - 98%	shading coefficient - .29	color - grey/grey
type - KL-3	VLT - 6%	total UV rejection - 98%	shading coefficient - .30	color - gold/grey
type - KL-4	VLT - 13%	total UV rejection - 97%	shading coefficient - .27	color - silver/grey
type - KL-5	VLT - 48%	total UV rejection - 98%	shading coefficient - .64	color - grey

description - "Kool-Lite" is an interior roll-up shade that uses 4-mil 3-ply thick Mylar (polyester) reflective sun control tinted film. The primary purpose of the solar reflective shade is for protection against solar heat. It also gives protection against glare and fading of furniture and carpets. The shades are semitransparent in duplex colors. It is available on spring rollers or as a bead chain and clutch shade. The shades are custom made to your specifications.

type - CV-5	VLT - 46%	total UV rejection - 98%	shading coefficient - .80	color - amber
type - CV-6	VLT - 74%	total UV rejection - 99%	shading coefficient - .88	color - diamond clear
type - CV-7	VLT - 10%	total UV rejection - 97%	shading coefficient - .78	color - smoke grey

description - A 3-mil thick non-reflective interior roll-up shade — "Clear-View", is primarily aimed against sun-fading and glare. Solar heat protection is the secondary purpose. These are solid and semitransparent color shades. It is available on spring rollers or as a bead chain and clutch shade. The shades are custom made to your specifications.

EGE SYSTEMS, 15203 N.E. 95th St., Redmond, WA 98052 - (800) 343-1003

| type - exterior screen | VLT - 8% to 16% | total UV rejection - 80% | shading coefficient - .16 to .26 |
| average openness - 6% to 9% | | width - custom | color - 15 colors to choose from |

description - These exterior screens are made of PVC-coated fiberglass. The screen is operated by a pull tape from the inside or by motorization. The hardware is clear, bronze anodized or white aluminum.

MIDWEST MARKETING, 2000 E. War Memorial, Peoria, IL 61614 - (800) 638-4332 (309) 688-8858

type - GS-35	VLT - 37%	total UV rejection - 96%	shading coefficient - .60	color - gray/silver
type - GSG-10	VLT - 10%	total UV rejection - 96%	shading coefficient - .57	color - gray/silver/gray
type - BSB-10	VLT - 10%	total UV rejection - 96%	shading coefficient - .57	color - bronze/silver/bronze

description - "Sun Shade" is an interior roll-up sun control tinted Mylar (polyester) film shade. It is 4-mil thick, 3-ply construction. The shades are custom made up to 145" in width and by any height. The shades are made with 1" or 1³/₈" steel rollers with a choice of ball bearing spring action or bead chain and clutch.

type - "SheerWeave" interior shades — see Phifer Wire Products "ShearWeave 2000 and 3000" for specifications

description - "SheerWeave" is an interior roll-up shade made of ribbed fiberglass, PVC coated fiberglass or a combination of fiberglass and polyester. The shades are made with 1" or 1³/₈" steel rollers with a choice of ball bearing spring action or bead chain and clutch.

PHIFER WIRE PRODUCTS, PO Box 1700, Tuscaloosa, AL 35403 - (800) 633-5955 (205) 345-2120

type - SheerWeave 1000	VLT - 31% to 32%	total UV rejection - 70%	shading coefficient - .50
average openness - 30%		width - 36" • 48" • 60" • 72" • 84"	color - white • antique white
type - SheerWeave 2000	VLT - 6% to 16%	total UV rejection - 95%	shading coefficient - .32 to .72
average openness - 5%		width - 72" • 96" • 3½" — vertical	

color - white • white/bone • bone • platinum • bone/platinum • white/platinum • bronze

| type - SheerWeave 3000 | VLT - 14% to 22% | total UV rejection - 86% | shading coefficient - .34 to .74 |
| average openness - 14% | | width - 72" | |

color - Spanish grey • pearl white • mushroom sand • custard cream • chocolate • honey umber • blue gray • china blue • sea mist • mauve • dusty grey • pale grey • ninja grey • soft slate

description - Interior sun control fabrics, can be used for shading systems. "SheerWeave 1000" is ribbed weave PVC-coated fiberglass fabric, gives good shading but still allows outward visibility, daytime privacy. Good choice for skylight shades. "SheerWeave 2000" is made of PVC-coated fiberglass yarns, has a basket-weave design, used for applications that require more opaque, nondirectional fabric. Ideal choice for Roman shades or vertical blinds. "SheerWeave 3000", combination of PVC-coated fiberglass and polyester yarns. Nice shading fabric, gives elegant appearance with some colors having linen-like weaves. Ideal choice for roller shades, Roman shades or other types of interior sun control applications where elegant appearance desired.

**VLT - visible light transmitted

PHIFER WIRE PRODUCTS - cont'd

type - SunTex (screening) VLT - 28% total UV rejection - 75% shading coefficient - .23 to .33
average openness - 25% width - 36" • 48" • 60" • 72" color - brown • black • grey • stucco
type - SunScreen VLT - 24% to 29% total UV rejection - 75% shading coefficient - .30 to .35
average openness - 25% width - 24" • 30" • 36" • 48" • 60" • 72" • 84"
color - silver gray • charcoal • bronze • dark bronze • gold
type - Solar/Insect Screen VLT - 37% total UV rejection - 68% shading coefficient - .37 to .40
average openness - 32% width - 24" • 30" • 36" • 48" • 60" • 72" • 84" color - silver grey • charcoal
description - "SunTex" is an exterior shading screen system made from vinyl-coated polyester that is mildew and fade resistant. It needs to be cleaned occasionally with mild soap and water. This screening can be used as an insect screen. "SunScreen" is a removable solar screen that is made of vinyl-coated fiberglass and it can be stored in the winter months if full heat gain is wanted. "Solar/Insect Screening" is 20×30 mesh that looks like a screen and works like a sun shade. It is made of vinyl-coated fiberglass. The screens work with windows open or closed.

SCREEN TIGHT, 407 St. James, Georgetown, SC 29440 - (800) 768-7325

description - This is a two part system that can be used to make solar screens. It consists of a cap, which serves as trim, and a base component which secures the spline and screen. The base attaches to wood framing with screws. Screen is rolled into base strip with spline and screening tool. Excess screen is trimmed, then the cap snaps onto the base strip. There are pre-punched slots on 8" centers. There are 1.5 or 3.5 inch base and caps .
color - standard cap colors — white • beige • gray • brown

SNAPSCREEN, 8922 Frey Rd., Houston, TX 77034 - (713) 941-6100

description - This is a heat tempered, extruded aluminum frame that is designed to hold solar screen mesh. The frame snaps together to hold the mesh in place. It is very easy to rescreen without any special tools if the solar screen needs to be replaced. The frame has a built-in thermal break which helps stop the transfer of heat through the frame. The frames can be curved at the factory to conform to special shapes such as arches. color - frame — bronze • tan • white • driftwood

SOLAR-SCREEN CO., 53-11 105th St., Corona, NY 11368 - (718) 592-8222

type	VLT	total UV rejection	shading coefficient	color
Solar Block	33.4%	98%	.29	silver/white
#7	8%	86%	.23	silver
#10	8%	96%	.33	smoke silver
#16	7%	96%	.33	bronze/silver
#11	11%	96%	.57	smoke/smoke
#12	14%	96%	.58	blue/blue
#13	7%	96%	.43	black/gold
#14	7%	96%	.43	blue/bronze
#15	10%	96%	.57	bronze/bronze
#17	12%	96%	.57	green/green
#18	35%	96%	.60	smoke tint
#19	12%	96%	.58	mauve/mauve

type - "SheerWeave" interior shades — see Phifer Wire Products "ShearWeave 3000" for specifications
width - 24" • 36" • 48" • 54" • 66" • 72" • 78" • 84" • 90" • 96" • 108"
description - "Solar Block" — interior shade syste, made of aluminum foil laminated to 12 gauge vinyl with a fiberglass base for dimensional stability. "Kool Vue #7, #10 and #16" are transparent interior roll-up shades that use 3-mil 2-ply thick reflective sun control tinted film. "Kool Vue #11, #12, #13, #14, #15, #17, #18 and #19" are transparent interior roll-up shades that use 4-mil 3-ply thick reflective sun control tinted film. The "Kool Vue" shades are laminated layers of metallized and dyed mylar. The "SheerWeave" shades are an interior roll-up shading system. These shades are available with a spring roller (best for small windows), chain roller that is also called clutch or springless (good for larger windows, patio doors) or with electric rollers.

VIMCO, 9301 Old Staples Mill Rd., Richmond, VA 23228 - (800) 446-1503 (804) 266-9638

type - "SheerShades" interior shades — see Phifer Wire Products "ShearWeave 2000 and 3000" for specifications
description - This is an interior roll-up shading system. There are several different operating systems to choose from — spring operated, bottom-up mechanism, crank operated or motorized sheer shade. See page 4 for more details. Other options include — decorator toggle and paddle switches, sun sensor control, remote control or a group control system. A complete blackout system is available where total darkness is desired. It features side channels and a fully enclosed head box allowing the shades to disappear into the pocket. There are also vertical blind systems available
type - Skylight Shade — see Phifer Wire Products "ShearWeave 1000" for specifications
sizes - up to 24" wide × 24", 36" 48" or 60" long • 22' to 30" wide × 36", 48" or 60" long • 36" to 48" wide × 48" or 60" long
description - This removable interior skylight shade uses sun control fiberglass screening. It is a simple spring-loaded attachment which requires no holes, brackets or tools. Simply measure the opening and trim your fabric to fit the opening width. Adjust lock screws on compression rods and place the rods into the pockets in the screen. Attach three clips on each rod and position rods in the skylight opening. The skylight shade blocks 70% of the sun's heat, glare, and fading rays.
type - SheerWeave 4000 VLT - 27% to 68% total UV rejection - 95% shading coefficient - .31 to .45
average openness - 5% color - chalk • alabaster • pebblestone • greystone • granite • ash • ebony • tobacco • pewter
type - SheerWeave 4100 VLT - 11% to 16% total UV rejection - 90% shading coefficient - .32 to .46
average openness - 10% color - see SheerWeave 4000 above
sizes - 20", 24", 28", 32", 36", 40", 44", 48", 60" or 72" wide × 36", 40", 44" 48", 52", 56", 60", 64", 68" or 72" long
description - The "Solar-Net" shading system is made of vinyl-coated polyester, "SheerWeave 4000 and 4100" or "SunTex" (see specifications under Phifer Wire Products) and consists of a series of solar screen fabric panels that are stretched over the outside of the opening by using stainless steel or solid brass springs and screws. It can be left up all year or easily removed without tools.

Definitions of Window Sun Contol Properties

Average Openness (applies to screen and fabric products, not films) — The openness factor describes weave density. Use these values to decide weave patterns for functions of privacy and view. Denser weaves allow greater privacy while more open weaves afford a better view. Colors of both weave patterns have a negligible effect on privacy and view. Denser fabrics from 0% to 15% openness factor in lighter colors are usually selected for interior moveable shades. For exterior shading, darker colors of lighter density fabrics from 15% to 32% openness factors are usually selected for their superior see-through visibility. Denser fabrics should be considered to shade overhead glazed openings because they are subjected to much more direct solar radiation than side wall windows.

Visible Light Transmitted — This is the percentage of the sun's light that actually gets through the shading system and into your house.

Total UV Rejection — The percentage of UV-A and UV-B solar energy that does not pass through window glass. Ultraviolet is the primary cause of fading and deterioration of colors and finishes exposed to sunlight and deterioration of the fibers of the materials.

Shading Coefficient — The fraction of solar heat that gets through a window insulating system. An example is how much heat comes through the glass before and after using window treatments. The numbers give protective values. A shading coefficient of 0.2 means only 20% of the solar radiant heat will go through the window and about 80% is rejected. Darker-tinted films usually have a lower shading coefficient.

Do-it-Yourself Instructions for Installing Static Cling Vinyl Window Film

Tools Required for Installation — Squeegee, Tape Measure, Straight Edge Ruler, Utility Knife, Razor Blades, Glass Cleaner, Lint Free Cloth

Avoid working in direct sunlight or wind. For best results apply when the temperature is between 45 and 90 degrees. Clean window thoroughly with a glass cleaner. Use a single edge razor blade to scrape excess build up. Make sure all corners and edges are as clean as possible. Wipe window dry with a lint free cloth.

1) Measure window glass. Unroll window film on a flat surface and cut ½ inch larger than the actual surface.

2) Spray the window thoroughly with a glass cleaner before applying window film. *Wet generously.* Never install on a dry surface.

For easier handling, spray the surface of the window film before applying. This will prevent the film from clinging.

3) Starting at the top, apply film to the inside window. There is no front or back so either side may be applied. Position and smooth out the film by using your hands to work out wrinkles until it overlaps the frame on all sides. Should the material wrinkle, crese or cling to itself, simply spray it with glass cleaner and reapply. On larger windows and doors some assistance will be helpful.

4) Spray the surface of the film. *Wet generously.* Beginning at the center of the window firmly squeegee out bubbles and moisture towards the sides, working in a side to side,

up and down direction.

5) After you have squeegeed out excess water and bubble, use a straight edge ruler to press the film to the inside edge of the window frame and trim excess with a sharp razor blade or utility knife. It is recommended to leave at least a ¹/₁₆ inch space around the perimeter of the window. This will allow any remaining moisture to escape and is necessary for the film to adhere properly to the surface.

6) Spray the film and firmly squeegee the edges toward the frame. Any remaining small bubbles or excess moisture should evaporate in a few days. During the first 10 hours after installation the window film should not be disturbed.

SIDE VIEW

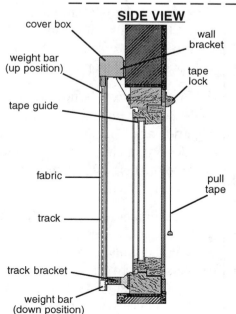

cover box
weight bar (up position)
tape guide
fabric
track
track bracket
weight bar (down position)
wall bracket
tape lock
pull tape

EGE Screen by EGE Systems

- An external sun blind.
- Eliminates glare while maintaining a clear and open view — almost total non-glare visibility from the inside.
- Effectively blocks 75% - 85% of the solar heat rays when installed on the exterior of the window.
- Comfort of extra insulation and it protects against cold penetration during chilly winter nights.
- Easily operated, maintenance-free, rot-proof and fireproof.
- Choose from many colors to match your exterior.
- Motorized or manual operation.
- 5-year warranty on screen and hardware.
- The slim box, track and fireproof screen can easily be built-in on original construction or retrofit to an existing house.

Solar Snapscreen

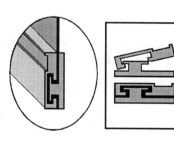

- Heat tempered, extruded aluminum frame
- Frame holds solar screening by snapping the pieces together
- Built-in thermobreak
- Mounts on exterior of any size or shape window

Geothermal heat pump saves money year-round

Q: Our heating and air-conditioning bills are busting the budget. I have heard about earth-friendly geothermal heat pumps that can cut our bills in half. What are they and are they good for any home?

A: A geothermal heat pump is an ideal year-round system for almost any home. Basically, a geothermal heat pump draws "free" extra heating and air-conditioning capacity from the ground. Over its life, a geothermal heat pump can save many thousands of dollars.

For example, in the winter, for each $1 on your utility bills, you get $4 worth of heat ($3 free from the earth). These systems also eliminate that "chilly" air feeling common to regular heat pumps in the winter.

If you have an old central air conditioner, installing the most efficient geothermal heat pump can reduce your cooling bills by two-thirds. Even more important is the superior dehumidification (for allergy sufferers) and steady cooling, even on the hottest summer afternoons.

Many geothermal heat pumps use a water/antifreeze-filled plastic pipe loop buried in your yard. This earth loop is used instead of the typical noisy outdoor condenser fan unit. This results in a very quiet system (all indoors) with less risk of damage and maintenance problems.

Geothermal heat pumps attain high efficiency because the ground temperature stays fairly constant year-round. It is much easier in the winter to "pump" heat from the warm ground at 50 degrees than from the frigid outdoor air.

In the summer, the situation is reversed. It is much easier to pump heat from inside your house to the

Typical horizontal ground loop

Pipes below ground level

Variable-speed blower motor for comfort and savings

Vertical loop - holes are drilled deep in the ground - requires less yard area

Two-speed or dual compressors for year-round efficiency

cooler 50-degree ground than to the oven-like outdoor afternoon air. For an additional savings, this waste indoor heat can be diverted to your water heater for free hot water all summer.

There are many designs of geothermal heat pumps to choose from depending on your budget, yard and specific needs. The ground pipes are normally buried in a very narrow trench. If your yard is small, the pipes can be placed in vertical holes drilled deep into the ground. Ponds or wells are also used.

The best geothermal heat pumps (for year-round comfort and savings) use multilevel heating and cooling outputs. These models use either two small compressors or a single two-speed one. They continually adjust the heating and cooling outputs to match the varying comfort requirements of your house.

Another, simplified, but highly efficient, single-level design uses direct exchange (DX). Instead of using plastic pipes buried in your yard, much shorter, tiny copper pipes are used. These are ideal for smaller yards.

Q: Even though we have not used our fireplace for over a month, the room still smells smoky on windy days. It seems worse in the summer. What can I do to stop this?

A: Your situation is not unusual. Under certain temperature and wind conditions, outdoor air is making its way down your chimney and out into your room. This not only smells bad, but it is inefficient.

It is important to seal off this source of outdoor air leakage, especially in the summer. Most chimney dampers do not seal well. Check at your hardware store for a special inflatable chimney sealer or just use rags.

Manufacturers of the Most Efficient Geothermal Heat Pumps

ADDISON PRODUCTS, 7050 Overland Rd., Orlando, FL 32810 - (407) 292-4400

| model - "Excel" | output levels - one | blower - see features | type - loop |
| cooling - 12,000 to 65,000 Btuh | EER* - 13.2 to 16.1 | heating - 8,900 to 48,000 Btuh | COP* - 3.0 to 3.7 |

features - Dual control thermostat/humidistat, one setting is for the temperature and one is a low dehumidifying speed. Multi-speed blower motor automatically switches to its lowest, dehumidifying speed when the home has been cooled to your preset temperature, but the humidity is still too high. Keeps running on a low blower speed until the humidity is reduced. Optional auxiliary backup electric heaters, internally mounted available. Include microprocessor controls. More compact than external heaters, lower installation costs and easier to service. Cabinet completely insulated with one-inch thick high density fiberglass insulation for quiet operation. Compressor compartment also has own additional layer of sound insulation. Very quiet.

ADVANCED GEOTHERMAL TECH., PO Box 511, Reading, PA 19607 - (610) 796-1450

| model - "Great Aire Comfort System" | output levels - one | blower - single-speed | type - DX |
| cooling - 18,000 to 61,000 Btuh | EER - **n/a | heating - 18,000 to 60,000 Btuh | COP - 4.5 |

features - This system uses copper tubes placed in 4 to 10 holes, depending on size of the system. The 3-inch diameter holes are drilled 65 feet deep. These are all drilled in one small area and angled out forming a conical shape under the ground. The tops of the copper tubes are all soldered to a manifold that is connected to the heat pump compressor. This manifold is buried three feet deep so you can plant grass or flowers over it. This system requires only a small yard and is extremely efficient. The earth tap system has a limited lifetime warranty. The compressor unit can be placed indoors or outdoors. There is a hot water heater available for heating household water. An optional variable-speed motor is available upon request. This design is the most unique and makes good engineering sense. ** The current ARI 330 test criteria do not cover DX systems. An equivalent EER of 18 to 20 is probably a good approximation to use.

BARD MFG. CO., PO Box 607, Bryan, OH 43506 - (419) 636-1194

model - "WQS"	output levels - one	blower - single-speed	type - loop
cooling - 31,600 to 41,500 Btuh	EER - 14.0 to 14.2	heating - 26,400 to 37,400 Btuh	COP - 2.8 to 3.1
model - "WPV"	output levels - one	blower - single-speed	type - loop
cooling - 21,600 to 54,000 Btuh	EER - 11.5 to 13.0	heating - 15,600 to 40,000 Btuh	COP - 2.8 to 3.0

features - The "WQS series" is a split system with a separate air handler and compressor unit. As an add-on compressor unit, this is ideal if you have a gas furnace and you want to use the geothermal heat pump primarily for air-conditioning. It uses your existing furnace air handler. "WPV series" is an integrated unit with the compressor and air handler in one complete system. This model would be used as the sole source of heating or cooling. This is a fairly basic, reasonably-priced unit.

CARRIER CORP., PO Box 4808, Syracuse, NY 13221 - (800) 227-7437 (315) 432-6000

| model - "Weathermaker" | output levels - two | blower - variable-speed | type - loop |
| cooling - 34,800 to 71,300 Btuh | EER - 14.2 to 17.6 | heating - 26,300 to 63,000 Btuh | COP - 3.3 to 3.8 |

features - The ICM-2 blower motor has the soft start and matches the system airflow with demand for highest operating efficiency and dehumidification. Carrier uses one of the most sophisticated blower motor speed controllers available. The two output levels are attained by using two separate smaller compressors.

CLIMATE MASTER INC., PO Box 25788, Oklahoma City, OK 73179 - (800) 299-9747 (405) 745-6000

| model - "Paradigm" | output levels - one | blower - single-speed | type - loop |
| cooling - 18,500 to 56,000 Btuh | EER - 14.0 to 15.2 | heating - 13,500 to 46,000 Btuh | COP - 3.1 to 3.4 |

features - The "Paradigm" is designed to be placed outdoors, where your existing heat pump or air-conditioner outdoor unit now is, and is connected to your existing interior blower unit. It is a dual-fuel unit so it can work in conjunction with a gas furnace. The compressor is mounted on vibrations isolators to reduce noise. The thermostat features an automatic heating-to-cooling changeover with a digital LCD display. There is a keypad lockout to prevent accidental access by children. An optional remote indoor or outdoor temperature sensor is available. This helps to maintain a comfortable and steady indoor temperature. An optional internal auxiliary heater can be added to provide supplemental heating during very cold weather. In September 1998, they will introduce an indoor model called "Genesis".

ECONAR ENERGY SYSTEMS CORP., 19230 Evan St., Elk River, MN 55330 - (800) 432-6627 (612) 241-3110

model - "Invision 3"	output levels - two	blower - variable-speed	type - loop
cooling - 51,000 to 64,000Btuh	EER - 11.6 to 13.7	heating - 47,000 to 61,000 Btuh	COP - 3.0 to 3.2
model - "Geo Source"	output levels - one	blower - single-speed	type - loop
cooling - 11,200 to 63,000 Btuh	EER - 10.5 to 14.5	heating - 11,100 to 64,000 Btuh	COP - 3.0 to 3.4

features - The "Invision 3" uses two small compressors for the two-level output. The "PumpPak" design incorporates all pumps and valves into one unit making it simple to install. It has a device called "TempSense" that precisely controls the pumping energy needed in the ground loop to reducing overall electricity usage.

FHP MFG., 601 NW 65th Ct., Ft. Lauderdale, FL 33309 - (954) 776-5471

model - "Geo Miser"	output levels - one or two	blower - variable-speed	type - loop
cooling - 25,800 to 70,000 Btuh	EER - 11.9 to 22.2	heating - 17,000 to 47,000 Btuh	COP - 2.8 to 4.0
model - "Geo Thermal"	output levels - one	blower - single-speed	type - loop
cooling - 11,200 to 60,500 Btuh	EER - 13.0 to 16.2	heating - 8,000 to 50,000 Btuh	COP - 3.0 to 3.3

features - "Geo Miser" can be set up as a single-or two-output level compressor model. Two-level unit has two compressors sized at 40% or 60% of total capacity. Depending on climate, installer will determine which compressor it starts on. It operates on the single compressor the majority of the time and the other compressor kicks in only during extremely hot or cold weather. Provides excellent comfort and summertime humidity control. It uses a variable-speed blower motor to provide soft start (quiet) and precision air flow to match each of the output levels. Also available is an optional factory-installed internal auxiliary heater.

* Ratings are for ground source closed-loop heat pumps (ARI 330). "EER" is cooling efficiency. "COP" is heating efficiency. A higher number is more efficient

GEO TECH SYSTEMS, INC., 439 Clark St., Middletown, OH 45042 - (937) 423-7907

model - "DX3000"   output levels - one   blower - singleor variable-speed   type - DX
cooling - 34,100 to 63,700 Btuh   EER - ** n/a   heating - 35,200 to 67,100 Btuh   COP - 4.0
features - Geo Tech Systems sells only the compressor units. Your heating contractor will attach it to either your existing furnace or heat pump indoor blower unit or install a new (Trane, Carrier, etc.) blower unit. ** The current ARI 330 test criteria do not cover DX systems. An equivalent EER of 18 to 20 is probably a good approximation to use.

HYDRO-TEMP CORP., PO Box 566, Pocahontas, AR 72455 - (800) 382-3113 (501) 892-8343

model - "Three Level"   output levels - three   blower - variable-speed   type - loop
cooling - 18,000 to 120,000 Btuh   EER - 18.3, 14.4, 12.6***   heating - 18,000 to 120,000 Btuh   COP - 4.1, 3.7, 3.3***
model - "Standard"   output levels - one   blower - single-speed   type - loop
cooling - 27,100 to 64,200 Btuh   EER - 11.2 to 14.4   heating - 17,791 to 53,604 Btuh   COP - 2.5 to 3.5
features - These heat pumps are custom built to meet your specifications. The three-level output model uses two different size compressors -- either the small, the medium, or both run. ***These efficiencies are estimates only and refer to heat level 1, 2 and 3 respectively. There is an optional hot water desuperheater available that produces hot water for household use whenever the unit runs in the cooling mode. There is an optional space-heating-priority water heating system. This means that, if both your house needs heat and your water heater needs heat, the heat from the heat pump first goes to the house until it is warm and then to the water heater. A zone control system is built internally into the unit and controls up to four different zones in your home.

TETCO (GEOTHERMAL PRODUCTS), 4059-E St. Rt. 36/37 East, Delaware, OH 43015 - (740) 363-5002

model - "ES II series"   output levels - one   blower - variable-speed   type - loop
cooling - 11,400 to 58,000 Btuh   EER - 13.0 to 15.1   heating - 8,400 to 73,000 Btuh   COP - 3.8 to 4.6
model - "ESX"   output levels - one   blower - single-speed   type - loop
cooling - 27,200 to 35,000 Btuh   EER - 11.7 to 12.2   heating - 35,600 to 41,500 Btuh   COP - 4.0
features - The "ES II" unit is just 36" high and has an optional electrostatic filter for filtering the air. Optional programmable thermostats (5/2 day or 7 day) are available. There are models available that can be added to your existing system — gas, LP, oil or electric. There is a direct cool air-conditioning coil option (for wells only). This circulates the cold water through an extra blower heat exchanger. This provides cooling very efficiently because the compressor is not running. Only a small water circulator pump runs.

TRANE CO., PO Box 7916, Waco, TX 76714 - (254) 840-3244

model - "GSUF series"   output levels - one   blower - single or variable-speed   type - loop
cooling - 20,000 to 70,000 Btuh   EER - 14.0 to 17.1   heating - 14,000 to 50,500 Btuh   COP - 2.9 to 3.1
model - "GSUG series"   output levels - two   blower - variable-speed   type - loop
cooling - 49,000 to 70,000 Btuh   EER - 10.8 to 14.9   heating - 33,000 to 52,000 Btuh   COP - 2.7 to 3.3
features - The ICM (Integrated Control Motor) variable-speed blower can vary its speed between zero and maximum. It starts quietly and then slowly speeds up, using very little energy. The "GSUG" model uses a two-speed Copeland compressor.

WATER FURNACE, 9000 Conservation Way, Ft. Wayne, IN 46809 - (800) 436-7283 (219) 478-5667

model - "Premier 2"   output levels - one or two   blower - variable-speed   type - loop
cooling - 9,900 to 67,000 Btuh   EER - 13.4 to 16.8   heating - 7,400 to 41,500 Btuh   COP - 3.0 to 3.6
model - "Northern Leader"   output levels - two   blower - variable-speed   type - loop
cooling - 22,400 to 39,000 Btuh   EER - 14.0 to 14.1   heating - 25,600 to 44,500 Btuh   COP - 3.2 to 3.3
model - "Spectra"   output levels - one   blower - single-speed   type - loop
cooling - 9,900 to 68,000 Btuh   EER - 12.0 to 15.7   heating - 7,600 to 53,000 Btuh   COP - 3.0 to 3.5
features - Two-level output models use a single two-speed compressor motor. Variable-speed "ECM2" motor features soft-start and quiet operation. An optional supplementary internal heater provides backup heat if it is required for any reason. An optional water heater with stage control and scald protection is available for heating household water. There is a dual fuel kit to replace electric resistance backup heaters, designed to work with natural gas, oil or propane water heaters. It is an internal add-on to the "Premier" and is to be used as a supplement to the heat pump. Kit includes a circulating pump, control box and internal plumbing. "IntelliZone" for use with the "Premier" is a zoning system that can control up to four zones in your home. "Premier Plus" add-on" (see below) is a small geothermal heat pump water heater that can run with or independently of the main geothermal heat pump.

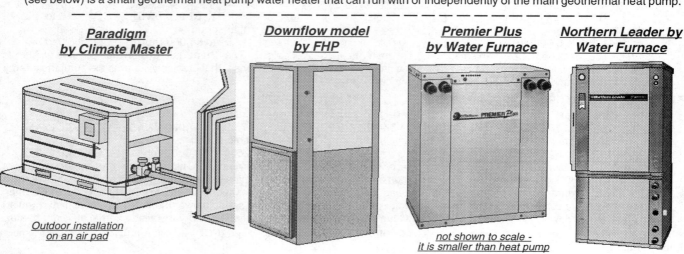

Paradigm by Climate Master
Outdoor installation on an air pad

Downflow model by FHP

Premier Plus by Water Furnace
not shown to scale - it is smaller than heat pump

Northern Leader by Water Furnace

Closed Loop Earth Coupled Applications

There are three standard methods of closed loop ground source installations — horizontal, vertical and pond loop.

diagram #1

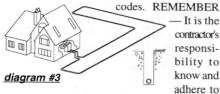

The method of installation should be chosen after considering the constraints of each application. All provide the same benefit; using the temperatures of the earth as a heat source/heat sink. The "appropriate" choice for an installation is the most cost effective method. Piping configurations can be either series or parallel, with pipe sizes ranging from ¾" up.

Series applications normally use 1¼", 1½" or 2" pipe. Parallel applications use ¾" or 1" pipe for the loops and 1¼", 1½" or 2" pipe for the headers and service lines. On parallel applications, headers should either be the "closed-coupled" short headers as shown in diagram #1, or a reverse return design as shown in diagram #2.

The following information is an example of good installation practice and will assist you in installing trouble free ground loops.

It is intended as a recommendation and shall not take precedence over local or state codes. REMEMBER — It is the contractor's responsibility to know and adhere to all applicable codes.

diagram #3

General

Prior to installation, be sure to locate and mark all existing underground utilities, piping, etc. If the installation is new construction, get there before sidewalks, patios, driveways and other obstructions are begun. After

diagram #4

the installation is complete, be sure to accurately locate the earth coupling on the plot plan. This location information will be very useful if additional construction takes place or maintenance is required.

Horizontal Application

Horizontal earth couplings can be installed using either a chain-type trenching machine or a backhoe. Trenches should be at least 5 feet apart, but can be curved to miss obstructions or turned around corners. If multiple pipes are used in a trench, care should be used during backfilling to ensure proper pipe spacing.

Diagrams #3, #4 and #5 are examples of narrow trench applications. Diagrams #6 and #7 illustrate typical wide trench applications.

Diagram #8 illustrates a wide trench application under a septic system. BE SURE to have the local health department approve this method prior to beginning work.

During layout and installation, remember that horizontal systems should be at least 5 feet from existing utility lines, foundations and property lines, and at least 10 feet from privies and wells.

Vertical Applications

Vertical applications can be installed using any size drilling equipment. The minimum diameter for 1" U-bend well bores is 4 inches. There is no problem if the driller's tooling cuts a larger diameter borehole unless local code requires some expensive method of backfilling. Most vertical applications require multiple boreholes which

should be spaced a minimum of 10 feet apart.

The U-bend assembly should be put together, filled with water and pressure tested prior to insertion into the borehole. Taping a length of conduit, pipe or reinforcing bar to the U-bend end of the assembly will assist in inserting the pipe down the borehole. It adds weight and prevents the

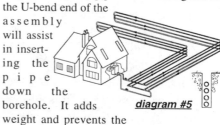

diagram #5

pipe from curving and digging into the borehole wall during insertion. The added weight helps sink the water filled U-bend assembly since water filled pipe is still somewhat buoyant in water or drilling mud solutions. Also, tape the pipes together every 10 feet or so. U-bend assemblies not taped will separate under downward pressure and bow out against the borehole wall.

diagram #6

diagram #7

Boreholes must be carefully backfilled. Backfill to within 10 feet of the surface or as code requires.

After all U-bends are installed, as shown in diagram #1, dig the header trench. Dig as close to the boreholes as possible to a depth of approximately 6 feet. Use a spade and break through into the borehole from ground level to the bottom of the trench. At the bottom of the trench, dig a relief to allow the pipe to bend for proper access to the header.

diagram #8

If no local code supersedes, remember that boreholes should be at least:

A. 5 feet from foundations and lot lines
B. 10 feet from utility lines and drain fields
C. 20 feet from non-public wells
D. 50 feet from public wells
E. 100 feet from cesspools, feedlots, lagoons, privies, seepage pits and septic tanks

---

Applications from Tetco

Forced Air System

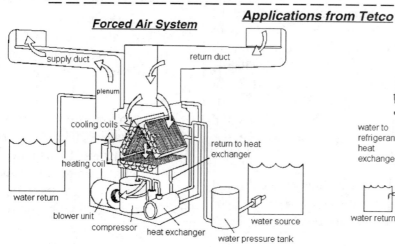

Hydronic System

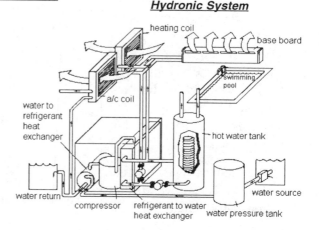

Solar deck and gazebo kits for savings, comfort

Q: I want to add a large deck or build a do-it-yourself gazebo kit. I have heard of attractive "solar" deck designs that can help reduce year-round utility bills. Can one really help and are they attractive?

A: When you have an attractive deck or an insect-free screened gazebo, it is much more pleasant to be outdoors in the evening. This allows you to set up the air conditioner thermostat earlier and save more money.

The design of a passive solar deck is not particularly unusual. To anyone other than a trained energy expert, it looks like just a very attractive two-level contemporary deck.

What makes a deck "solar" is the orientation of the top trim and the side details. In the summer, it should block the hot sun from baking your house. In the winter, it should slow the force of the cold winds striking your house, but allow the sun to shine through for free passive heating.

Although a solar deck can be designed for any side of your house, building it on the west side is most effective for year-round energy savings and comfort. The south side is the next best choice and the east comes in third. Unless you have no other option, avoid the north side.

A two-level west-facing solar deck is easy to design and build. The first design step is to cover the west side of one level (the one opposite the most windows) with 1x6 louvers. Actually covering both upper and lower levels is most effective, but you may feel closed in.

The trick to making it effective is slanting the louvers outward from top to bottom. Space them fairly far

Build a preassembled kit using only a screwdriver

Fasteners are hidden for a professional look

Precut gazebo kit with screen panel option

Typical octagon kit with two-level roof

Slanted louvers for sun control

West-facing solar deck

apart. This allows cool evening breezes through, yet slows ferocious winter winds. The proper slant varies with your area's latitude. Temporarily attach two louvers to test the shading.

Cover the top of the deck with louvers and slant them at the opposite angle (inward from top to bottom). This also allows the winter sun to shine through to your house, but blocks the steeper intense summer sun.

Building a gazebo kit will allow you to spend more comfortable time outdoors too. Depending on your level of skill and time available, you can select a precut or a preassembled kit. A precut kit includes all the lumber materials and hardware, but you must assemble it completely.

A preassembled kit is delivered in eight finished roof, wall and floor sections. You just need a screwdriver

to assemble it. An octagonal design made of western red cedar with a curved two-level cedar shake roof is my favorite. For about $600, you can add an insect screening option.

Q: I have a waterbed and I like it very much. My children are considering getting them too. I was wondering if the heaters for these big bags of water cost much to operate?

A: You ought to think again about getting waterbeds for your children. It can cost about $14 to $23 per month in electricity usage just to keep one waterbed comfortably warm.

If your children really want them, put a one-inch thick foam pad over the mattress. It insulates the mattress and separates their bodies from it so you can set the temperature lower. Cover it with a quilt during the day.

Instructions for Making Deck for West Side of House (diagram on page199)
(design modifications for decks on east and south sides of house are described in sections 13) and 14), diagrams shown.)

1) Before you begin to build your deck, carefully plan your project. Check all local codes and restrictions, zoning, and the location of any underground utilities. For a rough size estimate, plan on about 20 square feet times the maximum number of people that you will usually have on the deck.

2) Lay out your deck position and stake the corner locations. Also

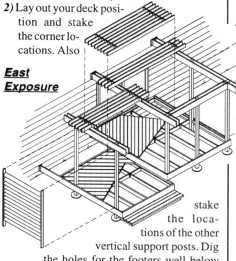

East Exposure

stake the locations of the other vertical support posts. Dig the holes for the footers well below the frost line. Most builders can tell you how deep to dig in your area. You can either set the posts in concrete or crushed rock. Although concrete provides the best support, the posts can expand and sometimes cause the concrete to crack.

3) In order to retard the growth of weeds and grass under the deck, cover area under deck with polyethylene plastic film. A dark-colored film is usually used. You can use the same type of 4-mil plastic film that is used for vapor barriers for wall insulation. Make small slits in plastic film to allow water to pass through it and not stand. Cover it lightly with gravel or bark to hold it in place.

4) Plan the size of the deck and height of the deck that you want. Try to balance its size with the size of your house and yard. Cut the 4x4 vertical supporting corner posts (**A**) to proper length plus the amount that will set in the ground plus an extra several inches.

5) Put some gravel in the post holes to make sure the tops of the support posts are slightly higher than you want them to finally be. Place the posts in the holes and pour concrete around them. Use a plumb line to make sure they are vertical and stake them in position. Wait several days for the concrete to set up thoroughly. If you just set them in crushed rock, wait several days for it to settle. Saw the appropriate amount off of the tops to get the desired height.

6) Cut and attach the upper level floor joists (**B,C**) to the support posts. Use joist hangers to secure them in position. Attach the floor joists (**D,E,F**) for the lower level in the same manner. For the most secure and stable deck, screws are best to use for attaching the joist hangers.

7) Attach 2x6 nailer (**G**) to your house with screws. Recess it the thickness of the decking material. You can also attach piece (**G-1**) across the frame's side members for additional support.

8) Attach 2x4 supports (**H,I**) and 2x6 supports (**J**) to the framing. Using nails or joist hangers, attach 2x6 joists (**K,L**) to form the support for the flooring. Repeat the same flooring method for the lower level, using 2x6 (**N,O**) and 2x4 (**P**) boards. Nail the 2x6 deck flooring to the joists (**M**).

9) Attach horizontal framing pieces (**Q,R**) to the tops of the support posts. Then bolt framing piece/support posts to your house.

10) Attach short 2x4 pieces (**S**) to the corner support posts. Bolt horizontal framing (**T**) to pieces (**S**) and to the posts.

11) Although the diagram shows vertical top louvers which are easier to build and attach, slanted louvers are more effective for energy savings. They should slant toward your house from the top to the bottom of the louver. Loosely nail (leave the nail heads extended so you can pull them out easily) several in place to determine the best angle and spacing for summer sun control. Don't position them too closely together or they will also block the winter sun. For slanted top louvers, cut spacer pieces (**W**) at the angle of slant that you desire. Toe nail the top louvers (**U,V**) to the upper framing member.

12) Cut the 1x6 side louvers (**X**) and nail them between the vertical framing members (**Y**). Loosely nail several of them in place first with various gaps between them. Hold it up vertically and select the positioning which gives adequate sun control in the summer. The wider you leave the gaps, the more solar heat your house will get in the winter. Attach the side louver assembly to the front of the deck.

13) For the east side of your house, follow

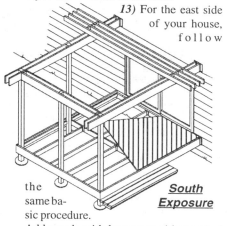

the same basic procedure.

South Exposure

Add panels with louvers at either end of the deck to block the blustery winter winds and to shade from the hot summer sun.

14) For the south side of your house, build the upper level of the deck only. Install only enough top louvers to block the midday sun. Since the sun is high in the sky when it is to the south, only a few top louvers will be needed. If you install too many, the lower winter sun will also be blocked. No side louvers are needed. Winter winds are seldom from the south.

Solar Positioning (Latitude Angles) Chart

City	Angle	City	Angle
Albuquerque, NM	35°	Los Angeles, CA	34°
Atlanta, GA	34°	Louisville, KY	38°
Atlantic City, NJ	39°	Madison, WI	43°
Billings, MT	46°	Memphis, TN	35°
Birmingham, AL	33°	Miami, FL	26°
Boise, ID	44°	Milwaukee, WI	43°
Boston, MA	42°	Minneapolis, MN	45°
Buffalo, NY	43°	New Orleans, LA	30°
Burlington, VT	45°	New York, NY	41°
Charleston, SC	33°	Oklahoma City, OK	35°
Cheyenne, WY	41°	Omaha, NE	41°
Chicago, IL	42°	Philadelphia, PA	40°
Cincinnati, OH	39°	Phoenix, AZ	34°
Cleveland, OH	41°	Pittsburgh, PA	41°
Columbus, OH	40°	Portland, ME	44°
Corpus Christi, TX	28°	Portland, OR	46°
Dallas, TX	33°	Providence, RI	42°
Denver, CO	40°	Roanoke, VA	37°
Des Moines, IA	43°	Salt Lake City, UT	41°
Detroit, MI	42°	San Diego, CA	33°
Dodge City, KS	38°	San Francisco, CA	38°
Greensboro, NC	36°	Seattle, WA	48°
Houston, TX	30°	Sioux Falls, SD	44°
Indianapolis, IN	40°	Spokane, WA	48°
Jackon, MS	32°	Springfield, MA	42°
Jacksonville, FL	30°	St. Louis, MO	39°
Kansas City, MO	39°	Syracuse, NY	43°
Las Vegas, NV	36°	Washington, DC	39°
Little Rock, AR	35°	Wilmington, DE	40°

Required Materials for Deck

4x4 pressure-treated wood posts
2×4, 2×6, 1×6, 1×4, 2×10 lumber
nails - stainless steel or plated
joist hangers and carriage bolts
screws - stainless steel or plated
polyethylene plastic film
crushed rock and concrete

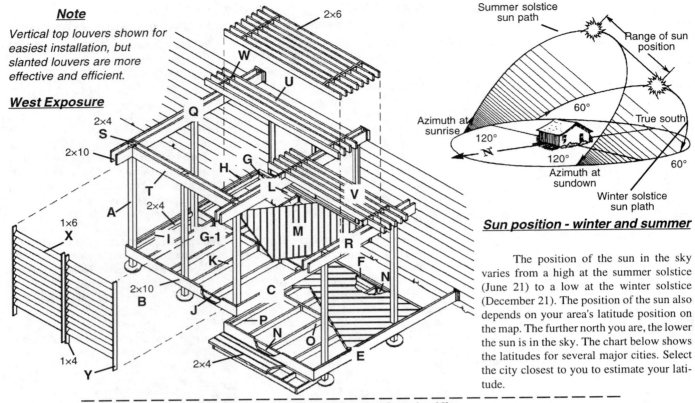

Note

Vertical top louvers shown for easiest installation, but slanted louvers are more effective and efficient.

West Exposure

2×4
S
2×10
1×6
X
2×10
B
1×4
Y
2×4
2×6
W
U
Q
G
H
L
V
T
A
2×4
I
G-1
K
C
J
M
R
F
N
P
N
O
E

Summer solstice sun path

Range of sun position

Azimuth at sunrise

60°

True south

120°

N

120°

60°

Azimuth at sundown

Winter solstice sun plath

Sun position - winter and summer

The position of the sun in the sky varies from a high at the summer solstice (June 21) to a low at the winter solstice (December 21). The position of the sun also depends on your area's latitude position on the map. The further north you are, the lower the sun is in the sky. The chart below shows the latitudes for several major cities. Select the city closest to you to estimate your latitude.

Selected High-Quality Gazebo Kits

AMISH COUNTRY GAZEBOS, 739 E. Francis St., Ontario, CA 91761 - (800) 429-3267 (909) 947-3095
material - southern yellow pine   sizes - 8' • 10' • 12' • 14' • 16' • 18' • 20' octagon
features - Includes — cedar-shingled cupola, one-tier roof with cedar shingles, straight facia, 2x6 header, regular braces, straight 4x4 posts and straight 2x2 balusters on seven handrail sections. Available with or without wood deck. Roofing options — cedar shingles, 20-year or 30-year composition shingles with tongue and groove, fire-treated cedar shingles or Hardishake roofing. Other options — Victorian braces that look like butterfly wings, turned posts, wrapped posts, electrical package (concealed wiring), gazebo painted a special color, heavy duty anchors, benches, pagoda roof, and site preparation which would be blocks, piers, slabs, etc. Custom built available. Limited lifetime warranty against rot, termite damage.

BELLA VISTA GAZEBOS, 3358 Monier Circle, Suite 3, Rancho Cordova, CA 95742 - (800) 600-0299 (916) 852-0299
material - redwood   sizes - 9' • 11' • 13' • 15' hexagon / 9' • 11' • 13' octagon
features - The kits are precut, with a smooth mill finish and come in easy to assemble sections. Includes — optional preassembled floor sections, optional center floor hub, preassembled rail sections, posts, post trim, main and secondary rafters, preassembled ceiling panels, ridge caps, arched collars and center king pin. Some kits will include a cupola and fascia trim depending on model. Included are easy to follow instructions and all the hardware required for assembly.

BOWBENDS, PO Box 900, Bolton, MA 01740 - (800) 518-6471 (978) 779-2271
material - southern yellow pine   sizes - 10' • 12' • 14.5' • 17' octagon
features - Available with or without a floor. Options include screen panels and doors, glass panels and doors, benches, electrical channels, weathervanes and cupolas. Different roof styles and other custom variations available.

DALTON PAVILIONS, INC., 20 Commerce Dr., Telford, PA 18969 - (215) 721-1492
material - western red cedar   sizes - 9' • 11' • 13' • 15' • 18' • 21' • 26' octagon
features - The prefab gazebo comes assembled in sections and predrilled for easy installation. Step by step illustrated instructions provided. Cover trim, stainless steel screws and finish nails and matching wood filler included. Available with or without floor. Options — small, medium or large tables, movable or fixed benches. Hidden electric channel with a light switch box provided. Screening package includes replaceable full size dark screen panels with bronze color frames. Screw on from the inside. Under floor also screened. Single or double doors provided depending on size. Doors swing outward. Screening package not available on units larger than 15'. Other options — steps and handrail, custom lengths or prefabricated deck railing to match the gazebo designs and lattice underpinning that is supplied with corner trim and fasteners. Also available are cupola and weather vanes. A finial is provided with the cupola unless a weather vane is ordered. Weather vane designs available — antique auto, eagle, goose, horse, owl, rooster, sea gull or sulky. Available in gold bronze color or hand painted. Has one-tier roof and pagoda available with two-tier roof. A pergola seat, trelliswork arbor, is also available.

GAZEBO CENTRAL, 1000 Ken-o-sha Ind. Dr. SE, Grand Rapids, MI 49508 - (800) 339-0288
material - aluminum   sizes - 11' octagon
features - Kit includes all bolts and fasteners and step by step instructions. There are 44 roof colors to choose for the canvas fabric roof. Roof can be easily removed for winter snow load. The frame is available in a white powder coat finish.

GAZEBOS LTD., 140 W. Summit St., Milford, MI 48381 - (800) 701-6767 (248) 685-8993

material - western red cedar   sizes - 9'9" octagon / 12'1" decagon / 14'5" dodecagon / 7'7" x 7'7" • 11' x 11' • 15' x 15' square / 7'7" x 11' • 11' x 15' rectangle

features - Kits easy to assemble — everything precut, predrilled, most parts preassembled. Cedar shingle roofing available — three-ply roof consisting of 3/4" thick cedar paneling, one layer of 15 lb. roofing felt and cedar shingles. Available with or without floors. Optional removable screen kits — prehung screened door, fiberglass screen panels. Some units have bronze-colored acrylic, track style sliding windows and/or acrylic skylights. Weathervane designs — cardinal (hand painted), rooster, country doctor or horse. Hand cast aluminum, finished in satin black baked enamel. Two sizes available, large and small.

IRON BEAR, 1509 Wiltsey Rd. SE, Suite 208, Salem, OR 97306 - (503) 581-3081

material - wrought iron frame • aluminum castings   sizes - 12' octagon

features - Measures 10' at its peak. Eight main panels come in three different designs — arbor rose, curly oak or vineyard. Each panel measures approximately 5' wide and 8' tall. The gazebo can be powder-coat painted (paint baked on) in any color for a rust-resistant finish. Detailed instructions are included for assembly. The entire gazebo can be made of bronze.

LEISURE WOODS INC., PO Box 177, Genoa, IL 60135 - (888) 442-9326 (815) 784-2497

material - western red cedar   sizes - 10' • 12' • 14' octagon / 14' • 16' decagon / 18' • 20' • 23' • 26' • 28' dodecagon / 10' x 14' • 12' x 16' oblong / 10' x 10' • 12' x 12' square / 10' x 15' • 12' x 16' rectangle

features - All hardware, fasteners are provided with preassembled, predrilled kits. Roof interior finished with clear, 1" cedar tongue and groove as standard option. Screen package available, includes top and bottom screens for each wall, upper roof wall section. Prehung door included. Removable screens are made with bronze aluminum frames and charcoal colored fiberglass screen. Bench package includes interlocking, preassembled bench sections. Two floor options — standard floor package includes precut structural joist, framework, bearing beams. Tri-floor package comes in triangular sections, completely precut, partially preassembled. Screen provided for placement under deck. Steel roof option in red, blue, charcoal, brown, evergreen or grey. Roof styles available in straight, double-straight, triple-straight, curved or double-curved.

OLD WORLD GAZEBOS, 41 N. Business Park, 1033 E. Mt. Pleasant Rd., Evansville, IN 47711 - (800) 877-3622

material - southern yellow pine   sizes - 8' • 10' • 12' • 14' • 16' octagon / 8' x 14' • 10' x 14' • 10' x 16' • 10' x 18' • 10' x 20' • 10' x 24' • 12' x 14' • 12' x 16' • 12' x 18' • 12' x 20' • 12' x 22' • 12' x 24' oblong

features - All models are available as preassembled or knock-down kits. The knock-down series kits are delivered as individual precut and predrilled components pieces. These kits are shipped with precut tongue and groove roof decking. The preassembled kit is delivered with completely finished component pieces. The roof is pre-shingled with cedar shakes. The kits contain complete assembly instructions for do-it-yourselfers. Offered with or without a prefabricated floor. The floor kit has pre-numbered floor sections. If gazebo will be installed on a concrete slab or on a deck, proper attachment hardware can be provided. Hand rail sections can be custom designed. Roofing options — cedar shake shingles, or the roof decking can be prepared for asphalt shingles, copper or slate. Prefabricated bench seating and removable screen sections are available. An optional hand-crafted cedar cupola is available for all sizes.

SAM'S GAZEBOS, 343 W. 130th St., Los Angeles, CA 90061 - (800) 376-7267 (310) 324-5363

material - redwood and Douglas fir   sizes - 8' • 9' • 10' • 11' • 12' • 13' • 14' • 15' • 16' • 17' • 18' • 20' • 21' • 22' • 23' octagon / 7' x 7' • 8' x 8' • 9' x 9' • 10' x 10' • 11' x 11' • 12' x 12' • 13' x 13' • 14' x 14' • 15' x 15' square / 6' x 8' • 7' x 9' • 7' x 10' • 8' x 10' • 8' x 11' • 8' x 12' • 9' x 11' • 9' x 12' • 9' x 13' • 10' x 12' • 10' x 13' • 10' x 14' • 11' x 13' • 11' x 14' • 12' x 14' • 12' x 15' • 12' x 16' • 12' x 17' • 12' x 18' rectangle

features - The gazebos are constructed with mortise-and-tenon joinery, and half-lapped joints. The interlocking tongue-and-groove construction gives the gazebo durability. There are 12 custom design roof options to choose from. All octagon gazebos come with the standard louver roof (1x3 open roof) unless custom ordered. Options available — high (33") or low (19") handrails, contour bench, lattice panel with strips all 1 1/2" wide, 3/8" thick with 2x2 square windows in between, redwood floor with or without steps — redwood 2-step or 3-step floor, shingle solid rood, 1x6 overlapped cedar solid roof, composition shingle roof (gray, brown, blue, green or red shades), colonial posts with wrapped edged, classic posts with heavier bases, columns, lattice arch panels, arch panel with sunburst cutout, Gothic arch panel, cupola, post anchor form which is preset post anchors mounted on an octagonal floor frame or concealed wiring ready for hookup.

SUMMERWOOD PRODUCTS, 190 Konrad Crescent, Markham, ON L3R 8T9 - (800) 663-5042 (416) 498-9379

material - western red cedar   sizes - 8' • 10' • 12' • 14' • 16' octagon

features - Available as precut or preassembled kits. Precut kit has all components precut, ready for assembly. Includes instructions, all required hardware. Does not include shingles. Ideal do-it-yourself project. Preassembled kit designed for quick, easy assembly. All wall and floor sections preassembled, roof panels are preshingled. Copper roofing available in the preassembled kit. Noncorrosive plated hardware is included in all kits. Step by step instructions are also included. An optional screen package includes screen panels with brown anodized aluminum frames and black fiberglass mesh. A cedar door and frame are provided for the entrance. Black mesh is used under the floor and inside the cupola to fully enclose the gazebo. Plastic clips secure the screens making them easy to remove for cleaning or storage. The kits are available with or without a floor. You can also omit rail sections. Optional seating benches and solid cedar tongue and groove rails available. There are several sizes and styles of cupolas and weathervanes. There are some models that have a pagoda top roof section. The "Garden House" is a structure that is designed for year-round use with windows and doors.

VIXEN HILL, Main St., Elverson, PA 19520 - (800) 423-2766 (610) 286-0909

material - western red cedar   sizes - 9' • 12' • 15' • 21' • 24' • 27' • 30' octagon / 8' x 11' • 11' x 14' • 14' x 18' oblong

features - Available as prefabricated modular kits. Comes with complete instructions and all necessary hardware. Can be purchased with or without the floor system and with either a single or two-tiered roof. The modular roofing material can be copper, cedar shingle or tongue and groove planking. There are three grades to choose from — "Pennsylvania Dutch" with less detailing and occasional tight knots. "Carpenter Grade" have full detailing, but allow for occasional knots and minor cosmetic milling defects. "Cabinet Grade" have no milling defects or visible knots. All units can be equipped with a switch/outlet and floodlight fixture in the cupola. The "GardenHouse" includes insect screens. Options available for the "GardenHouse" are — spring-loaded decorative trim panels, louvers, glass window panels and solid bottom panels for year round use.

House plants purify air naturally

Q: We have an efficient airtight house. We use room air cleaners, but they push up our electric bills. Are there really house plants that can remove cancer-causing and other pollutants from the air?

A: Running several room air cleaners helps remove particles from the air, but the fans use a lot of electricity (up to $50 per year per air cleaner) and the noise can be annoying.

Typical air cleaners are relatively ineffective at removing most of the carcinogenic chemical pollutants common in an airtight efficient house. These chemicals also often cause sneezing, itchy eyes and headaches.

The most common unhealthy chemicals include benzene, formaldehyde and trichlorocethylene (TCH) given off from furniture, carpeting, cleaners, plastics, paints, dry cleaned clothes, plywood, adhesives, etc.

Significant research has been done, much of it by the NASA space program, which shows houseplants are effective, non-energy using air purifiers. In addition, they increase the oxygen content indoors.

More than 20 common houseplants have been found to be useful. Each is particularly effective for specific chemicals. Select plants which fit your decor and tolerate your indoor lighting and moisture levels.

For example, Boston ferns and Dracaena are good for formaldehyde removal. English Ivy is good for benzene removal and Parlor Palm and Peace Lily are good for TCH removal.

A combination of selected plants is best. Including a few or-

chids and bromeliads (some are very easy to grow) is effective for nighttime purifying. Their leaf pores open at night.

Hydroponics is an excellent way to grow healthy plants indoors for effective air purification. With hydroponics, no soil is needed. The plants grow in an inert medium with water, air and special fertilizers. Many companies sell complete single plant and larger hydroponic planter kits.

This is ideal indoors for several reasons. The plants grow much faster and larger because not as much growth goes into root production. With no soil, there are less mold spores given off to cause allergies. Hydroponics is also effective for growing vegetables (tomatoes, lettuce) year-round.

To purify air with plants in rooms with little natural lighting,

artificial light is needed. High intensity discharge (HID) lights use the least amount of electricity. High pressure sodium and metal halide are the best for plants.

Q: I bought a house with a roof ridge vent. When I removed part of the vent to fix some leaky shingles, I noticed that some of the rafters have separated from the ridge beam. How can I fix this?

A: The problem you describe is typically caused by a combination of sloppy construction and shrinkage of the lumber over the years. Specifically, improper toenailing technique can result in a gap.

On a typical gable roof, this should not be a problem because the members are in compression and stable. With a cathedral ceiling, the roof is less stable, so you should call in an engineer to evaluate your specific problem.

General Information on Hydroponics

Hydroponics is the science of growing plants without soil. Plants thrive on a nutrient solution. The growing medium acts as a support for the plants and their root systems. It also helps hold moisture around the roots. The growing medium is totally inert. Common media includes — fired clay pebbles (Leca stone, Geolite, etc.) • rockwool • perlite • vermiculite • sand • etc.

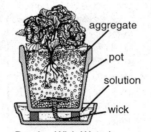
complete system

You need to use a complete nutrient in hydroponics. A complete nutrient has all the elements required for plant growth. These elements include nitrogen • phosphorous • potassium • calcium • copper • iron • zinc • boron • magnesium • molybdenum • cobalt • chlorine • sodium • nickel • carbon • oxygen and hydrogen. When the hydroponic nutrient is combined with air and water at the proper pH, level the elements are provided in the correct proportion.

Since the nutrients are dissolved into the water, they are readily available to the plant's root. Plants get all the elements they need all the time. The plants do not need to develop a huge root system to search for food so the growth energy is spent into growing the plants and fruits.

Plants maintain optimum nutrient and moisture levels in hydroponic systems. This will produce faster growing and healthier plants. This can result in up to 30% faster growth. There are no soil borne diseases or pests and no weeds to deal with.

If you grow hydroponically indoors, you need to address the problems of the indoor environment and lighting. Each plant has an ideal temperature. Lettuce prefers 60 to 70°F while tomatoes prefer 70 to 80°F. Most homes are kept around 70°F, so plants will do well. If it is comfortable for you, it will be comfortable for your plant. The easiest way to handle temperature, humidity and carbon dioxide requirements is with air flow from a fan.

Lighting requirements differ for each plant Some need direct sunlight, such as vegetables. Other plants need indirect light, such as tropical house plants or african violets. Growing indoors using natural sunlight requires a sunroom, greenhouse, solar room or good south-facing windows. If you do not have this type of sunlight, high intensity discharge lights will provide the intensity needed for vegetables at the most reasonable energy costs.

- **High Intensity Discharge Light**s — are cost efficient to operate. They provide the intensity of light needed to grow flowers and vegetables year round. They have an extremely long life. There are two HID lights suited for plant growth.

   1. **High Pressure Sodium** lights provide more of the red/orange spectrum. This is very helpful for fruiting and flowering. They are the most cost-efficient lights to operate. Some of the new lights also have more of the blue spectrum.

   2. **Metal Halide** light systems give more of the blue/green spectrun of light needed for vegetative growth. This type of lighting is recommended as the best all around garden light. High pressure sodium conversion bulbs allow changing to sodium spectrum in the metal halide fixtures.

- **Flourescent** — grow tubes work but are not as efficient. They need to be kept very close to the plants for vegetable growth. They work well for african violets, tropical houseplants or low growing crops such as lettuce, spinach and some herbs.

Description of the Different Types of Hydroponic Systems

Hydroponics systems are classified by the way the nutrient solution is made available to the plant's roots.

Passive Systems — This is a good system to begin with on a small scale or to just grow one single plant. This system does not use a pump but instead uses capillary actions by means of a wicking material. The wicks are placed in the water reservoir and draw moisture and nutrients upward into the growing medium to reach the roots. This is a good choice for house plants, herbs or other slow-growing plants.

Active Systems — There are several different types of active systems. These systems are used for larger hydroponic gardens, inside or outside, chosen by the most serious growers.

aggregate
pot
solution
wick

Passive Wick-Watering

- **Aeroponics System** — This system does not use a growing medium other than the seed starting cube. The roots are suspended in the air — the stems, leaves or flowers are all above the surface of the container. A pump produces a fine mist of air and nutrient solution that is sprayed onto the roots. The roots are constantly moistened by the solution that allows for an adequate supply of oxygen and excellent aeration. These systems must be closely monitored. If there is an electricity failure or a pump malfunction, the plants will die quickly.

- **Drip System** — This system operates with a pump and plumbing system that has a nutrient delivery tube to each plant. A timer turns the pump on and off which delivers the nutrient solution for a few minutes at each feeding. The growing media is usually perlite,

nutrient film

rockwool or a porous stone. The medium retains some of the nutrient solution but also allows for plenty of oxygen around the roots. This is popular with commercial growers but it works great for the hobbyist.

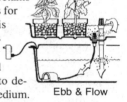

- **Ebb & Flow System** — This is also called the flood and drain system using a pump to deliver water from a reservoir to the growing medium.

Ebb & Flow

The pump is usually controlled by a timer and operates for a specified time to flood the medium. It then shuts off and the solution drains back into the reservoir. This action will draw oxygen into the growing medium. The process is repeated several times throughout the day. Usually a type of porous stone is used in this system. These systems are effective when propagating many cuttings in Rockwool or when irrigating plants in pots. This is a very popular system with orchid growers because potted plants may be moved in and out of the system at will.

- **Nutrient Film System** — A thin film of nutrient solution is circulated over the root system that allows plenty of air to reach the root system. You will need a very dependable power supply to keep the solution flowing. The roots will dry out quickly if they are left without water for a very long time. This is a very popular system for commercial lettuce and herb growers but it also works for the hobbyist.

- **Trickle System** — This system uses a small aquarium type air pump that continuously circulates a small amount of the nutrient solution through the growing medium. The water returns to the reservoir and is recycled over and over again.

- **Hybrid Systems** — There are many hybrid systems available, with minor variations of the systems described above. You may wish to design your own system with materials on hand or through a garden store or mail order business.

Cenotec Hydroponic Planters

1. Remove planter pot — it's the top of the column — a generous 7" deep and 11" square. Fill with perlite.

2. Rinse soil from roots of the plants you plan to use. Plant them in the pot.

3. Mix ½ teaspoon plant nutrients (year's supply included) and two gallons tap water. Pour into column. Repeat this step in a month.

4. Replace pot on top of column. Feeder tube fits easily through funnel at bottom of pot.

5. Place planter in sunny window or under artificial light.

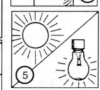

Complete System

• Reservoir tank in classic column styling
• 11" planter pot
• Built-in circulating pump
• 1 year's supply of house plant nutrients
• Perlite (feather light volcanic rock)
• Planter dimensions — 28" high × 11" square base and top Column diameter 8"
• Full one year warranty
• Made in the U.S.A.
• Available in five finishes — black onyx • alabaster • malachite • granite dark • granite light • redstone

Available from CropKing
5050 Greenwich Rd.
Sevill, OH 44273
(800) 321-5211

Do-It-Yourself Instructions for Building A Simple Hydroponic Unit

This is a very simple and small setup, but you can change the plans to fit your own design or modify it to make a larger system.

1) You need to make your system light tight. Paint the bucket, the hoses and the PVC pipe with a coat of black paint. Let the paint dry overnight. Now paint these surfaces with a coat of white paint. This makes it reflective and will help reduce the temperature of the nutrient solution.

2) Drill a 1" hole in the side of the PVC pipe. The hole should be about 1" from the end. Epoxy the caps to the ends of the PVC pipe.

outlet hole — 1" hole — inlet hole
PVC pipe with end caps

3) Drill inlet and outlet holes on the PVC pipe end caps. The outlet hole should be as high as possible and the inlet hole should be as low as possible. Make these holes as close to the wall of the PVC pipe as you can.

4) Cut two 5" holes (near the top) in the sides of the bucket and push the PVC pipe into these holes. Epoxy the PVC pipe in place and make sure that about 2" of the pipe and the outlet hole are inside the bucket. The 1" hole needs to be facing straight up.

1" hole — 1" hole
inlet hole — outlet hole — inlet hole
bucket

5) Place the airstone in the bottom of the bucket and find a location for the airpump. This is to dissolve oxygen into the nutrient solution.

6) Place the water pump in the bottom of the bucket and attach a hose to it. This needs to be long enough to reach the top of the bucket. Attach the T-fitting to the hose. Attach the hoses to the free ends of the T-fitting and run them to the inlet holes on the end of the PVC pipes. Use the clamps on the T-fitting and on the pump. Use epoxy to attach the hoses to the PVC pipe. This seal needs to be absolutely water tight. Let this dry for at least 24 hours.

7) You should check the system for leaks and to see if it is running properly. Put some water in the bucket and turn the pump on. The PVC pipes will fill with water and when they are full, they will begin to drain out the outlet holes back into the bucket. If there are any leaks, you need to fix them now. If water is coming out of the 1" hole on the top of the pipe, the outlet hole is too small or the pump might be too strong. You need to make any adjustments to take care of these problems at this time.

8) Remove the water from the system and replace it with a nutrient solution.

9) Place an aggregate and your plant(s) into the bucket. Turn on the air and water pumps.

Required Materials

one (1) 5-10 gallon bucket
two pieces of PVC pipe, 8-10" long, 5" or greater diameter
4 caps for PVC pipe ends
1 submersible water pump
4' of hose that will fit the water pump
1 T-joint that fits the water hose
4 clamps for the water hose
1 airpump, airstone and some airline (the type used for an aquarium)
1 can white epoxy-based spray paint
1 can black epoxy-based spray paint
epoxy and aggregate

Purifying House Plants

Aglaonema — Chinese Evergreen — high humidity is preferred, stand on trays of moist pebbles, a north-facing window is best
light - shade | temperature* - warm | water - water generously on soil, spray foliage

Aloe — Aloe Vera — avoid wetting the leaves when watering, the water lodged in the leaf axils can cause rot
light - full sun | temperature - medium | water - thoroughly in summer, sparingly in winter

Aspidistra elatior — Cast-iron Plant — ideal for a poorly lit situation, use small pots and only repot when absolutely necessary
light - shade | temperature - medium | water - moderately, allow soil to dry out

Dracaena deremensis — Striped Dracaena — stand pots on trays of moist pebbles for extra humidity, repot only when necessary
light - bright but filtered light | temperature - medium | water - plentifully, do not allow to stand in water

Dracaena marginata — Dragon Tree — stand pots on trays of moist pebbles for extra humidity, repot only when necessary
light - bright but filtered light | temperature - medium | water - water plentifully when in active growth

Chamaedorea — Parlor Palm — tolerates dry air but will do better when stood on pebble tray
light - bright but not direct light | temperature - medium | water - water plentifully summer, sparingly winter

Chlorophytum comosum — Spider Plant — dry air causes leaf tops to brown
light - bright, a few hours of sunlight | temperature - medium | water - generously in summer, sparingly in winter

Chrysanthemum morifolium — Pot Mum — may be planted outdoors as a flowering perennial
    light - bright light but not direct sun   temperature - cool   water - frequent, keep the soil damp

Ficus benjamina — Weeping Fig — does best when roots are a little restricted in what may appear too small of a pot
    light - bright but filtered light   temperature - medium   water - thoroughly, allow soil to dry between waterings

Gerbera jamesonii — Gerbera Daisy — may be planted outdoors as a flowering perennial
    light - bright light but not direct sun   temperature - cool   water - moderation, allow surface to dry out

Hedera helix — English Ivy — stand on trays of moist pebbles, move to larger pots two or three times a year
    light - bright light but not direct sun   temperature - cool   water - moderation, allow surface to dry out

Nephroplepis — Boston Fern — ideal for moist bathrooms or kitchens, spray foliage daily, place pot in moist pebbles
    light - bright but no direct sun   temperature - medium   water - plentifully, frequently so soil is always damp

Peperomia caperata — Emerald Ripple — stand pots on trays of moist pebbles, very little root so small pots are adequate
    light - bright but filtered light   temperature - medium   water - sparingly, let soil dry out between waterings

Philodendron domesticum — Elephant Ear — an east- or west-facing window is best, move into a larger pot every other year
    light - bright, indirect light   temperature - medium   water - water well then no more until the soil is dry

Philodendron scandens — Climbing Philodendron — pinch the growing tips to maintain within bounds
    light - bright, indirect light   temperature - medium   water - wet thoroughly, dry out before repeating

Sansevieria trifasciata — Mother-in-law's Tongue — no water for up to three months will not kill this plant
    light - bright light and direct sun   temperature - medium   water - moderation, roots rot easily

Schefflera — Umbrella Tree — move to a bigger pot size each spring
    light - bright light but not direct sun   temperature - cool   water - moderation, allow surface to dry out

Scindapsus — Pothos — stand on moist pebble trays, replant into the next size pot each spring
    light - bright, indirect light   temperature - medium   water - moderately in summer, sparingly in winter

Spathiphyllum — Peace Lily — stand on trays of moist pebbles and mist-spray foliage weekly, repot yearly
    light - bright light but not direct sun   temperature - medium   water - moderation, allow surface to dry out

Syngonium — Arrowhead Plant — needs high humidity, place pot on moist pebble trays
    light - bright light but filtered   temperature - medium   water - moderation during growing season

*Temperature range — cool is 55° to 64°F • medium is 64° to 75°F • warm is 75° to 80°F.

Purifying Plants to Remove Common Chemicals in Homes		
Pollutant Chemicals	**Source of Pollutant**	**Effective Houseplant**
Formaldehyde	foam insulation plywood particle board clothes carpeting furniture paper goods household cleaners water repellents	Aloe Vera Arrowhead Plant Boston Fern Chysanthemum Dracaena English Ivy Ficus Gerbera Daisy Parlor Palm Philodendron Pothos Schefflera Spider Plant Weeping Fig
Benzene	tobacco smoke gasoline synthetic fibers plastics inks oils detergents rubber	Cast-iron Plant Chinese Evergreen Chrysanthemum Dracaena English Ivy Gerbera Daisy Parlor Palm Peace Lily Peperomia
Trichloroethylene	dry cleaning inks paints varnishes lacquers adhesives	Arrowhead Plant Dracaena English Ivy Gerbera Daisy Mother-in-law's Tongue Parlor Palm Peace Lily

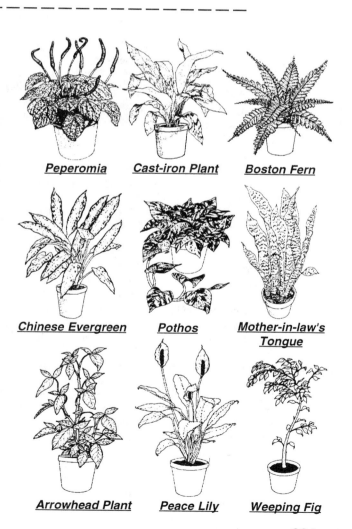

Peperomia   **Cast-iron Plant**   **Boston Fern**

Chinese Evergreen   **Pothos**   **Mother-in-law's Tongue**

Arrowhead Plant   **Peace Lily**   **Weeping Fig**

Index

A
Active water heating kits, 5
Adapter plug, 161
Air conditioner - room, 189
Air-type solar heater, 45
Anti-scald device, 109
Appliance electricity usage, 32
Attic
 foil, 65
 heat, 17, 25, 53, 65, 129
 insulation, 1
 pool solar systems, 129
 vent fan, 25
 ventilation, 17, 25, 55
Awnings, 185

B
Batch solar water heater, 1
Bay window, 161
Bio-gas generator, 157
Boiler - wood-burning, 69
Bow window, 161
Breadbox water heater, 1

C
Cardboard solar cooker, 108
Cathedral ceiling, 153
Caulk, 69
Ceramic tile
 adhesive removal, 49
 floor rigidity, 85
 solar floor/wall tile, 61
Chimney - solar, 53
Climbing vines, 141
Clothes dryer, 181
Concrete
 pavers, 137
 planter, 25
Continuous ridge vents, 18

D
Deck
 heater, 73
 solar, 197
Dimmer switch, 5
Dishwasher - clogged holes, 65
Door shutter, 57
Dryer vent, 113, 177
Dual fuel furnace, 70
Dwarf shrubs, 145

E
Electric generating windmill, 13
Electric tools, 89
Emergency generator, 29
Extension cord, 157
Exterior Solar Improvements, 133-140

F
Fading rays, 174
Fiberglass windows, 157
Filter for dryer vent, 177
Finnish fireplace, 81
Fireback, 90
Fireplace
 doors, 90
 firewood, 85

improvements, 89, 193
 manufactured logs, 85
 smoking, 45
 wood-burning, 81, 93
Firewood, 85
Firewood dryer, 97
Firewood tips, 83
Floor heating, 49
Floor plans, 114, 115, 116
Flower dryer, 101
Flowering vines, 141
Foam insulation board, 17
Food dryer, 101
Formaldehyde insulation, 21
Fuel cost comparison, 80
Furnace - wood-burning, 69

G-H
Garage door opener, 81
Garden window, 109
Gazebo kits, 197
Generator, 29
Greenhouse
 do-it-yourself construction, 121
 mini, 97
 window, 109
Ground source heat pump, 193
Gutter cleaning device, 13
Halogen light bulbs, 185
Hardiness zone map, 151
Hardwood fuel values, 84
Heat-circulating fireplace, 93
Heat-circulating grates, 89
Heat pump - ground source, 193
House plants, 201
Hydroponics, 201

I-J
Ice dam, 37
Indoor air pollution, 201
Insulating rolling shutters, 181
Ionization purification, 125

K-L
Landscaping, 141-152
 climbing vines, 141
 dwarf shrubs, 145
 tree selector guide, 149
Leaking toilet, 101
Lightwell, 172

M-N
Masonry fireplace, 81
Mirrored shutter, 177
Motion sensing lights, 21

O-P
Other Alternative Energy Topics, 193-204
Outdoor furnace, 69
Outdoor lights, 21
Oven
 gasket, 129
 window, 125
Passive Solar Houses & Sunspaces, 109-124
Passive solar house, 113
Passive water heating kits, 5

Patio door
 shield, 57
 shutter, 59
Pavers, 137
Pellet heater, 77
Permanent window film, 173
Photovoltaics/Electricity Generation, 21-36
Photovoltaic systems, 33
Plywood quality, 133
Plywood solar cooker, 105
Pool purification, 125
Portable windmill, 13
Pressure-balance valve, 109
Purifying house plants, 201

Q-R
Radiant barrier attic foil, 65
Radiant barrier coating, 68
Radiant floor heating, 49
Range hood, 121
Reflective window shutter, 177
Refrigerator
 frost-free, 169
 placement, 57
 transporting, 41
Removable window film, 189
Retaining wall, 133
Retractable awnings, 185
Ridge vents, 18
Rolling shutters, 181
Roof insulation panels, 153
Rusty water, 53

S
Security shutters, 181
Self-cling window film, 189
Shading with trees, 149
Showerhead, 173
Shutters, 177, 181
Skylight
 cathedral ceiling, 153
 high-efficiency, 169
 lightwell instructions, 172
 tubular kits, 165
Smoking fireplace, 45
Solar cell systems, 33
Solar cooker kit, 105
Solar deck, 197
Solar food dryer, 101
Solar Food Preparation, 101-108
Solar Heating/Cooling, 37-68
Solar lights, 21
Solar-powered attic fan, 25
Solar Water Heating, 1-12
Standby generator, 29
Sun-tracking racks, 33
Sun/wind door shield, 57
Sunlight tube, 165
Sunroom kits, 117
Sunshine chart, 34
Swimming pool
 deck, 129
 ionizer, 125

solar systems, 129
Swimming Pools, 125-132

T
Thermostat setting, 97, 141
Tile, 61
Tile adhesive removal, 49
Toilet
 flapper, 153
 leaks, 101
Tree selector guide, 149
Trombe wall, 39
Tubular skylight, 165
Turbine ventilator, 17

U-V
Vaulted ceilings, 153
Ventilation chimney, 53
Vented roof panels, 153
Venting
 attic, 25
 dryer vent, 113
 range hood, 121
 roof ridge vent, 18
Vines for shading, 141

W-Z
Wall heater, 45
Water heater noise, 73
Water heating
 breadbox water heater, 5
 solar water heating kits, 1
 water-type solar collector, 9
Water pressure, 93
Water-type solar collector, 9
Wall switch installation, 5
Warm water floor systems, 49
Waterbed heating, 197
Weatherstrip windows, 33
Wind Energy, 13-20
Wind speed chart, 16
Wind/sun shield, 57
Windbreak with shrubs, 145
Windmill, 13
Window
 bow and bay, 161
 fiberglass, 157
 garden/greenhouse, 117
 heater, 41
 shades, 190
 shutters, 177, 181
 storm, 33
Window Improvements, 173-192
Window film
 permanent, 173
 removable, 189
Windows & Skylights, 153-172
Whole-house fan, 55, 149
Wood-burning fireplace, 81, 93
 glass doors, 89
 improvements, 90
Wood-burning furnace, 69
Wood heat evaluation, 72
Wood Heating, 69-100
Wood siding, 117
Zoned cooling system, 189

Boldfaced heading indicates chapter topic